Stamp Duty Land Tax

NINTH EDITION

Other titles available from Law Society Publishing:

Commonhold
Gary Cowen, James Driscoll and Laurence Target

Conveyancing Checklists (2nd edn)
Frances Silverman and Russell Hewitson

Conveyancing Forms and Procedures (4th edn)
Annette Goss, Lorraine Richardson and Michael Taylor

Conveyancing Handbook (17th edn)
General Editor: Frances Silverman, Consultant Editors: Annette Goss, Russell Hewitson, Peter Reekie, Anne Rodell, Michael Taylor

Environmental Law Handbook (7th edn)
Valerie Fogleman, Trevor Hellawell and Andrew Wiseman

Leasehold Enfranchisement and the Right to Manage
Christopher Sykes

Property Development
Gavin Le Chat

Understanding Property Insurance
Gerald Sherriff

Understanding VAT on Property (2nd edn)
David Jordan

Titles from Law Society Publishing can be ordered from all good bookshops or direct (telephone 0870 850 1422, email **lawsociety@prolog.uk.com** or visit our online shop at **www.lawsociety.org.uk/bookshop**).

STAMP DUTY LAND TAX

A Practical Guide

NINTH EDITION

Reg Nock

The Law Society

Crown copyright material is reproduced with the permission of the Controller of Her Majesty's Stationery Office

ISBN-13: 978-1-85328-809-8

Published in 2011 by the Law Society
113 Chancery Lane, London WC2A 1PL

Typeset by Columns Design XML Ltd, Reading
Printed by TJ International Ltd, Padstow, Cornwall

The paper used for the text pages of this book is FSC certified. FSC (the Forest Stewardship Council) is an international network to promote responsible management of the world's forests.

FSC
www.fsc.org
MIX
Paper from
responsible sources
FSC® C013056

Contents

Preface to the ninth edition

This new edition continues the previous trend of the book looking not only at the technical law but also at the implications for both the practitioner and actual professional practice. The many developments in this tax not only change the law but also require changes in practice. These issues are commented on at relevant places in the text.

It is appropriate to express thanks to Sarah Foulkes and Ben Mullane at the Law Society for their assistance and co-operation in dealing with the developing text. A special thank you is due to Lynn Gower whose technological skills and patience were invaluable in preparing the materials.

The law is stated as at 1 January 2011.

Reg Nock
February 2011

Table of cases

Table of statutes

Table of statutory instruments

CHAPTER 1

Introduction and general principles

1.1 BACKGROUND

Stamp duty land tax (SDLT) replaced stamp duty upon land transactions with effect from 1 December 2003 subject to certain complex transitional provisions in Finance Act (FA) 2003, Sched.19 largely designed to exclude from SDLT transactions entered into before 11 July 2003. Subsequent amendments, some retrospective, are intended to bring into charge to SDLT transactions entered into between 10 July and 1 December 2003 which are 'completed' or performed on or after the latter date.

1.2 CHANGEOVER RELIEF

Although it is many years since the introduction of the tax this transitional relief is of considerable practical importance, for example:

- a considerable amount of tax can be saved and substantial costs avoided by investigating whether the transaction remains subject to stamp duty, which is usually considerably lower than the equivalent charge to SDLT;
- the fact that the transaction was entered into in the context of stamp duty may mean that reliefs such as relief for disadvantaged land remain available and many of the SDLT provisions relating to leases do not apply to leases that were originally granted within the stamp duty regime. For example, the complex rules relating to holding over and many of the charges arising upon rent reviews are not appropriate to stamp duty leases.

There may be considerable tax saving for a client in completing an existing arrangement. However, the transitional treatment is usually dependent upon the original contract not having been varied.[1] In consequence, where there is a transaction that is potentially subject to stamp duty rather than SDLT it may be much cheaper and more efficient in the longer term for the parties to complete the original agreement and then vary the lease or other documentation as appropriate. This latter

---

[1]   See, for example, FA 2003, Sched.19, para.3(3).

route will attract stamp duty and there may be little or no SDLT upon the transaction. This relief can apply to conditional agreements such as arrangements for the grant of a lease when planning permission is obtained and the building works completed.[2]

1.3 INTERACTION WITH STAMP DUTIES

1.3.1 Fixed duties

Certain fixed duties remained chargeable in respect of specified transactions involving stock, marketable securities and land. However, FA 2008, Sched.32 made some fundamental changes in this area. Fixed duties have been removed from transfers of shares, but may remain for certain land transactions.[3] This and the decision of the Land Registry to remove the exempt instruments certificates[4] from its documents has created practical problems for non-notifiable transactions and the abolition of the self-certificate (SDLT 60) (see **17.7**).

1.3.2 Shares

FA 2008, Sched.32 provided for the removal of the fixed duties and exempting certificates and introduced a nil rate in relation to transactions involving stock or marketable securities (including any linked transactions) where a certificate of value is inserted to the effect that the consideration does not exceed £1,000.[5] The effect of the repeal is that for transactions involving shares and marketable securities the Stamp Duty (Exempt Instruments) Regulations 1987[6] are no longer necessary.

1.3.3 Land

Certain fixed duties appear to have been retained in respect of land transactions[7] but the Land Registry has subsequently redesigned the forms omitting the facility to include the certificates pursuant to the regulations. This would mean that techni-cally the Land Registry transfer, etc. is subject to the fixed duty because it is not

---

[2] But see whether these are conditional agreements or there is some form of potentially taxable consideration as in *Eastham* v. *Leigh London and Provincial Properties Ltd* [1971] 2 All ER 887.

[3] FA 2008, Sched.32, para.22.

[4] Stamp Duty (Exempt Instruments) Regulations 1987, SI 1987/516.

[5] Since the exemption from the charge to stamp duty reserve tax requires the execution of a duly stamped stock transfer form there is a technical issue as to whether the nil rate is available for small transactions involving shares. It seems that certain fund managers of ISAs and unit trusts charge stamp duty land tax in respect of transactions notwithstanding they fall before the £1,000 limit, probably because it is easier to pass the cost to the taxpayer than to organise the necessary paperwork.

[6] SI 1987/516.

[7] FA 2008, Sched.32, para.22, which states that certain parts of the repealing provisions do not apply to land transactions.

certified as required.[8] In consequence, the parties may find it helpful to include some form of certification in the relevant Land Registry documentation since this may avoid any residual questions and challenges as to the payment of the fixed duty and may provide evidence to encourage the Land Registry to accept that the transaction is not notifiable for the purposes of SDLT.[9]

1.3.4 Stamp duty scope

In addition to such transitional reliefs, stamp duty or stamp duty reserve tax remains applicable to:

- transactions relating to shares and marketable securities:[10] the principal charge to stamp duty reserve tax also applies;[11]
- 'transfers' in writing of partnership interests where the partnership owns stock or marketable securities to the extent that the consideration or deemed consideration for the transfer is apportioned to shares and marketable securities where the 0.5 per cent rate will apply;[12]
- bearer shares and unit trust schemes and open-ended investment companies.

1.4 SDLT STRUCTURAL CHANGES

It is important to note that SDLT was introduced as a panic measure after a less than satisfactory consultation process intended to block certain very simple stamp duty mitigation techniques, such as the need for writing of a particular type. The charge

---

[8] FA 1985, s.87.

[9] For the problems in dealing with the Land Registry in the current regime see e.g. **1.12.3**. It is usually significantly better for the taxpayer to remain within the former stamp duty regime because the amount of tax, timing of payment, penalties and interest and the compliance obligations, including being audited by HM Revenue & Customs (HMRC) Stamp Taxes, are less onerous than in the new regime. It is important, therefore, to avoid any transaction that may cancel the transitional benefits such as variations of contracts, subsales and assignments or, importantly, surrenders and regrants of leases because many of the charges in the new regime do not apply to 'stamp duty leases' such as holding over but any variation that amounts to a surrender and regrant will bring the new regime into operation immediately, imposing not only a higher charge to SDLT but major compliance costs and long-term complications because of the lack of finality in this tax (see **1.11**).

[10] Stamp Act 1891, s.122.

[11] The special charge to stamp duty reserve tax for depository and clearance schemes has been declared in part unlawful by the European Court (see *HSBC Holdings Plc* v. *Revenue and Customs Commissioners (C-569/07)* [2010] STC 58; *HSBC Life (UK) Ltd* v. *Stubbs (HMIT)* [2002] STC (SCD) 9) so that the charges are undergoing modification. Guidance has been provided as to the attitude of HMRC Stamp Taxes in relation to claims for repayment of the tax. Similar problems apply in relation to bearer instrument duty pursuant to FA 1999, Sched.19, see *Kingdom of Belgium* v. *European Commission* (unreported, 2004), ECJ; FA 1986, s.87. The attempt to apply land rich company rules has temporarily been abandoned. The attack has been focused upon attempts to convert land into shares by imposing charges upon routine commercial transactions such as business incorporations or clawback of reliefs on an arbitrary basis not concerned with tax avoidance motives.

[12] FA 2003, Sched.20 (as amended).

to SDLT is complex and wide-ranging. It arises where there is a chargeable transaction, which is defined as the acquisition of a chargeable interest for chargeable consideration.

'Acquisition' and 'chargeable interest' are extensively defined and discussed elsewhere (see **2.5**) but the tax is more complex. It is a transaction tax and does not depend upon the existence of documentation.[13]

Also, although the definition of chargeable transaction does not refer to consideration it is a key ingredient in the charge[14] and, to a large extent, the notification obligations that there is 'chargeable consideration', since there is a wide-ranging exemption from tax and from notification[15] where there is no chargeable consideration.[16] Unfortunately, 'chargeable consideration' differs from 'actual consideration' as is discussed elsewhere (see e.g. **5.7.2.1**).

Since the tax is a transaction tax and does not require documentation it differs fundamentally from stamp duty as to the time when it arises. This introduces a new concept into the taxation of land transactions namely 'the effective date'.[17]

1.5 CONVEYANCING CHANGES: TRANSACTION TAX

It is actions (rather than documentation) that trigger the tax and this has given rise to fundamental changes in relation to appropriate conveyancing practice (see **Appendices A** to **D**). Changes relate to:

- investigations of title;
- due diligence because of problems where the tax runs with the land rather than staying with the taxpayer;[18]
- the need for solicitors to be more actively involved with the activities of their client, particularly between contract and completion (see **3.6.1**); and
- the obligations to the client when signing off on a transaction (see e.g. **14.7**) particularly since his tax return is unlikely to be final (see **1.11**) notwithstanding that he has obtained a Revenue certificate (SDLT 5) and his title has been registered.

Failure to deal with the situation properly can easily constitute a breach of duty to the client[19] and may expose the solicitor to potential penalties for participating in incorrect returns, which can involve a penalty of £3,000[20] or even imprisonment.[21]

---

[13] FA 2003, s.42(2).
[14] FA 2003, Sched.3, para.1; s.77A.
[15] FA 2003, s.77A.
[16] FA 2003, Sched.3, para.1; see **5.7.2.1**.
[17] FA 2003, Sched.10, para.2; ss.119, 76 (as amended) and 86.
[18] See, for example, FA 2003, Sched.17A, paras.12 and s.81A.
[19] See, for example, *Slattery* v. *Moore Stephens* [2003] STC 1379; *BE Studios* v. *Smith & Williamson* [2006] STC 358.
[20] FA 2003, s.95.
[21] FA 2003, s.96.

The detailed issues of the charging provisions and compliance obligations are considered elsewhere at appropriate parts of this book but solicitors who are anxious to 'process' their conveyancing may discover, to their cost, that their processes do not meet the stringent criteria of the new tax or their obligations to the client (see e.g. **1.14**, **3.6.1**, **6.9**, **14.7**).

1.6 KEY PRINCIPLES FOR PRACTICE

SDLT is very different from stamp duty not merely as regards enforcement and compliance but also as regards its nature and scope. It is a fundamental error to regard SDLT as simply stamp duty with SDLT 1 and related forms replacing the old 'PD' form. It differs from stamp duty in many ways:

- SDLT is a transaction-based tax not a document-based tax, i.e. a tax charge can arise even where there is no document.[22]
- The charging provisions for SDLT apply to a wider range of transactions than those that attracted stamp duty (see **1.18**).
- Third parties such as assignees of leases are made liable for the taxation liability and compliance of the original taxpayer.[23]
- The principles for the computation and payment are completely different (see **Chapter 4**).
- There is no real finality (see **1.25**). For example, the tax liability for a purchase with a clawback provision remains open for at least a century after the initial transaction on current conveyancing practice. There is no equivalent to adjudication and an Enquiry does not end the taxpayer's exposure to the tax; much of the tax operates retrospectively, complicating title investigation or other issues.
- It is a transaction tax liability and notification obligations potentially arise at different stages in the sale or lease process.[24]
- It is directly enforceable.[25]
- There is a limited form of wait-and-see dealing with the areas formerly within the contingency principle for stamp duty such as variable or deferred consideration such as overage and clawback payments and rent reviews but this is a retrospective tax (see **1.24**). This together with certain compliance provisions (such as the penalties for failing to correct a return, for which there is a 21-year limitation period[26]) produces a lack of finality which is creating problems for persons such as personal representatives of deceased persons and liquidators of companies. Unless the initial transaction has been properly prepared with an 'exit strategy',[27] that lack of finality will prevent the early termination of those

---

[22] FA 2003, s.43. See **1.18**.
[23] FA 2003, s.81A; Sched.17A, para.12; see **1.15** and **14.10**.
[24] See FA 2003, ss.119, 44, Sched.17A, para.12A; see **8.9**.
[25] FA 2003, s.75 and Sched.10. See **Chapters 14** and **18**.
[26] FA 2003, Sched.10, paras.31 and 31A.
[27] FA 2003, ss.81A, 90; Sched.17A, para.12; see **14.10**.

persons' administration of the assets. Considerable difficulty also arises for all parties when negotiating rent reviews, overage and clawback provisions where the 'costs' involved in the calculation of the payment include stamp tax liabilities that may never be finalised, particularly given the current practice of HMRC Stamp Taxes of enacting retrospective legislation by way of 'clarifying' earlier defective drafting.

- SDLT raises fundamentally different issues in relation to registration of title and the investigation of the vendor's title; failure to deal with these issues upon acquisition may make the title subsequently unsaleable (see **1.14**). For example, where a lessee does not pay the tax and cannot register his interest[28] any sublessee will be unable to register his interest and be unable to give security to his mortgagee (see **1.10.2**). Similarly, where a landlord refuses to deal with the surrender of a lease[29] so that it remains off the register, it may affect his reversionary interest and be a title issue for any new lessee who may be taking subject to the now surrendered lease affecting his title for a later sale.
- A wholly new set of warranties and indemnities for routine land transactions is required (see **Appendix C**).
- The warranties and indemnities required in relation to the acquisition of shares in companies, including companies incorporated outside the UK are totally different.
- Major changes are required in relation to the valuation of shares because of the nature of the tax and its lack of finality (see **Chapter 13**).
- Significant practical problems arise when purchasing interests in land from companies.
- Finally, SDLT has a different jurisdictional basis.

These issues are considered at various places in this book but the various comments, while covering a wide range of routine transactions where there are serious traps for the unwary practitioner, do not necessarily indicate all of the problem areas where difficulties exist,[30] especially where the parties' advisers seek by unorthodox means to provide commercial protection against minimal commercial risks without considering the enormous increase in the SDLT charges. The advisers of vendors or landlords may frequently seek to protect their client where relatively straightforward arrangements such as second mortgages for the payment of deferred consideration are not available because of the attitude of mortgagees such as banks. Provisions may be written into the contract that are designed primarily to provide some comfort to the vendor or landlord. Unfortunately, those inserting such

---

[28] FA 2003, s.79(1) (as amended); but this is less of a problem for third parties now that it is possible to obtain the Revenue certificate (SDLT 5) without payment when filing electronically.

[29] Because, for example, he is not relieved from tax by FA 2003, Sched.17A, para.16.

[30] But see e.g. **Appendix A** for certain guidance on due diligence, etc. for the practitioner.

provisions frequently overlook the definition of 'chargeable interests'. For example, FA 2003, s.48(1)(b) applies to certain contractual arrangements affecting the value of land.[31]

The most important practical change is the non-documentary nature of the tax. In consequence, liability to the tax and obligations to report and pay can arise notwithstanding that there is no document,[32] and this transaction basis affects the time at which the tax arises.[33] Although many transactions can be effective only if in writing[34] there are various situations where informal or oral arrangements can be effective to pass title,[35] and completion of an ineffective arrangement such as an oral agreement will be effective to pass title[36] and give rise to a charge to the tax. Although it was intended to deal with the problems of electronic conveyancing[37] even to the extent of creating the possibility of instant payment of the tax at the time of electronic completion,[38] with significant implications for the structuring of payment at completion and risks of personal accountability for client tax for solicitors, there are still unresolved issues of the legal effectiveness of electronic or telephone arrangements and the impact of the new tax regime upon such arrangements.

1.7 STAMP DUTY BAGGAGE

Moreover, this impression of SDLT as simply stamp duty is reinforced by the initial reading of the legislation: notwithstanding the attempt at a plain English style of drafting, many of the old stamp duty provisions, or something that looks like the old legislation, appear in FA 2003. There are considerable difficulties in practice with HMRC Stamp Taxes as to whether any, and if so which, of the practices and

---

[31] There is a similarly cryptic provision in relation to leasehold covenants affecting the market rent contained in FA 2003, Sched.17A, para.10(1)(c); see **8.56.3**.

[32] FA 2003, s.43.

[33] But note that in some cases, but not all, the charge is linked to the date of the documentation. This currently gives rise to significant problems in relation to agreements for lease and leases – see **Chapter 8**.

[34] See, for example, Law of Property (Miscellaneous Provisions) Act 1989 and that writing is in proper form and content (*Firstpost Homes* v. *Johnson* [1995] 4 All ER 355); but the contract may be contained in more than one instrument (see e.g. *Spiro* v. *Glencrown Properties* [1991] 2 WLR 931); and equitable principles may apply *Banner Homes Holdings Ltd* v. *Luff Developments Ltd (No.1)* [2000] 2 All ER 117; *Bannister* v. *Bannister* [1948] 2 All ER 133; *Hussey* v. *Palmer* [1977] 3 All ER 744. According to Walker LJ in *Yaxley* v. *Gotts* [1999] 3 WLR 1217, such equitable principles override the statutory requirements notwithstanding the intention of Parliament to escape from the problems associated with Law of Property Act 1925, s.40. Walker LJ has potentially overruled Parliament and brought back these issues; see also *RTS Flexible Systems Ltd* v. *Molkerei Alois* [2010] 3 All ER 1.

[35] See e.g. Law of Property Act 1925, ss.52 and 53(2); *Yaxley* v. *Gotts* [1999] 3 WLR 1217; *Henry* v. *Henry* [2010] 1 All ER 988 but see *Cobbe* v. *Yeoman's Row Management Ltd* [2008] 4 All ER 713.

[36] Tootal Clothing Ltd v. Guinea Properties Management (1992) 64 P&CR 452.

[37] See e.g. amendment in Finance (No.2) Act 2005, s.47.

[38] FA 2003, s.76(2).

interpretations of stamp duty are to be carried over to the new tax particularly since many solicitors still advise on the basis that SDLT is the same as the old tax. However, it is rarely obvious whether a word is used in its traditional technical sense or in a new 'plain English' meaning. This causes difficulties in a subject as technical as land law and conveyancing, which is not only beset with technical terms that have acquired specialised meanings, but is also based upon legislation drafted in the old practice of technical wording or provisions in identical terms to the old stamp duty provisions. For example, difficulties have emerged whereby 'excepting and reserving interests' is now treated by HMRC Stamp Taxes as a land exchange (see **Chapter 7**).

Yet these longstanding stamp duty terms do not necessarily continue to bear their former stamp duty meaning when construed in the context of the new legislation. Although it seems that, in practice, HMRC Stamp Taxes tends to carry forward the former interpretations, this presumption cannot be acted upon as a general principle since they are given, directly or indirectly, somewhat unusual meanings either expressly or impliedly. Even the new plain English provisions in the legislation have to be given very unplain meanings if the legislation is to work: for example, 'conveyance' must include leases, thereby providing a trap for the unwary. To approach the legislation upon the basis of stamp duty interpretations and practices is something that must be resisted.

At present much of the baggage of stamp duty continues to influence the practice of both HMRC Stamp Taxes and professionals in this area, such as the conduct of Enquiries which usually operate as though they were adjudications and are, in consequence, not conducted in accordance with the legislative requirements.[39] A cautionary note, however: both the charging provisions and the compliance obligations of both the taxpayer and HMRC Stamp Taxes are fundamentally different from those that applied to stamp duty but only the taxpayer is exposed to the risk of penalties and the costs of the Enquiries. Badly conducted Enquiries do not expose HMRC Stamp Taxes to financial sanctions although it may be a ground for applying to the relevant tier tribunal for an order that the Enquiry be terminated.[40] In addition, the power of HMRC Stamp Taxes to issue a 'discovery assessment' is protected notwithstanding an ineptly conducted Enquiry since included in the legislation are provisions limiting the knowledge of the transaction that HMRC is deemed to have[41] which might otherwise preclude it from effectively reopening the Enquiry.

---

[39] However, the high profile of promoters of aggressive tax mitigation arrangements has provided HMRC with an easy access to taxpayers through its power to demand information; see **Chapter 18**.

[40] FA 2003, Sched.10, para.24.

[41] FA 2003, Sched.10, para.30(4).

1.8 PLAIN ENGLISH

In some cases, the special 'plain English' meaning is made clear by a specific definition such as 'acquisition', although even here the definition frequently states that the word being defined 'includes' rather than 'means' various matters so that it is not exhaustive[42] and remains capable of expansion or modification by HMRC Stamp Taxes. In other cases the meaning of plain English words such as 'purchaser', 'completion' and 'conveyance' have to bear bizarre meanings such as 'purchaser' being a lessee or landlord depending upon context; and 'conveyance' and 'transfer' and 'assignment'[43] have to bear some very unusual meanings since 'conveyance' includes 'lease'[44] but 'transfer' *prima facie* does not. The special meanings for routine words have to be discovered from the overall context of the legislation. Moreover, as it is a transaction-based tax the interpretation of the legislation may be affected by the judicial adoption of a purposive construction principle[45] such as the comments of Carnworth J[46] in relation to stamp duty that in an area as technical as this the judge should not pay too much attention to the wording of the legislation but should seek to apply the 'spirit' of the Acts which no doubt will acquire a share of intellectual respectability and integrity as a 'purposive' construction of the legislation!

1.9 GENERAL PRINCIPLES

Although rushed into legislation after several previous legislative failures to block certain simple stamp duty mitigation arrangements, SDLT is not a stamp duty upon documents, it is, as noted above, a transaction-based tax governed by totally different principles and enforced in a totally different way. Unfortunately the background of attempting to block so-called loopholes by a totally new tax rather than deal with the particular arrangements[47] has dominated the drafting of the legislation and regulations, including attacks upon the basic subsale relief and the entire partnership regime which was considered essential to the fair application of

---

[42] *Oughtred* v. *IRC* [1960] AC 206.

[43] FA 2003, Sched.17A, para.12B.

[44] Compare *IRC* v. *Littlewoods Mail Order Stores Ltd* [1963] AC 135, HL; [1961] Ch 597, CA.

[45] *McGuckian* v. *IRC* [1997] STC 908.

[46] See also the judgment in *LM Tenancies (No.1)* v. *IRC* [1996] STC 880 (on appeal [1998] STC 326) where interestingly the Court of Appeal did not adopt the reasons for the decision of Lindsay J at first instance in refusing the appeal and decided this case on different but equally dubious grounds. The comments of the Court of Appeal are only slightly less perplexing than those of Lindsay J in *Parinv* v. *IRC* [1998] STC 305 to the effect that a document does not exist until properly stamped without considering how HMRC Stamp Taxes could stamp something that does not exist! Again the Court of Appeal wisely rejected all of his views, but were themselves in fundamental error.

[47] Which has clearly failed since HMRC Stamp Taxes has attempted to introduce statutory general anti-avoidance provisions (FA 2003, ss.75A–75C; see **1.33**) which are themselves defective.

stamp duty for over 200 years.[48] This means that it is difficult, if not impossible, to find anything approaching a coherent and consistent structure for the new tax. The following comments are, therefore, somewhat tentative and are merely intended to provide a limited tool for approaching the construction of the legislation, but the detailed applications and modifications of these principles are considered in later chapters.

1.10 BACKGROUND POLICIES: E-CONVEYANCING

The ostensible basis for the tax was fundamentally to deal with an oversight in relation to the investigation of electronic conveyancing. For a considerable time it was overlooked that where conveyancing was dealt with electronically there would be no document to stamp. It was, therefore, considered necessary to 'modernise' the tax in order to deal with the problems of a documentary tax applied to a non-documentary transaction. This had already been addressed by HMRC Stamp Taxes in relation to electronic trading of shares.[49] The initial consultation process was set up by HMRC Stamp Taxes, at which certain tax advisers were invited to divulge details of advice given to clients in relation to mitigation arrangements, to explain how the arrangements worked and how these could be countered by legislation. The process therefore appears designed more as a fishing expedition for anti-avoidance reasons rather than one to deal seriously with electronic conveyancing which was regarded as a long-term issue that could be dealt with subsequently. Some of the invited parties refused to continue to participate and the process was abandoned until there was an unfortunate disclosure of certain tax avoidance schemes in the *Financial Times* shortly before the Budget. This provoked a not unpredictable response from the then Chancellor of the Exchequer requiring properly effective anti-avoidance provisions, given the failures over several previous Finance Acts to deal with these situations.[50] The tax is, therefore, a panic response to certain anti-avoidance schemes and the basic legislation has been subject to subsequent amendments to deal with defects in the anti-avoidance nature of the original drafting. There are considerable problems because it is not a coherent simple tax built upon a structure but rather is a collection of anti-avoidance provisions not operating on a comprehensive basis.

---

[48] The relief is necessary to avoid the potential cascade effect of the cumulative tax costs on the price of land.

[49] See FA 1986, ss.86 and following dealing with stamp duty reserve tax where title could be transferred but without the need for writing such as by stock exchange transactions through CREST.

[50] Certain of these arrangements were very basic and had been subject to attack for many years, albeit unsuccessfully.

1.10.1 Main policy matters: anti-avoidance bases

Some background to the tax provides a useful guide to the stamp duty mitigation arrangements intended to be counteracted and how certain provisions are intended to deal with these arrangements. It may help explain how some of the many obscure charging provisions are meant to operate.

As indicated the legislation on various matters arising has to be viewed in terms of these policy considerations. Given the possible rise of a purposive construction to the legislation[51] the objectives of HMRC Stamp Taxes may become important techniques for construing the legislation; the parties and their advisers may therefore have to take the policy issues into account. Some of the types of arrangement targeted are listed below.

1.10.1.1 No document

As noted, the tax is a transaction tax and a document is not necessary. Informal or oral transactions may be effective notwithstanding Law of Property (Miscellaneous Provisions) Act 1989, s.2,[52] but for stamp duty purposes where a document could be avoided there was no tax charge.[53] The tax now applies to non-documented transactions. Surrenders of leases by operation of law are now chargeable transactions.

1.10.1.2 Deferring payment of tax by postponing the execution of documents

Stamp duty could not arise until the document was executed; it was, therefore, relatively straightforward to postpone the payment of tax by delaying documentation. In order to combat this routine device, a charge to tax now arises prior to the completion or other execution of the document. Obviously, merely making a contract the chargeable event would be too dramatic a change so events between contract and completion have to be monitored in order to determine whether a charge arises.[54]

1.10.1.3 Variable consideration

It was possible to mitigate the impact of stamp duty by arranging for consideration to be 'uncertain'. This arrangement is no longer possible because various rules now require the tax to be prepared on a provisional or estimated basis and to be retrospectively adjusted when the final circumstances are known.

---

[51] See, for example, Collector of Stamp Revenue v. Arrowtown Assets Ltd [2003] HKCFA 47.
[52] See *Yaxley* v. *Gotts* [1999] 3 WLR 1217; see **10.2**.
[53] Carlill v. Carbolic Smoke Ball Co [1892] 2 QB 484.
[54] FA 2003, s.44; see **Chapter 3**.

1.10.1.4 *Value shifting*

It was a useful technique for mitigating stamp duty to organise property in such a way that value could be moved without the need for writing. For example, a person acquiring land could enter into some form of a restrictive covenant which would depress the value of the land. There would be no charge to stamp duty upon the restrictive covenant. Subsequently, the purchaser would make a payment for the release of the restrictive covenant which was not a conveyance or transfer of property on sale. Likewise, dealings in licences and similar arrangements that can be cancelled without charge were not uncommon. Legislation relating to SDLT deals with this in two ways:

1. Many such arrangements are now 'chargeable interests'.[55] The definition includes interests in or rights over land such as rights of way and restrictive covenants. The definition is extended[56] to include obligations and rights affecting the value of land and this has been extended to certain covenants in leases.[57] In consequence, attempts to depress the value of land, by carving out rights or obligations, is likely to produce multiple charges to tax. Given the approach of HMRC Stamp Taxes to the limited scope for 'excepting and reserving' interests and treating these as being exchanges[58] there may be charges upon the creation of the rights and there will be payments for the 'acquisition' in the form of the release of the rights for a chargeable consideration.

2. Where the arrangements for depressing the value are not chargeable interests they may be caught by other specific anti-avoidance legislation. For example, mortgages and other forms of security are not chargeable interests,[59] but attempts to depress the value of land by creating a mortgage over the property prior to sale are likely to encounter difficulties because of the provisions deeming the chargeable consideration to include the amount of the mortgage liability assumed or rearranged after the transaction.[60] Licences (at least where they are true licences and not some form of *profit à prendre* such as mineral licences[61] or some form of tenancy) and tenancies at will are not chargeable interests. However, in relation to the statutory general anti-avoidance provisions[62] dealings in non-chargeable interests can be 'scheme transactions' and therefore any money paid for these arrangements will have

---

[55] FA 2003, s.48; see **2.12**.
[56] FA 2003, s.48(1)(b).
[57] FA 2003, Sched.17A, para.10.
[58] FA 2003, s.47; Sched.4, para.5; see **Chapter 7**.
[59] FA 2003, s.48(2).
[60] FA 2003, Sched.4, para.8 (as amended).
[61] See T&E Homes v. Robinson [1979] STC 351; Bocardo SA v. Star Energy UK Onshore Ltd [2010] 3 All ER 975.
[62] FA 2003, ss.75A–75C; see **1.33**.

to be taken into account when computing the deemed chargeable consideration for the notional transaction.[63]

1.10.2 Title issues

1.10.2.1 General

The fundamental change in the nature of the tax has considerable practical implications for routine conveyancing. Some of these are beneficial such as the fact that the landlord's counterpart lease is no longer taxable and can be utilised in court to enforce payment of the rent or other provisions in the lease. Others are not so beneficial and require major changes in practice, particularly in relation to completion arrangements. The provisions of contracts dealing with situations where the vendor has not yet obtained registration of the title, including but not limited to subsale situations,[64] will require modification, such as requiring the vendor to produce a land transaction return certificate (SDLT 5) since there will be no duly stamped transfer to produce. Major changes are also required in relation to investigations of title and the warranties, indemnities and undertakings required to be included in the contract.[65]

These policy (i.e. anti-avoidance) issues have produced considerable complications. The original idea for electronic conveyancing was that the payment of the tax should not be a precondition to registration and any disputes as to the amount of the tax, availability of exemptions or otherwise should be dealt with subsequently behind the registration. Unfortunately, there have been two key problems in relation to the introduction of this simple policy of removing the payment of tax as an obstacle to a person's ownership of property. These are, broadly:

1. Title may not be registered, electronically or otherwise, where there is a notifiable transaction unless an appropriate certificate is produced to the effect that some tax is paid.[66] This simple proposition has been complicated to deal with non-taxable transactions. It was originally provided[67] that where a transaction was not a notifiable and taxable or related transaction the parties could sign a certificate to this effect indicating the nature of the transaction which could be relied upon by the Land Registry. The former self-certificate (SDLT 60) and the certificates for exemption from the fixed stamp duty[68] provided a mechanism whereby the Land Registry could pass over the problem of whether the transaction was or was not taxable to HMRC Stamp

---

[63] FA 2003, s.75A(5).

[64] See Chapter 5.

[65] Additionally, major changes in relation to the warranties and indemnities and valuations on share purchase are required.

[66] FA 2003, s.79(1) (as amended).

[67] FA 2003, s.79 (as originally enacted); Sched.11.

[68] Stamp Duty (Exempt Instruments) Regulations 1987, SI 1987/516.

Taxes. Unfortunately, self-certificates were removed by FA 2008. This has created problems in certain Land Registry offices where some employees in the exercise of their 'local discretion' believe that they have powers to interfere with transactions if they believe that SDLT should be payable or insufficient SDLT may have been paid or even that the parties are embarking upon some tax avoidance arrangements. These powers claimed by the Land Registry which are considerably in excess of those available to HMRC Stamp Taxes (see **1.12.3**, **14.13** and **18.4**) mean that there can be considerable difficulties in obtaining registration.

2.   There are many situations where in order to obtain registration it is not sufficient to produce simply the appropriate Revenue certificate (SDLT 5). Other documentation may be required. The problem is, therefore, obtaining a Revenue certificate (SDLT 5) that will be accepted by a particular officer or employee in the Land Registry notwithstanding the clear terminology of FA 2003, s.79(1) or that will persuade the relevant employees that the transaction is not notifiable pursuant to FA 2003, s.77A.

1.10.2.2   Completion documentation

Title issues involve not only the question of what is required in terms of contractual obligations and documents to be delivered at completion (see **Chapter 3**) but also whether the activities of the vendor or landlord are themselves consistent with producing good title and what title documents and investigations are required from the vendor or landlord. There may be situations where, for example, the issue is very simple; namely whether the vendor or landlord is proposing to file the necessary land transaction return (SDLT 1), obtain the necessary certificate and secure registration of his title so that he can pass on a potentially registerable title to his purchaser or tenant.

1.11   LACK OF FINALITY

Much of SDLT is on a provisional or estimated basis requiring retrospective adjustment. In consequence, there is a 'lack of finality' and in many situations:

*   this lack of finality as far as the original taxpayer is concerned is passed over to successors in title;[69] therefore
*   the taxation issues for the successor in title, such as a purchaser of land or the assignee of a lease, may be dependent upon the taxation history of the vendor or landlord. The failure to produce the necessary information could make the title unsaleable because the purchaser cannot comply with or compute his tax liability in the future.

---

[69]   See, for example, FA 2003, s.81A; Sched.17A, para.12; see **8.60**.

For example, where there is the assignment of a lease after the expiration of more than five years from the grant of the lease the assignee may, at the expiration of the contractual term, hold over. Where the lease has not been excluded from the provisions of the Landlord and Tenant Act 1954 (as amended) his holding over will have SDLT consequences.[70] In such a situation the assignee of the lease will need to know the history because this will form a key factor in computing his taxation liability and whether he needs to notify. Similarly, a detailed history of all rent reviews during the first five years and thereafter will now be key documents of title.[71]

1.11.1 Mortgagees

The practice of retaining money pending the registration of title has been fundamentally altered. Mortgagees concerned about their security pending registration and perfection of their security no longer need to retain substantial sums for a significant period in case of HMRC challenges. Indeed, retention is, itself, not a particularly useful protection.

HMRC Stamp Taxes is no longer prepared to accept payment from a third party unless that payment is accompanied by a land transaction return (SDLT 1) with the appropriate declaration signed by the correct person. A mortgagee cannot, as such, sign the declaration on the land transaction return (SDLT 1). In consequence, where the purchaser or mortgagor has not completed the SDLT 1 HMRC Stamp Taxes has, hitherto, refused to allow registration to proceed upon payment of the tax from a third party. In this situation the Land Registry will not proceed with an application by the mortgagee to register the title since there will not be the necessary Revenue certificate (SDLT 5). There are dangers that in this, and other situations, the title will become 'blocked' and it is necessary to ensure that the appropriate documentation is available so that title registration can proceed and the security be perfected.

For example, where there is a sublease at a premium which is to form the basis of a charge to secure borrowing the sublessee will not be in a position to register his title until the immediate landlord has registered his title. Should there be difficulties with the landlord's paperwork or a refusal to pay the tax then his title cannot be registered; this blocks the title of the sublessee and means that the mortgagee cannot obtain a full charge over the legal title. The fact that the sublessee may have retained money from the premium and/or his mortgagee may have retained funds out of the loan will not assist because they are not entitled to pay the tax and cannot sign the landlord's land transaction return (SDLT 1) in order to obtain a certificate so that the Land Registry can proceed. They will need to retain only the amount shown as tax payable in Box 15 of SDLT 1 and can release those funds once the SDLT 5 has been produced and acted upon by the Land Registry.[72]

---

[70] FA 2003, Sched.17A, paras.3, 4, 9 and 9A; see **8.47**.
[71] FA 2003, Sched.17A, paras.13, 14 and 15; see **8.37**.
[72] However, the security issues are not all straightforward commercially. Since the tax charge can arise before completion and even when the rights of the purchaser remain conditional because of the

Essentially the Land Registry no longer has the power to investigate the stamping of the documentation and cannot challenge the certificate presented to it simply because it believes that insufficient tax has been paid,[73] although there can still sometimes be difficulties (see above). However, professional advisers would be wise to include terms in the contract calling for the production of the information relating to title and completion that is required to satisfy the Land Registry.

1.11.2 Sanctity of title

The fact that the incorrect amount of SDLT has been paid does not affect title. For example, the taxpayer may form the opinion that he is entitled to an exemption from the tax or that the market value/estimated rent upon which he calculates the tax is correct, file the land transaction return (SDLT 1) on that basis, and pay the tax shown in Box 15 on that return. Since the powers and resources available to HMRC Stamp Taxes to challenge the return are limited, other than for minor errors such as incorrect arithmetic, it is highly probable that eventually[74] an SDLT 5 certificate will be issued which can be acted upon. The taxpayer will then make the appropriate change to the register supported by the SDLT 5 certificate. Legal title will pass to the taxpayer, and the mortgagee will obtain good security, upon registration. The fact that subsequently HMRC Stamp Taxes on an Enquiry establishes that insufficient tax has been paid because, for example, the exemption claimed in SDLT 1 is not available or the market value included in Box 10 thereof was too low, does not affect the validity of the legal title of the taxpayer and his mortgagees and tenants. There is no power for HMRC or the Land Registry to remove the entry from the register in such circumstances.

This applies notwithstanding that there is, as considered later in this chapter (see **1.25**), no real finality in relation to many areas of SDLT; without unchallengeable registration rights titles would become extremely uncertain. The possibility that a title once registered, whether correctly or incorrectly, can be removed or modified

---

complexities of 'substantial performance' (see **Chapter 3**), taxpayers such as developers who need to raise money in order to fund the new tax charges that arise at an early stage in the transaction will find that the security which they can offer, such as a conditional agreement for lease, will frequently not be entirely satisfactory to potential funders. The lender of funds cannot protect himself by taking transfers in escrow or deposits of deeds and procure registration by executing the documents because he cannot obtain a Revenue certificate (SDLT 5) or registration simply by paying the tax. The parties therefore may have to consider as part of the funding arrangements powers to call for transfers of the legal title by the mortgagee and possibly an appropriate power of attorney to act as agent in the signing of the land transaction return (SDLT 1) pursuant to FA 2003, s.76; Sched.10, paras.1(1)(c) and 1A.

[73]   In practice, it seems certain offices of the Land Registry believe that their powers pursuant to Stamp Act 1891, s.17, etc. have survived and may seek to enlarge their power to investigate tax issues; see **1.10.2**.

[74]   HMRC Stamp Taxes has sought to blame solicitors for the delays in the system (see, e.g. *Daily Telegraph*, 15 August 2005), although it appears that many of the problems are its own errors, or arise because of incorrect advice provided by the 'helpline' which cannot be relied upon to bind HMRC Stamp Taxes or even to support an application for a mitigation of penalties. Moreover, it seems many of the rejected returns are rejected in error by HMRC Stamp Taxes.

by the Land Registry whether on its own initiative or at the instigation of HMRC Stamp Taxes for good reason would introduce chaos into the system of registration of title.

For example, if a lessee files a land transaction return (SDLT 1) in respect of his lease upon the basis that it is exempt for any of the permitted reasons but this claim for exemption or the market value taken into the self-assessment is successfully challenged by HMRC Stamp Taxes the suggestion that HMRC Stamp Taxes could, pending the payment of the tax, require the registration to be frozen would block title and cancellation would mean reinstating the original party to the transaction as the registered owner of the property. These problems would, of course, be even worse where the property has been sold to a third party. For example, if adopted as a principle of general application, the taxpayer would find himself deprived of title so that his mortgagee would suddenly lose his security and any persons who are successors in title will also find their title taken away. This would apply to subsequent purchasers or to lessees or sublessees. Should this be the situation then the original vendor of the property, for example, would become once again the owner of the property and will be required to deal with documentation in order to put the property in place once the SDLT position was resolved. This could be a considerable problem where the relevant party has been dissolved or has died. It is by no means obvious that the parties could rely upon the original documentation in order to restore the transaction to the register and to deal with all of the subsequent transactions relating to the property. For these reasons any suggestion that title once registered can be cancelled or modified would produce potential chaos in the system and cannot be right because it is completely unworkable.

1.12 COMPLETION ARRANGEMENTS AND DOCUMENTATION

It will have been noticed from the above comments that particular documents may be required from the vendor. The contract should specify these and require them to be delivered at completion to avoid difficulties later should the vendor disappear.

For example, where the vendor has not been registered in respect of his acquisition, such as in a subsale situation, the question of whether he has paid or is in the process of paying the tax is an issue and appropriate undertakings will be required as to the delivery of the land transaction return, payment of the tax and prompt procedure with the registration process. Until the vendor has become registered or can produce a land transaction certificate (SDLT 5)[75] he cannot deliver an instrument of transfer or lease that will be recognised as effective by the Land Registry since it will not be executed by a person whose name appears on the register.[76] This

---

[75] Formerly the Land Registry would usually act on the basis of a letter from the relevant party explaining why he is not required to file a land transaction return (SDLT 1) and does not need to produce a Revenue certificate (SDLT 5). This practice has been largely abandoned and the Land Registry requires the relevant party to file a return (and consequently face the risk of an Enquiry).

[76] But see **Chapter 5** on the machinery to be adopted in certain subsale situations.

may contain references to direct transfers from the registered owner to the subpurchaser so that intervention by the initial purchaser is not required to pass the registered title. The charge upon third parties who receive the directed grant of a lease depends upon the history of the transaction and, in particular, the state of substantial performance of any contract.[77]

1.12.1 Registration of title

Registration can only be achieved by production of an appropriate[78] certificate, namely an SDLT 5 certificate to the effect that a land transaction return has been completed. Non-payment of tax by a vendor or landlord may in consequence in many, but not all, cases provide a title issue for a purchaser or lessee where his title is registerable. It is not sufficient that the purchaser can produce an executed Land Registry transfer and an appropriate certificate if the unregistered person executing the transfer as transferor cannot produce the necessary documentation to enable his registration so that the transfer can be recognised by the Land Registry.[79] In consequence, it is important for solicitors to ensure that the SDLT 1 is properly completed and ready by completion in order to ensure prompt registration. The contractual provisions relating to completion should, therefore, require production of the necessary certificate at some stage and a prudent purchaser may prefer not to make payment until the paper chain is completed. It is no longer possible simply to retain a sum equal to the vendor's stamp tax liability because if the vendor has not completed, signed and delivered the necessary land transaction returns it is not possible for the purchaser to rectify the situation by paying the tax. In the absence of what appears superficially to be the correctly signed and completed return (SDLT 1) HMRC Stamp Taxes will refuse to accept the payment and to issue the appropriate certificate (SDLT 5). Where it is necessary to deal with the Land Registry an unregistered vendor should, it seems, be required to establish that he has delivered the appropriate returns, if any are needed, to HMRC Stamp Taxes together with payment and an undertaking to pursue such notification expeditiously so that the purchaser will be in a position to produce his complete documentation to the Land Registry within the registration time limits (note that the SDLT timetable is different from and not necessarily compatible with the registration regime).

These issues do, however, raise practical problems even in routine conveyancing since there has been no attempt to harmonise the SDLT compliance requirements with the Land Registry requirements, particularly where the SDLT documentation differs from the Land Registry documentation such as where the registered owners

---

[77] FA 2003, Sched.17A, para.12B; see **Chapter 8**.

[78] FA 2003, s.79(1) (as amended) but it is no longer necessary for any tax shown by that return to have been paid (FA 2003, s.76 (as amended)).

[79] These issues seem to be less of a problem in Scotland where it is possible to deal with the tax 'over the counter' in Edinburgh producing the necessary certificate in a few minutes. In England the target of HMRC Stamp Taxes is a turnaround time of five days. Filing electronically does, however, appear to produce a fairly rapid response, but lacks flexibility in dealing with possible errors in the return.

or applicants for registration are nominees so that the names on the Land Registry transfer and SDLT 5 certificate differ. Notwithstanding the detailed regime for tax, the real timetable is dictated by Land Registry requirements (see **1.12.2**).

1.12.2 Timetable: completion and other problems

The land transaction return (SDLT 1) has to be filed under penalty and payment made to HMRC Stamp Taxes within 30 days after the effective date; but this timetable is misleading. The deadline means that the cheque has to be received by HMRC Stamp Taxes by that date[80] so that earlier posting is required. The major practical problem is that the SDLT timetable pays no regard to the requirements of the land registration regime with its own timetables which frequently have shorter deadlines. It will be noted that it is necessary to file the land transaction return in time for it to be processed and the certificate (SDLT 5) to be returned in time for the documents to be submitted to the Land Registry on time. Electronic filing produces a rapid but unchecked response in the form of the SDLT 5.

In other cases of manual filing problems may arise. This type of filing puts great pressure on HMRC Stamp Taxes to process documents speedily which, of course, restricts the scope for scrutiny of the land transaction return and any covering letter or application for a post-transaction ruling. The initial undertaking was to turn all returns around within a maximum of five days. However, to cover the possibility that this time limit might not be achieved the Land Registry has continued its practice of provisional registration. If 20 working days have elapsed from the filing of the land transaction return and nothing has been received from HMRC Stamp Taxes the application for registration can be processed in order to protect priorities and timetables. In practice the ability to file electronically with virtual instantaneous return of the SDLT 5 has removed this issue, but where the filing is of return by post, this must not be delayed.

1.12.3 Land Registry issues

Fundamental issues of principle underlie the above comments. One of these is the power of the Land Registry to challenge the certificate produced by the parties (see further **1.10.2**). There is no equivalent to the stamp duty provisions of s.17 of the Stamp Act 1891 which imposed penalties for registering an insufficiently stamped document. In consequence, the Land Registry has no general power to refuse to act upon a document that appears to be correct, even though subsequently it may prove to be incorrect. For example, an SDLT 5 certificate based upon the intra-group relief has to be accepted and the Land Registry cannot require the person presenting the documents to justify the claim in support of that exemption. A frequent exercise of the Land Registry's powers in this area concerns subsales and surrenders and regrants of leases where it is provided that the new lease is not consideration for the

---

[80]   FA 2003, s.76.

surrender of the existing lease.[81] This means that normally the surrender will be for no chargeable consideration and will fall within the exemption contained in FA 2003, Sched.3, para.1. As a result, it is not a notifiable transaction requiring an SDLT 5 for registration.[82] It seems the Land Registry has not always acted upon this analysis or has sought to enforce the tax beyond the requirements of FA 2003, s.78A.

Moreover, it is not always necessary to require the immediate vendor to produce the SDLT 5 certificate. This will apply in cases where the registration of the vendor, or his nominee, is not required because he will not be a person executing the Land Registry transfer in favour of the purchaser. Examples include a routine subsale pursuant to a previous uncompleted contract, or an assignment of the benefit of a contract for sale or agreement for lease, where the relevant documentation will be executed by the original vendor who may be the registered owner of the property.[83] As there will be no transfer or grant by the immediate vendor there will be no need to produce the SDLT 5 certificate for the intermediate vendor who is not seeking registration. An explanatory letter to the Land Registry may be required because the SDLT 5 will have a different vendor from the transferor identified in the Land Registry documentation. This question of registered title can lead to mismatches between the stamp documentation and the Land Registry documentation. The Land Registry transfer will refer to the registered owner as vendor and identify the person into whose name the property is to be transferred.

There may be situations where nominees are involved (on the problems surrounding nominees and bare trustees see **Chapter 10**). However, the requirements of the legislation are that the land transaction return (SDLT 1) must identify the true vendor, i.e. the beneficial owner and the true purchaser or lessee (on many aspects of these issues see **Chapter 17**). Thus the purchaser who requires property to be transferred into nominee names will have filed a land transaction return (SDLT 1) in his own name as beneficial owner and the Revenue certificate (SDLT 5)[84] will refer to the beneficial owner. There will, therefore, be different names on the various documentation. It seems that in these situations the Land Registry will usually act upon the basis of a covering letter explaining the differences between the transfer and the certificate. It will be necessary for an adviser to investigate whether the title is actually registered in the appropriate name but it will also be necessary to check whether the person who appears on the document is the relevant party. This issue can arise in relation to subsales and similar arrangements of purchases from plan where the intermediate party will not appear on the register but the transaction to be reported is that between the first purchaser and the subpurchaser or assignee of the right to call for the lease. It is not necessarily possible, therefore, to rely upon the name appearing on the register or appearing on the contract since these may be nominees or undisclosed agents. The details will be required in order to make a

---

[81] FA 2003, Sched.17A, paras.9 and 16.
[82] FA 2003, s.77 (as amended).
[83] FA 2003, s.45 (as amended) and Sched.17A, para.12B.
[84] Stamp Duty Land Tax (Administration) Regulations 2003, SI 2003/2837, reg.5.

correct land transaction return (SDLT 1) and the co-operation of all parties will be required in dealing with the Land Registry such as some covering letter of declaration of trust or other power of attorney or documentation which enables the vendor to act as such.

This situation can also arise in relation to certain cases where the intermediate vendor has received a Land Registry transfer since there is a limited relief for subsales.[85] This relief for SDLT is not linked to the absence of transfers as was the case with the equivalent relief from stamp duty.[86] The relief is available notwithstanding that the first purchaser has received a Land Registry transfer from the original vendor. If the conditions for the relief are met there is no chargeable transaction, notwithstanding that the transfer has been delivered. In this situation it is sufficient to obtain registration of title by producing the two transfers so that the names of the parties match the land register, together with an SDLT 5 in relation to the sale to the ultimate purchaser/transferee together with a covering letter explaining that no SDLT 5 is required in respect of the transfer from the original vendor to the first purchaser because the conditions of FA 2003, s.45 are believed to have been satisfied. The fact that subsequently, upon an Enquiry, HMRC Stamp Taxes establishes that the subsale relief was not available is irrelevant to the Land Registry entries and cannot affect the validity of the entry of the ultimate purchaser.

It is assumed that similar practices will be applied where pursuant to the equivalent provision for leases[87] no charge arises upon the original tenant where there has been an assignment of the right to call for the lease (whatever that may mean) before the agreement for lease is substantially performed.[88] In this case the liability for the original SDLT passes to the assignee and is added to any other chargeable consideration that he may be providing directly or indirectly. It is expected that no SDLT 5 will be requested by the Land Registry in relation to the original tenant and that it will be satisfied by a covering letter explaining that no charge has arisen in respect of the original tenant pursuant to FA 2003, Sched.17A, para.12B.

1.13 TRANSITIONAL TITLES

For many years to come, vendors and, particularly, landlords, will be relying upon title based on the stamp duty regime.[89] This will apply not merely to titles acquired before 1 December 2003 but also to titles vested after that date pursuant to

---

[85] FA 2003, s.45 (as amended); see **Chapter 5**.

[86] Stamp Act 1891, s.58(4) and (5).

[87] FA 2003, Sched.17A, para.12B; see **8.9**.

[88] There are many technical problems with the drafting of these provisions which, if taken strictly, do not always match conveyancing practice in this area. Until the law is clarified, parties may be making errors but this should not affect the title registered for the new lease.

[89] This issue will also have substantive consequences. For example, holding over a lease is potentially a chargeable transaction for the purposes of SDLT but it is currently accepted by HMRC Stamp Taxes that, notwithstanding the technical issues in this area, no charge to tax arises where the

transactions entered into prior to that date which, although completed on or after that date, remain subject to stamp duty pursuant to the provisions of FA 2003, Sched.19 (as amended, in some cases retrospectively, so as to transfer transactions from stamp duty to SDLT). Since incorrect payment of SDLT will not produce a duly stamped instrument sufficient to satisfy the title and admissible evidence rules,[90] this will leave the purchaser and others vulnerable to attack upon their titles[91] and the need to pay stamp duty. HMRC Stamp Taxes is receiving land transaction returns (SDLT 1) and payment without investigating whether the transitional provisions apply and the document is strictly chargeable with stamp duty. This means that where it is a stamp duty transaction, professional advisers need to be aware of the transitional arrangements not merely for the completion of outstanding contracts because of the residual risk that the wrong tax may be paid, but also because the vendor may have paid the wrong tax or insufficient stamp duty or because the Land Registry is still obliged to challenge stamp duty payments but cannot challenge SDLT certificates.

1.14   TITLE INVESTIGATION AND DUE DILIGENCE

1.14.1   Payment of tax and title: third party problems

Although to some extent the payment of SDLT is essential in many routine situations in order to obtain registration of title so as to make certain entries in the land register in the relevant jurisdiction, the evidence and title issues of stamp duty do not apply. They have, however, been replaced with completely different and more complex problems:

1. Obtaining registration of title, including the pending change of the title where the vendor or landlord has not been registered at the time when he is required to complete and deliver legal title. There are now different documents required at completion to aid the registration process to satisfy the Land Registry.

2. Investigating the title of the vendor. In many cases the SDLT obligations of the vendor in relation to his previous acquisition or later dealings in relation to the property are dealt with initially only on a provisional basis (see **1.24** and **1.25**). In consequence:

    (a) there may be a statutory passing of the outstanding tax obligations from the vendor to the purchaser;[92] or

---

lease being held over is one that was within the former stamp duty regime. There may also be issues for linked transactions and other transactions; see FA 2003, Sched.19, paras.7 and 9.

[90]   Stamp Act 1891, s.14.

[91]   It may also mean that the SDLT has been paid unnecessarily so that it may be necessary for the purchaser to make an error or mistake repayment claim pursuant to FA 2003, Sched.10, para.34, which is subject to time limits.

[92]   FA 2003, Sched.17A, para.12.

(b)   special charges may apply, in effect, counteracting or cancelling any relief obtained by the vendor by taxing the transaction on a totally artificial basis so that the purchaser's tax liability is totally different from the actual transaction (see **1.23**). The third party may be affected by the vendor's tax notwithstanding that it does not pass, as such, with the property. This can apply in cases such as rent review or holding over (see **8.60**). This issue will be complicated where the vendor's tax position is not final; so that the purchaser's own tax position may be in limbo or subject to retrospective adjustment until the vendor's tax liability is revised.

3.   The third party's tax charge is influenced by the tax payable upon the original acquisition of the vendor or even his predecessors in title. The assignee of a lease is liable not merely for the filing of land transaction returns for the immediate transaction but also for any additional SDLT arising, for example, in respect of the vendor's acquisition. Moreover, the assignee may be entitled to a tax refund if the original tax estimate should prove to be excessive. In consequence, appropriate undertakings, warranties or indemnities as regards making the necessary returns, paying over underpaid or overpaid tax, dealing with late payment, interest and penalties and providing the necessary information to enable these and future obligations to be performed properly will be required in addition to the warranties that all land transaction returns relevant to the chargeable interest have been prepared on a proper basis and have been filed.

1.14.2   Post-transaction issues

In addition to the problems of inheriting the vendor's open tax position the purchaser's or lessee's tax position may be affected by subsequent actions of the vendor or landlord or even other persons not parties to the transaction such as other tenants of the landlord, or later linked transactions which retrospectively affect the purchaser's tax position (see **1.24**). This risk may require undertakings by the relevant party to produce full disclosure of the SDLT history of the chargeable interest concerned including potentially commercially sensitive information and, in certain cases, the purchaser or lessee may be required to supply information to the vendor or landlord in order to enable the latter to deal with his outstanding tax position. The assignee may also require information to be supplied by the vendor because certain obligations to notify HMRC Stamp Taxes and to recalculate and pay the tax pass to him.

1.14.3   Interaction of tax and title

As a transaction-based rather than a document-based tax, SDLT is not a title issue nor an issue for the rules of evidence in quite the same way as was the case with stamp duty. As noted above, the fact that a person has not paid SDLT or may have paid an incorrect amount should not affect the validity of his title and any registration of that title remains effective although there are difficulties in practice with the Land Registry and there will be difficulties in obtaining registration where the vendor has not obtained registration of his title because, for example, he has not received a Revenue certificate (SDLT 5). However, now that it is possible to obtain the certificate without payment (see **14.13**), non-payment of tax is a less significant problem in practice. For example, the fact that a transfer was registered on the basis that the transfer was exempt because of intra-group relief, which is subsequently successfully challenged by HMRC Stamp Taxes or is clawed back by subsequent degrouping, does not affect the validity of the original registration and any charge over that title remains effective. Neither the Land Registry[93] nor HMRC Stamp Taxes has power either to challenge the application for registration or to alter the register once the title has been changed.[94] This alleviates the problems surrounding the quality of the title offered to purchasers and lessees and provides better security for mortgagees and an easier situation for dealing with retentions for stamp taxes at completion.[95]

1.15 PARTICULAR PROBLEMS WITH LEASES

Title investigation within the new stamp taxes regime, unfortunately, creates a wide area of new problems for purchasers, particularly in the area of the acquisition of existing leases.[96] These problem areas arise because of the general lack of finality for many areas of SDLT even though the return has been the subject-matter of an Enquiry.

It must be noted that certain title investigation areas may require disclosure of highly confidential personal or business information such as details of business turnover or profits where the rent reserved by a lease is linked to such matters. Prudent advisers should therefore ensure that appropriate provisions are contained in the contract since there is no statutory power to demand the information. It is the taxpayer's own obligation to negotiate a contractual right to call for or to require disclosure of the information. It may be necessary in the absence of express provisions in the contract to test the limits of the usual types of covenant for further assurances or what is required pursuant to full title guarantee provisions. It is not

---

[93] In practice, certain employees of the Land Registry claim power to reject applications even where there is a Revenue certificate (SDLT 5).

[94] However, it is probable that HMRC Stamp Taxes will seek to develop the common law crimes of forgery and fraud by seeking to prosecute for obtaining registration by deception where incorrect returns are produced. This is in addition to the special sanction imposed by FA 2003, ss.95 and 96.

[95] The same principles will apply in relation to unregistered titles; the non-payment of the correct amount of SDLT is not generally a title issue.

[96] Problems can apply in other areas; a wide range of new warranties and indemnities is needed and there should be changes in valuation practices in relation to shares and company acquisition (see **Chapter 13** for further discussion of these issues).

possible to obtain the information from HMRC Stamp Taxes because much of the information will not be notifiable to it otherwise than by the taxpayer. HMRC Stamp Taxes will be dependent upon the taxpayer to supply the information notwithstanding that he is not a party to the transaction which gives rise to the notification obligation, i.e. the person who is under the obligation to produce the information is the very person who is dependent upon other persons to notify him of the relevant subsequent events to which he is not necessarily a party. Additionally, HMRC Stamp Taxes will not disclose the information because of taxpayer confidentiality and data protection. Moreover, since each notifiable event requires a separate land transaction return with its unique bar code reference number, rather than a transaction or property reference, any person seeking information will have to produce a complete list of all such bar code references.

1.16 INVESTIGATIONS, REQUISITIONS AND TITLE ISSUES

The areas for investigation and/or requiring the production of information and indemnities include the following.

1.16.1 Variable consideration

The following points should be borne in mind in transactions where the vendor acquired his interest in the land, whether the whole or only the part that is being sold or leased in the current transaction, for a variable consideration such as an overage payment or a long-term clawback arrangement (see **Chapter 4**).

1. In cases where the transaction involves a freehold or the assignment of a lease for a variable consideration[97] the vendor's tax position will have been dealt with on a provisional estimated basis until the variable consideration position is finally resolved, with consequent problems for executors, liquidators and others who may not be in a position to complete their administration of the estate or business because there are outstanding tax liabilities which pass to the successor in title to the chargeable interest in question. This open tax position remains with the vendor notwithstanding the disposal of all or part of that chargeable interest. In so far as the parties do not renegotiate the position with the original vendor or landlord, the vendor will require undertakings from the purchaser to provide information as to any dealings by himself or his successors in title that may have a bearing on the vendor's open tax position. Obviously the terms of any such renegotiation will have their own SDLT implications particularly if the purchaser in that transaction is, effectively, taking over the original purchaser's liability for the additional consideration. However, there are important practical issues if the legislation provides for

---

[97] The position differs where the variable payment is within the lease such as some form of overage premium; FA 2003, s.81A; Sched.17A, para.12.

the liabilities to pass to a person acquiring the chargeable interest. The personal representative, liquidator or other party will in theory cease to have any involvement with the tax. However, in practice, the person acquiring the chargeable interest may impose contractual obligations for notification and/or indemnities from the vendor which may be outstanding for many years so that the administration or liquidation cannot be concluded because of the possibilities of a claim under the contract.

2. Where the variable payment arose in connection with the grant of a new lease, whether in the form of a variable premium or variable rent (including rent reviews as well as turnover rents),[98] the position differs. It is provided that an assignee of such a lease takes over the outstanding tax position of the original tenant to deal with the variable premium or rent.[99] A full SDLT history will be required as well as provisions to deal with any overpayment or underpayment of tax made on the initial self-assessment by the original tenant and with any interest or penalties arising.

1.16.2 Assignees of leases

1. Since there is a deemed new lease liable to tax arising where there is an abnormal increase in the rent after the expiration of the fifth year of the term of the lease,[100] assignees of leases will require a full SDLT history of the lease, since the starting point for testing whether the increase is abnormal is not the passing rent immediately before the increase but the highest rent paid in any 12 consecutive calendar months during the first five years of the term of the lease. This is the assumed rent taken into account when calculating the tax due in respect of the grant of the lease.

2. A similar need for a full SDLT history is required by an assignee who may hold over a tenancy after the expiration of the contractual term by operation of law or who becomes entitled to a periodic tenancy which continues beyond the current period, because the holding over or continuation of the tenancy is treated as an extension of the original lease or tenancy for a period of one year.[101] This requires the current tenant to revisit the original self-assessment or any amended or subsequent adjustment of the tax relating to the grant of the lease or tenancy and to reassess the original or latest tax return upon the basis of a lease for the deemed longer term. The current tenant is liable to pay any additional tax arising. As this requires a retrospective adjustment of the previous assessments the assignee will need full details of these.

3. It is specifically provided that it is the responsibility of the assignee of a lease to make a return and presumably pay any additional tax arising in connection

98   See Chapter 8.
99   FA 2003, Sched.17A, para.12.
100 FA 2003, Sched.17A, paras.14 and 15.
101 FA 2003, Sched.17A, paras.3 and 4; see **8.49** and following.

with a later linked transaction.[102] This will require complicated mutual contractual obligations because of what appears to be HMRC Stamp Taxes' view that assignees can be affected by later linked transactions notwithstanding that the legislation[103] requires the transaction to be between the same parties or persons connected with them (see **Chapter 4**). Each party will require disclosure from the other of details of any transaction which may be linked, particularly as the later linked transaction does not have to relate to the same property or chargeable interest. For example, where there are linked leases the nil rate slice, applicable to the aggregate net present value of the rents of the linked lease, has to be allocated between the various linked leases in the proportion that the levels of the individual rent values bear to the aggregate rents.[104] This allocation of the proportionate part of the nil rate slice will, of course, be relevant in calculating the tax due in respect of the lease such as on the first rent review or holding over as well as retrospectively in relation to the original grant. The assignee will require disclosure of the relevant amount.

4. Since subsequent events may affect the tax calculation retrospectively, such as successive linked leases arising pursuant to the exercise of an option to renew,[105] this would require a reallocation of the nil rate slice between that and any other linked leases which may affect, for example, the position of an assignee. The same consequences would also appear to follow from any holding over of any one or more of the linked leases. The parties to an assignment will, in consequence, require notification of any transaction that might have an impact on this allocation of the nil rate slice.

1.17 WARRANTIES AND INDEMNITIES

The parties to the particular transaction may find it necessary to require indemnities relating to the tax liability. For example, as so much of the initial assessment of SDLT is made on a provisional estimated basis there will be crucial questions of initial overpayment or underpayment of tax, together with related questions of interest and penalties for inadequate payment or inaccurate returns to be dealt with and liabilities and refunds to be allocated between the parties arising for subsequent retrospective adjustments in the overall tax position.

---

[102]   FA 2003, s.81A.
[103]   FA 2003, s.108.
[104]   FA 2003, Sched.5, para.2 (as amended).
[105]   FA 2003, Sched.17A, para.5.

1.18 TRANSACTION TAX NOT DOCUMENTS

As noted above, unlike stamp duty, SDLT is based upon transactions and not documentation.[106] It is specifically provided that the tax arises notwithstanding that there is no document,[107] and a charge will frequently be triggered by events and the actions of the parties such as obtaining the keys or entering to fit out the premises (see **3.8**) prior to formal completion in the sense of the delivery of the written conveyance or lease.[108] This is reinforced by statutory provisions that the tax applies to transactions taking effect pursuant to statute, court order or by operation of law.[109] In many cases without written instruments in the appropriate form, whether deed, written contract or memorandum, there will be no valid and enforceable transaction,[110] but this is not an invariable principle.[111] The cases indicate that unwritten arrangements can be effective to pass title to land. This is not to state that documentation is irrelevant for the purposes of SDLT. In certain cases, 'completion' by a written instrument may be the event giving rise to the charge to tax[112] or to reporting obligations or even, as in the case of new leases, a second chargeable event in respect of the same transaction[113] and it may affect the rules for the effective date.[114] In addition, the drafting of the documentation may influence whether there is a charge to tax, such as whether this is a lease or a licence[115] or the extent of the charge, such as whether there is a payment by instalments or a periodical payment.[116]

This transaction basis of SDLT means that:

- although apart from options and pre-emption rights[117] the making of the contract is not, of itself, a chargeable transaction the liability to notify the transaction and pay the tax may arise early in the transaction and before completion. This can occur where the contract is still conditional such as where a prospective tenant goes into possession of the land to be demised in order to fit out the premises before the landlord has consented to the assignment or grant of the sublease;[118]

---

[106] FA 2003, ss.44(2), 45(2) and 45A(2).

[107] FA 2003, s.42(2).

[108] There are many potential problems arising from the gap between the effective date and completion. For example, it will not technically be possible to prove that the conditions for relief have been satisfied since these actions (such as the allotment of the consideration shares and their registration) have yet to be performed. HMRC Stamp Taxes has not yet addressed these issues; see **1.24** on 'wait and see'.

[109] FA 2003, s.43(2).

[110] Law of Property (Miscellaneous Provisions) Act 1989, s.2.

[111] See, for example, *Yaxley* v. *Gotts* [1999] 3 WLR 1217; *Henry* v. *Henry* [2010] 1 All ER 988; *RTS Flexible Systems Ltd* v. *Molkerei Alois* [2010] 3 All ER 1.

[112] FA 2003, s.44(8); but see **3.9.2** on issues of phased completions.

[113] FA 2003, Sched.17A, para.12A.

[114] FA 2003, s.119.

[115] FA 2003, Sched.17A, para.19 (as amended).

[116] FA 2003, s.52.

[117] FA 2003, s.46.

[118] *Warmington* v. *Miller* [1973] 2 All ER 372.

- it may be necessary to file at least two full land transaction returns, namely on the effective date and at 'completion' when the documentation is executed.[119] Filing at completion will usually be crucial because this will be the stage when the Land Registry documentation emerges;[120]
- since land transactions may continue over time and many initial returns are filed and tax paid only on a provisional basis (see below), it may be necessary to file several land transaction returns for the same transaction and the outstanding provisional obligations of the initial taxpayer may by law pass to third parties.

1.19 CANCELLATION OF CONTRACT

This acceleration of the obligation to pay the tax before legal title has been obtained means that there may be a claim for repayment of the tax where the transaction does not proceed to completion.[121] The early payment obligation can give rise to funding problems because at that time the security which the taxpayer can offer may not be acceptable to the lender, especially where the contract is still conditional or there are substantial obligations to be performed before he can obtain legal title to the property or outstanding interests such as restrictive covenants have still to be cleared off the title (see **Chapter 3**).

1.20 NON-DOCUMENTARY ARRANGEMENTS

Notwithstanding the numerous provisions in the Law of Property Act 1925 and the Law of Property (Miscellaneous Provisions) Act 1989 there are many situations where oral or informal arrangements are binding upon the parties and can pass interests in land.[122] This is reinforced by the provision that the tax can apply to transactions taking effect without writing or 'by operation of law'. These unwritten transactions which are valid can include the following.

- Certain leases and tenancies for less than three years.[123] Informal arrangements for the occupation of premises are a major problem for SDLT in practice. There is, of course, the basic issue of whether the relationship created is by way of a

---

[119] FA 2003, s.44(8). This has become an acute problem in relation to agreements for lease where pursuant to FA 2003, Sched.17A, para.12A there may be two separate chargeable events with only limited credit being available; see **Chapter 8**.

[120] FA 2003, s.79(1) (as amended).

[121] FA 2003, s.44(9).

[122] See, for example, Firstpost Homes v. Johnson [1995] 4 All ER 355; but see Tootal Clothing v. Guinea Properties Management (1992) 64 P&CR 452; North Eastern Properties Ltd v. Coleman & Quinn Conveyancing [2010] 3 All ER 528; RTS Flexible Systems Ltd v. Molkerei Alois [2010] 3 All ER 1.

[123] Law of Property Act 1925, s.52.

lease or a licence[124] since only the former is within the charge to SDLT. Since this is a matter of construing the rights and duties created[125] and, apart from perhaps residential property where the problematic statements of Lord Templeman in *Street* v. *Mountford*[126] that the sole test is exclusive possession may retain some slight credibility, the absence of a written record of the detailed arrangements between the parties makes an analysis of their relationship in legal terms extremely difficult.[127] Matters may ultimately turn upon assumptions and presumptions which seem, in practice, to be a matter of judicial whimsy and, therefore, a risky strategy. There is also the question of the terms upon which a person is allowed into occupation, albeit as licensee, since these rights of entry may amount to taking possession and so constitute substantial performance of another agreement triggering a tax charge and reporting obligations.[128]

- Oral exercise of an option.[129]
- Surrenders of leases and tenancies by operation of law. These will frequently arise in practice particularly where the tenancy is for a short term or is of periodic nature or terminated by notice to quit.
- Implied, resulting[130] and constructive trusts.[131] The area of constructive and similar trusts is likely to cause problems in practice since this will catch many informal arrangements (see **Chapter 10**). For example, the principles of proprietary estoppel may prevent parties from refusing to act upon their oral promises where these have been acted upon by other persons who have substantially changed their position.[132] Thus an oral statement by parents that their house will belong to the daughter if she pays off the balance of the

---

[124] See Chapter 8.

[125] Addiscombe Garden Estates v. Crabbe [1958] 1 QB 513.

[126] [1985] 1 AC 809. A more realistic approach has been taken in relation to commercial property and the parties' stated intention may be important; *Ogwr* v. *Dykes* [1989] 2 All ER 880. However, even in relation to residential property, domestic or family arrangements that are not normally intended to create legal relationships may produce licence rather than lease; see, e.g. *Facchini* v. *Bryson* [1952] 1 TLR 1386; *Perry* v. *IRC* [2005] STC (SCD) 474; but the parties' intention to have some form of protected interest may produce more significant legal consequences; see e.g. *Lloyds Bank* v. *IRC* [1998] STC 559.

[127] Note especially *Ogwr* v. *Dykes* [1989] 2 All ER 880 on the possible importance of a written provision that the arrangements are not intended to create a tenancy; see also *Ready Mixed Concrete (South East) Ltd* v. *Minister of Pensions* [1968] 1 All ER 433; *Massey* v. *Crown Life* [1978] 2 All ER 576.

[128] See Chapter 3.

[129] See, for example, *Spiro* v. *Glencrown Properties Ltd* [1991] 2 WLR 931 on the oral exercise of options over land.

[130] Resulting trusts by reason of their name suggest a transfer or a regrant and HMRC Stamp Taxes is likely to regard such arrangements as land exchanges notwithstanding that such trusts usually arise where there has been a failure to deal with the equitable interest; see, for example, *Vandervell* v. *IRC* [1967] 1 All ER 1.

[131] Law of Property Act 1925, s.53(2); see *Neville* v. *Wilson* [1997] Ch 144.

[132] *Binions* v. *Evans* [1972] Ch 359; *ER Ives (Investments)* v. *High* [1967] 2 QB 379; *Perry* v. *IRC* [2005] STC (SCD) 474).

mortgage or cares for them in their old age[133] may bind the parties and equitable title may pass eventually.[134] It will not be possible to regard these as conditional gifts exempt from the charge to SDLT[135] because the 'condition' is really the performance of the consideration for the 'gift' making it contractual.[136] This is, however, an area of great technical difficulty because of the debate as to whether such equitable intervention is a matter of rights or is merely some form of equitable remedy of a 'discretionary' nature. The analysis may differ so that proprietary estoppel may create interests (i.e. involve the acquisition of rights), or prevent property interests passing (such as constructive trusts imposed in transactions entered into in breach of trust or fiduciary duty), and other situations may involve pure remedies where the court is seeking to produce a reasonable result. Unfortunately, the remarks of Walker LJ in *Yaxley* v. *Gotts*[137] to the effect that equitable intervention in this area overrides the statutory requirement for writing muddies the waters for practitioners. This transaction basis of the tax and the attack on value shifting (see **1.10.1.4**) linked with the width of the types of consideration that are subject to tax[138] means that many transactions not subject to stamp duty are now taxable, such as extensions of options, variations of rights to light and release of restrictive covenants.

- A tax charge may arise in respect of certain transactions that do not necessarily directly involve the land in question notwithstanding the absence of writing, such as clawback of certain reliefs for charities or intra-group transactions where there is a sale of shares in a company or even a subsidiary company owning the land.

1.21   SIGNIFICANCE OF DOCUMENTS AND DRAFTING ISSUES

During the introduction of the legislation HMRC Stamp Taxes made confident statements that because SDLT is a transaction tax the drafting and structuring of documentation would no longer be effective to reduce the tax liability. It is, however, potentially misleading to regard the tax as a totally transaction-bound tax, since documentation does have a significant impact on whether and, if so, when the charge arises. Drafting may have an important effect upon the nature of the rights or interests involved in the transaction, and have a significant impact upon the tax charge. For example:

---

[133]   See *Henry* v. *Henry* [2010] 1 All ER 988. Such services would be chargeable consideration unless it can be argued that they do not have an open market cost: FA 2003, Sched.4, para.11.

[134]   *Errington* v. *Errington and Woods* [1952] 1 KB 290; *Yaxley* v. *Gotts* [1999] 3 WLR 1217.

[135]   FA 2003, Sched.3, para.1.

[136]   Eastham v. Leigh London and Provincial Properties Ltd [1971] 2 All ER 887; GUS Merchandise v. HM Customs & Excise [1981] STC 569.

[137]   [1999] 3 WLR 1217; see *RTS Flexible Systems Ltd* v. *Molkerei Alois* [2010] 3 All ER 1.

[138]   FA 2003, Sched.4; see **Chapter 4**.

- Whether the effective date is completion or substantial performance of the contract depends upon whether the contract is to be completed by a 'conveyance' so that the drafting of the completion arrangements may affect the timing of the tax charge. For example, a provision in the contract that the vendor will, as from payment of the purchase price, hold the property as a bare trustee for the purchaser[139] may in certain types of contract defer the time for paying the tax giving a cash flow/interest saving benefit for the taxpayer notwithstanding the taking of possession.[140]

- There is an issue with part completions where there are staged transactions. A purchaser may agree to acquire a substantial area of land which is to be drawn down in several tranches over several years. There will be questions whether there has been sufficient taking of possession or payment of the price to constitute substantial performance as each transaction is drawn down. In such cases the rules specifically require the purchaser to take possession of a substantial part of the land or to make payment of a substantial amount of the consideration (in practice 90 per cent). In consequence, each drawdown may fall short of substantial performance but may be completed at some stage by one or more transfers of the relevant part of the land such as on subsales of any residential property constructed on the part of the land. The legislation does not refer to the effect of conveyance of part of the land where there has not been prior substantial performance on the overall charge, notwithstanding, for example, that reliefs may be dependent upon the happening of the effective date for example to exempt the cost of works or subsale relief. It is theoretically arguable by HMRC Stamp Taxes that 'completion' in this context requires the conveyance of the full title to all of the land which would potentially jeopardise such reliefs. However, as a policy matter the rules relating to substantial performance are intended to accelerate the tax charge and prevent the parties from resting on contract. In consequence HMRC Stamp Taxes may seek to establish that the first transfer of any part of the land is 'completion' thereby accelerating the tax charge. However, this destroys subsale relief, the disposal of a house from plan and, hitherto in practice, HMRC Stamp Taxes does not appear to have raised this point. Unfortunately, silence on the issue is not necessarily a guarantee of acceptance of the former analysis.

- The execution of documents may be the 'transaction' which triggers the tax charge, such as where the parties perform a legally ineffective oral agreement by a formal conveyance[141] because in general 'completion' by writing is the basic effective date.[142]

---

[139] There is not to be a completion document or 'conveyance'; see *Peter Bone* v. *IRC* [1995] STC 921.

[140] FA 2003, s.119; s.44 thereof applies only where there is a contract to be completed by a 'conveyance' and does not override the basic provision where there is no 'conveyance' contemplated by the contract.

[141] *Tootal* v. *Guinea Properties* (1992) 64 P&CR 452.

[142] FA 2003, s.119; see **Chapter 3**.

- The drafting of the document may affect the nature of the transaction such as whether there is a lease or a licence[143] or whether there is payment by instalments or a periodical payment.[144]

- Whether fitting out arrangements are chargeable consideration, i.e. a form of premium being provided by the tenant, depends upon the terms of the agreement for lease.[145]

- Whether entry upon the land involves taking possession, operating as substantial performance of the contract depends upon the terms upon which such entry is made. The nature of the arrangements for fitting out and rent-free periods can affect whether the tenant's ability to enter on to the premises to fit out is part of the chargeable non-rent consideration for the grant of the lease taxable upon the open market cost.[146] It may be important whether the tenant is obliged to fit out so as to earn the rent-free period[147] or because the landlord is anxious to ensure that the tenant begins trading as soon as possible or whether the agreement merely permits the tenant to enter to fit out if he so wishes. Also, the terms upon which the tenant enters may affect whether he is a licensee taking possession of the whole or substantially the whole of the chargeable interest or merely has limited access to the premises; the former may be taxable events, the latter may not be taxable.

- The availability of various reliefs may depend upon drafting, particularly where VAT is involved. Since this is the vendor's risk the contract will usually provide for the payment of the tax.[148] For example, although the parties believe that they have a transfer of a going concern, the contract may provide that should the transaction not qualify as a transfer of a going concern the transferee company acquiring the assets will pay the VAT to the transferor company. This can affect the availability of certain reliefs.[149] The only safe procedure in such a situation is to provide that the initial issue of consideration is inclusive of VAT and avoid creating any right to a contingent or deferred consideration (see **Chapter 4**).

---

[143] Ogwr v. Dykes [1989] 2 All ER 880; Massey v. Crown Life [1978] 2 All ER 576; Ready Mixed Concrete (South East) Ltd v. Minister of Pensions [1968] 1 All ER 433; Dragonfly Consulting Ltd v. Revenue and Customs Commissioners [2008] STC 3030.

[144] FA 2003, s.52; see **4.31.4**.

[145] FA 2003, Sched.4, para.10; *Eastham* v. *Leigh London and Provincial Properties Ltd* [1971] 2 All ER 887; see **Chapter 9**.

[146] FA 2003, Sched.4, para.10.

[147] Ridgeons Bulk v. Customs & Excise [1994] STC 427.

[148] FA 2003, s.46; *Wood Preservation* v. *Prior* [1969] 1 All ER 364; *J. Sainsbury* v. *O'Connor* [1991] 1 WLR 963; *Wynn Realisations Ltd* v. *Vogue Holdings Inc* [1999] STC 524; *Hostgilt Ltd* v. *Megahart Ltd* [1999] STC 141.

[149] FA 2003, Sched.7, Part 2; see **Chapter 13**.

- A tax charge can arise by reference to 'payment' of a substantial part of the consideration.[150] The drafting of the contract may mean that there is a set-off involving payment rather than a deferred payment.[151]
- Entries in a share register may affect the availability of the relief.[152]
- The choice between an option and a conditional contract may affect the time of the tax and other issues.[153]
- The drafting and structuring of deferred consideration such as earnouts and clawbacks can affect the time of payment and the number of times that the taxpayer is required to file a return.[154] In relation to certain types of deferred consideration[155] tax becomes due and payable when any part of the deferred consideration becomes certain. There is, therefore, an important difference where the consideration only becomes 'certain' at the end of the project rather than when individual events happen. For example, where there is a sale of land to a retail housing developer with an overage payment of X per cent of the price per house over a specified figure there is a clear risk that part of the overage consideration will become 'certain' as and when any house is sold. This would require payment and a return on every relevant house sale. On the other hand, where the payment is to be made only out of the total consideration there will be only two payments and filings, namely the initial return on a guestimated basis and a final retrospective adjustment when the consideration is finally quantified.

1.22 DOCUMENTATION AND MULTIPLE REPORTING

Overall, therefore, structuring may be important as a safeguard against completion of a small part of the transaction jeopardising reliefs. The basic rule is that the tax arises at 'completion'[156] which is not defined, but there are many special rules. The most important special rule, in practice, is that when there is a contract which is to be completed by a 'conveyance' which is defined but only for these purposes in effect, as being any written instrument,[157] the tax event is the earlier of substantial performance of the contract and completion, i.e. delivery of the written instrument. Moreover, even if substantial performance precedes 'completion' there is an obligation following such completion to complete and file a full land transaction return

---

[150] FA 2003, s.44(5); see **3.8**; regarded by HMRC Stamp Taxes as 90 per cent, but this is a percentage of the total possible variable consideration not the basic price.

[151] *Coren* v. *Keighley* 48 TC 370.

[152] *Oswald Tillotson* v. *IRC* [1933] 1 KB 134; *Brotex Cellulose Fibres Ltd* v. *IRC* [1933] 1 KB 158; *Murex* v. *IRC* [1933] 1 KB 173; *National Westminster Bank* v. *IRC* [1994] STC 580.

[153] FA 2003, s.46; *Wood Preservation* v. *Prior* [1969] 1 All ER 364; *J. Sainsbury* v. *O'Connor* [1991] 1 WLR 963.

[154] They may have other major taxation consequences such as in *Marren* v. *Ingles* 54 TC 76; *Page* v. *Lowther* [1983] STC 799.

[155] FA 2003, s.51; see **4.38**.

[156] FA 2003, s.119; but note the amendments in FA 2005.

[157] *IRC* v. *Littlewoods Mail Order Stores Ltd* [1963] AC 135, HL; [1961] Ch 597, CA.

(SDLT 1) bearing a different transaction number (bar code) from the original return even though no further tax is payable and there may be a problem of filing for a part-completion (see **3.9.2** and **9.14**).

As the principle of completion by written instrument between the same parties will apply to virtually every contract relating to land,[158] the execution of the final documentation or possibly any part thereof will produce an obligation to notify the tax charge.

This time lapse between substantial performance of the contract and completion is particularly important in relation to leases, since in attempting to deal with certain inconveniences in the compliance system[159] HMRC Stamp Taxes claims to have created two separate chargeable transactions for the same legal/commercial transaction. The timing of the execution of the actual lease, which is frequently arbitrary, now has major taxation consequences.

1.23 FORM, SUBSTANCE AND LAND LAW

The antiquity and complexity of land law has produced many situations where the arrangement cannot proceed in a straightforward fashion but has to adopt certain mechanics. For example, subject to the rules of accepting and reserving interests, many transactions have to take the form of a transfer of one interest and a regrant of the relevant subordinate interests back. Thus what is, essentially, a sale of a part-interest in land may have to take the form of a transfer and a leaseback.[160] Although in *Sargaison* v. *Roberts*[161] Megarry J suggested that when dealing with taxation issues HMRC should not be over-zealous in relying upon conveyancing mechanics, HMRC Stamp Taxes is anxious to take advantage of these mechanics and will treat a transfer and a regrant as being some form of land exchange with potential double charges.[162] Similarly, certain variations of leases may only take effect as surrenders and regrants.[163] HMRC Stamp Taxes will treat such variations as the surrender and the grant of the new lease notwithstanding the parties merely implement it by a deed of variation.[164] The starting point of HMRC Stamp Taxes is

---

[158] This issue turns upon the terms of the contract.

[159] FA 2003, Sched.17A, para.12A; see **Chapter 8**.

[160] It may be possible to carve out the lease earlier by granting a lease to oneself or to a nominee as in *Ingram* v. *IRC* [1999] STC 37; but note, in Scotland, *Kildrummy* v. *IRC* [1990] STC 657; and note that leases to nominees are subject to a special charging regime: FA 2003, Sched.16, para.3 (as amended). Attempts to carve out the lease by granting it to a subsidiary company may qualify initially for the relief for intra-group transfers but this relief is subject to clawback if the lessee ceases to be a member of the group within the relevant three years (FA 2003, Sched.7, Part 1; see **Chapter 13**) or is subject to a special charge upon any assignment of a lease out of the group (FA 2003, Sched.17A, para.11).

[161] [1969] 3 All ER 1072.

[162] FA 2003, s.47; Sched.4, para.5; see **Chapter 7**.

[163] Friends Provident Life Office v. British Railways Board [1996] 1 All ER 336.

[164] See *Gable Construction* v. *IRC* [1968] 1 WLR 1426 for possible limits on this principle.

to treat these arrangements as exchanges but, fortunately, there are certain special but limited reliefs.[165]

The converse of this principle is if the parties can achieve the same economic or commercial result by different means within the principles of land law these alternative means have to be taxed accordingly and may be more efficient.[166] In consequence, rather than changing the term of a lease the parties may insert a break clause in order to be in a position to shorten the lease where appropriate or insert an option to renew or enter into an agreement for reversionary lease (see **8.58**). HMRC Stamp Taxes cannot treat these transactions as being surrenders and regrants although the same result could be achieved by those means. Similarly, changing the demised premises by deed of variation would be a surrender and regrant but entering into a partial surrender or a side-by-side lease in order to reduce or enlarge the demised premises would be taxable only as a surrender of part or the grant of a new lease but not a surrender and regrant of the entire lease.

1.24 PROVISIONAL TAX AND WAIT-AND-SEE

SDLT, unlike stamp duty, is not a once-for-all tax producing finality and certainty as to stamp tax costs shortly after the relevant event. The issues surrounding this problem for title have been simplified to some extent, in that the main process is to file the return and obtain the necessary certificate and obtain registration leaving the disputes, in general, to be decided behind the title.[167] However, much of SDLT is of a provisional nature being dealt with initially on the basis of 'reasonable estimates' which have to be reviewed retrospectively from time to time and, as described above, the obligations to deal with such reviews and pay any tax arising (or recover tax provisionally overpaid) may pass to subsequent owners of the land.[168] There is, therefore, an aspect of wait-and-see at least as regards the computation of the tax, but there is no statutory guidance upon the other more significant aspect of wait-and-see principles, namely whether there is a general principle that events other than linked transactions arising after the effective date can affect the *liability* to tax rather than the amount of the tax. There are many occasions in practice when a provisional return is required:

---

[165]   FA 2003, Sched.17A, paras.9 and 16; see **8.57**.

[166]   The choice of alternatives is not necessarily tax avoidance; see *IRC* v. *Willoughby* [1997] STC 995; *Sherdley* v. *Sherdley* [1988] AC 213; but note the statutory general anti-avoidance provisions pursuant to FA 2003, ss.75A–75C.

[167]   See **1.11.2**; note the difficulties sometimes encountered at the Land Registry which are endangering the effectiveness of this attempt at simplifying and speeding up the process of registration.

[168]   See e.g. FA 2003, s.81A and Sched.17A, para.12.

- Variable consideration and lease premiums such as overage payments or clawback arrangements require a provisional return,[169] but not variable annuities and periodical payments.[170] Since these arrangements can extend over a long period, including in current practice up to 80 years for clawback provisions, the initial tax position can remain open for many years, until the final payments have been agreed.

- Variable rents, including virtually all forms of rent reviews and rents subject to VAT, remain open for up to five years,[171] with implications for a longer period because of the charge arising where there is a subsequent abnormal increase in the rent.[172]

- Certain reliefs are subject to clawback and the transaction becomes retrospectively taxable should certain events occur within a specified period.[173]

- Where there is or may be a linked transaction the particular transaction is vulnerable to retrospective adjustment. Thus the initial assessment of SDLT in respect of the premium paid for the grant of an option will require adjustment if the option is exercised because the option premium and the purchase price may have to be aggregated[174] which is likely to have the effect of increasing the rate of SDLT applied to the option premium.

- Effectively every lease where the tenant can hold over by operation of law such as pursuant to the Landlord and Tenant Act 1954 (as amended) will require a provisional return.[175]

- Where there is a lease with options for one or more renewals the lease or leases arising pursuant to the exercise of the option may be a linked transaction with the original lease (a successive linked lease). The result is that the original lease is retrospectively treated as a single lease for a term for the aggregate terms of the original lease and all renewals thereof,[176] and the original application of the formula for the net present value of the rent has to be revisited retrospectively on the basis of a longer term with additional years of rent to be included in the revised calculation.[177] This will, at first sight, increase the SDLT payable over the sum originally paid, but without interest and penalty. The uncertainty extends beyond such simple situations because where there are linked leases the nil rate slice of the net present value of the rent has to be allocated between the various linked leases pro rata to the net present value of the rent.[178] In consequence, if there is a later linked lease including a later lease arising pursuant to the exercise of an option to renew another lease with a consequent

---

[169]   FA 2003, s.51.
[170]   FA 2003, s.52.
[171]   FA 2003, Sched.17A, paras.7 and 8.
[172]   FA 2003, Sched.17A, paras.14 and 15.
[173]   See e.g. FA 2003, Sched.6A, Sched.7, Sched.8 and s.86(2).
[174]   FA 2003, s.46(1) using the word 'may'.
[175]   FA 2003, Sched.17A, paras.3, 4 and 9.
[176]   FA 2003, Sched.17A, para.5 (as amended).
[177]   Similar problems arise for holding over; see **Chapter 8**.
[178]   FA 2003, Sched.5, para.2 (as amended).

increase in the net present value of the rent for that lease, there will have to be an adjustment of the allocation of the nil rate slice for all of the current linked leases. This reduction in the nil rate slice will, it seems, have to be separately notified since it will affect the initial self-assessment of the net present value subject to the 1 per cent rate, so it will affect the computation of SDLT in relation to that lease after the initial calculation including rent reviews that have taken place and been taxed between the original effective date and the effective date for the linked transaction.

These are, however, merely specific provisions dealing with particular sets of circumstances. There is a more general problem, i.e. whether the whole of SDLT is underpinned by a wait-and-see principle, and whether there is a general principle that all tax returns can be revisited in the light of the later events such as where there is a claim for breach of contract and the purchase price is effectively reduced. The problem for the relief for corporate reconstructions set out above is another illustration of whether the relief can be claimed retrospectively if the VAT is not payable (see **Chapter 13**). Similarly, there is a question of whether such relief can be claimed because the consideration shares will frequently not have been issued (i.e. registered) at the effective date or at the time when the land transaction return is filed because the parties may take a relaxed approach to tidying up the paperwork. The company may have entered into occupation of the land ahead of completion and will not 'issue' the consideration shares for some time thereafter. At that time the conditions for the relief may have not been satisfied. In practice, this latter point was not taken by HMRC Stamp Taxes for the purposes of the equivalent stamp duty reliefs but the whole timing policy and structure issues of SDLT raise different problems and there are expected to be significant problems in this area if there is not instant completion and all paperwork properly completed at that time.

The position is at present uncertain and there is a risk that because there are numerous specific provisions dealing with timing issues there cannot be a general wait-and-see principle since this would render many of the particular provisions redundant. In consequence, notwithstanding the extended nature of the time over which the SDLT has to be computed, it is unclear whether there is a fully developed wait-and-see principle or whether there is a degree of a once-for-all tax retained and brought over from stamp duty. It seems to be the view of HMRC Stamp Taxes that the wait-and-see aspects of SDLT are limited to dealing with the calculation only and are intended solely to address the problems of the stamp duty contingency principle whereby, with suitable drafting, certain parts of the consideration could escape tax. In its apparent view because there is, in general, only one relevant effective date,[179] the question of liability to tax and the availability of exemptions or reliefs is answered once and for all as at that date and subsequent events, although relevant for computing the SDLT, cannot affect the liability to the tax or eligibility to any reliefs.

---

[179] But see FA 2003, Sched.17A, para.12B.

1.25   NO FINALITY

There are other situations where, unlike stamp duty and adjudication, stamp duty land tax does not produce a point where the tax position can be regarded as closed without the risk of having to file further returns and pay additional tax which produces outstanding tax positions with the related uncertainty as to the costs of the acquisition[180] if only because of the extended periods during which HMRC Stamp Taxes can issue discovery assessments notwithstanding that there has been a full Enquiry.[181] This issue of open or provisional tax assessment may frequently affect third parties such as grantees and assignees of leases.[182] However, since personal representatives and liquidators and certain receivers take over responsibility for the unresolved SDLT position of the deceased or company in addition to possibly becoming liable for exercising options entered into by the deceased or the company prior to their taking office, they will have an obligation to investigate whether there is an outstanding position, including warranties and indemnities given where the chargeable interest has been transferred to or acquired by a third party. As noted above, it will in many cases be a potential obstacle to the final administration of the estate or conclusion of the liquidation since the circumstances where the SDLT can be finalised may not have occurred and may not occur for many years in the future.

Other arrangements may be affected by the lack of finality. For example, there may be a purchase price for land linked to the profits or earnings from the development of the land. The calculation is likely to involve a deduction for any stamp tax costs. Unfortunately, unless the documents are carefully drafted, these costs can never, in theory, be finally determined because of the potential 21-year period for discovery notices. The repeal of the obscure obligation of the taxpayer to rectify the situation, if an error in the return emerges, leaves an open question as to the obligations of the taxpayer where he becomes aware of an error, whether of fact or law, relating to his return if he does not correct the error.[183] Parties will have to take their chances on this lack of compliance finality by providing for an arbitrary cut-off date when the provisional tax computation will be deemed to be conclusive for the purposes of the calculation or by making a reasonable disclosure with the land transaction return (SDLT 1) which may preclude the making of a discovery.[184] At present, it is uncertain which is the appropriate cut-off date to select but it seems likely that a period of seven years (i.e. one year after the expiration of the basic

---

[180]   This will, of course, affect the purchaser's overall tax position such as the base cost for capital gains tax and the sums paid for capital allowances. While the SDLT position is unresolved or open to challenge, it may prove difficult to determine the amount upon which capital allowances may be claimed or what is the base cost for capital gains. There will also be issues as to whether there is a potential liability for SDLT against the estate of the deceased for the purposes of inheritance tax. These are complex issues (see e.g. the extremely difficult legislation for VAT and the capital goods scheme contained in Capital Allowances Act 2001, ss.546 *et seq.*).

[181]   FA 2003, Sched.10, paras.12(2A) and 30(4).

[182]   See Chapter 8.

[183]   See FA 2003, Sched.10, para.8 (repealed); paras.31 and 31A.

[184]   *Langham* v. *Veltema* [2004] STC 544; *Parinv* v. *IRC* [1998] STC 305.

period for discovery assessments) could be the most convenient in practice for the time being until the problem is sorted out by HMRC Stamp Taxes.

It might be thought that this problem of uncertainty as to tax costs and of the long-term possibility of a challenge by HMRC Stamp Taxes should end after the expiration of the nine months during which an Enquiry can be launched[185] into land transaction returns (SDLT 1). No Enquiry may be launched into a non-notifiable transaction unless an unnecessary land transaction return (SDLT 1) has been filed. The removal of self-certificates means there is nothing into which HMRC Stamp Taxes may enquire because of the consequential repeals of much of FA 2003, Sched.11. However, where HMRC Stamp Taxes makes a 'discovery', which is relatively easy given the deficiencies in the self-assessment regime and the design of the forms,[186] it may issue an assessment at any time up to six years after the effective date for the transaction. However, where there is evidence of fraud or negligence the discovery assessment may be made up to 21 years after the effective date of the transaction. Fraud is widely defined and includes wrongful allocation of the consideration between chattels and land. 'Negligence' not only refers to an error of law in deciding how the SDLT regime applies to the transaction such as whether there is an arrangement within the anti-avoidance provisions for the intra-group relief pursuant to FA 2003, Sched.7, Part 1, but also includes errors in the completion of the return such as not taking proper steps to determine the market value of the property or to obtain reasonable evidence as to future variable payments of contingent sums and rent reviews. There will therefore be ample opportunity for HMRC Stamp Taxes to extend the discovery assessment time limit to 21 years.[187]

1.26 SIDE EFFECTS

This lack of finality also affects transactions indirectly. For example, a company may be a tenant of a lease with variable rents, or a lease that was exempt when granted but which may have a negative value because of the special charge upon

---

[185] FA 2003, Sched.10, para.12(2).

[186] See *Langham* v. *Veltema* [2004] STC 544.

[187] Moreover, even if this were not enough of a problem, it was originally provided that where a taxpayer discovers that an error was made in the completion of the land transaction, including an error made innocently, without fraud or negligence, he would be under an obligation under a tax-related penalty to remedy the defect within a reasonable time after discovering the error (FA 2003, Sched.10, para.8). This provision was replaced by Sched.10, paras.31 and 31A, possibly creating an obligation to report errors of law and fact. This leaves an open question as to the obligations of the taxpayer in this situation. Should there be a general principle of confession where there is knowledge, there will be interesting questions as to what constitutes appropriate knowledge of such an error, particularly where it arises out of litigation to which the taxpayer is not a party and which relates not to SDLT but to the construction of documents relating to land. This obligation was apparently unlimited in time. It is not clear how such knowledge might affect persons other than the taxpayer such as his personal representatives and his professional advisers, nor is it clear whether they have a continuing obligation to notify clients of developments possibly affecting their tax return for a chargeable transaction filed many years previously.

assignment being taxed as a new lease,[188] or there are clawback risks. There are crucial issues in the pricing of the shares. Similarly, the valuation of interests in trusts may be influenced by open SDLT assessments such as where land has been acquired for a consideration including an overage payment. The adjustment of SDLT may affect the base costs for capital gains tax and capital allowances.[189]

1.27 SELF-ASSESSMENT

Unlike stamp duty where the obligation to assess the tax lies with HMRC Stamp Taxes, SDLT is initially and subsequently calculated by the taxpayer as part of the process of completing the land transaction return.[190] This assessment may be corrected by HMRC Stamp Taxes upon initial filing but only where there is a manifest omission or error in the arithmetic.[191] The issue of an SDLT 5 certificate is, therefore, not conclusive that the correct amount of tax has been paid and, as noted above, any additional tax can be assessed by HMRC Stamp Taxes by means of a 'discovery assessment' for up to 21 years after the effective date of the transaction where negligence is involved. There is now some uncertainty whether the taxpayer is exposed to an obligation to rectify the return including payment of additional tax, interest and penalties should he become aware of errors such as by way of subsequent litigation between parties with whom he is not associated concerning the valuation techniques adopted.[192]

The obligation of the taxpayer is to provide an accurate assessment of his tax liability. This entails an appreciation of:

- whether a land transaction return (SDLT 1) is required, i.e.:

  - when an initial return is required;[193]
  - when a further return is required for the same transaction, including situations where the taxpayer although not a party to the transaction is nevertheless required to file a return and pay additional tax such as the linked transaction charges; and
  - when amendments or corrective returns are required;[194]

---

[188]   FA 2003, Sched.17A, para.11 (as amended).

[189]   Compare the complex legislation in dealing with problems of capital allowances and VAT pursuant to Capital Allowances Act 2001, ss.233 and following. See further **Chapter 6**.

[190]   FA 2003, s.76.

[191]   FA 2003, Sched.10, para.7. On difficulties with the Land Registry whose employees may seek to challenge returns (see **1.12.3**, **14.13** and **18.4**).

[192]   FA 2003, Sched.10, paras.31 and 31A. The responsibility of professional advisers to keep the clients informed of such developments long after the association has ceased remains to be explored and the issue should be expressly addressed in any retainer letter.

[193]   Which may be a problem since a return is required by the statutory general anti-avoidance provisions.

[194]   A position left open by the replacement of FA 2003, Sched.10, para.8 by Sched.10, paras.31 and 31A imposing penalties for failure to rectify.

- when the tax charge arises since the effective date will be crucial for a variety of issues such as the date for determining market values or whether the option to charge VAT has been exercised;
- the nature of the transaction and how it fits into the plain English drafting of the legislation and the approach of HMRC Stamp Taxes to form and substance (see **1.32**);
- the precise conditions for the availability of any exemptions, whether these are satisfied and whether the transaction is bona fide commercial, etc. since there is no advance clearance procedure;
- the details relating to chargeable consideration (which is not the same as the actual consideration in many cases e.g. where connected companies or partnerships are involved, or works or services provide all or part of the consideration);
- whether the correct procedures for determining the market value or reasonable estimates of future payments or rents have been adopted or whether other 'guestimates' that are required when completing the return have been correctly determined.

In this the taxpayer or his advisers are very much left to their own devices.[195] There is no formal clearance procedure although HMRC Stamp Taxes has indicated that it would adopt the appropriate code of practice for assisting taxpayers in dealing with their returns. Unfortunately, this code of practice does not seem to operate in key areas such as the application of the tax avoidance and bona fide commercial tests and HMRC Stamp Taxes is frequently too slow in responding. Indeed, on occasion HMRC Stamp Taxes has refused to proceed with a pre-transaction clearance on the basis that the questions raised were too difficult. In addition, it is a longstanding policy of HMRC Stamp Taxes not to regard itself as bound by any advance ruling.[196] Indeed, it would appear to be keen supporters of the approach of Lord Nolan in the *Matrix* case[197] where he indicated that in order to bind the Revenue the ruling had to be the equivalent of a House of Lords or Supreme Court decision. This would require, as a minimum, the taxpayer to set out in full his arguments and any weaknesses therein and any arguments that HMRC Stamp Taxes might wish to rely upon.

1.28 NEGLIGENCE

It will be clear from the above list of potential areas of difficulty that a whole new area of negligence has been created. Merely being wrong or mistaken is not negligence, but failure to take the proper steps when advising on the return such as

---

[195] Note the comments of Russell LJ in *Crane Fruehauf* v. *IRC* [1975] STC 51 that in many valuation exercises the taxpayer must do the best he can.

[196] *J Rothschild Holdings Plc* v. *IRC* [1988] STC 645 (on appeal [1989] STC 435).

[197] R v. IRC ex p Matrix Securities Ltd [1993] STC 773.

asking the right question of the client is negligence.[198] The fact that a conclusion (whether of law or the methodology adopted for preparing the return) is not accepted by HMRC Stamp Taxes or is rejected by the court on appeal does not necessarily mean that the decision was negligent and if disclosure of the obtaining of professional advice is made HMRC Stamp Taxes may not be able to make a 'discovery' (see **18.12**). If the taxpayer and/or his advisers have prepared contemporaneous records of the decision-making process and can establish that all relevant issues have been properly investigated and that nothing has been overlooked, it will be extremely difficult for HMRC Stamp Taxes to establish 'negligence'. It will also be clear that such new negligence is important in relation to the client since it may extend the discovery assessment period from six to 21 years and may leave the client exposed to a theoretical duty to rectify the erroneous tax return (this, however, applies even where the return was not prepared negligently).[199]

In broad terms, self-assessment creates three areas of potential negligence:[200]

- negligence in relation to interpreting the charging or relieving provisions;
- negligence in computing the tax because, for example, the correct consideration was not utilised; and
- negligence in relation to the methodology adopted for the preparation of the land transaction return,[201] for example, no proper evidence as to market value was obtained.[202]

There may also be issues as to the imposition of penalties. These are the personal liabilities of the taxpayer although in the circumstances he or she would wish to be reimbursed by his professional advisers.[203] For some time HMRC took the view

---

[198]   *Slattery* v. *Moore Stephens* [2003] STC 1379.

[199]   A position left open by the replacement of FA 2003, Sched.10, para.8 by paras.31 and 31A thereof.

[200]   It may be that failure to point out tax efficiencies as opposed to aggressive schemes constitutes a breach of duty: *BE Studios* v. *Smith and Williamson* [2006] STC 358.

[201]   *Slattery* v. *Moore Stephens* [2003] STC 1379. There is also a possible issue of whether, should the client refuse to accept advice as to the proper procedures for preparing the land transaction return and may in consequence be acting fraudulently, i.e. knowingly submitting a return prepared on an incorrect basis, the professional adviser is exposing himself to criminal penalties for 'knowingly' (whatever that may ultimately be held to mean in this context) assisting in the preparation of an incorrect return.

[202]   Since many of the difficulties for taxpayers and self-assessment arise because of the problems of lack of space to set out the background, particularly to explain entries that appear on the forms described as 'other', this renders taxpayers vulnerable to discovery assessments. Attempts have been made to cover the deficiencies in the forms by submitting covering letters setting out the background to the form though it seems that such attempts are not likely to be successful. However, these letters may be helpful in combating allegations of fraud. It will be difficult for HMRC Stamp Taxes to maintain such allegations if the taxpayer has sought from the beginning to make full disclosure to it; fraud is likely to require a degree of concealment. However, the letters will not produce 'finality'. HMRC Stamp Taxes has indicated that it will not take notice of such letters and that the employees processing the land transaction return have no authority to consider or act upon such letters. In consequence, such letters will not bind HMRC Stamp Taxes because it will be beyond the authority of the recipients to deal with them.

[203]   There may be other difficulties involved e.g. in obtaining employment or visas in other countries where there are apparently 'tax penalties' upon a person's record.

that where a taxpayer was receiving professional advice this was a reason for not mitigating a penalty since the punishment would be visited upon the professional adviser who should have got it right. However, it may be that this approach will have to be modified and recognition given that the taxpayer should not be punished or have a significant penalty imposed because of its effect upon his position where relying in good faith on a professional adviser properly instructed.[204]

The first two areas fall within the adviser's traditional remit to provide proper advice relating to the transaction such as whether the taxpayer is entitled to a relief or exemption. The last area is totally new and has to be approached with circumspection, because the amount of information contained in the land transaction returns is limited and does not permit disclosure of the calculation or valuations or assumptions behind the final entry.[205] It is unbelievably easy for HMRC Stamp Taxes to issue a discovery assessment.[206]

In consequence of this new compliance regime, the question of completing the forms (SDLT 1 to 4) is now of major significance with real consequences of tax-related penalties and extended periods for discovery assessments if there are errors in the form (see **Chapter 18** and **Appendix D**). There is a need to give careful thought not only to the analysis of the transaction such as lease or a licence, conditional gift or contract for consideration but also to the methodology to be adopted in gathering the data and producing the information required by the land transaction returns such as the correct method for apportioning the consideration between the land and fixtures and chattels as required by the amended SDLT 4, or determining the market value or for making reasonable estimates of future rents and future overage or clawback payments.

1.29 POST-TRANSACTION RULINGS

It is theoretically possible to apply for a ruling after the transaction so as to reduce the risk of errors attracting substantial penalties and interest.

Post-transaction rulings are of little benefit since the transaction will have been carried out and the taxpayer has had to make his own decisions as to the contents of the land transaction return (SDLT 1). Moreover, HMRC Stamp Taxes tends to regard applications for post-transaction rulings designed to expedite clarification of the situation as being invitations for it to initiate an Enquiry with all the costs, expenses and powers associated with that. There can be no such post-transaction ruling to provide a speedy answer where a land transaction return has been filed. As mentioned above, the 30-day time limit is irrelevant because it ignores the Land

---

[204] *Moores* v. *Customs and Excise*, VAT Decision 19024.

[205] The situation is unlike the old-fashioned mathematics examinations where the candidate is advised to show his workings so that errors of arithmetic can be dealt with and credit given if the principles adopted are correct. The self-assessment system does not permit such 'workings' to be disclosed, only the final answer; see also FA 2003, Sched.10, para.30(4).

[206] *Langham* v. *Veltema* [2004] STC 544.

Registry time limits so that it is potentially imprudent to delay filing to obtain a ruling. At this stage the request for a ruling is converted into a full-blown expensive and time-consuming Enquiry.

1.30 SOURCES

The main provisions at present are contained in FA 2003, but these have been substantially amended by later legislation and statutory instruments. HMRC has an exceedingly large number of powers to issue regulations on a wide range of issues and these can change the tax by altering the charging and relieving provisions and the compliance requirements, including prescribing the land transaction return forms and arrangements for postponing tax payments.

HMRC Stamp Taxes has begun to publish a SDLT Manual, but at present this is far from complete and is little more than a précis of the legislation. Moreover, it is uncertain how far the Manual can be relied upon. HMRC generally is, it seems, seeking to limit the ability of taxpayers to rely upon statements in Manuals which it claims are not binding because they are intended purely for internal guidance and not as the equivalent of Statements of Practice. They are published merely as a courtesy to assist taxpayers as to the broad lines of the approach of HMRC and not intended to be exhaustive or definitive nor to restrict HMRC in any particular case. It remains to be seen how far this view is developed in practice.

HMRC Stamp Taxes has begun a practice of issuing bulletins or notices setting out its views and possible practices in certain areas, but since none of these has been formally issued as a Statement of Practice it may lack any binding power to prevent these views not being applied in practice where they prove to be inconvenient.

There is a helpline but at present this has high records of incorrect and inconsistent advice. Moreover, advice given over the telephone does not bind HMRC[207] and it seems that relying upon the helpline will not even be regarded as a reason for the mitigation of penalties.

It appears that past practice or previous dealings are not regarded as binding by HMRC Stamp Taxes. Additionally, it will be difficult to establish practice in particular areas[208] since HMRC can refuse to disclose details of previous dealings with taxpayers on the ground of confidentiality so that it is virtually impossible to produce evidence of the treatment of previous transactions that will convince the current judiciary.

It might be thought that, as much of the legislation is the same as or in similar terms to the old stamp duty, the former case law and Statements of Practice will be relevant in relation to the new tax. In certain cases this may be a correct assumption but it is one that has to be approached with caution. The 'one-size-fits-all' and plain English style of the drafting and structuring of the legislation mean that words have

---

[207] *J Rothschild Holdings Plc* v. *IRC* [1988] STC 645 (on appeal on other grounds [1989] STC 435).
[208] J Rothschild Holdings Plc v. IRC [1988] STC 645.

45

to be given unusual meanings in order to make the tax workable and their new meanings or the subtle effects of the 'one-size-fits-all' drafting, which can work against as well as for HMRC Stamp Taxes, may alter the meaning of both stamp duty and conveyancing terms. Nevertheless as there are some indications in practice that a certain amount of stamp duty baggage is being brought across the old stamp duty position may be a potential source for guidance.

1.31 JURISDICTION

1.31.1 Execution

SDLT is a global tax in that it applies in cases where there is an instrument effecting the transaction; it is irrelevant whether the instrument is executed in the UK or abroad.[209]

1.31.2 Taxpayers

More importantly, it applies whether or not any party to the transaction is present or resident in the UK. Thus non-residents such as foreign companies,[210] foreign partnerships,[211] foreign trustees and beneficiaries of such trusts and foreign estates will be subject to the tax. This gives rise to problems where, because of the need for personal signature by the taxpayer on the SDLT 1, it may be necessary to arrange for the return to be sent to several different countries for signature. Even if it is possible for a person holding a power of attorney or other authority to sign on behalf of the taxpayer, it may be necessary to obtain the appropriate power of attorney or company resolution for the representative to act for the party overseas.

1.31.3 UK land

SDLT is limited to chargeable interests in land situate in the UK;[212] foreign land is not subject to stamp taxes. However, it is clear that certain interests that appear to be foreign are to be regarded as interests in or over land in the UK. These are interests in trusts and estates of deceased persons which arise because of the rules providing for a look-through where a beneficiary is 'absolutely entitled' as against the trustee[213] and deeming foreign trusts as being the same as English trusts where the draftsman took the view that beneficiaries have a proprietary interest in the assets held by the trustees.[214] Two main areas in practice will be involved, namely:

---

[209] FA 2003, s.42(2).
[210] FA 2003, s.100(4).
[211] FA 2003, Sched.15, para.1.
[212] FA 2003, s.48(1)(a).
[213] FA 2003, Sched.16, para.2; see **Chapter 10**.
[214] Baker v. Archer Shee 15 TC 1; Archer Shee v. Garland 15 TC 693.

- foreign fixed interest (as opposed to discretionary) trusts because of the rules equating these with English trusts where the legislation works upon the basis that beneficiaries under such trusts have an equitable interest in the underlying assets (as a separate interest in the land held by the trustees this interest will be a chargeable interest).[215] Consequently, where a foreign trust holds land in the UK the equitable interests will be within the charge to tax even where the settlor is non-domiciled. Such trustees should consider holding land through a body corporate; and
- foreign partnerships where, although it is now accepted by HMRC Stamp Taxes that a share in a partnership wherever established is not itself a chargeable interest, there are provisions in FA 2003, Sched.15 (as amended) imposing a charge upon dealings in partnership interests. Participants in such arrangements should consider how either the land in the UK and/or the partnership share should be held to side-step these problems.

1.32 TAX AVOIDANCE

1.32.1 General

A potential payer of SDLT may seek to arrange his affairs so as to minimise his liability for the charge. There was a weaker presumption in the case of stamp duties than in other fields of taxation that there is a rational and coherent system of taxation. It was observed by Taunton J in *Morley* v. *Hall*[216] that stamp duty 'involves nothing of the principle or reason but depends altogether on the language of the legislature' although more recently Carnworth J stated that in stamp duty one should not pay too much attention to the wording of the legislation.[217] However, the peculiar nature of stamp duty as a documentary tax gave rise to numerous issues as to how far HMRC Stamp Taxes can go behind the documents and restructure the transaction and/or rewrite the documents where these have been designed to minimise stamp duty. The long-held principle generally applied to all taxing statutes was that avoidance was acceptable in that it was perfectly permissible deliberately to arrange one's affairs with a view to minimising the payment of tax.[218] The resultant mushrooming of tax avoidance in other spheres of taxation by the use of highly complex and artificial schemes resulted in a severe curtailment of the operation of the *Westminster* principle by the House of Lords[219] in the leading cases since then, and this principle has undergone significant revision in later cases. It does, however, permit the courts to take a more robust approach to the legal form of the transaction when analysing matters as regards the tax consequences and

---

[215] FA 2003, Sched.16, para.2.
[216] (1834) 2 Dowl 494.
[217] *LM Tenancies* v. *IRC* [1996] STC 880 (on appeal [1998] STC 326).
[218] IRC v. Duke of Westminster [1936] AC 1.
[219] *WT Ramsay Ltd* v. *IRC* [1979] 1 WLR 974; *Eilbeck* v. *Rawling* [1981] 2 WLR 449; *Furniss* v. *Dawson* [1984] STC 153.

notwithstanding the comment in *Westmoreland* v. *MacNiven*[220] that stamp taxes are different. These principles have been applied to stamp taxes in other jurisdictions. [221] They have also been applied by the much reversed Vinelott J in *Ingram* v. *IRC*.[222] However, HMRC Stamp Taxes has, hitherto, shown no great enthusiasm for applying these principles. The attack on various routine devices was abandoned shortly after the *Ingram* decision and there was only one very half-hearted attempt to apply these principles to stamp duty reserve tax. It has emerged informally that an attempt by HMRC Stamp Taxes to apply them to SDLT has been abandoned in one particular case for 'operational reasons' which have not been explained. In addition, there is the fundamental question answered in different jurisdictions as to whether the judicial anti-avoidance principles can co-exist alongside statutory general anti-avoidance provisions and where there are specific anti-avoidance provisions.

Historically stamp taxes have been regarded as a tax of wholly different nature from other taxes. A key issue is that the tax falls upon the purchaser. Most taxes fall upon the vendor. Stamp taxes are, in consequence, a cost of the transaction rather than a tax upon the disposal proceeds. Additionally, it is a tax upon the gross price whereas most taxes are upon the profits or gains of the taxpayer. Stamp taxes are a cost imposed upon individual transactions whereas most taxes fall upon the annual profits or gains of the vendor. It might be said that similar issues apply to VAT; but in regard to that tax the purchaser may be entitled to recover the input tax on his transaction. If he cannot recover the input tax, it is unlikely that the purchaser will be required to charge tax on his onward sale so that the cascade effect of transaction-based taxes is avoided to a significant extent. Unfortunately, there is no such relief for stamp taxes against this cascade effect of tax upon the same tax since subsale relief (which was designed to deal with such problems) has been severely truncated (see **5.8**). These issues applied to stamp duty as well as SDLT but the judiciary have not tackled the cascade problem, nor it seems have they always appreciated the basic distinction between tax avoidance and cost reduction. Moreover, since SDLT is a transaction-based tax this judicial stance makes it likely that the tax avoidance cases will be applied to the new tax regardless of the issues and consequences. The main issue is whether HMRC Stamp Taxes having traditionally not pursued this approach to tax efficiency in practice in relation to stamp duty will continue this practice of not relying upon the approach as part of the inevitable baggage of previous law carried over with the new tax. Previous cases have shown that the courts were only too ready in this field to tax the legal substance of the transaction rather than the form but in this context of a highly technical land law regime 'legal substance' has a particular meaning, namely the true legal effect of the transaction rather than any 'label' which the parties may attach to their document. Thus a

---

[220] [2001] STC 237.
[221] Collector of Stamp Revenue v. Arrowtown Assets Ltd [2003] HKCFA 47; Carreras Group Ltd v. The Stamp Commissioner [2004] STC 1377.
[222] [1995] STC 564.

transfer of assets to a company may be described as an amalgamation but in stamp tax terms it is an acquisition.[223]

In the same way, the grant of some rights over land will be taxable as a lease regardless of the fact that the parties term the instrument a licence, if the legal relationship which the instrument creates is one of lessor and lessee.[224] On occasion, the label used by the parties to describe their document may tip the balance when interpreting its effect[225] but, in general, the parties' intention is irrelevant in arriving at the legal effect or construction of the document.[226] Hence, the substance of an instrument has traditionally meant strict legal effect looking at all the circumstances rather than an alternative economic or commercial arrangement.

1.32.2 Sham transactions

The above examples concerned the artificial nature of the end result of the transactions, and provided that they were genuine in themselves it was considered allowable to arrive at their conclusion by a circuitous route provided that the steps taken genuinely had the effect intended. On the other hand, as Lord Wilberforce observed in *Ramsay*, a sham transaction is one which 'while professing to be one thing, is in fact something different'. This raises the question of whether the documentation setting out the various steps represents the true bargain between the parties. The normal principles of construction involve only the words in the instrument so that extrinsic materials such as the parties' intentions are irrelevant.[227] This can work both for and against the parties since they are not allowed to contradict their written words.[228] In consequence the nature of the transaction and its SDLT consequences depend upon the drafting and the parties' conduct is not relevant to the analysis unless such conduct shows that the drafting was misleading and intended to produce a tax result different from that which would have applied had the transaction been accurately described.[229]

1.32.3 Form and substance

There are questions as to whether HMRC Stamp Taxes can go behind the legal structure adopted by the parties to investigate whether the parties have correctly and accurately set this out in the documentation, and whether HMRC can charge SDLT upon the basis that the same economic and commercial result could have been

---

[223] *Great Western Railway Co* v. *IRC* [1894] 1 QB 507; *J&P Coats Ltd* v. *IRC* [1897] 1 QB 778, on appeal [1897] 2 QB 423.

[224] See Addiscombe Garden Estates Ltd v. Crabbe [1958] 1 QB 513.

[225] *British India Steam Navigation* v. *IRC* (1880–81) LR 7 QBD 165; *Ogwr* v. *Dykes* [1989] 2 All ER 880.

[226] *Peter Bone* v. *IRC* [1995] STC 921.

[227] West London Syndicate Ltd v. IRC [1898] 2 QB 507.

[228] *Peter Bone* v. *IRC* [1995] STC 921.

[229] Lloyds & Scottish v. Cyril Lord [1992] BCLC 609; Snook v. London and West Riding Investments Ltd [1967] 2 QB 786; Ingram v. IRC [1985] STC 835.

achieved by other means attracting a higher liability to tax. It is clear that in SDLT no such power exists. A taxpayer is entitled to choose between alternative routes to reach the same commercial end[230] and it is permissible for that choice to be made upon the basis of a better post-tax result.[231] Tax efficiency in choice of routes is not tax avoidance. This is important in the context of certain reliefs from SDLT for company reconstructions[232] where one of the conditions for relief is the absence of a stamp duty avoidance motive.[233]

1.33   STATUTORY GENERAL ANTI-AVOIDANCE PROVISIONS

There are certain specific anti-avoidance provisions in the legislation directed at particular transactions.[234] There are also 'general' anti-avoidance provisions where there are conditions within various reliefs such as requiring the transaction to be bona fide commercial or not for tax avoidance purposes. These restrictions apply to numerous particular reliefs.[235] In December 2006 HMRC Stamp Taxes introduced in what is now FA 2003, ss.75A–75C (as amended) certain general anti-avoidance provisions. These provisions apply where:

- there are a number of transactions. This means that there must be more than one step in the arrangement. However, it is unclear at present whether HMRC Stamp Taxes intends to take the view that, because of the transaction nature of the tax and the rules of substantial performance, in a routine sale and purchase or grant of a lease transaction there are at least two steps (namely contract and completion) with possibly a third step in the form of substantial performance. Moreover, 'transaction' is not limited to chargeable transactions and includes non-chargeable events and such activities are not limited to land transactions such as the purchase or issue of shares;
- the taxpayer, described in the legislation as 'P' acquires the property having paid less tax than he would have done in respect of a notional transaction. This, the lower tax condition, tests whether the SDLT paid by P upon his actual acquisition is lower than the tax that he would have paid on a direct acquisition from the vendor or landlord, described in the legislation as 'V'.

---

[230]   *Sherdley* v. *Sherdley* [1988] AC 213.
[231]   *Willoughby* v. *IRC* [1995] STC 143.
[232]   FA 2003, Sched.7.
[233]   Thus, for example, it has been accepted by the previous Special Commissioners (now the Upper Tribunal) that deciding upon a transaction and seeking to implement it with the minimum stamp duty is not a tax avoidance motive for these purposes.
[234]   See, for example, FA 2003, ss.44A and 45A dealing with certain types of building contract; see **Chapter 9**.
[235]   See, for example, FA 2003, Sched.7; see **Chapter 13**.

1.34 REPORTING TAX SCHEMES

There is a complex and developing regime for the disclosure of tax avoidance schemes (DOTAS). These provisions have been extended to SDLT and require taxpayers and promoters of tax schemes to disclose if they are entering into arrangements designed for the reduction of SDLT or certain other taxes.

1.35 FORWARD PLANNING

There appears to be a major issue of principle involved in this area. For there to be unacceptable tax avoidance there must be an actual avoidance of tax. Should no tax charge arise, no tax has been avoided and planning with a view to possible reduction of tax in the future is not tax avoidance.[236]

In the light of judicial observations in cases such as *Shepherd* v. *Lyntress*[237] there would seem to be no objection, for example, to transferring land to an offshore company with a view to finding a purchaser at a later date,[238] even though by passing the land into the company in this way a stamp duty liability may be avoided on what is the effective disposal of the land.[239] A series of transactions is not 'pre-ordained' unless it involves a degree of certainty and control over the end result at the time when the intermediate steps are taken.[240] Preparatory steps such as these cannot be censured as tax avoidance, because at this stage no tax charge has arisen so no tax has been avoided.[241] The parties have merely put themselves in a position whereby at a later date a transaction may escape a tax charge that might have arisen had not the steps been taken. In such situations the question is how the current judiciary will develop the need for a cut-and-dried or pre-arranged scheme as an integral part of the tax avoidance principle and if such a scheme or an 'arrangement' rather than the very different issue of hope or expectation[242] is required for these principles to apply, how this concept of a cut-and-dried scheme is to be interpreted.

---

[236] Where this is the case the questions of the seven-year rule and potentially exempt transfers, the previously owned assets regime, etc. would be redundant since the original gift here, intended to mitigate possible tax, would remain unacceptable tax avoidance and, therefore, ineffective to save tax.

[237] [1989] STC 617.

[238] But note the circumstances requiring disclosure of tax avoidance schemes and the formation of 'special purpose vehicles'; see **1.34**.

[239] HMRC has recognised the problems of land rich companies and foreign incorporated special purpose vehicles but it appears that technical and practical difficulties thwarted the intention to tax such arrangements.

[240] Shepherd v. Lyntress [1989] STC 617; Littlewoods Mail Order Stores v. IRC [1961] Ch 597; Fitzwilliam v. IRC [1993] STC 502.

[241] Compare *Times Newspapers* v. *IRC* [1971] 3 All ER 98. The decision of Vinelott J in *Combined Technologies Plc* v. *IRC* [1985] STC 348 was inconsistent with some of his own decisions in a similar context such as *Ingram* v. *IRC* [1985] STC 835 at the same time.

[242] See the attempt by HMRC Stamp Taxes to introduce such a concept when dealing with the meaning of 'arrangements' in the effectively abortive Statement of Practice SP3/98 in relation to stamp duty.

This could be important where the parties take steps to convert land into shares by vesting it in a company; but the importance of such forward planning has been substantially diminished by the three-year clawback provisions introduced by FA 2003 for corporate reliefs and subsequently as a long-term anti-avoidance measure of an extremely crude nature.[243] There is also a fundamental question of principle as to whether the judicial intervention is applicable to a wide range of tax mitigation techniques upon the basis that the arrangements are seeking to make use of a choice of routes for purposes not intended by what the judge believes to be Parliament's intention or is limited to transactions where the taxpayer seeks to reduce his taxation liability by generating losses or other reliefs as deducted which have no reality economically.[244]

Aggressive tax savings schemes were never within the scope of this book, but other straightforward – and hopefully still recognised – side-steps which can be legitimately and safely employed to avoid major pitfalls or to minimise or avoid tax, are dealt with as and when appropriate in the following chapters.[245] A key obligation owed to clients is to avoid pitfalls (by e.g. inappropriate drafting) which lead to an unnecessary large charge to tax and to suggest a structure that produces a reasonably tax efficient implementation of the transaction. This duty applies notwithstanding that the adviser may have indicated that he does not advise on tax as such;[246] it arises from the professional duty to draw the attention of the client to 'benefits' as discussed in *BE Studios* v. *Smith and Williamson*.[247] Attempts are made in the following chapters to indicate such pitfalls and possible alternatives.

The linked transaction rules exist solely for the purposes of fixing the rates of tax and are not a general principle that enables HMRC Stamp Taxes to introduce some form of associated operations principle. Unless the statutory general anti-avoidance provisions are potentially involved, the chargeable transaction has to be dealt with on its own terms; the fact that it is part of a larger transaction or arrangement cannot, of itself, affect the taxation consequences. Any challenge by HMRC Stamp Taxes must be founded, if at all, on the 'tax avoidance cases' based upon *Ramsay*[248] and *Furniss* v. *Dawson*[249] and the issue of form over substance or the purposive construction or however the principle is developed by judicial interpretation in the future. It must, however, be reiterated that stamp taxes differ fundamentally from most other taxes in that they are a cost of acquisition not a tax on the profit arising on

---

[243] There will also be major issues of evidence and principle for the statutory general anti-avoidance provisions (FA 2003, ss.75A–75C, as amended) and whether such forward planning means that the disposal into the forward planning makes it 'involved in connection with' the relevant acquisition which is required before these provisions can apply.

[244] Note the approach in *Burmah Oil* v. *IRC* [1982] STC 30; *Cairns* v. *MacDiarmid* [1983] STC 178.

[245] Moreover, such planning may involve advance disclosure to HMRC pursuant to FA 2004, Part 7; Stamp Duty Land Tax Avoidance Schemes (Prescribed Descriptions of Arrangements) Regulations 2005, SI 2005/1868.

[246] Hurlingham Estates v. Wilde [1997] STC 627.

[247] [2006] STC 358.

[248] [1979] 1 WLR 974.

[249] [1982] STC 267.

sale. Also there will be real transactions designed to reduce the tax charge not create an artificial tax loss (i.e. a technical tax loss but no real economic loss). These issues have not been raised by counsel adequately in the cases of stamp taxes but may represent a significant obstacle for HMRC Stamp Taxes which is not at present structured to investigate the evidence in order to find the facts necessary for these principles to apply. As noted above, notwithstanding the unsatisfactory decision of Vinelott J in *Ingram* v. *IRC*[250] HMRC Stamp Taxes has wisely not sought to rely upon these principles and has recently abandoned a challenge based upon these principles for unspecified 'operational reasons'.

The issue is considered elsewhere below, but there is a danger that the wait-and-see provision, if applicable to the particular chargeable transaction, might mean that later events could become relevant. There is therefore the risk that the tax avoidance cases could mean that the later facts could be utilised by the current judiciary to make the relief unavailable because the first transaction was simply a stepping stone to some larger avoidance arrangement not covered by the relief.

---

[250] [1985] STC 835.

CHAPTER 2

Chargeable transactions

2.1 GENERAL

The charge to SDLT arises in respect of 'land transactions', which includes the general charge to the tax[1] plus a whole range of specifically chargeable transactions. These include transactions deemed to be chargeable transactions such as certain building arrangements[2] or 'abnormal' increases in rent after the expiration of the fifth year of the term of the lease[3] or the clawback of previously taken reliefs.[4] However, it is provided[5] that, in general, entry into a contract does not give rise to a payment obligation at that stage. The contract may be the basis for a chargeable transaction, but it is necessary for there to be other events in order to give rise to an obligation to pay SDLT and notify.[6]

2.2 CHARGEABLE AND NOTIFIABLE TRANSACTIONS

The tax has an extensive compliance regime (see **Chapters 14, 17** and **18**) imposing *inter alia* a notification obligation upon taxpayers;[7] but there is not a total correlation between chargeable transactions and notifiable transactions. Consequently, where there is a chargeable transaction the mere fact that tax is not payable (such as where there is a relief) does not mean that some form of notification is not required by means of a land transaction return (SDLT 1).[8] Conversely, there are many situations where it is necessary to file a land transaction return (SDLT 1) in response to which a Revenue certificate (SDLT 5) will be issued notwithstanding that it is not necessary to trouble the Land Registry with the transaction. For example, the parties may be entering into a transaction where the legal title is held by a nominee and they are merely dealing with the equitable interest behind the bare trust. Such interests

---

[1] FA 2003, s.43.
[2] FA 2003, ss.44A and 45A; see **Chapter 9**.
[3] FA 2003, Sched.17A, paras.14 and 15.
[4] See, e.g. FA 2003, Sched.7, paras.3 and 9.
[5] See, e.g. FA 2003, ss.44(2), 45(2) and 45A(2).
[6] FA 2003, ss.119 and 44.
[7] FA 2003, s.77 and Sched.10, Part 1.
[8] See e.g. FA 2003, s.77A.

are chargeable interests and the relevant parties are the beneficial owners not the registered nominee.[9] Subject to any relevant thresholds and whether the interests concerned are major interests[10] the transaction is *prima facie* chargeable and tax may be payable. It will be necessary to notify the transaction to HMRC Stamp Taxes but any Revenue certificate (SDLT 5) received will be little more than an acknowledgement that a return has been received.[11] Similar issues can arise in many situations such as variations of interests in trusts, or variations of the estates of deceased individuals, or where there is substantial performance of a contract without 'completion'. There is, therefore, no direct correlation between chargeable and notifiable transactions.

There are specific provisions in FA 2003 dealing with situations where a Land Registry may be involved but filing an SDLT 1 is not required, such as:

- non-notifiable transactions and situations where entries may be made without any form of registration (e.g. entry of restrictions against title in certain circumstances);[12]
- where the entry is required to be made without any application;
- so far as the entry relates to an interest or right other than the chargeable interest acquired by the purchaser under the land transaction that gives rise to the application;
- a contract under s.44(4) or as that applies to s.45 or Sched.17A, para.12B;
- a contract within s.44A(3) or as that applies to s.45A;
- deemed grants of leases (including Scotland) upon substantial performance pursuant to Sched.17A, paras.12A(2) or 19(3); and
- deeds of variation increasing or reducing the rent or term pursuant to Sched. 17A, paras.13 and 15A.

2.3 NON-TAXABLE TRANSACTIONS

There are numerous reasons why a transaction is not taxable in the broad sense that no tax is payable (see **Chapter 5** and **17.7**) and there are many (not necessarily consistent) ways in which the draftsmen have made use of various terms for cancelling, excluding or reducing the charge to SDLT. Moreover, the reason why a transaction is not chargeable is important for compliance purposes such as where the transaction is for a consideration treated as nil or to be ignored.[13]

---

[9]   FA 2003, s.48 and Sched.16, para.3 (as amended).

[10]   FA 2003, s.77A.

[11]   In the current regime where filing and payment are not necessarily concurrent events it will not even operate as a receipt or proof of payment of the tax potentially due. FA 2003, s.76 (as amended) and the form of the Revenue certificate (SDLT 5) as specified by Stamp Duty Land Tax (Administration) Regulations 2003, SI 2003/2837, Part 1 as amended.

[12]   FA 2003, s.79(1) and (2).

[13]   See, for example, FA 2003, Sched.17A, para.16 on surrenders and regrants, etc.; Sched.3, para.1; s.77A.

2.4 THE BASIC CHARGE

The effect of the interaction of the various definitions[14] is that a chargeable transaction is one that:

- arises on the acquisition of a chargeable interest in land in the UK (excluding cases where the transaction is not chargeable because it relates to an exempt interest[15] or because the particular transaction qualifies for relief, such as a lease to a charity);[16] and
- is not a transaction that is exempt (which is an ambiguous term; see **2.10**) from charge.[17]

Although it is not expressly stated, there needs to be 'chargeable consideration', which can include deemed consideration.[18] Consideration is required in law to create a contract so no charge normally arises where there is no actual consideration unless the legislation deems there to be consideration.[19] Also, there is a general exemption for transactions where there is no chargeable consideration notwithstanding that there is actual consideration. Where there is no chargeable consideration the transaction is not chargeable but there may be notification obligations[20] (although there are considerable technical problems as to whether the charge applies where the title passes by reason of equitable principles[21] or by other operation of law because there may not be a 'contract' with actual or deemed consideration).

The transaction may be 'chargeable' although no tax is payable, which is an issue around the obligation to file a land transaction return (SDLT 1).[22]

There are several aspects of the basic charge outlined above each of which requires explanation and expansion and these will now be discussed in turn. There are other situations where there are deemed chargeable transactions.

---

[14] FA 2003, ss.49(1) and 43(1).

[15] FA 2003, s.48(1) and (2).

[16] FA 2003, Sched.8.

[17] FA 2003, s.49(1).

[18] There are three situations albeit of limited extent where actual consideration and chargeable consideration differ, namely: (i) where the legislation deems there to be consideration notwithstanding that there is no actual consideration (see e.g. FA 2003, s.53; Sched.15, Part 3); (ii) where the legislation deems the chargeable consideration to be of a different amount or value from the actual consideration (see e.g. FA 2003, s.53); and (iii) where the actual consideration is ignored (see e.g. FA 2003, Sched.17A, para.16).

[19] Such as in regard to the connected company and partnership regimes: FA 2003, s.53 and Sched.15, Part 3.

[20] FA 2003, Sched.3, para.1; see **Chapter 5**.

[21] FA 2003, s.43(2); *Yaxley* v. *Gotts* [1999] 3 WLR 1217; *Henry* v. *Henry* [2010] 1 All ER 988.

[22] FA 2003, s.77; Sched.10, Part 1.

2.5 CHARGEABLE TRANSACTIONS: 'ACQUISITION'

The charge is based upon 'acquisition' of a chargeable interest. 'Acquisition' has a plain English meaning but this is not in any way consistent with the legislation if this is to work as intended. Moreover, certain provisions providing 'reliefs' are indirect extensions of the meaning of 'acquisition' because the reliefs would not be necessary unless there would otherwise be a chargeable transaction.[23] There is no express statement that an 'interest' is acquired when purchased. This appears to be assumed and the 'plain English' meaning of 'acquisition' is artificially extended to 'include':[24]

- the creation of a chargeable interest;[25]
- the surrender of a chargeable interest;[26]
- the release[27] of a chargeable interest;[28]
- the variation of a chargeable interest other than leases;[29]
- certain variations of leases;[30] and
- deemed acquisitions. Certain transactions that would not fall within the above are treated as taxable and the deemed acquisition of a chargeable interest.[31]

Notwithstanding that the SDLT is based upon 'acquisition' of chargeable interests the tax charge, i.e. the effective date, can arise before any interest is 'acquired' by the purchaser in the traditional sense of property vesting even in cases where property is transferred, such as sales. It is, therefore, essential to note that the rules apply by reference to artificial dates that are essentially unrelated to either the passing of title whether legal or equitable or even the time when title passes. Any correlation between the passing of title, whether legal or equitable, and the charge to tax will be essentially a matter of coincidence rather than a matter of principle. For example, a constructive trust in favour of a purchaser arises and the equitable interest vests only where the purchase price is paid in full[32] and cannot arise where the contract is

---

[23] Compare *J&P Coats Ltd* v. *IRC* [1897] 2 QB 423; see, for example, FA 2003, Sched.3, paras.3A and 4, compare *Jopling* v. *IRC* [1940] 2 KB 282; Administration of Estates Act 1925, s.42.

[24] 'Include' means that the statutory definition is not exhaustive. It assumes a basic meaning but other events may be subject to the tax (*Oughtred* v. *IRC* [1960] AC 206). Indeed this construction is essential since the list of 'inclusions' does not refer to routine purchases which must be involved if the legislation is to work effectively.

[25] FA 2003, s.43(3)(a). It remains to be seen whether 'creation' includes an interest arising by reason of 'exception and reservation' in a conveyance or grant or whether such words operate as a transfer or regrant producing a land exchange; FA 2003, s.47; see **Chapter 7**.

[26] FA 2003, s.43(3)(b).

[27] It remains to be seen whether 'release' and 'surrender' includes actions such as 'waiver' or 'disclaimer' or 'renunciation' particularly in Scotland.

[28] FA 2003, s.43(3)(b).

[29] FA 2003, s.43(3)(c).

[30] FA 2003, s.43(3)(d) (as amended) and Sched.17A, para.15A (as amended); see **Chapter 8**. There are issues around break clauses.

[31] See, for example, abnormal rent increases pursuant to FA 2003, Sched.17A, paras.14 and 15 and certain variations of leases pursuant to FA 2003, Sched.17A, para.15A.

[32] Michaels v. Harley House (Marylebone) Ltd [1999] 3 WLR 229; Re Kidner [1929] 2 Ch 121; Musselwhite v. Musselwhite [1962] Ch 964; Langen and Wind Ltd v. Bell [1972] Ch 685.

conditional;[33] but the charge arises when only 90 per cent of the purchase price is paid as substantial performance of the contract.[34]

The basic charge will apply to sales of freeholds and leases and the grant of leases, although in some situations[35] such as where there is an 'acquisition' producing a chargeable transaction, that transaction may be taxed in a manner totally different from its correct legal analysis. For example, the assignment or variation of a lease may be taxed upon the basis that it is the grant of a new lease,[36] and a deed of variation of a lease may be taxed as a surrender and regrant.[37]

In consequence, the inappropriateness of this use of 'acquisition' is likely to mislead taxpayers in cases such as where on surrender or release interests disappear or cease to have a separate existence (as in the merger of interests or surrenders of leases or the termination of leases by notice to quit).[38] In many situations there is no obvious 'acquisition'. It is difficult to see who in plain English 'acquires' what when an option is varied or the property interest involved 'disappears' such as upon the release of a restrictive covenant. However, since the term is defined merely by what it 'includes' there is the potential for HMRC Stamp Taxes to seek to bring other types of transaction into charge. Problem areas could include disclaimers, waivers and renunciation.[39] In addition, and unhelpfully, the tax charge arises before, as a matter of law, any interest in the property vests in the taxpayer (as noted in the situation of constructive trusts and purchasers).[40]

There is also a question of whether 'acquisition' requires a bilateral transaction. A movement of an interest in land as a result of the actions of one person acting alone, such as giving a notice to quit[41] has the practical effect of returning the tenancy interest to the landlord but, it seems, may not be an 'acquisition'.[42] Arrangements involving break clauses may give rise to a notional chargeable transaction pursuant to the general anti-avoidance provisions.[43] Fortunately, it seems that there is no intention to treat 'mergers' of separate interests held by the

---

[33] Michaels v. Harley House (Marylebone) Ltd [1999] 3 WLR 229; Warmington v. Miller [1973] 2 All ER 372.

[34] FA 2003, s.44(7).

[35] FA 2003, Sched.17A, paras.11 and 14.

[36] FA 2003, Sched.17A, para.15A (as amended).

[37] Friends Provident Life Office v. British Railways Board [1996] 1 All ER 336; compare Gable Construction v. IRC [1968] 1 WLR 1426.

[38] Which raises fundamental issues as to whether a chargeable interest that disappears can have a value because there is nothing to be sold by the 'purchaser' in the open market.

[39] The inclusion of 'renunciation' in relation to the definition of 'transfer' involving partnerships (FA 2003, Sched.15, para.9(2)(c)) suggests that, because it was thought necessary to include in this definition so transactions such as renunciations, disclaimers and waivers are not acquisitions notwithstanding that the property transfers to or vests in another person because these dispose of property not owned by the person entering into the transaction. The word has a special meaning in Scotland which may not be within the legislation.

[40] Re Kidner [1929] 2 Ch 121; Parway Estates Ltd v. IRC 45 TC 135; Michaels v. Harley House (Marylebone) Ltd [2000] Ch 104; Warmington v. Miller [1973] 2 All ER 372.

[41] *Barrett v. Morgan* [2000] 2 AC 264.

[42] See also FA 2003, s.43(3)(d) and Sched.17A, para.15A (as amended).

[43] FA 2003, ss.75A–75C; see **1.33**.

same person as acquisitions because, notwithstanding the change in the nature of the reversionary interest of the owner, he does not 'acquire' any additional interest in the property.[44]

2.6 ABORTIVE ARRANGEMENTS

Since the charge can arise before completion or even by equitable 'acquisition', an effective date can occur at an early stage (for example where a purchaser goes into possession when the contract is still conditional such as where the assignment of a lease or the grant of an underlease is dependent upon the consent of the landlord where no equitable interest passes until the consent has been obtained).[45] It is for this reason that it has proved essential to provide that if the contract is cancelled or rescinded the SDLT can be reclaimed.[46]

2.7 EXTENDED DEFINITION: TYPES OF 'ACQUISITION'

This extended definition of 'acquisition' outlined above gives rise to several surprising consequences because of the implications derived from the legislation as to the construction of the various sub-aspects of acquisitions such as 'creation' and how this relates to 'excepting and reserving' interests and similar routine convey-ancing terminology or consequences. In *Sargaison* v. *Roberts*[47] Megarry J urged HMRC not to create tax charges on the back of antiquated conveyancing laws that are inconsistent with the economic or commercial reality of the transaction. For example, the word 'creation', which is not itself defined, may convert what appears to be a straightforward 'sale' into a land exchange because of the extended meaning given to that term by FA 2003, s.47 and the enlarged definition of chargeable interests pursuant to s.48(1)(b) thereof. It is not unusual for a developer of residen-tial or industrial sites involving several properties to convey each property subject to some form of 'estate covenant'.[48] On occasion this covenant or benefit may be

---

[44] However, this issue is less clear where there is a severance of a beneficial joint interest because the interests of the co-owners are 'enlarged' by the power to dispose of the property by the removal of the right of survivorship. It may also be a 'variation' taxable as a land exchange.

[45] *Warmington* v. *Miller* [1973] 2 All ER 372.

[46] FA 2003, s.44(9).

[47] [1969] 3 All ER 1072.

[48] Different issues may arise where the developer grants leases which contain appropriate covenants. Although there is a question of whether the giving of covenants in a lease constitutes entering into a land contract within the terms of FA 2003, s.47, which would appear to be the case, note the treatment of certain leasehold covenants as not being chargeable consideration pursuant to Sched.17A, para.10. It is understood that HMRC Stamp Taxes has not responded to an enquiry as to whether it will treat every lease containing appropriate covenants by the tenant as two taxable events within FA 2003, Sched.4, para.5. Fortunately, hitherto, no points have been taken in practice on this basis but in the absence of a formal statement, there are risks of it being the basis of a challenge should HMRC Stamp Taxes form the impression that any particular case is one where 'tax avoidance' is involved.

retained by the developer by means of provisions relating to the 'exception and reservation' of rights from the conveyance when it may be arguable that there is no 'creation' of a new right, simply a retention by the vendor of a part-interest in the land so that a part-interest does not pass to the purchaser. However, HMRC Stamp Taxes does not accept this analysis of routine transactions and claims that[49] such exception and reservation involves a transfer and regrant of a new right in exactly the same way as where there is an outright transfer with a regrant of the right back to the transferor by the transferee.[50] This approach represents the express creation of a new right rather than the retention of an existing right implicit in the ownership of the land.[51] Whenever the arrangement 'creates' a new right there will be a land exchange, probably of a major interest for a minor interest, thereby leading to two transactions deemed to take place at market value.[52] There will be considerable debate as to what rights, if any, may be excepted and/or reserved without the need for a regrant. It seems at present that only mineral interests and already existing separate rights over the land are regarded by HMRC Stamp Taxes as being capable of retention not requiring a 'regrant'.

2.8 PROCESS OF 'ACQUISITION'

The charge to tax applies whether the 'acquisition' is effected:

- by act of the parties, which will apply to routine contracts for sale, agreements for lease, grants of options, etc. (i.e. bilateral transactions for consideration);
- by order of the court or other authority such as where the court order creates or completes or sanctions a transaction;[53]

---

[49]   Except in relation to pre-existing rights or mineral rights which can be 'reserved'.

[50]   Relying upon *Johnstone* v. *Holdway* [1963] 1 All ER 432; HMRC Stamp Taxes has not addressed the issue of rights arising pursuant to Law of Property 1925, s.62 but as the tax applies to transactions taking effect by operation of law it seems that such transactions may be taxable and fall within the land exchange head of charge. A more challenging issue is that of 'resulting trusts' where the label suggests that the entire interest has passed and part thereof 'returns' to the transferee rather than there being a failure to dispose of the equitable interest (such as the presumptions in relation to true purchasers and nominees) or to dispose of part thereof (see e.g. *Vandervell* v. *IRC* [1967] 1 All ER 1). This may be a further reason for HMRC Stamp Taxes to raise unintended tax based on ancient land law and equitable principles.

[51]   Note the similar issues of 'resulting trusts' i.e. whether they represent a failure to dispose of the entire interest or an outright transfer with a re-transfer of the undisposed part of the interest (*Vandervell* v. *IRC* [1967] 1 All ER 1).

[52]   FA 2003, s.47 and Sched.4, para.5; see **Chapter 4** on the vexed question of the market value of minor interests.

[53]   Terrapin International v. IRC [1976] 1 WLR 665; Sun Alliance Insurance Ltd v. IRC [1971] 1 All ER 135.

- by or under any statutory provision such as a private Act of Parliament or the exercise of powers of compulsory acquisition;[54] or
- by operation of law.[55]

These definitions and the express statement that a document is not necessary[56] are the provisions that make the SDLT a transaction-based tax since the charge applies whether or not there is any instrument effecting the transaction,[57] and bring into the charge to tax many transactions entered into informally and without professional advice but which are nonetheless effective to constitute 'acquisitions'. This exposes the lay taxpayer to considerable risks of penalties and interest, particularly in family arrangements such as caring for elderly relatives. The tax is a major trap for taxpayers who tend not to seek advice unless they believe that documentation is required and may rely upon non-legal professionals who are not always aware of the subtleties of land law and the scope of the tax.[58]

Unfortunately none of the above sub-terms is itself defined so that problems lurk in areas such as transactions by operation of law.

2.9 BY OPERATION OF LAW

'Acquisitions' include transactions taking effect by operation of law because no writing is required. This includes surrenders of leases by operation of law and releases of life interests in settlements and easements. Variations of chargeable interests[59] other than leases will include any modification of a chargeable interest such as the extension of an option, moving a right of way or changes in rights to light. Variations of leases have caused HMRC Stamp Taxes considerable problems and have produced numerous changes so that variations of leases must be regarded as an extremely fluid matter requiring constant inspection of the legislation and regulations.[60]

'By operation of law' is a particularly ambiguous term and is a very obscure form of chargeable 'acquisition' within the legislation. There are many situations where

---

[54]   The effect of rights created by provisions such as Law of Property Act 1925, s.62 remains an open question particularly as the tax applies to transactions 'by operation of law'.

[55]   FA 2003, s.43(2).

[56]   FA 2003, s.42(2).

[57]   FA 2003, s.42(2)(a).

[58]   The introduction of the tax may have extended the duties owed by non-legal advisers because there is unlikely to be the expectation of other legal or tax advisers acting in relation to the transaction; see e.g. *Hurlingham Estates* v. *Wilde* [1997] STC 627 on the expectation of other tax advice as a defence to negligence.

[59]   This is a different issue from the variation of a contract which is not, in general, of itself a chargeable transaction but contracts to acquire land are clearly chargeable interests so that in the absence of specific provisions excluding dealings in contracts such as FA 2003, ss.44 and 45 modifications of contracts could be chargeable transactions especially where value shifting may be involved. Also such variations will be 'transactions' within the statutory general anti-avoidance provisions (FA 2003, ss.75A–75C). Moreover these activities may affect transitional relief for new changes in the tax.

[60]   See for details **Chapter 8**.

the transaction takes effect by operation of law giving a particular effect to the actions of the parties which may not be the same as that which they contemplated. For example, a deed of variation may by operation of law constitute a surrender and regrant.[61] A tenant may surrender a lease without writing by operation of law. In these cases the law operates to give effect to the agreement or contract between the parties but not in the way described in the parties' documentation. In other words the law gives a particular effect to the parties' agreement at variance with that which they may have believed was appropriate.

Alternatively transactions by operation of law[62] can arise where a transaction takes effect pursuant to statute such as holding over[63] or pursuant to certain reorganisations of insurance companies or certain types of administrative merger or demerger of companies pursuant to foreign law: i.e. the relevant law provides that certain consequences follow automatically upon the actions of certain persons. In relation to stamp duty HMRC Stamp Taxes accepted that such transactions were not conveyances on sale because the title, or at least the beneficial interest in the assets, passed by reason of the operation of foreign law and did not require any further act on behalf of the parties to transfer the title other than in the case of overseas transactions the purely administrative movement of legal title to assets in the United Kingdom such as registered land.

In other situations the law may operate in a different way to impose obligations upon parties where there is no prior agreement. The circumstances may by reason of the conduct of the parties give rise to some form of equitable relief such as a constructive trust.[64] In this situation there is no valid contract between the parties.[65] In consequence, there may not be chargeable consideration and, therefore, the transaction being non-contractual may not be a chargeable event. However, many of these arrangements will give rise to a preliminary argument as to whether there is some form of contract for consideration. There are numerous cases indicating that what appears to be a conditional arrangement may not be a conditional contract or a conditional gift but is a transaction for consideration and, therefore, *prima facie* contractual.[66] Such arrangements may also constitute an attempt by the party to create a contract for consideration but fail to satisfy the requirements for writing or deed such as Law of Property (Miscellaneous Provisions) Act 1989, s.2 or Law of Property Act 1925, ss.52 and 53. Here there is an agreement but it is not a contract

---

[61] *Friends Provident Life Office* v. *British Railways Board* [1996] 1 All ER 336 compare *Gable Construction* v. *IRC* [1968] 1 WLR 1426; see also *Donellan* v. *Read* (1832) 3 B & Ad 899.

[62] But HMRC Stamp Taxes may have it in contemplation to contend that such arrangements are either by order of any authority or under a statutory provision notwithstanding that the authority is situated within a foreign jurisdiction.

[63] Landlord and Tenant Act 1954; see **8.47**.

[64] *Binions* v. *Evans* [1972] Ch 359; *ER Ives (Investments)* v. *High* [1967] 2 QB 379.

[65] But note *Yaxley* v. *Gotts* [1999] 3 WLR 1217; compare *Henry* v. *Henry* [2010] 1 All ER 988.

[66] *Errington* v. *Errington and Woods* [1952] 1 KB 290; GUS Merchandise v. Customs and Excise [1981] 1 WLR 1309; *Eastham* v. *Leigh London and Provincial Properties Ltd* [1971] 2 All ER 887.

because the paperwork is inadequate.[67] In these situations equity may intervene to provide relief notwithstanding the absence of writing.[68] However, this line between invalid attempts at contracts that give rise to possible equitable relief 'by operation of law' and effective oral contracts notwithstanding the legislation as suggested in *Yaxley* v. *Gotts*[69] has been blurred. Possible arguments that passing of property by operation of equitable notions where there is no valid contract do not giving rise to a charge to tax are no longer quite so clear. Many arrangements will, therefore, where they turn upon equity potentially raise very difficult issues of the charge to tax.

2.10   NOT AN EXEMPT TRANSACTION

SDLT arises in relation to a land transaction that is a chargeable transaction but not a transaction that is 'exempt' from charge,[70] which refers[71] to the list of 'exempt transactions' within FA 2003 and, obviously, includes transactions involving exempt interests.[72] It seems that 'exempt' in this context is limited since the legislation refers to transactions 'exempt' for reasons other than as provided in Sched.3. Transactions not 'exempt' pursuant to Sched.3 remain *prima facie* notifiable notwithstanding that no tax is payable.[73] Since transactions are 'exempt' for a variety of reasons, not all of which are described in the legislation as 'exempt', it is important to note that the manner in which the relief is given can have significant consequences for the compliance regime and for subsequent transactions relating to that property. Great care is needed when seeking to construe the word 'exempt'.[74]

Transactions may be 'exempt' although no tax is payable such as where a relief applies but are notifiable or they fall within Sched.3.[75]

---

[67]   See on the requirements of s.2 cases such as *Firstpost Homes* v. *Johnson* [1995] 4 All ER 355; but note the oral exercise of options pursuant to *Spiro* v. *Glencrown Properties Ltd* [1991] 1 All ER 600; *Yaxley* v. *Gotts* [1999] 3 WLR 1217; *RTS Flexible Systems Ltd* v. *Molkerei Alois* [2010] 3 All ER 1.

[68]   See, for example, *Yaxley* v. *Gotts* [1999] 3 WLR 1217; but note the limits upon the possible scope of this decision in *Yeoman's Row Management* v. *Cobbe* [2008] 4 All ER 713.

[69]   [1999] 3 WLR 1217.

[70]   FA 2003, s.48(1).

[71]   FA 2003, s.48(2).

[72]   FA 2003, s.48.

[73]   FA 2003, ss.77(1)(b) and 77A(2)(b).

[74]   The restricted nature of this issue must be noted since not being liable to SDLT is based upon several different bases, not all of which qualify as 'exemption' within the peculiar terminology of SDLT. For example, a land transaction will remain a chargeable transaction for the purposes of deciding whether it is notifiable within FA 2003, s.77 notwithstanding that some provisions reduce the chargeable consideration to nil.

[75]   See, for example, FA 2003, Sched.15, para.30; s.53(4); but note this notification obligation does not apply to the exclusion within s.54, Sched.4, para.17.

2.11 SPECIFIC OR DEEMED CHARGEABLE AND NOTIFIABLE TRANSACTIONS: ANTI-AVOIDANCE

The general charge to tax arising upon 'acquisitions' has been progressively enlarged beyond the basic (albeit extended) definition of 'acquisition' described above with related extension of the compliance obligations by an ever-growing number of situations where a charge to tax arises that is not covered by the basic charging provisions. These charges are deemed to arise even in cases where there are no transfers of or modifications of titles or interests in land.[76] Again it is necessary to take into account serious deficiencies in the legislation regarding the difference between chargeable and notifiable transactions (see **Chapter 17**). In many cases an event will have taxation consequences. Frequently, because of the lack of finality in the tax structure, these events will not be chargeable transactions in their own right but events which retrospectively adjust the 'guestimated' land transaction returns filed for the earlier chargeable transaction. It is essential to bear this distinction in mind.

These extensions of the tax base include:

- rent reviews during the first five years;[77]
- increases of rent otherwise than pursuant to the terms of the lease;[78]
- abnormal increases in rent after the earlier of first review date or the expiration of the fifth year of the term of the lease;[79]
- certain variations of leases that are not surrenders and regrants;[80]
- the clawback of various reliefs as a consequence of subsequent transactions;[81]
- the formal grant of a lease subsequent to substantial performance of the agreement for lease.[82] Although this provision was introduced to deal with drafting errors which created problems in relation to compliance, it is being treated by HMRC Stamp Taxes as a separate chargeable transaction (not merely a second stage of a single transaction involving entry into possession and later grant), creating a wide range of problems for the conveyancer;[83]
- completion of a contract between the same parties not being an agreement for lease where there has been prior substantial performance which is regarded by HMRC Stamp Taxes as a separate chargeable transaction;
- holding over leases after the expiration of the contractual term by operation of law or continuation of periodic tenancies or similar arrangements where the aggregate net present value of rent exceeds the chargeable threshold so that tax

---

[76] See, for example, FA 2003, ss.44A and 45A; see **Chapter 9**.

[77] FA 2003, Sched.17A, paras.7 and 8. This is, however, not a separate chargeable transaction but a notifiable retrospective variation of the earlier transaction.

[78] FA 2003, Sched.17A, para.13; see **Chapter 8**.

[79] FA 2003, Sched.17A, paras.13, 14 and 15; see **Chapter 8**.

[80] FA 2003, s.43(3)(d); Sched.17A, para.15A.

[81] FA 2003, Sched.6, para.11; Sched.7, paras.3 and 8; Sched.8, para.2; see **Chapter 5**.

[82] FA 2003, Sched.17A, para.12A; see **Chapter 8**.

[83] Obviously the grant of the lease has to be notified in order to obtain the SDLT 5 required to obtain registration of the lease; FA 2003, s.79(1).

becomes initially payable or additional tax is payable by reason of the deemed extension of the lease or tenancy;[84]

- contracts with a power to direct a conveyance.[85] Measures are in place to combat mitigation arrangements such as building arrangements (see **Chapter 9**) designed to avoid multiple charges on new builds where a developer, rather than purchase the land, enters into a building agreement whereby he is to receive a specified percentage of the sale proceeds of the development. In these circumstances a charge to tax arises upon substantial performance of a contract whereby a person has the right to direct a conveyance (which will include power to direct the grant of a lease) to a third party or to the person himself or such a third party. This will apply, typically, to an agreement between A and B whereby B agrees to carry out works on A's land and A agrees to convey or lease the land either to B or to a third party at B's direction. If B substantially performs the contract with A there is a chargeable transaction even though B may not even have a licence to enter upon A's land;
- variation of chargeable interests[86] such as the modification of the exercise dates for options.

2.12 CHARGEABLE AND EXEMPT INTERESTS IN LAND

The charge is limited to chargeable interests in land in the UK. Other forms of property such as shares and chattels (see **2.15.1**) are not subject to the tax but special rules apply to dealings in interests in partnerships which own interests in land.[87]

2.12.1 Chargeable interests: basic

A chargeable interest is defined[88] as being:

- an estate, interest, right or power in or over land in the UK; or
- the benefit of an obligation, restriction or condition affecting the value of any such estate, interest, right or power;

other than an 'exempt interest'.

Exempt interest is defined[89] as:

- any security interest, which means an interest or right, other than a rent charge, held for the purpose of securing the payment of money or the performance of any other obligation.[90] This will include mortgages[91] and special reliefs that

---

[84] FA 2003, Sched.17A, paras.3 and 4.
[85] FA 2003, ss.44A and 45A.
[86] FA 2003, s.43(3).
[87] FA 2003, Sched.15 (as amended).
[88] FA 2003, s.48(1).
[89] FA 2003, s.48(2).
[90] FA 2003, s.48(3)(a).
[91] On mortgages in general see **Chapter 4**.

apply to other forms of financing property transactions (some of which are intended to assist persons who for religious reasons cannot be involved in borrowing at interest but the relief is not restricted to such persons);[92]

- a licence to use or occupy land. Apart from the question of whether there is a licence or tenancy and the problem of what restrictions upon the exemption arise from the words 'use or occupy',[93] there may be some other form of interest so that not all transactions described as 'licences' will be exempt. For example, a mineral licence is not a licence as such; it is a licence to enter upon land and remove minerals, i.e. it is a *profit à prendre* and a chargeable interest.[94] Licences and tenancies at will are exempt interests not chargeable as such, but they do have tax implications. For example, taking possession of land as a licensee or tenant at will may amount to substantial performance of another contract and produce an effective date;[95]
- in England and Wales and Northern Ireland a tenancy at will or an advowson, franchise[96] or manor and certain interests held by finance companies for the purpose of the alternative finance relief.[97]

This definition of 'chargeable interest' involves numerous problems of construction. The first part, namely estates or interests in or over land, would appear to encompass the normal range of interests or rights affecting land such as freeholds, leaseholds, easements and restrictive covenants. Other legislative provisions indicate that certain arrangements are assumed to be interests in land such as options[98] and pre-emption rights, interests of beneficiaries in trusts and estates.[99] Powers over land would presumably include powers of trustees to appoint or advance property out of a settlement and the powers of executors and personal representatives to appropriate land forming part of an estate of a deceased individual (see further **Chapters 10** and **11**). Without such wide interpretations, the provisions of FA 2003 dealing with exemptions or reliefs for transactions involving trustees and personal representatives[100] would not be necessary. However, the reference to 'power' leaves open many questions apart from powers of appointment or powers of appropriation. For example, it is frequently provided in the articles of a company that the liquidator can use his power to enter into various transactions and

---

[92] FA 2003, ss.71 and following.
[93] FA 2003, s.44.
[94] On questions of whether it is deemed to be a lease and whether the royalty payments are 'rent' see FA 2003, s.52 and Sched.17A, paras.1 and 6; *T&E Homes Ltd* v. *Robinson* [1979] STC 351; see **Chapter 8**.
[95] FA 2003, s.44(6)(b).
[96] Used in the technical sense and not including commercial arrangements to exploit a business name or concept.
[97] FA 2003, s.73B.
[98] FA 2003, s.46.
[99] FA 2003, Sched.3, paras.3, 3A and 4; see **Chapters 10** and **11**; *Baker* v. *Archer Shee* 15 TC 1; *Archer Shee* v. *Garland* 15 TC 693.
[100] FA 2003, Sched.3, paras.3A and 4.

these may in particular circumstances affect land owned by the company. Similarly, a mortgagee has a power of sale of the land held as security.[101]

There are many problems with this definition since, as with so much of the legislation, it is not clear whether it is intended to be so-called 'plain English' or bear its longstanding technical meaning in land law and stamp taxes in order to deal with the highly technical land law and conveyancing underlying land transactions. 'Estate' and 'interest' in or over land are well known, but 'rights' or 'powers' in or over land are not explained. Clearly, rights of way or rights to light will be rights over land, but it seems that the definition is intended to apply on a wider basis, because these aspects of the legislation are intended to block attempts at achieving a non-taxable value shift (see **1.10**). For example, powers of appointment or advancement whether of a general or a special nature will be regarded as chargeable interests.

2.12.2 Contracts as chargeable interests

Contractual rights such as options and pre-emption rights as well as contracts to purchase or lease land are chargeable interests, although many dealings in contractual rights are expressly made non-chargeable.[102] Contractual rights restricting the use of land falling short of restrictive covenants because there is no dominant land to be benefited,[103] such as restrictions related to some form of security for payments pursuant to an overage or clawback arrangement, are intended to be chargeable interests in order to impose a charge to tax upon anything that could facilitate a shift in value.[104] Attempts to create derivative interests in land such as contracts to account for a sum equal to a specified share in the proceeds of sale[105] or profits from the land may be chargeable interests where they affect the value of any estate or interest or right or power in or over land.[106]

---

[101] The power of sale by a mortgagee has given rise to many problems in stamp taxes. HMRC Stamp Taxes has indicated that when dealing with the question of possible changes of control for the purposes of relief for certain types of transactions within FA 2003, Sched.7 the fact that the property is secured with a power of sale will not be regarded as being an arrangement or similar circumstances within the anti-avoidance or restrictive provisions. However, the fact that FA 2003, ss.44A and 45A have specifically referred to a power to direct a conveyance and bring it into charge to tax suggests that there may be considerable restrictions upon the scope of the word 'power' where a person who does not own the land such as a mortgagee nevertheless has some right to intervene or deal with the land. There may also be important technical issues for the routine contract provisions which empower a purchaser to execute a conveyance, etc. if the vendor defaults after notice. Although this is not a conveyance because it is conditional, it is a conditional power to create a conveyance. It is, therefore, considered prudent for the power to be vested in the purchaser's solicitors (compare *Diplock v. Hammond* (1854) 5 De GM & G 320; *Roddick v. Gandell* (1852) 1 De GM & G 763).

[102] See e.g. FA 2003, ss.45 and 45A and Sched.17A, para.12B. Different issues may arise in Scotland where contracts do not create equitable interests.

[103] Which may mean that the retention of a ransom strip to support such an arrangement may not qualify as a restrictive covenant.

[104] This may raise questions whether payment of the overage is an 'acquisition' of a chargeable interest.

[105] Rights to the proceeds of sale may be an interest in land.

[106] See also FA 2003, ss.44A and 45A.

2.12.3 Indirect interests

It must, however, be noted that the draftsman assumes that certain indirect interests may be chargeable interests. It is assumed that under English law persons entitled to interests in non-discretionary trusts have an interest in the underlying assets.[107] There are certain technical problems in relation to estates (see further **Chapter 10**) and these may have far-reaching implications for the first time buyer relief.[108] It is well-settled law that, in certain cases, persons interested in unadministered estates of deceased individuals have no equitable or beneficial interest in the assets for the time being held by the personal representatives of the deceased.[109] Those cases apply where the interest is in residue or possibly for specific devises where the estate is insolvent and there may have to be abatement of interest. However, this exclusion from a proprietary interest appears to be regarded by HMRC Stamp Taxes as applying to all beneficiaries in an estate, including, it seems, specific devises of land where the estate is solvent until such time as the property is assented or the executors become trustees.[110] The point has not been tested in litigation[111] but the issue may depend upon whether the specific devises and legacies may be subject to abatement and the need to sell the assets where there are potentially insufficient assets of a suitable nature to meet the claims of creditors (including HMRC) and distribute the specific assets to the relevant devisee.[112] Notwithstanding such technical issues HMRC Stamp Taxes appears to regard devisees or persons entitled on intestacy as having no interest in the property. This will be important where any variation of the estate takes place which does not qualify for the exemptions contained in FA 2003, Sched.3, paras.3A and 4 (as amended) (see **Chapter 10**). It seems that the current official view would accept, for example, that no charge arises in relation to a variation outside the two-year period because the participants do not have 'chargeable interests' and the charge is restricted to cases where the deceased's estate has been fully administered. It is considered that the official view is incorrect and that it may be perilous to rely upon it so that the two-year time limit and other conditions for the availability of the relief should be carefully observed.

2.13 CHARGEABLE INTERESTS ILLUSTRATED

In consequence, transactions involving the following interests in or rights over land are chargeable transactions:

---

[107] FA 2003, Sched.16, para.7.
[108] FA 2003, s.57AA.
[109] See e.g. Commissioner of Stamp Duties (Queensland) v. Livingston [1964] 3 All ER 692.
[110] See *Re King's Will Trust* [1964] Ch 542 and the need for writing to formalise the situation.
[111] And is inconsistent with the longstanding 'practice' of HMRC Stamp Taxes that in the liquidation of a company the beneficial interest in the company' assets during winding up vests in the shareholders where creditors have been provided for (compare *Ayerst* v. *C&K (Construction) Ltd* [1976] AC 167).
[112] Compare Administration of Estates Act 1925, s.46.

- options and pre-emption rights where various special rules apply;[113]
- equitable interests in trusts which include interests in UK land in their assets (see **Chapter 10**);
- easements such as rights of way and rights to light;
- interests in estates of deceased individuals (see **Chapter 11**);
- *profits à prendre*, where it must be noted that certain interests such as mineral licences may not be licences exempt from the tax but profits which are chargeable;
- true fixtures, i.e. equipment that becomes part of the land but not chattels (see **2.15.1**); and
- possibly tenant's fixtures, i.e. those chattels which become part of the land but which the tenant may remove on the termination of the tenancy or which the tenant is obliged to maintain, repair and/or remove by the terms of the lease.[114]

These are, of course, separate issues from the superficially similar problems such as:

- whether equipment attached to the land has become part of the land and so taxable;
- whether any item referred to as 'goodwill' is really embedded land value;
- whether there is a single contract for the sale of land with a completed building or two separate contracts for the sale or leasing of the land and a construction contract which is not taxable.

2.14 LAND RICH COMPANIES AND LAND INTO SHARES

At present, shares in companies holding land in the UK are not chargeable interests but it is understood that HMRC Stamp Taxes is continuing to investigate the possibility of treating shares as land in order to counter planning opportunities whereby, for example, persons such as trustees hold their UK land through companies preferably incorporated offshore so that no stamp duty or stamp duty reserve tax should arise on the sale of such shares, representing a substantial tax saving which can be shared with the purchaser in the form of an increased purchase price for the shares.[115]

As part of the attack upon land-holding companies (see **13.3**), there are numerous anti-avoidance provisions which are available for HMRC Stamp Taxes to counter attempts to 'convert' land into shares such as the charge upon market value when a chargeable interest is acquired by a company connected with the 'vendor',[116] or the clawback provision for intra-group transfers and company reorganisations.[117]

---

[113] FA 2003, s.46; compare *George Wimpey Ltd* v. *IRC* [1975] 2 All ER 45.
[114] On the analysis of such equipment for stamp duty see *Hallen* v. *Runder* (1834) 1 CM&R 266.
[115] Compare *Henty and Constable* v. *IRC* [1961] 3 All ER 1146.
[116] FA 2003, ss.53 and 54.
[117] FA 2003, Sched.7, paras.3 and 9.

These rules do not require a tax avoidance purpose and so will apply to routine commercial transactions such as incorporating a family business or vesting land in a corporate trustee unless it is an exempt trustee.[118] There are, in addition, many special provisions producing traps where one of the parties to a transaction is a company.

In general an interest in a partnership is a separate chose in action so that even where the partnership owns land the partnership interest is not in whole or in part a chargeable interest. However, special rules apply to partnerships, including foreign partnerships, treating certain transactions in relation to partnership shares as chargeable transactions.[119] Notwithstanding the look-through provisions for all partnerships wherever established,[120] this would appear to apply only for the purposes of enforcing the tax and not to convert partnership interests into land (see **Chapter 12**). Consequently a partnership interest is not as such a chargeable interest and dealings in such interests are taxable only in accordance with the special charging provisions[121] and the statutory general anti-avoidance provisions. [122] Partnerships should therefore consider the feasibility of holding UK land through appropriate corporate vehicles, preferably incorporated outside the UK because there is no transparency for such companies.

2.15 LAND

'Land' is defined[123] in standard terms but the legislation extends the definition of 'chargeable interest' in order to make it apply to cases where land is not owned directly. Special rules apply to equitable and other interests in trusts and estates (see **Chapters 10** and **11**) notwithstanding that these involve non-resident, non-domiciled and non-national individuals. The special charges applying to partnerships (see **Chapter 12**) apply to partnerships established abroad, including vehicles established abroad that are not partnerships under the law of the place of their establishment but which would be partnerships if formed or established in the United Kingdom.[124] The key issue is whether the trust, estate or partnership has a chargeable interest in land in the UK.

2.15.1 Fixtures

The charge to SDLT does not apply to chattels so that, subject to a proper apportionment of the consideration[125] no charge will arise in respect of items other

---

[118] FA 2003, s.54.
[119] FA 2003, Sched.15, para.14 (as amended).
[120] FA 2003, Sched.15, para.1(1) (as amended),
[121] FA 2003, Sched.15, paras.14 and 15 (as amended).
[122] FA 2003, ss.75A and following; see **1.32**.
[123] FA 2003, s.121; Interpretation Act 1978, Sched.1.
[124] FA 2003, Sched.15, para.1(1). See, for example, *Dreyfus* v. *IRC* 14 TC 560.
[125] FA 2003, Sched.4, para.4(4); *Saunders* v. *Edwards* [1987] 2 All ER 651.

than land such as carpets and curtains or lifts, escalators and cables. In consequence, the issue of 'fixtures' gives rise to two problem areas for the conveyancer: determining what is a fixture and determination of price.

2.15.1.1 What is a fixture?

Not everything that is attached to land is a 'fixture'. The test for determining this is basic land law and turns upon two factors:

- the purpose of the annexation, i.e. whether it is fixed simply for its better use as a chattel (which may encompass industrial safety requirements) and not with the intention of making it part of the land; and
- the degree of affixation and whether it is possible to remove the chattel without substantial damage to the physical premises.

The former purpose test has become more relevant in the light of recent cases which look more to the reasons for the affixation and whether the equipment was attached to the land simply to permit the chattel to be used as a chattel rather than with the intention of making it part of the structure. This means that under the modern approach many items of equipment that are attached to land simply for the purposes of industrial safety are not fixtures but retain their character as chattels provided that they can be detached from the land without substantial harm to the premises with the consequent SDLT advantages of being outside the charge to tax.[126]

2.15.1.2 Allocating the price

Many contracts such as sales of businesses or even residential contracts may include property other than land, such as chattels or free goodwill, and in such contracts the parties may sell several assets for a single or global consideration. However, whether the consideration is global or allocated in the contract to the individual items, it has to be allocated on the land transaction return between the items on a just and reasonable basis.[127] This can cause practical problems of classification between chattels, intangibles (such as goodwill) and land. However, there is no general obligation to sell or apportion at market value, which is useful for sales at other than market value such as sales at 'cost' or 'book value'. This can be a problem for residential transactions where there are arrangements relating to carpets and curtains. In commercial contracts other professional advisers dealing with other taxes such as capital allowances will be allocating values and prices on an

---

[126]   In addition, the linked transaction rules do not apply so that the price properly allocated to the chattels is not taxable and does not affect the rate. Also the price so allocated is ignored for the purposes of the statutory general anti-avoidance provisions.
[127]   FA 2003, Sched.4, para.4.

acceptable basis.[128] As decisions such as *Saunders* v. *Edwards*[129] indicate, a totally artificial and unjustifiable allocation of the consideration between the assets in order to produce a particular taxation result may be a criminal fraud on HMRC[130] and lead to an unenforceable illegal contract.[131] Specific penalties are imposed[132] upon persons involved in the preparation of a return which they 'know'[133] to be incorrect or who know of tax evasion which includes improper allocation of the price. It may also be professional misconduct and conspiracy for the parties' advisers to assist in the exercise.[134] It is essential to note that a conspiracy to defraud HMRC requires conspirators – who can include the vendor's solicitors and advisers who agree to the valuation allocation or apportionment and they will probably 'knowingly' participate in tax evasion by so doing.[135]

2.15.2 'Goodwill'

Although goodwill proper is free of stamp taxes, except to the extent that its value affects the price for shares in a company, numerous issues have arisen in relation to what is goodwill.

2.15.2.1 Embedded or free goodwill

What is described as goodwill may, in law, be a premium price for the land because of its location and planning permission.[136] Proper advice should be sought when dealing with this issue, particularly on the sale of a business because such advice on allocating prices and values will frequently provide powerful evidence against a challenge by HMRC Stamp Taxes and will refute allegations by HMRC of negligence or fraud as part of the discovery and penalty process. This issue of embedded as opposed to free goodwill has become a potentially significant issue for SDLT, as

---

[128] There are, of course, many unresolved issues of the allocation of professional duties between advisers who become involved at different stages in the transaction as regards dealing with SDLT. Such advisers frequently seek to exclude, limit and/or delay the involvement of lawyers in their own interest. In so doing they may be creating professional duty problems for themselves; see *BE Studios Ltd* v. *Smith & Williamson Ltd* [2006] STC 358 on not pointing out issues to the client.

[129] [1987] 2 All ER 651.

[130] *Re Wragg* [1897] 1 Ch 796.

[131] See the discussion in *Lloyds & Scottish* v. *Prentice* (1977) 121 SJ 847 affirmed on other grounds in *Lloyds & Scottish* v. *Cyril Lord* [1992] BCLC 609; *Saunders* v. *Edwards* [1987] 2 All ER 651.

[132] FA 2003, ss.95 and 96.

[133] There will be key issues to be clarified between what a person 'knows' and what he 'ought to know' with problems where there is either negligence and failure to investigate or a deliberate decision to turn a blind eye to the problem.

[134] *Saunders* v. *Edwards* [1987] 2 All ER 651. Such an exercise may also have unforeseen taxation or contractual consequences; see e.g. *Re Hollebone* [1959] 2 All ER 152.

[135] Such persons may also be vulnerable to demands by HMRC Stamp Taxes that they produce their entire files and supply 'information' in non-written format pursuant to FA 2003, Sched.13 (as amended).

[136] See e.g. *Mullins* v. *Wessex Motors* [1947] 2 All ER 727.

well as other taxes such as VAT, where land is treated differently from other assets.[137] Two issues arise in this context:

- whether the payment described in the contract as 'goodwill' is to be regarded as free or true goodwill not subject to tax or whether it is to be regarded as premium value for the land (embedded goodwill) which includes a payment as a premium for the grant of a lease of the business premises; or
- where the item involves land, embedded goodwill and free goodwill or other non-chargeable interests, how the consideration allocated to 'goodwill' is to be apportioned between the free goodwill and the embedded goodwill or land value or other assets.

HMRC Stamp Taxes, along with other divisions of the Revenue has issued guidance notes.[138] Unfortunately, these concentrate upon the latter problem of apportioning the consideration between free and embedded goodwill and other assets. This is a well-trodden area and the guidance appears to be based upon the surveyor's 'Red Book'. Unfortunately, there is little guidance as to the principles to be adopted in making the fundamental decision of whether the item is embedded or free goodwill. It appears early in the guidance that HMRC's starting point is that all payments described as goodwill are embedded goodwill and there is unlikely to be any free goodwill. The onus is, therefore, upon the taxpayer to be able to defend the position, which depends upon getting proper advice. It is consequently important to obtain professional advice to determine the value of the property and the value of the goodwill separately. If the parties have given appropriate retainers and instructions to their advisers who have acted in accordance with the professional rules then it is, potentially, extremely difficult for HMRC Stamp Taxes to challenge the allocation of the consideration in the absence of some suggestion of fraud.[139]

The real issue will, therefore, be to identify the aspects of 'goodwill' in general and whether the item in the contract is free goodwill. In this context there is no statutory definition of 'goodwill' but parties may be dealing in goodwill without being aware of this. For example, it has to be noted that goodwill issues can arise where there is a covenant in restraint of trade such as the vendor agreeing not to carry on a competing business.[140] In addition the parties may not refer to goodwill but make arrangements for the name of the business and lists of customers to be passed to the purchaser.[141] There will, therefore, be important issues as to whether a covenant restraining the vendor from carrying on business within a specified radius

---

[137] See e.g. *Balloon Promotions Ltd* v. *Wilson* [2006] STC (SCD) 167.

[138] HMRC Guidance Note January 2009; Simon's Tax Intelligence (STI) 2009, p.460.

[139] Note *Re Wragg* [1897] 1 Ch 796.

[140] See, for example, *Eastern National Omnibus Co Ltd* v. *IRC* [1939] 1 KB 161; *Connors* v. *Connors Brothers* [1940] 4 All ER 179; *Kirby* v. *Thorn-EMI* [1987] STC 621.

[141] In relation to certain types of takeaway catering businesses which operate a home delivery service, the radius for free or other delivery and the retention of the telephone number could be crucial. The telephone number may be more significant than a change of name. A change of menu to a different cuisine is likely to be fatal to the claim.

means that the goodwill attaches to the premises rather than to the vendor.[142] In such a situation there will be an argument that because it restricts the activities of the vendor a certain element in the goodwill is personal and people might follow the vendor if within a convenient radius.[143] The instructions for the valuers will be important and it may be helpful to the taxpayer if the instructions are to value to relevant property in the context of the business as a going concern rather than as part of the valuation of the business as a whole.

2.15.2.2 Long-term contracts

Certain types of businesses such as computer support services may have long-term contracts and the question has arisen with HMRC from time to time as to whether such long-term contracts are separate assets or are in whole or in part aspects of the goodwill of the firm. In the latter case there will be problems as to whether the goodwill attaches to the premises from which the business is carried on because of the local nature of the clientele. However, since the internet enables service businesses to operate at a distance the embedded goodwill factor is likely to be negligible or nil.[144] This question becomes quite acute in relation to farming and similar activities where there may be a long-term contract to supply all relevant vegetables to a food manufacturer over a specified period. HMRC Stamp Taxes has been known to take the view that this represents additional value to land. While it is difficult to believe that farming activities can have 'goodwill' in general this argument for long-term supply contracts has been weakened for taxpayers by the current practice of farms producing their own produce and marketing them under their own names and the rise of local[145] farmers' markets, farm shops and the local sourcing of produce by shops and restaurants. The name or brand could clearly become part of the 'goodwill' and therefore part of the value of the farm because the name is located solely in relation to the farm.

2.15.2.3 Licences or planning permission

Where the business requires some form of licence such as betting shops or nursing homes the question may arise as to whether the availability of the relevant planning permission and the licence is part of the land value as being embedded goodwill.

---

[142] Although there may be challenging issues for sale of catering businesses which have a takeaway or, more interestingly, a home delivery business with a free delivery within a specified radius.

[143] Note the total rejection of the Revenue Capital Gains Tax Manual dealing with various types of goodwill in *Balloon Promotions Ltd* v. *Wilson* [2006] STC (SCD) 167. This total rejection was not accepted wholeheartedly by HMRC in general which modified its position only slightly and the new guidance deals predominantly with price apportionment rather than identifying 'free goodwill'.

[144] It may be necessary in the event of litigation with HMRC to provide a map showing the location of clients and their distance from the relevant premises and the base from which they are serviced.

[145] Not all participants in such arrangements are local but may be trading under a 'brand name' which could become 'goodwill' for their distant farm.

2.15.2.4 'Anchor' tenants in retail

A latent problem[146] is that of anchor tenants, i.e. those key tenants much desired by developers of retail precincts, etc. because they can attract other tenants to the development. Some major companies regard this as evidence of a good reputation. Deals for leases may be entered into on a favourable basis so that the developer has the access to 'goodwill' to 'advertise' the development.

2.15.2.5 Continuity

Also important is the subsequent conduct of the taxpayer. Clearly when acquiring goodwill, there may need to be some form of continuity. It could prove of great significance that the purchaser continues the name of the business and retains the same staff. A complete refurbishment or refitting of the premises, such as happens with change of ownership of supermarkets and similar operations, could point against free goodwill. For example, there may be a replacement of the name of the business. There may be different brands offered for sale, particularly own brands as well as changes in the uniform of the staff and the layout of the store. Clearly, where there are major restructuring operations of this nature, or the absorption of the new business into the purchaser's existing business, it may be difficult to find that there is any continuity of the business; and possible disappearance of those factors that represent a key part of goodwill is not helpful. However, the restriction upon the vendor's freedom to carry on a business may mean that the goodwill has been acquired notwithstanding that the purchaser does not utilise the goodwill. Continuity is, therefore, merely one of the factors involved.

2.15.2.6 Employees and staff

Also important in many respects is the question of employees and staff. For example, it may be a key issue in one of the major problem areas of nursing homes. HMRC Stamp Taxes is quite firm in its view that in relation to 'goodwill' this is part of the land value of the premises for the nursing home. However, it may be possible to counteract this contention, assuming that there have been proper instructions to the valuers to value the premises in the context of the business as a going concern. Obviously, where the business has a good reputation locally the retention of the staff who have proved to be a major factor in fostering that reputation is an indication that the goodwill may be related to something other than the premises. On the other hand, where the staff are all dismissed because the business has a poor reputation and much has to be made of the fact that it is 'under new management', this may indicate that there was no true goodwill and that the consideration allocated to goodwill should be allocated to other assets such as the premises. Similarly a change in the type of business or telephone number for a 'takeaway' or home delivery business could be important and almost certainly adverse. While in relation

---

[146] Although HMRC Customs and Excise has begun to explore these issues in relation to VAT.

to catering it may be possible to argue that there is goodwill in the sense that the quality of the chef and the service by waiters and others is an important factor and that imposing some area of restriction upon the opening of a similar business is free goodwill and not embedded goodwill, this argument is effectively undermined where the parties change the restaurant from an Italian to an Indian restaurant.

CHAPTER 3

Taxable events: effective date

3.1 TAXABLE DATE

Having established that there is a chargeable transaction, it is necessary to determine when the charge to tax arises, along with all related events such as notification which are indicated below. It is important to note that the 'effective date' which is the basic date for the computation of the tax is frequently but not necessarily the same as the 'notification date' which is the date at which the obligation to file a land transaction return arises (see **Chapter 17**).

The key basic time point for the purposes of SDLT is the 'effective date'. This is important for the following reasons.

- It establishes *inter alia* the time for assessing the tax. In particular, it is the date for determining the rate of tax applicable to the transaction (even for later stages of the same transaction where the tax is adjusted retrospectively) for or the recalculation of SDLT upon a variable rent or variable consideration.[1]
- It is the date from which the time for filing the initial land transaction return (SDLT 1) and for payment of the initial estimate of the tax begins to run.
- It is the date for determining whether the consideration is uncertain or unascertained.
- It helps to see the final date for applying to postpone the payment of tax upon certain payments.[2]
- It is the date for determining the market value of chargeable interests or consideration *in specie*;[3] but this does not apply necessarily to situations where the consideration consists of the carrying out of works[4] or the provision of services[5] when the question of 'cost' as the tax base arises which HMRC Stamp Taxes seems to regard as actual cost[6] which may raise other issues.

---

[1] FA 2003, ss.51, 87 and 90; Sched.17A, paras.7 and 8.
[2] FA 2003, s.80; Stamp Duty Land Tax (Administration) Regulations 2003, SI 2003/2837, Part 4; see **15.7**.
[3] FA 2003, Sched.4, para.7.
[4] FA 2003, Sched.4, para.10.
[5] FA 2003, Sched.4, para.11.
[6] Stamp Duty Land Tax (Administration) Regulations 2003, SI 2003/2837, Part 4.

- It is the date for determining whether the conditions for the potential exemption from tax are satisfied.[7]
- It is the date from which the periods for the clawback of reliefs begin to run such as clawback of certain reliefs for corporate reorganisations, intra-group acquisitions and charities[8] and the relevant rate.
- It is the basis for fixing the date from which penalties and late payment interest commence, including the time when the penalties increase.[9]
- It establishes the start date for HMRC Stamp Taxes' powers to launch an Enquiry or issue a discovery assessment (though as this may extend for 21 years the start date is unlikely to have much real significance).[10]
- The computation of the tax depends upon whether VAT arises after the effective date such as pursuant to the exercise of the option to tax or whether this is to be ignored in computing SDLT.[11]
- It is the start of the period during which records must be maintained even for non-notifiable transactions.[12]
- It is the start of the limited period during which a taxpayer may 'amend' a land transaction return.[13]
- Works carried out upon the land being acquired after the effective date are excluded from charge[14] subject to a special relief where there are two effective dates for the same commercial transaction.
- It is the date for the rate of conversion for foreign currency.[15]
- It is relevant for the computation of the amount of liabilities assumed as part of the consideration and the amount of interest accrued since only debt and interest outstanding at the effective date are chargeable.[16]
- It sets the temporal discount rate for the calculation of the net present value of the rent for both the initial and any subsequent reassessments of the rent (see **Chapter 8**).
- It is usually important for determining whether transitional provisions for the introduction of the tax, changes in rate or amendments in various Finance Acts apply.

---

[7] But see **1.24** on whether there is a 'wait-and-see' principle.
[8] FA 2003, Sched.7, paras.3(2) and 9(2) and Sched.8, para.2(2); Sched.6A, para.11.
[9] FA 2003, Sched.10.
[10] FA 2003, Sched.10, paras.12, 25(3) and 31.
[11] FA 2003, Sched.4, para.2; see **4.30**.
[12] FA 2003, Sched.11A, paras.3 and 3A.
[13] FA 2003, Sched.10, para.6.
[14] FA 2003, Sched.4, para.10.
[15] FA 2003, Sched.4, para.9.
[16] FA 2003, Sched.4, para.8.

3.2   ACTIONS NOT DOCUMENTS

SDLT is a transaction-based tax and not a tax upon documentation. Consequently, the time or times at which the charge to tax arises or there are notifiable events is not necessarily linked to paperwork. This is particularly important since events both before and after 'completion' in the traditional conveyancing meaning of the term give rise to obligations to pay tax and to file returns and, as described elsewhere (see **Chapter 17**), much of the tax is of a provisional nature so that subsequent events unrelated to the paperwork give rise to retrospective adjustments. The one major charging area where paperwork matters is the possible double charge (but with a credit) upon substantial performance of agreements for lease and the subsequent grant thereof[17] which in the opinion of HMRC produces two chargeable events. In other cases, paperwork may trigger a reporting obligation but it rarely triggers a separate chargeable transaction since it relates back to the effective date for the transaction. While the basic effective date is linked to 'completion',[18] i.e. paperwork, this is subject to numerous special provisions because one of the key policies behind the legislation is to prevent parties deferring the payment of tax simply by delaying the execution of documentation but otherwise carrying out their contract by taking possession of the land and paying the price. As a result, the actions of the parties between contract and 'completion' can operate to trigger a tax charge[19] with a further charge and notification obligation on the subsequent completion.[20] Solicitors who are expected to advise on the land transaction return or sign as agents will need to have confirmation that the client has not performed any act that might constitute substantial performance (see **3.6.1**) in order to avoid personal penalties.[21] Unfortunately there are no provisions dealing adequately with this time discrepancy between substantial performance and completion, although what happens at completion may be vital to the charge such as whether the condition for the relief can be satisfied early, and there may not be a general wait-and-see principle[22] to deal with the problems arising.

3.3   HOW MANY EFFECTIVE DATES: DOUBLE CHARGE AND RETROSPECTION

The rather bizarre structure of SDLT produces many practical problems in relation to 'the effective date'. Although, as a basic principle, it would seem reasonable to

---

[17]   FA 2003, Sched.17A, para.12A; see **Chapter 8**.
[18]   FA 2003, s.119.
[19]   Or make reliefs available see FA 2003, Sched.4, para.10(2).
[20]   FA 2003, s.44(8).
[21]   FA 2003, ss.95 and 96.
[22]   Which is relevant for the computation of the tax or the eligibility for reliefs; see **1.24**.

expect there should be only one effective date for each commercial transaction,[23] two strange consequences arise from the legislation:[24]

1. The same commercial transaction may give rise to more than one separate chargeable event each with its own effective date. This problem emerged primarily in relation to the provisions dealing with substantial performance of agreements for lease and subsequent grant of the lease[25] where these are two separate chargeable events each with its own effective date requiring a recalculation of the tax upon the basis of certain assumptions and with a credit in respect of the rent. This interpretation of FA 2003, Sched.17A, para.12A[26] drew attention to a similar problem in relation to all other chargeable transactions which are to be completed by way of completion. FA 2003, s.44(8) provides that where there has been substantial performance and the contract is subsequently completed between the same parties by conveyance[27] a further notification is required at the time of the subsequent completion and additional tax is expected to be paid;[28] but such notification is essential since this is the step in the transaction that usually produces the Land Registry documents. HMRC Stamp Taxes appears to take the view that this is a separate chargeable event with a credit for tax paid in respect of substantial performance, i.e. it is provided that only additional tax is payable.[29]

2. Much of SDLT, particularly in relation to leases, operates on a provisional or 'guestimated' basis. The initial return[30] will eventually require a subsequent retrospective revision in the light of events. This means that the later return is filed by reference to the original effective date; the filing and payment obligation does not create a separate chargeable transaction with its own effective date. Consequently any relief available as at the original effective date may be available when the subsequent event occurs and the return will be

---

[23]   There is a provision in FA 2003, Sched.10, para.33 to the effect that a taxpayer can complain if he is being charged twice in respect of 'the same transaction'. However, this is to be limited in the view of HMRC Stamp Taxes to double taxation in respect of the same chargeable transaction as opposed to multiple charges arising in respect of the same commercial transaction. Indeed, much of the tax would not work if the latter more reasonable view were basically incorrect.

[24]   These are separate problems from the situation of clawback of reliefs where the original transaction with its own effective date was relieved from tax in some way but subsequent events produce a forfeiture of the relief with a separate chargeable or clawback event. See, for example, FA 2003, Sched.7, paras.3 and 9; Sched.8, para.2.

[25]   FA 2003, Sched.17A, para.12A; see **8.9**.

[26]   Which was introduced to deal primarily with a compliance problem in relation to the original legislation but was used as an opportunity for increasing the scope of the tax.

[27]   Reference to the same parties raises interesting questions as to the effect of these contentions by HMRC Stamp Taxes where there are subsales and similar arrangements falling within FA 2003, ss.45 and 45A and Sched.17A, para.12B.

[28]   There is no suggestion of a refund of tax if as a result of the intervening event the overall tax charge has fallen, such as on a reduction of VAT on rents.

[29]   FA 2003, s.44(8)(b).

[30]   See, for example, FA 2003, Sched.10, para.1; see **1.24** and **1.25**.

eligible for relief.[31] It is, therefore, necessary to deal in some detail with many of the situations where there are subsequent filing obligations in order to determine whether it is a separate chargeable event or is simply a retrospective revision of an earlier filing.[32] This determines whether there is a new effective date or a continuation of the old effective date.

The argument that there can be more than one effective date in respect of the same commercial transaction has been reinforced by the fact that subsequent legislation has been enacted on this basis. For example, there is a relief in respect of building works or fitting out carried out before completion of the transaction.[33] It is provided that where the taxpayer is acquiring a major interest and substantially performs the contract prior to completion any building or fitting out works carried out after the effective date are not subject to tax. This would work well for actions carried out after substantial performance but since, in the view of HMRC Stamp Taxes, subsequent completion by the grant of the lease between the same parties is a separate chargeable event with its own effective date the building works would not have been carried out after the effective date of the grant of the lease but prior to its grant although after substantial performance. It is specifically provided[34] that works carried out prior to the grant of the lease but after substantial performance of the agreement for lease remain exempt. Similarly, the actual grant of a lease has a credit for the previously taxed rent[35] on substantial performance. Those reliefs would not be necessary if the later events were merely retrospective recalculations.

3.4 BASIC POSITION IN THEORY

It has been indicated (see **1.10**) that one of the policies of the tax is to prevent parties avoiding or deferring the tax charge by avoiding or delaying the execution of documentation. In consequence actions prior to 'completion' can operate to trigger the tax should they constitute 'substantial performance'.[36] This transaction-based nature of SDLT is emphasised by the fact that there are numerous provisions[37] which state that simply entering into a contract (or agreement for lease) is not, of itself, a chargeable transaction;[38] nor is it in general the effective date;[39] something more is required. In consequence, tax no longer arises upon contracts or agreements

---

[31] On the other hand, the fact that a relief might have been available at the time of the subsequent event does not mean that the notification will be free of tax since the transaction for which the relief might be available is taxable at an early date.
[32] Both types of event will usually be notifiable, even though the Land Registry will not be involved.
[33] FA 2003, Sched.4, para.10.
[34] FA 2003, Sched.4, para.10(2).
[35] FA 2003, Sched.17A, para.12A.
[36] FA 2003, ss.119 and 44.
[37] FA 2003, ss.44(2), 44A(2), 45(2), 45A(2).
[38] But this does not mean that contractual rights are not chargeable interests in land; see, for example, FA 2003, ss.46 and 48(1)(b) and Sched.17A, para.10.
[39] FA 2003, s.119; see **3.6**.

for lease other than options and pre-emption rights[40] and entries can be made at the relevant Land Registry to protect such contracts without the production of a certificate.[41]

3.5 EFFECTIVE DATE

3.5.1 Basic definition

The basic definition,[42] which is made subject to special provision,[43] of 'effective date' is 'completion' which is not generally defined;[44] but which appears to mean the date when the parties perform their obligations pursuant to the terms of the contract such as payment of the purchase price in full and delivery of the title documentation and delivery up of the premises with vacant possession. The legislation on this point gives a totally misleading impression of the times at which the payment obligations arise in at least two ways, namely:

- it defines the effective date in terms of completion, but then subjects this definition to special rules which, because they will apply in virtually every case that will occur in practice, deprive this provision of any practical effect; and
- it does not make clear that other events give rise to those payment and/or notification obligations.

3.5.2 Special provisions

Other specific provision where the basic effective date is an event other than 'completion' is made for:

- contracts to be completed by a 'conveyance' which is defined as any instrument.[45] Since standard form contracts provide for completion to require the delivery of an appropriate written instrument this special rule will apply in virtually every case in practice;
- options and pre-emption rights;[46]
- agreements to direct conveyances to third parties and subsales thereof;[47]

---

[40] FA 2003, ss.44(2) and 46; see **Chapter 6**.
[41] FA 2003, s.79(2).
[42] FA 2003, s.119.
[43] This may not be a problem where these various events are expressed to be simultaneous. There will be difficult problems where the contract provides for different payment dates and transfer dates. HMRC Stamp Taxes takes the view that an arrangement for postponing the delivery of vacant possession is a post-completion transaction involving a completion and regrant and has on occasion taken the point that the right to remain in occupation of the premises is the regrant of a lease producing a land exchange pursuant to FA 2003, s.47 and Sched.4, para.5; see further **Chapter 7**.
[44] FA 2003, s.44(10)(a) provides that for the purposes of that section 'completion' means in conformity with the contract between the same parties.
[45] FA 2003, s.44.
[46] FA 2003, s.46; see **Chapter 6**.
[47] FA 2003, ss.44A and 45A; see **Chapter 9**.

- agreements for lease and grants;[48]
- assignments of agreements for lease.[49]

Where there are specific charging arrangements such as clawback of reliefs these usually have their own arrangements for the 'effective date' for the arrangements.

3.6 BASIC POSITION IN PRACTICE

The basic definition of the effective date is subject to certain 'special provisions'. However, the nature of routine conveyancing means that the basic provision will rarely, if ever, apply in practice.

3.6.1 Routine contracts: substantial performance

Where, as will usually be the case, there is a contract or an agreement for lease which provides for completion by a written instrument between the same parties, which will include contracts with the usual power to subsell which provides that one form of completion contemplates a transfer to the original purchaser the effective date is the earlier of substantial performance of the contract or agreement or 'completion'.[50] There is a key special provision which in effect applies to all standard form contracts. The practical effect of these 'special provisions' is that in virtually every case the effective date will be the earlier of completion between the parties or substantial performance and means that persons assisting in the preparation of land transaction returns even in routine residential transactions need to monitor and be aware of events occurring between contract and completion.[51] Where these two events are not simultaneous, dual charges and notification obligations arise with extremely complex rules and problems for agreements for lease,[52] although, in general, there remains only one effective date.

Essentially, in virtually every case in practice, the tax charge will arise at the earlier of substantial performance or completion. In consequence, in normal practice:

1. There is, in general, no charge to SDLT simply upon exchanges of contracts for sale or agreements for lease or contracts to create or terminate rights

---

[48] FA 2003, Sched.17A, para.12A.
[49] FA 2003, Sched.17A, para.12B.
[50] FA 2003, s.45.
[51] Such events are also relevant when advising parties where subsale relief (FA 2003, ss.45 and 45A), the equivalent relief for new leases (FA 2003, Sched.17A, para.12B) or the reliefs for building or fitting out works (FA 2003, Sched.4, para.10) are involved. Without knowledge of the conduct of the parties correct advice cannot be provided and this is negligence: *Slattery* v. *Moore Stephens* [2003] STC 1379.
[52] FA 2003, s.44(8), Sched.17A, para.12A; see **Chapter 8**.

except options and pre-emption rights.[53] There will, therefore, be important issues as to whether the contract is a contract or is a 'conveyance' operating as completion.[54]

2. There is a charge to tax upon substantial performance of the contract[55] should this precede 'completion' such as where a tenant is allowed into possession early in order to fit out the premises.

3. There is a charge to tax upon 'completion' between the same parties.[56] However, where there has been prior substantial performance,[57] completion may mean that there is a further notification obligation and additional tax, if any, is payable[58] but there is no statutory right to a refund where the tax would have been lower at completion. Additional tax arising at completion will be unusual since, except for problems arising in relation to the grant of leases, the SDLT is payable upon substantial performance in respect of the whole of the chargeable consideration including any relevant VAT (although the rates many change between substantial performance and completion) and overage or similar payments or variable rents, albeit on an estimated basis.[59] The problem will be to determine whether there has been any change of circumstances requiring a recalculation of the SDLT between substantial performance and completion in accordance with the principles governing variable payment. Moreover, should there be a change after substantial performance and prior to completion this will normally require its own return and payment of tax.[60] The obligation arises even where a land transaction return (SDLT 1) has been previously filed and tax paid by reference to substantial performance. It is important, particularly for smaller transactions, that this double notification if possible be avoided in order to keep costs to a reasonable amount. Otherwise these costs may be disproportionate since the second land transaction return requires a new[61] fully completed SDLT 1 (with any necessary SDLT 2, 3 or 4 forms) with a new bar code reference notwithstanding this is merely repeating the information already produced to HMRC Stamp Taxes on the original SDLT 1 filed at substantial performance.[62]

---

[53] FA 2003, ss.44(2), 45(2) and 46; see **Chapter 6**.

[54] *Peter Bone* v. *IRC* [1995] STC 921; *West London Syndicate Ltd* v. *IRC* [1898] 2 QB 507; *Angus* v. *IRC* (1889) 23 QBD 579; note the potential problems for powers of attorney as assignments: *Diplock* v. *Hammond* (1854) 5 De GM & G 320; *Roddick* v. *Gandell* (1852) 1 De GM & G 763.

[55] FA 2003, s.44(4).

[56] FA 2003, s.44(5) and (10)(a).

[57] FA 2003, s.44(2).

[58] FA 2003, s.44(8).

[59] FA 2003, Sched.17A, para.12A.

[60] FA 2003, s.80.

[61] It is essential that a completely new return is filed rather than the original form 'amended' even if this were physically possible.

[62] In some situations where the time between the two events is short, in practice, HMRC Stamp Taxes may be prepared to accept an amendment to the return which is essentially an explanatory letter dealing with the changes to be made (see **Appendix D**). Unfortunately, this practice is not consistently applied.

3.7 SUBSTANTIALLY PERFORMED

These principles mean that in virtually every case in practice the rules relating to substantial performance will be areas for investigation and the practitioner who does not monitor the actions of the client is in peril (see **1.5**). The rules for substantial performance depend upon whether the contract involves a grant of a new lease or any other transaction.

3.7.1 Transactions not involving agreements for lease

Where the transaction is not one involving a grant or deemed grant of a lease such as a sale of a freehold or the sale or surrender of an existing lease, a lease or a release of an interest or variation of a restrictive covenant, then the contract is substantially performed on the earlier of:

- a substantial amount of the consideration being paid or provided;[63] or
- the purchaser taking possession of the whole or substantially the whole of the subject-matter of the contract. For these purposes the purchaser takes possession if he receives or becomes entitled to receive rents and profits.[64] It is immaterial whether a purchaser takes possession under the contract or under a licence or lease of a temporary character.[65]

3.7.2 Agreements to grant a new lease

Where the grant of a new lease is involved[66] the agreement for lease is substantially performed on the earliest of:

- a substantial amount of the premium being paid or provided;[67]
- the purchaser taking possession of the whole or substantially the whole of the subject-matter of the contract. For these purposes a lessee takes possession if he receives or becomes entitled to receive rents and profits and it is immaterial whether the lessee takes possession under the contract or under a licence or lease of a temporary character;[68] or
- the first actual payment of rent being made.[69]

Each of these potential tax triggers requires detailed investigation.

---

[63]   FA 2003, s.44(7)(a) provides, somewhat unnecessarily, that a substantial amount of consideration is provided or paid where the whole or substantially the whole of the consideration is paid or provided.

[64]   FA 2003, s.44(6)(a).

[65]   FA 2003, s.44(6)(b).

[66]   See also FA 2003, Sched.17A, para.12A for other problems relating to agreements for lease.

[67]   FA 2003, s.44(7)(c).

[68]   FA 2003, s.44(6).

[69]   FA 2003, s.44(7)(b).

3.8 SUBSTANTIAL PAYMENT OR PROVISION OF THE CONSIDERATION

Little guidance has been provided as to the official view upon when the consideration is substantially provided. It is stated in SDLT 6 (Notes for Guidance) that this is regarded as occurring when 90 per cent of the chargeable consideration is provided.[70] This is a simple test where cash is involved although problems can arise even in routine cases in practice, as follows.

3.8.1 Deposits/stage payments

The payment of a normal deposit of 5 or 10 per cent[71] will not amount to substantial provision of the consideration. However, where there are building or other arrangements involving stage payments this question will have to be considered more closely and payments for variations which may or may not be part of the land transaction may increase the amount paid towards the land price. For example, a purchaser or lessee may agree with the vendor or landlord for the installation of equipment or furnishings at the expense of the purchaser or lessee prior to completion so that it may form part of the chargeable consideration (see **Chapter 9**, especially **9.9** and **9.10**). Obviously, the first few stage payments will not amount to payment of 'substantially the whole' of the price but it is not unlikely that there will be anti-avoidance concepts developed. In consequence, where the developer enters into some form of pre-sale or pre-let as a means of financing the arrangement then the contract may have been substantially performed[72] or the deposit or loan may be part of the chargeable consideration.[73]

3.8.2 Loans

Similarly, where a prospective purchaser or lessee as part of the financing arrangements and in order to reduce the costs agrees to make a loan to the developer on favourable terms,[74] there will be questions as to whether the provision of such a 'soft loan' or a guarantee of any loan taken out by the developer from a bank might amount to 'indirect provision of the consideration' within the view of HMRC Stamp Taxes. These situations may be quite rare in relation to single dwelling transactions but where the residential construction is part of a larger project involving, for example, social housing or affordable housing with a local authority or housing

---

[70] On arrangements for providing the consideration see **4.16** and decisions such as *Customs and Excise* v. *Faith Construction* [1989] 2 All ER 938; *Coren* v. *Keighley* 48 TC 370. Note, however, there are problems with leases where the parties enter into a loan arrangement rather than an immediate payment; FA 2003, Sched.17A, para.18A; see **3.8.2**.

[71] On whether larger payments are deposits or penalties see *Workers Trust and Merchant Bank Ltd* v. *Dojap Investments* [1993] 2 All ER 370.

[72] Such arrangements also have to be viewed in the context of whether such arrangements might adversely affect the taxation of any related building contracts pursuant to FA 2003, Sched.4, para.10 (as amended); see **Chapter 9**.

[73] FA 2003, Sched.17A, para.18A.

[74] Compare the VAT position of *Faith Construction* v. *Customs and Excise* [1988] STC 35.

association, such financing may be more common. The implications for the timing of any transactions will be an important part of the structuring of such arrangements.

3.8.3 Anti-avoidance loans and deposits

The general principles referred to in the preceding paragraphs have been made the subject-matter of anti-avoidance provisions where leases are concerned. Fortunately, these anti-avoidance provisions have been designed primarily to attack certain aggressive avoidance schemes of limited compass but they need to be noted because, as they are widely drafted, they provide traps for the unwary in bona fide commercial arrangements.

It is provided that[75] where, under arrangements made in connection with the grant or the assignment of a lease, the lessee or any person connected with him or acting on his behalf pays a deposit or makes a loan[76] to any person and the repayment of all or part of the deposit or loan is contingent or anything done or omitted to be done by the lessee or assignee or on the death of the lessee or assignee, the amount of the deposit or loan is to be taken as chargeable consideration. There is no repayment of the tax if the loan is repaid.[77] In the case of the grant of a lease it is taxable as a premium and is a purchase price for the assignment of the lease.[78] The charge does not apply to a deposit[79] (but this relief does not apply to a loan) if the amount that would be chargeable in relation to the grant or assignment of the lease is not more than twice the relevant maximum rent (which is the highest amount of rent payable in respect of any consecutive 12-month period in the first five years of the term[80] or in the case of an assignment the highest amount of rent payable in respect of 12 consecutive months in the first five years of the term after the date of the assignment of the lease).[81] There are also certain exclusions from the charge. No charge arises in cases where there is a restriction upon the nil rate premium in those cases where the rent for non-residential property is not less than £1,000 per year.[82] The charge also does not apply in those cases where relief is available in respect of residential property in disadvantaged areas pursuant to Sched.6.

---

[75]   FA 2003, Sched.17A, para.18A.

[76]   It may be important to note the distinction between a 'loan' (i.e. a cash advance) and a 'debt' (an unpaid loan or purchase price). Note also that set-off arrangements can involve 'cash movements' as in *Coren* v. *Keighley* 48 TC 370.

[77]   FA 2003, Sched.17A, para.18A; s.80(4A).

[78]   There is an obvious problem where there is an arrangement that there is a payment in excess of the normal 10 per cent rules which may not be a deposit; see *Workers Trust and Merchant Bank Ltd* v. *Dojap Investments* [1993] 2 All ER 370.

[79]   Provided that other events that constitute substantial performance do not occur.

[80]   Note that this is a key factor in determining the charge to tax upon rent for all periods after the expiration of the fifth year of the term: FA 2003, Sched.17A, paras.7(3) and 14(4) and (4A).

[81]   FA 2003, Sched.17A, para.18A(4).

[82]   FA 2003, Sched.5, para.9A.

3.8.4 Consideration in kind

The 90 per cent test leaves open difficult issues where there is consideration in kind such as the issue of shares or the performance of services or carrying out building works. It seems that in the case of shares these are 'provided' when the board of directors resolves to allot the shares rather than when they are 'issued',[83] i.e. entered in the register of members.[84]

It is difficult to see how the 90 per cent test can be applicable to land exchanges or other consideration in kind which is unlikely to be provided piecemeal.

3.8.5 Variable payments

Other difficulties arise where the chargeable consideration is variable involving tax paid (or deferred) initially on an estimated basis.[85] The final figure may not be known for many years, so that it will be difficult to determine when the 90 per cent threshold has been crossed. Surprisingly HMRC Stamp Taxes appears to be prepared to wait until the parties have made payments close to the commercially anticipated maximum, i.e. the estimated figure included in the initial land transaction return (SDLT 1) notwithstanding that this offers the opportunity to postpone the payment of the tax without interest and penalties (see **14.21**). In such situations, it is probable that there will be an in-depth Enquiry as to whether there has been 'completion' in accordance with the contract or whether the purchaser has taken 'possession' of substantially the whole of the land. For example, where there is a sale of land with a basic price plus additional consideration for overage or clawback with a clawback period of 80 years, HMRC Stamp Taxes in practice treats substantial performance as taking place when the purchaser has either paid 90 per cent of the estimated figure (so that in most cases the practical issue will be whether the purchaser has taken possession of the whole or substantially the whole of the chargeable interest), or has received the 'conveyance'.

3.9 TAKING POSSESSION

Substantial performance occurs where a person takes possession of the whole or substantially the whole of the land.[86] This raises various technical issues such as what is 'possession' and what is substantially the whole of the land.

---

[83] Note the technical differences between a right to be allotted: *Pye-Smith* v. *IRC* [1958] 1 WLR 905; *Letts* v. *IRC* [1957] 1 WLR 201, a right to an allotment, i.e. shares previously allotted and the issue of shares: *Oswald Tillotson* v. *IRC* [1933] 1 KB 134; *Brotex Cellulose Fibres Ltd* v. *IRC* [1933] 1 KB 158; *Murex* v. *IRC* [1933] 1 KB 173; *National Westminster Bank* v. *IRC* [1994] STC 580.

[84] This raises 'wait-and-see' issues for certain reliefs; see **1.24**.

[85] FA 2003, ss.51, 80, 87 and 90. For the treatment of such payments and tax see Stamp Duty Land Tax (Administration) Regulations 2003, SI 2003/2837, Part 4; see **14.21**.

[86] FA 2003, s.44(5)(a).

3.9.1 'Possession'

There is no statutory definition of what constitutes 'possession' other than an extension to the terms whereby for these purposes a person is deemed to take possession if he receives or becomes entitled to receive rents and profits.[87] Basically it would seem, possession is taken when a person moves into physical occupation of the land with some degree of exclusivity and territorial control otherwise than for some possibly limited purpose. However, it must be possession pursuant to an agreement of some sort, such as a conditional agreement.[88] It is also essential that the taking of the possession in whatever capacity is related to the particular transaction for which the charge applies. Being in possession in some other capacity or for some other reason than as a form of performance of the chargeable contract will not constitute substantial performance. The rules of substantial performance are part of the anti-avoidance policies upon which the structure of SDLT is based. They are designed to impose tax where parties enter into a contract and, resting upon the contract, effectively perform their agreement but without taking a formal conveyance. In consequence, where the possession does not represent a form of performance of the relevant contract it cannot be substantial performance. For example, where a tenant under an existing lease exercises an option to renew the lease before the contractual termination date his continuation in occupation will be as tenant under the existing lease and will not be a taking of possession in connection with the grant of the new lease.[89] The continuation of the existing lease will, therefore, not be substantial performance of the new lease. However, there will inevitably be substantial performance of the agreement for the lease arising pursuant to the exercise of the option on the day immediately following the contractual termination date for the existing lease because, *prima facie*, at that point the tenant will be occupying pursuant to the agreement for lease. There will be a change of status sufficient to produce a tax charge. It should, however, be noted that this would apply only where the chargeable event is related to substantial performance and possession. Should the parties grant the new lease immediately upon the exercise of the option to renew the lease this will be a 'completion' and will be a chargeable event giving rise to an effective date. Such an execution of the lease will, therefore, accelerate the tax charge.[90]

It is immaterial whether the purchaser takes possession under the contract or under a licence or lease of a temporary character,[91] such as a tenancy at will.[92] Thus

---

[87] See FA 2003, s.44(6). Apportionment at completion would not be relevant for these purposes where a person purchases a reversion on a lease from the landlord.

[88] This could be a crucial point should, as expected, HMRC Stamp Taxes pursue the tax where an interest passes by equitable principles (see **2.9**). It will be important whether there is an effective oral contract (see *Yaxley* v. *Gotts* [1999] 3 WLR 1217) or there is no 'agreement' in equity merely a 'promise'.

[89] It is, however, important to avoid any suggestion of a surrender and regrant.

[90] There are problems with reversionary leases and leases in this situation assuming that they are not some form of surrender and regrant; see **8.64**.

[91] FA 2003, s.44(6) (as amended).

[92] These types of interest may also be important in relation to holding over; see **8.47**.

allowing a purchaser or tenant into 'possession' in whatever capacity may trigger an early tax charge and probably two reporting obligations.[93] Therefore, there may be dangers for purchasers going on to the land prior to payment of the purchase price or conveyance. This may give rise to difficulties where there is a lease and the tenant is allowed into occupation of the land for the purpose of carrying out fitting out or repairs or redecoration prior to actual completion in the sense of payment, but sometimes early possession can avoid a charge upon building works and fitting out.[94]

It is the view of HMRC Stamp Taxes that the obtaining of the key to the premises, is, of itself, sufficient to constitute taking possession even without physical entry. However, this ignores the fact that the key or access to the premises may be made available only upon a restricted basis such as for a limited time or for a limited purpose. Entry while at the same time the 'vendor' remains in physical occupation of the premises would not give sufficient control of the premises to constitute possession for that purpose. There is also a major issue of whether there can be 'joint possession' where a person who has title to the land or a prior right to possession allows another person on to the land at the same time. Permission to enter upon the land to investigate minerals or geological structures prior to development is unlikely to constitute taking possession, but entry for the purpose of demolishing existing buildings or preparing foundations or infrastructure works for new buildings will probably involve taking possession.

3.9.1.1 'Possession' and minor interests

Given the extended definition of 'acquisition' this test of 'possession' may not be applicable in many cases other than sales and leases. For example, where there is an agreement to release or vary a restrictive covenant or right to light it is difficult to see when the purchaser can take possession of the varied covenant since his conduct will not change. In such a case, notwithstanding that the contract will provide for the execution and delivery of a deed or other instrument, it seems unlikely that the rules of substantial performance relating to possession will be appropriate and the effective date may be linked to the payment of a substantial part of the consideration.

3.9.1.2 Fitting out and works

The circumstances of the case may suggest that although a person has access to the land on a limited basis this is not possession. For example, as discussed elsewhere,[95] fitting out and other works can be chargeable consideration but with relief for works carried out after the effective date. A prospective tenant may be allowed upon the

---

[93]   FA 2003, s.44(8), Sched.17A, para.12A.
[94]   FA 2003, Sched.4, para.10(2).
[95]   See **Chapter 9** and **4.16**; *Eastham* v. *Leigh London and Provincial Properties Ltd* [1971] 2 All ER 887; FA 2003, Sched.4, para.10.

land by the developer/landlord during the continuation of building operations with a view to commencing fitting out. This may be upon a restricted basis for security or safety reasons. The limited access would suggest that this is not 'possession' of the land since the prospective tenant is not in a position to do any acts that he wishes upon the land. However, in certain circumstances the tenant may be given relatively unrestricted rights of access notwithstanding that the landlord is continuing to build. These will raise questions as to whether there can be 'joint possession' between persons with different interests and carrying out different activities upon the same land.

3.9.2 'Substantially the whole': phased completions

The 'possession' must be of the whole or substantially the whole of the land within the contract. No guidance is provided as to the percentage of the land that amounts to substantially the whole, but as this does not refer to the major part of the land[96] it seems probable that this will require something like 90 per cent of the total area. This could be a problem where there is to be a phased completion with only parts of the land or building being made available to the purchaser from time to time. In such cases it would seem to be more tax efficient to have separate contracts each of which is separately completed in full, as opposed to a single contract with a phased completion. The fact that the contracts will be linked should not affect the question of whether each individual contract has been substantially performed or completed, since linking merely affects the rate of tax and does not amalgamate the contracts for the purpose of substantial performance.

3.9.3 Conditional and similar arrangements

Substantial performance can occur notwithstanding that the contract in question is not binding. For example, where a person who has executed an agreement for lease that is subject to the consent of the superior landlord which is yet to be obtained[97] enters upon the premises to fit out, this may amount to a taking of possession which triggers the tax charge upon the conditional agreement for lease.

However, there must be a contract or agreement for lease, including contracts that are conditional,[98] before this can occur. For example, where the parties have entered into an option arrangement there will have been a chargeable transaction on the

---

[96] Compare the clawback provisions relating to leases granted by charities which inconsistently refer to 'greater part': FA 2003, Sched.8, para.3(1).

[97] Such as where the landlord has indicated that he has no objections but the paperwork has yet to be completed.

[98] But note the key issue of whether there is a condition or it is consideration: *Eastham* v. *Leigh London and Provincial Properties Ltd* [1971] 2 All ER 887; *GUS Merchandise* v. *Customs and Excise* [1981] 1 WLR 1309. This is a major issue for domestic transactions since gifts or transactions without either chargeable consideration or intention to create legal relations are not taxable; FA 2003, Sched.3, para.1.

grant of the option;[99] taking possession before the option is exercised will not produce a tax charge in respect of the potential contract but there will be a charge upon substantial performance and/or completion of the contract arising pursuant to the exercise of the option, which 'may' be a linked transaction with the original grant.[100]

Where there is an existing lease with an option to renew the lease, the exercise of that option during the currency of the original lease will not give rise to an immediate charge to SDLT because although the tenant is in possession of the demised premises this will be possession in his capacity as the existing tenant and not a fresh taking of possession as a new tenant pursuant to the renewed lease. In such a case the effective date will be the earlier of 'completion', i.e. the grant of the new lease or the first actual payment of rent thereunder.[101] As this illustrates, the mere fact of being in occupation of the land which may or may not be 'possession' is not conclusive: it will be necessary to investigate the nature of the possession and the capacity of the occupier. Similarly, where a prospective tenant enters on to the land during the negotiations for a lease there will be no contract in place and so there is no agreement to be substantially performed.[102] However, where the person is already in possession under a prior arrangement, the subsequent exchange of a contract or the exercise of the option may mean that there is simultaneous substantial performance and an immediate tax charge, or the exemption for works to be carried out on the land may not be available because there was no possession sufficient to produce the necessary effective date.[103] Such informal arrangements, where there is no contract but a person has access to premises where there is a potential purchaser or prospective tenant and carries out works on the land during the negotiations, potentially raises considerable technical problems in relation to the tax. Such informal operations where the parties 'trust' each other or are closely connected frequently fall short of contracts although eventually interests may pass because of equitable remedies. In particular, there is the fundamental question as to whether the party carrying out the works is subject to tax upon the open market cost of the works.[104] There will be the question as to whether there has been an informal arrangement whereby the building works are part of the consideration in the absence of a contract,[105] or whether there is merely some arrangement 'subject to contract', or a temporary arrangement binding the parties while the lawyers sort out

---

[99]   FA 2003, s.46.

[100]   FA 2003, s.46(1).

[101]   The complications of FA 2003, Sched.17A, para.12A should not arise in the former case, but there are likely to be two chargeable transactions in the latter case.

[102]   There may, however, be a question of whether the terms upon which he has entered constitute a potentially taxable tenancy which may be some form of periodic tenancy that can be effectively created without writing: Law of Property Act 1925, s.52.

[103]   FA 2003, Sched.4, para.10.

[104]   FA 2003, Sched.4, para.10.

[105]   See, for example, Eastham v. Leigh London and Provincial Properties Ltd [1971] 2 All ER 887; Brewer Street Investments Ltd v. Barclays Woollens [1953] 2 All ER 1330.

the paperwork.[106] Also in these situations the parties may be related or connected such as members of the family when there may not be the necessary intention to create legal relations at a particular stage.[107] In consequence, acting upon the basis of a general promise in good faith where this is not intended to form the basis of a contract could raise the question as to whether it is taxable. There are risks, where the subsequent documentation refers to the transaction being in consideration of the works having been carried out, as to whether this is past consideration and therefore no consideration as a matter of contract.[108] Also, because of the uncertainty of the arrangements where there are no standard form provisions to apply[109] there may be difficulties in implying some form of oral contract that could give rise to some form of binding contract in equity or other arrangement.[110] This will depend upon the precise circumstances of each individual case. For example, entry during the negotiations for a lease may lead to substantial performance when the agreement is executed, but it is arguable that since there was a prior right to occupy the land, there is no 'taking possession of the subject-matter of the contract' unless there is some alteration in the pre-existing relationship which creates a new licence to occupy.

3.10 SUBSEQUENT RESCISSION OR CANCELLATION BETWEEN SUBSTANTIAL PERFORMANCE AND COMPLETION

As noted, 'substantial performance' can precede payment in full or 'completion' in the generally accepted sense of the word. Thus, where the contract has been substantially performed and is, to any extent, afterwards rescinded or annulled, or is for any other reason not carried into effect, the tax paid in connection with the substantial performance is to the appropriate extent to be repaid by HMRC Stamp Taxes.[111] Repayment must be claimed by amendment of the land transaction return in respect of the contract[112] and the contract must accompany the claim.[113]

3.11 OTHER SPECIAL RULES FOR THE EFFECTIVE DATE

3.11.1 Options and pre-emption rights: grant and exercise

Special rules apply to options and pre-emption rights (see further **Chapter 6**).

---

[106]   *Winn v. Bull* (1877–78) LR 7 Ch D 29; *Branca v. Cobarro* [1947] 2 All ER 101; *RTS Flexible Systems Ltd v. Molkerei Alois* [2010] 3 All ER 1.
[107]   *Balfour v. Balfour* [1919] 2 KB 517.
[108]   *Eastwood v. Kenyon* (1840) 11 Ad & El 438; *Re McArdle* [1951] 1 All ER 905.
[109]   Scammell v. Ouston [1941] AC 251; Sweet & Maxwell v. Universal News Services [1964] 3 All ER 30.
[110]   But note RTS Flexible Systems Ltd v. Molkerei Alois [2010] 3 All ER 1.
[111]   FA 2003, s.44(9).
[112]   FA 2003, s.44(9).
[113]   The procedure for amending returns by a taxpayer is contained in FA 2003, Sched.10, para.6. See **Appendix D**.

The effective date of the transaction in the case of the acquisition of an option or pre-emption right is when the right is acquired as opposed to when it becomes exercisable.[114] For example, where there is an option to acquire land *if* planning permission is obtained not *when* the planning permission is obtained, the SDLT arises upon the grant of the option.

It must also be noted that the grant of the option and its subsequent exercise are two separate but chargeable transactions each with its own effective date. There is one charge to tax when the option is granted and a separate chargeable event when the option to tax is exercised. *Prima facie*, because these are separate transactions there is no duplication of the tax,[115] and each transaction will be subject to its own charge to tax with the rate appropriate to the amounts involved. However, the draftsman has rather intriguingly left in the legislation the provision that while the grant of the option and its exercise are separate transactions they 'may' give rise to linked transactions. The use of the word 'may' indicates that there is no automatic linkage between the option and its exercise so that the option premium and the strike price or purchase price are not automatically aggregated. It will be a question of fact in each case whether the rules for linked transactions (considered elsewhere; see **4.12**) are satisfied. Should the option and its exercise be part of some pre-arranged plan or scheme the two considerations will be aggregated and there will be a retrospective increased charge to tax in respect of the option premium.

Options in relation to leases also raise a potential problem for effective dates. Where there is an option to renew a lease this may give rise to a successive linked lease.[116] It will be a question of fact whether in any particular case the grant of the original lease including the option to renew and the exercise of the option are part of a scheme or arrangement.[117] This means that the original lease and the lease arising pursuant to the exercise of the option to tax are treated as a single lease for the aggregate term. This will mean that there is not a linked transaction in general terms but a retrospective adjustment in respect of the original calculation. While the exercise of the option to renew will not, as indicated above, necessarily give rise to the immediate charge to tax when the event occurs, it will give rise to an obligation to notify and to pay, but the effective date for the purpose of computing the tax will be the effective date for the original lease or agreement for lease. The charge and the effective date are separate.

3.11.2 Agreements for lease and sale

FA 2003, Sched.17A, para.12A raises many problems for leases where there is a delay between substantial performance and formal grant because there appear to be

---

[114] FA 2003, s.46(3).

[115] But note the need for suitable drafting to avoid any double taxation of any premium for the grant of the option where this is not deducted from the consideration payable pursuant to the agreement as in *George Wimpey Ltd* v. *IRC* [1975] 2 All ER 45.

[116] FA 2003, Sched.17A, para.5.

[117] FA 2003, s.108; see **4.11**.

two separate chargeable transactions with a rent credit for tax paid (see also **Chapter 8**). The substantial performance is treated as the grant of the lease and the subsequent grant of the lease is treated as a limited form of surrender and regrant but with only a credit in respect of the rent for the overlap period. It is not treated as a land exchange as is the case with normal surrender and regrant. Although substantial performance of the agreement for lease is a chargeable transaction in its own right and gives rise to an effective date there is a computational issue in many cases. Where the agreement for lease is substantially performed after the term commencement date and it is fully operative the computation would seem to be based upon the passing rent. However, there are many situations where this may not arise, such as where there is a conditional agreement for lease (e.g. where the parties are awaiting the consent of any superior landlord) so that the terms of the lease itself are not operative.[118] Nevertheless, entry by the tenant upon the land to carry out repairs or fitting out would appear to be taking possession and therefore substantial performance of the conditional agreement. At this time, as the agreement for lease is still conditional or the commencement provisions have not been satisfied (because, for example, the building has not been completed) there will be no rent currently payable.[119] Entry as a licensee to fit out would not normally give rise to an obligation to pay rent under the lease. There is, therefore, an open question with HMRC Stamp Taxes as to the rent computation. It seems that in practice HMRC Stamp Taxes does not accept the argument that rent for the conditional period is to be treated as nil and that the five years commence at the relevant time of taking possession. It seems that HMRC Stamp Taxes expects the calculation to be carried out upon the basis that the rent to be included starts with the term commencement date or the date when the lease is to take effect and that the rent in respect of the first five years is rent from this projected date in the future. However, at substantial performance, such as where a tenant fits out under a conditional agreement, it may not be possible to predict when the conditions will be satisfied. It will not be possible to determine the start of the term, making the computation effectively impossible. There are obvious difficulties in dealing with such a computation where there are numerous outstanding conditions and it is uncertain precisely when the conditions will be satisfied so that the effective term can actually commence.

HMRC Stamp Taxes regards this as not merely a compliance amendment but as creating a totally separate chargeable event for the same lease, i.e. there are two separate taxable events (see further **Chapter 8**). This may affect, *inter alia*:

- the availability of reliefs;

---

[118] *Warmington* v. *Miller* [1973] 2 All ER 372.
[119] This raises various issues as to the rent to be included in the formula for determining the taxable amount. It seems that the initial 'rent' will not be nil because the lease has not become operative. It will be the rent for the periods arising after the lease becomes effective which may have to be estimated and revised late. There will also be problems in calculating the five-year period for variable rent.

- VAT where the option to tax has been exercised between substantial performance and grant. Although the existence of the option to tax and its exercise are to be ignored at substantial performance, it will be VAT actually payable as at completion;[120]
- the five-year period for rent reviews and rent reviews that would have fallen outside the five-year period; they may now be within that period affecting the computation and compliance;
- rent increases in the interim period because these will be the rent reserved as at the date of the grant;
- clawback periods;
- the computation formula in relation to the net present value of the rent when the lease is granted, as it will relate to a later date and a shorter term and the initial five-year period will also differ, providing fundamental issues of principle for rent credits;
- the rent taken into account for the charge upon abnormal increases in rent after the expiration of the fifth year of the term of the lease as it will be based upon a different 12-month period;
- whether the relief for rent reviews and backdating to the previous quarter day is effective because the actual grant is more than three months after the term commencement date.[121]

---

[120] FA 2003, Sched.4, para.2; see **4.30**.
[121] FA 2003, Sched.17A, para.7A. It seems that this period is not calculated by reference to any prior effective date which in principle may precede the term commencement date.

CHAPTER 4

Computation of tax

4.1 BASIC STRUCTURE

There are four basic regimes for the computation of SDLT, namely:

- the general regime for most 'acquisitions' such as sales, releases and variations other than variations of leases;
- a special regime for variable consideration other than rent;[1]
- a special regime for leases including variations thereof[2] whereby the rules for determining the tax charge upon premiums are generally calculated in accordance with the general regime, although the availability of the nil rate for premiums is restricted by reference to the level of rent, and there is a completely different regime for calculating the SDLT upon rents (see **Chapter 8**); and
- a special regime for partnerships.[3]

The two components of consideration and rates are interlinked.

4.1.1 The rate of tax

The rate of tax is, to a large extent, dependent upon two main factors:

- the amount of the chargeable consideration as affected by the linked transaction rules; and
- the property (whether residential or non-residential).[4]

4.1.2 The chargeable consideration

The tax is the application of the rate to the chargeable amount which also determines the level of the rate. The amount of the chargeable consideration itself involves many issues, namely:

---

[1]   FA 2003, s.52; see **4.38**.
[2]   FA 2003, s.43(3)(d), Sched.5 and Sched.17A, para.15A (as amended).
[3]   FA 2003, Sched.15.
[4]   FA 2003, s.55; see **4.3**.

- what is consideration;
- what types of consideration are chargeable since actual consideration and chargeable consideration are not necessarily the same in all cases;
- whether the transaction is governed by special rules such as deemed chargeable consideration;
- how is the amount or value of the consideration to be determined.

4.2 RATES

There is not a simple rate structure since the rate depends upon a variety of factors such as the amount of chargeable consideration which may be variable and require retrospective adjustment.[5] The rate of tax must, in consequence, initially be determined on a provisional basis. The rate of tax has to be computed by reference to the estimated consideration; this may produce a higher rate that may reduce when the final figures are known. As a result there will frequently be claims for repayment of overpaid estimated tax (such as variable consideration or overestimated rents; see e.g. **8.43**). Other factors that will affect the rate include:

- whether the property is residential or non-residential or 'mixed';
- whether the property is wholly or partially in a disadvantaged area;[6] although the significance of this has been much reduced by FA 2005;
- if leasehold the net present value of the rent;[7]
- the level of rent[8] in relation to the nil rate for leases with premiums;
- whether there are 'linked transactions' either currently or in the future.[9] It must be noted that the retrospective nature of the linked transaction rules means that the level of chargeable consideration can increase with a consequent increase in the rates;
- the impact of the linked transaction rules upon the nil rate slice for lease rents which rules can retrospectively increase the rate of tax.[10]

The computation process is complex. Not only are there questions of determining values because of the wide range of consideration in kind including services where the charge is based upon 'open market cost', but also in many areas of consideration such as rents and clawback payments the original land transaction return (SDLT 1) has to be prepared on a 'guestimated' basis and subsequently retrospectively adjusted in the light of actual events. Parties are, therefore, required to determine the

---

[5] But not all cases require revision such as annuities and periodical payments: FA 2003, s.52.

[6] FA 2003, Sched.6 (as amended). To identify disadvantaged areas see Stamp Duty (Disadvantaged Areas) Regulations 2001, SI 2001/3747; Stamp Duty (Disadvantaged Areas) (Application of Exemptions) Regulations 2003, SI 2003/1056.

[7] FA 2003, Sched.5, para.3.

[8] i.e. Whether greater than £1,000 per annum for non-residential property: FA 2003, Sched.5, paras.9 and 9A (as amended).

[9] FA 2003, s.108, Sched.5, para.2.

[10] FA 2003, Sched.5, para.2.

market value of certain assets, the cost of certain services[11] and try to make defensible guesses as to future values or the impact of rent reviews in the future.[12] Moreover, this provisional nature of much of SDLT has considerable title and due diligence issues because in certain situations the liability in respect of the estimated tax does not stay with the original taxpayer but by statute is passed to a third party such as a purchaser of the lease.[13]

4.3 BASIC PRINCIPLES

4.3.1 Residential property purchase price or premium

Generally see FA 2003, s.55 (as amended).

Relevant consideration or premium	Percentage
Not more than £125,000	0%
Not more than £250,000 for first time buyers*	0%
More than £125,000 but not more than £250,000	1%
More than £250,000 but not more than £500,000	3%
More than £500,000	4%
More than £1,000,000	5%**

*   FA 2003, s.57AA; until March 2012; see **Chapter 5**.
**   For transactions completed or performed on or after 1 April 2011.

Where only rent is involved in relation to residential property the position is:

Relevant rental value	Percentage
Not more than £125,000*	0%
More than £125,000	1%

*   It seems that there may be first time buyer relief for certain leases.

In relation to rents it is only the excess over the relevant nil rate slice that is taxable.

Where the property is in a disadvantaged area the residential nil rate band was increased to £150,000 for price, premium and rent. This may have a residual relevance for late completions but these are unlikely in residential transactions. Formerly there was a special rate structure for land within a disadvantaged area.[14]

---

[11]   FA 2003, Sched.4, para.11.
[12]   FA 2003, Sched.17A, paras.7 and 8; see **8.29**.
[13]   See, for example, FA 2003, s.81A and Sched.17A, para.12.
[14]   FA 2003, Sched.6; but see restrictions made by FA 2005.

This provided for certain modifications in the nil rate band for residential property and provided, in some circumstances, a total relief or exemption. This relief was severely restricted by FA 2005. However, this restriction was subject to transitional provisions which means that the relief is available for certain contracts and agreements for lease that were entered into prior to 16 March 2005.[15] This relief is available where the contract was conditional and so there may be transactions yet to be completed that are still within the former relief. This favourable treatment is, however, dependent upon the relevant contract not having been varied. It must also be noted that many aspects of SDLT are provisional subject to retrospective adjustment. Where there is such a retrospective adjustment the effective date may well be prior to 16 March 2005. In these circumstances if the original transaction was within the disadvantaged land relief the subsequent adjustment of the original return would also be within the relief. The adjustment is retrospective. This can be significant in relation to rent reviews being carried out over the next few years because the adjustment at the end of the fifth year of the lease relates back to the original effective date, i.e. the date of the grant and even though the lease was granted after 16 March 2005 if it was granted pursuant to a contract entered into prior to that date the relief may still be available for any rent reviews for several years to come. The former restriction on the nil rate premium level of rent exceeding £600 has been removed.

4.3.2 Non-residential property

4.3.2.1 Purchase price and premium

Relevant consideration/premium	Percentage
Not more than £150,000 where the rent does not exceed £1,000 p.a.*	0%
Not more than £150,000 where the rent exceeds £1,000	1%
More than £150,000 but not more than £250,000	1%
More than £250,000 but not more than £500,000	3%
More than £500,000	4%

*   FA 2003, Sched.5, paras.9 and 9A.

---

[15]   FA 2005, s.95.

4.3.2.2 Rents

Relevant rental value – net present value of rent	Percentage
Not more than £150,000*	0%
More than £150,000	1%

*   But this may impact upon the nil rate for any premium or deemed premium; FA 2003, Sched.5, para.9A.

4.3.3   Mixed property

'Mixed property' is property that includes both residential and non-residential premises such as a shop and flat.[16] This is normally treated as non-residential. Special rules apply to leases where the transaction is two leases and the consideration has to be apportioned between the two deemed leases on a just and reasonable basis.[17]

4.3.4   Special rates

Certain reliefs are available that affect the rates of tax:

- some corporate transactions qualify for a rate of 0.5 per cent;[18]
- first time buyers of residential property are exempt from the 1 per cent rate for purchase prices not exceeding £250,000 for periods on or after 25 March 2010 until 24 March 2012.[19]

4.4   RESIDENTIAL PROPERTY

Residential property has certain minor differences from non-residential property but subject to these limited differences routine residential property transactions are subject to the same regime as major complex commercial transactions.

4.4.1   Definition of 'residential property'

Residential property is defined[20] as meaning:

---

[16]   FA 2003, s.116; Sched.5, para.2, Table B; but see paras.9 and 9A.
[17]   FA 2003, Sched.5, para.2; Sched.7, para.4; Sched.5, paras.9 and 9A.
[18]   FA 2003, Sched.7, Part 2; see **Chapter 13**.
[19]   FA 2010, s.6(6); see **4.33**.
[20]   FA 2003, s.116.

- a building that is suitable for use as a dwelling (this is not itself defined);
- a building that is in the process of being constructed or adapted for use as a dwelling which is a key issue when selling or leasing from plan;[21]
- land that is or forms part of a garden or grounds of a building that is used or is intended for use or is being constructed or adapted for use as a dwelling; or
- an interest in or right over land that subsists for the benefit of a building or land suitable for use with a dwelling.

4.4.2 Actual use: not intentions

It is the actual use or suitability for use, not the proposed use, at the effective date for the chargeable transaction that governs the status of the property as residential or non-residential. For example, where there is the acquisition of commercial property with a view to redevelopment as residential, such as the conversion of a hotel into flats, then its non-residential status will be the factor governing the liability or level of the nil rate for SDLT for that transaction; the future intended use will not be appropriate. On the other hand, if the property acquired consists of several dwellings and does not meet the relief for six or more dwellings acquired under a single transaction because there are different vendors[22] the fact that the dwellings are empty and about to be demolished would indicate that the property is to be regarded as residential and the fact that the existing buildings are to be demolished or converted into offices is irrelevant.

4.4.3 Not in use at effective date

Where the building is not in use at the effective date but is suitable for:

- a purpose that *is* to be treated as use as a dwelling; and
- at least one of those purposes that is *not* to be regarded as use as a dwelling (such as a hall of residence for students in further or higher education),

---

[21] This part of the definition fails to indicate how far the building works need to have progressed such as whether it is sufficient that existing buildings have been demolished or whether it is necessary for actual works of construction such as foundations or other infrastructure works to have commenced. It seems that the latter is the true test, i.e. only at this stage is the building in the process of being constructed.

[22] Such acquisitions would be unlikely to be linked transactions because there are different parties; see **4.6**. This, of course, depends upon whether there is the acquisition of a block of seven or more flats, as the property will then be regarded as non-residential provided that acquisition from seven or more different vendors under potentially separate contracts can be regarded as a 'single transaction' (but see below). It is the nature of the land itself not the interest being acquired that matters. For example, where a management company is acquiring the landlord's interest in a block of flats this will be residential property even though the interest itself does not confer any power to dwell in the premises. This will require SDLT 4 to be filed.

then, if there is one such use for which it is more or most suitable, it is that use that is taken into account when deciding whether it is a dwelling or not;[23] but otherwise the building is to be treated as suitable for use as a dwelling.[24]

4.5 SPECIAL SITUATIONS

4.5.1 Multiple occupancy

As the legislation is basically in terms of single occupancy, it is necessary to deal with situations of multiple occupancy such as old people's homes, hostels for asylum seekers and temporary accommodation for the homeless. Detailed provision is made but it does not appear to convert all of these arrangements into dwellings. A building is used as a dwelling when used as:

- residential accommodation for school pupils;
- residential accommodation for students other than accommodation as a hall of residence for students in further or higher education;
- residential accommodation for members of the armed forces;
- an institution that is the sole or main residence of at least 90 per cent of its residents and which is not used as:

  - a home or other institution providing residential accommodation for children;
  - a hall of residence for students in further or higher education;
  - a home or other institution providing residential accommodation with personal care for persons in need of personal care by reason of old age, disablement, past or present dependence on alcohol or drugs or past or present mental disorder. It seems this would not necessarily cover the provision of hostel accommodation for unemployed or other homeless persons;
  - a hospital or hospice. This would seem to be limited to hospices providing accommodation with some form of medical treatment;
  - a prison or similar establishment;
  - a hotel, inn or similar establishment,[25] as hotels and inns are run for providing temporary accommodation[26] on a profit-making basis. It is

---

[23]   FA 2003, s.116(5)(a).

[24]   FA 2003, s.116(5)(b).

[25]   FA 2003, s.116(2) and (3); there is power to amend by statutory instrument in s.116(8)(a).

[26]   There is an open question of whether the mixed property rule will apply to hotels and similar buildings which provide not only temporary accommodation for guests but also accommodation for members of the staff on a longer-term basis, even though the staff may be on short-term or temporary contracts of a seasonal nature. There is no exclusion for residential accommodation of an incidental nature. It seems that the main argument will be that although there is a 'long-term occupation' the structure or rooms involved are not in themselves suitable for use as a 'dwelling' because they may lack basic facilities for dwellings, but this test may prove difficult to define in practice because of problems with shared facilities in multiple occupancy buildings.

considered that 'similar establishments' will not extend to hostels and similar accommodation for homeless and other persons because these are not likely to be operating on a profit-making basis in most cases.

Where at the effective date the building is actually being used for any of the institutional purposes that are not regarded as the provision of dwellings, it is that actual use that is taken into account and the fact that it is suitable for any other use is to be ignored.

4.5.2 Mixed property

For the purposes of whether the property is mixed property[27] building includes part of a building[28] so that issues will arise where there is sale[29] or lease of a single structure with mixed use such as a shop with a flat above or a public house with accommodation for staff[30] or a house with a paddock, or a farm with housing occupied by agricultural workers or a farmhouse.

4.5.3 Six or more properties

It is specifically provided that where there is a single transaction involving the transfer of major interests in or the grant of a lease over six or more separate dwellings, those dwellings are treated as not involving residential property.[31] Unfortunately there is no explanation of what is a 'single transaction' for these purposes; but fortunately it is of little practical significance and frequently a problem rather than a benefit. A single transaction is obviously not the same as a 'linked transaction' which links otherwise separate transactions,[32] and there is no provision that provides that linked transactions are to be treated as a single transaction. Although such transactions are aggregated for the purposes of deter-mining the total chargeable consideration or the length of a lease, the transactions remain separate transactions and are *prima facie* separately reportable[33] and apart from successive linked leases[34] have their own effective dates; they do not become a single contract or transaction. For example, a person proposing to redevelop by acquiring several adjacent properties with a view to demolition and construction of new premises or the refurbishment of existing premises will be dealing with separate vendors; technically, then, this would be several separate transactions and

---

[27]   Detailed rules were enacted (FA 2003, Sched.6, para.6; s.55(2), Table B) where the property related to land in a disadvantaged area. These rules may still be relevant for certain transactions which commenced prior to the abolition of the relief on 16 March 2005; see FA 2005, Sched.9.

[28]   FA 2003, s.116(6).

[29]   The rules as to linked transactions mean that it will be almost inevitable that such acquisitions are linked and aggregated. Separate sales each with their own lower rates will be extremely rare.

[30]   Rooms for hotel guests on a temporary basis will be governed by the exempting provisions.

[31]   FA 2003, s.116(7).

[32]   FA 2003, s.108.

[33]   FA 2003, ss.108 and 77.

[34]   FA 2003, Sched.17A, para.5.

not a single transaction,[35] which will usually benefit the purchaser. This consequence of being deemed to be residential property will also apply where the
purchaser is acquiring numerous properties from connected vendors so that these
transactions will be linked so as to attract the higher rate but would not qualify for
the benefit of the non-residential property reliefs.

4.6   LINKED TRANSACTIONS

4.6.1   Background

The question of linked transactions is important for:

- the availability of the lower rates of SDLT;[36]
- certain computational provisions;[37]
- determining the length of lease usually retrospectively in respect of the net
  present value of the rent.[38]

In consequence, the rules will apply to determine whether the chargeable consideration for the related transactions or the lengths of the related leases has to be
aggregated; but only chargeable consideration attributable to land transactions is to
be aggregated. Where there is a sale of several parcels of land and chattels or the sale
of land with a related building contract, or the sale of a business carried on from
several premises with a sale of goodwill, only the land prices are to be aggregated.
This, however, means that there are many problems in practice in identifying which
are and which are not chargeable interests and allocating the consideration between
them on a just and reasonable basis, such as:

- which are fixtures (land) and which are tax-free chattels (see **2.15.1**);
- whether any 'goodwill' is free or embedded in the land (see **2.15.2**);
- whether the allocation between the land and other parts of the contract has been
  apportioned on a proper basis.[39]

The rules, which have the potential for great practical difficulties, differ from
certificates of value for stamp duty in that they are much wider in their scope; but
they are subject to limitation in their application. Moreover, attempts have been
made by HMRC Stamp Taxes to put them to wider use than the legislation allows. It
is important to note that the concept of linked transactions is not:

---

[35]   As there are separate vendors the transactions are *prima facie* not linked unless the vendors are
'connected'.
[36]   FA 2003, s.55(4).
[37]   FA 2003, Sched.17A, para.14(5)(b).
[38]   FA 2003, Sched.17A, para.5.
[39]   FA 2003, Sched.4, para.4; see **4.27**; note the problems of *Saunders* v. *Edwards* [1987] 2 All
ER 651.

- a statutory equivalent of the anti-avoidance cases based upon *Ramsay* v. *IRC*;[40] or
- a form of associated operation provisions providing power for HMRC Stamp Taxes to amalgamate, merge or separate transactions;[41] or
- a power to recharacterise transactions. For example, it cannot convert legally separate contracts for building works and for the lease of the land into a single transaction for the lease of a completed building (see **Chapter 9**).

The following problems arise.

- The linked transaction principles apply on a retrospective basis.[42] In consequence, many transactions will to the surprise of taxpayers be initially dealt with only on a provisional basis because of the possibility of later linked transactions[43] and the initial land transaction return will have to be revised in the light of subsequent events. For example, the exercise of an option to renew a lease 'may'[44] produce a successive linked lease[45] so that the self-assessment of the tax upon the initial lease 'may'[46] have to be revised should the initial lease have to be treated as part of a single scheme and so retrospectively as a lease for a longer term. Thus the linked transaction principles require the original land transaction return to be retrospectively revised on the basis that it relates to the aggregate of the terms of the original lease and of the renewed lease so that net present value of the rent is to be recalculated by reference to a deemed longer term.[47] In addition to retrospectively affecting the initial calculation, this subsequent event constitutes a separate transaction requiring its own return which will be separate from the land transaction return required for the subsequent transaction.
- The land transaction return (SDLT 1) requires the taxpayer to indicate whether the transaction is linked with another transaction. This question will be irrelevant for the first transaction, as it has nothing with which to be linked and can only become linked retrospectively. It therefore will not, as at the initial filing date, be a linked transaction but a separate return correcting the situation will, inevitably, be required when dealing with the later transaction.[48]

---

[40] [1981] STC 174.

[41] This function may have been taken over by the statutory general anti-avoidance provisions: FA 2003, ss.75A–75C.

[42] This differs from the certificates of value for stamp duty whereby although later transactions might be vulnerable the earlier contracts were not retrospectively affected. There is still, however, the problem that a transaction cannot be linked with something yet to occur which is dealt with by the legislation imposing a retrospective adjustment for earlier transactions.

[43] FA 2003, s.81A.

[44] See FA 2003, s.46.

[45] FA 2003, Sched.17A, para.5.

[46] It is initially for the taxpayer to decide under penalty whether the later lease is 'linked' with the original lease and any other previously renewed leases. Usually it will be beneficial for the taxpayer to argue for successive linked leases; see **4.13**.

[47] This is intended to avoid taxpayers obtaining the benefit of several nil rate 'slices' for tax upon the rent; but it offers considerable opportunities for mitigating the impact of the tax; see **4.13**.

[48] FA 2003, s.81A; note also Sched.17A, para.12.

- The taxation of leases has to be aggregated and the relevant rate thresholds have to be apportioned between leases and subsequently adjusted.[49]
- Linked transactions involving the grant of new leases or renewals of leases as successive linked leases[50] may affect third parties such as assignees of leases.[51]
- The principles have a significant impact upon rent reviews because the rent reviews may affect the allocation of the net present value between the leases and other leases some of which may have been assigned to third parties.[52]

4.7 LINKED TRANSACTIONS: THIRD PARTIES' RISK AND DUE DILIGENCE

There is an open question, as far as HMRC Stamp Taxes is concerned, with third parties and linked transactions. Notwithstanding that the linked transaction rules apply only to transactions between the same parties,[53] purchasers of chargeable interests may find that their liability to tax is affected by the tax position of the vendor or landlord[54] not merely upon the immediate transaction, but also future linked transactions to which they are not parties.[55] This may arise because the later linked transaction, although relating to other property and involving other parties, retrospectively adjusts the tax calculation for the property which the third party holds, e.g. by reason of a reduction in the amount of the nil rate slice allocated to the net present value of the rent for the lease.[56] Such third parties who may be affected by subsequent dealings involving other parties will need to insist not only upon appropriate disclosure of all relevant information relating to the history of the chargeable interest in land which they are acquiring, but also upon appropriate undertakings from the vendor or landlord to disclose all subsequent events which may be linked with their transaction, including full details of transactions with third parties that may be commercially sensitive. As in many cases in other key areas, the obtaining of the essential protection for clients may prove extremely difficult, if not impossible, particularly where the third parties sensibly require undertakings against the disclosure of information without their consent in order to protect their confidential business information.

---

[49] FA 2003, Sched.5, para.2.
[50] FA 2003, Sched.17A, para.5.
[51] FA 2003, Sched.5, para.2(5) and (6) and Sched.17A, para.11.
[52] FA 2003, Sched.5, para.2.
[53] FA 2003, s.108.
[54] FA 2003, Sched.5, para.2; s.81A; Sched.17A, para.11.
[55] See, e.g. FA 2003, s.81A and Sched.17A, para.11.
[56] FA 2003, s.81A; Sched.5, para.2(5), note also Sched.17A, para.12.

4.8   AGGREGATING TRANSACTIONS

4.8.1   General principles

Transactions are linked if they form part of a single scheme, arrangement or series of transactions between the same vendor and purchaser or persons connected with either of them.[57] This definition leaves open many problems, particularly as the practice of HMRC Stamp Taxes is not supported by the legislation. For example, it is its automatic response that if the various separate transactions involve the same parties they must be 'linked'.[58] It has attempted to apply this approach even where several separate lots have been purchased at an auction.[59] Clearly, there is no linkage but the official, erroneous, view is that they are linked. This view ignores the basic requirement that there must be 'a' scheme, arrangement or series of transactions. The utilisation of the word 'a' clearly indicates that two or more unrelated transactions cannot be linked because there are two schemes or arrangements. The fact that two or more transactions are more or less simultaneous is not sufficient to link transactions; there must be essentially a pre-arranged deal not a coincidental or fortuitous timing relationship between the various transactions. In broad terms the test is whether the parties would have signed up to the deal on those terms such as discounts unless all contracts were exchanged.

It might be thought that it should be easy for HMRC Stamp Taxes to establish a 'series' from a succession of transactions. However, it has been held[60] that a series requires some form of contractual linkage such as a single option exercisable by instalments. In other words, to be a 'series' or 'arrangement' there must be a pre-arranged plan amounting to an 'arrangement' rather than a hope or expectation.[61] Broadly, one transaction would not arise unless the others were also entered into. It is not sufficient that there is a simple chronological sequence of transactions that are not part of such a plan.[62] The draftsman recognised this in that an option and its exercise only 'may' be linked transactions.[63]

It is no longer sufficient to try to obtain the benefit of the lower rates by fragmenting the overall transaction into separate legally independent contracts if it can be established that the parties would not commercially have signed one agreement unless the others were also signed. What matters is the commercial agreement or understanding between the parties, not the legal form into which it

---

[57]   FA 2003, s.108(1).

[58]   Questions have been raised on this issue where the same firm of solicitors files returns on behalf of different, unconnected clients.

[59]   Note, however, *Att-Gen* v. *Cohen* [1937] KB 478.

[60]   *Att-Gen* v. *Cohen* [1937] KB 478.

[61]   Note especially, *Times Newspapers* v. *IRC* [1971] 3 All ER 98 on the very important distinction between 'intention', 'expectation' and 'arrangement'. Note the definitions of 'arrangements' such as FA 2003, Sched.7, para.2(5); para.8(5C).

[62]   Compare *Clarke Chapman John Thompson Ltd* v. *IRC* [1975] STC 567. This may be a key factor in the possible application of the statutory general anti-avoidance provisions pursuant to FA 2003, ss.75A–75C; see **1.33**.

[63]   See especially FA 2003, s.46.

may be eventually reduced. If there is a commercial linkage, broadly a single negotiation for several properties (especially where there is a discount for a purchase of the multiple purchases) the purchaser cannot escape from these provisions simply by arranging for separate contracts to be signed by associates or connected companies, whether acting as nominees or beneficial owners in their own right, or by entering into separate contracts for each property with separate completion dates. This need to deal with such 'commercial linkage' will be a matter of detailed contemporaneous evidence as to the manner in which the negotiation developed. Clearly, if there is a discount for the purchase of several properties the transactions will be linked because there will be 'a scheme' for a multiple sale at a reduced price. Professional advisers may find it appropriately prudent before signing off the land transaction return (SDLT 1) to have a full statement of the background to the transaction from their clients and ideally seek confirmation from the vendor or lessor that this understanding of the preliminary negotiations corresponds with the statement provided by the taxpayer since it would prove embarrassing in an Enquiry if the two versions diverge.[64]

4.8.2 The same parties

It is specifically provided that the transactions must be entered into between the same persons or persons connected with either them[65] but relief is provided for exchanges between connected parties such as where parent and child exchange houses or flats.[66] Numerous problems frequently arise in practice, as discussed below.

4.8.2.1 Subsales

Where there is a subsale of part of the property originally agreed to be purchased, the sub-purchaser, if otherwise unconnected with the original purchaser, will not be a party to a linked transaction since his agreement will be with the original purchaser.[67] He will be entitled to the lower rates.

---

[64] HMRC Stamp Taxes has the power to demand information and documents from the vendor and the vendor's advisers, and advisers are personally vulnerable to serious penalties involving imprisonment where fraud in the wide sense of *Saunders* v. *Edwards* [1987] 2 All ER 651 is involved. See, for example, FA 2003, ss.95 and 96 the provisions of which apply to the vendor's advisers as well as the purchaser's advisers.

[65] Difficult questions will no doubt arise in practice in due course where the original party has died and the option is exercised by a person interested in his estate or his personal representative. These do not appear to be 'connected persons', but the position is not entirely clear.

[66] FA 2003, s.47 (as amended).

[67] It is, of course, essential that none of the other sub-purchasers is connected with the particular sub-purchaser which may help to link the transactions.

4.8.2.2 Connected parties

It must be noted that the connected person rules apply not only to connected purchasers but also to vendors. In general, where a single purchaser agrees to acquire several properties from different vendors these will not be linked transactions, notwithstanding that there may be a condition in each of the contracts that each of them will complete only if all of the other related contracts also complete simultaneously. The transactions will remain linked by reason of the contract term only if, and to the extent that, some or all of the vendors or lessors are connected. However, where there is a contract to acquire a leasehold interest or a freehold interest from a company and, as part of a single overall commercial arrangement, the reversion or an adjacent freehold is to be acquired from the shareholders, the fact that the parties are connected will help to link the transactions even where they are in separate contracts.

4.8.2.3 Multiple party transactions

Frequently there will be several vendors to a single purchaser or several purchasers from a single vendor. For example, a developer may buy several properties with a provision that one contract will complete only if all contracts complete so that there is a contractual linkage. Alternatively a syndicate may agree to purchase a block of flats from plan, each member of the syndicate agreeing to acquire the relevant part of the property individually.[68] The negotiations will no doubt involve a special price so that there is a commercial linkage. However, the contracts will be unlinked to the extent that the vendors and purchasers, as the case may be, are unconnected. The linked transaction principles apply only to the extent that individual vendors, purchasers or lessees are connected.

4.8.2.4 Assignees

The reference to the same persons or persons connected with them indicates quite clearly that transactions involving one or more different parties are not linked. However, it appears to be the view of HMRC Stamp Taxes that transactions involving third parties can be linked. For example, it is its view, almost certainly erroneous, that the exercise of an option, including an option to renew a lease, is linked with the initial grant of the option or lease notwithstanding that the option is exercised by the assignee of the option or the lease,[69] at least in those cases where the landlord and the tenant who exercise the option are connected notwithstanding that the original tenant was not connected with the original landlord. It is considered that, as a general principle, this is incorrect. Assignments of either the reversion or

---

[68] Should there be a single purchase whereby all of the properties are to be held jointly the linked transaction principles will not apply because there is only one transaction. In addition there may be a need to investigate whether there is a partnership.

[69] Assuming that the correct party to exercise the option can be identified; see *Brown & Root Technology Ltd* v. *Sun Life and London Assurance Ltd* [2000] 2 WLR 566.

the lease or both break the linked transaction rules. The legislation requires the same persons to be involved and it is difficult to establish 'a scheme or arrangement' where third parties are involved who could not be parties to a cut-and-dried arrangement between the original parties and were not involved in the original contract. It seems, therefore, that assignees are not affected by the linked transaction rules, which is crucial for assignees of leases with options to renew or extend the lease.

4.9 EXCHANGES AND LINKED TRANSACTIONS

HMRC Stamp Taxes has abandoned the attempt to aggregate exchanges because the same parties are involved, even where the parties are connected.[70] Each side of the exchange will be taxed as a separate transaction.

4.10 SIDE EFFECTS AND PROBLEMS FOR ASSIGNEES

This is a different issue from that of whether a surrender and grant of a new lease is between 'the same parties' for the purposes of the various reliefs. Much of SDLT is initially dealt with on a provisional or guestimated basis leaving the SDLT position of the original taxpayer open (see **1.11** and **1.24**). Unfortunately, by statute this open tax position follows the chargeable interest so that third parties who acquire an interest in the land may become liable for the original 'purchaser's' tax liability.[71] Although transactions entered into by assignees of chargeable interests are probably not linked transactions with transactions entered into by the assignor of the rights, this does not mean that the assignee will not be affected by transactions entered into by the assignor. The fact that the original taxpayer has sold on all or part of the originally acquired chargeable interests does not 'unlink' that transaction from subsequent transactions, notwithstanding that this may adversely affect the overall tax position of the assignee. For example, a subsequent linked lease, such as one created by the exercise of an option to renew another lease by the assignor, will reduce the amount of the nil rate slice for the net present value of the rent of a lease assigned to a third party, in relation to the first rent review or a possible abnormal increase[72] in the rent after the expiration of the fifth year of the term of the original lease. Appropriate investigations of the SDLT history will be required together with

---

[70]   FA 2003, s.47 (as amended).
[71]   Regrettably the legislation does not expressly state whether the original taxpayer is released from liability and/or whether the third party is solely liable or there is joint and several liability with a possible implied indemnity for the third party.
[72]   FA 2003, Sched.5, para.3, Sched.17A, paras.5, 14, 15 and para.11 (as amended).

appropriate undertakings from the vendor to supply detailed information of subsequent transactions which may affect the tax position of the purchaser of the chargeable interest so that he can comply with his obligations[73] and/or compute his future tax correctly.

4.11 LINKED LEASES: LEASE PREMIUMS AND RENTS

When dealing with leases there are numerous special issues which depend upon whether:

- the transactions relate to leases of different premises – when the basic rules apply; or
- the transactions relate to renewals or other dealings in leases of the same premises – when special rules apply[74] but which may retrospectively affect linked leases of other property.

The double structure of taxation of lease premiums and lease rents provides for complexities. It appears that where the chargeable transactions include leases which are linked, any premium will be aggregated with any premiums for other linked leases and the chargeable consideration for other transactions. However, where there is a lease at a rent which is a linked transaction, no account is to be taken of rent in determining the relevant premium.[75]

Where there are linked leases the nil rate slice has to be allocated between the linked leases in accordance with the proportion that the net present value of the rent for each individual lease bears to the total net present value of the rents reserved by all of the linked leases.[76] Since the linked transaction rules can include later leases and renewals of leases the initial allocation of the relevant proportion of the nil rate slice for the rent will be on a provisional basis subject to retrospective review as each subsequent linked transaction occurs. In consequence, assignees will require the basic disclosure of the history of the lease and related transactions and of any subsequent potentially linked transactions.

4.12 LINKED TRANSACTIONS: OPTIONS AND PRE-EMPTION RIGHTS

4.12.1 Options

Specific, but unclear, rules apply to deal with the link between the grant of options and the contract or lease arising from their exercise. It is provided that the grant of an option is a chargeable transaction in its own right distinct from any transaction

---

[73] FA 2003, s.81A.
[74] FA 2003, Sched.17A, para.5.
[75] FA 2003, Sched.5, para.9(5).
[76] FA 2003, Sched.5, para.2.

resulting from the exercise of the option.[77] However, the provision goes on to indicate that the grant and the exercise of the option only 'may be' linked transactions. This word 'may' indicates that there is, at least in the view of the draftsman, no automatic linkage between the grant of the option and the transaction arising pursuant to its exercise. This must be a matter of evidence in each case, i.e. whether there was an arrangement or understanding between the parties that the option would be exercised and possibly whether there is a realistic commercial possibility that it might not be exercised.[78] The consideration for the option should be retrospectively aggregated with the consideration payable upon the exercise of the option so that, if appropriate, the higher rates of SDLT will be applicable to both the contract price and the option price.

This issue of linkage means that it will be necessary to file a further land transaction return (SDLT 1) in respect of the initial grant of the option or pre-emption right because of an increase in the amount of tax payable by reason of a higher rate becoming applicable. This would seem to apply even where the premium for the option is a token sum of £1.[79] This return is in addition to the return on the grant of the option and the separate return required in respect of the contract or agreement for lease arising pursuant to the exercise of the option, i.e. at least three separate land transaction returns will be required in relation to the initial agreement for lease and the subsequent grant.

4.12.2   Pre-emption rights

The same legislation is applied to pre-emption rights but since such rights depend upon a decision by the landowner to sell and are, in effect, merely offers to sell entirely within the decision-making power of the landowner, it is less likely that there will be a scheme or arrangement with the degree of certainty to link the two events.[80] It is usually uncertain when the right will become effective because this depends upon the decision to sell and it is usually uncertain whether the rights will be exercised. Nevertheless the question of whether the grant of the rights and their exercise are linked transactions must be investigated when completing the return.

The initial return on a provisional basis has to be revised should the pre-emption rights be exercised if the grant and exercise are linked. In consequence it may be necessary to submit a land transaction return (SDLT 1) in respect of the contract arising from the exercise of the right.

---

[77]   FA 2003, s.46(1).

[78]   It may be prudent to keep a detailed file note where the parties are negotiating whether to have a long lease with a break clause or a short lease with an option to renew, to provide evidence on this key issue of fact.

[79]   But not, perhaps, a peppercorn or 99p because of rounding down.

[80]   In certain cases the pre-emption right is part of a sale with a buyback arrangement when the circumstances may point to a scheme for only temporary ownership, i.e. a scheme to repurchase which suggests a taxable land exchange specifically taxable (see **Chapter 7**) which is no longer a linked transaction, but the form of a land exchange may prevail over the substance of a dealing in a part interest.

4.12.3 Completion issues

Since cross-options are a form of land exchange, both parties will need to investigate whether their option has any market value because although options are minor interests there is a potential land exchange.[81] In consequence there is unlikely to be tax payable unless the market value exceeds £150,000 repayment of tax nor will filing be required by either party, but the purchaser/grantee may have tax issues should he exercise the rights.[82]

4.13 LEASE RENEWALS: SUCCESSIVE LINKED LEASES

It is not unusual for leases to contain an option to renew the lease or for leases to be held over and renewed whether pursuant to statute such as the Landlord and Tenant Act 1954 and Agricultural Holdings Acts or the similar form business legislation[83] which will fall within the provisions for successive linked leases.[84] Moreover, HMRC Stamp Taxes is anxious to prevent parties from entering into a series of short leases where the net present value of the rent is within the nil rate slice. Thus leases being subsequently renewed would also, *prima facie*, qualify for a nil rate treatment, although a lease for the aggregate term would have been taxable.[85] Under the present regime relating to the calculation of SDLT upon rents by reason of the nil rate 'slice' of the net present value of the rent always being free of tax,[86] there may be opportunities to mitigate the tax by taking short leases with options to renew, each of which may fall within the nil rates of SDLT. However, the legislation[87] indicates that the new lease may be linked with the original lease and any previous renewals thereof, so that the terms of the original lease and the renewal(s) thereof are retrospectively aggregated to become a lease for a longer (i.e. the aggregate) term.[88] This means that any premium for the new lease will be aggregated with the premium for any prior lease or leases, and the charge upon the rent reserved by the initial lease will have to be recalculated upon the basis that the original lease was for a term equal to the aggregate of the terms of the original lease and any linked renewals thereof.

---

[81] FA 2003, s.47; Sched.4, para.5.

[82] FA 2003, ss.77 and 77A.

[83] Which involves a key issue of principle as to the meaning of a charge applying to transactions by operation of law (FA 2003, s.43) and to the continuation of lease 'by operation of law' pursuant to FA 2003, Sched.17A, para.4.

[84] FA 2003, Sched.17A, para.5.

[85] Because of the benefit of deferring the payment of tax; but this depends upon whether the nil rate slice is significant so that a second or third nil rate will outweigh the benefits of the rent being discounted over time and the tax being deferred free of interest.

[86] FA 2003, Sched.5.

[87] FA 2003, Sched.17A, para.5; see also **4.11**.

[88] See FA 2003, Sched.19, para.9 on the transitional position of the exercise of options to renew leases granted within the charge to stamp duty, which may include leases granted on or after 1 December 2003 but pursuant to an agreement entered into prior to that date.

The issue is, however, whether there is a linked transaction within the general principles, which is a question of fact in each case. If there is a genuine commercial possibility that the option might not be exercised because of subsequent events, such as not renewing a lease because the trading activities at the demised premises might not have proved successful, it is an indication that the two stages are not linked. Moreover, the linked transaction principles apply only between the same parties, so the exercise of the option to renew the lease by an unconnected assignee is *prima facie* not a linked transaction.[89] Consequently the assignee exercising the option will qualify for a nil rate slice as regards the rent because of the leases not being linked since they are not between the same parties unless the assignee and assignor are connected parties.

The difficulty will be trying to predict when HMRC Stamp Taxes will accept that the original and the new leases are linked. It seems that if the lease has been assigned the exercise of the option will not be a linked transaction since the exercise and the contract arising are not between the same parties as those to the original lease.[90] Where it is the original tenant who exercises the option the outcome will depend upon the original negotiations and whether there were 'side arrangements'[91] relating to the renewal of the lease and whether these discussions were adequately documented at the time. In the absence of such direct contemporaneous evidence, the decision will depend largely upon inference from the facts. For example, where there is a long lease during which much can happen the renewal is less likely to be a linked transaction than where the parties began by negotiating a seven-year lease and agreed a three-year lease with an option to renew. It is unclear whether the exercise of the option will be 'linked' with the original and any other prior agreements for lease so that the chargeable consideration has to be aggregated for these purposes, particularly where the lease has been assigned so that the person exercising the option is not the same person as the original tenant.

4.14 DEEMED LINKED TRANSACTIONS

The legislation also deems certain transactions to be linked so that the deemed new lease arising upon an abnormal rent increase is deemed to be linked with the actual lease and no nil rate slice will be available.[92] This frequently arises because certain events are not in themselves chargeable transactions but are deemed to be such. It is,

---

[89] See FA 2003, s.108.

[90] Provided that the assignee is not connected with the assignor. However, HMRC Stamp Taxes has previously acted upon the basis that since the contract between the original vendor/landlord and the assignee is the same as that with the assignor, the assignor and the assignee are the same person. It is, however, difficult to justify this analysis as a matter of general principle, rather than a point depending upon the particular legislation.

[91] Note the decision in *Times Newspapers* v. *IRC* [1971] 3 All ER 98 on the important distinction between an 'arrangement', which requires a strong element of 'certainty' and 'intention' or 'purpose' as in *Combined Technologies Plc* v. *IRC* [1985] STC 348.

[92] FA 2003, Sched.17A, paras.14 and 15.

therefore, necessary to deal with such deemed transactions as new transactions where they are separate taxable events rather than retrospective revisions of the initial transaction. However, the deemed transactions may also be deemed to be linked transactions.

4.15 CHARGEABLE CONSIDERATION

The second stage of the computation involves the determination of whether there is consideration, whether this is chargeable consideration or there is deemed chargeable consideration, not the amount thereof. For example, in relation to deemed chargeable consideration there are three separate sets of principles, potentially applicable, namely:

- situations where there is no actual consideration but the legislation deems there to be chargeable consideration;[93]
- situations where the chargeable consideration is deemed to differ from the actual consideration;[94] and
- situations where there is actual consideration which is deemed to be non-chargeable, although the terminology for the treatment varies enormously. For example, the transaction may be 'exempt'[95] or such actual consideration is to be 'ignored',[96] treated as 'nil' or 'exempt'. These various concepts appear at various places in the legislation but it is unclear what, if any, are intended to be the general consequences of these differences in terminology although there are certain express differences in the compliance regime (see **Chapter 1**).

There are, significantly, situations where the notification obligations may have special rules notwithstanding the absence of actual or deemed chargeable consideration.[97]

Chargeable consideration, which is required by the charging provisions,[98] requires two elements, namely:

- the existence of either:
  - actual consideration since, in general,[99] the absence of actual consideration means that there is no chargeable transaction; or
  - deemed consideration since there are situations where there is a deemed

---

[93]   Such as connected companies or partnerships: FA 2003, s.53 and Sched.15, Part 3.

[94]   Such as land exchanges: FA 2003, s.47.

[95]   On the various meanings of this word and the differing consequences see **Chapter 5**.

[96]   There are problems as to the 'plain English' meaning of words such as 'ignored' and 'disregarded' in the context of the legislation which seem to require a bizarre construction.

[97]   FA 2003, ss.77, 53(4) and Sched.15, para.30.

[98]   FA 2003, Sched.3, para.1.

[99]   There is no general principle that transactions are to be taxed upon the basis that they are deemed to be taking place at market value. There are only certain specific instances; see **Chapter 15**.

consideration, most notably in relation to the connected company charge and the special regime for partnerships; and

- such actual or deemed consideration must be 'chargeable'. This clearly means that these situations must involve 'consideration' actual or deemed which is also chargeable and which is significantly wider than the categories of consideration that were required to create a charge to *ad valorem* stamp duty. There are also provisions such as the connected company charge[100] which deem there to be a chargeable consideration. This is important since not all actual consideration is within the definition of chargeable consideration.

There is also the question of the chargeable amount of consideration which involves numerous technical issues of statutory construction such as identifying the relevant chargeable consideration. For example, in relation to land exchanges the chargeable consideration is not the value of the chargeable interest disposed of but the market value of the interest received.[101]

4.16 CHARGEABLE CONSIDERATION: GENERAL ISSUES

This question of when the consideration whether actual or deemed is 'chargeable' raises some very fundamental issues affecting the scope of the tax and the computation thereof, namely:

- what is 'consideration';
- when is the actual consideration chargeable and so relevant for the purposes of the charge to tax;
- when the actual consideration or absence of consideration is to be replaced by a deemed amount of consideration;
- how the chargeable amount is to be calculated;
- where there is consideration in kind how the chargeable amount is to be determined, i.e. what are the 'valuation' principles to be adopted;[102] and
- how variable consideration is to be dealt with.

Unfortunately these are fundamental issues which those responsible for preparing the structure and drafting of the tax failed to appreciate and deal with adequately, leaving matters of highly technical taxation law to general principles of statutory construction which are not necessarily appropriate. As usual the taxpayer will have to do the best he can,[103] bear the risk of interest, penalties of incorrect interpretations and may have to incur the cost of litigating to get a decision in his favour simply to avoid penalties and interest charges.

---

[100] FA 2003, ss.53 and 54.
[101] FA 2003, s.47; Sched.4, para.5.
[102] FA 2003, Sched.4, paras.7, 10 and 11.
[103] See the dubious comments of Russell LJ in *Crane Fruehauf* v. *IRC* [1975] STC 51.

4.17 CONSIDERATION

There is no definition of what constitutes 'consideration' although there are certain general rules for determining the amount or value of the consideration that is subject to charge in relation to certain situations of the asset or service. Obviously where there are computational or valuation provisions dealing with the valuation of the tax this is a clear indication that the benefit or obligation referred to is 'consideration'.[104]

This requires professional advisers to be aware not only of the tax issues but also of the basic principles of the law of contract and their interaction with land law and conveyancing. In consequence, subject to specific provisions, 'consideration' must bear, at least, its general contractual meaning and all of the conditions relating thereto. Although it may be necessary for the consideration to move from the promisee (i.e. the 'purchaser' in SDLT parlance), it need not pass to the promisor (i.e. the 'vendor' for the purposes of SDLT). For example, a lease may be granted by a landlord at the direction of the other party to the agreement for lease to a third party who pays a sum of money to the original contracting party for the 'assignment of the right to call for the lease',[105] which may be paid directly to the landlord at the direction of the original contracting body in satisfaction of the building obligation; a payment to a developer for building works may also form part of the consideration.[106]

4.18 OPERATION OF LAW AND CONSIDERATION

The highly technical area of SDLT taking effect by operation of law will require detailed understanding of the basic law of contract but certain provisions raise doubts as to whether because of the imposition of the charge to SDLT taking effect by operation of law[107] 'consideration' is to be regarded as wider than its general meaning and includes 'benefits' or 'detriments' that would not rank as contractual consideration. This tax charge arises in relation to transactions 'taking effect by operation of law' where the passing of the property may be effected by equitable principles in favour of a person suffering a detriment such as the performance of services rather than making a payment. This concept of 'by operation of law' is one of profound obscurity and in the context of the SDLT legislation massively ambiguous and uncertain. For example, the concept may include:

- contracts or other binding arrangements that are perfected without intervention of the parties. This may occur where the land in the United Kingdom is owned by a foreign company that by reason of administrative arrangements is merged

---

[104] See *J&P Coats Ltd* v. *IRC* [1897] 2 QB 423 to the effect that because there are computational or relieving provisions the asset in question must by necessary implication be taxable.
[105] Compare FA 2003, Sched.17A, para.12B.
[106] *Att-Gen* v. *Brown* (1849) 3 Ex 662; FA 2003, Sched.17A, para.12B; see **Chapter 8**.
[107] FA 2003, s.43.

with another foreign company. The title to the assets of the first company which is absorbed into the new company pass under the relevant law of the jurisdiction of incorporation to the new company. This means that all that is left is for the United Kingdom courts to arrange for the transfer of the bare legal title to recognise the effect of the change of title to the property pursuant to the operation of the foreign law. This has always, hitherto, been accepted by HMRC Stamp Taxes, in practice, as a transaction not on sale;[108]

- arrangements governed by United Kingdom law where the title passes without intervention by the court. This includes situations such as equitable or promissory estoppel where 'by operation of equitable principles' an interest moves from A to B by reason of A's promise to B who acts upon the basis of that promise but which promise may fall short of a binding contract either for reasons of formality[109] or for other reasons. The issue is whether the reliance upon the promise and changing of position constitutes some form of 'consideration' that can convert an oral informal arrangement into a binding contract within the scope of the comments of Walker LJ in *Yaxley* v. *Gotts*;[110]
- a contractual arrangements where the legal mechanics for perfecting that arrangement may differ from the terms of the contract such as where the parties enter into a deed of variation of a lease that constitutes some form of surrender and regrant by operation of the general law;[111]
- surrender of a lease by operation of law; or
- continuation of a tenancy by operation of law, at least in the view of the draftsman.

The ambiguity around the meaning of 'operation of law' would seem to justify the attitude of HMRC Stamp Taxes to treat the type of transaction on its legal basis as opposed to taking it at face value or the terms of the contract. The deed of variation would, therefore, be taxed as some form of surrender and regrant. It is also possible that, notwithstanding the long-term practice, HMRC Stamp Taxes may claim that its longstanding practice is not a practice but a consistent series of mistakes which do not bind them, and contend that the arrangements between the shareholders in a

---

[108] HMRC Stamp Taxes has sought to reserve its position to attack such transactions upon the basis that there is a transfer, albeit by operation of law, that constitutes a sale because the title to the assets passes and by reason of the operation of the foreign law any liabilities of the existing company are novated to the new or continuing company. However, in practice, this point has never been pursued and there is a question as to whether this foreign novation by operation of law operates as the assumption of a liability for the purposes of the deemed consideration rules pursuant to FA 2003, Sched.4, para.8 (as amended).

[109] Law of Property (Miscellaneous Provisions) Act 1989, s.2; *Firstpost Homes* v. *Johnson* [1995] 4 All ER 355.

[110] [1999] 3 WLR 1217.

[111] See Gable Construction v. IRC [1968] 1 WLR 1426; Friends Provident Life Office v. British Railways Board [1996] 1 All ER 336; see **8.58**.

merger of foreign companies sanctioning the arrangement is a contract and therefore taxable notwithstanding that the passing of title is a matter of the operation of a legal regime whether foreign or domestic.[112]

The main practical difficulty will be in relation to the other category of equitable intervention should this prove to be not an effective oral contract but some form of equitable remedy. There will be significant issues as to whether the equitable remedy arising in such cases is a form of contract so that the reliance upon the promise is some form of performance of an obligation that constitutes the provision of consideration.[113] For example, there are key issues as to constructive trusts:

- whether these are merely equitable remedies in the discretion of the judiciary where a party has acted upon oral statements so as to give rise to a constructive trust by operation of law; or whether the terms of the promise (i.e. the oral promise to transfer the property 'if' certain actions were performed) may be effective to create a contract for actual consideration and are effective to pass or create property interests (see **Chapter 1**); or
- the fundamental question of whether in equity the 'conditions' of the promise constitute 'consideration' or whether 'consideration' requires a 'contract' in the narrow sense of a valid, legally enforceable agreement which meets all formal requirements arising solely from the agreement of the parties and complying with the formal and other legal requirements for a valid contract,[114] rather than from acting upon the basis of an otherwise unenforceable oral promise or statement.

Many arrangements, particularly those of a domestic nature, will be informal and not necessarily supported by any presumptions as to intention to enter into binding legal relationships,[115] but are effective to create a proprietary transfer simply because it would be 'inequitable' for the parties to insist or rely upon their strict legal position.[116] Consequently there may not be sufficient consensual element to make contractual consideration out of the oral statements or promises which may fall short of a formal 'offer'. It is probable that HMRC Stamp Taxes will take the view that such acts will be 'consideration' for the purpose of SDLT[117] notwithstanding

---

[112] See, for example, Insurance Companies Act 1982 (repealed), now Financial Services and Markets Act 2000, Part VII.

[113] Compare Errington v. Errington and Woods [1952] 1 KB 290; Eastham v. Leigh London and Provincial Properties Ltd [1971] 2 All ER 887; GUS Merchandise v. Customs and Excise [1981] 1 WLR 1309.

[114] Such as Law of Property (Miscellaneous Provisions) Act 1989, s.2; see *Firstpost Homes* v. *Johnson* [1995] 4 All ER 355; but note the statements of Walker LJ in *Yaxley* v. *Gotts* [1999] 3 WLR 1217 to the effect that judicial intervention in equity can overrule parliamentary legislation.

[115] See the presumptions in relation to domestic arrangements in cases such as *Gage* v. *King* [1961] 1 QB 188; *Balfour* v. *Balfour* [1919] 2 KB 517; *Parker* v. *Clark* [1960] 1 All ER 93.

[116] *Binions* v. *Evans* [1972] Ch 359.

[117] Relying upon FA 2003, Sched.4, para.11.

that there cannot, in law, be a contract because there is not the degree of writing required by legislation.[118]

Similarly, what might appear to be a conditional gift[119] or a conditional contract[120] may be an offer for a consideration which is constituted by 'satisfying the condition', i.e. the supplying of the consideration or part thereof consists of performing the requirement of the 'promise' such as paying off the mortgage or providing the care services required by the promisor.[121] This may be taxable as the supply of services.[122] It may be, therefore, that undertakings by the parties such as to apply for planning permission or to carry out the fitting out of premises or to construct a building may be taxable consideration, particularly where one of the parties undertakes to use reasonable endeavours to procure the satisfaction of the conditions. Additionally, it remains to be seen how far HMRC Stamp Taxes will pursue the argument that undertakings to use reasonable endeavours to bring about the satisfaction of conditions precedent by themselves represent the provision of chargeable services which may have an open market cost. It is thought that there is no substance in the point but, from time to time, other divisions of HMRC have sought to argue that agreeing to procure the happening of an event or the completion of a transaction is the provision of services.

4.19   REVERSE CONSIDERATION AND INDEMNITIES

The draftsman also has a theory of 'reverse consideration'. He has provided that reverse payments such as sums paid by landlords as inducements for the grant of a lease or by assignors to assignees of leases[123] where there are dilapidations are not to be taxable, and he assumes that where a tenant agrees to take a lease subject to the landlord constructing a building, the landlord's building works (as opposed to the cash paid for them) are consideration provided by the tenant in return for the landlord granting the lease. Notwithstanding these bizarre provisions, it is considered that they do not affect the general proposition that there is no such concept as reverse consideration; but the judiciary may be reluctant to strike the legislation down as meaningless should there be an attempt by HMRC Stamp Taxes to develop this theory of a 'reverse consideration'. In practice issues based around this area have already arisen. For example, where a developer agrees to pay the costs, etc. of

---

[118]   Law of Property (Miscellaneous Provisions) Act 1989, s.2; *Firstpost Homes* v. *Johnson* [1995] 4 All ER 355.
[119]   GUS Merchandise v. Customs and Excise [1981] 1 WLR 1309; Errington v. Errington and Woods [1952] 1 KB 290.
[120]   Eastham v. Leigh London and Provincial Properties [1971] 2 All ER 887.
[121]   Errington v. Errington and Woods [1952] 1 KB 290.
[122]   FA 2003, Sched.4, para.11; note especially *Henry* v. *Henry* [2010] 1 All ER 988.
[123]   Compare the VAT cases such as Gleneagles Hotel v. Customs and Excise [1986] VATTR 196; Russell v. Customs and Excise [1987] VATTR 194; Customs and Excise Commissioners v. Cantor Fitzgerald International (C-108/99) [2001] ECR I-7257.

the purchaser or lessee this is regarded as increasing the market value or price of the property over the initial asking price.

4.20 CHARGEABLE AMOUNT

Having determined that there is 'consideration', whether actual or deemed, it is necessary to determine:

* whether the consideration, actual or deemed, is 'chargeable'; and
* the amount of the chargeable consideration for the transaction (including any linked transactions) to which the rate is applied.

4.21 'PROVISIONAL TAX'

It should be noted that in a significant number of situations, because the consideration or rent is not finally determined, the computation of the tax for the first stage, and possibly later stages of the same tax computation related to the effective date will be provisional (only being based upon certain assumptions or estimates), and it will frequently be necessary to revisit the initial and later computations of the tax retrospectively and submit a fresh land transaction return with payments of any tax due.[124] This uncertainty of the amount of the consideration can arise even where the price or rent is fixed because there may be later linked transactions.[125] It will not be appropriate to 'amend' the original land transaction return (SDLT 1) because the required retrospective re-self-assessment is a separate notifiable transaction[126] and as such it requires a new land transaction return with a different bar code or transaction number. Nevertheless, the initial return requires the tax to be calculated upon the guestimated figures and subject to the limited power to defer payment of the tax as part of such guestimated figures,[127] must be paid in full. For example, where the transaction is prepared as a going concern for the purposes of VAT the SDLT must, in the view generally advanced by HMRC Stamp Taxes,[128] be calculated and paid upon the basis that the transaction is not a transfer of a going concern, i.e. the chargeable consideration is the estimated gross (VAT inclusive) amount which fixes the rate. This may mean that there may be a provisional higher rate[129]

---

[124] There are also practical difficulties in that the amendment does not consist of altering the original form but submitting a written 'notice' in the prescribed form; see **Appendix D**.

[125] FA 2003, s.81A.

[126] But not necessarily a separate chargeable transaction because usually, but not invariably, it relates back to the original effective date. There may be a separate chargeable transaction such as a later linked transaction increasing the chargeable consideration above a rate threshold. In consequence more than one return may be required for the same event.

[127] Stamp Duty Land Tax (Administration) Regulations 2003, SI 2003/2837, Part 4; see **1.24**.

[128] Which is probably incorrect; see **4.30**.

[129] And a higher tax sum payable which in the view put forward from time to time by HMRC Stamp Taxes cannot be deferred; see **4.30**.

when there will be a claim for repayment when it becomes clear[130] that the variable amount will not become payable.[131]

Moreover, even if it were possible to deal with the situation as an 'amendment' the 'amendment' will usually be outside the maximum amendment period of 12 months from the filing date,[132] i.e. 30 days after the effective date.

Those areas where the initial computation is provisional include:

- transactions where there may be later linked transactions which operate retrospectively, such as leases with options to renew or transactions where there are numerous related options to purchase. It should be noted that the linked transaction rules, although expressed to be limited to transactions between the same parties or persons connected with them, may directly or indirectly affect purchasers and assignees of the chargeable interest and provision is made imposing obligations upon such third parties[133] e.g. assignees of leases and for the allocation of the nil rate slice of rent;

- where there is variable consideration such as overage or clawback arrangements;[134]

- variable premiums and rents,[135] where the responsibility for dealing with the outstanding SDLT passes to the assignee of the lease;[136]

- all leases where there is a possibility of holding over pursuant to the Landlord and Tenant Act 1954 (as amended).[137]

In a practical sense, all chargeable transactions where the chargeable consideration consists of or includes consideration in kind, such as where market value or market costs are involved, will be provisional since HMRC Stamp Taxes does not, in theory, regard itself as bound by the figures produced by the parties in the completion of the land transaction return,[138] and so can challenge the parties' figures during an Enquiry even where they are backed by independent professional advice. Moreover, owing to the deficiencies in the self-assessment system generally and the land transaction returns and related form in particular, as no background information can be produced upon the return, HMRC Stamp Taxes is free to make a discovery assessment at any time within six years because the officer processing the form did not have information as to the basis upon which the valuation was prepared.[139]

---

[130]   It is unclear at present what evidence will persuade HMRC Stamp Taxes that the VAT is not payable.

[131]   FA 2003, s.80; Sched.11A; Sched.10, para.33.

[132]   FA 2003, Sched.10, para.6(3).

[133]   See e.g. FA 2003, s.81A; Sched.5, para.2.

[134]   FA 2003, ss.51 and 80.

[135]   FA 2003, Sched.17A, paras.7 and 8.

[136]   FA 2003, Sched.17A, para.12.

[137]   FA 2003, Sched.17A, para.4; see **8.47**.

[138]   See e.g. Lap Shun Textiles v. Collector of Stamp Revenue [1976] 1 All ER 833; Langham v. Veltema [2004] STC 544.

[139]   *Langham* v. *Veltema* [2004] STC 544. As the theory is that all land transaction returns should be processed by computer with the form scanned in, and not scrutinised by individual employees

4.22 DEFINITION OF CHARGEABLE CONSIDERATION

'Chargeable consideration' is defined[140] in addition to deemed consideration as any consideration given:

- in money or money's worth;[141]
- for the subject-matter of the transaction[142] (i.e. the chargeable interest being acquired plus any interest or right pertaining or appurtenant to the interest being acquired) but not rights or assets other than 'land';
- directly or indirectly;
- by the purchaser or a person connected with him;

but this is supplemented by various provisions in the legislation. For example, Sched.4 contains provisions for calculating the amount of tax where the actual consideration is not money or money's worth, which carries with it the clear implication that such consideration is chargeable.[143]

4.23 PROBLEM AREAS IN CHARGEABLE CONSIDERATION

Numerous problems arise upon this definition.

4.23.1 By the purchaser

The consideration must be provided directly or indirectly[144] by the purchaser or a connected person. It is, therefore, necessary to identify the 'purchaser', which can include persons who do not provide consideration such as donees of gifts,[145] and consideration provided by other persons may not be chargeable.[146] Inducement

---

who in any event have only limited power to correct the land transaction returns in respect of 'obvious errors or omissions' (FA 2003, Sched.10, para.7), the subsequently shown to be incorrect choice of a basis for valuing the consideration in kind will not be an obvious error in relation to the original return, and there is no procedure for the forms to be rejected by the scanners, should they ever work, where, for example, consideration in kind is involved. Every return having been electronically processed will be open to challenge by a discovery assessment for at least six years, not just nine months, being the period for Enquiries (see **18.12**).

[140] FA 2003, Sched.4, para.1.
[141] *Secretan* v. *Hart* 45 TC 701.
[142] FA 2003, s.43(6).
[143] Compare the analysis of similar stamp tax legislation in *J&P Coats Ltd* v. *IRC* [1897] 2 QB 423.
[144] See third party involvement such as *Crane Fruehauf* v. *IRC* [1975] STC 51; *Central and District Properties* v. *IRC* [1966] 2 All ER 433; *Shop and Stores Developments* v. *IRC* [1967] 1 All ER 42; *Curzon Offices Ltd* v. *IRC* [1944] 1 All ER 163 and *IRC* v. *Wachtel* [1971] 1 All ER 271.
[145] Such persons have to be treated as purchasers for the effectiveness of the compliance regimes, i.e. to identify the person to sign the relevant forms.
[146] FA 2003, Sched.4, para.1; but note the provisions of FA 2003, s.44A.

from a third party to enter into the contract may not be chargeable,[147] at least if the person providing the inducement is not connected with the purchaser.

4.23.2 To the vendor

Although the consideration must be provided directly or indirectly by the 'purchaser', it seems that it is not necessary for it to pass to the 'vendor', i.e. the person disposing of the subject-matter of the transaction.[148]

4.23.3 Directly or indirectly

In the context the word 'indirectly' will be significant in practice. No guidance as to HMRC Stamp Taxes' view has been given but it is likely to apply to situations other than where a person supplying the actual consideration is somehow reimbursed or indemnified by the person receiving the land. On the other hand, simply putting the person in funds, such as by making a loan or purchasing part of the property or other assets from the taxpayer, will not be the indirect provision of the consideration even though it puts cash into the taxpayer's hands.

4.23.4 Money or money's worth

Subject to statutory extensions[149] chargeable consideration must consist of money or money's worth. 'Money's worth' has been judicially explained by Buckley J:[150]

> The expression 'consideration in money's worth' is, of course, one which is very familiar to lawyers as being a way of expressing the price or consideration given for property where property is acquired in return for something other than money, such as services or other property, where the price or consideration which the acquirer gives for the property has got to be turned into money before it can be expressed in terms of money.

Anything that cannot be turned into money is not money's worth.[151] In consequence, special rules provide that non-saleable items of consideration such as 'services' or non-assignable interests, liabilities of the transferor, or the rights of shareholders which are satisfied in a winding up or on a return of capital, which are

---

[147]   Cf. Crane Fruehauf v. IRC [1975] 1 All ER 429; Central and District Properties v. IRC [1966] 2 All ER 433; Shop and Store Developments v. IRC [1967] 1 AC 472.

[148]   FA 2003, s.43.

[149]   Such as services and costs pursuant to FA 2003, Sched.4, paras.10 and 11.

[150]   *Secretan* v. *Hart* [1969] 1 WLR 1599, 1603; but there are possible defects in this statement.

[151]   This issue of realisation and conversion into money is likely over time to give rise to many issues. There are questions where the right is purely personal or non-assignable so that as a matter of contract it cannot be sold such as a lease for life made non-assignable. There may be a question whether this is money's worth because the restriction can be ignored which may be a different issue from the effect of such restrictions upon market value as in *IRC* v. *Crossman* [1937] AC 26; *Alexander* v. *IRC* [1991] STC 112. Alternatively it may be necessary to debate with HMRC Stamp Taxes whether money's worth extends to the person acquiring the asset and selling it thereby realising the value of the right indirectly.

in general no consideration in 'money's worth', are deemed to be chargeable consideration.[152] However, the limits on the concept of 'money's worth' of saleable property have to be modified since the chargeable consideration clearly indicates that actual consideration which would not be 'money's worth', such as services[153] and certain building arrangements which cannot be sold in the open market,[154] are chargeable and the tax is calculated on the basis of open market cost.[155]

It is clear from these definitions that the item constituting or deemed to constitute the consideration must be something that is capable of being sold as a separate asset;[156] the fact that the right or interest in question is valuable does not of itself make it money's worth.[157] This will be important where many minor interests are involved, such as where land is transferred in consideration of the grant of restrictive covenants that are valuable but cannot be sold separately from that land, except by way of releases of them in favour of the servient land, the owner of which cannot be regarded as an open market.

4.24 'EXCEPTING AND RESERVING'

One area of difficulty affecting a wide range of transactions relates to transfers of interests in land subject to obligations to grant new rights back to the transferor, such as where a freehold is transferred subject to the obligation to grant a restrictive covenant and, if the current views of HMRC Stamp Taxes should prevail, virtually every case where the words 'excepting and reserving' appear, as it contends that this can only operate as a regrant (see **Chapter 2**). This question of the correct analysis of the conveyancing effect of such words and whether a transfer and regrant although by operation of law[158] is an issue as to whether there is 'chargeable consideration' (see **4.18**). This will produce a land exchange taxable by reference to the market values but issues can arise in connection with the value of the main interest and the value of the 'regranted' or reserved interest.

---

[152] A dividend *in specie* will not be for a consideration: *Associated British Engineering* v. *IRC* [1940] 4 All ER 278; *Wigan Coal and Iron* v. *IRC* [1945] 1 All ER 392 and so within FA 2003, Sched.3, para.1; see **5.4**. This may differ from a transfer in satisfaction of the rights of members such as in a winding up or a return of capital.

[153] Notwithstanding the comments in *Secretan* v. *Hart* 45 TC 701; see *Nokes* v. *Doncaster Amalgamated Collieries* [1940] AC 1014; *O'Brien* v. *Benson Hosiery* [1979] STC 735.

[154] If these items were not intended to be chargeable consideration, it would not be necessary to include the computation rules.

[155] FA 2003, Sched.4, paras.10 and 11; see **15.18**.

[156] This is supported by the definition of 'market value' which requires a sale in the open market (FA 2003, Sched.4, para.7).

[157] These may be issues in relation to certain interests where the right itself cannot be separately sold directly but can be realised indirectly such as the sale of the interest to which it relates and the value of which it enhances.

[158] Such as certain variations of leases.

4.24.1   The value of the main interest

HMRC Stamp Taxes formerly maintained that the hypothetical terms of sale must prevail over the actual terms of sale, and notwithstanding that the taxpayer acquires the chargeable interest already encumbered by a binding and specifically enforceable obligation to regrant interests to the 'vendor' or a third party, the terms of the actual sale have to be ignored and the property valued free from the regrant obligations ignoring the obligation to grant rights back. For example, where the tenants in a block of flats acquire the landlord's interest which they transfer to a management company in return for the grant of new leases at a token ground rent,[159] the freehold subject to such leases has negligible value; but HMRC Stamp Taxes has contended that the market value of the reversionary interest has to be valued ignoring the leases back, i.e. the unencumbered freehold value which is significant. The leases back will also have a large value so that in effect the transaction will involve an 8 per cent charge upon the vacant possession value of the land.[160] These views are considered to be incorrect in principle[161] and HMRC Stamp Taxes appears to have changed its view and accepts the position that the interest has to be valued subject to the obligations to 'regrant' the interest back.

4.24.2   The value of the 'regranted' or reserved interest

The reserved interest will usually be a minor interest such as an easement, but it seems that as such minor interests are not capable of independent sale because they exist only as rights for the benefit of the dominant land, they do not have a market value. As the charge does not include the enhancement of the value of the dominant land, it is considered that the chargeable consideration, i.e. the market value of the restrictive covenant is nil.[162] Similarly, where the transaction involves the release or surrender of an interest in circumstances where this is taxed by reference to the market value of that interest rather than the actual consideration,[163] it is considered that since there is nothing to sell, there cannot be a market value in these terms.

---

[159]   Additionally, because this is connected with the transfer of the reversionary interests HMRC Stamp Taxes does not give the reliefs for surrenders and regrants.

[160]   In these situations the tenants should seek to organise matters as a surrender and regrant for which substantial reliefs are available pursuant to FA 2003, Sched.17A, paras.9 and 16.

[161]   Where there was a sale and leaseback qualifying for the relief in the original, now amended, FA 2003, s.57A, the transfer of the reversionary interest was taxable upon not less than the market value of the interest, which was to be calculated as if it were not part of a sale and leaseback transaction. Presumably this meant that the reversionary interest is to be valued ignoring the obligation to grant the leaseback. This may be a useful argument should HMRC Stamp Taxes persist in its current views, i.e. a specific provision to ignore the reciprocal obligation suggests that upon general principles it should be included in the valuation process, but recently the official view seems to be changing to the correct principles of valuing subject to the regrant obligations.

[162]   This may mean that there is not a chargeable transaction at all. However, upon either view formerly a self-certificate or currently a covering letter would support any change of the land register, subject to the vagaries of 'local discretion'.

[163]   Such as where the land exchanges rules or the connected company charges apply.

Two issues arise where minor interests are involved as part of the consideration for the chargeable interest such as where interests are reserved to the vendor. Since these may not be capable of separate sale because they can only exist as rights forming part of the dominant land,[164] it might be thought that they are not money's worth, and can be ignored. This argument, however, is countered by the land exchange definition[165] which applies where one party as part of the consideration for one land transaction is to enter into another land transaction so that in the view of HMRC Stamp Taxes there are two separate land transactions with the chargeable consideration being determined pursuant to FA 2003, Sched.4, para.5.

4.25 CONSIDERATION IN KIND AND MARKET VALUE

SDLT applies to a wide range of types of non-cash consideration and numerous provisions exist for attributing a value to these situations (see further **Chapter 15**). This means that advisers have valuation problems related not merely to land but to the valuation of any other property (e.g. shares or even equipment) provided by way of consideration. For example land may be transferred to a company in consideration of the issue of shares or as a premium for the issue or assignment of an insurance policy.

4.26 ACTUAL CONSIDERATION

In general SDLT is charged by reference to the amount or value of the actual consideration and there is no general provision substituting market value if higher than the actual consideration; but there are situations where the element of the chargeable consideration is treated as being the market value of a chargeable interest. This can be by way of:

- the procedure for determining the value of the actual consideration; or
- a deeming provision ignoring any actual consideration or the absence of consideration and imposing a charge be reference to the value of an asset.

These provisions apply basically to two broad contexts, namely determining:

- the market value of the land being acquired, which can apply to:

    - the connected company charge;[166]
    - special dealings involving partnerships;[167]
    - land exchanges;[168]

---

[164] But note FA 2003, s.48(1)(b).
[165] FA 2003, s.47; see **Chapter 7**.
[166] FA 2003, ss.53 and 54.
[167] FA 2003, Sched.15, Part 3.
[168] FA 2003, s.47; Sched.4, para.5.

- building works;[169]

• the market value (or cost) of the interest or other consideration being provided such as:

  - consideration in kind;[170]
  - services supplied as consideration.[171]

There will be, initially at least, a question of whether it may be possible to avoid a valuation by inserting a cash amount into the documents. In *Stanton* v. *Drayton Commercial Investment Co Ltd*[172] the consideration was expressed as a cash sum to be satisfied by the transfer of specified property. The House of Lords stated that, in the absence of any fraudulent or improper attempt to manipulate the tax position, the specified amount being bona fide was the taxable figure. However, that case was concerned with issues of 'value' rather than 'market value' and it was regarded as the price the parties put upon their bargain. Notwithstanding that stamp duty was occasionally concerned with 'market value', HMRC Stamp Taxes in practice tended to act upon the basis of such figures inserted in the contract, particularly where there was independent professional advice on value (largely because the costs of valuation disputes in many transactions are disproportionate to the extra tax likely to be produced).

However, at the same time, HMRC Stamp Taxes continued with the contention based upon *Lap Shun Textiles* v. *Collector of Stamp Revenue*[173] that the parties' figures were not conclusive of market value even when the parties were at arm's length.[174] The price may have been agreed for a quick sale or there may be discount for the purchase of several properties[175] and so not market value in accordance with the provision for fiscal valuations where the time of the sale is not a pressing factor relevant for consideration because the vendor is merely 'willing', not 'obliged', to sell.[176] This, of course, is likely to raise issues in relation to transactions where there is a discount; it is the official view that a discounted price whether for a quick sale or because several properties are involved is not a market price.

Nevertheless, while the parties' own figures are not necessarily conclusive they are likely to be important in practice, particularly in smaller transactions where the amount of tax is fairly small so that it is not economic for HMRC Stamp Taxes to mount a serious challenge. For example, in relation to exchanges or part-exchanges, in practice, it is likely that the price at which the property was originally offered for

---

[169] FA 2003, Sched.4, para.10.
[170] FA 2003, Sched.4, para.7.
[171] FA 2003, Sched.4, para.11.
[172] [1982] STC 585.
[173] [1976] AC 530.
[174] See also the power to issue a discovery assessment where it disagrees with the valuation methodology adopted by the parties or their advisers: FA 2003, Sched.10, Part 5; *Langham* v. *Veltema* [2004] STC 544.
[175] But note *Duke of Buccleuch* v. *IRC* [1967] AC 506 on sale in parcels to produce a better price; see, however, Taxation of Chargeable Gains Act 1992, s.272(2).
[176] See also Cowan de Groot Properties Ltd v. Eagle Trust Plc [1991] BCLC 1045.

sale will be taken by HMRC Stamp Taxes as the market value at least on a *prima facie* basis.[177] Figures supported by professional valuations are in many cases likely to be accepted as representing the market value, at least if the valuation is fairly close to the effective date.[178] Such independent valuations will, moreover, be advisable, if not absolutely necessary, in practice since in the absence of such a valuation it is questionable whether the taxpayer will have complied with his obligation to make a correct return. Approximations as to value are not necessarily the correct way to complete the land transaction return (see **Appendix D**). The preparation of the return requires not merely the 'correct' market value but also the adoption of the current methodology for valuation, if allegations of negligent returns are to be avoided.

4.27 GLOBAL CONSIDERATION AND APPORTIONMENT

It may be that the land is not the only element of property being acquired by the transaction but there may be a single consideration expressed for the whole package of assets and liabilities.[179] For example, where there is an acquisition of a business as a going concern there may be land, chattels, goodwill[180] and so on[181] (as well as a possible issue of VAT which may affect the tax charge and the availability of certain reliefs)[182] being acquired for a single price (which may include general liabilities of the vendor which are not specifically charged upon the land) or the issue of shares. In this situation the chargeable consideration is that which is limited to the subject-matter of the land transaction,[183] which is the chargeable interest being acquired together with any interest or right appurtenant or pertaining to it that is acquired with it.[184]

In such a case,[185] the actual consideration has to be apportioned between consideration which is 'chargeable', i.e. relates to the subject-matter of the land transaction, and other parts of the contract where the actual consideration is not

---

[177] It is possible to resist this depending upon the facts. For example, where the property had been on offer at that price but had not attracted any significant interest from prospective purchasers.

[178] For many decades in relation to stamp duty HMRC Stamp Taxes was prepared to accept a recent certificate prepared by independent advisers to the effect that the property was worth 'not more' than a specified value at least where the amount was not unduly large.

[179] Note that liabilities may affect the amount of chargeable consideration: FA 2003, Sched.4, paras.8 and 8A.

[180] But note the problem of whether the 'goodwill' is really part of the land value.

[181] In such case SDLT 4 (as amended) may have to be completed.

[182] FA 2003, Sched.7, Part 2; see **Chapter 13**.

[183] And any linked transactions; but the consideration for the non-land items does not have to be aggregated for the purposes of the lower rates of SDLT.

[184] FA 2003, s.43(6). It will be noted that this definition differs from that applied for the purposes of determining substantial performance, which relates to the subject-matter of the contract (FA 2003, s.44(5)(a)). It remains to be seen whether, in practice, HMRC Stamp Taxes will seek to exploit this difference which is important in relation to the scope of FA 2003, s.44A.

[185] This allocation of the actual consideration is not required where the chargeable consideration is the market value such as FA 2003, s.52 and Sched.15, Part 3.

'chargeable', on a just and reasonable basis.[186] This has to be done on the revised SDLT 4 in most cases. If the consideration is not apportioned the SDLT will apply as if it had been so apportioned.[187] Also HMRC Stamp Taxes can challenge the allocation[188] and any consideration given for what is, in substance, one bargain is attributed to all the elements of the bargain even though separate consideration is or purports to be given for different elements of the bargain or there are or purport to be separate transactions in respect of different elements of the bargain.[189] This seems to be intended to give HMRC Stamp Taxes power to reallocate consideration between what are technically legally independent contracts but which are part of a single overall commercial arrangement.[190]

No statutory guidance is provided as to what is a 'just and reasonable basis' and it is very likely that the views of HMRC Stamp Taxes will differ significantly from those of taxpayers and their advisers, but arbitrary attempts to allocate consideration simply to mitigate the tax charge by obtaining the lower rates of tax[191] will not be acceptable and will be regarded as attempts to defraud HMRC.[192] Seeking to reduce the tax by producing an artificially low consideration could be regarded as fraud[193] involving a conspiracy[194] by those co-operating in the preparation of documentation or return forms on the basis of improper allocation so that the vendor and the various professional advisers could be conspirators. Advisers may need to consider whether, having advised the taxpayer on the need to justify the allocation, it is prudent to continue to act if this advice is ignored because of the financial and criminal penalties potentially arising in relation to the completion of the land transaction return in these circumstances, i.e. knowing that it has not been prepared on a proper basis. In addition to any general criminal sanctions that may be applicable for attempts to defraud HMRC Stamp Taxes or conspiracy to achieve the same,[195] there was formerly a tax-related penalty for any person who fraudulently delivers a land transaction return and fails to make a correction.[196] In addition, a person who assists in or induces the preparation or delivery of any information, return or other document that he knows will be or is likely to be used for any purposes of SDLT and he knows to be incorrect is liable to a penalty not exceeding

---

[186]   FA 2003, Sched.4, para.4(1).

[187]   FA 2003, Sched.4, para.4(2).

[188]   But where the allocation has been made on the basis of recent independent professional advice suitably instructed it may be difficult for HMRC Stamp Taxes to challenge the parties' figures: *Re Wragg* [1897] 1 Ch 796.

[189]   FA 2003, Sched.4, para.3.

[190]   For example, this enables HMRC Stamp Taxes to reapportion the allocation of the consideration between the land price and any related building works but it has been advised that it does not enable it to make the two contracts into a single fully taxable contract.

[191]   See e.g. *Lloyds & Scottish* v. *Prentice* 121 SJ 847.

[192]   *Saunders* v. *Edwards* [1987] 2 All ER 651.

[193]   *Re Wragg* [1897] 1 Ch 796; *Saunders* v. *Edwards* [1987] 2 All ER 651.

[194]   *Saunders* v. *Edwards* [1987] 2 All ER 651.

[195]   See *Saunders* v. *Edwards* [1987] 2 All ER 651.

[196]   FA 2003, s.95; Sched.10, para.8 (now repealed); but no clear provision of a duty to rectify has been made to give guidance as to the obligations of the taxpayer to correct returns following the replacement of this particular penalty by paras.31 and 31A of Sched.10.

£3,000.[197] However, more significantly, a person who is knowingly concerned in fraudulent evasion of tax[198] by him or any other person[199] is guilty of an offence which carries with it:

- on summary conviction imprisonment for a term not exceeding six months or a fine not exceeding the statutory maximum, or both;
- on conviction on indictment imprisonment for a term not exceeding seven years or a fine or both.[200]

Any allocation of the consideration should, therefore, as a matter of prudence be supported by detailed contemporaneous documentation. Failure to obtain such supporting independent evidence could be regarded as 'negligence' in the preparation of the land transaction return, enabling HMRC Stamp Taxes to issue a discovery assessment for up to 21 years after the effective date.[201] and impose penalties upon the professional advisers for assisting in the preparation of a land transaction return which they knew to be incorrect[202] (because, for example, they knew that proper advice had not been obtained to support the data inserted into the SDLT 1). It should, however, be noted that the apportionment is not necessarily based upon relative or particular market values. In other cases, of course, there may be situations where there is consideration in kind when the market value is the chargeable consideration. This market value has to be determined on a proper basis and then suitably apportioned between the assets, i.e. by reference to their own individual market value.[203] There will be situations where the land element in the transaction is deemed to be acquired at market value, such as where the connected company charge applies, or the land exchange rules are relevant. In such a situation the market value rules will prevail over the apportionment obligation and the transaction will have to be returned as being for a market value consideration, notwithstanding that this exceeds the actual consideration given for the totality of the assets.

---

[197] FA 2003, s.96.

[198] Such issues are not limited to SDLT but will apply to any attempt to produce a favourable result by an arbitrary allocation of the price, and it should be noted that a wrongful allocation may have other taxation consequences (see e.g. *Re Hollebone* [1959] 2 All ER 152).

[199] As regards the statutory sanctions in FA 2003, the liability here is likely to be limited to the purchaser's solicitor because the vendor is not involved in the preparation and submission of the land transaction return, but he and his advisers may be parties to a criminal conspiracy should they agree to an artificial apportionment of the consideration in the contract. Mortgagees may, in consequence, be adversely affected by these arrangements particularly where the same solicitor is acting for both the purchaser and the mortgagee so that it may be easy for the court to impute knowledge of the illegality to the mortgagee through his agent where knowledge of impropriety affects the rights or liabilities of the parties in the context. The criminal aspects of such arrangements for the contract would be subject to the restriction imposed upon illegal contracts so that they would be unenforceable.

[200] FA 2003, s.95.

[201] FA 2003, Sched.10, para.31.

[202] FA 2003, ss.95 and 96 which may involve even the vendor and his advisers in a criminal conspiracy as in *Saunders* v. *Edwards* [1987] 2 All ER 651.

[203] Possibly in accordance with SDLT 4 (as amended) which is required when there is the transfer of a business.

4.28 BASIC COMPUTATIONAL PROVISIONS

4.28.1 Cash debt, etc.

Where the price is a straightforward payment of cash the calculation is easy but it has to be noted that there is no discount for deferred payment, although such a delay in payment may postpone the effective date (see **3.8**).

4.28.2 Market value

Subject to any specific provisions, the value of any chargeable consideration other than money, including foreign currency or 'debt',[204] is its 'market value' at the effective date of the transaction (see further **Chapter 3**).[205] 'Market value' is to be determined in accordance with ss.272–274 of the Taxation of Chargeable Gains Act 1992.[206]

'Market value' is the price which the relevant asset might reasonably be expected to fetch in a sale on the open market.[207] Unfortunately this simple statement hides a multiplicity of problems, and although it is likely that in practice SDLT valuation will follow capital gains tax valuation practice, there are potential difficulties in applying the latter to SDLT so that special rules may have to be developed.

The issues include:

- *Identifying the property to be valued.* Usually this will be the property being provided as consideration, but, for example, in relation to exchanges and part-exchanges involving major interests and in relation to dealings involving partnerships or connected companies it is the value of the property being received by way of consideration. These rules will frequently require the parties to value property other than land (see **Chapter 15**).
- *The meaning of 'open' market.* Many interests in or rights over property cannot exist except in relation to other land. It is not possible to sell the benefit of a restrictive covenant to any person other than the owner of the servient land. It is considered that such non-saleable assets, although they are potentially valuable and enhance the value of the dominant land, do not have a 'market value'. While the existence of special purchasers cannot be ignored and their possible presence on the open market if it should exist has to be taken into account, the fact that there is only one potential 'purchaser' cannot create an 'open' market.
- *The terms of the sale.* Fiscal valuations tend to work upon the basis of a willing purchaser and a willing vendor so that there is a hypothetical contract which may not be the same as the terms of the actual contract between the parties. A willing vendor, for example, is under no pressure to sell so discounts are irrelevant. There are basic issues to be debated with HMRC Stamp Taxes as to

---

[204] Defined in FA 2003, Sched.4, para.8.
[205] FA 2003, Sched.4, para.7.
[206] FA 2003, s.118.
[207] Taxation of Chargeable Gains Act 1992, s.272(1).

the terms of the sale and how far these differ from the actual terms of any sale or lease between the parties. There are few legislative provisions setting out the detailed principles to be applied,[208] such as the factors to be taken into account and the relative weight to be attached to the various factors. Where there is no sale but an exchange the terms of the sale will be largely hypothetical, but it is understood that HMRC Stamp Taxes takes the view that the market value includes VAT. This is debatable particularly where the option to tax has not been exercised or the hypothetical sale could be a transfer of a going concern.

4.29   FUTURE VALUES AND RENTS

SDLT does not seek to impose a charge upon market rents in the absence of detailed legislation because HMRC Stamp Taxes appears to have realised there are many unanswerable questions. Where there is a lease issued on favourable terms and a market value charge arises this is usually taxed in the form of a deemed premium.

The issue of future rents is not unique, there are many cases where future values are required such as overage and clawback arrangements[209] or future rents such as rent reviews. Here the taxpayer has to make a reasonable estimate of future value, payments and rents although it seems that he can prepare his return upon the basis of the rate of VAT current as at the effective date, unless the Government has announced an adjustment in the rate from a specified date; but the tenant must treat any subsequent variations as increases or reductions in the rent when conducting the retrospective revision of the initial return at the end of the first five years of the term.[210] Interest and possibly penalties can be imposed if the estimate turns out to be incorrect.

4.29.1   Practical issues

The practical difficulty is that professional advisers are justifiably reluctant to give advice that is essentially crystal-ball gazing and is not a valid professional exercise based upon valid data. Nevertheless, taxpayers are expected to make reasonable 'guestimates' of future values and future rents even though this can be a nonsensical exercise, such as seeking to predict the likely effect of obtaining some form of planning permission in relation to the land some half-a-century or longer after the immediate sale. Nevertheless, these exercises have to be carried out and failure to

---

[208]   FA 2003, Sched.15, para.38.

[209]   FA 2003, s.51; see below on such variable payments; *Akasuc Enterprise* v. *Farmar* [2003] PL SCS 127.

[210]   On changes in the VAT position after the expiration of the fifth year of the term see **8.27**; FA 2003, Sched.17A, paras.13, 14, 15 and 15A.

obtain and preserve the details of proper advice exposes the taxpayer or his estate to the risk of significant penalties.[211]

4.30 VALUE ADDED TAX

It is provided that chargeable consideration includes any VAT chargeable in respect of the transaction other than the VAT that may arise in respect of the transaction pursuant to the exercise of the option to tax after the effective date for SDLT, including VAT upon future instalments,[212] including variable consideration, and in effect, future rent.[213] The fact that the purchaser or tenant or other person paying the VAT may be able to recover the input tax in whole or in part is not a relevant factor.[214]

However, where the transaction is exempt from VAT as at the effective date, the fact that the option to tax is available is ignored.[215] In consequence:

- the fact that the transaction or subsequent payments could become taxable by reason of the exercise of the option to tax is ignored;
- the actual exercise of the option to tax after the effective date is ignored for the purposes of the original land transaction return (SDLT 1) even though this may affect the level of subsequent payments;
- the two-stage taxation of substantial performance of leases and the grant thereof[216] raises a particular difficulty where the option to tax is exercised between the substantial performance of the agreement for lease and the subsequent grant of the lease. The view of HMRC Stamp Taxes is that the taxable rent at the time of the grant includes the actual VAT notwithstanding that this possibly was required to be ignored at the time of the substantial performance of the agreement for lease; and

---

[211] Taxpayers and their advisers cannot rely upon the advice given by the helpline as it does not bind HMRC Stamp Taxes and so cannot use such advice as a negotiating counter in the mitigation of penalties. The interest charge is mandatory and cannot be mitigated.

[212] However, it seems that the fact that the rate of VAT may vary in the future does not make the consideration 'uncertain' for the purposes of FA 2003, s.51 because changes after the effective date are to be ignored but official confirmation from HMRC Stamp Taxes is awaited whether this is its view. There are, however, possible complications where there is a lapse of time between the agreements for lease and the actual grant; see **Chapter 8**. Cf. *Glenrothes Corporation* v. *IRC* [1993] STC 74.

[213] This appears to have the effect of making the rent variable for the special regime pursuant to FA 2003, Sched.17A, paras.7 and 8; see **8.42**.

[214] HMRC Stamp Taxes takes the same line of ignoring the actual or potential input tax credit when determining 'costs' such as for the purpose of FA 2003, Sched.4, paras.10 and 11. Since the cost is the price, i.e. the consideration payable pursuant to the contract the VAT content is, in its view, fully taxable.

[215] FA 2003, Sched.4, para.2. This modifies the former stamp duty argument that the VAT that might arise pursuant to the exercise of the option to tax was a *prima facie* sum within the contingency principle and was accordingly tax.

[216] FA 2003, Sched.17A, para.12A; see **Chapter 8**.

- it remains an open question whether the subsequent exercise of the option to tax can constitute a chargeable transaction in its own right. So, where there is a variation of the lease after the effective date by the exercise of the option to tax the rent there are various possibilities:

  - it is an increase of the rent taxable in its own right; or
  - the VAT arising is rent to be taken into account for the purposes of the retrospective review of the rent at the end of the first five years of the term; or
  - it is a factor to be taken into account for the purpose of applying the abnormal rent increase provisions after that date.

Several other significant practical issues arise in relation to VAT, as follows.

4.30.1 Transfers of going concerns

It is usual to provide in the contract (in order to protect the vendor) that, although the parties believe that the transaction is a transfer of a going concern, should this not be the case the vendor will deliver a tax invoice and the purchaser will pay the VAT.[217] Additionally, the contract usually requires that a payment of the VAT is conditional upon the delivery of a tax invoice. The general view[218] is that the VAT is a contingent sum which has to be declared in the chargeable consideration, but the tax on the VAT element can usually be deferred until the position is resolved. The problem is how such provision should be dealt with in relation to SDLT. It is clear that the undertaking to pay the VAT if the various conditions are satisfied is part of the consideration that is chargeable, since it applies because the tax is potentially chargeable as at the effective date and does not arise pursuant to the exercise of the option to tax. It would seem obvious that the chargeable consideration is not just the basic price but the VAT potentially payable should treatment as a transfer of a going concern not arise. At least three issues arise on this point:

1. The amount to be included in the land transaction return (SDLT 1) as regards chargeable consideration. It is considered that the amount to be included in the return is the total amount including the VAT.[219] The payment would appear to be a contingent sum, i.e. a fixed amount payable if something happens. HMRC Stamp Taxes has from time to time taken the view that the consideration is 'unascertained'. This view, however, turns upon many technical issues of VAT. In particular, this view is based upon the principle that the tax point for

---

[217] There may also be issues as to whether the purchaser should indemnify the vendor against misdeclaration and other penalties and interest where the treatment is not available because of actions of the purchaser. It is considered that because the liability to pay arises by reason of breach of contract, if suitably drafted, the compensation is not part of the consideration and so does not have to be added to the chargeable consideration for the purposes of SDLT; cf. *Western United Investments Ltd* v. *IRC* [1958] Ch 392.

[218] But this view is not always shared by HMRC Stamp Taxes.

[219] FA 2003, s.51.

VAT[220] is the same as or will precede the effective date for SDLT. That is not necessarily the case and the VAT may arise by reason of subsequent events such as where the purchaser of the business effects certain changes, which in the view of HMRC Customs and Excise mean that he is not carrying on the same business within the conditions for treatment as a transfer of a going concern. However, if the analysis of the consideration being 'unascertained' is correct then the taxpayer is merely required to make a reasonable estimate of the amount that may become payable.[221] This might justify the view that appears to be the widespread practice that in these situations the VAT can be ignored when computing and returning the SDLT return but the issues of interest and penalties remain if the VAT becomes payable.

2.   It appears to be the view of HMRC Stamp Taxes that the VAT must be included in the chargeable consideration. This has the effect that it fixes the rate. It may be that the land price in the transaction is below a particular rate threshold but if the potential VAT is included the chargeable consideration would exceed that threshold. HMRC Stamp Taxes considers that the tax has to be computed by reference to the higher figure. Obviously, if this view be correct and the practice adopted, then at some stage if the taxpayer is in a position to establish that the VAT will not become payable[222] the chargeable consideration will retrospectively reduce below the threshold. He will be entitled to make a claim for the repayment of the SDLT paid in respect of the potential VAT. On the other hand, should the taxpayer decide not to include the VAT in the chargeable consideration and the treatment as a transfer of a going concern is successfully challenged by HMRC Customs and Excise, additional tax will become payable not merely in respect of the VAT but also possibly at a higher rate in respect of the initial basic consideration. In this situation, since the taxpayer will not have included the VAT in his initial calculations, there are risks of penalties and interest.[223]

3.   Since the potential VAT[224] means that the consideration is variable there is a question as to whether the SDLT in respect of the potential VAT can be deferred. It should be noted that this merely enables part of the consideration to be deferred; it does not mean that the rate of tax can be calculated by

---

[220]   Value Added Tax Act 1994, s.6.

[221]   FA 2003, s.51.

[222]   The problem in practice is to persuade HMRC Stamp Taxes that this risk of VAT arising has terminated.

[223]   This approach also raises a significant issue for professional advisers. It would seem a necessary professional duty to notify the taxpayer of the VAT position and of the risks of further tax becoming payable or reclaims becoming possible. The taxpayer should be advised of the need to file further returns should the treatment adopted in preparing the initial land transaction return (SDLT 1) change. See **17.3**.

[224]   i.e. VAT that may arise because certain conditions may not be satisfied, as opposed to VAT that may become payable should the consideration vary by reference to the terms of the contract, bearing in mind that the legislation clearly requires a self-assessment to be made upon the basis that the sum is payable rather than the fact that it is unlikely to become payable. However, this depends upon the correct technical analysis of the possible payment as contingent or unascertained.

reference to the basic figure where the tax threshold is exceeded by the potential VAT in position.

It is currently the view of HMRC Stamp Taxes that this possible non-availability of the treatment as a transfer of a going concern means that because the VAT position is unresolved this produces 'unascertained consideration' (i.e. in the view of HMRC Stamp Taxes all of the information necessary for deciding whether the VAT is or is not payable exists on the effective date for SDLT).[225] In consequence, not all of the conditions will be necessarily satisfied as at the effective date. Moreover, the effective date for SDLT and the tax point for VAT will rarely be the same[226] and the liability cannot be affected by subsequent events.[227] In consequence, the taxpayer has to decide as at the effective date both whether the tax is or might be payable and into which category of variable consideration upon which the tax is computed, if any, falls;[228] and whether he takes the view that it is unascertained consideration as opposed to contingent consideration. He must then make a return of either the net or the tax inclusive amount. Should he take the view[229] that the tax may be payable he must calculate and pay the tax upon the gross amount including the VAT. It is not possible to defer the SDLT upon unascertained consideration. Should the taxpayer take the view that the VAT will not be payable the tax is calculated and payable by reference to the net price. Whichever view is taken, the SDLT position remains open until the VAT position is resolved with HMRC or cannot be challenged because the time limit for such challenges has expired. The practical problem is convincing HMRC Stamp Taxes that the VAT position has been finally resolved, particularly where a repayment of SDLT is involved. If fully paid and the taxpayer can achieve the difficult task of satisfying HMRC Stamp Taxes that VAT cannot be claimed by HMRC[230] the tax overpaid can be

---

[225] Which is not necessarily completion and substantial performance may not be the same as the VAT tax point.

[226] See the problems of VAT charges in e.g. *Higher Education Statistics* v. *Customs and Excise* [2000] STC 332.

[227] The revised Statement of Practice dealing with the interaction of stamp duty and VAT (SP11/91) proceeded upon the basis of unascertained consideration which justified a limited wait-and-see approach. However, the argument of the counsel for HMRC Stamp Taxes, which was surprisingly not challenged by counsel for the taxpayer in *Prudential Assurance* v. *IRC* [1992] STC 863, was to the effect that the potential VAT was a *prima facie* sum within the contingency principle. It seems that, in practice, HMRC Stamp Taxes preferred the former view, notwithstanding the way in which it presented its case to the court and that the dubious view has been carried over in practice into the SDLT regime.

[228] FA 2003, ss.51, 80 and 90. Since the parties have made provision in the contract for the possible payment of the VAT, it will be less than convincing for them to contend that they did not believe it might be payable when attacked for the numerous penalties for negligent or otherwise improper returns.

[229] This view will need to be based upon appropriate advice if the taxpayer wishes to avoid the long-term uncertainty arising from the fact that he has submitted a 'negligent return', i.e. one not prepared on a proper basis. Hopefully, the basic three-year limitation period applicable for VAT will help to produce a reasonable degree of 'finality'.

[230] Which is an area where HMRC Stamp Taxes has indicated, in practice, it will not be easy to persuade because of the uncertainties as to 'finality' in relation to VAT and its general position is that

reclaimed.[231] However, if it has not been fully paid because the taxpayer formed the view that the VAT would not be payable and the risk of payment was not included in the initial self-assessment, the SDLT will be payable with interest with effect from 30 days after the effective date and it is probable that HMRC Stamp Taxes will seek penalties for an incorrect return.

It is generally considered that this analysis that the potential VAT is 'unascertained' rather than 'contingent' which formed the basis for the incorrect practice in stamp duty,[232] is incorrect because, for example, it is a condition for the treatment as a transfer of a going concern that the purchaser continues to carry on the same business as the transferor.[233] In consequence, not all of the conditions will be necessarily satisfied as at the effective date. Moreover, the effective date for SDLT and the tax point for VAT will rarely be the same.[234] Additionally, the contract usually requires that a payment of the VAT is conditional upon the delivery of a tax invoice. The general view is that the VAT is a contingent sum which has to be declared in the chargeable consideration, but the tax on the VAT element can usually be deferred until the position is resolved. At that time the SDLT becomes payable but without interest or penalty, but to avoid interest and penalty charges the VAT must be declared on the initial return and a deferment of payment of the related SDLT must be sought.

4.30.2   VAT and rent

There is an issue whether actual VAT payable at the relevant effective date in respect of rent which is separately reserved as additional rent is taxable as rent or as a premium payable by instalments.[235] Current official practice[236] suggests that it is to be treated as 'rent' (see further **Chapter 8**) notwithstanding that it is reserved as a separate sum apparently upon the basis that 'consideration' including rent for the purposes of VAT includes the total amount payable including the VAT.[237]

---

because this is an error or mistake by the taxpayer the overpayment cannot be recovered after three years from the effective date pursuant to FA 2003, Sched.10, para.34.

[231]   In practice HMRC Stamp Taxes is suggesting that the tax will not be repaid because the VAT position can never be closed, particularly since there may be appeals to Europe. This view is not sustainable.

[232]   See points made in **note 227** above.

[233]   Although there is some debate as to whether this condition is consistent with the VAT directives and may be void.

[234]   See the problems of VAT charges in e.g. *Higher Education Statistics* v. *Customs and Excise* [2000] STC 332.

[235]   Pursuant to FA 2003, s.52.

[236]   It must, however, be noted that in SP 11/91 there is a statement that VAT would not necessarily be part of the rent but would be taxed as a premium payable by instalments. This point was rarely taken in practice for stamp duty but the same risk applies to SDLT.

[237]   Value Added Tax Act 1994, s.19. Since this is merely one of many issues in relation to VAT and rent, such as the effect of the option to tax and the charges upon increase of rent, these issues are more appropriate for consideration in **Chapter 8** on leases.

4.30.3 VAT and market value

In some situations (see **Chapter 15**) the SDLT is charged by reference to market value, which is the 'price' that would be obtained in the open market for the interest to be valued.[238] On ordinary principles of construction of stamp taxes the 'price' will include VAT if appropriate. This is the consideration, i.e. the VAT inclusive amount.[239] The question is whether the hypothetical terms of sale of the transaction in the open market would subject the transaction to VAT. This depends upon how the vendor is identified and whether he is to be assumed to be a taxpayer for the purposes of VAT or whether the transaction might qualify as a transfer of a going concern. Clearly the fact that the hypothetical purchaser might obtain full credit for the VAT as input tax is ignored since the tax inclusive figure is the price that he would pay. The issue is one of considerable complexity. It appears that, in practice, HMRC Stamp Taxes is prepared to act upon the basis that the market value is the price that would be obtained exclusive of any VAT that might otherwise arise. (See further **15.19**.)

4.30.4 VAT and costs as taxable consideration

Certain consideration is taxable by reference to its open market cost.[240] It appears to be the view of HMRC Stamp Taxes that the open market cost includes any VAT that might be payable upon the hypothetical sale, but this view ignores many issues such as the possibility of transfers of going concerns and recovery of input tax. There will be a need for preliminary negotiations as to whether the market price is the tax inclusive figure or the price net of VAT which has to be paid over to HMRC. The official view seems to be that the VAT is part of the consideration.[241] In consequence, notwithstanding that the vendor does not account for the VAT as such,[242] but simply includes the tax upon the particular transaction in his overall quarterly return, the cost is the tax inclusive figure. It will be necessary to press for treatment as a hypothetical transfer as a going concern or recoverable input tax if such treatments are available on the hypothetical facts. It is therefore open to challenge (see **15.18**).

The converse situation can arise, namely, where the taxpayer is assessed upon the open market cost whether 'cost' if determined upon a hypothetical basis should include VAT and, if so, whether the taxpayer's potential for recovering all or part of such VAT as a deductible input tax should be taken into account. It is considered that 'cost' is linked to cost less any recoverable input tax rather than the gross sum

---

[238]   FA 2003, Sched.4, para.7.

[239]   See e.g. *Glenrothes Corporation* v. *IRC* [1993] STC 74.

[240]   FA 2003, Sched.4, para.11; Stamp Duty Land Tax (Administration) Regulations 2003, SI 2003/2837, Part 4.

[241]   Value Added Tax Act 1994, s.19; see also *Glenrothes Corporation* v. *IRC* [1993] STC 74.

[242]   i.e. he is not a lay tax collector as such. The rules are simply computational principles, not a separate set of charging principles.

paid,[243] but the legislation does contain some assistance for the contrary view of HMRC Stamp Taxes because it refers to the 'price', i.e. tax inclusive consideration. There is considerable potential for a long debate over the meanings of 'price', 'cost' and 'value' in these contexts. It seems that, in practice (although the practice is not totally consistent) HMRC Stamp Taxes is prepared to accept a 'cost' net of VAT regardless of the individual taxpayer's ability to recover input tax in whole or in part.

4.31 POSTPONED CONSIDERATION AND INSTALMENTS

4.31.1 Basic rules

The parties will frequently enter into a transaction where payment of the consideration or premium is postponed in whole or in part, or may depend upon the outcome of specified future events, or is payable by instalments whether with or without interest at the market rate, possibly even secured by a charge on the property. The SDLT position depends upon the nature of the deferred consideration and this may depend upon the drafting. There may be a difference between a payment of £1 million by four equal instalments and four annual payments of £250,000 because the postponed consideration is simply payable by instalments or because it is some form of overage or clawback arrangement or is something like an annuity. The distinction between the three broad categories of deferred payment (namely: contingent; unascertained; uncertain) is crucial because totally different rules apply,[244] and these rules for variable consideration differ fundamentally from the rules applicable[245] to periodical payments[246] including certain types of premium for leases.

4.31.2 Delayed payment and instalment

Where the consideration is simply a delayed cash payment, such as where there is a deferred or phased completion, or even a deposit on contract with the balance payable at some future date, or the vendor agrees to leave the consideration outstanding possibly secured by a charge upon the property the chargeable consideration is the full amount of the purchase price and there is no discount for the postponed payment notwithstanding there may not be any interest running in the

---

[243]   However, the position is uncertain since the taxpayer's effective 'cost' may be lessened by other tax reliefs such as capital allowances. This could form the basis of an argument by HMRC Stamp Taxes that incidental tax reliefs or credits have to be ignored when determining the cost of a transaction. Moreover, the VAT rules as to capital goods schemes mean that the recovery may extend over a 10-year period in many cases providing a long-term continuous reporting and payment obligation (Value Added Tax Regulations 1995, SI 1995/2518, Part XV).

[244]   FA 2003, s.51 and Sched.4, para.3.

[245]   For example, see the issue of VAT and rent above.

[246]   FA 2003, s.52; *Blendett* v. *IRC* [1984] STC 95.

intervening period.[247] There is no right for the taxpayer to apply to postpone the payment of tax notwithstanding that the transaction takes place by instalments.[248] Since there is no right to apply to defer the payment of SDLT for instalment payments it does not appear to make any difference whether there is simply a deferred payment arrangement or the issue of loan notes for the payment of any consideration provided at completion; both are taxable immediately upon the amount ultimately payable.[249] This is because, unlike most other forms of tax, stamp taxes fall upon the purchaser and not upon the vendor.[250] Additionally, the compliance requirements of the various categories of deferred payment will differ depending upon the characteristics of the payment, in that the payment and compliance liabilities may pass to any person who acquires the relevant chargeable interest in the land.[251]

4.31.3 Variable consideration

The issues relating to variable consideration are complex and are discussed elsewhere (see **4.38**).

4.31.4 'Periodical payments' or 'instalments'

This difference between the computation rules for deferred or instalment consideration and periodical payments is clearly important and there may be a significant difference in tax liability between a fixed sum payable by instalments and a series of annual payments for a similar amount, particularly if the payment period exceeded 12 years when the difference in the computational principles might become important. It seems that this may ultimately be a matter of drafting.[252] For example:

- a consideration of £20,000,000 payable by 20 annual instalments if treated as a deferred consideration would be subject to SDLT upon £20,000,000; but
- a consideration consisting of £1,000,000 payable annually for 20 years would, it seems, be taxable upon a consideration of 12 years namely £12,000,000.

---

[247] FA 2003, Sched.4, para.3.

[248] Since this is the payer he will, unlike the vendor or payee, be faced with the cash flow problem of paying tax without receiving the money.

[249] There will be different issues where the loan notes may have a market value different from their face value because of the interest rate or absence thereof, or because the notes are convertible into shares of the company acquiring the chargeable interest.

[250] The fact that the consideration is payable by instalments may be relevant in deciding whether the contract has been substantially performed, see **Chapter 3**. The drafting may be important in deciding whether payment has been made with a loan back or is unpaid consideration: *Coren* v. *Keighley* [1972] 1 WLR 1556, a key issue for substantial performance.

[251] See **Chapter 1** above on title investigation and due diligence. Note the comments in *Stevenston Securities* v. *IRC* [1959] SLT 125.

[252] But see *Western United Investment Co* v. *IRC* [1958] 1 All ER 257 on the question of liquidated charges, etc.

However, even when drafted in this way there is still the question of whether there is a periodical payment. In relation to the equivalent stamp duty provisions,[253] it was held that where there was a 'distorted' payment arrangement this was not a true periodical payment because it lacked periodicity or regularity of payment.[254] Thus a payment of £1 per annum for 12 years and a payment of £1,000,000 in year 13 would not be treated as a periodical payment.[255]

In relation to stamp duty, an arrangement for periodical payments which contained the provision for payment of the balance forthwith upon default in any instalment was held not to affect the position since the payment of 'compensation' or damages for breach was not an item that could be included in the computation of stamp duty.[256] It remains to be seen whether a similar arrangement would be equally effective for the purposes of SDLT.

4.31.5 Periodical payments and annuities other than rent

Where the consideration, including any premium or payment treated as a premium, for a lease is not simply a payment delayed or by instalments, but is an annuity or periodical payment other than rent[257] payable either for life in perpetuity, for an indefinite period, or for a definite term exceeding 12 years,[258] the chargeable consideration is limited to the aggregate of 12 years' annual payments.[259] Although not specifically stated, it would appear that where there is an annuity or periodical payment payable for a fixed term not exceeding 12 years the chargeable consideration is the aggregate amount of the annuity or periodical payment.

4.31.6 Variable annuities and periodical payment

4.31.6.1 Index linked payments

The fact that the annuity or periodical payment is adjustable in line with the retail price index[260] is ignored, although linking to any other form of index such as stock exchange indices or a modified retail price index will bring the uncertain consideration rules into play. HMRC Stamp Taxes also appears to take the view that where the payment is to increase by, say, the greater of 50 per cent of the retail price index increases or 5 per cent of the amount or there is a ratchet effect (in that the payment can only increase and will not be reduced if the index falls) it is not within this relief

---

[253]   Stamp Act 1891, s.56.
[254]   *Quietlece Ltd* v. *IRC* [1982] BTC 8059.
[255]   Note also the charge in relation to loans and deposits in relation to the grant of leases and sales of property: FA 2003, Sched.17A, para.18A.
[256]   Western United Investment Co v. IRC [1958] Ch 392; see also Photo Production Ltd v. Securicor Transport Ltd [1980] 2 WLR 283.
[257]   FA 2003, s.52(6); see **Chapter 8** on the possible treatment of VAT payable in relation to rent.
[258]   FA 2003, s.52(1).
[259]   FA 2003, s.52(2).
[260]   But not consumer prices index (CPI) or other indices.

and the payment will be a variable payment (see following paragraph). However, the legislation refers to the adjustment being 'in line with' the index which is potentially ambiguous so that an adjustment of a percentage of the index movement may be within this treatment.[261]

4.31.6.2 Other variable annual payments

Where the annual amount varies otherwise than purely by reference to 100 per cent of the change in the retail price index then the consideration has to be paid upon the basis of a reasonable estimate of the amount expected to be paid over the 12-year period.[262] There is, however, a particular quirk in that where the amount payable varies, or may vary, the 12 years taken into account are the 12 highest annual payments. No guidance is provided as to how to determine the estimated 12 highest payments where consideration is 'uncertain' and the payment period extends or may extend beyond 12 years; presumably the parties have to make their reasonable estimate of the 12 highest amounts expected during the lifetime of the annuity but the right to apply to defer payment does not apply.

There is a related issue where the annuity is not for a fixed term[263] such as a life annuity. However, in this case although the initial return is prepared upon the basis of estimates there is no further obligation to revise the SDLT where the actual outcome differs from the original estimates.[264] This is a two-edged weapon in that there is no right for the taxpayer to recover tax should the original estimate prove to be excessive.

4.32 DEBTS, LIABILITIES AND MORTGAGES

Dealings involving debts and liabilities as consideration can take many forms, for example:

- The consideration may be left outstanding as an unpaid debt.[265] *Prima facie* the taxable amount is the face value of the indebtedness without any discount for the delay in payment.[266] However, where there is the issue of a debenture or loan note, it seems that the chargeable amount will be the market value of the debenture which may include a discount or premium as regards face value, depending upon the interest rate.

---

[261] On other potential problems of index linked payments see FA 2003, s.52(3); also **8.28.4**.

[262] FA 2003, s.51.

[263] See also *Stevenston Securities* v. *IRC* [1959] SLT 125 on the question of whether a fixed term arrangement is an annuity or insurance arrangement or a loan repayable by instalments with interest; but note also *Mersey Docks and Harbour Board* v. *IRC* [1897] 1 QB 786 to the effect that non-repayable loans may be annuities.

[264] A significant discrepancy may be regarded as negligence or fraud, i.e. if the return was not prepared on a proper basis.

[265] But note the drafting problems such as *Coren* v. *Keighley* 48 TC 370.

[266] FA 2003, Sched.4, para.3.

- The vendor may be indebted to the purchaser and the chargeable interest or lease premium may be treated as being in full or partial satisfaction of the debt, such as may occur on foreclosure. The chargeable amount is the amount of the debt outstanding and any accrued unpaid interest as at the effective date or the market value of the property whichever is the lower unless the connected company charge applies.[267]
- The acquisition of the land may be part of the purchase of a business including liabilities[268] (the chargeable amount will be the properly apportioned part of the liabilities and other consideration).
- The property may be subject to a charge or mortgage, including a mortgage to provide security such as a guarantee for a debt, i.e. a form of contingent liability. The chargeable consideration is the actual consideration plus the mortgage liability assumed by the purchaser (see **4.33**) (i.e. the amount of principal and accrued interest outstanding at the effective date) assumed by purchaser or the market value of the property if lower than the mortgage liability. This charge applies notwithstanding that mortgages are not chargeable interests. Before the charge arises there must be an assumption of liability so that if property is transferred subject to a mortgage the transferee will not have to pay tax upon the mortgage if he does not give a personal covenant to pay, notwithstanding that he may acknowledge that the property is subject to the charge. A charge arises if in connection with the transfer the rights and liabilities in relation to the mortgage are subsequently varied; this is deemed to be an assumption of liability.[269]

4.33 DOMESTIC ISSUES AND MORTGAGES

The answers to the issues discussed in this paragraph are fundamental to the availability of the limited first time buyer relief. A routine problem for practitioners will be when there is an assumption of liabilities such as occurs in many domestic situations where there is always the problem of determining the terms of the arrangement and whether there was an intention to enter into legal relationships.[270]

---

[267] There is, however, a longstanding debate with HMRC Stamp Taxes as to whether the market value is the value of the property, subject to the mortgage, i.e. the equity of redemption. This was initially accepted by it in relation to, e.g. FA 1965, s.90, but this position was later changed. The point is open for argument since the market value charge may override the charge upon the assumption of the mortgage.

[268] Care is needed with the drafting of 'liabilities' otherwise the purchaser may discover that he is responsible for the vendor's tax liabilities including any unpaid VAT. See, for example, *Re Hollebone* [1959] 2 All ER 152 and *Stevens* v. *Britten* [1954] 3 All ER 385.

[269] FA 2003, Sched.4, para.8 (as amended).

[270] See, for example, *Parker* v. *Clark* [1960] 1 All ER 93; *Balfour* v. *Balfour* [1919] 2 KB 517; *Spellman* v. *Spellman* [1961] 2 All ER 498; *Farina* v. *Fickus* [1900] 1 Ch 331; *Davies* v. *Sweet* [1962] 1 All ER 92; *Gould* v. *Gould* [1969] 3 All ER 728.

There may also be issues as to whether there is a contract or a conditional gift.[271] Also, it is unlikely that the parties will have sought professional advice at the inception of the transaction and the details emerge years later when there are obligations of the professional adviser to comply with the money laundering legislation and the professional adviser may face penalties for assisting in the preparation of incorrect land transaction returns including a claim for first time buyer relief which he did not investigate.[272] For example, parents and child may jointly acquire property but on the understanding that the child will discharge the mortgage and the property will belong to him.[273] There are difficult issues of analysis in this relationship with long-term consequences for the first time buyer relief, which will depend upon the facts of each case including whether this is an agreement to transfer the property in consideration of the child discharging the joint and several liability for the mortgage debt which at some stage becomes a chargeable transaction.[274] As constructive trusts are involved the absence of writing is irrelevant.[275]

In relation to the satisfaction of debts or assuming liabilities other than dealing with charges, the chargeable amount is the amount of the debt satisfied, released or assumed plus any accrued unpaid interest as at the effective date.[276] Where this is not the whole of the consideration the amount of such debt or liability satisfied or assumed is added to the other consideration.[277] This relates only to pre-existing liabilities of the vendor, or possibly persons connected with him, prior to the transaction; it does not apply to any debts owed by the purchaser as consideration for the acquisition such as unpaid or deferred consideration which is governed by the principles for deferred consideration or instalments considered above. However, if the amount of chargeable consideration would, as a result of the treatment of debts and liabilities, exceed the market value of the subject-matter of the transaction, the chargeable consideration is limited to the market value.[278] For these purposes 'debt' means an obligation, whether certain or contingent, to pay a sum of money either immediately or at a future date. It will therefore include items such as guarantees of other persons' debts charged upon the property when the guarantee represents a contingent liability to pay the full amount of the underlying debt such as a charge upon the family home to secure borrowings of the family company.[279]

---

[271] Eastham v. Leigh London and Provincial Properties Ltd [1971] 2 All ER 887; GUS Merchandise v. Customs and Excise [1981] 1 WLR 1309.

[272] FA 2003, ss.95 and 96.

[273] See e.g. *Errington* v. *Errington and Woods* [1952] 1 KB 290.

[274] Probably at the very beginning when the child moves into the house, unless the parents are in occupation when any licence to the child may not constitute possession.

[275] See below on the alternative risk that this is an agreement to transfer in consideration of services taxable, at some stage, on the open market cost of such services.

[276] FA 2003, Sched.4, para.8(1) and (3)(a) and (c).

[277] FA 2003, Sched.4, para.8(1).

[278] FA 2003, Sched.4, para.8(2).

[279] FA 2003, Sched.4, para.8(1) and (3)(a).

4.34 INDEMNITIES AND LIABILITIES

It is not possible to assign a liability, so the assumption of liabilities frequently takes the form of an agreement to give an indemnity in respect of outstanding debts and liabilities of the vendor, and such indemnity is, *prima facie*, taxable.[280] In this context, where a purchaser agrees to indemnify the vendor in respect of liability to a third party arising from breach of an obligation owed by the vendor in relation to the land that is the subject-matter of the transaction, neither the agreement to indemnify nor any payment made in pursuance of the indemnity counts as chargeable consideration.[281] In some cases the parties seek to deal with this situation by backdating the effect of the agreement and deeming all transactions in the intervening period to have been entered into by the vendor as agent for the purchaser.[282] Since the parties cannot rewrite history this is merely a mechanism for adjusting the consideration and can have adverse consequences for, *inter alia*, stamp taxes.[283] See also **4.32** on indemnities and liabilities.

4.35 SPECIAL SITUATIONS AND RELIEFS

The above general rules are modified in certain cases:

- Where property subject to a charge is transferred out of a single name into joint names or out of joint names into the name of one of the owners, only a part of the mortgage is brought into charge. This is the proportion of the property to which the incoming party becomes entitled or to which the outgoing party was entitled and, where appropriate, the lower rates of tax apply.[284]
- Where, as part of the administration of an estate, property subject to a charge is appropriated or assented to a legatee in full or partial satisfaction of a cash or similar legacy the assumption of liability in respect of the mortgage is ignored.[285]

---

[280] It is considered that the assumption that a liability that is inherent in the property, such as future rent reserved by a lease, is not chargeable consideration for the purposes of these provisions (cf. *Swayne* v. *IRC* [1900] 1 QB 172; *Halsall* v. *Brizell* [1957] Ch 169 to the broad effect that he who takes the benefit must also take the burden); but the fact that the draftsman regarded it as necessary to introduce specific relieving provisions indicates that he clearly regarded this other provision as overriding these basic general principles.

[281] FA 2003, Sched.4, para.16.

[282] This is different from arrangements where the parties seek to backdate the execution of documentation or the date when the arrangement was performed which is, *prima facie*, fraud and forgery; see e.g. *Saywell* v. *Pope* [1979] STC 824; but this may affect reliefs, see e.g. *Metal Box Plastic Films Ltd* v. *IRC* [1969] 1 WLR 1620.

[283] *Metal Box Ltd* v. *IRC* [1969] 1 WLR 1620.

[284] FA 2003, Sched.4, para.8.

[285] FA 2003, Sched.3, para.3A and Sched.4, paras.8 and 8A.

- Where the assumption of the liability is part of a variation of the estate of a deceased individual within two years of his death, the mortgage is ignored in computing the amount of chargeable consideration.[286]
- Where the purchaser agrees to indemnify the vendor in respect of any liability arising from breach of an obligation owed by the vendor in relation to the land that is the subject of the transaction, neither the agreement nor any payment made in pursuance of it counts as chargeable consideration.[287] This is potentially helpful in practice in relation to the type of indemnity required, probably unnecessarily, by vendors where there is a 's.106 development agreement' with the local authority relating to planning consents. For example, a developer may enter into a conditional agreement or option to acquire land if planning permission acceptable to the parties is obtained.[288] The conditional or optional nature of this arrangement may require the participation of the current landowner as a party to the planning agreement with the local authority and he may be advised to insist upon some form of indemnity in relation to possible failures to comply with the planning agreement although he will not be the person in default. The required undertaking to indemnify the vendor against such default will *prima facie* be part of the chargeable consideration for the acquisition of the chargeable interest unless this provision for the exclusion of the indemnity from the amount of the chargeable consideration applies. However, the point is far from settled since this indemnity will not be in respect of any breach taking place before the assignment or conveyance of the land. It represents an undertaking by the purchaser to make a payment in respect of his breach after he becomes the effective owner of the property and, in effect, the beneficiary of the planning permission. Such an arrangement may not be regarded as falling within the exemption. In consequence, it will become a highly technical debate with HMRC Stamp Taxes as to whether the utilisation of the terminology of the indemnity can convert what is essentially a payment of damages into chargeable consideration. The difficulty in the way of such an argument is that the draftsman clearly regarded an agreement to indemnify against future liabilities as chargeable consideration otherwise he would not have made undertakings to pay future rents reserved by a lease exempt from that which he regarded as a chargeable consideration.[289] If the basic arrangement were not taxable the relief would not be necessary. If chargeable, the form of the 'indemnity' may be important, since it would appear that, upon basic principles, the payment of damages, even liquidated damages, is not part of a consideration of the transaction.[290] A payment for breach is not the same as performance of the

---

[286] FA 2003, Sched.4, para.8A; Sched.3, paras.3A and 4.
[287] FA 2003, Sched.4, para.16.
[288] Care may be needed in drafting since a 'condition' that is essentially an obligation upon the party to use reasonable endeavours or to procure the planning permission may be services that constitute chargeable consideration.
[289] FA 2003, Sched.17A, para.10.
[290] Western United Investments v. IRC [1958] Ch 392.

obligation.[291] It is expected that, although its position is technically somewhat weak, HMRC Stamp Taxes will seek to develop this argument. Prudence suggests that, for the time being pending clarification of the point in practice, striving for the strongest position to resist the claim by suitable drafting is appropriate.

- Where there is an assignment of a lease the usual covenants by the assignee to pay the rent and to observe the covenants in the lease are not taxable;[292] but where the lease being assigned was exempt for certain reasons when granted there may be a special charge overriding these reliefs.[293] The assignment is taxed as if it were the grant of a new lease.[294]

4.36 FOREIGN CURRENCY

Where the consideration for the transaction consists wholly or partly of non-sterling currency the tax is charged upon the sterling equivalent which is calculated by reference to the London closing exchange rate on the effective date of the transaction unless the parties have used a different rate for the purposes of the transaction.[295] Where there are two effective dates changes in the exchange rate may increase the tax charge.[296]

4.37 WORKS AND SERVICES

The massive extension of the tax base means that many new detailed rules are required for calculating the chargeable consideration where the value of money's worth or market value are inappropriate.[297] These apply where the chargeable consideration cannot be sold or otherwise turned into cash, or if saleable their value would be insufficiently large to produce a 'worthwhile' tax yield.[298] The main areas are works[299] and services.[300] These are taxed upon an amount equal to the cost of such services or works on the open market,[301] a novel concept in fiscal valuations in many respects.

---

[291]   Photo Production Ltd v. Securicor Transport Ltd [1980] 2 WLR 283.
[292]   FA 2003, Sched.17A, para.17.
[293]   FA 2003, Sched.17A, para.12.
[294]   FA 2003, Sched.17A, para.12; see **8.61**.
[295]   FA 2003, Sched.4, para.9.
[296]   FA 2003, Sched.17A, para.12A.
[297]   FA 2003, Sched.4, para.1; *Secretan* v. *Hart* [1969] 3 All ER 1196.
[298]   See, for example, *Nokes* v. *Doncaster Amalgamated Collieries* [1940] AC 1014; *O'Brien* v. *Benson Hosiery* [1979] STC 735.
[299]   FA 2003, Sched.4, para.10 (as amended); see **Chapter 9**.
[300]   FA 2003, Sched.4, para.11; see **4.37.2** and **15.18**.
[301]   See Stamp Duty Land Tax (Administration) Regulations 2003, SI 2003/2837, Part 4.

4.37.1 Carrying out works

Where the carrying out of works, including building or construction operations or fitting out the premises by the tenant, is part of the chargeable consideration and is not merely a condition of the transaction[302] then the chargeable consideration includes the value of the works.[303] The chargeable amount of the works is the amount that would have to be paid on the open market for the carrying out of the works in question.[304]

There are two sets of charges potentially involved, namely:

- where the works are to be carried out by the landlord or vendor and so are not consideration provided by the tenant where the question is whether the regrant by the tenant or purchaser for the works are chargeable consideration; and
- where the works are to be carried out by the purchaser or tenant at his expense.

These issues of building operations are very complex and may form part of a larger development arrangement. In consequence they are considered in more detail in the overall context of building and fitting out works in **Chapter 9**.

4.37.2 Services

The provision of services, other than the carrying out of building works or works of a similar nature, is expressly brought into charge and the tax is to be calculated upon the 'open market cost' or the amount that would have to be paid on the open market to obtain those services. No guidance is provided as to how to determine the 'open market cost' of the services[305] and whether this has to take into account the possibility of VAT upon the actual or hypothetical costs.

Among the difficulties of these provisions is that there is also no guidance as to what is meant by 'the provision of services', which is an issue of major technical importance given the comments by Walker LJ in *Yaxley* v. *Gotts*[306] and whether the services in question are chargeable consideration if they are not available as a package in the open market (see further below). No doubt HMRC Stamp Taxes has in mind some sort of transaction such as where a person is granted some right in or over land in return for architectural services such as designing a building or for acting as selling agent,[307] or situations such as *Yaxley* v. *Gotts*[308] where a builder was to be rewarded by being granted a lease of one of the flats, which would now be a taxable transaction. There is a question as to whether the giving of a guarantee by a

---

[302] See Eastham v. Leigh London and Provincial Properties Ltd [1971] 2 All ER 887.
[303] FA 2003, Sched.4, para.10.
[304] FA 2003, Sched.4, para.10(3)(b).
[305] See *Giambrone* v. *JMC Holidays (No.2)* [2004] 2 All ER 891 on some of the problems relating to cost.
[306] [1999] 3 WLR 1217.
[307] But note the possible effect of FA 2003, s.44A.
[308] [1999] 3 WLR 1217.

parent company that its subsidiary company will carry out its obligations in relation to land is a 'service' that would be part of the consideration for a land transaction.[309]

Also, a key issue for practitioners is whether domestic arrangements fall within these provisions, which may raise issues of intention to create legal relations.[310] For example, an aged person may agree, probably orally,[311] with a child or other relation that if the latter should move into the property and care for the property owner, the property will pass to the latter on the death of the former. It is understood that HMRC Stamp Taxes regards this as a chargeable transaction but so far no adequate guidance has been produced on how it believes the open market cost of such arrangements is to be determined in advance on a provisional basis and on the final basis when the 'services' are completed.[312] Moreover, there are two fundamental issues for HMRC Stamp Taxes to address; namely:

- whether the services have to be regarded as a single composite package (which in practice means that the 'package' has no 'open market cost' because there is no generally available package of services) or have to be individually 'unpacked' and costed; and
- whether a charge arises if the package of services or individual items therein are not purchasable in the open market (see further below).

4.37.2.1   Services and 'costs'

Several basic issues arise in practice. There is a fundamental question in relation to the taxability of services, however, there may also be questions as to whether there can be chargeable services where there is no comparable market for the services. For example, there will be a major issue as to whether a charge to tax arises in connection with the provision of caring services which, notwithstanding the absence of formality, can produce a situation where property interests arise by

---

[309]   *Curzon Offices* v. *IRC* [1944] 1 All ER 163; *IRC* v. *Wachtel* 46 TC 543. There may be a question as to whether the consideration is being provided directly or indirectly by the purchaser in this transaction as required by FA 2003, Sched.4, para.1. This is, of course, unless HMRC Stamp Taxes states that the question of provision by the purchaser is limited to those situations where the consideration consists of money or money's worth within para.1 and the restriction as to provision of the consideration directly or indirectly by the purchaser or a connected party has no relevance to any other provision for calculating the chargeable amount.

[310]   *Parker* v. *Clark* [1960] 1 All ER 93; *Balfour* v. *Balfour* [1919] 2 KB 517.

[311]   But legally effective as a constructive trust provided that admissible evidence can be produced of the promise, etc. *Binions* v. *Evans* [1972] Ch 359. However, the SDLT consequences of such an informal arrangement will ultimately depend upon the answers to immensely difficult questions of principle such as whether the equitable intervention produce a valid contract notwithstanding the absence of writing (*Yaxley* v. *Gotts* [1999] 3 WLR 1217) but this may depend upon the facts and the nature of the 'promise' (*Yeoman's Row Management* v. *Cobbe* [2008] 4 All ER 713) and whether equitable intervention is a right or a remedy and whether the interest passes by operation of law or the judgment is merely a declaration of rights rather than a vesting of property as such.

[312]   See e.g. Stamp Taxes Manual 4140 referring to the hypothetical rather than the actual transaction.

reason of equitable intervention.[313] There will be interesting questions as to whether there can be a 'package' of services and whether the charge to tax is based upon the equivalent cost of hiring a full-time live-in helper who provides similar services. Obviously, certain of the services may be provided by social services and may not have a 'market cost' in the sense that they are services uniquely provided. Also, where there are packages of services some of which are freely available in the open market and others of which are not readily purchasable, there will be the question as to whether the arrangement has to be taxed upon the basis of a package of services which is an item that cannot be obtained in the open market and so cannot have an open market cost, or whether the individual components thereof have to be broken down. Hitherto no really worthwhile guidance has been provided by HMRC Stamp Taxes on these fundamental issues which clearly extend beyond merely caring for elderly relatives and include many commercial activities where services are remunerated by an interest in land as in *Yaxley* v. *Gotts*.[314] The following need to be considered.

- As these computational provisions are based upon the 'open market cost' it is clear that the actual costs incurred by the taxpayer are not necessarily the correct figure.
- In many cases there is likely to be no cost unless the loss of other income is regarded as a 'cost' (but since this offers HMRC Stamp Taxes a windfall bonus of revenue it may well wish to pursue this dubious point).
- Moreover, even such lost income will not necessarily be open market cost, i.e. the price which the other party would pay for the services on a stand-alone basis with a third party seeking to make a profit on the transaction. For example, the cost to a builder employing his own labour force will almost certainly be different from the price that a third party seeking to make a profit might charge if the building work or other services were a separate transaction unrelated to the acquisition of an interest in land.
- The practical difficulty for taxpayers will be to obtain information from competitors as to their possible charges, particularly since this might reveal confidential business information; but, in the absence of such alternative quotations for the work or services on a stand-alone basis the land transaction return (SDLT 1) will not have been properly prepared pursuant to the rules relating to self-assessment with the consequences of extended Enquiry periods and the risk of discovery assessments plus interest and penalties.
- Although the comments it makes vary from time to time it seems that HMRC Stamp Taxes may require the costs to be determined upon the basis that they include VAT regardless of whether the taxpayer is able to recover all or any part of his input tax or would be so entitled if actual costs were incurred, or the

---

[313] See also *Errington* v. *Errington and Woods* [1952] 1 KB 290 (with all the problems related to first time buyer relief related to cases such as that); *GUS Merchandise* v. *Customs and Excise* [1981] 1 WLR 1309.

[314] [1999] 3 WLR 1217.

taxpayer or other supplier of the service would not be required to charge VAT, or other possible suppliers might be taxable persons for VAT purposes. There appears to be some statutory justification for this view since the charge is upon the price (i.e. total consideration) which would have to be paid on the open market. However, in relation to open market value it seems that HMRC Stamp Taxes takes the view that VAT can be ignored, and the market value is the net price at which the property could be sold. It may be that eventually a similar view will be taken for the cost of services but since many service providers are not subject to VAT this may be a tax benefit.

- Since works and services are supplied over a period of time they may be uncertain within the various categories of variable consideration. In this situation the taxpayer has to make a reasonable estimate of the open market cost[315] which has to be adjusted as the transaction proceeds.[316] It is possible to apply to defer the payment of the tax upon the uncertain element provided that the transaction is likely to take more than six months to complete;[317] but in certain cases the application to postpone the tax must be accompanied by a timetable indicating when HMRC Stamp Taxes may expect payments of tax pursuant to FA 2003, s.80.[318]

- As noted above, the services in question may not be available on 'the open market'. There is at present no explanation of which 'services' HMRC Stamp Taxes regards as subject to the charge to tax. In consequence, 'services' supplied in the form of caring for elderly relatives are chargeable consideration for the eventual acquisition of the house but while the equivalent of certain of these services may be available through welfare and social services departments not every activity involved will be so covered. There may be issues as to whether supplying lunch has to be equated with meals on wheels, but other activities are not so clearly matched by outside suppliers. Moreover, there will be the need to report the chargeable transaction at some stage which will be very difficult to determine otherwise than retrospectively. Although many such transactions will be informal they will be effective as constructive trusts (see **10.8**) or even valid contracts notwithstanding the absence of writing[319] but the intention is that the relevant party will ultimately receive the legal title to the property so that the effective date will be substantial performance. But because this is potentially an open-ended arrangement, the final consideration will not be known and it is unlikely that, where the current owner remains in occupation of the premises, there will be taking of possession (see further **3.9**).

This raises certain issues in practice. The reference to 'open market cost' suggests a fixed price contract should such arrangements be available in the open market; but

---

[315] FA 2003, s.51. See Stamp Taxes Manual 4140.
[316] FA 2003, s.80, leaving open the issue of 'stage payments' as the transaction progresses and 'instalments' fall due or become ascertained at least in part.
[317] FA 2003, s.90.
[318] Stamp Duty Land Tax (Administration) Regulations 2003, SI 2003/2837.
[319] *Yaxley* v. *Gotts* [1999] 3 WLR 1217; *Binions* v. *Evans* [1972] Ch 359.

HMRC Stamp Taxes treats such arrangements as involving variable consideration involving estimated returns. The application to postpone the relevant tax requires a timetable and estimated 'costs' but these are to be revised retrospectively by reference to actual cost.

4.38 VARIABLE CONSIDERATION

Unlike stamp duty which is a once-for-all tax assessed at the time of the execution of the document with the issue of variable consideration being dealt with by the so-called contingency principle,[320] SDLT seeks to deal with the problem by a form of wait-and-see or a multi-stage process by means of many returns, the tax being calculated initially on an estimated basis (but subject to interest and penalty risks if the estimate is incorrect) with subsequent adjustments as the uncertainties or variable elements are resolved. Regrettably for professional advisers this is merely one aspect of the fundamental provisional nature of SDLT (see **Chapter 1**).

It is, therefore, necessary to:

- produce an initial assessment and payment, with application to defer the payment of tax where possible to avoid interest charges and penalties; and
- make arrangements for the obligatory retrospective revisions of this provisional assessment from time to time.[321]

However, it is first necessary to determine into which category of variable consideration the arrangement falls since this affects not only the manner in which the initial self-assessment has to be made, but also the time of payment including the power to apply to defer payment of tax and the subsequent reporting and payment obligations.[322] Three types of variable consideration are prescribed by the legislation as described below. However, it has to be noted that the nature of the consideration may change as the transaction progresses. This is a particular problem where there are two separate effective dates, such as where substantial performance precedes completion (see **3.6**). What was *uncertain* consideration at substantial performance may have become *unascertained* at completion. For example, there may be an agreement to sell a building being constructed for a price linked to the square footage. Substantial performance during the building works such as entry to fit out is likely to involve uncertain consideration. However, at the time of the grant after completion of the building the size of the building will be known. HMRC Stamp Taxes appears to be undecided as to how far the payment and

---

[320] For continued extensions of this principle see Lindsay J and Millett LJ in *Parinv* v. *IRC* [1996] STC 933 and [1998] STC 305 respectively; and especially the comments of Carnwath J in *LM Tenancies* v. *IRC* [1998] STC 326. See also Lord Millett's judgment in *Collector of Stamp Revenue* v. *Arrowtown Assets Ltd* [2003] HKCFA 47.

[321] The number of returns may depend upon the drafting as each instalment may become 'certain'.

[322] Professional advisers must bear this in mind when agreeing the terms of their retainer with the client.

compliance obligations change in such circumstances. These types of variable consideration also apply to rent but special rules for computation and payment apply.[323]

The tax consequences depend upon the type of variable consideration.

4.38.1 'Contingent consideration'

A contingent element is a fixed sum payable if a particular event happens or which ceases to be payable or the *prima facie* price reduces upon the happening or non-happening of a future event, such as a sale of land for a fixed price with a specified additional sum if planning consent is obtained.[324] It does not apply to variable sums payable where there is not a fixed amount, notwithstanding that there may be a maximum or cap.[325] Different rules apply where, for example, there is an obligation to pay 50 per cent of any resale profit with a maximum amount. In such a case:

- initially, the SDLT has to be calculated and paid upon the basis that the contingent sum is payable;[326] but
- although it is necessary to pay the SDLT upon any fixed or minimum amount when filing the land transaction return (SDLT 1), except where rent is involved[327] it is possible to apply to defer the payment of the part of the tax attributable to the contingent element in the overall sum,[328] subject to satisfying certain conditions (e.g. the contingent payment may not fall due until at least six months after the effective date) and obtaining the agreement of HMRC Stamp Taxes after a written submission containing the prescribed information.

The importance of applying to defer is that:

- it avoids suggestions likely to be made by HMRC Stamp Taxes that there has been fraudulent concealment of a potential tax liability if the contingent consideration is not disclosed at the beginning of the transaction;
- it can avoid an interest charge for late payment which normally begins to accrue shortly after the effective date rather than the date when the contingent sum

---

[323] FA 2003, Sched.17A, paras.7 and 8.

[324] FA 2003, ss.51, 80 and 90. It is currently in dispute with HMRC Stamp Taxes whether the VAT charge, if there is not a transfer of a going concern, falls within those relatively favourable provisions.

[325] FA 2003, s.80, plus the possibility of paying by instalments pursuant to FA 2003, s.90; this may affect the interest provisions for late payment: FA 2003, s.87(5); Stamp Duty Land Tax (Administration) Regulations 2003, SI 2003/2837, Part 4.

[326] FA 2003, s.51.

[327] And for the professional adviser who may be liable if the client is subsequently challenged by HMRC Stamp Taxes who impose penalties and the client was not advised as to these issues.

[328] FA 2003, ss.80 and 91; Stamp Duty Land Tax (Administration) Regulations 2003, SI 2003/2837, Part 4.

falls due,[329] provided that the initial estimate is not less than the amount ultimately payable. Interest will accrue only upon any excess over the estimated figure; and

- there is a refund if the contingency does not happen or the sum ceases to be payable; and any postponed tax upon the amount ceases to be payable.

This prudent treatment which is essential for the protection of the client will be initially expensive because it will require the notification to HMRC Stamp Taxes as and when the contingency cannot be satisfied so that the sum will never become payable; as well as the obligation to unwind the deferred payment situation if the contingency is satisfied and the additional sum becomes payable; but it avoids interest and penalties.[330] Moreover, in such situations the obligation to deal with the contingency occurring passes with the land and failure to deal with the initial situation properly may adversely affect title (see **14.7**, **15.4** and **15.8**) especially now that it is possible to obtain a Revenue certificate (SDLT 5) permitting registration without ever paying the tax.

4.38.2 'Uncertain consideration'

For these purposes, the consideration, whether the purchase price or premium for the grant of a new lease,[331] is 'uncertain'[332] if the whole or part of the amount payable depends upon future events.[333] A typical situation will be where there is a sale for an overage or clawback payment, where the amount payable is uncertain and/or the tax when it becomes payable is uncertain. This will apply, for example, to the grant of a lease where the premium is a percentage of the proceeds of sale of the property in due course, or a multiple of the rent or profits in accordance with some algebraic formula, or is a sum linked to the actual square footage or net lettable area of a building to be constructed to be determined when it is finally completed.[334] Essentially this differs from the preceding comments only because the amount payable or the reduction in the *prima facie* consideration is uncertain even where limits are imposed. These rules will apply even where there is a maximum potential amount or 'cap' on the payment. Such a sum is not 'contingent' because the amount potentially payable is variable albeit within certain fixed parameters. In these cases,

---

[329] FA 2003, s.91.

[330] Fortunately, the liability to deal with the unresolved SDLT position for contingent payments does not directly pass to the purchaser except in cases of assignment of leases; but there are, for the professional advisers, practical problems of how to deal with these potential liabilities upon any assignment or sale or lease or sublease of land which will involve their own SDLT consequences for both the vendor and the purchaser or lessor in the current transaction, and the original landowner/ lessor and purchaser/lessee in the transaction which produced the contingent liability.

[331] Different problems arise for assignees of leases where the variable elements of the consideration, whether premium or rent, have not been finally resolved by the original tenant at the time of the assignment.

[332] FA 2003, ss.51, 80 and 90.

[333] FA 2003, s.51(3).

[334] Such consideration may also be 'unascertained' at the time when the lease is finally granted: FA 2003, s.51.

the SDLT has to be paid initially upon the basis of a 'reasonable estimate' of what will ultimately be payable[335] which will not necessarily be the maximum or cap. There is an inherent potential ambiguity in the legislation namely:

- the likelihood of any payment having to be made; and
- the amount of the consideration potentially payable should the relevant event differ no matter how unlikely this may be.

The context of the provision is such that the likelihood of the event happening is irrelevant. The key issue is the latter interpretation, i.e. the return refers to the potentially chargeable amount no matter how unlikely it is that any payment may have to be made. In consequence, there is an obligation to calculate the tax upon the basis of guestimates as to future payments that may never have to be made. Failure to complete the return upon this basis is negligent. In consequence tax may be overpaid or higher rates than those applicable to the final payment will have to be applied; but there is an obligation to review and adjust the initial estimate retrospectively (see **1.24** and **4.38**) in the light of later events or as any part or instalment of the variable element becomes settled and payable. This requires the taxpayer to report and pay tax (or claim a refund) as the final price or instalments become fixed and payable.[336] Interest is payable if the initial estimate is below the final amount payable but only on the excess over the estimated figure, and penalties may be imposed if the estimate is not properly prepared so that the return is 'negligent'.

4.38.3 'Unascertained consideration'

Unlike the previous two categories of variable consideration which are dependent upon future events this category looks to the past where events have occurred but details have yet to be agreed.[337] This is a consideration where all of the information for determining the consideration is available but has to be processed, such as where the price is the market value on the day of completion or the premium is a multiple of the net lettable area of a building which has been completed but not measured. It also appears to include the purchase of a reversion which is subject to a lease that is undergoing a rent review and the price depends upon the revised rent as finally agreed. Tax is payable in full on the estimated total; no deferral is allowed.[338]

Where the consideration is 'unascertained',[339] i.e. all of the facts relevant to the determination are available but their effect has not been agreed, the tenant must

---

[335] FA 2003, s.51(2).

[336] FA 2003, s.80, plus the possibility of paying the tax by instalments pursuant to FA 2003, s.90; Stamp Duty Land Tax (Administration) Regulations 2003, SI 2003/2837, Part 4.

[337] But note the possibility that the status or category of the consideration may change as the transaction progresses especially where there may be two effective dates; see **4.38**.

[338] FA 2003, s.90(1)(a) is limited to contingent and uncertain consideration, i.e. does not include 'unascertained' consideration or rent since unlike other forms of variable consideration this refers not to the future but to the past even where negotiations or disputes are in progress in order to finalise the figure.

[339] There is no definition but by default and elimination the explanation in the text appears to be the correct interpretation.

make a reasonable estimate of the amount expected to be payable. Tax must be paid upon the whole of such an estimate since there is no power to apply to postpone the payment of SDLT for such unascertained consideration.[340] The tax position is recalculated and adjusted when the facts are 'ascertained'. For example, where a lease is granted of a completed building for a premium of £X per square foot of net lettable area[341] there must be a reasonable estimate of the expected premium, tax paid in full and adjusted when the premium is agreed. The most frequent area of difficulty, in practice, is likely to be transfers of going concerns and VAT for reasons set out above (see **4.30**).

4.38.4 Fortune teller tax

The problem with these arrangements for deferred or contingent consideration is that they are intended to deal with many situations relating to the possibility of development value or marriage value. There are situations where land may be sold without the benefit of planning permission but the vendor suspects that such permission could be obtained at some future date. Similarly, there may be situations where the land could be sold on its own but, when combined with adjoining land, or other interests such as tenancies to which the land is subject are acquired, the value of the land will increase significantly. This type of 'hope value' is a key factor.[342] The attempt to arrive at some estimate of the current use and hope value of the land price has been replaced by various forms of deferred consideration. These may be short-term operations such as where additional consideration is payable if the original purchaser disposes of the land within a relatively short period; this involves payment of a proportion of the additional enhancement in the value of the land. Other vendors may require a longer-term participation or slice of any future action. In consequence, where the initial consideration is not related solely to the onward sale of the land by the original purchaser but relates to the fate of the land itself over an extended period of time the liability will not terminate with the disposal of the land. The original purchaser is, therefore, faced with many taxation issues,[343] including a long-term contractual position where, in a sense, the liability for the additional consideration is dependent upon the fate of the land notwithstanding it may no longer owned by the original purchaser. As the original taxpayer's tax liability will not necessarily be closed by the onward sale this means that when negotiating the arrangements the purchaser's advisers need to provide for some form of mechanism whereby while the liability, as it were, follows with the land, the

---

[340] FA 2003, ss.51(4) and 90; Stamp Duty Land Tax (Administration) Regulations 2003, SI 2003/2837, Part 4.

[341] If the arrangement takes effect before the building is completed the consideration will be 'uncertain' when different rules apply.

[342] There are many issues as to how far 'hope value' can now form part of fiscal valuations since the parties do not seek to arrange for a fixed price because of the uncertainties.

[343] Which can also affect the vendor unless the transaction is properly structured; see, for example, *Marren* v. *Ingles* 54 TC 76 (but note the numerous statutory interventions in this area for capital gains tax purposes); *Page* v. *Lowther* [1983] STC 799.

original purchaser or any successors in title who subsequently dispose of the land cease to be contractually liable (see further **4.40**).

In addition, the vendor may be reluctant to accept the second purchaser as the primary debtor in respect of the deferred consideration and seek to impose some form of indemnity or guarantee upon the original vendor. This is clearly unsatisfactory since it leaves the vendor and his estate or its liquidator with an open-ended contractual, albeit conditional, obligation under the guarantee.

4.39 CALCULATION

As with much of routine SDLT, the filing of the initial return (SDLT 1) and payment do not represent finality (see **1.11** and **1.24**). Variable consideration computations work upon initial 'guestimates' with retrospective revisions, provided of course, that the taxpayer has been advised of his outstanding obligations by his professional advisers pursuant to their contractual duties (see e.g. **15.4** and **15.8**). In consequence, as noted above, a minimum of two stages is required:

- the initial estimated return possibly involving an application to postpone part of the tax provisionally payable; and
- a subsequent retrospective return on the basis of the actual events which replaces the estimated figures upon which the original return was based.

4.39.1 Initial calculation

The initial calculation is a strange exercise, even by fiscal standards, since for uncertain or contingent consideration it involves a considerable element of trying to forecast the future and even for unascertained consideration or rents it requires what is essentially a prediction of the ultimate outcome of negotiations, which may not be between the parties to the transaction.[344] It is not simply a question of how much the taxpayer thinks that he may have to pay, which may be nil because it is unlikely that the obligation will arise. This is because there are two components:

- how likely it is that the purchaser will have to pay further consideration; and
- upon the assumption that such a liability arises, the amount which it is expected will be payable.

It seems that HMRC Stamp Taxes does not regard the former as a relevant issue; it is concerned only with the latter question of the amount potentially payable. The taxpayer cannot take the view that it is unlikely that anything will ever be payable; he must act on the basis that if, no matter how unlikely it is, the obligation arises, money will be payable and it is this sum that matters. In the case of a contingent sum,

---

[344] Such as where a reversionary interest is sold where there is a review of the rent of the lease in progress between the landlord and the tenant not necessarily involving the assignee of the reversion.

since there is a fixed amount, guesswork is not required; for unascertained consideration the amount which is currently under negotiation will be reasonably firm in that there may be negotiations and a fact basis, but the ultimate outcome is still to a degree a matter of guesswork.

For uncertain consideration there is no such safety net. Any figures will be purely speculation, both as to the possibility of payment and, especially, the amount thereof. No doubt if the taxpayer prepares the return upon the basis that the additional consideration will never become payable and this proves to be a correct assumption, no tax will have been lost, but HMRC Stamp Taxes may seek other penalties for incorrect returns. If money does become payable, the taxpayer will have under-declared the tax and will be liable to late payment interest as from 30 days after the effective date and possibly penalties for an incorrectly, i.e. negligently, prepared land transaction return. The taxpayer's professional advisers are also exposed to a penalty of £3,000 if they have helped the taxpayer to prepare the land transaction return without explaining these issues or being aware that appropriate advice has not been obtained.

Some of the issues around uncertain consideration can be adequately dealt with by proper planning. Clearly a figure must be included in the land transaction return (SDLT 1) and taken into account in fixing the applicable rate. However, if an amount is included for the variable payment, the tax thereon may be postponed. In such a case the interest runs only from 30 days after the later instalment of the consideration becomes payable.[345] The problems of interest arise only if there is more tax payable than the amount deferred. Parties should therefore:

- include a generous estimate of the total consideration in Box 10 of SDLT 1;
- show the full amount of tax payable upon that sum in Box 14;
- enter the figure for only the tax upon the actual initial consideration in Box 15;
- complete SDLT 4; and
- make an application to defer the payment.

The deferral does not affect the tax payable upon the basic price which might be subject to a higher rate of tax. Any additional tax so paid can be recovered should the additional sum not become payable or for any reason the rate of tax applicable falls below the rate taken into account in the initial return.

A severe practical difficulty exists in relation to preparing the initial 'reasonable' estimate of future payments,[346] particularly when the payment is linked to an event many years in the future, such as a percentage of the increase on the market value should planning permission be obtained at any time in the 80 years following completion. It will also be noted that these wait-and-see rules are based upon estimates of future values and planning permission or future rents. Professional advisers are rightly refusing to make such predictions and the HMRC Stamp Taxes helpline is giving out the risky advice to use the current values or rents and ignore

---

[345] FA 2003, s.91.
[346] These problems also apply to the need to predict future movements in the rent and related rates of VAT upon rents reserved by leases.

the variable element. Such advice cannot be relied upon and leaves the taxpayer exposed to penalties and interest for a negligent return because he has either not made any attempt to 'guestimate' the future figures or not taken proper steps to produce a reasonable estimate, i.e. notwithstanding the helpline advice, the tax-payer *prima facie* has not sought up-to-date independent professional advice[347] and thus will be penalised.[348] As Russell LJ stated[349] in relation to estimating the market value of shares yet to be issued, 'the parties must do the best they can'; scarcely a scientific or reasonable basis for a tax system with a harsh compliance regime. A crude but hopefully acceptable approach for HMRC Stamp Taxes is to take reasonable evidence of the impact of the planning permission for the relevant event at current values and to project this figure into the future at an inflation indexed amount plus, say, 5 per cent. This ignores the existing problems of the planning permission being unobtainable and the possibility of resale but these have to be ignored in making the self-assessment of the tax.

Moreover, where there are two separate effective dates for the transaction (see **3.3**) there will be two separate estimated returns[350] but only the second will require adjustment since the second estimated return will replace, with credit, the original return.[351]

4.39.2 Subsequent notifications

This initial calculation (or two calculations where there is a separate completion) unfortunately constitutes only the first steps in a long, tedious and expensive process. As and when all or any part or instalment of the variable consideration is ascertained and falls due for payment, the purchaser must submit a new land transaction return and pay the postponed tax relevant to the amount involved.[352] Where the consideration is 'contingent', i.e. a fixed amount so that the maximum figure will be known in advance, there are none of the problems of the original provisional 'guestimate' requirements of the legislation. The figure will be known. This means that if the contingency happens and the tax has been deferred the tax upon the contingent sum will be payable but without interest where the deferral arrangements apply.[353] If the tax has not been deferred and has been paid in full then there will be nothing further to do other than to notify HMRC Stamp Taxes that the event has happened and the tax file can be closed. If the correct procedure has not been adopted in relation to the inclusion of the contingent sum in the chargeable

---

[347] Which is frequently not available because prudent professional advisers do not risk negligence claims and refuse to participate in guessing games.

[348] It might be a question of a tax-related penalty.

[349] *Crane Fruehauf* v. *IRC* [1975] STC 51.

[350] But the basis for the estimates may change because the status of the consideration has changed between the two dates; see **4.38**.

[351] However the date of the ruling estimated return in these circumstances, i.e. whether the first or the second provisional return is the 'proper' return, may be relevant for the purpose of reliefs and other matters in many contexts.

[352] FA 2003, s.80.

[353] FA 2003, s.87(3)(b).

consideration and the tax dealt with accordingly and, provided that the taxpayer has been warned of the risks and obligations associated with non-payment, the tax will become due and payable together with any interest or penalties for not dealing with the situation correctly on the filing of the initial return. Where tax has been paid and not deferred there will be an entitlement to a refund. In some situations the existence of the contingent sum may have taken the provisional chargeable consideration above a relevant threshold producing a higher rate of SDLT. In these situations where a rate has been applied to the basic price that is higher than the rate that would have applied had the contingent sum not been relevant the taxpayer may be entitled to a refund in respect of the basic price because the lower rate is applicable. It will be noted that in these situations where a higher rate is applicable because of a further consideration, it is not possible to defer the higher rate of tax upon the basic price; this must be dealt with by a claim for a refund together with any interest that may be appropriate. Where the tax has not been postponed the estimated figures will require adjustment with additional tax payable with interest should the initial return be too low or a possible refund with interest if the taxpayer can establish that there was an initial overestimate. If the amount deferred exceeds the estimated figure for which the tax was postponed that excess will be taxable together with interest running from 30 days after the effective date; if the amount deferred exceeds the tax chargeable no interest will arise. This process and the number of returns required will depend upon the drafting and machinery contained in the contract for the payment of these amounts.

Professional advisers will need to take these issues into consideration when negotiating the arrangements, particularly as this can have a significant effect upon the client's cash flow and costs. For example, in relation to a residential development involving the construction of numerous houses or blocks of flats, if the overage takes the form of a single payment when the final proceeds or profit of the development are agreed, then only one additional land transaction return will be required at the end of the project. However, if the overage takes the form of a payment equal to a specified percentage of the sale proceeds of each house in excess of a target figure, then when each house is sold or each flat let and an instalment of the additional or overage consideration can be calculated and becomes due and payable, the developer will be required to make a fresh return, recalculate the tax and file and pay accordingly[354] (i.e. there will be a land transaction return for each house from the purchaser or lessee dealing with his outstanding liability for the original purchase or lease of the land).

---

[354] FA 2003, s.80. There are at present no proposals for periodical block returns from developers faced with multiple reporting and payment obligations.

4.40   EXIT STRATEGIES

It will be noted that the taxation position may remain open for many years, particularly given the current tendency to seek clawback arrangements that as a matter of the terms of the contract may extend over an 80-year period. For instance, there may be an arrangement whereby if certain events occur in relation to the land in question during a period of up to 80 years from the specified date, regardless of whether the chargeable interest is within the ownership or control of the 'purchaser' in the original transaction, additional consideration equal to a specified percentage of the proceeds or 'profits' of the transaction, or of the increase in the value of the land (which is hopefully defined by the agreement), will be payable by the original 'purchaser' or lessee to the original vendor. This type of arrangement represents serious practical problems over and above the SDLT issues. It seems to arise because valuers cannot handle the issue of 'hope value', marriage value or nuisance value and the courts (perhaps without a full understanding of the practical issues especially the tax and commercial consequences involved) have held that, notwithstanding the extremely complex tax issues involved for both the vendor and the purchaser[355] the vendor's advisers must use reasonable endeavours to obtain a clawback or similar possible additional payment.[356] There is, in consequence, for the purchaser or lessee as party to the original transaction an open tax position which may continue for up to 80 years plus any extensions available to HMRC Stamp Taxes to issue assessments, etc. for a further 21 years. This means that a liquidator of a company[357] or the personal representative of a deceased may not be able to close the liquidation or administration of the estate because the overage or other provisional tax arrangements are unresolved as matters of contract. Also since the contractual payment cannot be determined the tax position cannot be closed leaving a potential debt against the company or the estate. Furthermore in numerous situations the open or provisional SDLT position of the original taxpayer is by statute passed to any persons acquiring the chargeable interest.[358]

Apart from the special provisions passing certain of the outstanding obligations relating to lease premiums and rent (but not variable payments relating to earlier assignments of the lease), the original taxpayer remains liable for the tax, notwithstanding that he no longer owns the interest, unless the position is renegotiated at the time of the sale. There are various practical consequences and each solution has its own set of problems.

---

[355]   See e.g. *Page* v. *Lowther* [1983] STC 799; *Marren* v. *Ingles* [1980] STC 500.

[356]   *Akasuc Enterprise* v. *Farmar* [2003] PL SCS 127.

[357]   On the need for suitable warranties when purchasing shares in a company which may be affected by such a provisional SDLT situation, see **Chapter 13**.

[358]   But without making it clear whether this releases the original taxpayer and leaves the third party solely liable and in need of a contractual indemnity (with a counter indemnity for windfall refunds) or produces a joint and several liability with implied indemnities. Unfortunately the drafting points strongly towards the former situation, leaving third parties seriously exposed; see **8.61**.

4.40.1 Novation

Essentially the original contract for purchase should contain some form of effective novation arrangement whereby the original purchaser or his successors will cease to be liable when they cease to own the land provided that they obtain from the second or subsequent purchasers an undertaking to make the payment if the events happen during their period of ownership. This could take the form of a draft deed of undertaking attached to the original contract to be signed by the second or subsequent purchasers of the property. This means that provided that the appropriate deed of undertaking is executed by the transferee of the property, the relevant party ceases to be contractually liable and once the contractual liability ends the deferred taxation liability ends. This may mean that the party becomes entitled to a tax refund or, where the tax has been effectively postponed, his liability to pay the additional tax ceases because no further consideration is payable under the contingency arrangements. The latter set of circumstances may merely require a simple notification to HMRC Stamp Taxes cancelling the postponed tax arrangements because no tax can become payable.

4.40.2 Undertakings and indemnities

Unless he somehow negotiates the passing of the liability to the purchaser in such a way as to cancel his own outstanding tax liability (an exit strategy), the original taxpayer will require undertakings to supply information so as to be able to complete the notification and payment obligations as the deferred consideration becomes payable. Alternative arrangements might be possible where these safeguards have not been built into the arrangements, such as an express novation, although in these circumstances vendors and their advisers tend to be somewhat nervous about the larger taxation implications of the release of the first purchaser's undertaking to make the payment, since this may have been a taxable event in its own right and may have other consequences.

An indemnity from the third party will leave the taxpayer's contractual obligation unchanged and so his tax position remains unaffected. He will, however, need suitable undertakings from the third party and his successors in title to keep him informed of events over the relevant period.[359] On the other hand, a novation of the liability will bring his tax liability to an end without further payment since he will not be making any payment pursuant to the original contract.[360]

---

[359] There is no statutory power to demand such information; it is left to commercial negotiation. It is unclear at present how far HMRC Stamp Taxes expects the taxpayer to police future events.

[360] Moreover, such onward movements of the property are likely to have SDLT problems even where the original contract or transfer was subject to stamp duty because, for example, it was entered into prior to 1 December 2003.

4.40.3 'Cascade of covenants'

It is sometimes suggested that there could be a 'cascade of covenants' whereby the second purchaser covenants to make the payment to the first purchaser and/or to supply all information that is necessary in order to enable the first purchaser to deal with his obligations as regards the original vendor and HMRC Stamp Taxes. This is totally unsatisfactory in practice since it means that the original purchaser or any other relevant party in the chain or cascade of covenants remains contractually liable and therefore for example his business or estate cannot be finally liquidated or distributed. It also means that the tax position is compounded since each party will be liable for the tax in these circumstances. It is, therefore, an essential part of the professional adviser's obligation not merely to use reasonable endeavours to obtain a covenant but also when acting for the counterparty to ensure that there is a workable arrangement for dealing with the property or dealing with the estate or business of the first purchaser and his successors in due course.

In the case of a cascade of covenants each party will remain contractually liable to make the payment with a debt outstanding against his estate and a related taxation liability even though the tax may have been postponed. Additionally, the liability of the initial purchaser and any subsequent purchasers is likely to depend upon actions of other parties. Their fate is in the hands of any subsequent purchaser or lessee of the property in respect of transactions to which they are not parties and which may occur long after they have died. This will require a further cascade of covenants. In addition to the need to cascade the covenant which simply multiplies the tax charge for each stage of the transaction since the consideration will be payable up the chain instead of directly to the original vendor, it will be necessary for each purchaser who sells on to require an undertaking from his immediate purchaser to notify him of any relevant event.[361]

4.40.4 Renegotiating with original vendor

Ideally, the original contract should contain an exit strategy as an integral part of the arrangements. The clawback arrangements should provide that the party is liable only while he holds the property, provided that he obtains suitable undertakings in the form of a deed from his successor in title and so on down the line. In this situation the obligation to pay additional consideration will terminate and with it the related taxation liability, although the second purchaser and so on will have his own particular tax problems which will need to be resolved in due course. Where, as is frequently the case in respect of old covenants of this nature, there is no built-in exit strategy it may be necessary for the first purchaser or his successor to approach the original vendor with a view to renegotiating the contract. The structuring of such exit arrangements becomes more complex where the variable consideration arises in connection with the grant (as opposed to the assignment) of a lease. It is

---

[361] This may require entries upon the land register in order to ensure that any appropriate dealings with the land are notified.

provided[362] that these liabilities to deal with deferred consideration become the obligations of any assignee of the lease. In effect, the tax liability runs with the land.[363] It is unclear whether the effect of these provisions is to release the original taxpayer from all obligations as regards the unwinding of the consideration or whether there is some form of joint and several liability. In consequence, there is no statutory provision providing any form of assignment and taxpayers who will be affected by this and will need to investigate it as part of their due diligence and title requisitions are forced to rely upon contractual indemnities.[364]

Regrettably, attempts to deal with the situation are being met with nervousness or obtuseness by the original vendor's advisers who are afraid that the original valuations may be challenged or negligent and, more in an attempt to cover themselves rather than protect the client,[365] may insist that any such reasonable attempt to deal with the situation takes the form of a novation involving the release of the original obligation and the re-imposition of a similar obligation upon the third party with the start of a fresh 80-year period and an indemnity against any tax which may affect the vendor. Since such an indemnity will usually be required from the initial purchaser, his estate is not relieved of a contractual liability, so that the long-term issue remains. He has merely replaced one liability with another for the same period.[366] This exposes the new purchaser to a charge of SDLT upon the variable or clawback amount because as part of the chargeable consideration he is assuming an uncertain liability, but it means that the original taxpayer can inform HMRC Stamp Taxes that as far as he is concerned the amount in question will not become payable and close his provisional tax position.

4.40.5 Requirement for delivery of complete SDLT history

Where the liability for the outstanding deferred consideration and outstanding tax passes effectively to the purchaser of the interest, whether pursuant to statute or

---

[362] FA 2003, s.81A and Sched.17A, para.12.

[363] Unfortunately, HMRC Stamp Taxes has not seen fit to include in the legislation provisions dealing with the nature of these arrangements.

[364] There may not be any form of implied indemnity. Although in some situations there is an indemnity where one person is obliged to make a payment in respect of some other person's liability this would not apply in the present situation. The effect of the legislation is that the third party is meeting his own liability which may be his alone and not some form of joint liability with the original taxpayer in respect of which he could expect to be reimbursed.

[365] Professional advisers acting for the vendor or landlord in such cases must also consider their position in relation to e.g. the administration of the vendor's estate. There will be an asset in the form of the chose in action representing the right to the deferred payment, which will have to be valued for inheritance and other tax purposes and appropriated or assented in the administration of the estate with potential tax charges upon the beneficiary in due course. Liquidators and receivers of companies who are not advised upon how to deal with such assets will also face potential claims should they dissolve the company before assigning or otherwise dealing with such rights to payment, and the tax consequences thereof.

[366] There may also be issues in any particular case as to whether the arrangements relating to the additional consideration involve a chargeable interest (FA 2003, s.48(1)(b); see **2.12**). The release of this for a consideration is, in itself, a chargeable transaction (FA 2003, s.43(3)).

otherwise such as by assignment of a lease,[367] the purchaser may need to negotiate for the delivery of the complete SDLT history of the lease so that he can deal with any possible future reporting and/or notification obligations.

Notwithstanding that the SDLT in respect of the vendor's outstanding tax liability relating to his acquisition does not pass with the land, there may be circumstances where subsequent purchasers need to have the SDLT history passed to them. For example, although the SDLT upon the initial grant of a lease with a variable rent will normally be resolved after the fifth year of the lease,[368] an assignee of the lease even after that date will need the SDLT history of the lease. In order to determine whether any subsequent increase in the rent is an abnormal increase which is measured by reference to the assumed rent and not the passing rent,[369] the assignee will need to have details of the assumed rent, i.e. the highest 12 months' rent paid during the first five years.

4.41 SUBSEQUENT SALES OF THE PROPERTY

Where, as will often be the case,[370] the initial tax assessment is provisional only and is subject to adjustment notwithstanding that the original land transaction return has been the subject of an Enquiry and agreed by HMRC Stamp Taxes (which is merely to the effect that attempts at reasonable estimates have been made and does not mean that the final tax position has been resolved), there will be an outstanding liability for the original purchaser when he comes to deal with the land. As a contractual or commercial matter this needs to be dealt with as part of the negotiations for the sale of the property in the context of his contractual obligations to the original vendor.[371] Legislative arrangements provide, *inter alia*, that where a lease is granted for a variable premium or variable rent, the SDLT obligations as to payment and reporting pass to the assignee.[372] The legislation does not make it clear whether this is a sole liability of the assignee with the assignor being released from liability or whether it is a joint and several liability. Prudence suggests that assignees should ask for an express indemnity in the contract.

Unfortunately, no such statutory provision exists in relation to transfers or chargeable interests subject to such variable consideration which arose otherwise than in connection with the grant of leases. For example, upon transfers of freeholds or leases purchased with such a consideration it remains essentially the liability of

---

[367] FA 2003, Sched.17A, para.11.
[368] FA 2003, Sched.17A, paras.7 and 8 bearing in mind the effect of a delayed 'grant'; para.12A see **Chapter 8**.
[369] FA 2003, Sched.17A, paras.14 and 15.
[370] Which may also include risks of additional liability by reason of the linked transaction rules.
[371] Attempts to attach the overage or clawback to the land as some form of restrictive covenant or other arrangement is not likely to be successful since the original vendor may not have any adjacent land of sufficient size (ransom strips are probably not adequate for these purposes) to be the dominant land benefiting from the right.
[372] FA 2003, s.81A and Sched.17A, para.12.

the initial purchaser or tenant of the land in question.[373] This means that when the initial purchaser or tenant assigns the lease or sublets the property he must consider both the impact of the transaction upon the obligation itself and, if this continues notwithstanding the immediate transaction, the implications of attempts to pass on the original contractual arrangements with the original vendor or landlord to the third party who will in consequence have complex SDLT issues of his own to resolve as 'a purchaser'. Where the onward sale triggers the liability to pay the additional consideration, the original purchaser must retrospectively recalculate the tax upon the basis of the actual figure and pay any additional tax falling due or claim a refund if tax has been overpaid. Usually, however, the taxpayer will have deferred the liability to pay.[374] In such a case the postponement will cease and the appropriate amount of tax will have to be paid. Where the final figure is below the estimated figure there will be no penalty or interest;[375] but if the estimate is below the final payment interest will be due upon the excess over the estimated figure.[376]

4.42 REVERSE PAYMENTS

As a general principle of the law of contract, consideration must move from the promisee. In consequence, promises or undertakings by the promisor (i.e. vendor or lessor of the chargeable interest) cannot be consideration for the acquisition of the interest of which he has promised to dispose. Nevertheless those responsible for the legislation prepared it on the bizarre basis that the undertakings of the vendor can be chargeable consideration.[377] Reliefs have been provided on the basis that such a charge can exist.

Reverse payments (i.e. sums paid by the assignor to the assignee of a lease as an inducement for the assignee to enter into the assignment, or by a landlord as an inducement to the tenant to take the lease or by a tenant to the landlord as an incentive to accept an early surrender of the lease) are not chargeable consideration. These sums include[378] traditional types of payments moving from the assignor to the assignee in relation to the assignment of a lease, such as where there are dilapidations that have to be dealt with, or the current rent exceeds the market rent

---

[373] This may cause considerable practical difficulties for personal representatives and liquidators and receivers who cannot complete their administration while the contractual and SDLT positions remain unresolved. Specific statutory provisions apply to the assignment of leases with such built-in liability.

[374] FA 2003, s.90; Stamp Duty Land Tax (Administration) Regulations 2003, SI 2003/2837.

[375] FA 2003, s.87(6).

[376] FA 2003, s.87(3)(b) referring only to the relief for the tax deferred.

[377] For example, the abortive attempt to charge upon building works for works carried out by the vendor or landlord was believed by HMRC Stamp Taxes to be effective because the works were consideration for the disposal, i.e. the landlord provided consideration for his disposal. This reverse consideration concept has been applied by HMRC Stamp Taxes to promises by landlords or developers to pay the purchaser's costs and SDLT and because it is consideration provided in the open market it enhances the market value of the chargeable interest.

[378] FA 2003, Sched.4, para.16 and Sched.17A, para.18.

for equivalent premises, or the terms of the lease are particularly onerous or restrictive. The need for such payments has been increased by the introduction of SDLT to deal with cases such as the assignment of leases where these are to be taxed as if they were the grant of a new lease.[379] Consequently, the assignee's advisers will require a contribution towards the additional cost of acquiring the lease as compared with adjacent premises,[380] or because there are significant long-term difficulties of SDLT associated with variable rents and the assignee requires some protection against the problems arising because of the terms of the lease when granted. These difficulties include overage and clawback provisions. Failure to deal with such issues upon the assignment and to take account of the many other taxation problems which may affect the assignee will expose the advisers to justifiable claims for breach of professional duty.

---

[379] FA 2003, Sched.17A, para.11; see **8.61**.

[380] In these cases the lease may have a negative value, an important point when valuing assets or the shares in companies holding such leases.

CHAPTER 5

Exemptions and reliefs

5.1 EXEMPTIONS: BACKGROUND

It is the view of HMRC generally, not just HMRC Stamp Taxes, that exemptions from tax of a general nature are a 'bad thing'.[1] The attitude seems to be that exemptions are a springboard for wholesale mitigation of tax, and that merely claiming the benefit of a relief in accordance with the legislation is tantamount to tax avoidance, and borders on fraudulent evasion.[2]

In consequence, any reliefs from SDLT are of a highly focused and technical nature. Some reliefs are essentially simply ineffective reliefs,[3] or appear to be 'political gimmicks' such as disadvantaged land relief,[4] zero carbon homes and the unworkable first time buyer relief (which is a major problem for professional advisers where there are many highly restrictive conditions for eligibility and the costs of testing the client's eligibility are disproportionate). Other reliefs are usually hedged about by numerous anti-avoidance provisions including general anti-avoidance provisions[5] so that the reliefs are rarely available in practice. The conditions for the relief must be scrupulously considered and observed when implementing the transaction providing both short- and long-term problems and serious complications for investigations of title and due diligence. In order to avoid

---

[1] There is increasing legislation restricting reliefs where they are part of a tax avoidance arrangement; see e.g. FA 2003, Sched.7 (as amended); see **Chapter 12**.

[2] For example, during the less than satisfactory consultation process prior to the introduction of SDLT a senior representative of HMRC described the utilisation of the 200-year-old subsale relief in general and 'resting on contract' as a criminal offence moving on from the comments of the then Chancellor of the Exchequer in 1986 that a necessary relief from the cascade effect of stamp taxes was an unacceptable 'loophole' for share transactions.

[3] This may become a principle of statutory construction. The author was involved in a case where a claim for a newly introduced tax relief was submitted. The Inspector urged that when introducing the relief the Chancellor had stated that the cost of the relief would be £X, so as claims in excess of that figure had already been received the claim was inadmissible and the relief would not be allocated proportionately among the claimants – this becomes an exercise in first come first served.

[4] Such political gimmick reliefs are usually on the basis that few, if any, taxpayers will qualify as with first time buyer relief and zero carbon homes or are available for an extremely limited period; they are likely to be of a temporary nature and will be repealed if taxpayers actually benefit, i.e. tax is lost (as with disadvantaged areas relief which was removed earlier than the original projected date).

[5] FA 2003, ss.75A–75C (as amended).

suggestions of fraud or failure to report 'tax avoidance schemes' in routine commercial transactions for which the relief was intended, it will be essential to ensure so far as possible that the background to the transaction is properly and contemporaneously documented.

As a general point, the possibility that certain aspects of the tax may be unlawful pursuant to European law or human rights legislation must not be overlooked.

5.2 'EXEMPTION' AND 'RELIEF': TERMINOLOGY AND CONCEPTS

This approach has produced bizarre drafting in FA 2003 which is particularly significant, raising acute problems in relation to questions of reliefs from SDLT. Not only does the one-size-fits-all plain English drafting provide relief for a wholly new set of transactions which were not exempt from stamp duty, such as leases granted in connection with divorce or variations of estates of deceased individuals (see **5.7.2.3** and **5.7.2.4**) or possibly in connection with company reconstructions, but there are a variety of words setting out the ways in which a transaction is relieved in whole or in part from the charge to tax. In other words, there is no consistency in the legislation to situations where the full charge to SDLT is not imposed and/or the compliance obligations are modified.[6] Relief may, for example, also take the form that any actual consideration is not to be treated as chargeable consideration (such as actual consideration being treated as 'nil' or 'exempt', or to be ignored).[7] The strange terminology adopted means that the precise nature of the relieving legislation and, in particular, the compliance consequences of the relieving provision, will have to be carefully noted. Certain exemptions provide for relief from the notification obligation and the transaction can be submitted to the Land Registry unsupported by a Revenue certificate (SDLT 5);[8] in other cases the transaction is notifiable even though exempt.[9] For example, a relief where the actual consideration is ignored or treated as 'nil' means that there is no chargeable consideration so that the transaction is not notifiable and not taxable.[10] Unfortunately, the policy is not consistent, in that even in respect of those exemptions where there is a relief from notification, there are exclusions giving rise to notification obligations such as disadvantaged land and private finance initiative (PFI) projects.[11] Since reliefs take

---

[6] FA 2003, s.77A.

[7] There are, in these cases, issues relating to the linked transaction rules, depending upon the difference between actual consideration being ignored or treated as 'exempt', i.e. the latter has to be aggregated whereas the former does not. Notification obligations where the level of consideration is involved are also affected by the outcome of the debate on these issues.

[8] Although certain employees of the Land Registry dispute this analysis in practice (largely those reliefs contained in FA 2003, Sched.3); see **1.12.3**.

[9] FA 2003, s.77 (as amended).

[10] FA 2003, Sched.3, para.1; s.77A

[11] See e.g. FA 2003, Sched.6, para.13; Sched.4, para.17(4A) (as amended).

a variety of forms, there is no general principle; it is necessary to check the notification obligations which are scattered randomly throughout the legislation and regulations.

Often terms are used to provide a relief from the tax, apart from the provisions fixing the rate; but such terms must be construed in context because they cannot always be regarded as bearing their normal 'plain English' meaning. The list includes:

- ignored;
- disregarded;[12]
- consideration treated as nil or exempt; or
- a special rate is applied.

5.3 RELIEFS AND ANTI-AVOIDANCE

This dislike of exemptions and reliefs is also reflected in the complex anti-avoidance rules applicable to the individual reliefs which, in many cases, means that, consistent with the lack of finality of the tax in general, the relief is available initially only on a provisional basis. This arises because of the form that relief takes. Rather than submitting a claim for relief, the taxpayer prepares his land transaction return (SDLT 1) upon the basis that the relief is available and waits for HMRC Stamp Taxes to challenge the return in an Enquiry[13] or to make a discovery and issue an assessment after the expiration of the Enquiry period.[14]

The issues for the professional adviser are not merely the conditions that have to be satisfied before the relief can be taken into account in making the initial self-assessment, they also include provisions cancelling the relief, such as a clawback if certain events happen within a prescribed time period after the effective date. They also take the form of special charges upon subsequent dealings in the chargeable interest.[15] These provisions generally apply on an objective basis. The mere fact of the transaction occurring is sufficient to trigger the tax liability; there is no subjective element requiring some tax avoidance purpose or motive, and there is no need for any causal link between the exempt transactions and the anti-avoidance charge, which frequently falls upon unsuspecting third parties. Even routine commercial transactions are potentially vulnerable, notwithstanding that they are not connected with the relief being clawed back. Since these anti-avoidance provisions can affect third parties, the absence of any need for tax avoidance motives and, in

---

[12]   FA 2003. s.45(3); but note the bizarre meaning that this term must bear as a consequence of the statutory general anti-avoidance provisions and the attitude of HMRC Stamp Taxes to subsales.

[13]   Title is registerable and registration once obtained is not affected by a successful challenge by HMRC Stamp Taxes; but certain employees in the Land Registry claim that their local discretion empowers them to investigate the claim for relief. This claim, which seems to be developing into a consistent overall policy of requisitioning whenever certain reliefs are taken by the applicant, is unfounded, because it requires greater powers than those conferred upon HMRC Stamp Taxes.

[14]   FA 2003, Sched.10, paras.28 and following; see **18.13**.

[15]   FA 2003, Sched.17A, para.12; s.81A.

some cases, the absence of any time limit upon the occurrence of the offending arrangement, means that a taxpayer is vulnerable to traps as is a third party dealing with the taxpayer, such as a person purchasing the shares in or the business of a company.

It is, therefore, necessary to determine why the transaction is 'exempt' and the effect upon notification obligations.

5.4 'EXEMPT'

The word 'exempt'[16] has given rise to problems in relation to stamp duty over many years. On a broad view, a transaction is 'exempt' if it falls altogether outside the charge to tax[17] such as the grant of a simple licence to use or occupy land which is not a chargeable interest;[18] or it could mean a transaction that would be a chargeable transaction but for a specific relieving provision. Given the subtleties, or ineptness, of the drafting and the implications turning upon such 'plain English' terminology, this is an area where taxpayers need to tread warily and, no doubt, much cost will be incurred before the pitfalls have been identified and can be routinely dealt with in practice without the related penalties and interest.

Although the approach is not supported by the legislation, this chapter will refer to transactions as 'exempt' where they either fall outside the scope of the tax or are excluded from the tax and notification obligations; and refer to 'reliefs' for transactions that are within the charge to tax but there is either no actual charge to tax or a reduced charge to tax although the transaction remains a notifiable transaction.

5.5 PROCEDURE: 'CLAIMING AN EXEMPTION'

HMRC Stamp Taxes refers to the process as 'claiming' an exemption; but this is a misleading description of the process. It is important to note that, unlike the stamp duty regime, where adjudication is frequently required in order to obtain an exemption or mitigation of a charge in respect of a particular instrument, there is no equivalent procedure for SDLT and the position has been completely revised. It is no longer a case of asking HMRC Stamp Taxes to confirm that the relief is available[19] through the adjudication process; the taxpayer has to take the decision as

---

[16] This is recognised to some extent by the legislation such as FA 2003, s.77A which deals with situations where no tax is payable for notification purposes, dividing it into different categories, so that notification depends upon why no tax is payable.

[17] But see *IRC* v. *Henry Ansbacher* [1963] AC 191.

[18] This is a potential problem because tenancies at will are stated to be not chargeable interests (FA 2003, s.48); but for other purposes are treated as a form of yearly tenancy (FA 2003, Sched.17A, para.3).

[19] Asking for a post-transaction ruling does not produce finality, and, if a land transaction return has been filed this automatically in practice becomes a full tardy and expensive Enquiry. Even an Enquiry is not final since a discovery assessment can be issued after an Enquiry.

to whether the relief applies and take the risk of the enhanced penalty and interest regime[20] should HMRC Stamp Taxes disagree with this view in performing its downgraded role as auditor of tax returns in the course of an Enquiry. There has been a significant outsourcing of resources, cost and risk in this area from HMRC Stamp Taxes to the professions. As the tax is based upon self-assessment,[21] the taxpayer and his advisers must take a reasoned view of the transaction[22] and decide whether the relief is available. The taxpayer will then complete the return and take this view into account by not accounting for tax in whole or in part. No doubt details of this taking rather than claiming of the relief will require the making of appropriate entries in the land transaction return.[23]

This need for a reasoned view of the relief imposes a new area of professional risk and a potentially significant extension of professional duties, because of the need to make the decision *ab initio* and the structure of penalties for errors has changed dramatically. The penalty for error is no longer a short delay during adjudication but a risk of penalties upon a virtually unlimited time basis because of the decision taken.[24] On lack of finality, see **1.11**, **1.24** and **1.25**.

5.6 REDUCED RATES

In certain cases the relief takes the form of a lower rate of tax, as follows.

5.6.1 Small transactions

There are nil and lower rates for transactions below certain levels of chargeable consideration including rent; and there is a slightly higher nil rate threshold for land in disadvantaged areas where this is still available because of the transitional reliefs, but the nil rate does not apply for lease premiums for non-residential property where

---

[20] The parties must submit the return upon the basis that they think the relief is available and take their chances with Enquiries and penalties for incorrect returns in due course. The important principle to bear in mind is that it is essential to have well-documented records of the steps taken to decide upon the availability of the relief.

[21] FA 2003, s.76(3)(a).

[22] And it will be important to keep records of the debates concerning the issue of the availability of the exemption. Failure to keep such records will mean that there will not be any contemporaneous evidence either that the issues were considered or for the basis for the decision being taken, which will mean that there is a significant risk that a claim for penalties in respect of the submission of a negligent return will be made. It will be necessary to establish that such a review took place and to show that the issues were fully and properly considered. The absence of contemporaneous records will make it extremely difficult to substantiate these points.

[23] Various codes exist for identifying the exemption taken or claimed but as it is not easy for the prescribed forms to be amended the modification of the scope of exemptions will require increasing utilisation of the code for other exemptions. This makes it extremely easy for HMRC Stamp Taxes to make a discovery because there is no disclosure of the information behind this entry (see *Langham* v. *Veltema* [2004] STC 544).

[24] The time limits may be affected by negligence which can apply to errors in the legal analysis and in the preparation of the data for inclusion in the return as well as to the preparation of the return itself.

the rent exceeds £1,000 per annum.[25] These lower rates are subject to the linked transaction rules which make the initial self-assessments provisional only and subject to subsequent review.

5.6.2 Company reconstructions

There is a very prescribed relief for company reconstructions which will rarely be available for taxpayers.[26]

There is a narrowly defined reduced rate of 0.5 per cent for certain corporate reorganisations known as 'acquisitions relief'.[27] The conditions for these reliefs are not so strict. Unfortunately both reliefs are subject to forfeiture retrospectively if certain events occur, notwithstanding that the original transaction and the trigger event for the clawback are not connected by any planning motive or purpose.

5.6.3 Collective enfranchisement

Where there is a qualifying collective enfranchisement by tenants, the tax is charged at an average rate.[28] A similar relief applies to Scottish crofters.[29]

5.7 OUTSIDE THE TAX

This section deals with transactions that are not subject to tax and are not, in general, notifiable.

5.7.1 Exempt property

The tax applies only where there is the acquisition of a chargeable interest.[30] The definition of chargeable interest provides for 'exempt interests', i.e. those interests in property which are not subject to the charge (see further **2.12**). These are:

- any security interest, which means an interest or right (other than a rent charge) held for the purpose of securing the payment of money or the performance of any other obligation;[31]
- a licence to use or occupy land;[32]

---

[25]   FA 2003, Sched.5, paras.9 and 9A; for shared ownership transactions see FA 2003, Sched.9, para.2(4A).

[26]   FA 2003, Sched.7, para.8; see **Chapter 13**.

[27]   FA 2003, Sched.7, Part 2; see **Chapter 13**.

[28]   FA 2003, s.74.

[29]   FA 2003, s.75.

[30]   FA 2003, s.43(1).

[31]   FA 2003, s.48(2)(a) and (3)(a).

[32]   FA 2003, s.48(2)(b).

- in England and Wales or Northern Ireland, a tenancy at will, an advowson, franchise or manor;[33]
- land held by a financial institution as part of alternative finance arrangements.[34]

5.7.2 Chargeable property: exempt and non-notifiable

There are situations where the transaction is 'exempt' from SDLT and there is no basic obligation to report the transaction,[35] although specific provisions require notification for certain transactions where no tax arises, including: transactions involving non-residential land in disadvantaged areas (which still apply on a transitional basis);[36] dealings between partnerships and connected persons;[37] transactions between persons and connected companies[38] and certain PFI projects.

5.7.2.1 Transactions where there is no chargeable consideration

The exemption where there is no chargeable consideration[39] appears to be a wide one and it is fundamental to possible non-filing of a land transaction return (SDLT 1)[40] since it would appear to apply not only to gifts or appointments or advances by trustees or distributions by liquidators but also to situations where there is actual consideration which is stated by the legislation to be not 'chargeable consideration'. There are situations where there is no actual consideration unless some deemed consideration rules apply to override the relief (e.g. in respect of connected companies or the special regime for partnerships). The exemption also applies where there is actual consideration which is ignored, such as by being treated as non-chargeable in some form or is treated as nil.

The basic relief will be in respect of gifts including dividends *in specie*[41] and returns of capital.[42] It also covers assents by personal representatives[43] and most distributions by liquidators of companies.[44] It can now apply to certain gifts of property subject to a mortgage (see **4.34**) but this will remain a problem for liquidators since these will usually require some form of indemnity from the

---

[33] FA 2003, s.48(2)(c).

[34] FA 2003, s.73C.

[35] FA 2003, s.77A.

[36] FA 2003, Sched.6, para.4.

[37] FA 2003, Sched.15, paras.10 and 18.

[38] FA 2003, s.53(4); but note that the notification obligations do not appear to apply to excluded situations pursuant to s.54 thereof.

[39] FA 2003, Sched.3, para.1.

[40] FA 2003, s.77A.

[41] Wigan Coal and Iron v. IRC [1945] 1 All ER 392; Associated British Engineering v. IRC [1940] 4 All ER 278.

[42] Which are in satisfaction of the rights of members so they are for a consideration but one which is not chargeable.

[43] FA 2003, Sched.3, paras.3A and 4; see **Chapter 11**.

[44] But it must be noted that there are charges upon transactions involving connected companies: FA 2003, ss.53 and 54 and where liabilities or mortgages are involved FA 2003, Sched.4, para.8; see **11.8**.

shareholders.[45] Other exempt transactions include many of those where no beneficial interest passes, such as appointments and changes of trustees,[46] and transfers to or from mortgagees.

5.7.2.2   Dealings involving leases granted by registered social landlords

Leases granted by registered social landlords are exempt if granted to one or more individuals for an indefinite term or terminable by notice of a month or less.[47] This is pursuant to arrangements between a registered social landlord and the housing authority under which the landlord provides for individuals, nominated by the authority in pursuance of its statutory housing functions, temporary rented accommodation which the landlord has obtained on a short-term basis, i.e. the accommodation is leased to the landlord for a term of five years or less.

The housing authority is a principal council within the meaning of the Local Government Act 1972 or the Common Council of the City of London, a council constituted under s.2 of the Local Government etc. (Scotland) Act 1994 or the Department for Social Development in Northern Ireland or the Northern Ireland Housing Executive.[48]

5.7.2.3   Transactions in connection with matrimonial and civil partnership breakdown

A transaction between parties to a marriage or a civil partnership[49] is exempt from SDLT if it is effected:

- in pursuance of an order of a court made on granting in respect of the parties a decree of divorce, nullity of marriage or civil partnership or judicial separation;
- in pursuance of an order of a court made in connection with the dissolution or annulment of the marriage or civil partnership or the parties' judicial separation at any time after the granting of such a decree;
- in pursuance of an order made at any time pursuant to Matrimonial Causes Act 1973, ss.22A, 23A or 24A or Family Law (Scotland) Act 1985, ss.8(2) and 14(1) or equivalent provisions in Civil Partnership Act 2004, Sched.5;
- at any time in pursuance of an agreement of the parties made in contemplation of or otherwise in connection with the dissolution or annulment of the marriage or civil partnership, their judicial separation or the making of a separation order in respect of them.[50]

---

[45]   FA 2003, Sched.4, paras.8 and 8A; see **Chapter 4**.

[46]   But special rules apply to certain transactions involving bare trustees or nominees for certain periods: FA 2003, Sched.16, para.3; see **8.60** and **10.11**.

[47]   On reliefs for acquisitions by registered social landlords see FA 2003, s.71; see also Sched.3, para.2.

[48]   FA 2003, Sched.3, para.2.

[49]   FA 2003, Sched.3, paras.3 and 3A.

[50]   FA 2003, Sched.3, para.3.

It will be noted that the relief either requires or contemplates the making of a court order. This relief applies to 'transactions', i.e. all forms of acquisitions and will now include new leases.

5.7.2.4 Variations of estates of deceased persons

There is exemption[51] from SDLT in respect of a transaction following an individual's death that varies any disposition, whether effected by will or intestacy or otherwise, of property of which the deceased was competent to dispose,[52] provided that:

- the transaction is carried out within a period of two years after the person's death. The relief is, in consequence, frequently jeopardised where the parties are involved in a bitter family dispute; and
- no consideration in money or money's worth, other than the making of a variation of another such disposition, is given for it. If there is consideration, there is a partial relief in that the chargeable consideration does not include the giving up or varying of any interests in the estate.[53] This is to deal with the situation where the person acquiring the chargeable interest has to provide an equality payment. For example, a person may be entitled to a half share in the residue valued at £400,000 and comprising a house of £250,000 and the balance in shares. The estate may be varied for the individual to take the house but in order to achieve equality the individual has to pay £50,000 in cash to the other legatees. The tax charge is limited to the £50,000 equality. Frequently the property will be subject to a mortgage which would be potentially chargeable consideration. The chargeable consideration does not include the making of the variation.[54]

This relief applies whether or not the administration of the estate is complete or the property has been distributed in accordance with the original dispositions.[55] It also applies to leases granted as part of the variation of the estate, but the issue of rent as 'other consideration' will introduce a taxable element into the transaction.

5.7.2.5 Assents and appropriation by personal representatives

The acquisition of property in or towards satisfaction of entitlement under or in relation to the will or upon the intestacy of a deceased individual, including the grant of a lease or a release of property, is exempt provided that the person acquiring the chargeable interest does not give consideration other than the assumption of a debt,

---

[51] FA 2003, Sched.3 para.4.
[52] Which can include property where the deceased had a general power of appointment.
[53] FA 2003, Sched.3, para.4; Sched.4, paras.8 and 8A.
[54] FA 2003, Sched.4, para.8A(2).
[55] FA 2003, Sched.3, para.4. For the view of HMRC Stamp Taxes on testamentary arrangements relating to the matrimonial home and inheritance tax see Guidance Note 12 November 2004.

including a guarantee of a debt, charged upon the property.[56] Where there is consideration other than the assumption of a mortgage liability, the chargeable consideration does not include the mortgage debt assumed.[57] This indicates that the lower rates of tax are available where the other consideration does not exceed £500,000.

5.8 SUBSALES

This relief has formed the basis of many aggressive mitigation arrangements and is expressly identified as a target for the general statutory anti-avoidance provisions. Highly restricted forms of subsale relief are available[58] with a special relief for the grant of new leases.[59] These two forms of subsale relief are totally different from the stamp duty equivalent since the relief is no longer linked to the absence of a conveyance or the grant of a lease. The relief may, with care, be available notwithstanding completion of the initial contracts; but, more importantly, the relief is not necessarily available simply because there is no conveyance or lease to the first party, so that issues with standard conditions of sale prohibiting subsales, etc. are no longer inconsistent with this relief.[60] It is vitally important to appreciate that the reliefs are related to the effective date, which makes understanding substantial performance and keeping a watchful eye on the conduct of the clients key issues for practitioners.

5.8.1 'Disregarded'

The relief takes a somewhat unusual form in the case of subsales and assignments in that it is stated that the simultaneous substantial performance and completion of the various contracts in the chain is to be 'disregarded'.[61] This is a potentially unusual use of the word 'disregarded'.[62] On its plain English meaning the transaction being 'disregarded' would mean that it is not regarded as taking place therefore there is no chargeable transaction. However, it appears to be the view of HMRC Stamp Taxes and the Land Registry that the word 'disregarded' in the overall context of the legislation means that the transaction is 'disregarded' for the purposes of imposing an actual charge but is still 'regarded' if only for the purposes of imposing an obligation to notify the transaction. It seems that this requires any transaction where the first party is seeking to take advantage of relief for subsales and assignments will

[56] FA 2003, Sched.3, para.3A.
[57] FA 2003, Sched.4, para.8A(1).
[58] FA 2003, ss.45 and 45A (as amended).
[59] Sched.17A, para.12B.
[60] But it may create problems for VAT; see, e.g. *Kwik Save v. Customs and Excise Commissioners* [1994] VATTR 457.
[61] FA 2003, s.45(3).
[62] See also the similar bizarre use of the word in relation to the general anti-avoidance provisions in FA 2003, s.75A(4)(a); see **1.33**.

have to be notified. The unusual nature of the drafting has given rise to problems with the Land Registry and means that persons who suspect that there is some form of subsale arrangement or who are taking an assignment of the benefit of an existing contract may need to take this into account when dealing with the completion arrangements for their contract and require the production of a Revenue certificate (SDLT 5) from all intermediate vendors, particularly where they have taken a transfer which needs to be presented to the Land Registry.[63]

The issues differ in relation to the specific relief for the grant of new leases. In this case it is provided[64] that there is a form of statutory novation. The agreement for lease is deemed to have been made with the assignee not the original party.[65] This will, of course, change the nature of the documentation required at completion and may require indemnities because there may be an increased liability to tax upon the third party since he is completing the original contract between the landlord and the original party and not completing the contract for the assignment of the property or the benefit of the lease.

5.8.2 Subsales and assignments

The basic relief (i.e. that applicable for transactions other than arrangements relating to agreements to grant a lease)[66] applies, according to the legislation, to three situations. These are: subsales; assignments; and other transactions as a result of which a person other than the original purchaser becomes entitled to call for a conveyance to him. While the concepts of subsales and assignments are well established there is no guidance as to the circumstances when the provisions relating to other transactions could apply. Since subsales and assignments are fundamentally different, the traditional *ejusdem generis* principles are not appropriate. It may apply to novations in certain circumstances. It would seem that the basic application is for subsales, however, novations may give rise to problems where equitable interests may have passed since the novation may involve the 'release' (i.e. acquisition) of an equitable interest in land which is a chargeable interest.

Where A agrees to sell land to B and B subsells the land or assigns the contract to purchase the chargeable interest or assigns part thereof[67] to C, which seems to have created problems upon part assignments, no charge to SDLT arises upon B provided that he does not complete or substantially perform his contract with A prior to the

---

[63] For a discussion of the practical difficulties arising, particularly with the Land Registry, see **1.12.3**.

[64] FA 2003, Sched.17A, para.12B; see **8.9** and **8.13**.

[65] It seems that this is a statutory novation of the contract so that there is no joint and several liability which might create a right to an indemnity.

[66] FA 2003, Sched.17A, para.12B; see **8.9**.

[67] There may be difficulties in assigning part of a contract; the transaction may have to be a subsale or a sale of an equitable interest or by means of a declaration of trust. However, there is a major issue of principle which suggests that the relief is not available in cases other than the onward sale of the entire interest of a physical part of the land.

completion or substantial performance of his contract with C. The simultaneous performance of his contracts with A and with C is ignored. In consequence, that payment of the outstanding balance by C directly to A does not impose a charge upon B. In many cases there will be a transfer from A directly to C. This does not constitute a chargeable transaction for B provided that there has been no prior substantial performance by B. The relief is available notwithstanding that there is a conveyance to B or payment of the balance of the purchase price by B, provided that there is simultaneous payment of the purchase price by C to B and a conveyance from B to C. Although B is not taxable he may have to file a land transaction return.[68]

C is taxable on the balance owing by B to A plus the consideration paid by C to B. It seems that, in practice, many transactions are improperly reported. In many cases this will be because of the erroneous belief that B is not liable because he has not received a conveyance. This is a fundamental error and since it involves non-reporting of the transaction it can be expected that HMRC Stamp Taxes will seek to impose maximum penalties for failure to file a return.

5.9 RESTRICTIONS UPON SUBSALE RELIEF

In addition to the technical conditions for the relief such as the problems in relation to part subsales, specific anti-avoidance provisions mean that subsale relief is not available in some circumstances:

- certain alternative finance arrangements that involve a sale and saleback but not a sale and leaseback;[69]
- transactions within the intra-group relief;[70] namely, where A Ltd agrees to sell a chargeable interest to B Ltd which subsells the property to its wholly owned subsidiary C Ltd;[71]
- special principles may apply where the general statutory anti-avoidance provisions pertain since these are aimed principally at subsales.[72]

---

[68] The absence of an SDLT 5 in respect of the transfer to B was initially explained in a covering letter to the Land Registry informing it that B is not taxable because of subsale relief. For C the notifiable transaction is his acquisition from B ('the secondary contract') which may produce a mismatch between the Land Registry documents (executed by A) and the Revenue certificate (SDLT 5) identifying B not a party to the transfer. However, some employees of the Land Registry now require a letter from HMRC Stamp Taxes.

[69] FA 2003, ss.72A and 73.

[70] Compare FA 1967, s.27(3)(b) and *Escoigne Properties Ltd* v. *IRC* [1958] AC 549.

[71] However, HMRC Stamp Taxes does not, in practice, take this point where there are two completions rather than one direct transfer from the original vendor to the ultimate acquiring subsidiary company.

[72] FA 2003, ss.75A–75C; see **1.33**.

5.10   PART-SUBSALES AND PROBLEMS

There are many situations where a person can agree to acquire land and dispose of part of what he is agreeing to acquire, whether in geographical parts or technical legal parts. FA 2003, s.45(5) seeks to deal with this situation. This is, however, more concerned with allocating the chargeable consideration between the various sub-sales, particularly where the original purchaser retains an interest in the property such as where a developer of a block of flats grants leases but transfers the freehold interest subject to the leases to a company owned by the tenants.

Situations may arise where a person agrees to acquire land and to transfer part-interests in the land. The most obvious illustration of this situation is where a residential developer acquires a large plot of land and having built several houses on the plot subsells each item of property. Obviously, in such a situation subsale relief would not be available since the developer will have substantially performed the contract by entering upon the land in order to carry out the building works.[73] However, a person may be eligible for relief where, having contracted to buy the land but before having completed or entered into possession of the property, he subsells the various plots and houses from plan. This, however, is only one illustration of the sale of part-interests, namely a sale of a physical part of the land passing the entire interest to a specific area. Other situations might arise such as where a developer agrees to acquire the freehold in land in order to construct a block of flats which he intends to lease to third parties[74] and dispose of the freehold interest to a company owned by the tenants. Again, as the developer has entered upon the land to construct the block of flats, subsale relief would not be appropriate. In this situation, however, the question is whether having agreed to enter into the leases before substantially performing his contract he might be eligible for subsale relief as regards the leases. This may depend upon the time at which the freehold is conveyed to the management company. Yet another situation is where there is a part-disposal of the land in the form of an undivided interest. This may occur where a husband agrees to purchase land and agrees to sell a 50 per cent undivided equitable interest to his wife.

As regards the major question as to whether subsale relief is available for such leases, or partial undivided interests, traditionally subsale relief has been available only to the extent that the land has been physically sold onward and the first purchaser has not received any interest in the land or has received only part of the geographical area. The official view is that the 'secondary contract' must relate to the same estate and interest in the land as were comprised in the initial contract. In these situations the traditional stamp tax position was determined by the amount of consideration to be allocated to the part of the land retained and transferred to the original purchaser.[75] Much will, therefore, depend upon whether the reference in

---

73   FA 2003, s.44.
74   Not a transaction within FA 2003, Sched.17A, para.12B.
75   *Maples v. IRC* [1914] 3 KB 303.

s.45(5) to 'part only of the subject-matter of the original contract'[76] relates to other situations. It would seem reasonably certain that where a purchaser agrees to acquire the freehold in land, for example, and enters into an arrangement to grant a lease of the property subsale relief would not be available so that the charge would be upon the full price being paid for the freehold interest and not upon the value of that interest as reduced in accordance with s.45(5). This would suggest that the words 'part only' refer to a physical part and not a part or undivided interest in the property. In consequence, it is considered that although assignments may be a form of transfer of rights within the subsale relief this is not a transfer of part. In consequence, where a husband agrees to acquire a residential property and enters into a contract to assign a 99 per cent interest to his wife for a token sum, this would not be regarded as a transfer of rights within the relieving provisions, so that the husband would remain taxable upon the full purchase price and not merely the proportionate part of the consideration paid for his limited interest in the joint ownership.

5.11   AGREEMENTS FOR LEASE AND NEW LEASES

A similar relief is available for leases granted to third parties provided that the right to the lease is assigned before the original party substantially performed the agreement (see **8.9**).

5.12   RELIEVED TRANSACTIONS REQUIRING NOTIFICATION

This part of the chapter relates to those transactions where no tax is payable but the transaction has to be notified.[77]

5.12.1   Right-to-buy and shared ownership

FA 2003, Sched.9 (as amended) provides for a relief for right-to-buy, rent-to-mortgage schemes and shared ownership arrangements, including arrangements involving staircasing.[78] It also restricts the first time buyer relief.[79] Since these are

---

[76]   Note the definition of this in FA 2003, s.44.
[77]   FA 2003, ss.77 and 77A.
[78]   Usually these reliefs require not only that there is an election made in the land transaction return that the relief is claimed, but also that the relevant documents contain certain statements. Where the statement is omitted it may be possible to persuade the court to rectify the document (see *Re Slocock's Will Trusts* [1979] 1 All ER 358). It is necessary to seek a court order since HMRC Stamp Taxes is reluctant in practice to accept voluntary rectification. Should the parties rectify the document voluntarily and find that this is rejected by HMRC Stamp Taxes, the court has no jurisdiction to rectify the document; see *Whiteside* v. *Whiteside* [1949] 2 All ER 913. The other practical problem is the loss of the original documents by the parties. In this case it seems that in general, but not necessarily in all cases, HMRC Stamp Taxes may be prepared to accept Land Registry copies of the documents.
[79]   FA 2003, s.57AA; Sched.9, para.15.

transactions that may run for a longer period there are special transitional provisions for arrangements entered into within the previous stamp duty regime (FA 2003, Sched.19).

5.12.1.1   Right-to-buy transactions

In the case of a right-to-buy transaction any grant under Housing Act 1996, ss.20 or 21 does not count as part of the chargeable consideration where the vendor is a registered social landlord.[80] Also any consideration that would be payable only if a contingency were to occur or that is payable only because a contingency has occurred does not count as chargeable consideration.[81]

5.12.1.2   Shared ownership leases

Where a lease is granted by a qualifying body in pursuance of the preserved right to buy, and certain conditions are met and the purchaser elects for tax to be charged in accordance with the relieving provisions, the chargeable consideration for the grant of the lease is the amount to be stated in the lease as being the market value of the dwelling, or a sum calculated by reference to that market value.[82] For this relief to apply the lease must be of a dwelling and give the lessee or lessees exclusive use of the building. The lease must provide for the lessee or lessees to acquire the reversion and be granted partly in consideration of rent and partly in consideration of a premium calculated by reference to the market value of the dwelling or a sum calculated by reference to that market value, and a statement of the market value or sum so calculated must be contained within the lease. The taxpayer may elect for this treatment to apply and any such election must be included in the land transaction return (SDLT 1) made in respect of the grant of the lease or any amendment of that return. It is irrevocable.[83] Also where these provisions apply no account is to be taken for the purposes of SDLT of the rent that forms part of the consideration.[84] Where there is a shared ownership lease and a valid election for market value treatment has been made, the transfer of the reversion to the lessee or lessees under the terms of the lease is exempt, provided that an appropriate election for the market value treatment was made and any tax chargeable in respect of the grant of the lease has been paid.[85]

---

[80]   FA 2003, Sched.9, para.1(5).
[81]   FA 2003, Sched.9, para.1(1).
[82]   FA 2003, Sched.9, para.2.
[83]   FA 2003, Sched.9, para.2(3).
[84]   FA 2003, Sched.9, para.2(4A).
[85]   FA 2003, Sched.9, para.3.

5.12.1.3 Staircasing

In relation to such a lease granted by a qualifying body or pursuant to the preserved right to buy where the lease is of a dwelling which gives the lessee or lessees exclusive use of the dwelling, the lessee or lessees may on the payment of a sum require the terms of the lease to be altered so that the rent payable pursuant thereto is reduced. A special relief is provided[86] if there is an initial premium obtainable in the open market or the sum is calculated by reference to such a premium. The taxpayer may elect for the treatment but such election must be made in the land transaction return (SDLT 1) made in respect of the lease, which is irrevocable. Where the conditions are satisfied and the appropriate election is made, the chargeable rent in consideration of which the lease is granted is taken to be the minimum rent stated in the lease and the chargeable consideration for the grant other than rent (broadly the premium) is taken to be the amount of the premium or sum calculated by reference to the premium stated in the lease.

Where there is a lease providing for staircasing and the lessee exercises the right to alter the rent on payment of a sum, the acquisition of the additional interest is exempt from SDLT provided that:

- an election was made for the tax to be charged by reference to market value[87] and any tax payable in respect of the grant has been paid; or
- immediately after the acquisition the total share of the dwelling held by the lessee or lessees does not exceed 80 per cent.

The linked transaction rules are modified since it is provided that the grant of a lease qualifying for the market value treatment is not linked with the acquisition of any interest within the staircasing arrangements or the transfers of the reversion to the lessee or lessees under the terms of the lease.[88]

5.12.1.4 Rent-to-mortgage or rent-to-loan transactions

In the case of a rent-to-mortgage or rent-to-loan transaction the chargeable consideration is equal to the price that would be payable pursuant to Housing Act 1985, s.126 for a transfer of the dwelling to the person or the grant of a lease of the dwelling to the person concerned if the person were exercising a right to buy pursuant to Part 5 of that Act. For these purposes a rent-to-mortgage transaction means the transfer of a dwelling to a person or the grant of a lease of a dwelling to a

---

[86] FA 2003, Sched.9, para.4. For the relief to apply the lease must be granted partly in consideration of rent and partly in consideration of a premium calculated by reference to the premium obtainable in the open market for the grant of a lease containing the same terms as the lease but with the substitution of the minimum rent for the rent payable under the lease or a sum calculated by reference to the premium. The lease must contain a statement of the minimum rent which means the lowest rent which could become payable under the lease if it were altered in accordance with the power of the tenant as set out in the lease.

[87] Pursuant to FA 2003, Sched.9, para.2 or para.4.

[88] FA 2003, Sched.9, para.4B.

person pursuant to the exercise by that person of the right to acquire on rent-to-mortgage terms pursuant to Housing Act 1985, Part 5.

5.13 SHARED OWNERSHIP TRUSTS

A shared ownership trust means a trust of land within Trusts of Land and Appointment of Trustees Act 1996, s.1, which meets the conditions that the trust property is a dwelling in England and Wales and one of the beneficiaries described as 'social landlord' is a qualifying body. It is required that the terms of the trust:

- provide for one or more of the individual beneficiaries (the purchaser) to have exclusive use of the property as the only or main residence of the purchaser;
- require the purchaser to make an initial payment to the social landlord and to make additional payments to the social landlord by way of compensation;
- enable the purchaser to make other additional payments to the social landlord;
- determine the initial beneficial interests of the social landlord and the purchaser by reference to the initial capital;
- specify a sum equating or relating to the market value of the dwelling by reference to which the initial capital was calculated; and
- provide for the purchaser's beneficial interest in the trust property to increase and the social landlord's to diminish or to be extinguished as additional payments are made by the purchaser.

A qualifying body includes a registered provider of social housing provided that the purchase or construction of the trust property by the registered provider of social housing or a person connected with him (or the adaptation of the property by such a person) was funded with the assistance of a grant or other financial assistance pursuant to Housing and Regeneration Act 2008, s.19.

In this situation the 'purchaser' for the purposes of SDLT is the purchaser of the property and not the social landlord or any other beneficiary. Where there has been a declaration of a shared ownership trust and the purchaser elects for tax to be charged in accordance with these provisions, the chargeable consideration for the declaration of the shared ownership trust is the amount of the sum equating or relating to the market value of the dwelling by reference to which the initial capital was calculated, and no account is to be taken for the purpose of SDLT of any further payments enhancing the beneficiary's interest. The election must be included in the land transaction return (SDLT 1) for the declaration of the shared ownership trust or any amendment of that return; but may not be revoked. The transfer to the purchaser of an interest in the trust property upon the termination of the trust is exempt from SDLT, provided that an election was made in accordance with these provisions and any tax chargeable in respect of the declaration of trust has been paid.[89]

---

[89]   FA 2003, Sched.9, para.9.

Any additional payment made by the purchaser to the social landlord and the consequent increase in the purchaser's beneficial interest are exempt from charge if an election has been made and any tax has been paid in respect of the declaration of trust. Such a payment and the consequent increase in the purchaser's beneficial interest are also exempt from charge if, following the increase, the purchaser's beneficial interest does not exceed 80 per cent of the total beneficial interest in the trust property.[90]

In relation to a shared ownership trust where no election has been made for the 'market value treatment' the initial capital payment by the purchaser is treated as chargeable consideration other than rent, and any subsequent payments by the purchaser are to be treated as the payment of rent.[91]

Any payments made pursuant to the declaration of the shared ownership trust or any subsequent payments for the acquisition of additional interest or the transfer of the interest in the trust property are not treated as linked transactions.[92]

5.14 RENT-TO-SHARED OWNERSHIP LEASE

The linked transaction rules are modified for transactions forming part of a rent-to-shared ownership lease scheme. This is a scheme or arrangement pursuant to which a qualifying body grants an assured shorthold tenancy of a dwelling to a person or persons and subsequently grants a shared ownership lease of the dwelling or another dwelling to the tenant or one or more of the tenants.

The linked transaction rules do not apply to the grant of the assured shorthold tenancy, the grant of the shared ownership lease, and any other land transaction between the qualifying body and the tenant or tenants, or any of them entered into as part of the scheme. Moreover, the effective date rules are modified so that the effective date of the grant of the shared ownership lease has the effect that the possession of the dwelling by the tenant or tenants pursuant to the shorthold tenancy is to be disregarded.[93]

5.15 RENT-TO-SHARED OWNERSHIP TRUST

The linked transaction principles are modified in relation to a rent-to-shared ownership trust scheme. This is a scheme or arrangement under which a qualifying body grants an assured shorthold tenancy of a dwelling to a person or persons and the person or persons subsequently become the purchaser under a shared ownership trust of the dwelling or another dwelling under which the qualifying body is a social landlord.

---

[90]   FA 2003, Sched.9, para.10.
[91]   FA 2003, Sched.9, para.11.
[92]   FA 2003, Sched.9, para.12.
[93]   FA 2003, Sched.9, para.13.

The linked transaction rules do not apply to the grant of the assured shorthold tenancy, the declaration of a shared ownership trust and any other land transaction between the qualifying body and the tenant or any of the tenants entered into as part of the scheme. Also, the effective date of the declaration of the shared ownership trust is modified in that taking possession of the dwelling by the tenant or tenants pursuant to the shorthold tenancy is to be disregarded.

The conditions are similar to those that applied for stamp duty. The arrangement must relate to a dwelling and involve a qualifying body. The lease must be for a premium and a rent, and a statement of the market value or a sum calculated by reference thereto must appear in the terms. The election for the special treatment of tax upon the market value must appear in the land transaction return.

5.16 REGISTERED SOCIAL LANDLORDS

Registered social landlords may be eligible for the general relief for acquisitions by charities;[94] but there is also a special relief where the transaction is publicly funded which is not subject to the same restrictions, clawback and anti-avoidance provisions.

An acquisition of a chargeable interest in land is exempt from charge where the person making or deemed to make the acquisition is a registered social landlord, which is controlled by its tenants and:

- the vendor is a qualifying body; or
- the transaction is funded with the assistance of a public subsidy.

A body is controlled by its tenants if the majority of its board of members are tenants occupying properties owned or managed by it. A board member means:

- a director of the company;
- if it is a body corporate whose affairs are managed by its members, a member;
- a trustee; or
- a member of the committee of management.[95]

A qualifying body for the purpose of being the 'vendor' means:

- a registered social landlord;
- a housing action trust under Part III of the Housing Act 1988;
- a principal council under the Local Government Act 1972;
- the Common Council of the City of London;
- the Scottish Ministers;
- a council established under s.2 of the Local Government etc. (Scotland) Act 1994;

---

[94] See **8.66.1**. For the relief for leases granted by registered social landlords pursuant to FA 2003, Sched.3, para.2 see **5.7.2.2**.
[95] FA 2003, s.71(2).

- Scottish Homes;
- the Department for Social Development in Northern Ireland;
- the Northern Ireland Housing Executive.

A public subsidy is a grant or other financial assistance made under:

- National Lottery Act 1993, s.25 or given by way of distribution under that provision;
- Housing Act 1996, s.18;
- Housing Grants, Construction and Regeneration Act 1996, s.126;
- Housing (Scotland) Act 1988, s.2;
- Housing (Northern Ireland) Order 1992, SI 1992/1725, art.33;[96]
- Housing and Regeneration Act 2008, s.19.

5.17 RESIDENTIAL PROPERTY

There are a number of reliefs for residential property contained in FA 2003, Sched.6A which are relevant to part-exchanges involving new dwellings; chain-breaker companies; and purchases from personal representatives. These reliefs are highly technical and subject to clawback if the slightest error in implementing the transaction occurs.

5.18 EMPLOYEE RELOCATION RELIEF

There is an exemption from charge where a dwelling is acquired from an employee by his employer or by a relocation company in connection with the change of his or her place of employment. Numerous conditions are imposed. It is necessary that the individual occupied the dwelling as his or her only or main residence at some time in a period of one year ending with the date of the acquisition and the acquisition is made in connection with a change of residence resulting from a relocation of employment. The consideration for the acquisition must not exceed the market value of the dwelling and the area of the land must not exceed 0.5 hectares or such larger area as is reasonable for enjoyment with the house.[97] It is interesting that this relief takes the form of an 'exemption' whereas the relief for exchanges of residential property is a reduction in the chargeable consideration.

---

[96] FA 2003, s.71(4).
[97] FA 2003, s.59.

5.19 COMPULSORY PURCHASE FACILITATING DEVELOPMENT

A compulsory purchase facilitating development, defined as an acquisition of a chargeable interest in respect of which the person acquiring the interest has made a compulsory purchase order for the purpose of facilitating development by another person, is exempt from SDLT.[98] It does not matter how the acquisition is made, so that the relief applies where the acquisition is effected either by agreement or by vesting order.[99]

This relief, which will be key to many transactions involving 's.106 agreements' and their equivalent in other legislation, is subject to many restrictions. In the view of HMRC Stamp Taxes, the relief is simply designed to provide a form of subsale relief for local authorities where they are assisting in assembling a site, as is frequently the case because the local authority will wish to retain nominal control of the site through the reversion and granting only leases to the developer or its nominee. However, this is not a pure subsale relief, since there will usually only be a part disposal by the local authority (see **5.10**). As a consequence of considering this a form of subsale relief, HMRC Stamp Taxes appears to be applying the timeframe applicable to the basic subsale relief.[100] This has raised difficult questions in relation to the meaning of the words 'for the purpose of' facilitating development. Obviously, HMRC Stamp Taxes is reluctant to provide the relief where there is a possibility that the development may not proceed and the local authority then acquires the land free of SDLT. It would appear that there is an important difference between 'intention' and 'purpose'.[101] It seems that 'purpose' requires something that is cut-and-dried and is not being set up but is actually being performed. In consequence, there will be considerable doubt as to the availability of the relief when the s.106 agreement is itself conditional or has not been finalised.

Also HMRC Stamp Taxes has taken a narrow view of the definition of 'development'; a compulsory acquisition of property with a view to its refurbishment because it has been neglected and dilapidated would not be within this relief. Since it is a form of subsale relief it is not available where the local authority itself intends to carry out the development but it would seem that it would be available where the local authority is acquiring the freeholds and granting long leases to the developer so that the local authority can have a technical interest in the land and exercise more control over present and future arrangements.

Moreover, the compulsory acquisition process has given rise to problems as regards the effective date and the treatment of transactions where there is merely a threat of compulsory purchase rather than negotiation and acquisition by private treaty or a vesting declaration. It is the view of HMRC Stamp Taxes that the tax charge arises when the initial compulsory purchase notices are sent out. However, it

---

[98]   FA 2003, s.60(2).
[99]   FA 2003, s.60(3) and (4).
[100]   FA 2003, s.45; see **5.8**.
[101]   Compare *Times Newspapers* v. *IRC* [1971] 3 All ER 98 and *Combined Technologies Plc* v. *IRC* [1985] STC 348.

is considered that this is incorrect and that the effective date is only when the transaction is completed after values and prices have been fixed, including any appeals to the Lands Tribunal or challenges to the compulsory purchase orders themselves have been resolved. It is considered that the transaction is substantially performed only when possession is taken or the purchase price as agreed is paid or is completed when the general vesting arrangements are implemented.

5.20 COMPLIANCE WITH PLANNING OBLIGATIONS

There is an exemption from SDLT in respect of a transaction entered into in order to comply with a planning obligation or modification of a planning obligation provided that:

- the planning obligation or modification is enforceable against the vendor;
- the person making the acquisition is a public authority;[102] and
- the transaction takes place within a period of five years beginning with the date on which the planning obligation was entered into or modified.[103]

A 'planning obligation' means a planning obligation either within:

- the meaning of Town and Country Planning Act 1990, s.106 that is entered into in accordance with subsection (9) of that section; or
- the meaning of Town and Country Planning Act 1990, s.299A that is entered into in accordance with subsection (2) of that section. A planning obligation is 'modified' where there is a modification in accordance with Town and Country Planning Act 1990, s.106A(1). These provisions are also applicable in Scotland and Northern Ireland where the relevant provisions are Town and Country Planning (Scotland) Act 1997, ss.75 or 246 and Planning (Northern Ireland) Order 1991,[104] art.40 that is entered into in accordance with para.10 of that article.

Public authorities for these purposes are:

- Ministers of the Crown or government departments;
- the Scottish Ministers;
- a Northern Ireland department;
- the Welsh Ministers, First Minister for Wales and the Counsel General to the Welsh Assembly Government;
- a county or district council in England constituted under Local Government Act 1972, s.2;
- the council of a London borough;
- the Common Council of the City of London;

---

[102]   FA 2003, s.66.
[103]   FA 2003, s.61.
[104]   SI 1991/1220 (NI 11).

- the Greater London Authority;
- Transport for London;
- the Council of the Isles of Scilly;
- a county or county borough council in Wales constituted under Local Government Act 1972, s.21;
- a council in Scotland constituted under Local Government etc. (Scotland) Act 1994, s.2;
- a district council in Northern Ireland within the meaning of the Local Government Act (Northern Ireland) 1972;
- a Strategic Health Authority in England and Wales established under National Health Service Act 2006, s.13;
- a Special Health Authority established in England and Wales under National Health Service Act 2006, s.28 or National Health Service (Wales) Act 2006, s.22;
- a Primary Care Trust established in England and Wales under National Health Service Act 2006, s.18;
- a Local Health Board established in England and Wales under National Health Service (Wales) Act 2006, s.11;
- a National Health Service Trust established in England and Wales under National Health Service Act 2006, s.25 or National Health Service (Wales) Act 2006, s.18;
- the Common Services Agency established in Scotland under National Health Service (Scotland) Act 1978, s.10(1);
- a Health Board established in Scotland under National Health Service (Scotland) Act 1978, s.2(1)(a);
- a National Health Service Trust established in Scotland under National Health Service (Scotland) Act 1978, s.12A(1);
- a Special Health Board established in Scotland under National Health Service (Scotland) Act 1978, s.2(1)(b);
- a Health and Social Services Board established in Northern Ireland under Health and Personal Social Services (Northern Ireland) Order 1972, art.16;[105]
- a Health and Social Services Trust established under Health and Personal Social Services (Northern Ireland) Order 1991, art.10;[106]
- any other authority that is either:
  - a local planning authority within the meaning of the Town and Country Planning Act 1990; or
  - the planning authority for any of the purposes of the Planning Acts within the meaning of the Town and Country Planning (Scotland) Act 1997.

In addition, the Treasury has power to prescribe by order any person to fall within this relief.

---

[105] SI 1972/1265 (NI 14).
[106] SI 1991/194 (NI 1).

5.21   TRANSFERS INVOLVING PUBLIC BODIES

There is an exemption from SDLT in respect of a transaction entered into on, or in consequence of, or in connection with, a reorganisation effected by or under statutory provision involving the establishment, reform or abolition of one or more public bodies, or the creation, alteration or abolition of functions to be discharged by them.[107] In addition, the Treasury may by order provide that a land transaction that is not entered into within the basic exemption is exempt from charge if the transaction is effected by or under a prescribed statutory provision and either the purchaser or the vendor is a public body.[108]

The public bodies within this relief are:

- a Minister of the Crown;
- the Scottish Ministers;
- a Northern Ireland department;
- the Welsh Ministers, the First Minister for Wales and the Counsel General to the Welsh Assembly Government;
- the Corporate Officer of the House of Lords;
- the Corporate Officer of the House of Commons;
- the Scottish Parliamentary Corporate Body;
- the Northern Ireland Assembly Commission;
- the National Assembly for Wales Commission;
- a county or district council in England constituted under Local Government Act 1972, s.2;
- the council of a London Borough;
- the Greater London Authority;
- the Common Council of the City of London;
- the Council of the Isles of Scilly;
- a county or county borough council in Wales constituted under Local Government Act 1972, s.21;
- a council constituted in Scotland under Local Government etc. (Scotland) Act 1994, s.2;
- a district council in Northern Ireland within the meaning of the Local Government (Northern Ireland) Act 1972;
- a Strategic Health Authority established in England and Wales under National Health Service Act 2006, s.13;
- a Special Health Authority established in England or Wales under National Health Service Act 2006, s.28 or National Health Service (Wales) 2006, s.22;
- a Primary Care Trust established in England and Wales under National Health Service Act 2006, s.18;

---

[107]   FA 2003, s.66.
[108]   This power has been exercised by Finance Act 2003, Section 66 (Prescribed Persons) Order 2005, 2005/83; Finance Act 2003, Section 66 (Prescribed Transactions) Order 2005/645; Finance Act 2003, Section 66 (Prescribed Statutory Provisions) Order 2007, SI 2007/1385.

- a Local Health Board established in England and Wales under National Health Service (Wales) Act 2006, s.11;
- a National Health Service Trust established in England and Wales under National Health Service Act 2006, s.25 or National Health Service (Wales) Act 2006, s.18;
- the Common Services Agency established in Scotland under National Health Service (Scotland) Act 1978, s.10(1);
- a Health Board established in Scotland under National Health Service (Scotland) Act 1978, s.2(1)(a);
- a National Health Service Trust established in Scotland under National Health Service (Scotland) Act 1978, s.12A(1);
- a Special Health Board established in Scotland under National Health Service (Scotland) Act 1978, s.2(1)(b);
- a Health and Social Services Board established in Northern Ireland under Health and Personal Social Services (Northern Ireland) Order 1972, art.16;[109]
- a Health and Social Services Trust established under Health and Personal Social Services (Northern Ireland) Order 1991, art.10;[110]
- any other authority that is either a local planning authority within the meaning of the Town and Country Planning Act 1990 or is the planning authority for any of the purposes of the Planning Acts within the meaning of the Town and Country Planning (Scotland) Act 1997;
- a body other than a company[111] that is established by or under a statutory provision for the purpose of carrying out functions conferred on it by or under a statutory provision.

The Treasury is given power to prescribe other persons within this list.

For these purposes references to a 'public body' include both a company in which all of the shares are owned by such a body and a wholly owned subsidiary of such a company.

5.22 REORGANISATION OF PARLIAMENTARY CONSTITUENCIES

There is a relief where an Order in Council is made and there is a transfer of chargeable interests in land from an existing local constituency association to a new association that is its successor.[112]

---

[109]   SI 1972/1265 (NI 14).
[110]   SI 1991/194 (NI 1).
[111]   See FA 2003, s.100(1).
[112]   FA 2003, s.67.

5.23 ACQUISITIONS BY BODIES ESTABLISHED FOR NATIONAL PURPOSES

A land transaction is exempt if the person/body making the acquisition is:

- a Historic Buildings and Monuments Commission for England;
- the National Endowment for Science, Technology and the Arts;
- Trustees of the British Museum;
- Trustees of the National Heritage Memorial Fund; or
- Trustees of the National History Museum.[113]

5.24 ALTERNATIVE FINANCING FOR PURCHASER

Sale and leaseback will not normally be a method of financing the initial acquisition of a house but may form part of a fundraising exercise such as an 'equity release' arrangement or a form of disguised borrowing and provided that the conditions are satisfied the leaseback will be exempt.[114] A form of first time buyer relief is available.[115]

Special financing does, however, qualify for a limited form of relief in one narrow area designed to cope with problems of financing where parties are restricted by rules usually of a religious nature against usury or the taking of interest, and the financing must take the form of some mode of participation in the profits or gains of the property, and ordinary mortgages are not appropriate. However, the anti-discrimination principles mean that the relief is available to all persons not just those who subscribe to particular religious views.[116] This area of relief has been the basis for certain aggressive mitigation arrangements and in consequence has been made the target of anti-avoidance legislation such as exclusion from subsale relief in certain cases[117] and special rules apply for the purposes of excluding most such transactions from the general anti-avoidance provisions where they might otherwise fail the lower tax condition.[118]

5.24.1 Sale and lease arrangements

A purchase of a major interest is exempt where it is pursuant to an arrangement between:

---

[113] FA 2003, s.69.
[114] FA 2003, s.57A (as amended); see further **8.59**.
[115] FA 2003, ss.57A and 73CA.
[116] It is, therefore, incorrect to describe this as 'Sharia financing' which covers religious overtones and the author has encountered situations in practice where parties have refused to make use of this relief because some professional advisers have misdescribed the relief and offended their own religious sensibilities.
[117] FA 2003, s.45(3); see also s.45(5A)(a).
[118] FA 2003, s.75A(7).

(a)   a person[119] or a financial institution which acquired its interest under this type of transaction; and

(b)   a financial institution being a bank,[120] a building society pursuant to Building Societies Act 1986 or a wholly owned subsidiary of either, or a consumer credit company subject to many qualifying conditions[121] and there must not be any arrangement for the change of control of the financial body.

The relief is available where the institution acquires a major interest in land or an undivided interest so that the land is held for the person and the institution as beneficial tenants in common.[122] The institution must grant a lease or sublease out of that interest to the person, the lease or sublease being exempt. It is necessary for the parties to enter into an arrangement under which the individual has a right to require the transfer of the major interest purchased by the institution.

The transfer of the freehold or head leasehold interest back to the individual is exempt from charge provided that the additional acquisition of the major interest and the lease is exempt and, at all times between then and the transfer of the reversionary interest, the interest purchased by the institution is held by it and the lease or sublease granted is held by the person.

The requirements for relief are now satisfied if the person[123] enters into an arrangement or holds the lease or sublease as trustee and any beneficiary of the trust is not an individual or the individual enters into the arrangements and holds the lease or sublease as a partner and any of the other partners is not an individual.[124]

The reliefs are also available in Scotland and specific provisions deal with the equivalent terms and practices in that country.

5.24.2   Purchase and resale

There is an exemption for the acquisition of a major interest by a financial institution pursuant to an arrangement whereby the financial institution purchases the major interest in land and sells that interest to a person.[125] Both the acquisition by the financial institution and the onward sale to the individual are exempt from SDLT. The person grants the institution a legal mortgage over that interest.[126]

Subsale relief is not available for the person initially acquiring the property in these circumstances.[127]

---

[119]   This relief was originally not available to corporate purchasers but this restriction has been removed.

[120]   Income Tax Act 2007, s.991 and Corporation Tax Act 2010, s.1120.

[121]   FA 2003, s.72A(8).

[122]   The interest held by the institution is an exempt interest: FA 2003, s.73B.

[123]   Individual includes his personal representatives: FA 2003, s.72(9).

[124]   The restrictions in FA 2003, s.72(6) are now repealed.

[125]   Which includes his personal representatives after his death: FA 2003, s.73(6).

[126]   For definition of legal mortgage see FA 2003, s.73(5)(b).

[127]   FA 2003, s.45(3).

5.25 SPECIAL RELIEFS FOR LEASES

Certain reliefs are not available for leases such as those relating to residential property pursuant to FA 2003, Sched.6A. Other reliefs are available only for leases such as sale and leaseback.[128] These specific reliefs are considered in **Chapter 8**.

5.26 RESIDENTIAL PROPERTY

Certain reliefs are available only for residential property and are considered in **5.17**.

5.27 CHARITIES

Relief is available for acquisitions of chargeable interests by a charity for use for the purposes of the charity or by another charity or as an investment, e.g. to produce income to be used for charitable purposes.[129] However, the acquisition must be bona fide and not for the purpose of avoiding taxation. It seems that the acquisition of a charity shop is exempt provided that the proceeds of the shop are applied for charitable purposes.

The relief is clawed back if within three years after the acquisition and while the land is still owned by the charity it ceases to be used for charitable purposes. The relief is not lost where the charity disposes of the land.

The initial relief gave rise to problems where the land was initially acquired by the charity with the intention of participating in a joint development such as where part of the land was made available to a developer to construct a supermarket in consideration of the construction of a new school on land held by the charity. Pursuant to an amendment,[130] in such a situation the relief can be claimed but it is subject to clawback if the charity applies the land to non-charitable purposes within the three-year period. The clawback does not operate provided that the charity retains a major part of the land and any lease granted meets certain stringent conditions.

5.28 HISTORICAL HANGOVERS

A large number of ancient stamp duty reliefs for highly specialised transactions have been discovered and been carried over into SDLT by regulations,[131] usually by inserting relieving provisions into the relevant legislation. However, where leases

---

[128]   FA 2003, s.57A.
[129]   FA 2004, Sched.8.
[130]   FA 2003, Sched.8, para.2.
[131]   Stamp Duty Land Tax (Consequential Amendment of Enactments) Regulations 2003, SI 2003/2867.

are granted within the relief, special charges may apply to the first taxable assignment of the lease which is treated as the grant of a new lease.[132]

Regulations[133] issued pursuant to FA 2003, s.123(2) bring forward certain specialised reliefs from stamp duty. These are reliefs pursuant to:

- Inclosure Act 1845, s.163A;
- Metropolitan Commons Act 1866, s.33;
- Chequers Estate Act 1917, s.3A;
- Finance Act 1931, s.28(3), including land transaction returns within the list of instruments;
- Chevening Estate Act 1959, s.2A;
- Finance Act 1960, s.74A (visiting forces);
- Friendly Societies Act 1974, s.105A (amalgamations);
- Welsh Development Agency Act 1975, Sched.1, para.20A;
- National Health Service (Scotland) Act 1978, ss.12DA and 104A;
- National Heritage Act 1980, s.11A;
- Industry Act 1980, s.2A;
- Highways Act 1986, s.281A;
- Airports Act 1986, s.76A;
- Building Societies Act 1986, s.109A (mergers pursuant to ss.93 and 94);
- National Health Service and Community Care Act 1990, s.61A;
- Ports Act 1991, s.36A;
- Water Resources Act 1991, Sched.2, para.8(3)–(5);
- Further and Higher Education Act 1992, s.88A;
- Further and Higher Education (Scotland) Act 1992, s.58A;
- Friendly Societies Act 1992, s.105A;
- Museums and Galleries Act 1992, s.8A;
- Finance Act 1994, s.245(4);
- Health Authorities Act 1995, Sched.2, para.5(2A)–(2C);
- Merchant Shipping Act 1995, s.221(2A);
- Broadcasting Act 1996, Sched.7, para.25;
- Education Act 1997, s.53A;
- Regional Development Agencies Act 1998, s.39A;
- School Standards and Framework Act 1998, s.79A;
- Access to Justice Act 1999, s.34A;
- Criminal Justice and Court Services Act 2000, s.19;
- Learning and Skills Act 2000, s.94A;
- Transport Act 2000, Sched.26, para.40A;
- Communications Act 2003, Sched.2, para.5A; and
- Ports (Northern Ireland) Order 1994, art.23A.[134]

---

[132] FA 2003, Sched.17A, para.11.
[133] Stamp Duty Land Tax (Consequential Amendment of Enactments) Regulations 2003, SI 2003/2867.
[134] SI 1994/2809 (NI 16).

CHAPTER 6

Options and rights of pre-emption

6.1 GENERAL

Options and pre-emption rights are not expressly mentioned in the definition of chargeable interests but since specific provisions deal with how they are to be taxed it is clear that they must be chargeable interests.[1] In many respects options and conditional contracts are similar commercial vehicles but have different legal consequences.[2] There are, however, important differences in the SDLT treatment of options and conditional contracts:[3]

- The effective date in relation to options is the date of the grant whereas the normal rules for substantial performance or completion will apply in relation to a conditional contract. There will, therefore, be an immediate charge to tax upon the grant of the option but the charge to tax will not arise in respect of any deposit paid in relation to a conditional contract until completion or substantial performance if earlier.
- It is provided that an option and its exercise are two separate transactions but they 'may' be linked.[4] This means that if the two transactions are not linked part of the consideration will benefit from the lower rates where the option premium is below £500,000.[5]

---

[1] Compare the analysis in *J&P Coats Ltd* v. *IRC* [1897] 2 QB 423. Note: the legislation does not deal with the situation of an option to acquire a chargeable interest which is granted as part of a larger transaction such as an option to renew a lease or to acquire the reversionary interest. It seems that it may not be necessary to treat the transaction as involving two separate acquisitions, i.e. the lease and the option with apportioned consideration. This may occasionally be a relevant issue for the linked transaction rules in relation to the subsequent exercise of the option.

[2] However, there are numerous judgments discussing whether options are irrevocable offers or are some form of conditional contract and it seems that they may move between the two categories depending upon the purpose that is perceived to lie behind the legislation; see e.g. *Varty* v. *British South Africa Co* [1965] 2 All ER 395; *Spiro* v. *Glencrown Properties Ltd* [1991] 1 All ER 600. This analysis may also be important in relation to the effectiveness of the option because of the need for writing and land transactions pursuant to Law of Property (Miscellaneous Provisions) Act 1989, s.2.

[3] Assuming that 'condition' is a condition and is not some form of consideration as in *Eastham* v. *Leigh London and Provincial Properties Ltd* [1971] 2 All ER 887.

[4] FA 2003, s.46.

[5] But note the need for careful drafting in order to avoid the option premium being taxed twice as option premium and as part of the strike price as in *George Wimpey Ltd* v. *IRC* [1975] 2 All ER 45.

- Where the option and its exercise are linked it will be necessary for the taxpayer to make a retrospective return in relation to the grant of the option by aggregating the price with the strike price pursuant to the contract arising and paying any additional tax due because of the option premium being taken above the relevant thresholds.
- In relation to a conditional contract there will be only one transaction when the tax will be charged upon the total price.

There is, therefore, a possibility of reducing by a small amount the overall tax liability by the use of options; but this may be offset by the fact that the tax has to be paid at a much earlier stage in the transaction.

Options may have other benefits in relation to SDLT. For example, in order to obtain the benefit of the exclusion for building works on the land to be acquired, the taxpayer has to take possession of substantially the whole of the land being acquired. This may give rise to problems where there is a staged completion such as where a person agrees to purchase 20 acres of land to be completed in four stages of 5 acres each. There is, therefore, a single contract for the acquisition of the whole 20 acres for the purposes of substantial performance of the contract.[6] In such situations there is a danger that, where a person enters upon the first parcel of land to be drawn down in order to commence building or other works, there will not be the taking of possession of sufficient land for the benefit of the relief.[7] In such circumstances it may be preferable to have either a series of separate contracts or a contract with several options which can be separately exercised over time. In such a situation there will be a series of contracts, but each will be fully performed and possession fully taken at each stage for the purposes of the relief for building works.

6.2   OPTION OR CONDITIONAL CONTRACT?

There are frequently questions as to whether the parties should enter into an option or a conditional contract and a number of practical issues arise for the choice, namely:

- if a premium is paid for the option this will be taxable upon grant; a deposit paid under a conditional contract will not normally[8] be taxable until the contract is substantially performed or completed;
- entry upon the land will not involve substantial performance producing an immediate tax charge where there is an option, but may do so where there is a conditional contract;
- the premium for the option may, but not necessarily, have to be aggregated with the price payable in respect of its exercise.[9] This depends upon whether the two

---

6   i.e. taking possession of substantially the whole of the land.
7   FA 2003, Sched.4, para.10; see **Chapter 9**.
8   Since it is unlikely to exceed the 90 per cent threshold for substantial performance.
9   But the drafting may matter; cf. *George Wimpey Ltd* v. *IRC* [1975] 2 All ER 45.

stages are 'linked transactions'. However, the deposit pursuant to a conditional contract will always be part of the total chargeable consideration.

6.3 OPTIONS

There are three types of option: put, call and mutual or cross-options, but the legislation fails to address these issues expressly although they have important differences as to who has the power to control the time of the disposal of the land. There are also certain (probably incorrect) assumptions in the legislation that all forms of options are chargeable interests since the charge applies to an option binding the grantor to enter into a land transaction or to discharge his obligations under the option in some other way.[10]

6.3.1 Mutual or cross-options

Cross-options, i.e. the grant of a right to call for the sale or lease of the land in consideration of the grant of a right to require the other party to purchase or to take a lease of the land are within the definition of 'land exchange'.[11] However, the charge will be limited since the 'exchange' of options is an exchange of non-major interests taxable only upon any equality money paid.[12] However, it seems that cross-options are not contracts for the acquisition of land[13] for the purposes of the main charge to tax so that entry upon the land will not be substantial performance.

6.4 SPECIAL RULES FOR OPTIONS AND PRE-EMPTION RIGHTS

6.4.1 Effective date

The effective date of the transaction in the case of the acquisition of an option is when the right is acquired as opposed to when it becomes exercisable.[14] For example, where there is an option to acquire land if planning permission is obtained, the SDLT arises upon the grant of the option, not when the planning consent is obtained. There will be a separate chargeable transaction (possibly linked) with its own effective date for the contract arising.

---

[10] FA 2003, s.46(2).
[11] FA 2003, s.47.
[12] FA 2003, Sched.4, para.5(4).
[13] The position can be reinforced by providing for different exercise dates or different strike prices.
[14] FA 2003, s.46(3).

6.4.2 Options and exchanges

Where, as happens from time to time, land is sold by A to B who grants A an option or pre-emption right to re-acquire the land, A is acquiring a chargeable interest in land as part of the consideration for the disposal. In consequence there is technically a land exchange.[15] Should this point be taken, as is likely to be the case, both A and B would be potentially subject to tax and notification obligations upon the market value of the chargeable interests involved.[16] In the official view this could have a distorting effect where the strike price for the option is not the market value of the land at the time when it is exercised, i.e. such as where the option or pre-emption right has a significant value. Much may depend, however, upon the nature of the option. Where the grant of the option and the chargeable interest move in the same direction, such as where there is the grant of a lease which includes an option to renew, the option will form part of the subject-matter of the transaction and, in so far as the tenant pays a separate consideration for the option, it will form part of the chargeable consideration for the grant of the lease. However, this would be unusual and such option would rarely, if ever, have a separate market value in excess of the nil rate threshold and so will be neither taxable nor notifiable.[17]

6.4.3 Options and lease renewals

In order to prevent tenants obtaining multiple nil rate slices of rent, anti-avoidance provisions relating to successive linked leases have been introduced.[18] The renewal of leases by means of the exercise of an option may be linked transactions for these purposes.[19]

6.4.4 Options and reversions

Leases sometimes contain an option whereby the tenant may acquire the reversion. The option will not be separately taxable. The exercise of the option may be linked with the grant of the lease.[20]

6.5 PRE-EMPTION RIGHTS

The acquisition of a right of pre-emption preventing the person granting the right from entering into or restricting the right of the grantor to enter into a land

---

[15] FA 2003, s.47.
[16] FA 2003, Sched.4, para.5.
[17] FA 2003, s.77A.
[18] FA 2003, Sched.17A, para.5.
[19] FA 2003, Sched.17A, para.5; see **4.13**.
[20] FA 2003, Sched.17A, para.5; see **4.13**.

transaction, is a land transaction distinct from any land transaction resulting from the exercise of the pre-emption right.[21] This produces two stages in the tax computation:

- there is a charge in relation to the creation of the pre-emption right; and
- there is a charge in relation to the substantial performance and completion of the contract arising from the exercise of the right.

Although the grant of the pre-emption right is a land transaction in its own right, it may also be a linked transaction with the contract arising from the exercise of the right in due course.[22]

The effective date in the case of the acquisition of a pre-emption right is when the right is acquired as opposed to when it becomes exercisable.[23] Thus a right of pre-emption is acquired when granted, although it is not effective unless and until the person granting the right enters into the appropriate situations concerned with a potential sale or other disposition of the relevant property.

6.6 LINKED TRANSACTIONS

The grant of the option and the substantial performance or completion of the contract arising pursuant to its exercise 'may' be linked transactions. There is also a special problem for lease renewals such as pursuant to the exercise of an option to renew (see **Chapter 8**) and successive linked levies.[24] There may also be issues of linked transactions where a tenant exercises an option in the lease to acquire the reversionary interest. However, since this is merely a specialised application of the general linked transactions principle, there will not be a linked transaction where the lease or the reversion have been assigned by the original parties to persons unconnected with either of them because the exercise will not be between the same parties as the parties to the grant of the option or pre-emption rights.[25]

6.6.1 Options and their exercise

The general practice is that in order to constitute a 'linked transaction' there must be 'a' scheme or arrangement or series of transactions.[26] This means that there must be some form of pre-arranged and cut-and-dried understanding that an option will be exercised (see further **Chapter 4**). The legislation clearly recognises that there is no

---

[21] On the nature of pre-emption rights, see *Pritchard* v. *Briggs* [1980] Ch 338; FA 2003, s.46(1)(b).
[22] FA 2003, s.46(1).
[23] FA 2003, s.46(3).
[24] FA 2003, Sched.17A, para.5.
[25] This is subject to the question of whether the parties to the exercise of the option are connected with the parties to the grant when the link may be maintained.
[26] FA 2003, s.108; see **4.12**.

automatic linking of the grant of options and their exercise.[27] If there are genuine commercial reasons why the option may not be exercised there will be no linkage.[28] In practice, however, it will be appropriate for both sides of the transaction to make contemporaneous notes of their understanding of the transaction and the reasons for adopting the option route,[29] and, hopefully, such file notes will be mutually consistent. In the absence of contemporaneous documentation the dispute with HMRC Stamp Taxes will depend upon the evidence of the parties but the credibility of this will almost certainly be challenged by HMRC Stamp Taxes upon the basis of inference, i.e. the surrounding circumstances with the benefit of hindsight are not consistent with the explanation put forward by the taxpayer who is, in its view, in effect, seeking to mislead it and the tribunal. Since there is no control over subsequent events, contemporaneous written records will be vitally important.

Where the option and its exercise are linked transactions because those rules operate retrospectively, it will be necessary to file a land transaction return not only in respect of the chargeable transaction arising by reason of the exercise of the option but also in respect of the revision of the grant of the option.[30] For example, where an option is granted for a premium of £250,000 to acquire land for £2,500,000, the charge upon the option will be 1 per cent of £250,000. If the exercise is linked, the option premium will be aggregated with the strike price[31] so that retrospectively the rate applicable will become 4 per cent. This means that a further 3 per cent of £250,000 has to be paid and a separate return is required; therefore effectively at least three returns are required.

6.7 PRE-EMPTIVE RIGHTS AND LINKED TRANSACTIONS

It is possible that the grant of pre-emptive rights and the making of a contract pursuant thereto could be linked transactions; but it is considered that this will be a rare event in practice because the pre-emptive right is dependent upon the demise of the owner to sell and there is unlikely to be a pre-arranged plan or timetable or understanding and the grantor of the pre-emptive right may reject the opportunity to purchase the property.

6.8 SALES OF OPTIONS

An option is a chargeable interest so that a sale of the right will be a chargeable transaction. However, the subsequent exercise of the right by the purchaser of the

---

[27] FA 2003, s.46.

[28] On the question of assignees of options, see **4.10** on linked transactions which is particularly important for assignees of leases renewing the lease.

[29] Such as preference for the benefit of possible renewals rather than a longer lease with break clauses; see **8.51.2.3**.

[30] FA 2003, s.81A.

[31] Note the drafting problems in this area referred to in *George Wimpey* v. *IRC* [1975] STC 248.

option will not be a linked transaction with the purchase of the option (subject to the rules of linked transactions where the parties are connected) because the two contracts of the purchase of the option and that arising upon exercise will be between different persons. Nor, it is thought, will the subsequent exercise of the right by the purchaser of the option be linked with the original grant because the person exercising the right is not the same person as the original grantee.

6.9   DUE DILIGENCE

Parties acquiring the benefit of options or land with the benefit of pre-emption rights or options to renew leases should obtain details of the background to the option in case HMRC Stamp Taxes establishes, contrary to the wording of the legislation, that the exercise of the right by an unconnected assignee can be linked with the initial grant to the assignor or his predecessors in title.

6.10   COMPLIANCE ISSUES

The effective date for options and pre-emption rights is the date of grant of the right rather than the date of exercise of the right.[32] However, as options are minor interests there will be a notification obligation only where the premium for the option exceeds the nil rate threshold.[33] There may be further filing and payment obligations upon the effective date for any contract subsequently arising pursuant to the exercise of the option where there is a linked transaction.

Failure to investigate the background to the arrangement arising pursuant to the exercise of the option means that making the entry in Box 13 on SDLT 1 to the effect that there is not a linked transaction will be open to allegations of negligence or fraud, and the possible imposition of the statutory penalty[34] for knowingly assisting in the preparation of an incorrect land transaction return. As with so many entries on the SDLT 1 there is no opportunity to supply the detailed information behind the entry as to linked transactions so that it will be easy for HMRC Stamp Taxes to issue a discovery assessment,[35] effectively extending the Enquiry period from nine months to six years.[36]

---

[32]   FA 2003, s.46.
[33]   FA 2003, s.77A.
[34]   FA 2003, s.95.
[35]   FA 2003, Sched.10, para.5.
[36]   See FA 2003, Sched.10, para.31.

CHAPTER 7

Exchanges and partitions

7.1 GENERAL

The extension of chargeable consideration from the limited stamp duty charge by FA 2003, Sched.4 and other provisions has produced a complex compliance and self-assessment regime (see **Chapter 17**). In particular, where there is a transaction involving land and other forms of assets, the rules relating to consideration in kind rather than cash produce two sub-regimes and it is necessary as a preliminary step to determine into which category the transaction falls because the computation and reporting obligations differ significantly. The two regimes are:

- land exchanges; and
- acquisitions of chargeable interests for consideration in kind other than land. This is described elsewhere (see **Chapter 15**).

An acquisition of land for a consideration in kind that does not include chargeable interests in land is taxable upon ordinary principles upon the value of the consideration determined where appropriate upon the provision for valuation in the legislation.[1] However, where a land exchange is involved the position is very different and the rules depend upon whether a major or a minor interest is involved. A major interest is a freehold or a term of years absolute whether subsisting in law or equity or the equivalent in Scotland and Northern Ireland.[2] All other interests are minor interests. Thus a life interest in a settlement holding a freehold or leasehold interest will be a minor interest because of its limited nature. Similarly, it is the nature of the interest being acquired not what the person holds at the end of the transaction that matters. Thus the acquisition of a life interest by a remainderman is the acquisition of a minor interest notwithstanding that the purchaser becomes a freeholder; the 'merger' of the interests producing something different from the two previous parts does not alter the nature of the chargeable interest acquired.

---

[1]   FA 2003, Sched.4, para.7; see also **Chapter 15**.
[2]   FA 2003, s.117.

7.2 EXCHANGES: GENERAL

A 'land exchange' is defined[3] as a land transaction entered into by the purchaser (either alone or jointly) wholly or partly in consideration of another land transaction being entered into by him (either alone or jointly) as vendor where an obligation to give consideration for a land transaction is met wholly or partly by way of entering into another transaction as vendor. This will clearly apply where A agrees to transfer or lease land to B in consideration of B transferring or leasing land (whether or not the same land) to A. It is also a sufficiently wide definition to apply to trilateral arrangements such as where A transfers land to B in consideration of B entering into a land transaction with C.[4] Partitions of jointly held interests also involve 'exchanges' but these are governed by special rules (see **7.8**). A major area of land exchange will be lease variations where these involve surrenders and regrants. Since the entering into the land transaction as vendor need be only part of the consideration to be provided there will be an exchange where there is an equality payment or other adjustment where interests in land are moving in opposite directions.

7.3 EXCHANGES ILLUSTRATED

7.3.1 Excepting and reserving

The question of what is a land exchange has taken on a potentially enlarged meaning because of the attitude of HMRC Stamp Taxes to the word 'creation' and the conveyancing terms such as 'excepting and reserving'.[5] It is the view of HMRC Stamp Taxes that, in all cases other than those where the interest reserved was in existence before the conveyance in question, all rights excepted and reserved can take effect only by way of transfer and regrant.[6] Since the regrant is the creation of a new right, rather than a retention of an interest from the sale, many routine conveyances will be converted into land exchanges. Although the transferor is, in the view of HMRC Stamp Taxes, acquiring a chargeable interest, it is unlikely that he will be subject to tax since he will be acquiring a minor interest which has no or little market value and because of this low market value there will be no notification obligation.[7] This approach is, however, likely to have serious implications for the

---

[3] FA 2003, s.47.

[4] There are, however, difficult conceptual questions as to whether all of the transactions in such arrangements are individual land exchanges and there may be issues where there are related subsales or assignments and there are potential exchanges in relation to the 'secondary contract'.

[5] But note the comments of Megarry J in *Sargaison* v. *Roberts* [1969] 3 All ER 1072 to the effect that HMRC should not be over-zealous to distort the tax system by taking technical land law points when these are conveyancing mechanics in order to charge tax in circumstances where Parliament did not intend them to arise.

[6] See, e.g. *St Edmundsbury and Ipswich* v. *Clark (No.2)* [1973] 3 All ER 903 (ChD), [1975] 1 All ER 772 (CA); *Johnstone* v. *Holdway* [1963] 1 All ER 432.

[7] FA 2003, ss.77 (as amended) and 77A.

purchaser of a major interest. He will be taxed upon the market value of what he is acquiring, which will not necessarily be the same as the price that he is paying.[8] For example, it is the view of HMRC Stamp Taxes that a discounted price for a quick completion or because several properties are being acquired is not a sale at market value, which is the undiscounted price.[9] Thus what appears to be a straightforward sale of a new house becomes a double transaction by way of exchange because the developer/vendor reserves estate covenants.

7.3.2 Variations of trusts and estates

There will be an 'exchange' where there are dealings in equitable interests held by beneficiaries in a trust such as, for example, where a life tenant in a trust fund, which includes both land and other investments, agrees to 'exchange' his life interest in part of those underlying assets in return for a transfer of the interest of the remainderman in other assets. Here there will be an exchange of mixed funds.

7.3.3 Business de-structuring and joint ventures

It is considered that such arrangements, which can also arise where there are mutual transfers of businesses as going concerns, such as an exchange of a hotel business with assets including goodwill[10] and chattels for a transfer of a public house business which may have goodwill and fixtures and fittings plus trading stock,[11] are likely to be regarded as involving land exchanges. However, the land elements are likely to form only part of a total package on both sides which will produce extremely complex arrangements for the apportionment of the mixed consideration and the isolation of land where the market rules apply, which may ease the apportionment exercise because 'equality payments' are to be ignored in such cases (see e.g. **Chapter 4**). However, as will frequently be the case in situations such as the variation of trusts, the market value principles do not apply because 'minor interests' are involved where the tax is charged only upon the equality considerations however that may be determined in this context of mixed assets and

---

[8] There will, of course, be extremely important issues as to the principles of valuation to be applied, such as whether the special position of the taxpayer can increase the chargeable amount. For example, there may be a surrender of a lease which confers a substantial benefit upon the landlord because it unlocks the marriage value and releases 'benefit' to the taxpayer which may be greater than the mix of the property. This will require a lengthy negotiation with HMRC as to the parties to the hypothetical sale in the open market and the terms of such sale. It is considered that this is not the correct basis for determining the amount of chargeable consideration; see **15.13**.

[9] Lap Shun Textiles v. Collector of Stamps [1976] AC 530; Cowan de Groot Properties Ltd v. Eagle Trust Plc [1991] BCLC 1045.

[10] Bearing in mind that a covenant against competition may be a transfer of goodwill, and what is frequently described in contracts as goodwill may actually be a premium payment for the land with relevant planning permission and because of its location.

[11] Requiring at least two sets of fairly sophisticated form SDLT 4 (as amended) if penalties are to be avoided.

investments. These apportionment issues which can affect both parties for other tax purposes will often require the investment of a significant amount of time and resources.

7.4 MULTI-PARTY ARRANGEMENTS

Another issue is whether the land exchange principles are applicable to multi-party arrangements, such as where A is to transfer land to B who is to transfer or lease land to C. Although the legislation states that the consideration must be the entry by B into a land transaction as 'vendor', it does not require A to be the 'purchaser' pursuant to that contract. In consequence, an arrangement whereby B is to vest property in C could be a land exchange.

A typical illustration of such an arrangement would be a development or PFI project whereby the developer is to procure the transfer or surrender of existing interests to a local authority for a cash consideration to be provided by the developer as part of the costs. Part of the arrangement may involve a lease of the site to the developer at some stage. Obviously each case will depend upon its own facts, drafting and structure which are likely to be influenced by its own particular tax and commercial considerations.[12] Nevertheless, certain of these structures may involve possible land exchanges but part of the problem, where third parties are involved, will be determining whether any consideration is provided by an appropriate person because of the basic requirement that in order to be chargeable the consideration must be provided by the purchaser or a person connected with him or a party to the transaction.[13]

7.5 THE CHARGE

Where there is a land exchange within the definition, there are two chargeable transactions; both the persons involved are subject to a market value charge and a possible obligation to file land transaction returns. There is, therefore, a charge of potentially 8 per cent and possibly more if the VAT is included in the market value computation as well as the cost of preparing so many land transaction returns (see **Chapter 4**).

The special charges will, subject to a few limited and very specific reliefs, apply to all acquisitions that are exchanges, e.g. mutual release of covenants, surrenders and regrants of leases, changes of rights to light or alterations in easements such as rights of way and sale and leaseback arrangements of the kind that occur in equity release schemes.

---

[12] Such as the possible reliefs for acquisition pursuant to compulsory powers or for certain PFI projects as in FA 2003, s.60 and Sched.4, para.17 (as amended).
[13] FA 2003, Sched.4, para.1 and s.43 (as amended).

Where parties are exchanging chargeable interests, these are treated as two separate transactions each attracting the full charge to SDLT.[14] By statute, exchanges are no longer linked transactions. It is no longer possible to avoid the double sale charge, as it was in stamp duty, by appropriate drafting. The computational rules depend upon the nature of the interest being exchanged. Subject to various special rules the basic charging provisions are set out below.[15]

7.6   COMPUTATIONAL RULES

The amount of tax chargeable and the reporting obligation depends upon whether the chargeable interest involved in the exchange includes one or more major interests.

7.6.1   Major interest for major interest

Where there is an exchange of major interests, i.e. a freehold is being transferred in consideration of a lease or there is a variation of a lease that amounts to a surrender and regrant, the chargeable consideration for each of the transactions is the market value of the interest being acquired, plus the net present value of any rent that may be payable where there is the acquisition of a lease. Any cash being paid or other consideration provided as equality is ignored.

7.6.2   Major interest for minor interest

Where there is a transfer of a major interest and the consideration for the transfer consists of or includes a non-major interest such as the grant of an easement the chargeable consideration for each of the transactions is the market value of the interest being acquired, including any rent that may be payable where there is a lease. It would seem that any cash being paid or other consideration provided as equality is ignored. This typically might occur where a person sells part of his land to a developer and is granted rights such as access to the mains services or rights of way over the land being sold and developed for the benefit of the dominant land being retained, or some other chargeable interest is regranted,[16] as where the transferee agrees to a release of a restrictive covenant over land retained by the vendor or modification of rights to light. It seems that the market test applies even to the minor interests being acquired since the part of FA 2003, Sched.4, para.5 dealing with minor interests applies only where none of the transactions involves a

---

[14]   However, each transaction is separate for the purposes of the lower rates. HMRC Stamp Taxes has abandoned the argument that exchanges are linked transactions. Currently, the two transactions are not linked so that mutual exchanges of property valued at £200,000 are both taxed at 1 per cent and not as a single transaction for £400,000 at 3 per cent.

[15]   FA 2003, Sched.4, para.5.

[16]   FA 2003, s.48(1)(b); see **2.12**.

major interest. These current provisions must apply since these refer to 'any' (but not all) of the transactions relating to major interests. However, this may not be a significant problem since minor interests will frequently not have a market value because they cannot be sold separately from the dominant land on the open market. As the acquisition will be for a negligible consideration, it will not be notifiable[17] and any entries upon the land register can be supported by a self-certificate (SDLT 60). This will not always be the case since certain minor interests such as life interests in trusts may be both valuable and saleable.

7.6.3 Minor interest for minor interest

Where the exchange consists of or includes chargeable interests that are all non-major interests on both sides of the transaction, such as where one party agrees to release a restrictive covenant in return for the grant of rights to light, or the parties are beneficiaries in a trust which includes chargeable interests in the investment fund, the chargeable consideration ignores any land interests being 'acquired'[18] and the tax is charged only upon any consideration other than land being provided for the acquisition. In other words, the land exchange elements are ignored in determining the nature of the transaction so that there is no 'creation' of a new chargeable interest for the purpose of the charge to tax so that there is not a 'land exchange'. The charge is therefore effectively limited to the equality adjustment, if any.

7.7 SPECIAL SITUATIONS

There are special rules modifying the charge or providing relief in situations where there are technically land exchanges in relation to:

* part-exchanges involving new dwellings;[19] and
* a limited range of surrenders and regrants and variations of leases.[20]

The details of these reliefs are considered elsewhere (see **Chapters 5** (exemptions) and **8** (leases)).

Additionally, special charges apply to partitions and similar dealings involving land held by a partnership.[21]

---

[17] FA 2003, s.77 (as amended).
[18] FA 2003, Sched.4, para.5(4).
[19] FA 2003, Sched.6A, paras.1 and 2. There are similar provisions in relation to arrangements for the relocation of employees which are, hopefully, not land exchanges. These are described in **Chapter 5**.
[20] FA 2003, Sched.17A, paras.9 and 16.
[21] FA 2003, Sched.15, para.16; see **Chapter 12**.

7.8 PARTITION

A partition of land involves a land exchange since one joint owner is transferring his undivided interest in part of the land in return for a similar transfer in another part of the land by another co-owner. However, it can apply only to deals in concurrent interests; it does not apply to dealings in successive interests such as those involving a life tenant and a remainderman in a trust (see **Chapter 10**). This provision applies except in relation to partnerships[22] where the full land exchange charging provisions apply. In the case of a partition or division of a chargeable interest between persons who are jointly entitled,[23] the mutual exchange of any undivided interest in the land is ignored and is not chargeable consideration. The charge is limited to any equality adjustment being made.[24]

7.8.1 Scope of 'partition'

The precise scope of this provision is uncertain. It is clearly related to the physical partition of jointly owned land,[25] but there have been conflicting views expressed from time to time by HMRC Stamp Taxes in relation to the division of a pool of assets between joint owners. There may also be issues where there is a single geographical area of land that is jointly owned but held under several different registered titles where the plots were acquired at different times from different vendors (especially where some of the titles are freehold and others are leasehold). In practice the equivalent provisions were reasonably applied for the purposes of stamp duty. Notwithstanding the expression of doubt by the technical representative in HMRC Stamp Taxes there has been no major challenge to the treatment of the division of such pools of land interests as partitions for these purposes.

---

[22] FA 2003, Sched.15, para.16 (as amended).
[23] On joint tenants see FA 2003, s.120.
[24] FA 2003, Sched.4, para.6.
[25] It will, in consequence, not provide relief if HMRC Stamp Taxes attacks severance of beneficial joint tenancies as exchanges which may be technically open to them as land exchanges of major interests.

CHAPTER 8

Leases

8.1 GENERAL

Unlike a freehold, which continues indefinitely, a lease, to create an estate in land, must be for a term of years absolute as defined by Law of Property Act (LPA) 1925, s.205(1)(xxvii).[1] The conveyancing problems affecting freeholds, and in their wake the SDLT considerations, relate primarily to the change of ownership of the same estate. Each lease, however, is a separate interest[2] with its own birth, life and inevitable death – albeit with possibilities of variations that are either merely variations or changes in the rent or surrenders and regrants,[3] and a possible continuation of the relationship of landlord and tenant (or possibly licensor and licensee) after the expiration of the fixed term of the lease by holding over or similar arrangements, or possibly resurrection by means of an option to renew. Thus tax will normally be payable on the creation of a lease or even earlier where a tenant takes possession pursuant to the agreement,[4] and may well be payable on subsequent events such as rent reviews and assignment, or a variation of the terms of the lease, and may even be payable on surrender or on continuation after termination of the original lease by holding over or renewal. Although the exercise of an option to renew a lease or the negotiation of a new lease, whether pursuant to the Landlord and Tenant Act 1954 (as amended) or otherwise, represents in general law a completely new term, the SDLT legislation contemplates situations where the new term is 'linked' with the original lease in such a way that the deemed two or more terms are aggregated retrospectively into a single term for the combined terms. In consequence, the initial tax calculation and any revision, such as following the

---

[1] But note that although when defining a major interest FA 2003, s.117 refers to a term of years absolute, the definition of lease in Sched.17A, para.1 thereto is very different and much wider. It remains to be discovered in practice just how HMRC Stamp Taxes intends to exploit and develop these two differences in definitions, one being technical the other perhaps being plain English but which may be intended to extend the definition of the term. This difference also raises questions as to whether 'rent' has a much wider meaning than its normal usages (see *T&E Homes Ltd* v. *Robinson* [1979] STC 351).

[2] But may be affected by the linked transaction and linked lease provisions (FA 2003, s.108 and Sched.17A, para.5).

[3] See *Gable Construction* v. *IRC* [1968] 1 WLR 1426; *Friends Provident Life Office* v. *British Railways Board* [1996] 1 All ER 336; FA 2003, s.43(3)(d); Sched.17A, paras.7 and 8, 13–15A.

[4] FA 2003, s.44; Sched.17A, para.12A.

revision of the rent at the end of the fifth year of the term of the lease, may need retrospective recalculation, returns and payment because rent reviews and fluctuations within the first five years of the term of the lease have to be recalculated or re-recalculated by reference to the new longer deemed lease.

The attempts to deal with the complexities of leases have produced more than five sets of major amendments to the original proposals in FA 2003 which effectively have been totally replaced more than once and, it seems, HMRC Stamp Taxes is not satisfied that the current legislation operates as intended. In particular, in the context of rent reviews, HMRC Stamp Taxes is, it seems, considering whether there would need to be more changes, specifically with regard to rent variations,[5] so that amendments will continue to emerge before the ink is dry on the previous changes, and there is little transitional relief.[6] In addition, certain major amendments operate retrospectively so that solicitors will find that the perfectly correct advice that they gave in relation to a lease some years ago is now totally incorrect and the client may be exposed to penalties and additional tax charges by relying upon the original advice.

8.2 TRANSITIONAL ISSUES

Details of transitional arrangements affecting leases fall into two categories.

8.2.1 Continuation of stamp duty charges

There are transitional arrangements concerning the grant or performance of agreements for lease where the agreement was entered into prior to 1 December 2003. Since this will apply to conditional agreements[7] there may still be leases granted that are subject to stamp duty rather than SDLT.[8] Also many areas of SDLT operate retrospectively so that, for example, there may be a rent review involving a stamp duty lease or a holding over of such a lease which may have been granted at a time when the relief for land in a disadvantaged area, such as Lincoln's Inn, was available. This retrospection may mean that the review is not taxable. It is, however, important to check the terms of FA 2003, Sched.19 since this transitional relief or exclusion from SDLT may be dependent upon any contract not having been varied on or after 1 December 2003.

---

[5] FA 2003, Sched.17A, paras.13, 14 and 15.
[6] Note the problem in relation to leases to nominees: FA 2003, Sched.16, para.3; especially certain transitional provisions dealing with the many changes to these charges.
[7] But not options; compare *Swallow Hotels* v. *IRC* [2000] STC 45.
[8] See FA 2003, Sched.19; see **1.2**.

8.2.2 Changes in SDLT regime

Each of the many various amendments to the legislation relating to SDLT leases will have its own set of transitional provisions. In general the completion or substantial performance of an agreement that was entered into prior to the change date will be governed by the preceding law; but this is generally subject to qualification that there has been no alteration or amendment of the agreement.

8.3   RESTRICTIONS UPON TRANSITIONAL RELIEFS: CHANGES IN CONTRACT

The exclusion from the changeover from stamp duty to SDLT for agreements for leases exchanged prior to the changeover date and especially those exchanged prior to July 2003, does not apply where there is any alteration to the agreement. As HMRC Stamp Taxes takes an aggressive view on this point, anything other than a totally trivial amendment such as modification of the covenant relating to pets on the premises destroys the transitional relief, regardless of the state of commercial negotiations, which may mean that it is too late to go back and renegotiate the basic principles or heads of terms because these are now too expensive to pursue. There are major problems where the agreement for lease is to grant a lease in the form of the draft in the appropriate Schedule to the agreement with such amendments as the parties may agree. Such agreements to change or modify the terms even to a small extent may well destroy the transitional relief. Similarly, where there are building agreements, modifications of these building specifications or asking for 'extra' when purchasing or leasing a new building could, on the current HMRC Stamp Taxes view, produce a significantly increased tax charge which has not been factored into the commercial pricing of the overall viability of the deal. Professional advisers face serious risks in assisting in the preparation of the relevant documentation if they do not give detailed advice on the risks of extra cost being undertaken by the client in such matters, even in routine purchases of newly constructed houses. Parties should, therefore, investigate whether any amendment of an agreement for lease could have adverse consequences or whether it may be more efficient to complete the agreement, obtain the benefit of the favourable treatment and deal with any SDLT in respect of the amendment to the lease.

8.4   GUESTIMATES AND RETROSPECTION

In addition much of the SDLT applicable to leases is on a provisional or estimated basis which has to be revised retrospectively in the light of subsequent events. In consequence, and in general, the subsequent events may be governed by law that has been repealed or amended in the intervening period and exemptions that were available at the time of the agreement for lease may still be available notwithstanding that changes have been made in relation to those reliefs (see **8.29**). This is not a true aspect of 'wait-and-see' since it is not a question of waiting to see whether a tax charge arises or a relief is available, it is simply a machinery for adjusting the charge upon the initial transaction with the benefit of data arising from subsequent events.

8.5 'LEASE'

SDLT is charged by reference to 'leases'.[9] Unfortunately, there are two provisions dealing with leases. One of these is a minor provision as part of the definition of 'major interest' which is defined as including a term of years absolute whether subsisting at law or in equity.[10] It may be that this limits the definition of 'major interest' to those cases where there is a lease that meets the test of being a term of years absolute. On a more general level and presumably providing the basic definition for all purposes of the charge to tax, it is provided[11] that in England and Wales and Northern Ireland a 'lease' means an interest or right in or over land for a term of years (whether fixed or periodic) or a tenancy at will[12] or other interest or right in or over land determinable by notice at any time. Although there are certain provisions[13] which are attempts at adapting English legislation to Scottish land law, there is no separate definition of 'lease' as such for Scotland.

The fact that there is not only a reference within the legislation to the traditional definition of 'lease' as a term of years absolute but also a completely different working definition normally means that there will, obviously, be many questions as to whether there is a 'lease' whenever there is any form of temporary interest in land which, in traditional terms, is not an occupation of the land for a rent with exclusive possession, etc. In consequence, at some stage there will inevitably have to be a debate with HMRC Stamp Taxes as to whether temporary arrangements are 'leases'. This will apply to transactions such as an agreement by a purchaser of land to grant temporary rights in or over land, such as interim regrants and rights of way over land being sold to the vendor of the land as to involve the grant or the creation of a 'lease' and, in consequence, whether any payments thereunder are dealt with by the 'rent' regime[14] or whether such payments are to be taxed as periodical payments.[15] Much may depend upon the drafting.[16] This could become an acute problem where, in connection with the assignment of a lease, the assignee regrants

---

[9]   Which can include substantial performance of 'agreements for lease'.

[10]   FA 2003, s.117(2)(b).

[11]   FA 2003, Sched.17A, para.1.

[12]   Currently tenancies at will are not chargeable interests although they are included within the provisions relating to leases for an indefinite period (FA 2003, Sched.17A, para.4(5)(b)). Also holding as a tenant at will may constitute some form of taking of possession for the purposes of substantial performance and the triggering of a charge to tax (FA 2003, s.44).

[13]   FA 2003, Sched.17A, para.19.

[14]   See, for example, *T&E Homes Ltd* v. *Robinson* [1979] STC 351.

[15]   FA 2003, s.52; see **4.31.4** and **4.31.5**.

[16]   See **8.22** and **8.21** on whether service charges and VAT are 'rent'. Note especially FA 2003, Sched.17A, paras.6 and 10.

rights to the assignor. Such rights[17] will be effective only against the leasehold interest and may not affect the freehold reversion. In consequence, such rights will be of a temporary nature and the grant of such rights by the assignee may consist of the grant of a 'lease' and the nature of any payments being made or, in relevant circumstances, the market value of such rights may depend upon the nature of any rights and whether they are interests in land or simply contractual arrangements.[18]

The question will be how far the general land law will apply to help resolve these issues.

8.6 BASIC LAND LAW DEFINITION OF 'LEASE'

A lease, to take effect at law, must be by deed[19] which constitutes the 'grant' of the lease.[20] An agreement to grant a lease must also be made in writing – a written memorandum of an oral agreement is no longer effective,[21] and the technical requirements may be a key issue as to when the tax charge arises and numerous other problems such as the five-year period for rent reviews and the length of the term. An option for the grant of a lease may now have to be exercised in writing,[22] but this is by no means clear since the terms of the lease will be the written option contract which may become or form the basis of a contractual document.

However, where the lease is to take effect in possession for a term not exceeding three years at the best rent reasonably obtainable without a fine, it may be granted in writing, or even orally.[23] In such cases informal arrangements may amount to a yearly or other periodic tenancy, but the question of whether it is a lease or a licence, while important, may be difficult to determine in the absence of writing.

---

[17] FA 2003, s.48(1)(b).

[18] Ideally, such payments should not be described as 'rent' since this may be sufficient to turn them into 'rent' so that there is a tax upon the total net present value as opposed to the special rules for giving a 'capital value' to periodical payments; see **8.20** and **4.31**.

[19] LPA 1925, s.52.

[20] An agreement for lease is not a 'grant': *City Permanent Building Society* v. *Miller* [1952] Ch 840. A point not understood by those preparing FA 2003. This technical error gave rise to considerable problems, particularly in relation to compliance when different notification obligations applied to substantial performance, agreements for leases and the subsequent grant of the lease. An attempt to deal with the fundamental problems of taking possession under an agreement for lease prior to taking the grant (FA 2003, Sched.17A, para.12A; Sched.4, para.10 (as amended)), has given rise to even greater problems and increased tax liability in practice.

[21] Law of Property (Miscellaneous Provisions) Act 1989, s.2; but see *Yaxley* v. *Gotts* [1999] 3 WLR 1217, but there may be problems where no terms have been agreed: *Scammell* v. *Ouston* [1941] AC 251; *Sweet & Maxwell* v. *Universal News Services* [1964] 2 QB 699; *Yeoman's Row Management* v. *Cobbe* [2008] 4 All ER 713.

[22] *Spiro* v. *Glencrown* [1991] 2 WLR 931.

[23] LPA 1925, s.54.

8.6.1 Indefinite terms and periodic arrangements

Although the SDLT legislation refers to a lease for an 'indefinite term' a lease must also be for a term of years absolute; the length of the term must be fixed and certain before it starts,[24] even though it may thereafter be brought to a premature end by, for example, the operation of a break clause[25] in the lease, or by forfeiture. If, however, there is a lease which in other circumstances is to continue until the happening of an uncertain event, it is invalid,[26] and the fact that the 'agreed lease' is invalid means that entry into possession and the payment of rent may produce a tax charge totally different from that expected by the parties, who will undoubtedly be exposed to penalties for filing a negligent return.[27] This does not apply where the lease is granted for a maximum term which is expressed to be terminable on the happening of an earlier event: this is taxed as a lease for the maximum term without refund if terminated earlier by the happening of the specified event.[28] A sublease granted for a term of the same length as the lease out of which it is purported to be granted operates not as the grant of a new lease but as an assignment of the existing lease.[29]

8.7 LEASE OR LICENCE?

The charge is *prima facie* limited to leases or agreements for lease of land; it does not apply to licences to use or occupy land or tenancies at will which are exempt interests[30] but entry pursuant to such arrangements may operate as substantial performance of some other agreement.[31] In consequence, the distinction between a lease and a licence, so important to the question of security of tenure, has equal significance in the SDLT context of the transaction. Whether or not the parties have created a licence or a lease is a matter of construction in each case.[32] It should be remembered that the courts look at the substance of the transaction, not necessarily at the name that the parties have chosen to give it,[33] but a statement in the document to the effect that the parties do not intend to create the relationship of landlord and

---

[24]   See *Lace* v. *Chantler* [1944] 1 All ER 305.

[25]   Which is not the same as a surrender: *Barrett* v. *Morgan* [2000] 1 All ER 481.

[26]   *Lace* v. *Chantler* [1944] KB 368 where a tenancy for the duration of the war was held to be invalid and note the effect on such drafting of Landlord and Tenant Act 1954 and whether there is a lease for a fixed term, which may influence the taxation consequences of holding over; see **8.47**.

[27]   It is important to note that within the overall context of tax self-assessment HMRC has imposed major penalties where the taxpayer has incorrectly overpaid tax. His 'sin' is to seek a repayment of the tax overpaid which is something not regarded as acceptable by HMRC. The penalty imposed in one case was a multiple of the tax overpaid!

[28]   But see below on break clauses and notices to quit at **8.51.2**.

[29]   *Milmo* v. *Carreras* [1946] KB 306.

[30]   FA 2003, s.48.

[31]   FA 2003, s.44(3).

[32]   *Addiscombe Garden Estates* v. *Crabbe* [1957] 3 All ER 563; but subject, according to Lord Templeman, to certain presumptions in relation to residential arrangements (*Street* v. *Mountford* [1985] 1 AC 809), or domestic arrangements where the parties may not intend to create legal relationships of landlord and tenant as in *Facchini* v. *Bryson* [1952] 1 TLR 1386.

[33]   Addiscombe Garden Estates v. Crabbe [1957] 3 All ER 563.

tenant may tip the balance in borderline cases.[34] This is in accordance with general principles of construction that parties cannot enter into an agreement containing such a statement and then contend for the contrary position unless the contract is clearly inconsistent with the provisions[35] or there is a clear legislative policy contrary to such an arrangement.

HMRC Stamp Taxes starts from the proposition that if the arrangement confers exclusive possession upon the occupier and otherwise contains terms appropriate to a lease, it may be held to have created a tenancy, even though called a licence.[36] There may, however, be differences between arrangements relating to business property and those affecting domestic arrangements, since in relation to the former category the judiciary have generally rejected Lord Templeman's rigid formulation and have been prepared to pay some attention to commercial needs and the wishes of the parties since issues of social policy such as security of tenure for individual tenants are not involved.

However, difficult issues of classification can arise under building arrangements where a developer who is entitled to the benefit of an agreement for lease is allowed into occupation of the premises in order to carry out the building works. In practice he may have the equivalent of exclusive occupation and if he is paying a fee or fees HMRC Stamp Taxes may claim that the licence to enter and to build is some form of tenancy.[37] Moreover, such an arrangement may involve the prospective tenant taking possession and so substantially performing the agreement for lease triggering an effective date with a tax charge and an obligation to notify the transaction. Fortunately, an early effective date may operate to exclude from charge many building contracts and fitting out arrangements, provided that the taxpayer ensures that any licence he has to enter upon the land amounts to taking possession of the whole or substantially the whole of the land[38] (see **Chapters 3** and **9**).

8.8 DEEMED LEASES

Certain transactions are treated as giving rise to the grant of a new lease which differs from their analysis and effects as a matter of general land law and conveyancing. These transactions include the following.

---

[34] *Ogwr Borough Council* v. *Dykes* [1989] 2 All ER 880.
[35] Massey v. Crown Life [1978] 2 All ER 576; Ready Mixed Concrete v. Minister for Pensions [1968] 1 All ER 433.
[36] *Street* v. *Mountford* [1985] 2 WLR 877; *Ogwr Borough Council* v. *Dykes* [1989] 2 All ER 880.
[37] Such argument arose from time to time when licences were subject to stamp duty pursuant to the 'Bond Covenant' head of charge. The removal of the charge in 1971 has meant that the argument has lain dormant because of the lack of opportunity to attack such arrangements; but the point arose from time to time. It is likely to resurface significantly and FA 2003, ss.44A and 45A represent an intention to attack such arrangements.
[38] FA 2003, Sched.4, para.10.

8.8.1 Assignments

Assignments of leases (see further **8.60** and following) are treated as involving the grant of a new lease by the assignor[39] where the original lease was exempt because:

- it was part of a sale and leaseback arrangement;[40]
- group relief or reconstruction or acquisition relief applied;[41]
- it was a transfer involving public bodies;[42]
- charities relief applied;[43]
- it was a lease granted to nominees between the Finance Act 2004 and Finance (No.2) Act 2005;[44] or
- it fell within any such regulations as are mentioned in FA 2003, s.123(3) (regulations reproducing in relation to SDLT the effect of enactments providing for exemption from stamp duty).[45]

The grant is treated as being:

- for a term equal to the unexpired term of the original lease; and
- on the same terms as those on which the assignee holds that lease after the assignment.

In consequence, the assignee will be taxed upon any consideration paid for the assignment that is properly allocated to the land and fixtures, plus the net present value of the rent for the balance of the term. There will be the obligation to adopt the complex multiple reporting requirements for dealing with variable rent. It seems that the five-year period and abnormal rent increase provisions apply with full force to the deemed new lease with the relevant date commencing on the effective date for the actual assignment.

This charge does not apply where the relief in question is group relief, reconstruction or acquisition relief or charities relief which has been withdrawn as a result of a clawback event occurring before the effective date of the assignment.

8.8.2 Variations other than rent: surrender and regrant

Certain variations of leases operate as deemed surrenders and the grant of a new lease;[46] this applies even where the arrangement is set out as a deed of variation. The conveyancing consequences applying by operation of law prevail over the form of

---

[39] FA 2003, Sched.17A, para.11.
[40] FA 2003, s.57A.
[41] FA 2003, Sched.7, Part 1 or Part 2.
[42] FA 2003, s.66.
[43] FA 2003, Sched.8.
[44] FA 2003, Sched.16, para.3 (as amended).
[45] Stamp Duty Land Tax (Consequential Amendment of Enactments) Regulations 2003, SI 2003/2867; see **5.28**.
[46] Friends Provident Life Office v. British Railways Board [1996] 1 All ER 336.

the document *prima facie* producing a chargeable transaction. Fortunately there are certain but very restricted reliefs from the tax charge in such cases.[47]

8.8.3   Increase of rent

A variation of the rent does not operate as a surrender and regrant even where this is by a deed of variation and not pursuant to a rent review.[48]

Two areas of rent increase (but not rent reduction which is treated differently)[49] produce deemed new leases, namely:

- an increase in the rent otherwise than in accordance with the terms of the lease such as where a landlord pays a sum to the tenant to agree to an increase in rent;[50]
- where after the expiration of the fifth year of the term of the lease there is an abnormal increase in the rent.[51]

These issues of rent variations are considered later in this chapter (see **8.27**), but it should be noted that it is not expressly provided that the actual lease and the deemed lease merge for all purposes so that these deemed new leases may remain separate from the original lease for the purposes of calculating the rent duty and for general compliance purposes.[52]

8.9   GRANT OF LEASES, SUBSTANTIAL PERFORMANCE AND COMPLIANCE

A number of practical problems exist in relation to agreements for lease and the grant thereof relating to the filing of the land transaction return (SDLT 1) and the computation of the tax.

- It appears that as a result of the changes made in FA 2004[53] the same lease arrangement may have at its commencement two effective dates[54] producing two separate chargeable transactions, i.e. substantial performance of the agreement and the grant of the lease; but with a credit for the sums paid as rent.[55]
- In virtually every case the tax will be required to be calculated initially on an estimated basis under the sanction of interest and penalties if the estimate is unsatisfactory.

---

[47]   FA 2003, Sched.17A, paras.9 and 16; see **8.58**.
[48]   *Gable Construction* v. *IRC* [1968] 1 WLR 1426.
[49]   FA 2003, Sched.17A, para.15A and s.43(3)(d).
[50]   FA 2003, Sched.17A, para.13.
[51]   FA 2003, Sched.17A, paras.14 and 15.
[52]   But see FA 2003, Sched.17A, para.14(6).
[53]   Inserting what is now FA 2003, Sched.17A, para.12A.
[54]   Query whether other transactions have two effective dates and separate chargeable transactions or are one chargeable transaction with one effective date but two or more notification dates: see FA 2003, s.44(9).
[55]   FA 2003, Sched.17A, para.12A.

- Assignees of leases may have to take over the original tenant's outstanding tax liability.[56]
- Assignees of leases may find that, although they are not, as such, obliged to resolve the provisional tax position of the original tenant or any intermediate assignee of the lease, the SDLT position is dependent upon or affected by the tax position of the original tenant and/or intermediate tenants, such as when dealing with rent reviews and other variations after the expiration of the fifth year of the term of the lease as this is determined for the purposes of the tax but which is not the same as the fifth year after the term commencement date (see for example **8.50** and **8.60**). Similar dependence upon the tax record of the original tenant will occur upon holding over pursuant to the Landlord and Tenant Act 1954 (as amended) (see further **8.47** and **8.61**). These actions of the current tenant are dependent upon the tax history of the lease and there may be problems in resolving the current tax issue where the previous tenants are in dispute with HMRC Stamp Taxes as to the new tax liability.
- Special linked transaction rules apply which can affect assignees of the lease and even other leases and deemed new leases[57] which are linked because of the need to apportion the nil rate slice for rents between linked leases and because of the possibility of linked successive leases.

8.10 'DOUBLE CHARGE'

8.10.1 Effective date for leases

The effective date for leases is now split. The starting point is that virtually every agreement for lease will contain a provision that it is to be completed by a 'conveyance', i.e. by the formal grant of the lease so that substantial performance of the agreement becomes an issue.[58] There is an effective date at substantial performance with another at grant but with credit if these two events have the misfortune to be separated. There is now a potentially significant downside in resting upon the agreement for lease and postponing the actual grant because the tax charge can increase over the intervening period.

8.10.2 Substantial performance of agreement for lease and later grant

The charge to tax arises upon the grant of the lease and, if earlier, the substantial performance of the agreement for lease (see also **3.7**). The failure of the draftsman of FA 2003 to understand conveyancing practice, and the meaning of key technical terms such as 'grant' has produced amending legislation which is defective in

---

[56] FA 2003, s.81A, Sched.17A, para.12.
[57] FA 2003, Sched.17A, paras.14 and 15.
[58] FA 2003, ss.119 and 44.

concept but the defects are being exploited by HMRC Stamp Taxes to enlarge the tax base and compliance obligations significantly, namely:

- substantial performance of an agreement for lease (where the actual lease has not been previously granted or is not granted simultaneously with such substantial performance) is to be treated as the grant of a lease; and
- when the lease is formally granted there is a deemed surrender of the deemed lease arising upon substantial performance of the agreement for lease, but the tax in respect of the rent has the benefit of a credit for the rent, but only the rent, taxed at the time of substantial performance.[59]

8.10.3 Substantial performance: deemed grant

The basic rules of substantial performance apply to agreements for lease (see also **Chapter 3**), namely when there has been no prior or simultaneous actual grant of the lease, substantial performance occurs at the earliest of:

- when the lessee takes possession of the land such as where he enters upon the land before the deed is executed;
- payment of the whole or substantially the whole of any premium (i.e. 90 per cent of the premium where this is a cash payment);
- first payment of rent. This applies when rent is actually paid rather than the quarter or other date when it becomes due.

8.10.4 Two effective dates and notifiable transaction amendments

While this change to the consequences of substantial performance of the agreement for lease was apparently intended to remove the compliance problems arising from the manifest defects in the drafting of the original different reporting obligations for leases and for agreements for lease, it is currently being exploited as creating two chargeable events in relation to the same lease. For example, HMRC Stamp Taxes has already stated that where the substantial performance of an agreement for lease is exempt because it is an intra-group transaction within FA 2003, Sched.7, Part 1, this exemption no longer automatically carries over to the actual grant of the lease (see further **Chapter 13**). The exemption has to be reassessed by reference to the facts, intentions and circumstances existing as at the date of the grant of the lease. It is questionable whether the interpretation is correct given the apparent purpose of the amendment but there is limited support for the aggressive approach in the legislation.[60] If the interpretation is correct, a wide range of consequences follows from the official position including:

---

[59] FA 2003, Sched.17A, para.12A.

[60] Such as the rent credit mechanism which would not be necessary if the grant of the lease related back to substantial performance of the agreement for lease in para.12A itself; and the specific backdating of the relief for works such as building and fitting out works to the substantial performance of the agreement for lease by FA 2003, Sched.4, para.10 (as amended).

- a new effective date creating a new five-year review period for variable rents.[61] This is a key issue for assignees of leases to investigate;
- the possibility that there is a new assumed rent for years after the fifth year of the new term arising from the grant affecting linked transactions and subsequent abnormal rent increases;
- any exercise of an option to renew which is a linked transaction will be linked with the actual lease rather than the agreement for lease, since linked successive leases relate back to the effective date for the renewed lease;
- a different discount rate may apply for the net present value of the rent;
- the tax upon the rent has to be recalculated from the date of the grant by reference to the then passing rent subject to the limited credit mechanism. The net present value will almost certainly be different because different rent periods will be involved and there will be a shorter term;
- where the option to tax the rent for VAT has been exercised after substantial performance[62] but before the grant of the lease, the tax computation will have to include the VAT upon the rent although it was ignored at the time of substantial performance because the VAT after the exercise of the option to tax will be tax actually payable at the second and operative effective date for the actual grant of the lease;[63]
- changes in the rate of VAT will have to be taken into account when calculating the net present value of the rent;
- the rates, exemptions and charging provisions may differ from those applied to the substantial performance of the agreement for lease, subject to any transitional provisions where the law is changed;
- the term of the lease will differ from the term taken into account for the agreement for lease (i.e. it will be shorter, from a later date) which will be a complicating arithmetical factor when calculating the new tax on the rent;
- although rent payable under the agreement for lease would be 'rent' and taxed initially as such, it may be regarded as rent paid in respect of the lease but prior to its effective date and so taxed as a premium,[64] but this is subject to a relieving provision.[65] However, it seems that HMRC Stamp Taxes' argument is vulnerable because of its view that the grant is a new lease so that the rent is paid in respect of a different lease;
- dates for rent reviews may be fixed by reference to the term commencement date which will almost certainly precede the grant of the lease and frequently will precede substantial performance such as where a prospective tenant enters prior to the formal consent of the landlord to the lease[66] and the tax charge

---

[61] FA 2003, Sched.17A, paras.7 and 8.
[62] See also **4.30** and **8.21** on whether the exercise of the option to tax contributes to an abnormal increase in the rent.
[63] FA 2003, Sched.4, para.2.
[64] FA 2003, Sched.5, para.1A.
[65] FA 2003, Sched.17A, paras.9 and 9A.
[66] Note *Warmington* v. *Miller* [1973] 2 All ER 372.

arises early in the transaction.[67] In consequence, the first rent review may arise within the first five SDLT years of the lease. There is a relief for rent reviews in the last quarter of the fifth year of the term.[68] Although this special treatment is available for the agreement for lease it will almost inevitably not be available in respect of the later grant of the lease which will be much closer to the first review date than the prior substantial performance and be well after the three months from the term commencement date.

There may be arguments against certain of these potential applications of the charge by HMRC Stamp Taxes but it will be clear that given the relatively relaxed approach, in practice, to the actual grant of the lease, particularly for shorter terms, the taxation consequences can be arbitrary and capricious but severe. Professional advisers who do not discuss with their client the desirability of ensuring that substantial performance and grant coincide may, justifiably, find themselves in difficulty.

8.11   RELIEFS FROM THE DOUBLE CHARGE

Two reliefs against the separate double charges for substantial performance and grant of the lease are provided, but unhelpfully these also provide support for the argument that the same transaction now has two separate effective dates. These reliefs are:

- the chargeable rent reserved by the new lease is reduced by reference to the rent payable under the agreement for lease.[69] It is important to note the nature of this relief, namely merely deeming it to be a transaction with the rent credit relief;[70] and
- the exemption for works including fitting out executed after the effective date applies where this is substantial performance to all works carried out after the effective date for the agreement for lease, notwithstanding that they are carried out before the effective date for the grant of the lease.[71]

It is considered that, because the deemed surrender is not expressed to be in consideration of the grant of the lease and vice versa, so notwithstanding a surrender and regrant is a land exchange no charges arise by reference to the value of the

---

[67]   The legislation is silent on *inter alia* the problems if the effective date for SDLT precedes the term commencement date or the lease taking effect in possession.

[68]   FA 2003, Sched.17A, para.7A(c).

[69]   FA 2003, Sched.17A, para.12A. On issues relating to the computation of rent credits see **8.26**.

[70]   FA 2003, Sched.17A, para.9; see **8.26**.

[71]   FA 2003, Sched.4, para.10 (as amended).

interests involved which could be quite substantial because of the works carried out in the interim period.[72]

8.12   GRANT OF LEASES TO THIRD PARTIES

A frequent practical situation is where a person such as a developer enters into an agreement for lease with the freeholder and subsequently enters into arrangements with a third party pursuant to which he directs the grant of the lease to the third party.[73] Alternatively a person may agree to take leases of several flats,[74] hoping to dispose of the lease without paying stamp taxes. For such persons the stamp tax planning strategy has fundamentally altered, but the one-size-fits-all drafting means that leases are now eligible for a form of subsale relief[75] and a special albeit limited relief is now available.[76]

8.13   SPECIFIC RELIEF

The specific relief for leases to third parties applies where a person enters into an agreement for lease and before he substantially performs that agreement he assigns his interest as lessee to a third party. In such a case the original agreement takes effect as if it were with the assignee who is treated as providing as part of the consideration under that agreement for lease including any consideration given for the assignment.[77] A consequence of this relief for the original party to the agreement for lease is that the third party will pay tax upon the rent as well as any premium for the lease (i.e. as part of the charge he takes over the original party's contractual

---

[72]   Since the legislation does not deal with the situation as involving surrenders for consideration for the grant of the new lease, the relieving provisions of FA 2003, Sched.17A, para.16 could not apply so that it is vital that the deeming provisions do not provide for a surrender and regrant.

[73]   Cf. *Att-Gen* v. *Brown* (1849) 3 Exch 662. Obviously a key planning issue will be seeking to reduce the charge to tax upon the costs of the building works; see **Chapter 9**.

[74]   Which will be linked transactions even if embodied in separate legally independent contracts.

[75]   FA 2003, s.45 (as amended). Unfortunately, although because of the potential double charge upon the deposit by the original tenant the specific relief may be less favourable in many cases, it is provided that the original relief pursuant to s.45 cannot be claimed where the specific Sched.17A, para.12B is available, but where the para.12B relief does not apply the basic relief of FA 2003, s.45 (as amended) may be available (see **Chapter 5**).

[76]   FA 2003, Sched.17A, para.12B.

[77]   This provision will be somewhat random in its effect. It will apply where a person agrees to acquire several flats intending to sell them on at a profit. Normally he will not substantially perform his contract and he will escape the charge to tax. However, a developer will frequently have substantially performed his contract by taking possession in order to commence construction, if only to protect his building costs from tax. The assignee runs the risk of an element of double taxation. He will usually reimburse the original tenant for any sums such as deposits paid to the lessor. Unless HMRC Stamp Taxes is prepared to treat the new contract as being modified to exclude sums paid by the assignee prior to the assignment such sums will be effectively brought into the computation twice.

obligations such as premiums and rent)[78] and any consideration paid for the 'assignment'. Where the original contract has been substantially performed prior to the assignment, the assignment is a separate chargeable transaction. In consequence, the original tenant pays tax when he substantially performs and the assignee pays tax upon the sum paid to the original tenant for the lease, possibly including building works.[79] The third party in this case will need to investigate the original party's position since this fundamentally affects his tax liability; suitable indemnities may be required.

It is a condition for the relief that the person 'assigns' his interest as lessee under an agreement for lease. On certain analyses the direction to grant the lease to the third party can be an assignment[80] but this will usually occur after substantial performance and the tax charge has arisen, and the relief under discussion will not be available. These reliefs do not apply where there is a sublease granted by the original party to the agreement for lease, such as where the developer grants occupational subleases,[81] or directs the landlord to grant what are, in effect, subleases to the occupational tenants[82] prior to dealing with the headlease. That apart, the scope of the provision is unclear. 'Assign' would, in context, seem to require a formal transfer of the right, i.e. sufficient documentation to vest the right to call for the lease to be granted in the third party.[83] This will be a potentially limited situation since these tripartite arrangements are usually part of a development arrangement, whether of building new houses or flats or constructing commercial premises. An outright assignment would be therefore be difficult until the end of the construction phase because there will be outstanding building arrangements and obligations which the third party will not wish to take over. Moreover, at this early stage the right to call for the lease is likely to be conditional upon the satisfactory completion of the buildings so that an outright assignment is not really possible. The normal arrangement would seem to be for the original lessee to agree to procure the grant of a lease to the third party, as and when the right to call for the lease becomes unconditional.[84]

Although the legislation does not deal with the situation clearly, it is tentatively suggested that 'assign' includes 'agrees to assign' which will include 'agrees to

---

[78]   However, those responsible for the structuring of this provision have overlooked numerous technical issues such as the payment of a deposit by the original party which is recouped on the assignment consideration and the problem of building or fitting out obligations as part of the chargeable consideration: *Eastham* v. *Leigh London and Provincial Properties Ltd* [1971] 2 All ER 887; see **9.6**.

[79]   FA 2003, Sched.4, para.10.

[80]   *Att-Gen* v. *Brown* (1849) 3 Ex 662.

[81]   See **5.10** on whether the general subsale relief is available where the first purchaser takes a transfer of the freehold and grants a lease out of that interest.

[82]   The grant of such subleases may amount to substantial performance of the headlease if the head tenant becomes entitled to the rent: FA 2003, s.44(4).

[83]   It is interesting to compare the drafting of FA 2003, s.45 (as amended) which refers to a person becoming entitled to call for a conveyance.

[84]   But note the potential application of FA 2003, ss.44A and 45A; see **Chapter 9**.

procure the grant of the lease' and also applies to dealings in part of the land.[85] Unless the legislation is stretched in this way, the provisions of Sched.17A, para.12A are effectively redundant and FA 2003, s.45, will continue to apply to most cases.

8.13.1 Residual relief

Where the strict conditions for the specific relief are not satisfied, particularly if there are problems as to whether there has been an 'assignment', the general relief for subsales and assignments may be available.[86]

8.14 LEASES AND NOMINEES

Certain tax planning and commercial joint venture arrangements involve either the transfer of an interest to a nominee who grants a lease back to the transferor, or the grant of a lease to a nominee to hold absolutely for the landlord. It was held that in Scotland a lease to a nominee is invalid[87] but it seems that in England and Northern Ireland[88] a lease to a nominee for the lessor or a lease by a nominee to the beneficial owner is valid.[89] Such leases are *prima facie* taxable upon their terms, but in debates the Government has indicated that because the legal title alone has no value, the connected company charge[90] will not apply to deem a market value premium at least for a lease to a nominee.[91] The assignment of such a lease was, between the Finance Act 2004 and the Finance (No.2) Act 2005, taxed as the grant of a new lease by the

---

[85] There is also the difficulty in that the draftsman has failed to deal with the routine situation of a residential or industrial site developer dealing with several third parties who may each require separate leases of their house or business premises. There is no provision dealing with the assignment of the right to call for a part lease. It would seem prudent to include express provision in the original agreement for lease to call for or assign the leases separately or in parts.

[86] FA 2003, s.45; see **5.8**.

[87] *Kildrummy* v. *IRC* [1990] STC 657.

[88] See *Belaney* v. *Belaney* (1866–67) LR 2 Ch App 138; *Rye* v. *Rye* [1962] 1 All ER 146; *Ingram* v. *IRC* [1999] STC 37.

[89] A question has arisen as to whether this specific provision dealing with leases to nominees applies in all situations where a lease is granted to a nominee or whether it is limited to situations where the lease is granted to the nominee which is to hold it for the benefit of the beneficial owner lessor. In most cases where the nominee is acting for a third party there will be an arm's length transaction with full consideration, but there may be situations e.g. development on a joint basis, where the parties intend to hold their land through leases granted to nominees or acquired by nominees from third parties. In these situations a substantial charge may arise although in other situations a relief may be granted. HMRC Stamp Taxes seems to take the view that the provision applies to all situations even where the nominee is acting as nominee not for the lessor but for a third party. Thus, where a lease has been granted by a company to a nominee for an associated company the relief for intra-group leases (FA 2003, Sched.7, Part 1) has been refused where the nominee was not beneficially owned by the lessor or lessee so as to fall within the SDLT grouping definition.

[90] FA 2003, ss.53 and 54 and Sched.16, para.3; see **Chapter 4**.

[91] This view may be incorrect since, subject to any contrary legislation a transaction involving a nominee is a non-event for SDLT: FA 2003, Sched.16, para.3 (as amended).

assignor to the assignee;[92] but a later lease is currently taxed upon grant as if the nominee rules do not apply.[93] This new charge also applies where the freehold is transferred to a nominee which grants a lease back to the beneficial owner. When investigating title on the purchase of a lease not only is the status of the lessee and lessor a key consideration, the dates are also important because of the special charge for leases granted between the Finance Act 2004 and the Finance (No.2) Act 2005.

8.15 THE CHARGE TO TAX ON LEASES: GENERAL

There are two basic elements to tax upon leases:

- a charge upon the rent; and
- a separate charge upon consideration other than rent (for convenience described as 'premium').

The tax upon the rent is payable in addition to any tax upon the premium[94] which includes not only cash payments but also consideration in kind, works[95] and services (see **Chapter 15**) as well as deemed premiums such as where market value rules apply.[96] Moreover, for non-residential leases the rent reserved may affect the availability of the nil rate for any 'premium'.[97]

8.16 DUE DILIGENCE AND RENT

To some extent SDLT runs with the land in relation to leases. Third parties can be affected in two main ways but in a variety of situations, namely:

- assignees of leases are made liable for the tax in certain situations such as during the first five years of the lease and where there are variable premium payments (see further **8.61**); and
- the assignee of a lease may find that his tax liability is dependent upon the tax position of previous tenants such as in connection with rent reviews after the fifth year of the term, holding over and assignments of exempt leases.

It is in consequence a serious risk to buy a lease without a full history of the taxation of the rent. Detailed copies of the calculations not the final figures are required (see **Appendix A**).

---

[92] FA 2003, Sched.17A, para.11 (as amended).
[93] FA 2003, Sched.16, para.3 (as amended).
[94] FA 2003, Sched.5, para.9(4).
[95] Note Eastham v. Leigh London and Provincial Properties Ltd [1971] 2 All ER 887.
[96] FA 2003, s.53; Sched.15, Part 3.
[97] FA 2003, Sched.5, paras.9 and 9A; for shared ownership see FA 2003, Sched.9, para.2(4A).

8.17   TAXATION OF RENTS

8.17.1   Chargeable events affecting rent

SDLT is chargeable upon the net present value of the rent.[98] However, where there are linked transactions the net present value is not taken into account when determining the chargeable consideration for those transactions.[99] Although the nil rate band for lease premiums is not available for non-residential property if the average annual rent exceeds £1,000, where there is a lease of mixed property such as a shop with a flat above it is treated as two leases and the rent and premium have to be apportioned on a just and reasonable basis.[100]

The charge upon rents is not imposed solely upon the grant or deemed grant of a lease; there are numerous charges and reporting obligations arising in relation to:

- substantial performance of the agreement for lease;
- the grant of the lease with a rent credit for rent payable pursuant to the previously substantially performed agreement for lease;
- variations of rent during or at the end of the first five years of the term including routine rent reviews;
- 'abnormal' increases in the rent after the end of the first five years of the term;[101]
- increases of rent other than pursuant to the terms of the lease;[102]
- reductions in the rent;[103]
- assignments of leases that were within certain exemptions when granted.[104] These are taxed as the grant of a new lease taxable, *inter alia*, upon the then passing rent.[105]

It must also be noted that certain variations of lease operate as surrenders and grants of new leases which will be taxable in respect of the rent but with certain credits for previous tax charges upon the rent.[106]

---

[98]   FA 2003, Sched.5, para.2; Sched.6, paras.5 and 9.
[99]   FA 2003, Sched.5, para.9(5).
[100]   FA 2003, Sched.5, para.9 and Sched.4, para.4.
[101]   FA 2003, Sched.17A, paras.14 and 15.
[102]   FA 2003, Sched.17A, para.13.
[103]   FA 2003, Sched.17A, para.15A.
[104]   Certain leases granted to nominees between 17 March 2005 and 19 July 2007 are subject to special charges. The provisions have been amended but the charge appears to remain.
[105]   FA 2003, Sched.17A, para.11.
[106]   FA 2003, s.43(3)(d) and Sched.17A, para.15A (as amended) and para.9.

8.18   THE INITIAL CHARGE UPON THE RENT

The initial taxation of lease rents is in most cases[107] made upon a provisional basis which has to be retrospectively revised in the light of the actual payments immediately after the expiration of the fifth year of the term.[108]

8.18.1   Provisional tax

Moreover, many of the assessments and returns have to be prepared on an estimated or potentially temporary basis particularly where rent is concerned and, broadly, almost every land transaction will be subject to subsequent charges throughout and beyond its life (see **Chapter 1**). Matters that trigger retrospective adjustments to the previous rent calculations include:

- variable rents during or at the end of the first five years of the term including changes in the rate of VAT;
- later linked leases possibly including renewals of existing leases whether of the same or other premises;
- exercise of options to renew leases where these are linked transactions;[109]
- holding over by operation of law which produces a deemed extended lease;[110] and
- continuation of periodic and similar tenancies.[111]

This virtually continuous process of taxation of leases can pass over to third parties who need to obtain full disclosure of the SDLT history of the lease.[112] It also means, in practice, that the lease is constantly subject to possible scrutiny by HMRC Stamp Taxes which is given the power to launch Enquiries into previous returns or the absence thereof, notwithstanding that the basic nine-month period has expired.[113] It also offers HMRC Stamp Taxes a rare opportunity to make a discovery and to issue an assessment.[114]

---

[107]   For practical purposes the only lease likely to be unaffected by this problem is a lease for a rent which cannot change during the first five years of the term or is adjusted only in line with the RPI and in both cases is not subject to VAT or the possible exercise of the option to tax the rent.

[108]   The legislation (FA 2003, Sched.17A, para.8) is drafted upon the basis that the rent will cease to be variable during the first five years; however, since HMRC Stamp Taxes has included possible changes in the rate of VAT among the factors that make a rent variable for these purposes and since most non-residential rents are subject to VAT, almost all commercial leases will have a rent that is not totally certain until the first five years of the term have expired.

[109]   FA 2003, Sched.17A, para.5.

[110]   FA 2003, Sched.17A, para.4.

[111]   FA 2003, Sched.17A, para.3.

[112]   FA 2003, Sched.17A, para.12.

[113]   FA 2003, Sched.10, para.12(2A).

[114]   FA 2003, Sched.10, para.30.

8.18.2 Recession issues

The question of reclaiming overpaid tax in respect of rents is currently a significant issue in practice because of the recession and the fact that upon reviews rents are not being increased or rent reviews are being postponed or even where there is no provision for a downward rent review the parties are negotiating a variation of the rent outside the terms of the lease whereby the rent is reduced. In these situations the basic principle requiring rents to be estimated initially over a five-year period may mean that because the recession had not been taken into account in the initial calculation the estimated figures may exceed the actual rents payable. In consequence, at the expiration of the fifth year of the term (or earlier where the rent is not subject to VAT) there is a duty to file a retrospective return which may now involve a refund claim if only because the rate of VAT has reduced over five quarters of rent. HMRC Stamp Taxes has accepted that refunds of tax are available in respect of the reduction in the rate of VAT,[115] although it may be necessary to wait until the expiration of the first five years of the term before the rent becomes 'certain' for these purposes particularly as the rate of VAT has been increased twice from 15 per cent to 17.5 per cent and to 20 per cent in 2011.[116] The overestimated rent will, normally at the expiration of the fifth year of the term where the rent is subject to VAT, provide the taxpayer with a repayment claim because the actual rent will be below the estimated rent so that tax will have been overestimated and overpaid and the excess will be repayable together with interest.[117]

8.19 TAXABLE AMOUNT: NET PRESENT VALUE OF THE RENT

SDLT is charged upon the net present value of the rent which is essentially the aggregate of the rent or assumed or deemed rent over the whole term of the lease, suitably discounted.

There are, however, many oddities in the calculation of this amount where certain special or deeming provisions override the actual situation where the initial calculation is subject to retrospective adjustment.

The formula for determining the amount of the rent upon which the SDLT is to be charged is given below.[118]

In this formula:

---

[115] Although its Statement on changes in the rate of VAT and SDLT on rents (February 2009) indicates that it regards the amounts likely to be payable as so small that taxpayers will not bother to claim them, it is probable that HMRC Stamp Taxes would seek to recover the tax and impose penalties and interest upon taxpayers who did not effect similar small amounts in the increase of the taxable rent.

[116] It is necessary that the guestimated rent takes account of any changes in the rate of VAT that have been announced even though these are not effective until a future specified date.

[117] FA 2003, Sched.17A, paras.7 and 8.

[118] FA 2003, Sched.5, para.2.

$$v = \sum_{i=1}^{n} \frac{r_i}{(1+T)^i}$$

v is the net present value of the rent for the purposes of SDLT, i.e. the taxable sum;

Σ is the mathematical symbol generally utilised to denote the sum or aggregate of the various elements in a series of numbers. In this case it means the aggregate of the rent (or deemed rent) for each year of the term of the lease after it has been discounted, at the specified rate, i.e. $(1 + T)$;

r_i is undefined but is generally treated as the rent or estimated or assumed rent where there is a 'variable rent' payable in respect of year 'i';[119]

i is first, second, third, etc. years of the term producing r1, r2, r3, etc. being the rent in respect of[120] years 1, 2 and 3 respectively;

n is the term of the lease;[121] and

T is the temporal discount rate,[122] i.e. the rate at which each year's rent is discounted over time. The current rate is 3.5 per cent giving a starting figure for $(1 + T)$ of 1.035.

Although not specifically stated, it appears from the general computational provisions in relation to the relevant 'effective date' (see **8.9**), which appear to apply to only one of the possible dates, that the temporal discount rate at the effective date applies to all subsequent computations which 'relate back' to the initial computation of the SDLT as at the relevant effective date. In consequence, the original rate will apply to any recalculation of the SDLT upon the grant of the lease or where an uncertain rent becomes 'less uncertain' and further payment (or refund) notification and calculation are required,[123] notwithstanding that the temporal discount rate may have been changed by regulations in the intervening period.[124]

---

[119] It appears that this was inserted to deal with rent in relation to different years from that in which it was paid, such as rent in arrears or where there are complex negotiations each year to determine profits or turnover.

[120] This utilisation of the words 'in respect of' a year appears to be extended to charges upon the tax eventually paid for that year rather than any provisional or estimated figure used by the parties which are revised when the actual data for precise calculation is available.

[121] It must be noted (see **8.51**) that there are special rules and numerous deeming provisions for determining the length of the lease, which may at any particular time merely be a provisional factor in the calculation requiring subsequent retrospective adjustment.

[122] Assuming a lease for five years at a fixed rent of £100 the net present value of the rent would be the aggregate of: £100/(1.035) + £100/(1.035)² + £100/(1.035)³ + £100/(1.035)⁴ + £100/(1.035)⁵. The position for variable rents is somewhat more complicated and is described below.

[123] See e.g. FA 2003, s.80(2)(c).

[124] Persons seeking to utilise the online facility for calculating the SDLT may need to investigate whether the rate has been changed and that they are accessing the correct facility. Unless HMRC Stamp Taxes preserves the existing facility, notwithstanding the introduction of new rates, the facility will rapidly become useless. Nevertheless, as the point may be overlooked in the updating process the appropriate due diligence will be required. The online facility for rent increases has been generating a significant number of erroneous calculations usually, surprisingly, in favour of the taxpayer. HMRC Stamp Taxes stated that it will not challenge or penalise taxpayers in this situation provided that they

As indicated above, the calculation of the net present value of the rent may prove to be a title issue. Production of the total figures as inserted in the land transaction return (SDLT 1) is useless for these issues. It is prudent to keep a copy of the actual calculation, such as a printout of the page from the online facility provided by HMRC Stamp Taxes. However, even these pages may not be sufficient because the assumed rent that forms the basis of many tax calculations is based upon 12 calendar months, which is not the same as the years of the lease or rent periods taken into account in determining the net present value. The relevant data is not set out necessarily in the screen printout because the two sets of dates may relate to different lease years.

It will still remain necessary for the taxpayer to input the correct data[125] which will involve identifying the term of the lease (albeit provisionally) and the 'rent' for the premises and making the necessary estimates and calculations of the 'assumed rent' for periods after the fifth year, as well as making acceptable assumptions as to the rent during the first five years. It is essential that these estimates are carried out on a proper basis in order to avoid penalties for incorrect returns such as ignoring the effect of rent reviews.[126] Substantial interest costs for tax underpaid will be incurred.

There are certain key elements in the application of the formula to determine the net present value of the rent which require detailed explanation, as follows.

8.20 'RENT'

8.20.1 Basic position

'Rent' is not defined as such and so it would appear that the normal meaning of the term is applicable, i.e. a payment made by a tenant to a landlord for the exclusive possession of the land,[127] and is officially regarded as including mineral royalties. If the payment is not reserved out of the land, it is not rent.[128] It is provided that a single sum expressed to be payable either:

---

can prove that they relied upon the facility. It is, therefore, prudent to take a printout of the actual screen showing the calculation.

[125] A printout of the screen is also useful as a defence against allegations of fraud or negligence by HMRC Stamp Taxes where the calculation is incorrect which happens with the online calculator. It will provide contemporaneous evidence of the inputting of the correct data.

[126] As noted, HMRC Stamp Taxes has provided an online facility to enable solicitors and other professional advisers to calculate the tax.

[127] See e.g. *T&E Homes* v. *Robinson* [1976] STC 462; see also *Bocardo SA* v. *Star Energy* [2010] 1 All ER 26 on mineral arrangements; *Gable Construction Co* v. *IRC* [1968] 1 WLR 1426.

[128] *Hill* v. *Booth* [1930] 1 KB 381. This lack of statutory definition is important since 'lease' is defined (FA 2003, Sched.17A, para.1) in such a way as possibly to include rights such as easements granted for a limited time; see **8.5**. The SDLT charge will depend upon whether any annual 'fees' or royalties paid for such a right are 'rent' in the strict sense or some form of annual or other periodic payment (taxable pursuant to FA 2003, s.52) which may constitute some form of periodic consideration for the grant of the right taxed upon a chargeable consideration derived by 'capitalising' the annual payment pursuant to FA 2003, s.56. It is considered that on general principles such

- in respect of rent; or
- in respect of rent and other matters but not apportioned,[129]

is to be treated entirely as 'rent'.[130]

8.20.2 Drafting issues

This suggests that the reservation of various items as 'rent' for service charges and similar payments,[131] in order to provide the landlord with possible additional powers in relation to the enforcement of the covenant to pay the rent may have adverse effects upon the tenant, possibly sufficient in some cases to make the proposed lease commercially unattractive. It seems that a separate reservation of a charge as additional rent is not taxed as rent but is taxed as consideration other than rent unless exempted.

8.21 VAT AND RENT

8.21.1 Option to tax and charge to SDLT

Only VAT contractually payable at the effective date is taxable.[132] Where the lease rent is exempt at that date because the option to tax has not been exercised, both the possible and subsequent actual exercise of the option to tax are ignored when initially calculating the net present value of the rent because VAT arising after the effective date is to be ignored.[133] However, since HMRC Stamp Taxes has introduced two effective dates for leases,[134] there will be a charge upon the VAT where the option to tax is exercised after substantial performance of the agreement for lease but before the grant thereof.

There are, nevertheless, fundamental problems as to whether the subsequent exercise of the option to tax after the grant of the lease has tax consequences. For example:

- it may have to be taken into account in the retrospective revision of the rent at the end of the fifth year. However, since this is a retrospective revision of the initial calculation which precedes the review it is considered that the VAT

'fees' are not 'rent' but the description of them as 'rent' may mean that they are 'rent'. In many cases it may be that the SDLT charge as 'rent' is lower than an annual payment taxed at 4 per cent.

[129]   Where the sum is apportioned between various items such apportionments must be made on a 'just and reasonable' basis: FA 2003, Sched.4, para.4.

[130]   FA 2003, Sched.17A, para.6(1).

[131]   Which may be excluded from the charge if not reserved as rent; see FA 2003, Sched.17A, para.10(1); see **8.22**.

[132]   FA 2003, Sched.4, para.2.

[133]   FA 2003, Sched.4, para.2.

[134]   FA 2003, Sched.17A, para.12A.

arising pursuant to the exercise of the option to tax by the landlord can be ignored for these purposes because it is not VAT payable as at the effective date;[135]

- there is a question whether the exercise of the option to tax is a taxable rent increase in its own right generally; and
- there is an issue whether the exercise of the option to tax after the expiration of the fifth year of the term can represent an abnormal increase in the rent and/or has to be taken into account for ordinary rent reviews in deciding whether there has been an abnormal increase in the rent.

8.21.2 Rent or premium

The effect of FA 2003, Sched.17A, para.6(1) may be that where the VAT and the rent are not expressed as a single sum but are reserved as two separate items, the VAT is not 'rent', notwithstanding that it may be described as additional rent or may be enforced as if it were reserved as rent. In this case it would seem that the VAT not being reserved as 'rent' may constitute a periodical premium.[136] HMRC Stamp Taxes has publicly stated that where VAT was reserved separately from rent in relation to stamp duty it was a periodical premium within the provisions equivalent to s.52.[137] Since the basic structure of the legislation has not changed, the risk of treatment on this basis remains. Where VAT is treated as rent which generally produces a reasonably favourable result for taxpayers, HMRC Stamp Taxes does not appear at present to challenge this treatment in practice.

8.21.3 Variable rent

It is, however, the view of HMRC Stamp Taxes that where rent is subject to VAT and VAT forms part of the rent, this means that the rent is a variable rent because the rate of VAT may change during the first five years of the term. Unfortunately, HMRC Stamp Taxes has not indicated when it will regard the VAT as part of the rent, but has indicated that the initial estimate of the rent should include an element for the current rate of VAT as at the effective date and taking into account any variations in the rate already announced. In consequence, if the rate of VAT increases or reduces during the first five years of the term, this will mean that the actual passing rent is higher or lower than the estimated figure so that there may be additional tax to pay at the end of the five-year period, or the possibility of a refund where the rate has reduced.[138]

---

[135] FA 2003, Sched.4, para.2.
[136] FA 2003, s.52(6).
[137] Stamp Act 1891, s.56; SP11/91, para.9.
[138] Since the rate of VAT may change at any time, part of the rent will remain technically uncertain until the first five years of the term have expired. However, when making the initial estimate it must take into account any increase or reduction in the VAT where it has been officially announced that the rate will take effect from a future date.

8.21.4   Other issues

Other problems exist in relation to VAT and rent when the first five years of the term have expired. There are questions, considered elsewhere, as to whether any increase in the rate of VAT is to be taken into account in deciding whether subsequent reviews after the expiration of the fifth year of the term produce abnormal increases. This is a particular issue where the lease was originally granted for an exempt rent but the landlord has retained the option to tax the rent. It is as yet unresolved with HMRC Stamp Taxes whether the exercise of the option to tax is a chargeable event in its own right and outside the excluding provisions relating to the option to tax being exercised after the effective date pursuant to FA 2003, Sched.4, para.2. Clearly conversion of an exempt rent into a rent taxable at the full rate of VAT would represent a substantial proportion of the 20 per cent per annum, which is the broad test for deciding whether there has been an abnormal increase (see **8.37**).

8.22   SERVICE AND OTHER CHARGES AND PAYMENTS

The exclusion from rent applies to other routine payments and applies to both the covenants under the lease and underlease and any payments made, whether by way of performance of the covenants, such as a payment towards landlord's insurance premiums, or in respect of a breach of covenant such as damages for dilapidations. The excluded matters are considered later in this chapter in relation to 'premiums' (see **8.56**).

8.23   'BACKDATED RENT'

Some leases reserve sums as rent payable from some date prior to the grant of the lease. Such sums are taxable not as rents but as 'premium';[139] but there may be a relief where a new lease is granted during holding over and its term commencement date is backdated to the contractual termination date of the expired lease.[140]

8.24   DEEMED RENT

8.24.1   After fifth year

There is a special rent for all leases which are initially granted for a term exceeding five years or which are retrospectively extended beyond five years such as periodic tenancies, holding over by operation of law or successive linked leases. In the case of charges arising in relation to rent after the expiration of the fifth year, such as

---

[139]   FA 2003, Sched.5, para.1A.
[140]   FA 2003, Sched.17A, paras.9 and 9A; see **8.47** and following.

where there is an abnormal rent increase or because the lease is extended by reason of holding over or otherwise, the passing rent is ignored. The rent that is taken into account as the base figure in the retrospective recalculation of the 'rent' is either:

- the rent taken into account in the initial land transaction returns (SDLT 1) during the first five years of the term; or
- for the period after the fifth year of the term, the certificated or 'assumed' rent that was taken into account for the lease period after the expiration of the fifth year on the initial return or the subsequent review thereof at the expiration of the fifth year of the term.

This is the highest rent actually paid in any 12 consecutive months during the first five years of the term.[141] It will be noted that this rent is not calculated by reference to rent periods, as such, or by reference to years of the lease. In the case of most leases where the rent is payable quarterly it is possible that it may include rent from one or more quarters but these may extend over two rent years. Because of the importance of this rent the figures and the calculation thereof are almost documents of title, although because the 12 calendar months can straddle more than one lease year they do not necessarily provide all of the information that is required.

An assignee of the lease will require this information because it will form the basis of his tax computations in the future. It is also taken into account in determining any rent credits that may be available for surrenders and regrants or backdating of new leases in holding-over situations. This deemed rent will, of course, be eligible for the discounting when it is taken into account in any of the computations, although it is somewhat unclear whether it is the discounted assumed rent that is taken into account when determining rent credit (see **8.48**).

8.24.2 Employment situations

Where a lease is granted in consideration of a person's employment or the employment of a person connected with him which generates a benefit in kind within Income Tax (Earnings and Pensions) Act 2003, Part 3, Chapter 5, there is a charge to SDLT upon an amount equal to the cash equivalent of the benefits chargeable under that Act as if it were a sum of rent.[142] This sum is added to any actual rent reserved. As this charge is based upon a notional rent equal to the cash equivalent charged to income tax and that cash equivalent is variable,[143] this notional rent would appear to be 'uncertain' within FA 2003, s.51, so that the initial payment of SDLT will be based upon a reasonable estimate of the amount of the chargeable consideration, i.e. the estimated notional rent with obligations to notify, recalculate the tax and pay the

---

[141] FA 2003, Sched.17A, paras.7, 8, 13, 14 and 15.
[142] FA 2003, Sched.4, para.12.
[143] See Income Tax (Earnings and Pensions) Act 2003.

additional tax[144] at the end of the fifth year, taking into account the income tax calculation charges.[145]

Fortunately this provision is unlikely to have a significant impact in practice since, in general, the interest of the employee is likely to be an exempt interest as a licence[146] or as a tenancy at will.[147] Even where the interest created is a lease, it is likely that the level of the actual and/or notional rent will not exceed the nil rate threshold so as to give rise to a positive charge to tax, and as the contractual term is likely to be for less than seven years the grant of the lease will not be notifiable[148] as the nil rate applies. The problem will be how the term of such a lease is to be computed. Such tenancies are unlikely to be for a fixed term, but will be linked to the duration of the employment[149] or be of a periodic nature. The tenancy will be, in most cases, treated as being a tenancy for one year when the taxable sum will be the deemed rent with a discount which applies even for the first year's rent. Should the tenancy continue it will become a two-, three- or four-year lease with the net present value of the rent correspondingly increasing. There is therefore a risk that, notwithstanding the increasing impact of the discount, the net present value of the rent may exceed the nil rate slice and tax become payable and notifiable. However, unless the rent is taxable the lease is not notifiable simply because it is deemed to become a lease for seven years.[150] At this stage and every year thereafter there will have to be a retrospective recalculation of the tax to take account of any additional tax due and a need to file a complete land transaction return.[151] Once the rent exceeds the taxable threshold there is an annual payment and filing obligation.

8.25 DEEMED NEW LEASES

Two events give rise to a deemed lease, namely:

- abnormal rent increases[152] are treated as being the grant of a new lease. The rent for the new term is, broadly, the additional rent (although this varies between the different situations[153]) and the tax is charged upon the net present value of the deemed rent in accordance with the above formula; and

---

[144] Or possibly a claim for repayment of overpaid tax.
[145] It may be necessary to investigate and keep copies of Form PIID or its equivalent.
[146] FA 2003, s.48(2)(b).
[147] FA 2003, s.48(2)(c)(i).
[148] FA 2003, s.77A(1), item 5.
[149] If such arrangement is not void for uncertainty as may well be the case: *Lace* v. *Chantler* [1944] KB 368.
[150] FA 2003, Sched.17A, paras.3(4) and 4(4A).
[151] Fortunately, as a result of amendments it will no longer be necessary to notify the existence of the lease after the end of the fifth year when the tenancy becomes a lease for a term of seven years or longer. Notification is required only when tax is payable.
[152] FA 2003, Sched.17A, paras.13 and 14.
[153] Cf. FA 2003, Sched.17A, paras.13(1) and 14(3).

- assignments of certain leases exempt when granted,[154] which are described at appropriate places in this chapter.

8.26 RENT CREDIT

Certain variations of leases are taxed as surrenders and regrants and the varied lease, i.e. the new lease or deemed new lease where the parties effect the arrangement by a deed of variation, is, *prima facie*, taxable upon any premium paid for the lease and the rent reserved and will be treated as an exchange with market value issues arising.[155]

In certain cases,[156] including:

- actual grants of leases where there has been a prior substantial performance of the agreement for lease,[157]
- surrenders and regrants of leases of substantially the same premises;
- the grant of a new lease pursuant to Part II of the Landlord and Tenant Act 1954 (as amended), which relates back to the end of the contractual term of the original lease but SDLT has been paid in respect of the holding over,[158]

the rent reserved by the new lease is, broadly, reduced by the original rent payable in respect of the balance of the term surrendered or during the holding-over period, but the latter provision is not particularly well drafted.

This rent credit is highly restricted. It is available only where the new lease is between the same parties. This appears to refer to the persons who were landlord and tenant at the time of the variation or other event, i.e. the latest assignees of the lease. It is not limited to the original landlord or tenant. The major problem is the need for substantial identity of the premises. It is not known in practice how much variation in the demised premises HMRC Stamp Taxes will accept.

There are also deficiencies in the legislation in the machinery for the calculation of the rent credit because there is a difficulty in many cases in determining the amount to be deducted by way of credit from the new rent,[159] as well as determining the amount of the new rent where either or both of these are variable. In some situations the provisions state that the rent to be credited, i.e. the base rent to be deducted, is the amount of the rent that was previously subject to tax. It is this reference to the 'amount' of the rent that was previously taxed that causes confusion. It introduces a degree of ambiguity because the 'amount' of the rent is not necessarily the same as the passing rent. In most cases it is stated that the rent will be the estimated rent or the amount of adjusted rent at the end of the fifth year of

---

[154] FA 2003, Sched.17A, para.12; see **8.61**.
[155] FA 2003, s.47; Sched.4, para.9; see **4.36**.
[156] FA 2003, Sched.17A, para.9; see **8.58**.
[157] FA 2003, Sched.17A, para.12A; see **8.9**.
[158] FA 2003, Sched.17A, para.3.
[159] Where the new rent is itself variable in some way it may be difficult to find the amount from which the credit is to be deducted.

the term or the assumed rent taken into account for computations after the fifth year of the term. This is 'rent' that is taxed. The question is whether the 'amount' means that it is the rent as discounted over the relevant period. It does not seem to be a simple case of comparing the net present value of the previously taxed rent for the relevant period for which the credit is available against the net present value of the new rent for the same period. It may be that HMRC Stamp Taxes will, in the interests of simplicity, allow a deduction of the new rent, so far as this can be ascertained, whether it is a variable or turnover rent to be reduced by the face amount of the base rent, and will not require the comparison to be made on a yearly basis taking into account the appropriate discounts. It may, however, be necessary to review the rent credit at the end of the relevant five-year period where the new rent is variable.

8.26.1   Rent credit and old leases

However, it seems that this credit is available only where the original lease being surrendered or held over was within the charge to SDLT and does not apply to leases granted within the stamp duty regime even when granted on or after 1 December 2003[160] because the definition of the amount of the rent available for credit refers to the rent previously taxed, i.e. subject to SDLT.

8.27   VARIABLE RENTS: GENERAL

Rents are likely to change during the course of a lease in a variety of ways whether because they are subject to VAT (the rate of which can change), or by reason of rent review arrangements, or because they are linked to an index or interest rates, or to some form of turnover or participation figure in relation to sublease rents received or receivable possibly net of expenses on maintenance and repairs from occupational tenants.[161] The SDLT regime becomes immensely complicated in relation to both compliance and the initial calculation and recalculation required retrospectively in relation to such leases. There are two sets of problems, namely:

- how such rents are to be taxed initially because on the effective date the rent may change during the term of the lease; and
- whether any variation in the rent subsequently gives rise to either a liability to pay further tax or the taxpayer's entitlement to a refund of overpaid SDLT[162]

---

[160] Special rules are required for dealing with whether there are abnormal rent increases for stamp duty leases granted on or after 1 December 2003 in order to provide a base rent for making the comparison but this is somewhat obscurely drafted; see FA 2003, Sched.17A, para.14(4) and 9(2) and (4).

[161] There may be considerable delays in dealing with the SDLT at the end of the fifth year where there is a rent-sharing arrangement or the parties are negotiating a notional market rent for void lettings, etc. and disputing whether expenses are deductible.

[162] For the mechanics for reclaiming overpaid tax see FA 2003, Sched.11A; but note the particular problems as to the time for reclaiming overestimated tax and rents because of the impact of potential changes to the rate of VAT – see **8.32**.

and/or an obligation to notify HMRC Stamp Taxes of the variation. This includes rent changes during the first five years of the term as well as rent variations after that date which are governed by many separate and differently based regimes.[163]

8.28 'VARIABLE RENT' DEFINED

There is, obviously, the question of what is a 'variable rent' for these purposes. There are different regimes relating to the taxation of rent variations depending on e.g. whether these take place during the first five years of the term as this is determined for the purposes of the tax or arise after the expiration of the fifth year of the term or take effect by reason of some arrangement outside the lease such as a deed of variation[164] negotiated by the parties. Therefore the question as to what is the nature of a change in the rent needs to be determined and how any tax may be computed will vary.[165]

The basic definition for the purposes of the first five years of the term refers to three situations, namely:[166]

- the rent varies in accordance with a provision in the lease;
- the rent is contingent, uncertain or unascertained;
- there is a statutory extension which applies to rents where there is a possibility of the rent being varied pursuant to: Agricultural Holdings Act 1986, ss.12, 13 or 33; Agricultural Tenancies Act 1995, Part 2; Agricultural Holdings (Scotland) Act 1991, ss.13, 14, 15 or 31; and Agricultural Holdings (Scotland) Act 2003, ss.9, 10 and 11.

8.28.1 In accordance with the lease

The question is what is intended to be within the scope of rents which vary in accordance with the provision of the lease. It would seem that this is intended, primarily, to apply to rents where the increase is fixed in advance. It will apply to situations where there are stepped rents such as where the rent is to increase to a fixed amount after a particular time or the rent is to increase by the higher of increases in the RPI or by a specified amount. This will apply, for example, to ground rents for leases of residential premises and retirement homes where the rent is to increase by a specified amount after a specified period such as the rent doubling

---

[163] FA 2003, Sched.17A, paras.7 and 8 and 14 and 15 respectively.
[164] Which is not necessarily a surrender and regrant; *Gable Construction* v. *IRC* [1968] 1 WLR 1426; *Donellan* v. *Read* (1832) 3 B & Ad 899.
[165] However, there is a problem which HMRC Stamp Taxes is currently refusing to address of the effect of a deed of variation reducing a reviewable rent because the rent reviews do not provide for a reduction to market rent; see **8.42**.
[166] FA 2003, Sched.17A, para.7. Some of these issues may be relevant in determining the £1,000 rent for non-residential property: FA 2003, Sched.5, paras.9 and 9A.

every 25 years. Clearly, such rent will not vary during the first five years of the term and where the property is residential there will be no complications because this cannot be subject to VAT.[167] Nevertheless, the rents do vary in accordance with the terms of the lease, i.e. are variable rents.[168] Fortunately, generally this type of rent will be limited in practice to residential property and the figures will be fairly small, so that it is unlikely that the preordained increases in the rent will produce a net present value in excess of the nil rate slice for rents not exceeding £125,000.[169] In addition, such increases over time are unlikely to provide an abnormal increase of such an amount that a tax charge is likely to arise.[170] However, virtually every other type of rent will be taxed as a variable rent if it is capable of alteration during the first five years of the term. The fact that it may be changed after that date is ignored when making the initial provisional estimated return but any variations after that date may involve an abnormal increase in the rent.[171] Thus a ground rent which doubles every 25 years will be a variable rent but the initial calculation will be based upon the rent for the first 25 years being treated as the rent for the whole term. The subsequent adjustments are ignored unless they are 'abnormal'.

8.28.2 Contingent, uncertain or unascertained for non-residential properties

It is considered that the provision for rents varied in accordance with the lease is limited to such preordained increases. The principles do not apply to other types of rent even where the amount is itself uncertain. The question of whether rent is contingent, uncertain, or unascertained is to be determined in accordance with FA 2003, s.51 and is discussed below (see also **4.38**). This will include routine situations such as rent reviews and turnover rents or the possible changes in the rate of VAT (see **8.21**). The most obvious cases of variable rents that are contingent, uncertain or unascertained (e.g. rent reviews to future market rent or rents linked to turnover such as where the rent includes the 'landlord's share' of the rents received by the head tenant from occupation tenants and subtenants) will be within the contingent or unascertained or uncertain rents. In the circumstances, therefore, it is necessary to consider the scope of these provisions since an increase in the rent will be in accordance with the provisions in the lease as well as being potentially 'uncertain'. These words are taken from FA 2003, s.51; but unlike variable consideration including variable premiums, the tax due in respect of rent even though estimated has to be paid in full within 30 days after the effective date, with a right to a refund if the initial guestimate of future rents is high or an obligation to pay

---

[167] Value Added Tax Act 1994, Sched.8, Group 5, Items 1 and 2; Sched.10.

[168] This appears to be the view of HMRC Stamp Taxes so that the online calculator facility can be utilised rather than having to make a manual calculation of the chargeable amount of rent for each year which for a lease of a flat for 150 years could be a tediously time-consuming and costly exercise.

[169] FA 2003, Sched.5, para.2.

[170] FA 2003, Sched.17A, paras.14 and 15; see **8.37**.

[171] FA 2003, Sched.17A, paras.14 and 15; see **8.38**.

additional tax with interest and possibly under penalty if the estimate is low. There is no power to postpone the payment of tax upon any form of variable rents.[172]

8.28.3 Residential property

Residential property may be leased for a full market rent which may be variable and subject to the normal principles. In many cases, however, the lease of residential premises will be granted for a premium and a ground rent[173] which may be variable but is at such a level that its net present value will never exceed the nil rate threshold and any steps or increases in the rent will not be abnormal increases.[174]

8.28.4 Non-variable rents

To some extent the computation procedure depends upon the nature of the variation of the rent since rents index linked to the retail price index (RPI) are ignored.[175] There is a doubt from the drafting as to whether an upwards only indexation increase is within this provision, since this exclusion applies only where the rent adjustment is 'in line with' the RPI.

Various problems may arise.

- Adjustments related to a modified version of the index may not be accepted as excluded by HMRC Stamp Taxes. Rent reviews linked to some factor other than the RPI such as a review to indexation, or 5 per cent, whichever is the greater are not covered by these provisions. This will cause a significant compliance problem for finance leases, *inter alia*, where the rent is linked to movements in interest rates which is likely to be the case where there are sale and leaseback and similar arrangements intended as a fundraising exercise, although there is an exemption for leases in certain sale and leaseback arrangements on the initial grant.[176]
- Also not addressed by the legislation is the question of VAT and the RPI. HMRC Stamp Taxes regards possible changes in the rate of VAT as creating a variable rent (see **8.28**). It is uncertain whether the exclusion of rent linked solely to RPI means that the rent is not variable because it increases by reference to the VAT or the RPI increase. It is unclear whether the additional VAT related to the RPI increase is within the exclusion from the tax on variable rents. In theory it might seem that where there is a fixed rent for the entirety of the term this is not a variable rent because it does not change or is not uncertain and so on. However, even a fixed rent of commercial premises may be subject to VAT. Since there are potential fluctuations in the rate of VAT whether up or down this, in the view of HMRC Stamp Taxes, makes the rent variable,

---

172 FA 2003, s.80(5).
173 With the service charges not being included in the rent; see **8.22**.
174 FA 2003, Sched.17A, paras.14 and 15.
175 FA 2003, Sched.17A, para.7(5); but links to other indices such as the CPI are not ignored.
176 FA 2003, s.57A (as much amended).

notwithstanding that the extra VAT arises because of the adjustment by reason of the linkage to RPI.

8.29 TAXATION OF VARIABLE RENTS

8.29.1 Initial procedure: status of 'rent'

The procedure for dealing with such rents is:

1. Variations in accordance with the terms of the lease will usually be pre-agreed increases such as stepped rents. *Prima facie* such rents will be known in advance. However, they may nevertheless be uncertain where they are subject to VAT because the rate of VAT may change. These will fall under the procedure for uncertain rents set out below.

2. Where there is a contingent rent, i.e. a basic rent which is to increase or reduce by a fixed amount should a specified event happen or not happen, the tax is calculated initially upon the basis that the contingent rent is payable with adjustment in the tax charge should the contingency not occur. The prediction for the future is not the amount of the increase or reduction in the rent but the relevant rental period when this adjustment may take effect. This may also be a situation where the rent will increase or reduce retrospectively as and when the event happens. The legislation indicates[177] that the calculation should be made on the basis that the event has happened but it would be potentially imprudent to work upon the basis that the figures may reduce since this could result in the underpayment of tax with interest and penalties.

3. Where the rent is 'unascertained', such as rent based upon the square footage of a building which has been completed but not measured, the rent is taxed upon the basis of a reasonable estimate of the amount of rent expected to be paid. This will involve a certain degree of speculation and the position has to be revisited with the tax recalculated and the transaction notified again when the uncertainty is resolved such as the square footage being agreed.[178] Where there is a rent that is 'unascertained' this refers to previous data and it is merely a question of the time taken to determine and agree the relevant data. This should provide a firm basis early during the five-year period and so be fairly easy of estimate.

4. Where the rent is 'uncertain', such as a turnover rent or rents subject to reviews or subject to VAT the tax on the rent has to be calculated initially upon a reasonable estimate of the rent during the first five years and the position reviewed during or at the end of the fifth year of the term.[179] The problem is in

---

[177] FA 2003, s.51.
[178] FA 2003, s.80.
[179] See **8.33**. Where the rent is subject to VAT the retrospective review will in practice be at the end of the fifth year of the term because of the possibility that the rate of VAT may be changed at any time (see, for example, Value Added Tax Act 1994, s.2(2)).

relation to 'uncertain rent' such as rent reviews or turnover rents where the future events are completely incapable of precise determination. In this situation the tenant may find it prudent to overestimate since, although the tax may have to be paid, the overpayment would mean that there is a possibility of repayment with interest as opposed to the situation where there is an underestimate which will require additional tax to be paid together with interest and the possible penalty for negligently preparing a return.

8.30 INITIAL ASSUMPTION FOR RENT AFTER THE FIFTH YEAR

This means that there is a lease for five years which is held over.[180] It will be noted that where the lease is granted initially for a term in excess of five years[181] the calculation of the net present value of the rent requires a figure to be included in the formula for the net present value of the rents for the sixth and subsequent years. This will also be involved in the two-stage process. It will be necessary to make some form of guestimated figure when making the initial return which will be subsequently revised at the expiration of the fifth year of the term or any deemed term or extension thereof. This is the highest rent paid in any 12 consecutive calendar months during the first five years of the term[182] which means that it will initially be the highest estimated figure subject to review in the light of the actual rents at the end of the fifth year of the term. This may give rise to problems as regards the initial estimation of the rent because it will not be rent in respect of any year of the lease; it will be, broadly, any four consecutive rental periods for most leases which may straddle more than one year of the term of the lease. For example, the lease may have a commencement by reference to the 25 December quarter day but the rent variation may start by reference to the midsummer quarter day so that the 12 consecutive months will run from June to June notwithstanding the lease year starts from December. The issue is, therefore, the question of whether the nature of the rent may affect the manner in which estimates are made.

8.31 THE EFFECTIVE DATE ISSUES FOR THE INITIAL PROCESS

The status of the rent as uncertain or unascertained may change over time since the initial self-assessment calculation of the SDLT upon the rent has to be carried out as at the effective date when the rent, although not variable, may be uncertain such as where the rent is expressed to be a fixed sum per square foot of 'lettable area' when

---

[180]   There will be several calculations required including the calculation of the deemed rent for years after the fifth year of the term which will be required for the retrospective adjustment of the initial return. Hence the need for detailed documentation of the tax calculations in the due diligence process for the assignee of a lease; see **8.61**.

[181]   Special provisions apply to situations where the lease is granted for an initial term less than five years but grows beyond that term; see **8.47**.

[182]   FA 2003, Sched.17A, para.7(3).

the building is completed or as a percentage related to the final development costs. It may be that the effective date is either before the completion of the building so that the rent cannot be ascertained because the square footage or final cost has not been agreed and/or costs remain to be incurred. In the former situation, because the building has not been completed the formula is looking to future events, so the rent will be 'uncertain', whereas in the latter case the building having been constructed, or its square footage cannot be changed and the costs of the development cannot be increased because the appropriate operations have ceased, the rent will be 'unascertained'. In the latter case the return has to be prepared upon the basis of an estimate of what the rent is expected to be but since the parties are in negotiation relating to the size or costs they should have a reasonably accurate estimate of the amounts likely to be involved. However, since there can apparently be two separate effective dates for leases[183] the nature of the rent may change between the time of substantial performance and the grant of the lease.

An issue arises where at the relevant effective date the rent has the status of 'uncertain', i.e. it is dependent upon the outcome of future events but at some stage it could fall into the category of 'unascertained'. For example, where there is a rent that is reviewable to market rent as at the initial effective date such as the grant of the lease the rent will be uncertain. At the date of the rent review the parties will, for example, be looking to the market rent as at the review date. In consequence, the rent will be looking at historical data not future speculation. It will, at this point, become 'unascertained'.[184] It appears to be the view of HMRC Stamp Taxes that in this situation a return prepared on an estimated basis is required together with the payment of any tax. However, since the legislation requires the rent to become 'certain' as opposed to 'unascertained' it is considered that this view is clearly incorrect and that no return and payment will be required until the rent review has been agreed.[185] Since the legislation requires the rent or part of the rent to become 'certain' the fact that it is 'unascertained' clearly does not meet this condition. Moreover, there is a question as to whether the rent becomes even partially certain.[186] Where the rent is subject to VAT, although the 'basic rent' (i.e. exclusive of VAT) may become fixed, the total rent is still uncertain because the rate of VAT applicable to the basic rent may change during the balance of the five-year term.

---

[183]   FA 2003, Sched.17A, para.12A; see **8.9**.

[184]   This is a different issue from that as to whether the rent has ceased to be 'uncertain' for the retrospective adjustment provisions pursuant to FA 2003, Sched.17A, para.8; see **8.34**.

[185]   It is the date of the agreement of the new rent that represents the payment and reporting date and not the date when the parties seek to have the new rent endorsed by way of memorandum upon the lease which may be more than 30 days after the rent is agreed.

[186]   This can also be a significant issue as to filing and payment in relation to the retrospective review required at the expiration of the fifth year of the term.

8.32 'UNCERTAIN RENTS', RENT REVIEWS TO MARKET RENT AND SIMILAR ARRANGEMENTS

In general, the most frequently encountered variable rents in practice will be uncertain rents and these require an extended discussion because of the variety of rents involved and the complexities of the relevant legislation. Rents linked to turnover, rents subject to VAT, shares of occupational rents received from subtenants or rents receivable in such circumstances,[187] overage arrangements and so on are likely to fall into the definition of 'uncertain' consideration since the amount of rent payable depends on uncertain future events and cannot be predetermined.[188] The rate of VAT may be changed, the level of future profitability, turnover or rents received and payments made by tenants may change; or there may be a period of uncertainty when there are no sublettings in place and the future market rent may be substituted for the rent received in the rental formula. There may also be adjustments required in calculating the amount of the payment for the deduction of relevant expenditure by the tenant such as insurance or cost of providing services or repairs to and maintenance of the premises.[189] Such rent is totally dependent upon future events. Such rents have to be dealt with initially upon the basis of reasonable estimates of future rent, so far as there is no fixed rent for the particular year, and subject to review of a retrospective nature at some time during or at the end of the fifth year of the term of the lease.

For these purposes, however, it has to be noted that there are potentially two such five-year periods producing different calculations, but with a credit. There is:

- the initial five-year period from substantial performance of the agreement for lease; and
- a replacement five-year period starting from the date of the actual grant which terminates and supplants the initial five-year period.

With regard to the second calculation, credit is available by reference to the rent taxed at substantial performance of the agreement to lease and usually there will be no need to review the rent calculation for substantial performance at the end of the first five-year period since the deemed lease is deemed to be surrendered and cannot be in existence at the relevant five-year period.[190]

This need for review (and the double effective date which generates a second five-year period which appears to replace the five-year period commencing upon

---

[187] Such rents are likely to be uncertain because agreements for subleases may not be effective from the relevant period, i.e. there is no rent receivable. Also in these situations of shared rents there are the questions of costs and the parties having to agree 'market rents' for periods when all or part of the property is unlet.

[188] Even predetermined rents such as stepped rents may be variable pursuant to the terms of the lease (FA 2003, Sched.17A, para.7(2)) but the predetermined increase being outside the first five years of the term should not affect the initial calculation and the subsequent increases in practice are unlikely to be 'abnormal' since these are usually ground rents for residential property.

[189] FA 2003, Sched.17A, para.10.

[190] Unless the lease has not been granted during those five years. Unfortunately the provision suggests that there is no refund of tax where a lease is terminated early.

substantial performance of the agreement for lease) produces a complex multiple reporting obligation, as follows.

8.33 TWO STAGES

8.33.1 Initial calculation: at both effective dates

There will be two effective dates should there be a temporal separation between entry into possession, i.e. substantial performance and 'completion' in the technical sense.[191] As at the effective date for the agreement for lease or date of grant,[192] it is necessary to put into the formula set out above (see **8.19**) the actual or estimated rent for the first five years of the term and an assumed rent for all years after the expiration of the fifth year.[193] Where there is an initial fixed rent or a rent holiday for a few months or a low rent for a few years followed by a review to, say, market rent, it is necessary to insert the initial rent (or nil or the reduced figure for a rent holiday). This will initially be the agreed base rent plus VAT if appropriate at the rate in force as at the effective date but taking account of any imminent changes in the rate of VAT where these have been announced in advance by the Government. If the first review date falls after the expiration of the fifth year of the term or within the final three months of the five-year period[194] there will, subject to the question of VAT changes, be a fixed rent and this is also the assumed rent for the remainder of the term.[195] In addition the *prima facie* term of the lease will be shorter so that the rent for the period after the grant will be eligible for a lower discount overall when calculating the new net present value.

---

[191] The initial return will effectively lapse and have to be replaced by a totally new return with the limited rent credit relief. There will, therefore, be a new and provisional return for the same lease with the timeframe of five years moved. There is no express legislation dealing with the double taxation of the same lease since FA 2003, Sched.10, para.33 requires two separate commercial transactions and does not provide relief for two distinct chargeable transactions for the same commercial transaction, so that there is no statutory guidance for example where the market value rules apply. While there is credit for the rent there is no express credit for the deemed premium where the rent is below market rent or the tenant may have generated embedded goodwill between the two dates.

[192] For convenience the double chargeable transaction will be referred to as the effective date but it must be remembered that there is a second effective date as of the grant of the lease pursuant to FA 2003, Sched.17A, para.12A.

[193] There may or may not be a minimum rent payable. However, the existence of a minimum rent would appear to be no longer the sole relevant factor in determining the net present value of the rent. The existence of the minimum rent is merely one of the elements to be taken into account in making the necessary estimates of future rent. In consequence, the general provisions concerned with variable consideration would appear to be applicable.

[194] FA 2003, Sched.17A, para.7A.

[195] FA 2003, Sched.17A, para.8 but there is a high risk of taxable abnormal increases thereafter; see paras.13, 14 and 15 and **8.38**.

Where the first review is to occur during the first five years of the term,[196] because the legislation requires the 'amount' of the rent, not part thereof, to become certain which is unlikely to occur because of the changeable nature of the rates of VAT for each year in the period after the first review date it is necessary to make a reasonable estimate expected to be payable during the relevant five years including the expected effect of any review until the end of the five-year period. For periods after the expiration of the fifth year of the term, the rent to be taken into account ('assumed rent') is the highest amount of rent expected to be paid in any 12 consecutive months during the first five years. It has to be noted that this is any 12 consecutive months and is not necessarily linked to rent periods which may lead to inconvenience in practice, particularly for leases at a monthly rent reserved by reference to turnover if HMRC Stamp Taxes takes a strict view of this requirement. The SDLT is, therefore, calculated by reference to the initial actual rent as adjusted for changes in the rate of VAT until review and subsequent estimated rents for the first five years,[197] and for the balance of the term it is the 'assumed' rent.[198]

8.33.2 Reasonable estimates

The 'rent' for the purposes of calculating the tax and completing the return form is a reasonable estimate of the amount or value of the rent.[199] To avoid allegations of fraud and negligence the parties will, therefore, be required to make a reasonable estimate of the rents they expect to receive over the first five years of the term of the lease in order to apply the formula for determining net present value. This will involve additional complexity when applying the formula since there will need to be a separate reasonable estimate of the future rent for each of those five years. Simply inserting the current rent, as frequently suggested by the helpline operated by HMRC Stamp Taxes (which usually advises callers to ignore the variation provisions, but this is incorrect and inconsistent with the statements relating to changes in the rate of VAT), as an estimate of future rent for the calculation will clearly not be acceptable. In preparing the land transaction tax return the reasonable estimate of the future rent levels must be prepared on a reasonable basis, i.e. supported by such professional advice, economic and other analysis as is regarded appropriate by HMRC Stamp Taxes. Notwithstanding the difficulty of obtaining professional advice because advisers are not fortune tellers, failure to carry out a 'proper' exercise will undoubtedly be regarded as producing a 'negligent' return with all the

---

[196] But it seems to be acceptable to ignore the possibility of changes in the rate of VAT upon the rent no matter how likely an increase or reduction may be politically because of the economic situation, unless the rate variation has been announced in advance.

[197] FA 2003, s.51.

[198] FA 2003, Sched.17A, paras.7 and 8.

[199] FA 2003, s.51.

appropriate penalties imposed including the possibility that HMRC may raise an assessment against the taxpayer and his professional advisers for a period of up to 21 years.[200]

8.34   FIRST FIVE YEARS

Where the rent varies during the first five years of the term so that the rent for the balance of the five years becomes 'certain' during the first five years, the tax is recalculated as from the effective date on the basis of the actual rents paid in the past and fixed for the future, i.e. upon the basis of the reviewed rent. However, few, if any, commercial rents will cease to be uncertain during the first five years. The reference is to the 'amount of the rent' becoming 'certain'. This refers to the ambiguous undefined term 'amount' (see **8.48**) and does not refer to 'part' of either the 'amount' or the 'rent' becoming certain. The problem is when the rent becomes certain because of the inherent potential for changes in the rate of VAT (see **8.21**). The basic rent may become fixed on a review but the VAT applicable thereto may still vary so that the rent varies. The rent does not, therefore, become 'certain'. The actual rent paid to the review date and the reviewed rent for the period between review dates are inserted into the formula for the first five years and, in general, the reviewed rent will form the basis of the assumed rent for the balance of the term.

8.35   FIFTH YEAR CUT-OFF

Where the rent does not become 'certain' during the first five years of the term, as will be the case in turnover or similar rents, or where the rent is subject to VAT, a retrospective reassessment of the position is required after the end of the fifth year of the term of the lease. This is carried out upon the basis of the rent actually paid during that period,[201] and as regards the rent for each year of the term of the lease after the fifth year this is assumed to be an amount equal to the highest amount of rent payable in respect of any consecutive 12-month period during the initial five years. This 'assumed rent' is a key factor in relation to the taxation of the lease and is involved in many subsequent charges and calculations such as holding over and abnormal rent increases; assignees will require its details.

---

[200]   FA 2003, Sched.10, para.31(2).
[201]   When this has been finally 'ascertained' or ceased to be 'uncertain' or become 'certain' which may be a process taking a considerable time because the parties have to agree costs and expenses or the deemed rent for unlet premises where there is some form of rent-sharing or turnover lease. This is likely to give rise to problems with HMRC Stamp Taxes as to when the notification and payment obligations (or repayment entitlement) arise and the questions of interest and penalties assessment.

8.35.1 Estimates and refunds

Many returns should have been filed on the basis that the rent will be likely to increase. The estimated figures will, in consequence, exceed the actual rent producing an overpayment of tax. The rate of VAT may have been overestimated with the same consequences. However, the potential fluctuation in the rate of VAT means that the repayment claim cannot be made until after the expiration of the five-year period.

8.36 RENT 'REDUCTIONS' DURING THE FIRST FIVE YEARS

It is possible for rent to reduce in accordance with the terms of the lease. This will apply where there is an actual reduction in the rent because turnover falls or deductible expenditure increases. The rent may also reduce because of the reduction in the rate of VAT[202] and a produce situation where the actual rent is lower than the guestimated figure included in the provisional initial return. The issues arise in circumstances such as where there is a decline in turnover during the first five years or because of the recession rents may not increase and may be reduced. It is important to note that for these purposes the question of whether there is a reduction is measured by reference to the estimated rent on the initial return not a reduction in the initially agreed rent prior to the review. This will be taken into account on the revision calculation at the end of the fifth year. Although upwards and downwards rent reviews are currently rare, where they do exist the downward movement may mean that tax has been overpaid. In these situations a repayment claim is possible, together with interest from the date of payment.[203] Different principles apply where there is a rent reduction not pursuant to the terms of the lease.[204]

8.37 PERPETUAL REVIEW: AFTER THE FIFTH YEAR

Although the basic provisional SDLT position is intended to be terminated at the end of the fifth year of the term of the lease and subsequent reviews or variations are to be ignored,[205] this applies only for the initial assessment and there are situations where the rent after the expiration of the fifth year of the term can produce a tax charge.

---

[202]   On the position of negotiating downward rent reviews operating pursuant to a deed of variation outside the lease (which is not a surrender and regrant – *Gable Construction* v. *IRC* [1968] 1 WLR 1426) during the recession because the review procedure does not allow for a downward review, see **8.45**.

[203]   FA 2003, s.80(4).

[204]   FA 2003, Sched.17A, para.15A(1); compare para.13.

[205]   Provided that these are obligations pursuant to the terms of the lease.

8.37.1 Abnormal increase risk

Where there is a rent increase[206] pursuant to the provisions in the lease there is an anti-avoidance provision[207] whereby an abnormal increase of rent after the expiration of the fifth year of the term including increases operating outside the lease[208] such as a deed of variation of the rent[209] is deemed to be the grant of a new lease[210] for the increased rent and the balance of the unexpired term of the original lease.[211] It is, apparently, the view of HMRC Stamp Taxes that this applies not merely to rent reviews, but also to fluctuating rents such as profit-sharing or turnover rents. This 'blip' in the rent appears to have been intended to apply where the rent changes by reason of other factors. There are potential problems for turnover rents where there may be a freak year for turnover such as the Olympics in 2012 affecting business turnover or profits, hotel occupation rates where these form the basis of the rent reserved or there is a significant increase in the landlord's share of the rents from subletting.

It can apply even in commercial situations such as where there is a lease initially granted on favourable terms in a new development which proves to be successful so that rents soar upon review. This may be for only one or a few years of the term of the lease but the full consequences of taxation will apply. This means that reviews and other variations in rent such as exceptional fluctuations in turnover, or rents received from subleases, need to be regularly monitored, possibly annually, in order to be able to comply with this obligation to calculate the tax and notify HMRC Stamp Taxes should it produce an abnormal increase.

This trap exists in many routine situations; for example:

1. Although rent holidays or rent-free periods appear to offer a reasonably low SDLT charge it is virtually inevitable that the first review of the rent after the rent-free period will produce an abnormal increase in the rent giving rise to a deemed new lease at the new rent but, fortunately, few leases will operate rent-free, etc. for five years.[212]

2. Rents are frequently linked to a percentage of the net or gross rents received from subtenants or to turnover or business profits arising from a development and similar factors and may be calculated after the deduction of relevant expenses with problems for estimated (net) rents for void lets (i.e. periods when relevant property is not sublet). Such rents and expenses do not have an

---

[206] Different rules apply to rent reductions; see FA 2003, Sched.17A, para.15A; s.43(3)(d). The problem is determining whether there is an increase or reduction in the rent.

[207] FA 2003, Sched.17A, paras.14 and 15.

[208] FA 2003, Sched.17A, para.13. This is not a surrender and regrant: *Gable Construction* v. *IRC* [1968] 1 WLR 1426.

[209] Not a surrender and regrant: *Gable Construction* v. *IRC* [1968] 1 WLR 1426; *Donellan* v. *Read* (1832) 3 B & Ad 899.

[210] But this is linked with the original lease: FA 2003, Sched.17A, para.14(5).

[211] There would appear to be no carry forward of the discounting under the existing lease.

[212] FA 2003, Sched.17A, paras.14 and 15.

element of stability and change frequently by reference to future circumstances which will require frequent notification of transactions and recalculation of the SDLT payable or reclaimable.

3.   The lease may contain provisions whereby one party has the power to change the rent basis such as an election to switch from a profit-sharing to a market rent where there is an assignment of the lease to take account of the different activities of the assignee. The exercise of this power may produce an abnormal increase for these purposes.

There are problems for calculating whether there is an increase in the rent. The base rent is not the previous passing rent but usually the assumed rent for all years after the fifth in the initial calculation or the previous abnormally increased rent but there is little guidance as to the future rent.

8.38   ABNORMALITY

A rent increase is abnormal if it is greater than, broadly 20 per cent per annum. The precise figure is determined in accordance with the application to the rent increase of a formula which is

$$\frac{R \times Y}{5}$$

where:

R is the rent previously taxed ('the base rent'); and
Y is the number of whole years determined in accordance with the provisions of the charge.[213]

R depends upon whether there has been a previous abnormal increase in the rent. Where there is an abnormal increase it resets the base figure for future increases.

8.38.1   Base rent: R

It is, of course, necessary to determine the base figure to be included in the formula since this represents the amount by reference to which the increase is measured. Basically, where there has been no previous abnormal increase in the rent the 'rent previously taxed' is the amount of rent payable under the lease taking into account that it is a variable or uncertain rent. In consequence, since this charge is dealing with events after the expiration of the fifth year of the term it is the rent that is assumed to be payable after the expiration of the fifth year of the term, i.e. the highest rent paid in any 12 consecutive calendar months during the first five years of the term.[214] Where the rent has been varied not in accordance with the terms of the

---

[213]   FA 2003, Sched.17A, para.15.
[214]   This is one of the reasons why a person considering purchasing an existing lease will require a full SDLT history. It will be necessary to know what was the rent that was entered into the calculation in respect of all years after the fifth year of the term. If the detailed information, which may include details of the actual rents during the first five years of the term, is not available then it

lease but by means of a deed of variation or other arrangement operating outside the lease then the relevant base rent is the rent payable as a result of a last increase in the rent. However, when applying these provisions it is necessary to disregard any rent credits that may have been available for the taxation of the lease when granted.[215] In consequence, where there has been a surrender and regrant, for example, then the base rent will be the full rent and not the amount of the rent reduced by reference to the rent previously payable in respect of the surrendered lease. This is intended to ensure that it is not merely the excess rent but the total rent that is taken into account. Were it not for this provision then only the new rent increase would be taken as the base rent. In consequence, the rent to be taken into account will include not merely rent under the current lease but also rent payable under a previous lease as this is computed for the purposes of SDLT. This means that expired leases or surrendered leases may still retain a significant role in relation to title. Without the history of any preceding lease where a rent credit has been claimed the taxpayer will not have information as to the full base rent for the purposes of determining the factor R in the above formula.

8.38.2 New rents

Having determined the factors to put into the equation it is necessary to determine the new rent and deduct from this the base rent, i.e. the rent previously taxed as determined above. This increased amount of rent is then subjected to the formula set out above which is applied by reference to the base rent (i.e. the amount of rent previously taxed).

Unfortunately, the draftsman has totally failed to deal with the situation of how to determine the new rent. Frequently the new rent will be subject to rent review, changes in the rate of VAT, the exercise of the option to make the rent subject to VAT or subsequent reviews and other factors. The new rent will, therefore, itself be variable so that the rent payable as a result of the increase (the new rent) may not be ascertained or certain.

HMRC Stamp Taxes has provided an online facility for calculating whether a rent increase is abnormal. However, this calculator is deficient and frequently produces incorrect results. Surprisingly these tend to operate in favour of the taxpayer. HMRC Stamp Taxes has indicated that where a taxpayer can prove that he has made use of the online calculator it will accept the result even though incorrect and not

---

may be prudent to advise the potential assignee not to take the transfer since he will not be able to determine whether a charge arises in respect of any subsequent rent review of increase in turnover nor will he be able to calculate the amount of tax payable. Professional advisers who fail to make the necessary enquiries and require, as a matter of contract, the necessary information from the vendor of a lease face considerable risks since these issues can have a substantial impact upon value. It is necessary to have the information included in the additional box in the calculator for rent payable after year five. It is also necessary to require the data that was utilised to provide the information inserted in that box in the online calculator. Since this refers to 12 calendar months it does not refer to years of the lease since the highest rent may straddle two rent periods such as where there is a temporary increase in the rate of VAT.

[215] FA 2003, Sched.17A, para.7(3) and paras.9 and 9A.

seek to claim additional tax or interest and penalties. This, however, still leaves the difficulty of determining what the 'new rent' is in order to determine the amount of the increase.

8.39   STAMP DUTY LEASES: DUE DILIGENCE

In this context of determining the base rent there is a further title investigation problem. It is provided that the abnormal rent increase provisions apply to all leases granted on or after 1 December 2003. The draftsman[216] clearly overlooked the situation that certain leases granted on or after 1 December 2003 remain within the stamp duty regime.[217] Such rents will not have borne SDLT but the increase in the rent is taxable. It would seem that in these situations the base rent will be the actual passing rent when the lease was granted.[218]

8.40   TIME FACTORS

The other factor in the formula is Y – the number of whole years involved. This is an attempt to determine the period over which the increase is to be spread. The determination of the start date is itself a complex matter.[219] It is necessary to determine the start date of the period as well as end date. Basically the start date is the beginning of the term of the lease; but there is no explanation as to what that date is. This might either be the term commencement date or it may be the effective date in the form of substantial performance of the agreement for lease or it may be the date of the grant which is particularly important since stamp duty leases started after 1 December 2003 are within this charge. However, where the rent under the lease was initially variable then the start date is the beginning of the period by reference to which the rent assumed to be payable after the fifth year of the term of the lease is determined. If there has been a subsequent abnormal increase in the rent after the expiration of the fifth year of the term by some arrangement outside the terms of the lease the start date is the date of the variation. If there has been more than one such variation the start date is the most recent date. Having determined the start date it is necessary to find the number of whole years in the period between the start date and the date on which the new rent first becomes payable. Where there is a rent review or other increase operating part-way through a year the part year appears to be ignored.

---

[216]   The draftsman is not solely to blame; one of the advisers to HMRC Stamp Taxes on the issue reluctantly admitted to the author that they, too, have missed this fundamental point whereby they converted an 'exempt transaction' into a chargeable transaction.

[217]   FA 2003, Sched.19; see **8.2**.

[218]   It is necessary to ignore subsequent increases in the rent whether pursuant to rent reviews or other arrangements: FA 2003, Sched.17A, para.14(4)(a).

[219]   FA 2003, Sched.17A, para.5.

8.41   PROFESSIONAL RESPONSIBILITY: RETROSPECTION AND PREVIOUS ADVICE

It is crucial to note for client handling that the current abnormal rent increase test retrospectively replaced different tests so that the rules applicable to current rent variations will almost certainly differ from those potentially applicable when the lease was granted or the agreement for lease was substantially performed and the advice given at that time will be incorrect. There is, therefore, a problem for professional advisers who may have advised on the basis of the law as it applied at the effective date but are not in a position to identify clients who may be on risk in the current regime.[220]

8.42   OTHER VARIATIONS OF RENT NOT IN ACCORDANCE WITH THE TERMS OF THE LEASE INCLUDING DEEDS OF VARIATION OF RENT

Rent increases may operate outside the terms of the lease and so outside the terms of FA 2003, Sched.17A, para.7(1); but the question remains of how such a variation interacts with the variable rent rules. The parties may enter into some form of deed of variation. In general variations of rent will not, as such, operate as surrenders and regrants;[221] but they may have taxation consequences since an increase of rent is made subject to specific provisions imposing charges and notification obligations. Such deeds of variation are not infrequent especially in a recession where it is necessary to reduce the rent but standard rent review provisions allow only for the continuation of the current rents or an upwards review.

In some situations the possibility of a rent increase or reduction may be fairly obvious. For example, a landlord wishing to increase the value of his reversion may make a payment to the tenant in order to increase the rent or he may purchase the tenant's improvements for the purposes of calculating the rent on future reviews. In these situations it will normally be possible to identify that there is an increase. The problem is, as indicated above, whether determining the amount of such increase where the former rent and new rent are themselves variable. Similarly, there are arrangements whereby the rent reserved under the headlease is a percentage of the net rent received by the tenant from the occupational subtenants. In these situations the tenant may have the effective management of the property and in determining the landlord's share of the rent will be entitled to deduct various payments such as insurance, costs of repairs and so on. There may also be difficulties in rent-sharing

---

[220]   In addition, it is understood that HMRC Stamp Taxes is not satisfied that the current legislation produces the results and tax charges that it intended, so further legislation can be expected. It may be prudent to advise clients that the rules may change retrospectively and that they should seek advice from time to time.

[221]   *Gable Construction* v. *IRC* [1968] 1 WLR 1426; *Donellan* v. *Read* (1832) 3 B & Ad 899.

arrangements about notional rents and notional expenses where the premises may be void for part of the time and there is no subtenant in occupation paying rent at any relevant time.

Alternatively, the structure of the rent may change. The landlord may wish to take over the management obligations or, where the landlord has the management obligations and receives a percentage of the gross rents received or receivable because he bears the expenses, the parties may wish to transfer the repairing and maintenance and other management obligations to the head tenant.[222] In these situations, since much may depend upon the rents received and the level of expenses, it will be difficult to determine whether there has been an increase or a reduction in the rent and the amount thereof and this may be made even more difficult where the rent adjustment takes the form of an increased service charge separately reserved and apportioned[223] so that it is not a variation of the 'rent'. There will be movements from variable rents which are dependent upon future facts such as the actual rents received as opposed to the rents contractually payable. Moreover, expenses that are deductible at any particular level of landlord or head tenant will also fluctuate from year to year. While it may be possible to determine the 'base rent' because this is defined as the rent previously taxed, as discussed above it will be less obvious to determine the 'new rent'. Unless it is possible to determine the new rent it is difficult to determine whether the 'new rent' is greater than or less than the base rent. In consequence, it may not be possible to determine whether there is a reduction or increase in the rent.

8.43   CONSEQUENCES OF RENT VARIATIONS

However, assuming that guidance is provided[224] as to determining the new rent and other factors relevant for determining whether there is an increase or reduction, there are numerous provisions that need to be noted.

8.43.1   Reduction in rent

Where a lease is varied so as to reduce the amount of the rent the variation is treated for the purposes of SDLT as an acquisition of a chargeable interest by the lessee. There is no indication as to the nature of the chargeable interest being deemed to be acquired. This may be an important factor as to situations where the tenant is making a payment to commute the rent which is of a relatively small amount. Should the transaction be a dealing in a major interest, i.e. a freehold or a deemed

---

[222]   But note that with suitable drafting such items may not form part of the 'rent' and therefore are not taxable: FA 2003, Sched.17A, paras.6 and 10.

[223]   FA 2003, Sched.17A, para.6 and para.10; see **8.20** and **8.22**.

[224]   HMRC Stamp Taxes has provided a defective online facility for determining the existence or otherwise of an abnormal increase. Unfortunately it has not provided guidance as to the correct date to be inserted on any meaningful level.

new lease, the notification obligation may start if the consideration exceeds £40,000. However, if the new chargeable interest is a minor interest there will be no notification unless tax is payable because the consideration provided by the tenant exceeds the nil rate threshold for that particular type of property.

8.43.2 Increase in rent

Where a lease is varied so as to increase the amount of the rent otherwise than pursuant to the terms of the lease, and the variation takes effect before the expiration of the fifth year of the term of the lease the variation is treated as if it were the grant of a lease in consideration of the additional rent payable. Again, there is no guidance in the legislation as to how to determine whether there is an increase or a reduction. It would seem that the deemed new lease is intended to be for the balance or unexpired portion of the term of the lease being varied. This could be a significant problem where there is only a temporary increase in the rent. It would seem that where the deemed new lease is for a period exceeding five years and the rent increase is for only two years the first five years' rent may be the amount of the increase for years one and two, and nil for years three, four and five when the increase ceases to take effect but the rents for years six and subsequently will be the rent payable in years one and two for the deemed new lease. There is, therefore, a significant charge upon rent that will never become payable. Great care may be needed in entering into such arrangements in order to avoid excessive charges to tax.

8.43.3 Variation after the expiration of the fifth year of the term

Where the variation of the rent takes effect after the expiration of the fifth year of the term there is a charge if the increase in the rent pursuant to the deed of variation or otherwise is abnormal within the rules considered above.[225]

8.44 INCREASE OF RENT OUTSIDE THE LEASE: DEED OF VARIATION

As a matter of general law a variation of the rent is not a surrender and regrant.[226] A lease can be varied by deed such as where a landlord makes a payment to a tenant to purchase the benefit of the tenant's improvements and increase the rent accordingly, or simply pays cash to increase the rent in order to enhance the value of the freehold reversion. Where there is an increase of rent that is not within the variable or abnormal rent legislation,[227] the variation is treated as if it were the grant of a new lease in consideration of the additional rent made payable by it.[228] There are major

---

[225] FA 2003, Sched.17A, para.14.
[226] *Gable Construction* v. *IRC* [1968] 1 WLR 1426.
[227] FA 2003, Sched.17A, paras.8, 14 and 15.
[228] FA 2003, Sched.17A, para.13.

holes in this legislation. For example, there is no indication as to the nature of the terms of the deemed new lease so that the application of the provisions for leases and low rents to be taxed upon the basis of any notional market value premium whether involving connected companies or partnerships or otherwise is not dealt with. Since there is nothing indicating the terms and covenants in the new lease that is deemed to arise it is difficult to deal with the theoretical issue of potential market value premium.

More significantly the term of the new lease is not specified. This raises important questions as to where there is a temporary increase in the rent which will not necessarily carry forward until the contractual termination date for the lease whose rent is being increased. For example, the parties may as part of some arrangement agree that the rent is to be increased but only for a limited period. It seems that HMRC Stamp Taxes will not accept that the deemed new lease is to apply only for the period of the temporary increase in the rent. This will mean that there is a variable rent which will fall in due course but this may in its turn be subject to the impact of future rent reviews. This will be a particular problem since there is no attempt to deal with the interaction of these provisions and the increased rent in the context of the abnormal rent review provisions for the main lease. There is no statutory arrangement for the deemed new lease and the actual lease to 'merge' for the purposes of subsequent abnormal increase liability.

It seems that the deemed new lease is to be for the balance of the term although in this particular context it is not expressed to be the case[229] and there will be complex issues as to how to calculate the net present value of the rent for those years in respect of which the rent increase does not operate and the rent falls back into the normal rent review or other variable rent pattern of the main lease. Also, as discussed in more detail below (see **8.46**), there is a conspicuous lack of legislative guidance as to how to calculate the amount of the increase or, indeed, whether there is an increase in the rent at all because the parties move from one form of variable rent to another form of variable rent.

8.45 REDUCTION AND COMMUTATION OF RENT

A reduction of rent if made for consideration provided by the tenant will be a chargeable transaction. It is a variation of the lease within the basic definition of 'acquisition'.[230] There is, however, no express provision for a refund of tax paid upon the basis of the former rent.

It may be, however, that where there is a reduction during the first five years of the term and the lease is within the variable rent regime[231] the reduction in the rent may indirectly produce a tax refund. It is provided that at the end of the relevant period which is when the rent for the first five years of the term becomes 'certain' (which in

---

[229] Compare FA 2003, Sched.17A, paras.14 and 15.
[230] FA 2003, s.43(3)(d) and Sched.17A, para.15A (as amended).
[231] FA 2003, Sched.17A, paras.13, 7 and 8.

practice means the end of the fifth year of the term where the rent is subject to VAT as will usually be the case), it is necessary to revise retrospectively the initial return by inserting the actual rents paid for the estimated figures included in the original return. It would seem, on principle, that because the rent is variable and therefore within FA 2003, Sched.17A, para.7, the reduction in rent can be taken into account notwithstanding it arises by reason of a deed of variation outside the lease rather than pursuant to the terms of the lease. Since most commercial leases likely to be affected by these situations are, obviously, where there is no variable rent during the first five years of the term then para.8, which permits the refund of tax overpaid because the rent falls below the estimated levels, would not apply. However, as stated, most commercial leases will be affected by VAT and will therefore be variable rents within para.7. The manner in which the variation in the rent occurs may not be relevant although much of the benefits with the reduction in the rent would be lost by reason of the increases in the rate of VAT from 15 per cent to 20 per cent. HMRC Stamp Taxes appears to be taking the view that under no circumstances can a reduction of the rent taking effect outside the terms of the lease qualify for a refund.

8.46 INCREASE OR REDUCTION: A PRACTICAL PROBLEM

Unfortunately, the draftsman has not been adequately advised by those structuring the tax with the result that the draftsman has missed major issues of principle and, *inter alia*, has not been adequately advised to provide any test for determining whether there has been an increase or reduction in the rent which is not always obvious. It is necessary to provide a formula or mechanism for determining the nature of the rent variations which requires a machinery for determining both the base rent and the new rent especially where these are variable. There is occasionally guidance as to the base rent but no machinery for fixing the new rent.

This is important since there are fundamental differences in the manner in which the provisions relating to increases and reductions in rent operate. It is, therefore, frequently unclear into which regime the rent variation may fall. An increase in rent is taxable whether or not there is chargeable consideration and the tenant is always taxable even where the landlord pays the consideration; reductions are taxable only if there is consideration.[232]

There are also computational and compliance problems since it is not clear how to calculate the new rent. For example, there may be calculation complications since it is not always the passing rent that is involved in the comparisons. This rent may be the artificial 'assumed rent' for years after the fifth year.[233] In some cases whether the rent variations increase or reduce rent will be fairly obvious but others will be a source of uncertainty. For example, it is not clear whether there is an

---

[232] FA 2003, Sched.17A, paras.13 and 15A.
[233] Which has effectively turned many SDLT documents and related matters into complex title issues; see **1.14**.

increase or a reduction where there is a change in the review date.[234] In some cases the parties may negotiate a change in the rent basis from a turnover rent to a profit-sharing rent or switch to a market rent or during the recession the parties may reduce the rent by a deed of variation outside the lease because review provisions in current leases are usually upwards only. Since many of these rent bases will be uncertain in their own right, it will be difficult if not impossible to carry out a realistic comparison of the situation before and after the change, or to assess whether any variation involves an abnormal increase. It seems, although there is no guidance in the legislation, out of the possibilities available the comparison should be carried out upon the basis of the net present value of either the preceding rent or the assumed rent and the net present value of the new rent. These calculations will involve estimates but since the two rents themselves will or may be commercially uncertain, this provides as reasonable a basis as any other in the absence of an official policy.

8.47 HOLDING OVER AND RENT

There are, currently, in practice two forms of holding-over regime;[235] but there is a charge only where a lease for a fixed term[236] has expired and the tenant is holding over 'by operation of law'.[237] The other regime is holding over not by operation of law. The suggestion of 'by operation of law' means that this legislation may not apply to contracted-out tenancies[238] and it seems by implication from the legislation that the charge does not apply where the held-over lease was granted within the stamp duty regime.[239] It is important, therefore, to avoid converting a stamp duty lease into a SDLT lease.

The charge arises at the start of the first year of holding over, i.e. the first day after the contractual termination of the existing lease.[240] The original lease is deemed to have been extended by one year. There is a retrospective extension of the lease so

---

[234] Which is not a surrender and regrant and may affect the initial 'guestimate' because it produces an actual rent different from the estimated rent and possibly the assumed rent because it spreads the rent adjustment over a different 12 calendar month period from that within the original land transaction return calculations.

[235] Similar rules apply to the continuation of periodic and similar tenancies pursuant to FA 2003, Sched.17A, para.3; see **8.49**.

[236] Which in the context of Landlord and Tenant Act 1954, Part II has become a major issue as to the meaning of 'fixed term' where the lease itself refers to holding over as part of the term.

[237] Which probably means pursuant to a statute or legislative protection continuing the tenancy such as Landlord and Tenant Act 1954, Part II (as amended) or its equivalent for agricultural and farm business tenancies.

[238] Although recent decisions suggest that these may be fewer than advisers expected because for X years and thereafter by statute are not fixed terms.

[239] There will be no rent 'previously taxed'.

[240] Where the original lease is for five years (or less in certain cases) the commencement of holding over can provide some complex calculations. It will be necessary, *inter alia*, to deal with the retrospective review for the first five years. It will also be necessary to calculate the highest rent paid during any 12 consecutive months during the first five years of the term to determine the assumed rent for subsequent years pursuant to FA 2003, Sched.17A, paras.7 and 8.

that the initial return has to be revised on the basis of the statutorily extended lease term.[241] If the holding over continues beyond one year the original lease is deemed to have been for a term equal to the original term plus two years, or three or four years and so on.

The SDLT paid upon the original lease has to be recalculated on the basis of a lease for the longer deemed term at the end of each extended term, i.e. every year of the holding over.[242] This may become an annual event should tax become payable and holding over or the periodic tenancy continues for a sufficiently long period. Tax may become payable for the first time or the transaction become notifiable on a different basis if the term exceeds seven years but there is no obligation to notify simply because the effect of the holding over is to produce a lease for seven years or longer. Notification is, in this case, restricted to situations where tax becomes payable or additional tax is payable.[243]

The rents payable under the holding-over arrangements may initially be a continuation of the rents payable during the final years of the contractual term, but may be subject to variation such as an order for interim rents. However, where the initial rent is variable the rent taken into account during the holding-over period is the assumed rent for all years after the fifth year not the passing rent.[244] It remains to be seen whether, as is likely, HMRC Stamp Taxes intends to charge orders for interim rents as a deemed new lease for the notional increase over the assumed rent. It seems that if the lease was originally for more than five years or has 'grown' to such a term the interim rents will be taxable only if they constitute an abnormal increase[245] being an increase taking effect otherwise than pursuant to the terms of the lease.

A tenant may hold over at the expiration of the contractual term of a lease for a fixed term otherwise than 'by operation of law' which it seems will include holding over at common law and where the lease is not a contracted-out tenancy for the purpose of the Landlord and Tenant Act 1954. This, in general law, may be treated as a new lease of a periodic nature giving rise to a potential charge to SDLT. HMRC Stamp Taxes has indicated that it does not intend to take the point and will not treat this as a holding over by operation of law as described above so that no charge to tax arises. It is considered that this view may be incorrect but it will usually be

---

[241] Where the lease was for a term of five years not only is there a retrospective recalculation required, the legislation requires the parties to determine the highest rent paid over any 12 consecutive months during the first five years so as to determine the assumed rent for the lease after the expiration of the fifth year of the term.
[242] This means that where the held-over lease is for a fixed term of five years the tenant will be faced with considerable arithmetic problems. It will be necessary to: (i) carry out the review of the variable rent (VAT implications are obvious) at the end of the fifth year of the term (FA 2003, Sched.17A, paras.7 and 8); (ii) calculate the assumed rent for the additional deemed year of the lease (FA 2003, Sched.17A, paras.3 and 8); and (iii) make further revision of the initial calculation on the basis that it is for a lease of six years not for five years.
[243] FA 2003, Sched.17A, paras.3(4) and 4(4A).
[244] However, any arrangement for interim rents may have to be reviewed in the context of abnormal rent increases (FA 2003, Sched.17A, paras.14 and 15 (or possibly para.13 during the first five years); see **8.37**.
[245] FA 2003, Sched.17A, paras.13, 14 and 15.

beneficial to the taxpayer. The practice may change, but since the general level of rents it produces will be below £150,000 for the first few years of the holding over, especially since the continuation would be treated as a tenancy from year to year, there will normally be no tax loss to HMRC Stamp Taxes. It is, in consequence, not likely to take up this point with all the issues of finding the evidence. In effect, therefore, there will be no new tenancy since HMRC Stamp Taxes regards a person holding over without statutory protection as a licensee, tenant at will or a trespasser, none of which are chargeable interests producing chargeable transactions.[246] Continuation of occupation as licensee or tenant at will may be substantial performance where there has been a prior agreement to renew the lease or an option to renew has been exercised.

8.48 NEW LEASE AND RENT CREDITS

There are issues where there is an element of backdating of any new lease negotiated. *Prima facie*, 'backdated rent' is taxed as a premium.[247] However, in certain circumstances this is 'reconverted' into rent. Moreover, SDLT may have been paid as rent for part of a year that overlaps with the new lease. Rent credits may be available.

Where the new lease is granted pursuant to the Landlord and Tenant Act 1954 and is to be treated as relating back to the contractual termination of the original lease,[248] the taxable rent for the new lease is reduced by the amount of the rent taken into account for SDLT in the interim period between the termination of the old lease and the actual grant of the new lease.[249]

Taxpayers need to exercise care during a holding over including statutory tenancies such as agricultural holdings. During any negotiation the parties may modify the terms of the arrangement which may be a form of surrender and regrant, and thereby create a new tenancy for the purposes of SDLT.[250]

8.49 THE TERM OF THE LEASE: GENERAL

The term of the lease is important in relation to the tax for various reasons including:

- the calculation of the net present value of the rent;[251]

---

[246] FA 2003, s.48.
[247] FA 2003, Sched.5, para.1A.
[248] FA 2003, Sched.17A, para.9.
[249] FA 2003, Sched.17A, paras.9 and 9A; see **8.26**.
[250] And, for the time being, taxpayers crucially lose the benefit of no taxation when holding over a stamp duty lease.
[251] FA 2003, Sched.5 (as amended).

- whether the lease is for less than seven years or for seven years or longer when different reporting obligations apply.[252]

There are at least five important dates in relation to the start of the term which is one element in determining the length of a lease:

- the date from which the term is to be computed (the 'term commencement date') which may frequently be earlier than any agreement for lease, substantial performance or the actual grant;[253]
- the date of the agreement for lease which may depend upon the date of the exercise of any option to call for or to renew a lease. Such agreements are not taxable,[254] but the date of the agreement for lease may be information required for the purposes of completing the land transaction return;
- the date at which any agreement for lease becomes unconditional;[255]
- the date of the substantial performance of the agreement for lease which is a deemed grant of the lease;[256] and
- the date of the grant of the lease itself.[257]

However, these dates are relevant, if at all, only for the start date of the lease. The other issue for determining the term of the lease is the termination date. Unfortunately, the rules for determining the termination date of a lease are complex and are fundamentally merely provisional so that terms of leases may 'grow', i.e. be deemed to continue beyond the contractual termination date or some other date that is provisionally identified as the possible termination date such as certain forms of holding over or lease renewal.

8.50 START DATE FOR TAX CALCULATION

Three of the above dates may be important in relation to the charging and reporting obligations for SDLT.

1. *The 'start date' or term commencement date.* This is the date from which the term of the lease is calculated; it has no bearing on the length of the lease but it may have implications as to whether any backdated rent is a premium,[258] or in respect of the availability of relief from the treatment and a possible rent credit when holding over.[259] Its main practical significance is in determining whether a rent review takes effect during the final three months of the first five

---

[252] FA 2003, s.77A (as amended).
[253] Alan Estates Ltd v. W.G. Stores Ltd [1981] 3 All ER 481.
[254] FA 2003, s.44(2).
[255] But note *Eastham* v. *Leigh London and Provincial Properties Ltd* [1971] 2 All ER 887 on condition or consideration; *GUS Merchandise* v. *Customs and Excise* [1981] 1 WLR 1309.
[256] FA 2003, Sched.17A, para.12A.
[257] City and Permanent Building Society v. Miller [1952] Ch 840.
[258] FA 2003, Sched.5, para.1A.
[259] FA 2003, Sched.17A, paras.9 and 9A.

years of the term.[260] However, it has to be noted that the legislation does not deal in express terms with the not infrequent situation in practice of the effective date for substantial performance preceding the term commencement date. This may occur when a tenant of a new building enters into possession early to carry out construction or fitting out works. The issue in practice will be to determine the rent 'in respect of' the first five years of the tenancy.

2. *The date of substantial performance of the agreement for lease.* This is the effective date which starts certain of the notification and payment provisions; it is the relevant date for fixing the term in calculating the SDLT initially[261] and is the provisional start date for the term of the lease until the lease is actually granted when this takes over as the main base date.

3. *The date of the actual grant of the lease.* This is the date from which the 30-day notification and payment provisions run[262] even where there has been prior substantial performance of an agreement for lease.[263] This appears to supplant the date of substantial performance as the eventual base date for calculating the return of the lease for all subsequent situations where the start date is important such as holding over.

8.51 TERM OF THE LEASE FOR RENT DUTY CALCULATION

One of the key factors in the calculation of the net present value is 'n' (the number of years) namely, the term of the lease. *Prima facie* this is the period starting with the 'start date' as described above and ending with the termination date. This is an issue which has numerous special rules and frequently operates on a provisional basis because of retrospective increase arising from routine situations such as successive linked leases and holding over.

Where an agreement for lease has been entered into[264] and the agreement is substantially performed otherwise than by 'completion' so that an effective date has been triggered and subsequently the actual lease is granted pursuant to an agreement, the term of the lease is:

* initially the period from substantial performance until the end of the contractual term specified in the lease; or
* where there is a subsequent grant, from the date of the grant until the end of the contractual term.

---

[260] FA 2003, Sched.17A, para.7A.
[261] Originally set out in FA 2003, Sched.5, para.6(2), but amendment and repeal of these provisions by Sched.17A leaves this position unclear in theory. However, the comments in the text are believed to represent the official view, which is it seems based upon the repealed para.6(2).
[262] FA 2003, ss.44(8) and 77.
[263] FA 2003, s.44(8).
[264] Where the parties do not adopt the unusual course of proceeding directly from negotiation to the actual grant.

8.51.1 Fixed terms

Where there is a lease for a fixed term,[265] the problem is to determine whether the lease is for a fixed term, because of the principles of SDLT and the effect upon the term of the lease by the exercise of an option to renew the lease. This raises many questions where the effective date occurs before the lease takes effect such as where the agreement for lease is conditional at the effective date. There is an issue as to whether the term runs from the effective date or from the date when the lease becomes unconditional which itself is a problem since this is uncertain and is not necessarily a factor in determining the contractual term.

Another problem is that a lease that appears to be for a fixed term when granted may 'grow' retrospectively so that the contractual term is merely provisional and potentially subject to retrospective adjustment. Some guidance is provided in that no account is taken, at least initially, of any contingency as a result of which the lease may terminate prior to the termination date as stated in the lease,[266] or any right of any party either to terminate the lease or to renew it. In consequence, break clauses and options to renew are initially ignored, but the termination or renewal of the lease may have SDLT consequences in their own right when the rights are exercised.

8.51.2 Special cases

8.51.2.1 Renewals of leases

The existence of an option to renew or extend the lease is to be ignored when initially determining the contractual term of the lease for calculating the SDLT upon the rent.[267] Where a lease is renewed such as by the exercise of an option it may be a linked transaction, i.e. a successive linked lease and the original and new terms have to be aggregated,[268] so that the initial tax has to be reviewed on the basis of a lease for the combined term of the two leases as described later in this chapter.

8.51.2.2 Holding over

The holding over of a fixed-term lease which has expired or continuation of periodic tenancies is, in certain cases (depending upon whether the holding over is by operation of law; see **8.47**), treated as a retrospective extension of the term by at least one year. Although such a possibility of holding over or continuation is ignored in making the initial calculation, that initial assessment has to be revisited and

---

[265] Note FA 2003, Sched.17A, para.3.
[266] FA 2003, Sched.17A, para.2.
[267] FA 2003, Sched.17A, para.2(b). This raises the question of the effect of an option to extend the lease which appears to be different from an option to renew; see *Baker* v. *Merckel* [1960] 1 QB 657.
[268] FA 2003, Sched.17A, para.9.

revised when holding over commences and the tax recalculated on the basis of the term increased by one year, with a subsequent revision every year thereafter while the lease is held over or the periodic leasing continues. This will affect assignees of the lease who will be responsible for the taxation issues arising by reason of the growth of the lease and will be liable to pay the extra tax arising.

Where a new lease is granted by order of the court under the Landlord and Tenant Act 1954 or other legislation, the new lease may be treated as if it began on the expiration of the previous lease,[269] for the purposes of obtaining a credit in respect of the charge upon the rent and avoiding any interim rent being taxed as a premium.[270]

8.51.2.3 Break clauses and notices to quit

For the purposes of the calculation, no account is taken of any right of either party to determine the lease such as by notice to quit, forfeiture or otherwise. A potential area of difficulty would be break clauses since it is provided that a lease terminable by notice is a lease for an indefinite term,[271] but it is provided that, *inter alia*, break clauses are to be ignored, to counteract any suggestion that a lease terminable by notice is a lease for an indefinite term, although the drafting is less than helpful.[272] The tax is calculated on the basis of the maximum term[273] and there is no refund if the break clause should be exercised.[274]

8.51.2.4 'Indefinite' terms

For the purposes of computing the SDLT upon the rent, a lease for an indefinite term[275] is treated wholly on a provisional basis as if it were a lease for one year. Where there is a lease for a fixed term and thereafter until terminated by notice, it is for an initial term equal to the fixed term plus one year. A lease for an indefinite term is treated[276] as being initially a lease for a fixed term of one year. If it continues into a second, third or subsequent year it is treated 'retrospectively' as a lease for two, three, four years and so on, and the tax calculation will have to be revised on the basis of a longer term. In such cases at the start of each new year of the lease, i.e. at

---

[269] FA 2003, Sched.17A, paras.9 and 9A; see **8.26** for rent credits.

[270] FA 2003, Sched.5, para.1A; Sched.17A, paras.9 and 9A.

[271] FA 2003, Sched.17A, para.4(5)(c).

[272] FA 2003, Sched.17A, para.2(b). See *Baker* v. *Merckel* [1960] 1 QB 657.

[273] In these situations there may be considerable tax benefits in having a short lease with options to renew rather than break clauses; see **8.51.2.7**.

[274] There is an open question of how this provision interacts with the variable rent regime where the lease is terminated during the first five years of the term, i.e. whether there is an effective refund because there will be no rent to be paid during what might have been the balance of the first five years and the assumed rent for periods after the expiration of the fifth year of the term.

[275] If valid; it must not be overlooked that a lease for an unascertainable term is void for uncertainty; see e.g. *Lace* v. *Chantler* [1944] KB 368.

[276] Pursuant to FA 2003, Sched.17A, para.4(1).

the end of the current deemed fixed-term lease, it is necessary to reassess 'retrospec-tively' as from the original effective date taking it into account as an initial grant of a lease for the current deemed fixed term.

8.51.2.5 Statutory terms

The legislation was originally expressly applied to, *inter alia*:

- a perpetual lease, which is treated by the Law of Property Act 1925 as a lease for 2,000 years;
- a lease for life, which is treated by the Law of Property Act 1925 as being a lease for 90 years;[277] or
- a lease determinable on the marriage of the lessee.[278]

A lease at a rent or premium or for a mix of rent and premium determinable on death or marriage is, in general law, not a lease for an uncertain term, as the provisions of LPA 1925, s.149(6) turn such a creature into a fixed term of 90 years determinable by notice after the unhappy event.[279] However, these rules are not applied for SDLT where such a lease is treated as a lease for an indefinite term which begins life as a deemed lease for a year but which 'grows' into a longer lease on each anniversary as the arrangement continues.[280]

Although these provisions were repealed and do not reappear expressly in the inserted Sched.17A, it seems clear that such leases are to be treated as being for an indefinite term because of the provision excluding the effect of other legislation upon the term of the lease which is applied to:

- a periodic tenancy or other interest or right[281] determinable by a period of notice;
- a tenancy at will in England and Wales or Northern Ireland. Although a tenancy at will is not a chargeable interest,[282] it is treated initially as a lease for one year with the potential to 'grow' if the occupation continues for a sufficiently long period (this is presumably necessary to identify those interests that may be exempt); and

---

[277] Subject to determination upon the relevant death: Law of Property Act 1925, s.149(6); see e.g. *IRC* v. *Lloyds Private Banking* [1998] STC 559. Such leases may form part of home annuity and equity release schemes. It should be noted that the principles in the main text apply for the purposes of the rent. They do not apply where the issue is the market value of the lease. Actuarial and other issues may then be relevant.

[278] These three types of lease appear to fall within FA 2003, Sched.17A, para.4(2).

[279] See Skipton Building Society v. Clayton (1993) 66 P&CR 223.

[280] Cf. the position of yearly and other periodic tenancies at common law (FA 2003, Sched.17A, paras.3 and 4).

[281] On the meaning of the words 'interest or right' in this context see **Chapter 2** above.

[282] FA 2003, s.48(2)(c)(i).

- any other interest or right determinable by notice at any time.[283] This along with the definition of a lease[284] means they are not major interests and terms of years absolute[285] but are merely rights over land, as easements for a limited period are 'leases' that are not major interests but are subject to the complex rules relating to leases because the plain English drafting is replaced by inadvertent drafting that displaces both plain English and longstanding technical terminology with a very special meaning.

8.51.2.6 *Linked transactions and renewals of leases*

The basic linked transaction rules[286] apply to leases as regards premiums and rents, but there are special problems for leases which can retrospectively grow the term of the lease.[287]

- There are two sets of linked transaction regimes to leases, namely:
  - situations where leases are granted of several different premises to the same person or connected parties. This regime for 'concurrent linked leases' can apply where one person takes or several connected persons take separate leases of several different premises; and
  - situations where a lease is renewed.[288] This successive linked lease regime not only affects the renewed lease but may retrospectively affect any concurrent linked leases.

- In certain situations such as an abnormal increase in rent and the assignment of leases exempt when granted[289] the transaction is taxed as the grant of a new lease which, by statute, is linked with the actual lease.

CONCURRENT LINKED LEASES

Where there are concurrent linked leases, i.e. linked leases granted initially in relation to separate demised premises, the nil rate slice for the rent has to be apportioned between them.[290] This apportionment is made on the basis of the proportion that the net present value of the rent for the particular lease bears to the total net present value of the rents for all linked leases.[291]

Since the linked transaction rules apply on a retrospective basis the allocation of the nil rate slice of the net present value of the rent to any particular lease may be reduced subsequently. For example, the grant or substantial performance of the first

---

[283]   FA 2003, Sched.17A, para.1(b).
[284]   FA 2003, Sched.17A, para.1.
[285]   See FA 2003, s.117(2)(b).
[286]   FA 2003, s.108; see **Chapter 4**.
[287]   FA 2003, Sched.17A, para.5.
[288]   FA 2003, Sched.17A, para.5.
[289]   FA 2003, Sched.17A, paras.14, 15 and 12 respectively.
[290]   FA 2003, Sched.5, para.2(5).
[291]   FA 2003, Sched.5, para.2(5) and (6) (as amended).

lease will qualify for the full nil rate slice; but this will be retrospectively reduced when the second lease is granted. The latter will be chargeable for only a proportion of the nil rate for the rent. Should there be a third or further linked lease all prior leases will progressively and retrospectively have their allocation of the nil rate slice reduced. This reduction in the allocation of the nil rate slice is on a retrospective basis. This is likely indirectly to affect assignees of leases that are linked who are bound to notify[292] and who, since they will not be parties to the later linked transaction, will require an undertaking from the vendor to supply relevant information to enable them to recalculate his tax in respect of the lease by reducing the proportion of the nil rate slice provisionally allocated to the assigned lease[293] or which may affect the abnormal increase calculation. However, for linked leases, he may require an indemnity against any additional tax arising.

SUCCESSIVE LINKED LEASES

The basic planning strategy for leases is to operate upon the basis of short-term leases possibly with options to renew exploiting the possibility of new leases and the multiple use of the nil rate slice upon rents. Such options are ignored initially in determining the term of the lease when making the initial estimated calculation of the net present value of the rent[294] and the short term will mean in many cases that the amount by reference to which the SDLT is to be charged will fall within the nil rate band or slice. Anti-avoidance rules were introduced to deal with a succession of short leases and cancel the benefit of multiple nil rate slices. These apply where the renewal of the lease is linked with the grant of the original lease which will be an issue governed by the general law[295] as a matter of evidence (see **4.6**). However, where successive linked leases are granted of the same or substantially the same premises, the leases are treated as a single lease granted at the time of the grant of the first lease for a term of the aggregate of the terms of all the leases in the series for the time being in consideration of the aggregate net present value of the rent payable under all such leases.[296]

8.51.2.7 Options to renew leases

Options to renew leases are useful mitigation tools in relation to SDLT and leases. An option to renew may avoid a disadvantageous surrender and regrant when extending a lease (see **4.13**) and avoid an early effective date in general. However,

---

[292] FA 2003, s.81A and Sched.17A, para.12.

[293] It is unclear at present whether HMRC Stamp Taxes regards the rules as providing for a sole liability or some form of joint and several liability. This is important since there is no statutory indemnity provided for the assignee so that joint and several liability might provide a possible claim for indemnification where the assignee's professional advisers have failed to include the necessary safeguard in the contract.

[294] FA 2003, Sched.17A, para.2(b).

[295] FA 2003, s.108.

[296] FA 2003, Sched.17A, para.5.

options are outside the transitional reliefs.[297] Also the option may not be linked with the contract or lease arising upon its exercise.[298] The practical problem will be most frequently encountered in relation to options to renew leases. The general position would appear to be governed by FA 2003, ss.46(1) and 108. As the linked transaction rules apply only as between the same parties or connected persons, it seems that the new lease arising upon the exercise of an option in an existing lease cannot be linked with the original lease where the original lease has been assigned to some persons unconnected with the original tenant, because the exercise of the option to renew is not between the same parties. The view of HMRC Stamp Taxes is not known but any suggestion that assignees could be directly affected is generally considered to be incorrect. However, as discussed elsewhere (see **8.61**) the exercise of an option to renew a lease of other premises may indirectly affect the tax position of an assignee of another linked lease and require him to report and pay additional tax. He should insist upon suitable indemnities. Where the option is exercised by the original tenant, it appears to be necessary to investigate the grant of the original lease and whether there was an arrangement or understanding between the landlord and the tenant that the option would be exercised. If there is established on the evidence that there was a postponed genuine commercial decision as to whether the option would or would not be exercised the original lease and the new lease are not linked (see further **Chapter 4**).

8.52   THE PREMIUM

Subject to certain exclusions mentioned later (see **8.56**), where there is chargeable consideration other than rent in respect of a lease then not only the rent but also the other consideration is subject to SDLT.[299] A premium will therefore include everything that falls within the general definition of 'chargeable consideration' contained in FA 2003, Sched.4, as well as any rent paid in respect of a period before the grant of the lease,[300] unless there is a lease received or holding over when rent credits may be available.[301]

It is a fundamental question as to what is consideration for the grant of a lease. This can include building works and services, fitting out[302] and land exchanges including surrenders of other leases. As *Eastham* v. *Leigh London and Provincial*

---

[297]   See e.g. FA 2003, Sched.19, para.3; *Swallow Hotels* v. *IRC* [2000] STC 45.

[298]   FA 2003, s.46.

[299]   Where the lease for a rent or a variation is a linked transaction with another transaction for the purposes of FA 2003, s.55 no account is taken of the rent in determining the relevant consideration: FA 2003, Sched.5, para.9(5) and para.9(1).

[300]   FA 2003, Sched.5, para.1A. There is no attempt in the legislation to deal with the problems arising where rent is payable in respect of a period prior to substantial performance and the subsequent actual grant of the lease and for the intervening period when it is 'rent' for the deemed lease but a premium for the actual lease.

[301]   FA 2003, Sched.17A, para.9A; see **8.48**.

[302]   Timing of events is crucial in mitigating the tax charge on building or fitting out costs; see **9.9**.

Properties Ltd[303] clearly shows, what is described as a 'condition' may in fact be the consideration for the grant of the lease.[304] Subject to special rules, the basic computational rules will apply with the right to apply to defer payment of the tax in cases of variable premiums.[305] In theory, when calculating the premium, any lessor's costs paid by the lessee should be included, but as a matter of practice, HMRC Stamp Taxes ignored them for beneficial stamp duty.[306] It is not yet clear whether the practice is to continue into SDLT.

However, there is a major practical difference between sales and leases in that the liability to deal with the open or provisional estimated initial assessment of the vendor who was the initial tenant, will pass to the assignee in the case of a lease premium.[307] In consequence, he is vulnerable to the problems arising in connection with the resolution of this open tax position even though he may not contractually assume the liability for the payment of the deferred consideration to the landlord.

A grant of a lease or substantial performance of an agreement for a lease for an inadequate consideration, such as where the premium is below market value or the rent is low[308] is, in general, taxable only upon the actual premium and/or rent unless the connected company charge or other provisions such as the partnership regime expressly impose tax upon a deemed market value premium plus the net present value of the actual rent.[309] It is important to note that the market value charge applies only to the premium. HMRC Stamp Taxes seems to have abandoned its previous attempt to find a 'market rent' for leases which is an immensely complicated exercise because of the difference between a fixed rent for the entire term[310] which is commercially unusual so that there are no 'comparables' and the more usually reviewable or turnover rents where it is impossible to predict the future rent although HMRC Stamp Taxes has strenuously maintained that there is a scientific and precise process for determining future market rents! The test for future variable notional market rents is, clearly, virtually impossible to apply in practice for tax

---

[303]   [1971] 2 All ER 887.

[304]   See also GUS Merchandise v. Customs and Excise [1981] 1 WLR 1309; Errington v. Errington and Woods [1952] 1 KB 290.

[305]   FA 2003, s.51; see **4.38**.

[306]   [1959] *Gazette* 95.

[307]   FA 2003, Sched.17A, para.11. There is no indication as to whether the assignor remains liable on a joint and several basis with some form of equitable indemnity for the assignee or whether there is a form of statutory release and novation; compare FA 2003, Sched.17A, para.12B.

[308]   HMRC Stamp Taxes has great difficulty in dealing with what appear to be low rents which it, and other divisions of HMRC, seem to think is more or less automatically not a market value situation. However, low rents can be commercially agreed such as rent holidays where the tenant is incurring the fitting out or similar expenses and prefers a low rent to a reverse premium to reimburse him for carrying out the works. These commercial issues will need to be carefully documented in case HMRC Stamp Taxes contends that the low rent produces a market value charge for SDLT purposes in those situations where market value is involved such as with connected companies, partnerships or land exchanges.

[309]   FA 2003, s.53.

[310]   And the ancillary problem of such fixed market rents and whether VAT should be taken into account and whether the VAT upon the notional market rent makes it a variable rent with all of the problems relating thereto.

purposes even with the limited SDLT wait-and-see rules for rents since any actual variation in the rent will be irrelevant when determining a fixed notional market rent for the entire term.

8.53 PREMIUMS: PARTICULAR SITUATIONS – WITH SPECIAL LEASE MODIFICATIONS

The following situations apply the normal rules for computation of SLDT but with significant modification.

8.53.1 Variable premiums

Where a lease is granted for a variable premium the normal rules of the tax for contingent, unascertained or uncertain consideration (see **4.38**) apply including the right to apply to defer payment.[311] In consequence, the tax will be paid initially on an estimated basis with an obligation to notify and reassess the tax retrospectively as the contingencies occur or the consideration becomes ascertained;[312] but the obligation to deal with the subsequent adjustment in the tax passes to the assignee of the lease,[313] notwithstanding that he may not be personally affected by or assume all or any part of the liability to pay the outstanding or deferred consideration to the landlord. Assignees of leases will need to investigate these issues and require express indemnities in any contract because there is no express legislation setting out whether the original taxpayer is released from liability[314] or whether there is some formal joint and several liability with equitable remedies between the parties such as an indemnity.

8.53.2 Instalments and periodical payments

Where the premium consists wholly or partly of sums other than rent payable by instalments or periodically,[315] the SDLT is payable upon the total payment of the instalments or aggregate of the periodical payments; but where the periodical payments are payable for life, in perpetuity,[316] an indefinite period or a definite period exceeding 12 years, the amount is limited to the amount payable over 12 years[317] ignoring linking to the RPI.[318]

---

[311] There is no right to defer tax in relation to variable rent: FA 2003, s.90; Stamp Duty Land Tax (Administration) Regulations 2003, SI 2003/2837.

[312] FA 2003, ss.51, 80 and 90 on instalments; see **Chapter 4**.

[313] FA 2003, Sched.17A, para.12.

[314] Compare FA 2003, Sched.17A, para.12B.

[315] FA 2003, s.52(6). See also **Chapter 4**.

[316] Although this is unlikely in relation to leases which should have a definite or ascertainable date for termination.

[317] FA 2003, s.52(1) and (2).

[318] FA 2003, s.52(3).

One particularly important 'periodical payment' will be VAT where this is not reserved as part of the rent or additional rent. In relation to the equivalent provisions for stamp duty HMRC Stamp Taxes indicated that it regarded such VAT as consideration not rent which is payable periodically, i.e. a 'premium' (see further **4.31**). Unfortunately its statement dealing with changes in the rate of VAT as applied to rents[319] merely refers to the situation where the VAT is part of the rent. It deals with the situation upon the basis that the VAT is a 'rent'; it fails to address the question of when VAT is rent and when it is to be regarded as a premium payable by instalments. This is a crucial issue in practice since whether the VAT it is to be taxed as a periodical premium or as 'rent' could substantially affect the SDLT liability. The main issue in practice will depend upon the drafting and whether, where the VAT is not reserved as rent or an additional rent, it is taxable as a periodical premium pursuant to FA 2003, s.52 as outlined above. However, as described elsewhere, at present in practice HMRC Stamp Taxes does not appear to be pursuing this point and does not appear to be challenging or enquiring into land transaction returns which treat such VAT as 'rent'.[320]

8.53.3 Works

Chargeable consideration includes 'works'[321] which are not restricted to building works but include improvements, repairs[322] fitting out by a tenant, and other items (see **Chapter 9**) chargeable upon open market cost with relief for works to be carried out on the land being demised where these are carried out at the cost of the tenant provided that these are carried out after the effective dates.[323] Works carried out on the land to be demised before the effective date will be taxable where the carrying out of the works is part of the chargeable consideration[324] and the tenant is not making use of the landlord or anyone connected with the landlord as a builder.[325]

These provisions raise two important problems for the professional adviser; namely:

1. Whether the arrangement relating to the works constitutes consideration for the contract. *Eastham* v. *Leigh London and Provincial Properties Ltd*[326] is a case that indicates what might appear to be a condition could be consideration in the sense that the tenant is 'earning' the right to the lease by satisfying the

---

[319] HMRC Guidance Note January 2009; STI 2009, p.460.
[320] Obviously failure to deal in some way with such actual VAT will mean a possible attack for a negligent or fraudulent return and leave the taxpayer open to a discovery assessment.
[321] FA 2003, Sched.4, para.10 (as amended); see **Chapter 9**.
[322] But note the exclusion for repairs in FA 2003, Sched.17A, para.10(1).
[323] FA 2003, Sched.4, para.10(2A). The problem of FA 2003, Sched.17A, para.12A creating two effective dates where substantial performance of the agreement for lease precedes the grant of the lease is specially provided for (FA 2003, Sched.4, para.10(2A)) and works executed before the grant of the lease but after substantial performance of the agreement for lease are within the exemption.
[324] As in Eastham v. Leigh London and Provincial Properties Ltd [1971] 2 All ER 887.
[325] FA 2003, Sched.4, para.10(2).
[326] [1971] 2 All ER 887.

condition and carrying out the works in question.[327] There will be difficult drafting issues between what might be a mere permission for the tenant to enter upon the land to fit out if the tenant thinks fit and situations where there is some form of obligation upon the tenant to carry out the fitting out works before the lease can be granted. This might arise, for example, where the landlord is making a contribution towards the fitting out or the lease is granted with some form of rent holiday because of the tenant doing the fitting out. Similarly, where there is a sale of land with some form of overage or similar arrangement the vendor may impose an obligation upon the purchaser/developer to carry out the works since he will want to ensure that he will obtain the benefit of or require some protection against possible defaults in relation to any s.106 planning agreement.[328] There will be a very fine line for tax purposes between a permission to enter and carry out works and an obligation to do so. In the latter case it seems inevitable that HMRC Stamp Taxes will claim that the works whether construction or fitting out are chargeable consideration.

2.   Where the arrangements relating to the construction or fitting out works are possibly consideration[329] it will be necessary to ensure that any permission given to the purchaser or tenant to enter upon the land amounts to a taking of 'possession' creating an effective date by reason of substantial performance so that the tenant will have the additional argument that the works were carried out after the effective date and are therefore excluded from charge.

However, it has to be noted that this exemption applies only where the person is acquiring a major interest. Construction works may be involved in other projects such as the construction of underground pipelines or the installation of gas or electricity facilities. These will usually be the grants of easements or wayleaves which are not major interests[330] and are projects that may fall outside the relief unless they are ancillary to the grant of a major interest or the arrangement is structured as a term of years absolute for the relevant structure of the land in question (i.e. as a major interest). In consequence, if there is any suggestion that the construction of the hole in the ground is part of the consideration for the grant of the easement not related to the acquisition of a major interest there will be a full charge upon the total and rather high costs of the construction works. In these situations it may be necessary to consider whether it is possible to grant some form of lease of the substructure or airspace rather than an easement and that this lease is granted early and rent paid in order to create an effective date. To rely upon substantial

---

[327]   This is a wide-ranging issue of whether there is a premium for tax purposes where there are building covenants imposed upon a tenant.

[328]   The obligations imposed upon the purchaser by the tenant, who is technically the party to the s.106 planning agreement, may convert the planning gains of the local authority into chargeable consideration for the acquisition of the land.

[329]   See e.g. Eastham v. Leigh London and Provincial Properties Ltd [1971] 2 All ER 887.

[330]   FA 2003, s.117; see **7.1**.

performance may be difficult since HMRC Stamp Taxes may have some challenging views for taxpayers in relation to whether it is possible to take possession of a hole in the ground that has yet to be constructed.

8.53.4 Enfranchisement costs

There is an exemption from charge in relation to the payment of costs on a leasehold enfranchisement.[331]

8.54 LAND EXCHANGES INVOLVING LEASES

The definition of 'land exchange' is extensive[332] and includes a situation where A enters into a land transaction with B and the consideration provided by B is his entering into another land transaction whether with A or C.[333] There is no requirement of reciprocity in the movement of the chargeable interests although this may include merely contractual restrictions and routine conveyancing covenants.[334] In consequence, there will be many situations where routine land transactions involving leases are land exchanges[335] which means that there is a *prima facie* charge upon the market value of any lease or other interest involved.[336] There are, however, many exemptions and reliefs in this situation in order to recognise the commercial nature of the transaction rather than the archaic land law and conveyancing structures that have to be adopted.[337] The effect is that transactions such as surrenders and regrants, including deemed surrenders and regrants where there is a variation in the terms of the lease;[338] sale and leaseback transactions[339] are exchanges.

Land exchanges will, subject to the availability of reliefs in particular situations, involve a charge upon a consideration equal to the market value of any of the leases

---

[331] FA 2003, Sched.4, para.16C.

[332] FA 2003, s.47; see **Chapter 7**.

[333] This appears to produce a bizarre situation that A's transaction with B is a land exchange at least as regards B, but is not a land exchange by C who is not required to enter into a land transaction as consideration. His acquisition of the land is not consideration but is consideration of C's obligations which do not involve the disposal of land as all or part of the consideration. Also there would be problems for A and C since they may not receive land within the computation provisions. The fact that the computational rules cannot apply indicates strongly that not all of the transactions can be exchanges; compare *J&P Coats Ltd* v. *IRC* [1897] 2 QB 423.

[334] FA 2003, s.48(1)(b); see **2.12**.

[335] The exclusion of certain leasehold covenants and the specific reference to leasehold covenants affecting rent are clear indications that HMRC Stamp Taxes regards leasehold and other covenants as chargeable consideration and chargeable interests. HMRC Stamp Taxes has refused to confirm that routine covenants in leases would not mean that every lease is treated as a land exchange.

[336] FA 2003, Sched.4, para.5.

[337] Note the comments in *Sargaison* v. *Roberts* [1969] 3 All ER 1072 to the effect that when applying a rigorous tax regime HMRC should not rely too heavily upon conveyancing technicalities in order to produce multiple and inappropriate charges.

[338] See, for example, *Gable Construction* v. *IRC* [1968] 1 WLR 1426.

[339] But see FA 2003, s.57A (as much amended).

being acquired plus any rent reserved by that lease. Therefore, the tax is charged upon the market value of the property received, not the property transferred as consideration.[340] In consequence, where a lease is granted in consideration of the transfer of other land the lessee is liable to tax upon a notional premium equal to the market value of the lease, if any, after taking into account the rent, if any, reserved by the lease which is specifically part of the taxable consideration. If the lease is at a full rent it is unlikely to have a market value[341] and the tax charge will be limited to the net present value of the rent.

This charge upon the premium arising from the land exchange rules is subject to exceptions where the premium is not taxable such as:

- a relief for leaseback transactions entered into as part of an exempt sale and leaseback or sublease arrangement but these leases are subject to a special charge to tax on assignment;[342]
- a relief whereby two categories of surrender and grant of new leases are taken out of the land exchange charge; namely:

   - surrenders and grants of new leases of the same or different premises between the same parties;[343] and
   - surrenders and regrants of leases of substantially the same premises between the same parties;[344] and

- certain reliefs exist for land transactions entered into in connection with a limited range of PFI projects.[345]

---

[340] It should be noted that in such transfer and leaseback class of transactions it has for a decade been the view of HMRC Stamp Taxes that the value of the land transferred is determined upon a vacant possession basis ignoring the obligation to grant the lease back: FA 2003, s.47; FA 2003, Sched.4, para.5.

[341] However, it must be noted that even interests that have restricted 'marketability' because of covenants against assignments, etc. may nevertheless have a market value because they have a 'nuisance value'; see, for example, *Alexander* v. *IRC* [1991] STC 112. In addition, leases may have a 'marriage value' as well as a 'hope value' (although currently professional advisers are reluctant to commit themselves to a marriage or hope value because of the possibilities of future development and have forced clients into the unholy mess of overage, earnouts and clawback arrangements; see, the professional obligations as set out in *Akasuc Enterprise* v. *Farmar* [2003] PL SCS 127). It is, therefore, no guarantee that because a lease is at a full reviewable rack rent it does not have some form of 'value' and this may be important where there has been a review in the preceding year or so and the rents have risen in the intervening period so that the lease does have some sort of capital value because the assignee or hypothetical assignee would obtain the benefit of a rent slightly below market rent until the next review date.

[342] FA 2003, s.57A; see **8.67**

[343] FA 2003, Sched.17A, para.16.

[344] FA 2003, Sched.17A, para.16 with a limited additional relief for rent in the overlap period: FA 2003, Sched.17A, para.9.

[345] FA 2003, Sched.4, para.17 (as amended).

8.55   DEEMED PREMIUM

While, in general, SDLT operates upon the basis of the actual consideration provided, albeit with obscure principles for calculating the chargeable consideration, there are certain situations where the chargeable consideration is not the actual amount provided but may be the market value. Unfortunately, these issues will usually be influenced by the nature of the rent reserved by the lease and, in particular, whether such rent is a full market rent as affected by the terms and conditions contained in the actual lease, but HMRC Stamp Taxes and its valuation advisers have no real understanding of the nature of rent and what is a market rent. Problems have arisen where there is a rent holiday because a rent holiday cannot be a market rent and arguments based upon the commercial background are frequently challenged. These views are manifestly incorrect and fail to take into account the fact that variable rents are attempts to cope with the problems of producing a market rent rather than an old-fashioned fixed rent for the whole of the term. These issues will be resolved on an objective basis. It will not be sufficient that the parties genuinely believe that they are acting at market value levels.[346]

These potential deemed market value premium charges include the following.

8.55.1   Connected companies

An arrangement involving a lease to a connected company is deemed to take place at market value[347] so that where a lease is granted to a connected company or to or by a partnership in a transaction between connected parties,[348] it will be subject to tax upon the net present value of the actual rent reserved by the lease and, if appropriate, be a deemed premium equal to the market value, if any, for a lease on those terms. Reliefs have been made available for leases to connected companies where:

- the lease or agreement is with a corporate trustee[349] and immediately after the transaction the corporate trustee is, in effect, a professional trustee, i.e. it holds the property as trustee in the course of a business that it carries on that includes or consists of the management of trusts; or
- immediately after the transaction the corporate trustee holds the property as trustee and the lessee is connected with the corporate trustee only by reason of the lessor being the settlor.

---

[346]   See e.g. Lap Shun Textiles Industrial Co v. Collector of Stamp Revenue [1976] AC 530; Brown v. Cork [1985] BCLC 363.

[347]   FA 2003, s.53. Note that this is not market rent, although there are immensely complicated issues of what is a market rent and how this relates to the actual rent arrangements in order to determine whether the lease is granted at an undervalue.

[348]   FA 2003, Sched.15, Part 3.

[349]   The position is obscure where there are both corporate and individual trustees. It is thought that the charge is not intended to apply in such cases.

There are exemptions for certain transactions[350] including distribution or dividends *in specie* such as returns of capital and in a liquidation of a company[351] but it is most unlikely that these transactions will involve the grant of leases by a liquidator. There are also restrictions where the company making the distribution acquired the chargeable interest with the benefit of intra-group relief within the three years preceding the distribution.[352]

8.55.2 Partnerships

Leases between partnerships and connected persons within FA 2003, Sched.15, Part 3 are taxed at market value which may produce a deemed premium where the rent is potentially on favourable terms (see **Chapter 12**).

8.55.3 Leases, loans and deposits

Where in connection with arrangements[353] for the grant of a lease the lessee is a connected person or an agent pays a deposit or makes a loan to any person and the repayment of a loan or deposit is contingent on anything done or to be done or omitted to be done by the lessee or on the death of the lessee the amount of the deposit or loan (ignoring possible repayment) is to be taxed as a premium. The charge does not apply where the deposit is not more than twice the maximum rent, namely double the highest rent payable in respect of any 12 consecutive months during the first five years of the term.[354]

8.56 EXCLUSIONS FROM THE CHARGE ON PREMIUMS

A number of items of actual consideration are excluded from the scope of chargeable consideration other than rent. These include the following.

8.56.1 Reverse premiums

Upon basic contract principles a reverse payment by a landlord as an inducement for the tenant to take the lease is not consideration for the grant of the lease because it is moving in the wrong direction. To be consideration upon the basis of longstanding law of contract principles the consideration is what is provided by the promisee as the price for the promise; the promisor cannot be regarded as providing consideration for his own promise; he is providing an inducement for the promisee to agree to

---

[350] FA 2003, s.54.
[351] Provided that there is no assumption of debts by the members which constitutes a 'sale' for the debts or liabilities: FA 2003, Sched.4, para.8; see **4.32**.
[352] FA 2003, s.54(1); Sched.7, Part 1.
[353] See e.g. *Clarke Chapman John Thompson Ltd* v. *IRC* [1975] STC 567; *Times Newspapers* v. *IRC* [1971] 3 All ER 98.
[354] FA 2003, Sched.17A, para.18A.

provide the consideration. However, HMRC Stamp Taxes takes the opposite view and regards such payments as taxable.[355] The draftsman has provided reliefs for such reverse payments. Inducements paid by a landlord to a tenant to take the lease are not taxable.[356]

It must, however, be clear that the payment is an inducement for the tenant to take the lease and does not represent a payment for some other arrangement or transaction. For example, such payments may frequently be made where the landlord is a developer seeking to persuade the tenant to relocate from his existing premises to new premises. For other tax or commercial reasons the parties may wish to express the payment by the landlord to the tenant as being some form of compensation for relocation, damage to goodwill and related expenses. There is, therefore, a danger that HMRC Stamp Taxes might seek to argue that all or part of the reverse payment was not an inducement to take the new lease but was consideration for the surrender of the old lease, which is taxable (see **8.63**). Certain reliefs may be available where the landlord and the tenant to the existing and the new leases are the same parties. However, if the arrangement involves a payment by a landlord to the tenant of some other landlord the payment may not be an inducement to take the new lease but some form of consideration for the assignment of the existing lease to the developer landlord or consideration to encourage the tenant to surrender since this may require some form of reverse payment by the tenant to the landlord. While reverse payments paid in connection with the surrender (i.e. inducements for a landlord to accept and early termination of the lease) are exempt pursuant to these provisions where the inducement payment is being reimbursed by another landlord or developer it may mean that the reimbursement is itself taxable consideration for the surrender. For the purposes of SDLT while it is necessary to have chargeable consideration it is not necessarily necessary that the consideration is provided by the person who is acquiring the chargeable interest. The charge can, therefore, apply to a payment by a developer to a tenant in connection with a surrender of the lease by the tenant to a third party landlord. Moreover, such a tripartite transaction involving the grant of a new lease and the surrender or termination of the existing lease would, at least in part, constitute some form of land exchange and certain aspects of the transaction, depending upon its structure, may be taxed at market value rather than by reference to the actual consideration being provided.

Furthermore, it must not be overlooked that a reverse premium, i.e. an inducement to the tenant to take the lease will usually mean a higher rent because the landlord may recover the payment through the rent. Such rent will be subject to the heavy charge to SDLT upon rents.[357] In these situations it is likely to be more SDLT efficient for the tenant to choose a rent holiday rather than a reverse premium (which

---

[355] Issues have arisen in practice where the vendor or the landlord has agreed to pay the costs of the other party. Also such arrangements are regarded by HMRC Stamp Taxes as increasing the market value of the land – a bizarre view but one that may have to be contested by the taxpayer if selected for an Enquiry or discovery assessment.

[356] FA 2003, Sched.17A, para.18.

[357] FA 2003, Sched.5.

would be subject to tax as income); the lower rent would attract a lower charge to SDLT and no charge upon the capital benefit of the rent-free period.

8.56.2 Indemnities given by tenants

Where a tenant agrees to indemnify the landlord in respect of liabilities to a third party arising from breach of an obligation owed by the landlord in relation to the land that is the subject-matter of the transaction, neither the agreement nor any payment made in pursuance of it counts as chargeable consideration.[358]

8.56.3 Covenants and miscellaneous obligations under the lease

Certain covenants and obligations affecting the value of land are chargeable interests notwithstanding they are not interests in or rights over land in the traditional conveyancing sense,[359] but may be contracts affecting the value of land. Leases will usually contain mutual covenants in that the landlord will provide covenants to the tenant which will not be separately taxable because they are an integral part of the terms of the lease and the tenant may enter into appropriate covenants with the landlord such as the covenant to pay rent and undertakings to put the premises into repair, to maintain them in repair and to make other payments whether as additional rent or otherwise.[360] On a strict analysis of the legislation such covenants by the tenant in favour of the landlord could create chargeable interests and convert a lease into a land exchange with the inevitable problems of market value charges. Clearly, the covenants being embedded in the reversion to the lease interest are unlikely to have a separate market value (see **Chapter 15**) but they may have some impact upon the value of the lease.[361] Indeed, as indicated in the following section it is recognised by the legislation that covenants are not only potentially chargeable interests in their own right but also they can have an impact upon the value or rent and may have a value in their own right. It seems, however, that HMRC Stamp Taxes does not intend to take the point that every lease is a land exchange and there are various provisions in the legislation that would reduce the impact of this problem in many cases but because they exist to provide a relief it means that such arrangements are chargeable consideration as a general principle. However, since these merely exclude certain items and covenants from the realm of chargeable consideration they do not override the problems of market value which it seems means that the deemed premium is influenced by the contact terms relating to the actual rent notwithstanding that such actual rent is not chargeable.

---

[358] FA 2003, Sched.4, para.16 and Sched.17A, para.17; but note the anti-avoidance provisions of FA 2003, Sched.17A, para.11 imposing a special charge in certain cases which override the basic principles.

[359] FA 2003, s.48(1)(b); see **2.12**.

[360] Note the risks that such covenants may constitute works, etc.; *Eastham* v. *Leigh London and Provincial Properties Ltd* [1971] 2 All ER 887.

[361] Note, for example, the extremely cryptic charging provision in FA 2003, Sched.17A, para.10(1)(c).

It is provided[362] that the following do not count as chargeable consideration.

(a)   Any undertaking by the tenant to repair, maintain or insure the demised premises or, in Scotland, the leased premises. The reference to 'repair' rather than to 'keep in repair' and the additional reference to 'maintain' suggests that works undertaken by the tenant to put the property into a proper state are not taxable notwithstanding FA 2003, Sched.4, para.10 (see **Chapter 9**). Repairing a previous tenant's dilapidations may not be taxable.[363]

(b)   An undertaking by the tenant to pay any amount in respect of services, repairs, maintenance or insurance or the landlord's costs of management.[364] It is provided that if a single sum is expressed to be payable by way of rent then it should be treated as entirely rent even though it may relate to other matters such as services. The benefit of this exclusion of service charges from tax as a premium may be lost if the payment of rent wraps up the service charges as part of a single unapportioned sum. See further the discussion of 'rent' earlier in this chapter (**8.20**).

(c)   Any other obligation undertaken by the tenant that is not such as to affect the rent that a tenant would be prepared to pay on the open market. This is an extremely cryptic provision since virtually every restrictive covenant or restriction in a lease may have some effect on the rent that a tenant on the open market might be prepared to pay. This impact is usually hidden since the initial pricing and rent will be made on the basis that certain routine covenants are to apply to the transaction. For example, the rent may be set upon the basis of restrictive user covenants that are general in that shopping mall. During the due diligence process unusual covenants, etc. may lead to adjustments in the price or rent. However, the initial figure will be influenced by the proposed or expected covenants. The negotiations may remove or clarify covenants and the price or rent be increased when the impact upon the rent will emerge; but if the covenant is accepted its effect on the rent will not be obvious. A user covenant of commercial premises affects value, otherwise tenants would not be prepared to pay substantial sums for their release or relaxation. Moreover, the structure of this provision suggests that the giving of a covenant is part of the consideration for the lease. Since a covenant is, *prima facie*, a chargeable interest this points to a normal lease transaction which is technically a land exchange taxable upon market value.[365]

---

[362]   FA 2003, Sched.17A, para.10.

[363]   Such activities may also be relieved as works to be carried out after the effective date on the major interest to be acquired.

[364]   This will need to be considered in connection with the provisions of FA 2003, Sched.17A, para.10(1).

[365]   This clause illustrates a fundamental problem in relation to the legislation relating to valuation issues. It overlooks the fact that at the time a property is offered for sale or lease the initial price, premium or rent will be fixed upon the basis that there are standard terms and no difficulties in relation to the title. In other words, the impact of covenants or other rights in or over the land are taken into account and therefore influence the price. No doubt the issues may arise where it is discovered upon appropriate investigation that there are particular circumstances such as unusual or

(d)   Any guarantee of the payment of rent or performance of any other obligation of the tenant under the lease.[366] Without this provision the charge upon services pursuant to FA 2003, Sched.4, para.11 would include a charge to SDLT upon the market cost of obtaining a third party guarantee on the tenant's obligations. It seems bizarre that the draftsman of the legislation thought that a payment by a third party, i.e. a non-tenant, could be consideration for the 'acquisition' of a chargeable interest. The consequence of this view is that third parties can provide chargeable consideration, but only if they are connected with the purchaser or they are parties to the transaction both of which are likely to be satisfied in most such cases in practice.[367] A bank guarantee could be within these provisions because the provision of the guarantee will be required by the landlord and so will be chargeable consideration.[368]

(e)   Any penal rent, or increased rent in the nature of penal rent payable in respect of any breach of an obligation of the tenant under the lease.

The assumption or release of any such obligation in relation to the assignment of the lease is not chargeable consideration.[369] However, various points should be noted:

1.   If the sum is drafted as part of the 'rent' and not separately apportioned then it may be chargeable as rent notwithstanding this exemption.[370]

2.   The exclusion from charge applies not merely to assuming the obligation but also to any payment made in discharge of the obligation.[371] However, as *Banning* v. *Wright*[372] indicates, a payment in respect of a breach of covenant may also be in whole or in part a payment for a variation of the covenant which is a chargeable transaction.[373] For example, the acceptance of the compensation is potentially a release of the tenant from the covenant.[374]

3.   This has become a significant issue following the reinstatement of a charge upon all variations of leases for a consideration paid for by the tenant. There is

---

special covenants and the price is adjusted accordingly. It is, however, potentially a fundamental misconception to assume that it is only in respect of those covenants where the parties may seek to adjust the price because they do not fit the normal pattern that these problems as to valuation can arise. A lease that is granted on more relaxed terms may have a different value from a lease that is granted upon those that would normally be included in a lease for those premises (see **15.20**).

[366]   But special relief applies to leases granted to the guarantor: FA 2003, Sched.17A, para.9(1)(d).

[367]   FA 2003, Sched.4, para.1.

[368]   The fact that it was believed to be necessary to provide this relief means that there are many situations where it is believed by HMRC Stamp Taxes that a chargeable consideration can exist although there may be difficult technical issues in deciding the amount of the chargeable consideration although this may be within the uncertain consideration regime.

[369]   FA 2003, Sched.17A, para.17.

[370]   FA 2003, Sched.17A, para.6; see **8.20**.

[371]   FA 2003, Sched.17A, para.10(2).

[372]   48 TC 421.

[373]   FA 2003, s.43(3)(c) and (d); Sched.17A, para.15A.

[374]   But note *Photo Production Ltd* v. *Securicor Transport Ltd* [1980] 2 WLR 283 on the difference between the primary liability to perform the contract and the secondary liability to pay damages in the event of breach or non-performance. This fundamental distinction is not always

also a question of whether HMRC Stamp Taxes intends to challenge settle-ments of disputes involving breaches of leasehold and other covenants as a release of all or part of a chargeable interest. This exclusion would apply to the extent that the payment was not merely compensation for the breach but was for a modification of the covenant. The problem for practitioners also remains of whether HMRC Stamp Taxes will wish to contend that payment for the release of a restrictive or other covenant which might affect the amount of the rent is a taxable variation of a lease as a release of a chargeable interest for a chargeable consideration. This is a highly likely line of attack since one of the main policy justifications for the SDLT legislation was the need to charge tax upon anything that looked like a value shifting.

8.57 VARIATIONS OF LEASES

It is provided that 'acquisition' of a chargeable interest includes the 'variation' of a chargeable interest (see **Chapter 2**); but this has been modified in relation to leases.[375] In consequence, a variation of a lease is taxable only where:

- it involves a surrender and regrant which is a land exchange but with certain limited reliefs (see **8.58**);
- it reduces the rent (see **8.46**). It is, however, frequently difficult to determine whether the variation of a variable rent involves a reduction or an increase or neither of these;
- it increases the rent otherwise than pursuant to the terms of the lease. This is not a surrender and regrant, but it is frequently difficult if not impossible to determine whether the rent has been increased or reduced;[376]
- it involves an abnormal increase in the rent;[377]
- it reduces the term of the lease;[378] but such a variation will be a surrender and regrant which is chargeable as a land exchange with limited certain reliefs.[379] It is difficult to find any routine situations where this might apply since a termination of a lease by means of a notice to quit or break clause is difficult to regard as a variation which suggests that the lease continues albeit in a modified form rather than ceases to exist altogether. Similarly, inserting a break clause although potentially shortening the lease does not actually vary the term;[380] or

---

understood by HMRC Stamp Taxes who frequently regard damages and especially liquidated damages as consideration; see their unsuccessful argument in *Western United Investment Co* v. *IRC* [1958] 1 All ER 257.

[375] Different rules apply for periods prior to March 2005; FA 2003, s.43(3)(d) and Sched.17A, para.15A (as amended).

[376] FA 2003, Sched.17A, para.13; see **8.46**.

[377] *Gable Construction* v. *IRC* [1968] 1 WLR 1426.

[378] FA 2003, Sched.17A, para.15A (as amended).

[379] FA 2003, s.47; Sched.17A, paras.9 and 16.

[380] Inserting a break clause after Finance (No.2) Act 2005 is chargeable if for a consideration provided by the tenant.

- it is any other variation[381] made for a consideration in money or money's worth other than an increase in the rent provided that:

    - the consideration is provided by the lessee. This means that variations arising where the tenant receives a payment from the landlord will not be chargeable transactions; or
    - the variation is a variation of the rent which has its own regime (see **8.42**); or
    - it is a variation of the term of the lease. However, apart from the fact that there is a special charge as indicated immediately above in relation to the reduction of the term of the lease, any variation of the term of the lease will involve a form of surrender and regrant which is itself governed by a specific provision.[382]

8.58 VARIATIONS: SURRENDERS AND REGRANTS

Many variations of leases can constitute surrenders and regrants. These may arise by operation of law (see **2.9**) such as where there is a variation in the term of the lease[383] or there is a modification of the demised premises such as by including additional premises or excluding certain of the existing demised premises. Where a tenant enters into a deed of variation increasing or reducing either the term or the demised premises, it is a surrender and regrant. A typical situation will be where a tenant of a flat enlarges the term of the lease.[384] Occasionally a landlord and tenant agree to what purports to be a variation in the terms of the lease, but which, in the probably unwitting eyes of the parties, has the effect of a surrender of the old lease, followed by a regrant. The best example is where the parties agree to a variation in the length of the lease as simply extending the lease term is likely to be within the reliefs but changes in the demised premises are *prima facie* unlikely to be eligible for the reliefs for rent because they may not related to substantially the same premises. A variation of the rent by deed of variation will only result in an implied surrender and regrant if that is the intention of the parties.[385] There may also be an express surrender and regrant such as where there are variations in the terms of the lease that do not amount to automatic surrenders and regrants but the parties decide it would be much neater and tidier to consolidate the original lease and all relevant

---

[381] But see *Banning* v. *Wright* 48 TC 421 on whether the variation involves a release, etc. in whole or in part where this may be chargeable.

[382] And with the benefit of various reliefs under very narrow circumstances; see FA 2003, Sched.17A, paras.9 and 16; see **8.58**.

[383] Friends Provident Life Office v. British Railways Board [1996] 1 All ER 336; Gable Construction v. IRC [1968] 1 WLR 1426; Donellan v. Read (1832) 3 B & Ad 899.

[384] However, if the tenant takes an overriding lease and merges the existing lease the merger does not give rise to a chargeable transaction. The overriding lease will be taxable upon any premium paid and rent reserved. This may not be as efficient as on a surrender and regrant since the latter may qualify for a rent credit pursuant to FA 2003, Sched.17A, para.9.

[385] *Gable Construction* v. *IRC* [1968] 1 WLR 1426.

deeds of variation into a new lease. There will be a deemed surrender or deemed surrender and the deemed grant of a new lease which will be a land exchange and, therefore, there are potential charges:

- upon the landlord in respect of the market value of the existing lease that is being surrendered plus any cash paid by the landlord to the tenant for the variation;[386] and
- upon the tenant in respect of any actual or deemed premium for the grant of the lease plus the rent reserved.

There are, however, certain reliefs available under strict conditions. Where the new lease is between the same parties and for the same premises there is a reduction in the taxable rent and there is an exclusion from the land exchange charge;[387] but there is no rent credit. Where a lease is surrendered for the grant of a lease of other premises there is only an exclusion from the land exchange rules.[388] These are considered in more detail elsewhere (see **8.54**).

It should, however, be noted that these reliefs are subject to stringent conditions and, in general, are available only where the lease being varied is a lease that was subject to SDLT, at least as regards the credit for the rent already taxed.[389] This means that where the parties are seeking to vary a lease that was subject to stamp duty certain of the credits may not be available and the parties will be paying tax upon rent that has already borne stamp duty. When embarking upon a variation of an existing lease that may involve a surrender and regrant by operation of law or there is to be a formal deed of surrender and regrant in these or other circumstances the parties should consider the impact of the potential land exchange charges and the charge upon any new rent plus any cash that may be being paid by either the landlord or the tenant for accepting the variation and whether simple alternative arrangements are available to save large amounts of SDLT.[390] The parties should consider, therefore, whether in relation to the variation of the demised premises it would be more appropriate to have a separate lease of any new premises to be incorporated in the lease which will be taxable in its own right but not bring into charge the rents and other payments in respect of the existing lease. Where the parties are seeking to reduce the demised premises it may be more efficient to enter into some form of partial surrender which would not involve a surrender and regrant of the entire lease. Where the parties are considering varying the term numerous possibilities are available. For example, the parties may wish to shorten the term of the lease but rather than entering into a deed of variation as a surrender and regrant may consider the possible benefits of inserting a break clause which does not, of itself, shorten the term of the lease and the exercise of a break clause is not a surrender even though

---

[386] Such as compensation for disturbance during the refurbishment phase.
[387] FA 2003, Sched.17A, paras.9 and 16.
[388] FA 2003, Sched.17A, para.16.
[389] The exclusion from the land exchange charge appears to apply to surrenders of stamp duty leases.
[390] But this is *prima facie* not within the charge pursuant to FA 2003, Sched.17A, para.15A; **8.57**.

compensation may be paid.[391] Where the parties wish to extend the lease there may be possibilities of entering into a deed of variation that creates an option to renew the lease which would not be a surrender and regrant and in the circumstances the new lease would be unlikely to be a linked transaction with the existing lease so as to create a successive linked lease. Alternatively, the parties may enter into an agreement for a reversionary lease to commence in possession upon the termination of the existing lease.[392]

8.59 RELIEFS FOR LEASES

There are various reliefs but these are expressed in a variety of ways some of which may mean not only that the transaction is not taxable but also that it is not notifiable. For example, on a surrender and regrant the new lease is not consideration for the surrender of the old lease. In consequence, unless the landlord is making other payments he will be entering into a transaction for no chargeable consideration which is not notifiable.[393]

8.59.1 'Premium' issues

It is provided that in the case of a surrender of a lease and the grant of a new lease between the same parties,[394] whether of the same or different premises or a mixture of the old demised premises and new premises, the exchanges of the property interests are ignored even where the existing lease is a stamp duty lease. The general effect for most cases appears to be:

---

[391] *Barrett* v. *Morgan* [2000] 1 All ER 481.

[392] In these circumstances it is important to avoid entering into a formal reversionary lease. In the case of an agreement for a reversionary lease no charge to SDLT can arise until the lease takes effect on the termination of the existing lease since the tenant will be in possession of the land under the existing lease and will not be taking possession under the agreement for lease until the current lease expires. HMRC Stamp Taxes takes the view that where there is a formal grant of the reversionary lease there is an immediate charge and this charge is to be calculated by reference to the actual or estimated rent that would arise in the first five years, etc. of the reversionary lease taking effect; it is not a situation where there is nil rent payable between the grant of the lease and its taking effect in possession.

[393] FA 2003, s.77A; Sched.3, para.1.

[394] The question is sometimes raised with the author by solicitors as to the meaning of 'the same parties'. This could mean the same parties to the original grant of the lease, i.e. the original landlord and the original tenant so that this relief is not available where there has been an assignment of the tenancy so that there is a different tenant or the landlord has disposed of all or part of his interest such as by granting an overriding lease or selling the reversion. This interpretation would effectively nullify the benefit of the relief in the vast majority of cases in practice. In consequence, it would seem that the reasonable interpretation is that the reference to the same parties means to the parties who are currently landlord and tenant under the existing lease. This would mean that any assignee of the lease dealing with a new mesne landlord would be eligible for the relief since the new landlord and the assignee of the lease would be the same parties as those to the new lease.

- the landlord will not be providing any chargeable consideration, so his 'acquisition' will be exempt and not notifiable;[395] and
- the tenant will not be regarded as 'exchanging' land, so his acquisition will not be at market value but for the actual consideration,[396] if any, supplied to the landlord for the variation of the lease.

In these cases any cash payments made such as a sum paid by the tenant for the extension of the term will be taxable but because the values of the leases are ignored the eligibility for the nil or lower rates of tax will be tested solely by reference to the costs or other actual consideration[397] provided.

8.59.2 Rent issues

Prima facie, the tenant will be taxable upon the rent reserved by the new lease but he will be entitled to a form of credit where he has or his predecessors in title have paid SDLT upon the original[398] lease being surrendered provided that the new lease relates to substantially the same premises as the original lease. The 'credit' takes the form of reducing the amount of rent reserved by the new lease to be included in the rent formula by an amount equal to the rent for each particular year of the unexpired balance of the term of the original lease. Where the premises are the same, the chargeable rent is reduced by reference to the amount of rent payable for the balance of the surrendered term. This relief is, however, subject to numerous conditions:

- Because of the terms in which the rent credit is expressed the existing lease must have borne SDLT. It is important to note for many years to come that this relief is not available where the existing lease was subject to stamp duty which can include leases granted on or after 1 December 2003.[399] In such cases the new lease will be taxable in full upon the rent reserved notwithstanding stamp duty may have been paid at a fairly high level in respect of the rent for the overlap period, i.e. the period from the date of the grant of the new lease to the contractual termination date for the existing lease. In these circumstances parties should consider whether certain of the possibilities for managing the SDLT cost of such arrangements outlined above are appropriate. These are not aggressive planning techniques but simple possibilities of taxpayer choice

---

[395] FA 2003, Sched.3, para.1 which will have important implications for his reporting obligations, see FA 2003, s.77.
[396] Unless the landlord and tenant involve connected companies.
[397] Obviously the actual consideration may be ignored where the charge is by reference to market values.
[398] FA 2003, Sched.17A, para.9.
[399] FA 2003, Sched.19, para.7(2); Sched.9, para.3.

which is not tax avoidance[400] but rather is a bona fide commercial way of making a decision.[401]

- The lease must be between the same parties which, it is considered, means the parties to the immediate transaction and not the original landlord and tenant.[402]
- The new lease must relate to the same or substantially the same premises as the existing lease. There is no guidance as to how much flexibility is allowed where there is a modification of the demised premises.[403] It would seem that, until some widespread practical experience has been obtained as to the views of HMRC Stamp Taxes on the acceptable scope of these provisions, the parties should operate upon the basis that only a *de minimis* variation will be within the relief. In broad terms, where the parties are seeking to extend the term then it is likely that the parties will be the same and the premises will be the same so that the relief is potentially available, subject to the original lease having borne SDLT upon the rent. However, where the variation arises by reference to changes in the demised premises then, by definition, there will be different premises in the new lease whether additional new or reduced old premises or a combination of both and a risk that HMRC Stamp Taxes will take the view that the premises are not 'substantially the same'. In these situations a new side-by-side lease or a partial surrender may be the prudent way to proceed.

It will be seen that in some situations there can be a completely full charge to SDLT where the original lease was subject to stamp duty and all of the consequent problems for rent reviews and holding over will apply. It is, therefore, usually prudent to consider whether the parties can avoid surrendering the existing stamp duty lease since this will save the charge in full because no credit is available. It is also usually prudent to avoid the creation of a new SDLT lease since this is subject to a much higher level of charge to tax and to many more situations where charges to tax can arise such as holding over of a SDLT lease pursuant to the Landlord and Tenant Act 1954 since HMRC Stamp Taxes accepts that there is no charge where the original lease being held over was subject to stamp duty.

---

[400] *IRC* v. *Willoughby* [1997] STC 995; *Sherdley* v. *Sherdley* [1988] AC 213 but it will be necessary to consider whether there are 'tax schemes' that should be disclosed pursuant to the disclosure of tax avoidance schemes regime now that it has been extensively applied to SDLT.

[401] *IRC* v. *Brebner* 43 TC 705.

[402] See **note 394** above.

[403] Unfortunately, this is a frequent problem in SDLT as the draftsman appears to think in two dimensions only and has not made provision for potential differences between the land area occupied by the building and its volume.

8.60   ASSIGNMENT OF LEASES

8.60.1   General position

The assignment of an existing lease is an 'acquisition' by the assignee of a chargeable major interest generally notifiable.[404] Tax will be chargeable upon any actual or deemed consideration provided by the assignee, but the undertaking by the assignee to pay all future rent is not normally chargeable consideration and any covenant by the assignee to perform the covenants in the lease and, presumably, indemnify the assignor against any liabilities in respect of a breach of covenant is ignored in computing the tax.[405] There is, however, a special charge where the original lease was exempt from SDLT.[406]

If the assignee pays a lump sum to the assignor which is part of the consideration where the lease forms an asset of the business being purchased attributable to the land as opposed to, for example, chattels,[407] this is taxable consideration. There is a major issue of principle as to whether a payment for goodwill is in law an additional sum payable for the land rather than true goodwill.[408]

Where the assignor makes a payment to the assignee as an inducement to take the assignment, a 'reverse premium', such payment is not chargeable consideration.[409]

8.60.2   Loans and deposits

Where in connection with arrangements[410] for the assignment of a lease the assignee or a connected person or an agent pays a deposit[411] or makes a loan[412] to any person and the repayment of a loan or deposit is contingent on anything done or to be done or omitted to be done by the lessee or on the death of the lessee, the amount of the deposit or loan (ignoring possible repayment) is to be taxed as a premium. There is no refund if the deposit or loan is repaid.[413] The charge does not apply where the deposit is not more than twice the maximum rent, namely the highest rent payable in respect of any 12 consecutive months during the first five years of the term.[414]

---

[404]   FA 2003, ss.77 and 77A; see **Chapter 17**.
[405]   FA 2003, Sched.17A, para.17; see also Sched.4, para.16.
[406]   FA 2003, Sched.17A, para.12; see **8.61**.
[407]   On fixtures and chattels see **Chapter 2**.
[408]   Whiteman Smith Motor Co v. Chaplin [1934] 2 KB 35; Mullins v. Wessex Motors [1947] 2 All ER 727.
[409]   FA 2003, Sched.17A, para.18.
[410]   See e.g. *Clarke Chapman John Thompson Ltd* v. *IRC* [1975] STC 567; *Times Newspapers* v. *IRC* [1971] 3 All ER 98.
[411]   On what is a 'deposit' see Workers Trust & Merchant Bank Ltd v. Dojap Investments [1993] AC 573.
[412]   On loans and unpaid consideration see *Coren* v. *Keighley* 48 TC 370; see also *Faith Construction* v. *Customs and Excise* [1989] 2 All ER 938.
[413]   FA 2003, s.80.
[414]   FA 2003, Sched.17A, para.18A.

8.61 PROBLEM AREAS FOR ASSIGNEES OF LEASES: GENERAL

8.61.1 Tax running with the lease

The assignment of leases is, however, not entirely straightforward because the fundamental nature of SDLT is that it is usually provisional, subject to retrospective review and possibly open tax positions running with the land rather than remaining with the original taxpayer. For example, it is specifically provided[415] that where there has been an assignment of a lease and subsequently there is an event or transaction which:

- requires an adjustment in respect of a variable premium such as a premium that is linked to the profits or proceeds of the development by the tenant; or
- requires an adjustment of uncertain rent[416] during the first five years of the lease;[417] or
- requires a further return retrospectively 'correcting' an earlier land transaction return filed on a guestimated basis because there is a later linked transaction so that an earlier transaction becomes notifiable and/or tax or additional tax payable[418] which seems to include the exercise of options to renew,[419]

the assignee is liable for the obligations of the assignor. It is not clear whether this makes the original taxpayer's open tax position the sole responsibility of the assignee or whether there is an implied joint and several or similar liability with the original taxpayer. This is a key issue on the question of indemnities and the prudently advised assignee will seek an express indemnity against the liability to pay more tax than would normally arise in these circumstances. It seems clear that any interest arising upon tax underpaid by the assignor is the liability of the assignee but the issue of penalties for the defective earlier return remains an open question.

8.61.2 Assignee's tax affected by assignor's tax

In some situations, while the assignee is not as such liable for the assignor's open tax position his own tax liability may depend upon the tax previously paid by the assignor. This includes:

- where the assignee's transaction requires a return because of the provisions relating to holding over;[420] or

---

[415]   FA 2003, Sched.17A, para.12.
[416]   FA 2003, s.86; Sched.17A, para.7.
[417]   FA 2003, Sched.17A, paras.7 and 8.
[418]   FA 2003, s.81A; but as the lease has been assigned there is a fundamental question as to whether the later transaction can be linked because it will not necessarily be between the same parties or persons connected with them. See **Chapter 4**.
[419]   FA 2003, Sched.17A, para.5.
[420]   FA 2003, Sched.17A, para.4.

- where there is a linked lease of other premises reducing the amount of the nil rate slice allocated to the original lease;[421] or
- where there is a successive linked lease,[422] or
- where there is a retrospective adjustment of the calculation of the net present value of the rent during, or probably at or after (because of the problems of finding the necessary data) the expiration of the fifth year of the lease;[423] or
- where the tax upon 'abnormal' rent increases.

8.61.3 Assignee's position

The responsibility for dealing with these situations is passed to the assignee of the lease.[424] In consequence, it will be necessary for the assignee to obtain undertakings from the assignor to disclose the relevant information. As there is no express statutory right for non-taxpayers to demand the information that they may require notwithstanding that the legislation converts them into persons responsible for other people's tax, any contract may require express terms for an indemnity and the supplying of information.[425] For example, should a rent review or increase in the rate of VAT during the first five years of the term produce a higher rent than that used in estimating the rents upon the initial assessment this would affect the overall tax liability and require the reallocation of the relevant proportion of the nil rate slice to all linked leases, whether past, present or future.[426] The original tenant will, therefore, need to know what the assignee is doing in relation to the assigned lease and/or whether he is seeking to obtain planning permission or perform some other action that may retrospectively trigger a tax liability for the original party.

8.61.4 Assignor's position

Assignors will require undertakings to disclose relevant information where the liability to deal with their outstanding tax liability is not passed to the assignee because, for example, their advisers failed to include an effective exit strategy when agreeing to a clawback consideration (see **4.40**) or they have agreed to indemnify the lessee, when they may wish to have the conduct of the negotiations with HMRC Stamp Taxes. Provision in the contract may also be required to deal with issues of additional tax being payable or tax being refundable because of the assignor overestimating or underestimating the relevant rent levels, such as on the five-year

---

[421] FA 2003, Sched.5, para.2(5).

[422] FA 2003, Sched.17A, para.5; s.81A.

[423] FA 2003, Sched.17A, para.8; but the risk of and the responsibility for dealing with the possibility of an abnormal rent increase lies with the assignee (FA 2003, Sched.17A, paras.14 and 15).

[424] FA 2003, s.81A; Sched.17A, para.12.

[425] It would seem to be stretching the usual covenants for further assurance.

[426] The recession may mean a lower rent with a tax refund and an enhanced share of the £125,000 or £150,000 nil rate slice for the future. Assignors might wish to claim the 'windfall' from the assignee.

adjustment. Assignees will not wish to bear tax[427] over and above the tax that they pay upon their acquisition of the lease[428] and late payment interest because the assignor underestimated or relied upon the advice of the helpline to prepare the return upon the basis of the actual rent and ignore the possible effect of the rent review. Conversely the assignor may be reluctant to allow the assignee to recover overpaid tax as a windfall if he overestimated the possible increase in the rent.

8.62 OTHER PROBLEMS FOR ASSIGNEES

8.62.1 Consideration

In general an assignment of a lease will attract SDLT only upon any consideration paid by the assignee for the acquisition of the lease. This will involve a need to distinguish between items that are being acquired that are chargeable interests in land and those which are other items. These include key matters potentially of a significant amount in relation to equipment related to the land that has retained its character as chattels and therefore outside the charge to SDLT[429] and whether any item described as 'goodwill' is in fact free or genuine goodwill or is embedded goodwill in the sense of additional value for the land (see **2.15.2**).

8.62.2 Exemptions on grant: special charge on assignments

It is specifically provided that covenants by the assignee in relation to potential breaches and agreements to indemnify and, in particular, undertakings to pay the future rent are not part of the chargeable consideration.[430] However, there are certain provisions concerned with the assignment of leases where a special charge arises, usually in the form of the assignment being taxed not as an assignment but as the deemed grant of a new lease.[431] Some of these are transitional and apply only in relation to leases granted between certain dates particularly where nominees are involved.[432] It is a rather tedious exercise for persons acting on behalf of potential assignees of leases to bear in mind these very narrow dates in order to determine their clients' tax liability.

The most important of these arises where the original grant of the lease or substantial performance of the agreement for lease was exempt from SDLT because it was granted:

---

[427]   The position on penalties is uncertain in this case. It is thought that they remain a problem for the original tenant but this is unclear.

[428]   In accordance with the basic principles such as FA 2003, Sched.17A, para.17, but note the existence of special charges upon assignments such as FA 2003, Sched.17A, para.12; see **8.62**.

[429]   And may be ignored for certain purposes in relation to the statutory general anti-avoidance provisions pursuant to FA 2003, s.75B(3)(b).

[430]   FA 2003, Sched.17A, para.17.

[431]   FA 2003, Sched.17A, para.11.

[432]   FA 2003, Sched.16, para.3(3); for leases granted during the period between FA 2004 and Finance (No.2) Act 2005; see **8.8.1**.

- in connection with a sale and leaseback transaction;[433]
- in connection with an intra-group transaction;[434]
- in connection with a scheme of reconstruction or reorganisation of a company;[435]
- to an exempt public body;[436]
- to a charity;[437]
- within regulations bringing old, very specialised stamp duty reliefs into the SDLT regime.[438]

In the case of such leases, the first assignment[439] of that lease that is not also exempt from SDLT by reason of those exemptions and where there has not been a clawback of the relief in the intervening period is deemed to be the grant of a new lease to the assignee as tenant for the unexpired term of the original lease at the rent reserved (presumably with all of the problems of variable rents during the first five years of the term or thereafter where the rent is subject to VAT, is subject to review, or is a turnover or similar rent that falls within the variable rent regime).[440] This charge applies even though there was no tax avoidance motive relating to the original grant and the lease was granted upon a full commercial basis. There is no need for a causal link or arrangement between the grant of the lease and its assignment. In addition, there is no time limit so that an assignment of the lease which takes place say 15 years after the initial grant and is totally unconnected therewith is taxable under this provision which raises due diligence obligations for a professional adviser. Assignees need to investigate the tax history of the lease, even where this lease is acquired as simply one of the assets in a bona fide purchase of a business.[441]

---

[433] FA 2003, s.57A.

[434] FA 2003, Sched.7, Part 1.

[435] The provision operates particularly harshly where the lease is granted in connection with a scheme of reorganisation which is not exempt but qualifies only for the reduced rate of 0.5 per cent, which, it seems, is available in relation to both premiums and rent. There is no credit for the reduced rate of SDLT paid pursuant to this provision so that there is an approximate charge of 1.5 per cent upon the rent in such a case: FA 2003, Sched.7, Part 2.

[436] FA 2003, s.66.

[437] FA 2003, Sched.8 (as amended).

[438] Stamp Duty Land Tax (Consequential Amendment of Enactments) Regulations 2003, SI 2003/2867; see **5.28**.

[439] This charge may precede the actual assignment where the assignee substantially performs the purchase contract such as by being allowed into possession before completion to fit out or make alterations to the premises; this risk applies even where the agreement is still conditional upon landlord's consent.

[440] FA 2003, Sched.17A, paras.7 and 8 since these provisions appear to apply to deemed leases; see **8.8**.

[441] This charge does not apply if the exemption or relief in respect of the original grant of the lease has been withdrawn as a result of a clawback within the relevant three-year period.

8.63 TERMINATION OF A LEASE

8.63.1 Termination of leases by lapse of time

Prima facie the termination of a lease by lapse of time is not, as such, subject to SDLT. This does not involve a release or surrender and, in general, there will be no consideration when the lease expires.[442] This does not mean that no payments will be made. For example, the tenant may be making payments to the landlord in respect of dilapidations or the landlord may be making payments to the tenant by way of compensation pursuant to the Landlord and Tenant Act 1954 (as amended). Many such payments such as the payment of compensation will not be chargeable consideration since they are not the price being paid for the termination of the lease but are being paid pursuant to statute or as compensation for breach of an obligation. In addition, FA 2003, Sched.4, para.10 provides that both entering into covenants to repair premises and payments made in pursuant of such a covenant and possibly as damages for breach do not count as chargeable consideration.

However, the termination of a lease by lapse of time, i.e. because it has reached its contractual termination date does not mean that there are no SDLT implications. A charge may arise where, for example, the tenant under a SDLT lease holds over pursuant to statutory provision, i.e. by operation of law such as the Landlord and Tenant Act 1954 (see **8.47**). There may have been negotiations prior to the termination of the lease for the grant of a new lease or the exercise of an option to renew the lease in circumstances where there was not a surrender and regrant. In such a situation it may be that if the tenant continues in occupation pursuant to the new agreement for lease there is substantial performance of that agreement involving the deemed grant of a lease and so a charge to SDLT.[443] In consequence, the interaction of the arrival of the contractual termination date of an existing lease and the arrangements for the negotiation or grant of a new lease will need to be investigated in order to determine whether a charge arises.

8.63.2 Notice to quit and break clauses

Termination by notice to quit or the operation of a break clause would not seem to be within the charge to SDLT even though the landlord giving the notice to quit may be required to pay some form of compensation either under the terms of the lease or otherwise. A surrender and a notice to quit are different forms of legal operation[444] and so termination by notice to quit cannot be included under a 'surrender' or 'release' since these require the participation of the tenant whereas a notice to quit is a unilateral action of the landlord or of the tenant, not the joint action of both; but HMRC Stamp Taxes is apparently considering its position.

---

[442] Payments of statutory compensation for not relying upon statutory protection are not regarded as chargeable consideration because they are payments for forgoing statutory rights.

[443] FA 2003, Sched.17A, para.12A; s.44; on the position where the lease was granted before the contractual termination date see **8.64.1**.

[444] *Barrett* v. *Morgan* [2000] 1 All ER 481.

Two points nevertheless need to be noted for consideration when a lease is terminated by notice to quit, namely:

- the term of the lease for the purpose of SDLT is determined without regard to the existence of a break clause, i.e. the term of the lease for the purposes of the formula for determining the net present value is the maximum length of the term; but there is no right to a repayment of tax if the lease is terminated early by the exercise of such powers; and
- arrangements relating to break clauses have been singled out as potential targets for the statutory general anti-avoidance provisions.[445]

8.63.3 Surrenders

HMRC Stamp Taxes spares the dying lease on its deathbed from natural causes or, where the lease is forfeited for breach of covenant, from any further exactions. Not so, however, where there is a surrender to the landlord of a fixed term before its expiry by effluxion of time. A surrender of a lease whether by operation of law[446] such as where the tenant hands over the keys and vacates the premises or by deed[447] by a tenant in consideration of a payment or other property or services by the landlord will give rise to a charge to SDLT in respect of which the landlord will be the 'purchaser'. Tax is escaped where there is a 'reverse premium' and the tenant pays the landlord to relieve the tenant of the lease.[448] Where the other property is a chargeable interest in land there will be a land exchange with each party being subject to tax upon the market value of what he receives.[449] In some cases where the lease of one set of premises is being surrendered in return for the grant of a new lease of other premises between the same parties this is a land exchange but there is a relief which excludes the land exchange charge in such cases,[450] so that the tenant is taxable only upon the rent reserved by the new lease and any premium he is paying for the new lease. If the landlord is making a payment to the tenant, it may be important whether this payment is regarded as consideration for the surrender such as payment by the landlord to induce the tenant to surrender; or the grant of a new lease of different premises when it appears to be taxable; or a reverse premium or inducement to take the new lease when it is not taxable;[451] or it is a payment as a contribution to removal expenses, disturbance of business or to fitting out when it appears to be outside the scope of SDLT.

---

[445] FA 2003, s.75A(2) setting out the illustrative list of possible targets.
[446] FA 2003, s.43(2).
[447] LPA 1925, s.52.
[448] Re Duke of Westminster's Settled Estates (No.2) [1921] 1 Ch 585.
[449] FA 2003, Sched.4, para.5.
[450] FA 2003, Sched.17A, para.16.
[451] FA 2003, Sched.17A, para.18.

8.63.4 Forfeiture

No charge will arise where there is a forfeiture by the landlord for breach of covenant by the tenant since there is not an 'acquisition' which requires a vesting of an interest or a release, variation or waiver. Also there is unlikely to be any chargeable consideration which is a necessary condition for there to be a chargeable and a notifiable transaction.[452] A lease granted to a person who has guaranteed a lease may be eligible for a rent credit provided that it relates to the same or substantially the same premises.[453]

8.63.5 Merger

The extinction of a lease by a merger into the reversionary interest is not, of itself, a chargeable transaction, although the tenant may be facing a tax charge in respect of the transaction(s) by means of which he became entitled to the two interests involved. It would seem, however, that the rules against non-merger where a leasehold interest and the immediate reversionary interest become vested in the same person remain unaffected,[454] and the merger of the two interests is not, at present, itself a chargeable transaction.

8.64 DEALINGS IN REVERSIONARY INTERESTS

8.64.1 Reversionary leases

Rather than enlarge the term of the lease or enter into an option to renew the lease in due course[455] the parties may enter into some form of reversionary lease, i.e. a lease that is to commence shortly after the contractual termination of the existing lease. There are restrictions in LPA 1925 upon the creation of leases that are to take effect only in the future and there have been issues with HMRC Stamp Taxes. Obviously, where the reversionary lease is granted before the expiration of the current term, there is no form of surrender and regrant; there will have been a completion and therefore an effective date will have arisen. It is the view of HMRC Stamp Taxes that when calculating the tax in respect of such a reversionary lease the relevant rent for the first few years of the term is not nil even though no rent is payable until such time as the lease takes effect in possession. In its view it is necessary to include in the calculation the rent payable in respect of the first effective year of the lease notwithstanding this is many years into the future. It is questionable whether this is a correct analysis of the legislation unless the reference to a year refers to something other than the term commencement date. However, it seems that it is possible to defer this charge by not proceeding to completion and relying upon an agreement to

---

[452]   FA 2003, Sched.3, para.1; s.77A.
[453]   FA 2003, Sched.17A, para.9(1)(d).
[454]   See LPA 1925, s.185; *Ingle* v. *Vaughan Jenkins* [1900] 2 Ch 368.
[455]   But these issues may not affect options to renew leases.

grant a lease at some stage in the future. In this situation the fact that the tenant is already in occupation of the premises would not be substantial performance of the agreement for the reversionary lease. The tenant would be in occupation as tenant under the existing lease and would not be entering into possession as regards the new lease as the prospective tenant.

8.64.2 Acquisition of reversion

Reversionary interests are chargeable interests and 'acquisitions' of such interests are chargeable transactions in accordance with the general principles. However, the removal of stamp duty has removed many of the problems affecting landlords and persons acquiring reversionary interests[456] in that there is no longer any need for any form of denoting upon the transfer of the reversion that any lease to which it is subject has been duly stamped or SDLT has been paid. Where the lease is registered, it can be assumed that some form of SDLT return has been filed. Fortunately, if the tax has not been paid or insufficient tax has been paid and a successful challenge has been mounted by HMRC Stamp Taxes, this has no effect on the title of the person acquiring the reversion or a landlord seeking to sue in respect of the lease.

On the other hand problems have arisen for prospective tenants. Where a person has acquired a reversionary interest or has acquired the freehold or other interest out of which he is proposing to grant a lease the prospective lessee or underlessee may have a major title issue. Where the landlord has not paid SDLT upon his acquisition of the land, as appropriate, he may not be able to produce a Revenue certificate (SDLT 5) to the Land Registry which is a prerequisite to his being able to register his title.[457] Since the landlord's interest will not be registered any person deriving title under the landlord such as a tenant or subtenant will not be able to register his interest. Tenants may encounter a charge to SDLT such as where they take possession under an agreement for lease which will have to be paid notwithstanding that they will not be in a position to register their leasehold title as and when the lease is formally granted by the landlord since he does not have a registered title recognised by the Land Registry to form the basis for the title to the new lease. It is, therefore, a key issue for prospective tenants that they investigate whether they will be able to procure registered title of their lease. This could be important where the lease is to form the security for a mortgage or loan. Any lender may be less than happy at the prospect that his charge does not exist against a legal title and cannot be entered at the Land Registry.

---

[456] Note that where there are issues of market value the fact that the person acquiring the interest is the sitting tenant may affect the normal fiscal valuation principle.

[457] FA 2003, s.79 (as amended); but the inability to register title is no longer the same size of problem in practice now that it is possible to obtain a Revenue certificate (SDLT 5) without simultaneous payment (FA 2003, s.76 (as amended); Stamp Duty Land Tax (Administration) Regulations 2003, SI 2003/2837, Part 1 (as amended)).

8.65 EXEMPTIONS FOR LEASES

8.65.1 General

There are certain leases and agreements for lease which are exempt from SDLT. These exemptions are predominantly the same as the general range of exemptions because the one-size-fits-all drafting of the reliefs applies to both conveyances and leases in the absence of contrary provisions, although certain of the anti-avoidance rules apply only in the case of leases. The basic details of the general exemptions which include several reliefs that are potentially available are considered in detail in **Chapter 5** and the special reliefs for leases granted within a group or in connection with a corporate reconstruction or reorganisation[458] are described in **Chapter 13**. There are, however, certain points that require special comment.

The exemptions for leases fall into three broad categories. These are:

- exemptions that are available for all chargeable transactions and will apply to disposals of leases, grants of options and dealings in leases. The main question in these cases is determining how the relief which was drafted in relation to sales of freeholds fits into the somewhat different regime relating to dealings in leases. These are considered in this section of this chapter; and
- reliefs that are specifically available only for leases; and
- those reliefs that are *prima facie* generally available but are not available in respect of leases.

These reliefs may be granted initially upon a provisional basis and affect either the premium or deemed premium or the rent or deemed rent such as the rent credit mechanism.

8.65.2 Rent credits

There are certain situations largely concerned with the reduction of the tax on chargeable rents where there is an 'overlap' between the old tax and the new lease and the new rent has been taxed as rent for the old lease, e.g. where the old lease included part of the term for the new lease such as in an overlap arising out of the statutory extension of the expired lease for one year and backdating of the other lease with a relief from the 'backdated rent' being treated as a premium.[459] These include:

- surrenders and regrants of leases applying to the same premises;[460]
- grants of new leases pursuant to the Landlord and Tenant Act 1954 (as amended);[461]

---

[458] FA 2003, Sched.7.
[459] FA 2003, Sched.17A, paras.1(a) and 9A; see **8.23** and **8.48**.
[460] FA 2003, Sched.17A, para.9.
[461] FA 2003, Sched.17A, para.9.

- the grant of a lease where there has been a deemed grant upon the substantial performance of the agreement for lease.[462]

The problem is the calculation of the rent credit (see also **8.48**). This requires guidance in the legislation as to two elements:

- the identification of the amount of the new rent reserved by the new lease or deemed new lease; and
- the base rent in respect of the old lease.

It will not have escaped notice (see e.g. **8.42**, **8.44** and **8.46**) that these are also issues that are concerned with the question of variation of leases and whether there has been an increase in rent or a reduction in rent since these are governed by different regimes when they fall outside the statutory regime for variable rents.

8.65.2.1 New rent

It is regrettable that there is no guidance whatsoever as to determining the amount of the 'new rent'; the experts advising HMRC Stamp Taxes clearly overlooked the point that new or revised rents could themselves be variable or uncertain in some fashion. Also the parties may change the repairing obligations so that the landlord takes over these obligations from the tenant who agrees, otherwise than as part of the rent, to make a payment to the landlord which is *prima facie* not taxable[463] and such payments can be ignored in deciding whether there is an increase in the rent. For example, there may be a lease granted initially upon the basis that the rent is linked to turnover but within the lease the landlord has the power to elect to change the rent basis from the turnover figure to some form of profit figure or to a market rent. In this situation the new rent will be uncertain and provision is not made for the purpose of setting off relevant net present values of the old and the new rent regimes. Technically, it would seem, therefore, that the new rent would have to be determined upon an estimated basis which may require an estimated credit because the base rent itself is uncertain. This would produce a situation of having to calculate the net increase or reduction in the rent for each year of the overlap period. Similarly, since the new rent would itself be variable and, *prima facie*, within the five-year review period[464] the review may have to take effect retrospectively with substitution of whatever figures may be appropriate in respect of actual rent paid as opposed to notional rent that might have been paid.

8.65.2.2 Base rent

The second figure required in the calculation, namely the base rent, is also surrounded by numerous difficulties. This is usually, but not invariably, referred to

---

[462] FA 2003, Sched.17A, para.12A.
[463] FA 2003, Sched.17A, para.10.
[464] FA 2003, Sched.17A, paras.7 and 8.

as the 'amount of the rent that was previously subject to SDLT'. This 'plain English drafting' referring to the 'amount of the rent' that was previously taxed raises a fundamental ambiguity with the potentially obvious conclusion that it produces a requirement that will be very difficult to apply in practice. It is not a simple statement that this refers to the 'rent' brought in for the purposes of computing the tax which would be the passing or assumed rent. This clearly cannot be the situation because it refers to the 'amount' of the rent that was taxed. The amount of the rent that was taxed will be affected by *inter alia* the discounting factor. It will also be affected by the fact that in many cases where there is a variable rent the rent that is taxed will be the assumed rent taken into account for all years after the expiration of the fifth year of the term namely the highest rent paid in any 12 consecutive calendar months during the first five years of the term. This is, however, only the 'rent' that is brought into the computation. It is not the 'amount' of the rent that was subject to tax because this will require to be discounted. This leaves the taxpayer or his professional advisers with the difficult problem as to the determination of the amount of the new rent, particularly where this is variable. It has to be decided whether it is necessary to calculate this on a year-by-year basis because that rent, as taxed, will be subject to retrospective adjustment after five years and be the subject-matter of discounting. After the five years that discounted rent will be itself an assumed figure determined only after the expiration of the first five years of the term of the new arrangement. Since it is not a question of a deduction of reserved rent against reserved rent, or net present value against net present value of the rent for the overlap period, but of 'amounts' of rent it would seem that it would be necessary to determine what is the 'rent' to be taken into account in respect of any particular year especially those years after the expiration of fifth year of the term and the amount of discount that was applied to those rents.

Since the original lease and the new rent regime will have different start dates the level of discounting for the rent in any particular year will be completely different. This would seem to require a calculation on a year-by-year basis. It may be that in many cases such as where there is a holding over by operation of law which is backdated for part of a year the arithmetic may not be too horrendous. However, where there is a substantial variation of a lease that amounts to a surrender and regrant and there are, for example, 20 unexpired years, as these problems are only just beginning to emerge there is little practical experience of how HMRC Stamp Taxes will approach the problem or whether it will be prepared to accept a calculation based upon deductions of relevant net present values which will take into account the discounting terms of the lease and possibly be subject to retrospective adjustment subsequently.

8.66 GENERAL EXEMPTIONS AS APPLIED TO LEASES

8.66.1 Charities

The two forms of relief from SDLT upon an agreement for lease or lease granted to a charity are available pursuant to FA 2003, Sched.8 provided that the numerous conditions are satisfied. These are the same conditions for charitable relief considered elsewhere (see **5.27**).

Two points need to be noted in relation to the relief for leases:

- the relief will be subject to the forfeiture of the relief if the property is retained by the charity but ceases to be used for charitable purposes within the three-year clawback period;[465] and
- where a lease is being granted to a charity and at any time the lease is assigned in a non-exempt transaction the assignee is taxed upon the basis that he is being granted a new lease of the unexpired term at the current rent.

8.66.2 Gifts

A grant of a lease for no chargeable consideration is exempt[466] and not notifiable.[467] HMRC Stamp Taxes considers that a lease for a peppercorn rent is for no chargeable consideration and is within the exemption; but a token rent of £1[468] is chargeable consideration. There are, however, situations where such nominal consideration is ignored and a market value premium imposed such as where the lease is granted to a connected company when the market value is taxed as a premium[469] or the lease is between a partnership and connected persons.[470]

8.66.3 Matrimonial and civil partnership breakdown

A lease granted in relation to a divorce or judicial separation or the equivalent for a civil partnership may be exempt.[471]

8.66.4 Variations of estates of deceased persons

There would seem to be no reason why the 'exemption' for certain variations of the estates of deceased persons should not extend to a lease granted as part of those arrangements provided that the other conditions are satisfied.[472]

---

[465] FA 2003, Sched.8, paras.2 and 3(2).
[466] FA 2003, Sched.3, para.1.
[467] FA 2003, s.77A.
[468] A cash rent of 1p to 99p is ignored because of rounding down. The lease remains exempt.
[469] FA 2003, s.53.
[470] FA 2003, Sched.15, Part 3; see further **Chapter 12**
[471] FA 2003, Sched.3, paras.3 and 3A; see **5.7.2.3**.
[472] FA 2003, Sched.3, para.4; see **Chapter 5**.

8.66.5 Intra-group transactions

The relief for intra-group transactions applies to leases.[473] Such relief is, however, subject to several important restrictions:

- intra-group transactions can jeopardise the relief for sale and leaseback transactions;[474]
- it is not available where there is a subsale arrangement; but this may not apply to the special regime for the grant of new leases pursuant to FA 2003, Sched.17A, para.12B (see **8.12**);
- it is subject to the normal rules for clawback of the relief where certain events, such as degrouping, occur during the prescribed three-year period (see **13.25**); and
- there is a special charge upon the assignments of the lease at any time which are treated as the deemed grant of a new lease for the balance of the term at the then rent arrangements.[475]

8.66.6 Reconstructions and reorganisations of companies

The reliefs for reconstruction and reorganisation of companies[476] have been enlarged probably inadvertently to exempt leases. The reliefs are for land transactions entered into for the purposes of or in connection with[477] the transfer of the undertaking (see **13.19**). Subject to the issue of whether there is an undertaking where a lease is granted, it may no longer be necessary to transfer the entire land interests of the company whose business is being transferred in order to qualify for the relief. Granting a lease of the premises utilised or occupied for the purpose of carrying on the activities may now be eligible for relief because the lease is granted pursuant to or in connection with the reorganisation or reconstruction of the company. This may be helpful where the purpose of the reorganisation is to separate the trading activities of the company from its land but grants of leases do not necessarily qualify as transfers of going concerns for VAT and payment of such tax will cancel the reliefs unless appropriate steps in the structuring of the transaction are taken (see **4.30** and **1.24**).

This relief applies not merely to the total exemption for certain company reconstructions but also to the reduced rate of 0.5 per cent for certain company reorganisations. However, as a consequence it is subject to two major restrictions which have to be noted not only for dealings in respect of the lease but also in respect of any warranties and indemnities to be required in connection with the acquisition

---

[473] FA 2003, Sched.7, Part 1; see **Chapter 13**.

[474] FA 2003, s.57A.

[475] FA 2003, Sched.17A, para.11; see **8.62**.

[476] FA 2003, Sched.7, Part 2; see **Chapter 13**.

[477] See *Clarke Chapman John Thompson* v. *IRC* [1975] STC 567. HMRC Stamp Taxes has an incentive to give the words a wide meaning since they are a key component in the statutory general anti-avoidance provisions.

of the shares in any company that may have been part of a group where there have been these types of reconstruction. These areas for investigation include:

- the normal clawback of the relief where there is a change of control within the prescribed three-year period.[478] It should be noted that this three-year period runs from the effective date for the transaction and given that HMRC Stamp Taxes has introduced a provision that imposes two effective dates for leases any delay in actually granting the lease notwithstanding prior substantial performance will restart the time clock for computing the three-year clawback period. Intra-group or associated company arrangements should, therefore, not be conducted upon a relaxed basis; and

- where at any time the lease is assigned as part of a subsequent non-exempt transaction there is a special charge and the assignment is treated as the deemed grant of a new lease to the assignee for the balance of the term at the current rent arrangements.[479] This applies notwithstanding there is no pre-arranged plan or arrangement or causal connection between the creation of the lease and its subsequent assignment. There is no three-year limitation period.

8.66.7   Lease and underlease back

It is provided that the relief for sale and leaseback transactions[480] applies to a lease granted as part of a lease and sublease back transaction such as where one party wishes to keep certain capital allowances. In consequence, the lease or sublease back is not subject to SDLT[481] where:

1.   A transfers or grants a major interest in land to B, i.e. a lease wholly or partly as consideration out of that major interest. It seems that this does not require the leaseback to be of the entirety of the major interest acquired by B.

      However, the relief will be jeopardised if the leaseback includes other land. In such a case a separate lease of the additional land would seem prudent for the time being.

2.   B grants a lease or sublease to A, and:

   - the transaction is not part of a subsale arrangement;[482]
   - the consideration for A's transfer to B other than the lease or sublease back does not consist of or include anything other than the payment of money[483] or the satisfaction, assumption or release of a debt, which means an obligation whether certain or contingent to pay a sum of money either immediately or in the future; and

---

[478]   FA 2003, Sched.7, para.3.
[479]   FA 2003, Sched.17A, para.11.
[480]   FA 2003, s.57A.
[481]   Although 'exempt' the leaseback is fully notifiable: FA 2003, s.77.
[482]   This is limited to FA 2003, s.45 relief, it is not affected by the relief for new leases pursuant to FA 2003, Sched.17A, para.12B.
[483]   Whether sterling or a foreign currency.

- the parties are not members of the same SDLT group.

However, B is taxable upon the transfer of the major interest including the grant of any new lease. Since this form of sale and leaseback or lease and sublease back will be a land exchange then the charge will be by reference to the market value of the major interest being transferred to B.[484] HMRC has accepted that the market value of the major interest being acquired, including the grant of the new headlease, can be determined upon the basis that its value may be depressed by the terms of the leaseback or sublease back that B is required to grant.

8.66.7.1 *Assignment of leaseback*

The assignment of the lease or sublease back is taxable as the deemed grant of a new lease which represents a potential problem for assignees since there is no time limit on the clawback of the relief.[485]

8.66.8 Right-to-buy and shared ownership and similar transactions

Reliefs are available[486] for leases granted in relation to right-to-buy transactions and shared ownership leases, including staircasing transactions.

8.66.9 Rent-to-mortgage

Rent-to-mortgage transactions qualify for relief.[487]

8.66.10 PFI projects

Reliefs are provided for certain leases granted in relation to a limited range of PFI projects but these transactions have to be notified.[488]

8.66.11 First time buyers

Special restrictions apply to right-to-buy and similar transactions for first time buyers.[489] Such buyers may be eligible for the temporary extended nil rate relief for first time buyers.[490]

---

[484] FA 2003, s.47; Sched.4, para.5.
[485] FA 2003, Sched.17A, para.11.
[486] FA 2003, Sched.9 (as amended); see **5.12** and following.
[487] FA 2003, Sched.9, para.6.
[488] FA 2003, Sched.4, para.17; see **17.3**; **5.12**.
[489] FA 2003, Sched.9; see **5.12**.
[490] FA 2003, s.57AA; see **4.3.4**.

8.67 SPECIAL RELIEFS AVAILABLE ONLY FOR LEASES

8.67.1 Nil rate for premiums

Where the premium for a lease of residential premises does not exceed £125,000, the SDLT upon this premium is nil. If the term of the lease is for less than seven years it is not necessary to notify HMRC Stamp Taxes and such a lease is not registerable. Where the lease relates to non-residential property the nil rate for the premiums not exceeding £150,000 does not apply if the rent exceeds £1,000.[491]

Subject thereto the lower rates of SDLT and the linked transaction rules apply to agreements for lease and leases (see **8.9**).

8.67.2 'Assignments' of agreements for lease

A form of subsale relief is introduced[492] for leases to deal with the situation where A enters into an agreement for lease with B who directs A to grant the lease to C. In certain situations B is not subject to tax but many problems pass to C.[493] The details of this relief are described in detail elsewhere (see **8.12** and **8.13**).

8.67.3 Registered social landlords

Limited reliefs are available for short leases granted by registered social landlords as part of an arrangement to provide short-term accommodation with a housing authority.[494] Leases granted to registered social landlords may be eligible for a specific relief where the transaction is publicly funded (see **5.16**) and in other cases may be eligible for the less generous general relief for charities (see **5.27**).

8.68 RELIEFS NOT AVAILABLE FOR LEASES

Certain reliefs are not available for the grants of leases, namely:

- part-exchange of new houses;[495]
- relocation relief for employees;[496]
- certain exemptions involving compulsory purchase;[497]
- reorganisations of public bodies[498] and parliamentary constituencies.[499]

---

[491] FA 2003, s.77 (as amended).
[492] FA 2003, Sched.17A, para.12B.
[493] See also FA 2003, s.45.
[494] FA 2003, Sched.3, para.2.
[495] FA 2003, Sched.6A; see **5.17**.
[496] FA 2003, Sched.6A; see **5.18**.
[497] FA 2003, s.60.
[498] FA 2003, s.66.
[499] FA 2003, s.67.

Other reliefs appear to require outright transfers so that the grant of a lease would seem to be an unlikely event and may not be exempt. The exemption for land transactions in compliance with planning obligations[500] may include the grant of leases.

8.68.1 Alternative finance relief

Alternative finance relief is not available except where the relevant transactions involve a purchase of the interest in land.[501] Unless the words 'purchase' or 'sold' are given an extended meaning,[502] the relief may not apply for example to a lease and underlease back arrangement. It would seem to be contrary to the policy of this relief to restrict its availability where the first party is taking the grant of a new lease which he sells and leases back but allow the relief on the purchase of a freehold or existing lease which is, for example, sold and repurchased or sold and underleased back.

---

[500] FA 2003, s.61.
[501] FA 2003, ss.72 and 73.
[502] Compare, for example, sale and leaseback relief pursuant to FA 2003, s.57A which refers to 'transfers or grants'.

CHAPTER 9

Construction, fitting out and other 'works'

9.1 BACKGROUND

Land transactions frequently occur in the context of arrangements for the development or improvement or repair of land and buildings which activities may be upon the land being acquired or other land. Broadly, three[1] areas of difficulty arise in relation to construction operations for the purposes of SDLT, namely:

- the sale or lease of land where the parties enter into a more or less simultaneous agreement whereby the vendor or landlord is to carry out works on the land in question at the cost of the purchaser or tenant;
- the sale or lease of land with arrangements pursuant to which the purchaser or tenant is to carry out building or fitting out works on that land being acquired; or
- the sale or lease of land where the purchaser or tenant is to carry out works on land other than that to be acquired such as land owned by the vendor or landlord.

In each of these cases there is the question of whether the works to be carried out form part of the chargeable consideration for the acquisition of the land so as to form part of the purchase price or taxable premium for the grant of the lease.

HMRC Stamp Taxes has consistently targeted[2] sales and leases of land and related building agreements seeking to charge tax upon the building works or related services as part of the consideration provided for the acquisition of the land. The fundamental approach for the purposes of traditional stamp duties over many decades was that the purchaser or tenant was paying the vendor or landlord[3] a total sum for carrying out works and acquiring the fully developed land not the site

---

[1] There are, of course, problems other than construction operations, for example, the interaction of SDLT with s.106 agreements and whether the planning gain is taxation and arrangements with local authorities where CPOs may be involved in the assembly of the site (FA 2003, ss.60 and 61).

[2] But has excluded the longstanding techniques of separating the land and building contracts (see *Prudential Assurance Co Ltd* v. *IRC* [1992] STC 863; *Kimbers & Co* v. *IRC* [1936] 1 KB 132).

[3] Based upon *McInnes* v. *IRC* 1934 SC 424 HMRC Stamp Taxes contended that the charge applied where the builder was connected with the vendor or landlord. Embarrassingly, this case overlooked the need to refer to the terms of the various contracts (see *Kimbers & Co* v. *IRC* [1936] 1 KB 132). Moreover the decision was treated as incorrect by the same judges in the later case of *Paul* v. *IRC* 1936 SC 443.

without the buildings. The charge did not apply where the costs were incurred by the purchaser or tenant who employed an independent third party contractor to carry out the works. The basic issue was, where the landlord or possibly a person connected with the landlord was to carry out the construction works, whether there was a single contact for the land and buildings that could only be completed when the works were completely carried out or whether there were two separate contracts for the land and the buildings. In the latter case only the land price was taxable;[4] the problem did not arise where work had been carried out by the purchaser or tenant not using the landlord. In such situations the view was that the obligation, if any, imposed upon the tenant or the purchaser to carry out the building works was not consideration. This was not necessarily a correct analysis of the situation since such an obligation could be consideration rather than a condition.[5] However, this point was not fully appreciated by HMRC Stamp Taxes and its view was if the purchaser or tenant was employing an independent third party contractor the costs of the works would not be chargeable consideration. In general, where the purchaser or tenant employed an independent contractor to carry out the work it would be difficult to argue that there was an obligation to carry out the work although it would be not unusual for a lease agreement to contain provisions to the effect that the grant of the lease was dependent upon the works being carried out satisfactorily.

This was intended to be changed by FA 2003, Sched.4, para.10 rather than deal with a significant analysis of basic law of contract as to when what appeared to be a condition might be the performance of consideration, i.e. when the right to call for the property by carrying out specified works was consideration. The challenge by HMRC Stamp Taxes sought to produce a situation that where the purchaser or tenant employed the vendor or landlord to carry out the building or fitting out works this would automatically be chargeable. HMRC Stamp Taxes thought that the 2003 legislation had reversed the stamp duty position completely and made building works automatically taxable but the advice is[6] that the arguments were totally unsustainable upon the legislation. It has, however, produced massive tax charges for developers of new residential and commercial property and tenants fitting out. The effect has been to bring into charge to tax fitting out works carried out by the tenant at his own expense or by independent third parties at his cost. There is, therefore, a continuation of the charge where the landlord carries out the works at the expense of the tenant or purchaser and where there is an obligation upon the tenant or the purchaser to carry out the works as a 'condition' of earning the right to call for the lease or the transfer of the chargeable interest. The whole focus of the tax charge has moved in a manner increasing the costs, particularly for first time buyers and for local authorities and others desirous of providing social or affordable

---

[4] For transfers of partially completed buildings see *William Cory & Son Ltd* v. *IRC* [1965] AC 1088.

[5] Eastham v. Leigh London and Provincial Properties Ltd [1971] 2 All ER 887.

[6] See Statement April 2004; carrying forward SP8/93.

housing. This is because, unless care is taken,[7] purchasers and tenants may have to pay tax upon their own construction costs or fitting out expenditure. Fortunately, there is a highly technical exclusion from the charge to tax upon costs incurred by the purchaser or tenant which should, with care, ensure that in most cases the purchaser or tenant will escape tax on his costs. The relief should apply to a person buying land for a single residential dwelling or a commercial developer intending to construct a large-scale shopping precinct as well as a tenant of retail premises or offices who is intending to fit out the premises according to his needs. It is, however, important to note the limitations upon this possible relief from the charge to tax:

- It relates to works being carried out only on the land being acquired. In consequence, there is no exemption where a person is acquiring land and as part of the consideration is carrying out construction works or infrastructure works upon land that is owned by or for the benefit of land owned by the vendor or landlord.
- The relief is available only where there is the acquisition of a major interest in land, namely a freehold or a leasehold.[8] There are considerable problems where works are to be carried out in connection with the acquisition of minor interests in land such as wayleaves, underground pipelines and drains which are likely to constitute some form of easement.
- The works must be carried out after the effective date for the transaction, so it is important to ensure that entry upon the land in order to carry out the works in question operates as substantial performance,[9] if some other event has not been engineered to achieve this result before significant expenditure is incurred. It is, however, difficult to generate an activity that constitutes substantial performance of certain rights in land.

9.2 PRACTITIONER PROBLEMS

This regime imposes significant obligations upon the professional adviser since he has to consider two main issues when preparing the contracts or agreements for lease where these relate to major interests in land, namely:

- whether the arrangements relating to the building works constitute some form of chargeable consideration;[10] and

---

[7] The problems are increased because of the effective abolition of subsale relief for bona fide developers but retained for pure speculators.

[8] FA 2003, s.117.

[9] Provisions have been enacted to deal with HMRC Stamp Taxes' argument that there can be more than one effective date for each commercial transaction; but this is not eligible for the relief for multiple taxation of the same transaction (FA 2003, Sched.10, para.33).

[10] Eastham v. Leigh London and Provincial Properties Ltd [1971] 2 All ER 887.

- if there should be any risk that the works are consideration whether the arrangements allowing entry on to the land or payment of the price or otherwise constitute substantial performance so as to create an effective date and so exempt the costs.

The problem is increased where the arrangements involve the construction of works and the interest being acquired is only a minor interest. This can be a particular problem where a person is disposing of land and as part of the arrangements and building works there is to be some form of easement or right enabling the vendor or lessor of the land to have a right of way or right to light over the land to be developed or to link into the infrastructure or other works to be carried out on the land being acquired.

9.3 ANTI-AVOIDANCE

A further attack upon attempts to mitigate this new charge to tax upon building works was introduced by FA 2004.[11] This is intended to apply where, in order to avoid a charge, the developer does not agree to purchase the land but enters into a building agreement with the landowner for a consideration related to the disposal proceeds of the development. This avoids the double taxation of transactions arising upon the acquisition or the disposal of the developed land because of the substantial restrictions upon subsale relief for bona fide commercial developments since there was no acquisition of land for the purposes of SDLT. Where a person enters into a contract which gives him a power to direct a conveyance either to himself or to another person, it is now provided that if the contract is substantially performed, which has a limited meaning in the context,[12] a charge to SDLT arises (see further **Chapter 2**). This legislation is defective and somewhat haphazard in its application,[13] so that it is a potential but easily avoidable trap for all persons entering into building contracts and its terms should be checked as a matter of prudence in all such cases.

There are also anti-avoidance provisions imposing charges upon deposits and loans in connection with the acquisition of land.[14] Given the penal nature of these charges,[15] the terms of any funding arrangement for building works will need to be carefully considered as well as the details of the legislation excluding certain loans and deposits from the charge.

---

[11] Now FA 2003, ss.44A and 45A.
[12] FA 2003, s.44A(6).
[13] See also FA 2003, s.45A for its application to 'subsales' or assignments of the right to direct the conveyance; **Chapter 2**.
[14] FA 2003, Sched.17A, para.18A (see **8.55.3**).
[15] There is no recovery of the tax should the loan be repaid: FA 2003, s.80(4A).

However, normally the segregation of the acquisition of land and any related building contract will not be subject to attack pursuant to the statutory general anti-avoidance provisions.[16]

9.4 SALE OR LEASE OF LAND AND RELATED BUILDING CONTRACTS: VENDOR/LESSOR AS BUILDER

A person may agree to sell or lease land and, at the same time, enter into a contract to construct a building upon the land at the cost of the purchaser/tenant. The question is whether there is a single contract for the sale/lease of a completed building when the SDLT is chargeable upon the aggregate consideration for the land and the building works or there are two separate contracts with SDLT chargeable only upon the land contract. The former stamp duty position[17] has not been altered by FA 2003, Sched.4, para.10.[18] The position for SDLT is that, provided that the land and the works contracts are legally independent and not 'contractually interdependent', only the land price is taxable. The linked transaction rules do not apply to aggregate the two contracts but the consideration must be apportioned between the land and the works upon a just and reasonable basis.[19] Attempts to reduce the SDLT by loading the consideration on to the works may be fraud.[20]

9.5 WORKS TO BE CARRIED OUT BY THE PURCHASER/TENANT

Works to be carried out by the purchaser or tenant at his own expense may now be chargeable consideration even where he engages independent contractors and not the vendor or landlord.[21] Consequently, it must not be overlooked that what appears to be a conditional arrangement may be in law the provision of the consideration.[22] The effect is that an agreement for lease that is expressed to be 'conditional' upon the tenant completing the construction of a building is potentially taxable upon a 'premium' equal to the cost of the works.

---

[16] FA 2003, s.75B.
[17] *Prudential Assurance Co Ltd* v. *IRC* [1992] STC 863; this has been confirmed by HMRC Stamp Taxes; *Kimbers & Co* v. *IRC* [1936] 1 KB 132. The decision in *McInnes* v. *IRC* 1934 SC 424 was generally regarded as perverse in law and on its facts; see the comments of the same judges in *Paul* v. *IRC* 1936 SC 443, and the comments in *Kimbers & Co* v. *IRC* [1936] 1 KB 132. See also SP8/93 and its predecessors which still contain much helpful guidance.
[18] See HMRC Statement April 2004 applying SP8/93.
[19] FA 2003, Sched.4, para.4.
[20] *Saunders* v. *Edwards* [1987] 2 All ER 651.
[21] Note the restriction in the computation provision in FA 2003, Sched.4, para.10(2)(c) referring to the vendor or a person connected with the vendor.
[22] Eastham v. Leigh London and Provincial Properties Ltd [1971] 2 All ER 887.

9.6   CHARGEABLE CONSIDERATION

As indicated above, there are three areas for investigation; namely:

- what are 'works' for these purposes;
- whether the carrying out of the works is consideration; and
- if the works are chargeable consideration, the amount that is subject to tax.

9.7   WORKS

'Works' as chargeable consideration include:[23]

- construction of a building;
- improvement of a building;
- repair of a building;[24] or
- other works to enhance the value of land; but this is apparently not limited to the land being acquired or land retained by the vendor or landlord. Works carried out upon adjoining land may enhance the value of the land being acquired such as by providing access to a road or mains services.

'Works' is, in consequence, a word of wide application in this context and includes fitting out and possibly certain activities putting right a previous party's dilapidations. The word is not limited to the infrastructure costs but may also include the costs of implementing planning agreements with the local authority such as the provision of social housing or swimming pools and schools.[25] There is also a special restricted relief for acquisitions by charities such as registered social housing landlords where such bodies acquire land for development for social housing as part of a joint project.[26] There are also difficult issues arising from the financing of such arrangements which may add to the SDLT costs of the transaction, as well as of compliance costs of multiple notifications.[27]

---

[23]   But note the exclusion for certain leasehold covenants pursuant to FA 2003, Sched.17A, para.10, which includes certain building operations such as repairing the premises.

[24]   But not FA 2003, Sched.17A, para.10.

[25]   There is a fundamental issue of technical legal analysis of whether any stipulations as to the construction of works contained in a s.106 agreement are merely (non-taxable) conditions related solely to the implementation of the planning consent or are consideration for the acquisition of chargeable interests in land from the local authority. It is considered that any indemnity given to the vendor/lessor of land relating to failure to observe the stipulation in the s.106 agreement is not taxable (FA 2003, Sched.4, para.16 – the argument is reinforced by the terms of FA 2003, Sched.17A, para.17). If the local authority is not contributing land the stipulations in the s.106 agreement as to social housing or swimming pools are not part of the taxable consideration; but the position is less clear where the local authority is transferring land to the developer since there is an argument that construction obligations are consideration. That position can be helped where the s.106 agreement and the land contract are separate documents and do not cross-refer to each other.

[26]   See FA 2003, Sched.8 (as amended).

[27]   See FA 2003, ss.51 and 80.

9.8   THE CHARGE

The issues differ depending upon whether the works are to be carried out upon land to be acquired, for which a limited relief is provided, or upon land owned by the vendor as landlord or a third party (see below). Where a purchaser or tenant is to carry out works the open market cost of those works may be subject to tax as part of the charge upon the land transaction.

9.8.1   Works on land not being acquired

It will be relatively easy for HMRC Stamp Taxes to establish chargeable consideration where the purchaser or lessee is to construct works on land retained by the vendor such as where there is a lease from a local authority on terms, *inter alia*, that the lessee will construct a new school on other land owned by the local authority.[28] This will raise many technical issues for debate with HMRC Stamp Taxes since local authorities are a single legal entity notwithstanding that they have many departments which may have conflicting interests.[29] In many cases there is the problem of whether conditions imposed in the planning part of the agreement for the benefit of one department are consideration for the whole agreement and subject to tax. A major potential problem in practice is likely to be acquisitions of land which has planning permission and the vendor or lessor of the land requires indemnities from the purchaser or lessee to carry out the conditions in the planning agreement.[30] This may convert what is merely a condition for the local authority into a binding obligation with the vendor or lessor and so part of the chargeable consideration for the acquisition of the land. Consideration can be chargeable notwithstanding that it is being provided for the benefit of the person other than the vendor or lessor of the land. This can be a major issue where, pursuant to a planning agreement, the developer is required to make payments in cash such as towards the costs of the local authority; such payments cannot be exempted because they are not 'works' to be carried out by the developer.

9.8.2   Works on land being acquired

It may seem rather a strange concept that an arrangement under which a person acquires land in circumstances where he is to carry out works on the land to be acquired is regarded as providing consideration for the acquisition of the land such as where there is an agreement to grant a lease subject to the construction of a satisfactory building. This derives some support from the decision in *Eastham* v. *Leigh London and Provincial Properties Ltd.*[31] This line between a condition and

---

[28]   But note the possibility of relief for PFI transactions pursuant to FA 2003, Sched.4, para.17.
[29]   There is frequently an impression that the inter-dependent 'negotiations' are conducted more aggressively than those with third parties such as developers.
[30]   But see FA 2003, Sched.4, para.16.
[31]   [1971] 2 All ER 887.

the provision of part of the consideration is one that is likely to prove to be of considerable importance in practice and much will depend upon how the attitude of HMRC Stamp Taxes develops once it begins to understand the tax raising potential.

The drafting and structuring arrangements will affect the outcome. A tenant may simply be given permission to enter upon the land to fit out if he wishes. *Prima facie*, where there is no obligation to fit out and, in effect, the tenant merely has permission to enter on to the land in question, the costs of the works are not taxable and it is immaterial whether the limited access given to the tenant amounts to taking possession. If the agreement merely provides that the tenant may, if he wishes but is not obliged to, enter upon the land the fitting out works will probably not be chargeable consideration. On the other hand, if the tenant is required by the contract to fit out because, for example, the landlord is making a contribution to the costs or the lease is 'conditional' on fitting out within a specified time and to a good standard, this is likely to be regarded as chargeable consideration other than rent for the lease, i.e. a premium.[32] The charge is avoided where the works are carried out after the effective date for the transaction as described below.

Other arrangements may create tax problems; although taking possession ahead of the grant of the lease may accelerate the tax charge,[33] it may be prudent to consider early possession to protect the costs of the works from tax (see **Chapters 3 and 4**).

9.8.3 Infrastructure works

Often the developer agrees to the vendor having access to infrastructure works being constructed by the developer on the land to be acquired. Such rights are likely to be some form of easement or similar chargeable interest in or over land and the tax position may depend upon the form in which the rights are brought into existence. If the land is transferred to the developer who grants[34] new rights to the vendor then such rights are, *prima facie*, consideration in kind for the transfer of the land or part of a premium for the lease. This produces a land exchange and SDLT will, where major interests are involved, be chargeable upon the market value of such rights.[35] Strictly, the land exchange ignores the actual or other chargeable consideration and is taxed upon the market value of the interest received. This suggests that costs of works or variable consideration are to be ignored. Where land

---

[32] Compare Corporation Tax Act 2009, ss. 217 and following on deemed premiums and repairs.

[33] For reversionary leases see **8.64**, as potentially more efficient than extensions of the lease term.

[34] There are also issues where such rights are excepted and reserved. Such exceptions and reservations are regarded by HMRC Stamp Taxes not as excluding property from the sale, but as involving a full transfer and a regrant of the rights 'reserved' or retained, i.e. a land exchange. See e.g. *Johnstone* v. *Holdway* [1963] 1 All ER 432; *St Edmundsbury and Ipswich* v. *Clark (No.2)* [1973] 3 All ER 903 (ChD), [1975] 1 All ER 772 (CA); *Shannon, The* v. *Venner Ltd* [1965] 1 All ER 590; see also **Chapter 2**.

[35] FA 2003, Sched.4, para.5. This will be a difficult issue to determine since the rights themselves are not capable of realistic sale separate from the land, although they may substantially enhance or support the value of the land retained by the vendor.

is transferred to a developer for a cash sum plus a leaseback of one of the flats to be constructed, this is a land exchange and the building costs are ignored along with the cash sum. It may be that by suitable timing the developer's tax can be mitigated since the land has a low market value because it is undeveloped and the leaseback to the vendor may be of small value if granted before the works are started. This may in some cases be more tax efficient than a transfer of land for a cash sum plus an obligation to build a house upon the land retained by the vendor when the building costs would become an issue for the developer, particularly if the lower rates are available to the vendor on an exchange or leaseback arrangement. There is, however, the important underlying but as yet unexplored question of whether HMRC Stamp Taxes can assert that there is more than one relevant charging provision and it can choose whichever head of charge produces the higher or highest tax charge.

9.9 RELIEF FROM CHARGE UPON OWN WORKS ON OWN LAND

HMRC Stamp Taxes intends to target what it clearly regards as an avoidance arrangement where a person acquires an interest in land for a consideration that includes carrying out works upon the land of the vendor or lessor of the land or enters into arrangements such as for the construction of drains on the land of the vendor or lessor intended to benefit the developer's own land which will potentially provide a benefit in the form of enhanced value of the land retained by the vendor or lessor. In this context it is, therefore, important to note that the charge applies to works 'to enhance the value of land'.[36] This can include situations where the purchaser may construct an access road over the land of the vendor which would be a non-cash consideration and was therefore something that fell outside the scope of the former charge to stamp duty or it may consist in the grant of some right that is not a major interest within the exclusion from the charge that would enable the vendor to access infrastructure facilities such as mains drainage that was being constructed upon the land being acquired. This is a wide-ranging provision since, as indicated above, there is no explanation of what is the 'land' whose value is to be enhanced. This will presumably apply not merely to the land being purchased and actually built upon but to other adjoining land that may acquire an enhanced value. This enhancement of value being a form of value shift would not under normal circumstances be a chargeable consideration. However, HMRC Stamp Taxes seems anxious to avoid any situation where there is a form of value shift or value enhancement without a movement of a chargeable interest thereby escaping tax. In consequence, it can be expected that HMRC Stamp Taxes will pursue a potentially aggressive line in relation to situations where there are disposals of land with surrenders and regrants or covenants[37] granted back to the lessor where a new lease

---

[36] FA 2003, Sched.4, para.10(1).
[37] Note FA 2003, s.48(1)(b).

317

is granted which provides an enhancement of the value of the land retained by the vendor or lessor but which increase in value might otherwise not be taxable.[38] However, the legislation is unclear as to whether the enhancement of value has to be subjective, i.e. intentional or is objective, i.e. 'accidental'. There may therefore be problems for HMRC Stamp Taxes in dealing with situations where the purchaser of the land would be carrying out the relevant works such as the construction of roads upon the site which could, over time, improve the access to land retained by the vendor and, therefore, enhance the value of the land. This would be an incidental and not directly intended benefit. The legislation is unclear on this point but it does mean that HMRC Stamp Taxes has been forced to introduce a relief from the tax to avoid bringing into charge the cost of works that only incidentally benefit the vendor or lessor.

Such works to be carried out on the land being acquired are not subject to SDLT where:[39]

- the taxpayer is acquiring a major interest in the land;
- the works are carried out on land acquired or to be acquired under the transaction or on other land held by the purchaser or a person connected with him;
- it is not a condition of the transaction that the works are carried out by the vendor or lessor or a person connected with him;
- the works are carried out after the effective date of the transaction.[40]

The first three points are further elaborated below.

9.9.1 Where taxpayer is acquiring major interest in land

Works will not be subject to SDLT where the taxpayer is acquiring a major interest in the land, but this means that there is a high risk situation where the parties are *not* dealing in major interests. For example the parties may enter into an arrangement for a wayleave in order to construct a radio mast for mobile phones or to construct an underground pipeline for the flow of water or, even, the construction of underground railways for major events. In these situations the parties will potentially not be acquiring a major interest but some form of easement or other right that is not a freehold or leasehold (unless HMRC Stamp Taxes accepts that an arrangement for the grant of an easement for a limited term is a 'lease' although not a term of years absolute and is, therefore, a lease that qualifies as a major interest although this would not appear to be supported by the legislation).[41] In consequence, therefore, the relief for building on land to be acquired is not available in such cases. Also

---

[38] Since 'transactions' for the purposes of the statutory general anti-avoidance provisions (FA 2003, ss.75A–75C) include activities or events that would not normally be regarded as transactions. Value shifting may be a 'transaction' within these provisions.

[39] FA 2003, Sched.4, para.2.

[40] Note the extension of the relief where there are two effective dates: FA 2003, Sched.4, para.10(2A).

[41] See **8.5** on what is a 'lease'.

although there may be a possible effective date before completion this will be difficult to establish this since it will be difficult to take 'possession' of a hole in the ground that has yet to be constructed and it will not be taking possession of a major interest. In consequence, where parties are dealing with situations where HMRC Stamp Taxes is likely to take the view that the construction operations are part of the consideration for the grant of the easement[42] and the parties are dealing in minor interests the whole construction costs of a lengthy pipeline for transmitting water from a reservoir to a town some tens of miles distant will be subject to tax. It may be necessary for the parties to investigate whether they can grant leases of airspace or underground rights yet to be developed where the lease can be granted and/or rent paid before significant expenditure is incurred.

9.9.2   Works on land acquired or to be acquired or on other land held by purchaser or a person connected with him

Works carried out on land acquired or to be acquired under the transaction or on other land held by the purchaser or a person connected with him are not subject to SDLT. This leaves the charge applying to situations where the chargeable interest is acquired for building works that constitute 'consideration' even though they are to be constructed upon land not being acquired. Indeed, this situation is more likely to be productive of chargeable consideration than cases where the arrangement relates to construction by the purchaser or tenant upon the land that he is acquiring. It may be easier to persuade a court that a person carrying out works upon his own land employing independent contractors is not supplying consideration notwithstanding the comments in *Eastham* v. *Leigh*.[43] It would seem much easier for HMRC Stamp Taxes to persuade the current judiciary to impose a tax charge where a person acquires a chargeable interest in land and agrees to carry out work on land retained by the vendor or lessor. In this situation the right to call for the land to be transferred or leased is clearly being 'earned' by the undertaking to carry out work upon other land owned by the vendor or lessor. Moreover, these issues are likely to cause considerable difficulties in acquiring land where the arrangements relate to the obtaining of planning permission. For example, a property developer may enter into an arrangement with a landowner for the grant of an option that can be exercised if suitable planning permission is obtained. The planning application will be in the name of the grantor of the option as the legal owner of the land. This acquisition of the benefit of the land and the s.106 agreement in this situation creates a potential tax trap for purchasers where the solicitors to the grantor of the option require 'boiler-plated' indemnities. There may be issues as to whether there is a charge to tax in respect of the performance of the obligations imposed by the planning

---

[42]   Noting the possible enthusiasm for HMRC Stamp Taxes for decisions such as *Eastham* v. *Leigh London and Provincial Properties Ltd* [1971] 2 All ER 887; *Errington* v. *Errington and Woods* [1952] 1 KB 290; *GUS Merchandise* v. *Customs and Excise* [1981] 1 WLR 1309 where 'conditional gifts' were actually contracts for consideration.

[43]   [1971] 2 All ER 887.

agreement such as the construction of public spaces or new schools on part of the land or on land retained by the local authority.[44] In general, it could be argued that indirect dealings between the developer and the local authority would not be consideration but would be conditions imposed to the effect that if the developer were to proceed the work had to be carried out in a particular fashion. This is not the type of condition that was considered in *Eastham* v. *Leigh*.[45] Such a planning condition is not a chargeable liability pursuant to FA 2003, Sched.4, para.8, and while it is arguable that an indemnity is merely a contingent liability to make a payment if there is a default with no tax payable if no payment is made[46] this might not be accepted by HMRC Stamp Taxes. In consequence, there may be a 'contingent' or uncertain consideration which might be taxable if a payment were made, although this is probably unlikely in most commercial circumstances, and the only question is whether it would be appropriate for parties to apply to postpone payment in respect of any s.106 indemnities. However, where the vendor's solicitors insist upon a positive obligation to carry out and to observe the terms of the planning agreement this may convert a potential 'condition' into the price for obtaining the land and therefore chargeable consideration. The purchaser's solicitors should, therefore, consider very carefully the terms upon which they commit their client when entering into the contract. A positive obligation to the vendor to carry out the terms of the planning agreement could be construed as chargeable consideration even though the works benefit the local authority with the result that the costs of any planning gain for the local authority or other person will be fully chargeable because they are not being carried out on the land to be acquired by the purchaser/developer.

9.9.3 Works not a condition of the transaction

SDLT will not apply to works where it is not a condition of the transaction that the works are carried out by the vendor or lessor or a person connected with him,[47] i.e. it must not be a term of the lease or sale contract that the builder is to be the vendor. The reference to 'transaction' is to the contract for the sale or lease of the land not the overall commercial arrangement, so that separate contracts are outside this restriction.

To avoid the charge the developer must take possession of substantially the whole of the land before commencing operations. This can be a problem where he is acquiring the land in phases. Such arrangements should be structured as separate contracts rather than as a single contract with phased completion, because in the latter case there may be major problems in establishing substantial performance.

---

[44] There can be no relief where the planning obligation consists of something other than works such as a cash payment.

[45] [1971] 2 All ER 887; compare also the nature of conditions and contracts and consideration in *Wood Preservation* v. *Prior* [1969] 1 All ER 364.

[46] Compare *Western United Investment Co* v. *IRC* [1958] 1 All ER 257.

[47] But note the criticism of *McInnes* v. *IRC* 1934 SC 424 by the judges in that case in the later decision in *Paul* v. *IRC* 1936 SC 443.

9.10 FITTING OUT ISSUES

9.10.1 Chargeable consideration

Frequently, leases of commercial premises will be granted upon the basis that either the landlord or the tenant is to fit out the premises. Such fitting out works can form part of a chargeable premium.[48] For example, where the tenant is to pay for the fitting out but this is to be carried out by the landlord then subject to the structuring of the documentation the fact that the fitting out works are to be carried out by the landlord excludes them from the relief so that the costs paid to the landlord in respect of the fitting out works would be taxable.[49]

9.10.2 Terms of entry, timing and relief

Should the fitting out be a premium for the grant of the lease,[50] it will be necessary to ensure that the commencement of the fitting out works or any other initial entry by the tenant constitutes substantial performance of the agreement for lease so as to be within the exclusion from the charge to SDLT for the cost of building or other works carried out on the major interest with land to be acquired after the effective date.[51] This key issue will depend upon the terms upon which the tenant is permitted to enter although entry as a licensee or tenant at will may be sufficient to constitute the necessary substantial performance.[52] It must be noted when structuring and drafting these arrangements that the tenant must take possession of at least substantially the whole of the land. There will, in consequence, be difficulties where only partial access is granted such as access to only part of the land to be demised or access limited as to time, especially in cases where the landlord remains in occupation of the land because the main building works have not been completed.

9.11 ILLUSTRATIVE PROBLEM FOR NEW DEVELOPMENT

The person concerned will quite often need to acquire the land to be developed. There are certain possible arrangements under which rather than purchasing the land the person intending to undertake construction operations may simply enter into some form of profit-sharing agreement with the landowner. *Prima facie* in such

---

[48] FA 2003, Sched.4, para.10.

[49] Subject to the possibility of postponing the payment of tax where this is a variable payment related to costs.

[50] See e.g. Ridgeons Bulk v. Customs and Excise [1994] STC 427.

[51] The problem of the double effective date for agreements for lease and leases arising pursuant to FA 2003, Sched.17A, para.12B is specifically covered by a provision that in relation to the grant of the lease the cost of the works carried out prior to the grant of the lease but after the effective date for the agreement for lease is taxable.

[52] Subject to the commercial issues, the parties may be able to put this matter beyond dispute by early completion. On completion of partly developed sites with related building contracts see *William Cory & Son Ltd v. IRC* [1965] AC 1088.

a situation because there is no contract to acquire an interest in land there is simply an agreement to carry out building works for a consideration related to their sale proceeds or value or costs. In consequence, there is not a chargeable transaction. However, HMRC Stamp Taxes has introduced some rather defective anti-avoidance provisions as FA 2003, ss.44A and 45A in order to address such arrangements. These provisions deem certain such contracts, i.e. those where the developer has a power to direct a conveyance or lease in certain circumstances, to be the acquisition of chargeable interests although quite how the provisions will apply to most cases is uncertain because the concepts of the charges are not necessarily compatible with the commercial and legal structures that have to be adopted (see **9.3**).

Subject to dealing with such anti-avoidance provisions which are not universal since there are exclusions from the statutory general anti-avoidance provisions for the segregation of land and building contracts,[53] the problem for a developer is the curtailed subsale relief because entry upon the land in order to commence the development will usually constitute taking possession of the whole or substantially the whole of the land and therefore have the double effect of constituting an effective date giving rise to a tax charge but, at the same time, excluding the building costs from the charge to tax. There is, therefore, effectively a double taxation upon the new development namely a charge upon the acquisition of the land prior to its development and a further charge upon the onward sale or leasing of the land after the completion of the development. The latter is particularly harsh since the price or premium fixed for the onward movement will usually, in effect, include any SDLT paid in respect of the acquisition of the land plus a charge to tax upon the building works. It is, therefore, important to consider the structuring of new development arrangements and, as indicated above, to avoid any risk that indemnities given by the developer to the vendor or landlord in respect of planning obligations pursuant to any s.106 agreement are not included as part of the chargeable consideration.

9.12 RESTRICTED SUBSALE RELIEF

Previously, it was possible to control the stamp duty costs by not taking a transfer; but the previous stamp duty device of resting on contract and dealing with the matter by way of subsale transfer is no longer a realistic option in most cases (see **Chapter 5**). Although there is a highly limited form of relief for subsales and assignments[54] or the grant of leases to third parties[55] these reliefs are not available where the first purchaser or tenant has substantially performed the contract. In effect, the relief is available only for the speculator (see **Chapter 5**). The developer who enters upon land to commence the works will almost certainly not escape a new and early charge to tax because he will have substantially performed the contract by either providing about 90 per cent of the consideration, or going into possession such as by

---

[53] See FA 2003, s.75B(3).
[54] FA 2003, s.45.
[55] FA 2003, Sched.17A, para.12B; see **Chapter 8**.

commencing building or fitting out works operations; or where the interest being acquired by the developer is a lease the taxpayer has made the first payment of rent, even if this is only a token £1 rent during the development phase.[56]

Even though the developer or prospective tenant is only a licensee,[57] during the development phase it will be difficult to create a situation where the terms of the licence avoid the licensee entering into 'possession' so as to trigger a charge to SDLT and the consequent payment and compliance obligations.[58] On the other hand, a speculator who has no interest in developing or refurbishing the land and obtains a discount from the developer[59] can avoid SDLT altogether. He may take an option to purchase or call for a lease or a contract conditional upon obtaining planning permission. Alternatively, he may enter into an agreement to acquire leases of several flats intending that the leases will be granted to individual purchasers. Provided that he avoids substantial performance of his contract, which should be relatively easy because he merely intends to profit by turning his contract in these situations, he will not be subject to tax. The true developer cannot normally escape the charge to tax except by selling the land or assigning his right to call for the lease prior to or at the same time as he substantially performs his contract before commencing the works because of the effect of entering upon the land to carry out the development or refurbishment.

9.13   SUBSALE RELIEF AND SITE ASSEMBLY

A key element in the costs of any development is the taxation of the assembly of the land to be developed from the existing owners, whether or not with the assistance of a local authority or other body having compulsory acquisition powers.[60] This is

---

[56]   FA 2003, s.44.

[57]   It should also be noted that HMRC Stamp Taxes takes the view that where there is any licence to enter upon land to carry out building works and under the terms of the licence the landlord granting the licence has a right to enter upon the land in question in order to ensure that the building works are progressing satisfactorily, it is an indication that the licence confers exclusive possession upon the developer and may amount to some form of tenancy although this is merely an indication of tenancy. It may be possible to minimise this risk by making the licence non-exclusive, see the comments in *Street* v. *Mountford* [1985] 1 AC 809; but later cases have tended to restrict these typically enthusiastic comments by Lord Templeman to residential transactions within a statutory regime providing protection for residential tenants and the parties are not equally balanced in negotiating power; *Addiscombe Garden Estates Ltd* v. *Crabbe* [1957] 3 All ER 563; but note the decision in *Ogwr* v. *Dykes* [1989] 2 All ER 880 where there is the suggestion that the inclusion of a provision in the agreement that the arrangement is not intended to create the relationship of landlord and tenant may be effective to prevent the creation of a tenancy.

[58]   Attempts to escape from this restriction are possibly vulnerable to FA 2003, s.44A mentioned above.

[59]   But such a discount will almost inevitably produce linked transactions, cancelling the lower rates that should be chargeable with the tax.

[60]   For which there may be relief from SDLT pursuant to FA 2003, s.60; but this relief is subject to many restrictive conditions and HMRC Stamp Taxes has already taken points in practice which clearly indicate that this relief will be restricted whenever and as far as possible. For example, difficulties have arisen in relation to both the meaning of the word 'development' and the nature of

likely to be subject to the highest rate of SDLT which may include an SDLT charge upon VAT.[61] This can add significantly to the overall cost of the development as a factor in fixing the price or premium for the eventual disposal of the property which can add to the problems of first time buyers or other purchasers or tenants of newly constructed buildings.

Traditionally, this additional cost in the prices of new houses and commercial developments was mitigated by subsale relief;[62] but one of the major policy objectives of the introduction of SDLT was the removal of this key relief[63] regarded as vital to the reasonable operation of the tax over two centuries ago. The effect is that although the relief remains available, with careful planning for the short-term speculator, the person who is the developer of the land such as the constructor of houses for first time buyers, is now to be hit by the new tax in situations where previously no tax would normally arise. Moreover, this hit occurs at an early stage in the transaction so that as well as the new tax charge there is an additional carrying cost in the form of an interest charge incurred upon the borrowing to pay the tax[64] enhancing the cascade effect of stamp taxes in this area. This cascade effect is also increased because of:

- the charge to SDLT upon VAT even where there is a recoverable input tax;
- the acceleration of the time of the tax charge from documents to transactions and to substantial performance rather than 'completion' cancelling the cost benefit of resting on contract;
- the extension of the scope of taxable transactions, in particular in this context the potential charge to SDLT upon works to be carried out by the person acquiring the interest in the land;[65] and
- any overage or other arrangements which increase the tax charge and the compliance costs (see **Chapter 4**) because of the need to prepare and file several land transaction returns.

---

the development arrangements which have to be in place as at the effective date of the acquisition in question. There are also difficulties of analysis and the effect of arrangements where the local authority will be acquiring the land under compulsory powers and will be granting leases out of the land so acquired to the developer. These issues include whether payments made by the developer to the existing landowners are chargeable consideration for the acquisition by the local authority as required by FA 2003, Sched.4, para.1, and whether any arrangement for the grant of leases by the local authority out of the land acquired to the developer involves land exchanges chargeable in accordance with the provisions of FA 2003, s.47 and Sched.4, para.5.

[61] Treatment as a transfer of a going concern seems unlikely since the developer by intending to construct new buildings on the land is unlikely to be carrying on the same business as the vendor.

[62] Stamp Act 1891, s.58(4) and (5) (as amended) generally known as 'resting on contract'; see **1.10**.

[63] This attack upon subsale relief has been extended by the anti-avoidance provisions upon similar arrangements in FA 2003, ss.44A and 45A.

[64] There is also a commercial issue since the status of the contract to acquire the land may be conditional upon completion of the construction works and so there may be difficulties in providing acceptable security to the lender.

[65] FA 2003, Sched.4, para.10 (as amended).

CONSTRUCTION, FITTING OUT AND OTHER 'WORKS'

9.14 DEVELOPER TRAP: PHASED DEVELOPMENT

It is provided that, in general,[66] works effected on the land acquired or to be acquired for the improvement of the land are excluded from the charge to SDLT but, *inter alia*, only where these are carried out after the effective date for the agreement, i.e. after the date of substantial performance or taking possession.

Substantial performance requires taking possession of the whole or substantially the whole of the land in question. Entry into possession of part of the land will not necessarily operate as substantial performance. This should be noted, particularly where there is to be a staged development and the land is to be drawn down in tranches by the developer from time to time. While this may operate to delay the effective date for the transaction and so postpone the payment of tax, it represents a trap where the works in question are part of the chargeable consideration since in many cases what may appear superficially to be a condition may prove to be part of the consideration.[67] The relief for building works by the developer upon what is effectively his own land is not available in these circumstances since having access to only a limited part to the land the purchaser or tenant is not taking possession of substantially the whole of the land. As a result of the changes, taxpayers may find themselves subject to tax upon their own building works.

9.15 LAND BANKS AND JOINT DEVELOPMENTS

It may happen that developers combine to acquire land for eventual development. This may be part of a process of building up a land bank which is to be established as part of a joint proposal with possible plans for land being physically partitioned between the participants in order to share out the benefits and disadvantages of any planning agreements with the relevant local authority or authorities. Alternatively, the parties may already own land which they intend to 'pool' and partition when the combined application for planning permission is obtained, possibly with cash payment to provide equality and cross-easements, etc. which may create exchanges.[68] Obviously, where the parties combine to acquire land there will be the normal charges to SDLT. The pooling of land already owned will involve numerous taxable land exchanges.

There may be certain technical issues as to whether the participants as joint venturers constitute some form of partnership or they are simply some form of investment syndicate that is not a partnership. Under most circumstances whether or not they are a partnership should not have significant problems for the purposes of SDLT since the normal rules apply where the land is being acquired from a person who is not connected with the partnership or syndicate but there are frequently situations where connected persons do contribute land into the syndicate and run the

---

[66] FA 2003, Sched.4, para.10; see above.
[67] Eastham v. Leigh London and Provincial Properties Ltd [1971] 2 All ER 887.
[68] FA 2003, s.47; Sched.4, paras.5 and 6.

325

risk of potential market value charges pursuant to FA 2003, Sched.15, Part 3 (see **13.4**). This can arise where the parties already own land within the prospective project site and agree to pool such land. Obviously, there are many issues that need to be investigated in relation to the structure of the transaction such as whether the pooling constitutes some form of real property unit trust scheme with its own regime for SDLT as regards the acquisition of the land and stamp duty reserve tax as regards adjustments in the rights of the participants which may constitute changes in the unit scheme structure.[69]

Where there has been co-operation in acquiring a site on a joint basis and the site is then allocated to the various participants in accordance with the pre-agreement and the terms of any planning consent there will, *prima facie*, be a partition of the land. This is subject to a special relief that excludes it from the land exchange rules so that tax is charged only upon any equality payment.[70] However, the main trap for such arrangements is the initial assembly of the site since, as indicated in the preceding paragraph, there may be contributions of land already held by certain of the participants. This could easily involve simple land exchanges of part-interests or undivided interests in the land contributed into the arrangement whether or not as a partnership. Where there is a land exchange even of part-interests in land into joint names there will be multiple charges upon relevant market value because of the exchange of the undivided interests.[71]

9.16 CALCULATION AND PAYMENT: OPEN MARKET COST

The tax is charged upon the open market cost of the works or services, i.e. the amount that would have to be paid for the works on the open market.[72] No statutory guidance is given as to how this novel fiscal test is to be applied although, probably inconsistently with the concept of 'open market cost' which implies a notional fixed-price contract on arm's length terms, HMRC Stamp Taxes regards the open market cost as being within the variable consideration regime and has issued regulations[73] enabling the taxpayer to defer the payment of the tax upon the costs. Nevertheless, it seems that, strictly, actual costs are to be ignored and the tax calculated upon the prices that would be charged by contractors or subcontractors operating for a profit and on an arm's length basis. It seems probable that the tax will be charged upon the price that would have been charged for the supply of the

---

[69]   See, for example, FA 2003, s.101; FA 1999, Sched.19 (as amended).

[70]   FA 2003, s.47; Sched.4, para.6; see **7.6**.

[71]   It should, however, be noted that where land is jointly owned or put into joint ownership and market value issues arise there can be, as with shareholdings, a discount for a minority interest so that where the land is held on a 50:50 basis the value of the interest of each participant, whether as joint tenant or tenant in common, is not one-half of the market value of the unencumbered site but may be that one-half of the value as reduced by a discount of 10 to 15 per cent. See, for example, *Re Wight* [1982] 2 EGLR 236.

[72]   FA 2003, Sched.4, para.10(3).

[73]   Stamp Duty Land Tax (Administration) Regulations 2003, SI 2003/2837, Part 4; see **14.12**.

building works upon a stand-alone basis and not as part of the overall land acquisition arrangement. There will, therefore, have to be a profit element included in the 'cost' which may include VAT.

There are many issues concerned with the question of 'open market cost' in this context. Where the person concerned is a developer and is making use of his own labour force and not necessarily contractors and where he already owns equipment the 'cost' to him may be fairly small. This can be a key issue where, for example, the vendor sells a parcel of land to the developer and part of the consideration consists of the developer demolishing existing buildings on land owned by the vendor and the construction of a new building or the renovation of existing buildings. In these situations since the personnel and equipment will be on the adjoining land being purchased the 'cost' to the developer of dealing with the demolition and building obligations or infrastructure costs in relation to the project for the benefit of the vendor will be relatively small because everything is in place for the main development. Clearly, these actual costs will be very different from the 'open market cost' and there will be potential challenges by HMRC Stamp Taxes upon the basis that the price paid for the land being acquired has been manipulated in order to reduce the tax by writing down the purchase price and hiding this as cost of the new works. It may, however, be difficult for HMRC Stamp Taxes to establish this and the numbers may be defensible commercially; moreover since manipulation of the price with a view to mitigating tax is a criminal offence such as conspiracy to defraud HMRC there will be a criminal burden of proof upon HMRC should it seek to challenge the actual figures put forward by the parties.[74]

9.17 VAT AND 'COST'

As discussed elsewhere (see **Chapter 4**), there is some doubt as to the meaning of 'cost' but HMRC Stamp Taxes' position is that 'cost' is the price on the open market excluding VAT even where it is recoverable as input tax and ignoring the issue of the capital goods scheme. It seems that, in practice, HMRC Stamp Taxes may prefer to work on the basis of actual cost at least in those cases where subcontractors are engaged. The treatment of situations where an in-house labour force is employed remains problematic but this is likely to be an area where the open market cost will be relied upon by HMRC Stamp Taxes, i.e. the price that would be charged simply for the building works unrelated to the overall transaction.

---

[74] See *Re Wragg* [1897] 1 Ch 796.

CHAPTER 10

Trusts

10.1 JURISDICTION

The issues discussed in this chapter apply to both trustees and beneficiaries in trusts established within and outside the United Kingdom and governed by a foreign law. SDLT does not make any distinction between these two situations and seeks to bring as many foreign arrangements into charge as possible by deeming certain attributions to apply to foreign trusts.[1] Trustees should consider holding United Kingdom land through foreign companies.[2]

10.2 CREATION OF TRUSTS, CONSTRUCTIVE TRUSTS AND EQUITABLE REMEDIES

The whole concept of a trust is based on equity's insistence that a man follows the dictates of his conscience (as interpreted by equity). Looking, as ever, at the substance of the transaction rather than the form, equity (as opposed to statute) does not require any formalities to be observed on the creation of a trust.[3] All that is necessary for a trust to arise is the presence of the three certainties of intention, subject-matter and objects. If the property and interest therein to be the subject-matter of the trust are ascertainable, the beneficiaries identified or identifiable by reference to a sufficiently certain formula, and, above all, it is clear from the words or deeds of the person making the disposition that a trust is intended, a trust will come into being. These issues of oral arrangements and the need for writing may be of crucial importance in relation to many domestic transactions which almost certainly will not be adequately documented; such as where a child agrees to care for an elderly parent on the 'understanding' that the house will pass at some stage to the child. Such arrangements may not have the necessary evidence as to the parties' intention to create legal relations[4] and there may be issues as to whether there is

---

[1] FA 2003, Sched.16, para.2.
[2] As a general point it must not be overlooked that the existence of trusts may render the taxpayer ineligible for first time buyer relief; see **4.33**.
[3] *Paul v. Constance* [1977] 1 WLR 527.
[4] See e.g. *Facchini v. Bryson* [1952] 1 TLR 1386 on the presumptions for domestic agreements.

some form of trust created with a life interest to the parent and remainder to the child. The fact that the transaction is oral will not necessarily render the arrangement legally ineffective. Indeed, equitable notions may intervene to override statutory requirements for writing. In *Yaxley* v. *Gotts*[5] an oral promise that was acted upon was held to be effective notwithstanding the absence of writing required by Law of Property (Miscellaneous Provisions) Act 1989, s.2. Walker LJ stated that where equitable notions such as proprietary estoppel or constructive trust applied these overrode the need for writing in any statute.[6] Thus an oral declaration by the settlor that he intends thenceforth to hold stated property upon trust for stated beneficiaries will create an immediate and valid trust, as in *Paul* v. *Constance*[7] where there was an oral declaration of trust concerning money in a bank account by the use of the words, uttered by the settlor to the beneficiary, 'The money is as much yours as mine'.

Equity's permissive view has, however, long been modified by statutory provisions requiring the observance of written formalities in many cases, and in practice an oral declaration of trust is only unaffected by statute when limited to personalty. Section 53(1)(b) of LPA 1925 states: 'a declaration of trust respecting any land or any interest therein must be manifested and proved by some writing signed by some person who is able to declare such trust or by his will'. Like s.40 of the same Act before its repeal by Law of Property (Miscellaneous Provisions) Act (LP(MP)A) 1989, s.2(8), the above provision is evidential only, and does not require that the trust should necessarily be declared by writing. There must, however, at some stage, be written evidence of the declaration signed by the competent party or, probably, some act of reliance upon the oral arrangement which can be utilised to establish a constructive or similar trust which does not require writing.[8] It remains to be seen how far the judges who were trained upon the now repealed doctrine of part performance[9] will bring back a similar set of principles re-labelled 'constructive trust' which as Walker LJ stated[10] overrode the statutory requirement for writing and in consequence can operate to pass an equitable interest in land without writing. It is immaterial when the written memorandum is produced, but until there is a written declaration, the trust remains unenforceable by court action, although not invalid and ineffective. HMRC Stamp Taxes may seek to contend that even in the absence of a written memorandum such arrangements are valid, albeit unenforceable by the court[11] and the position differs from that of a

---

[5] [1999] 3 WLR 1217.

[6] There are limits on this approach because there must be a degree of certainty in the oral arrangements for the trust to arise; see *Yeoman's Row Management* v. *Cobbe* [2008] 4 All ER 713.

[7] [1977] 1 WLR 527. See also *Binions* v. *Evans* [1972] Ch 359; *T Choithram International* v. *Pagarani* [2001] 2 All ER 492; *Henry* v. *Henry* [2010] 1 All ER 988.

[8] LPA 1925, s.53(2); LP(MP)A 1989, s.2(6); *Yaxley* v. *Gotts* [1999] 3 WLR 1217; *Binions* v. *Evans* [1972] 2 All ER 70, where, in effect, the trust arose in favour of a person who was not a party to the transaction.

[9] LPA 1925, s.40 (repealed by LP(MP)A 1989).

[10] In *Yaxley* v. *Gotts* [1999] 3 WLR 1217.

[11] See *Forster* v. *Hale* (1798) 3 Ves 696; *Rochefoucauld* v. *Boustead* [1897] 1 Ch 196.

transaction which is void unless effected in writing.[12] However, although there may be a tax charge in the meantime, the beneficiaries will not, in the case of land, be able to enforce the trust by court action.

LPA 1925, s.136 requires transfer of legal title to choses in action to be in writing and legal choses in action can be chargeable interests since these include covenants and obligations affecting the value of land.[13] Section 53(1)(c) thereof requires writing to dispose effectively of equitable interests,[14] but the Court of Appeal in *Neville* v. *Wilson*[15] has reversed the House of Lords and held that the provisions of LPA 1925, s.52(2) prevail over s.53(1)(c) thereof.[16] If the settlor does not do all in his power, according to the nature of the property given, to vest the property in the trustees,[17] equity will not interfere to perfect the trust because, in the absence of consideration[18] given by a beneficiary, there is an imperfect gift and (in the absence of an estoppel or the creation of a constructive trust which does not require writing), as was said in *Milroy* v. *Lord*,[19] 'there is no equity in this Court to perfect an imperfect gift'. In certain situations trustees may be ordered by the court not to enforce a deed of covenant unless there is separate consideration as party within the marriage consideration.[20] This line of cases may be helpful for two reasons in practice, namely:

- there is no 'acquisition' of a chargeable interest because there is no transaction; and
- the absence of consideration may mean there is no chargeable consideration which makes the transaction 'exempt' (see **5.4**).

10.3 TESTAMENTARY TRUSTS

The position may differ where the proposed trustees are the personal representatives of the deceased settlor who thereby become vested with the legal estate[21] or the legal title otherwise 'accidentally' vests in them.[22] See also **Chapter 11**.

---

[12] This also means that the legislative requirement may be invalid pursuant to the human rights legislation as an obstacle to the protection of validly created property rights. This is a fundamental issue as to how far the rules of evidence and procedure can continue to regulate property ownership and its protection.

[13] FA 2003, s.48(1)(b).

[14] See, for example, *Grey* v. *IRC* [1959] 3 All ER 603; *Oughtred* v. *IRC* [1960] AC 206; *Vandervell* v. *IRC* [1967] 1 All ER 1; *Escoigne Properties Ltd* v. *IRC* [1958] AC 549.

[15] [1961] 3 All ER 769.

[16] Confirming once again a longstanding theory of the author that the answer to a problem depends upon whether the case is concerned with tax or with routine conveyancing and the right answer will emerge only in the latter situation.

[17] As in *Re Rose* [1949] Ch 78.

[18] Undertakings to pay inheritance tax or capital gains tax arising are not taxable: FA 2003, Sched.4, paras.16A and 16B.

[19] (1862) 4 De GF & J 264.

[20] See e.g. Re Kay's Settlement [1939] Ch 329; Re Cook's Settlement Trusts [1965] Ch 902.

[21] See e.g. *Strong* v. *Bird* (1874) LR 18 Eq 315.

[22] See e.g. *Re Ralli* [1964] Ch 288.

10.4 LAND ISSUES

These issues of the creation of trusts particularly those affecting land where there may be movements of equitable or beneficial interests[23] which are chargeable interests has a considerable practical significance for SDLT. Unlike stamp duty where documentation was required before a tax charge could arise it is specifically provided that SDLT applies notwithstanding the absence of writing and applies to transactions that take effect 'by operation of law' (see **2.9**). This may include situations where equitable notions apply to create a valid oral contract[24] or some form of trust[25] or fiduciary relationship between the parties whereby a person who appears to be the owner of land is simply in a representative capacity, the interest in the property having passed to some other person as a result of oral or other informal arrangements. Therefore, while there is no charge, as such, upon the execution of a trust instrument this may be part of an operation of law or other 'oral' arrangement that operates in such a way that a person 'acquires' a chargeable interest in land in the United Kingdom. In many cases the transaction may involve movement of a chargeable interest but there will be questions as to whether there is consideration for the creation of the beneficial interest that is transmitted by operation of law or act of the parties or otherwise. In such circumstances there being no chargeable consideration[26] there will be no chargeable transaction and the arrangement will not require notification.[27] There is now specifically a charge upon 'services'[28] so that arrangements under which property is transferred or to be transferred in return for certain activities may now be a chargeable transaction and what appears to be a conditional gift may, upon technical analysis, prove to be some form of arrangement that is for a consideration and therefore potentially taxable.[29]

Unfortunately, SDLT has a broad basis not only for the types of transactions that fall within the scope of 'acquisition' but also for the width of the definition of 'chargeable interest' which can include contracts and covenants that affect the value of land.[30] The area of 'chargeable consideration' has been significantly extended. It will include situations where there is a land exchange such as where parties are modifying trusts which can be a potential area of difficulty since the reallocation of the interests of the beneficiaries in particular assets would appear to be *prima facie* taxable but there is a relief available in certain circumstances.[31]

---

[23] Subject to the requirement of Law of Property Act 1925, s.53; Law of Property (Miscellaneous Provisions) Act 1989, s.2.

[24] *Yaxley* v. *Gotts* [1999] 3 WLR 1217.

[25] *Henry* v. *Henry* [2010] 1 All ER 988; *Binions* v. *Evans* [1972] Ch 359.

[26] Unless the promise which is relied upon can be taken as a request which constitutes consideration in any particular case.

[27] FA 2003, Sched.3, para.1; s.77A.

[28] FA 2003, Sched.4, para.11; see **15.18**.

[29] See, for example, Binions v. Evans [1972] Ch 359; Henry v. Henry [2010] 1 All ER 988; Errington v. Errington and Woods [1952] 1 KB 290; Eastham v. Leigh London and Provincial Properties Ltd [1971] 2 All ER 887; GUS Merchandise v. Customs and Excise [1981] 1 WLR 1309.

[30] FA 2003, ss.43 and 48(1)(b); Sched.17A, para.10(1); see **2.12**.

[31] FA 2003, Sched.16, para.8.

10.5 DOMESTIC ARRANGEMENTS

The problem is that many of these arrangements that lack formality and situations where equity may intervene are likely to be domestic arrangements between members of the family. Since the parties will not appreciate the need for their transaction to be recorded in writing to be accurately implemented they are unlikely to seek legal advice. Even where they seek legal advice such as upon the purchase of property in the names of parents and child they may not draw the attention of the professional adviser[32] to the fact that there is e.g. an arrangement as regards the discharge of the mortgage that could involve a creation of some form of trust and the eventual passing of an interest pursuant to what is essentially a contractual arrangement. The professional adviser in situations where he or she is dealing with residential property as part of a process may not raise the questions that are necessary in order to complete a correct and accurate land transaction return (SDLT 1). In these situations the charge to tax may arise immediately. For example, where the parents participate in the acquisition of the property but leave the discharge of the consideration to the child and the child takes possession of the property there will be an immediate charge to SDLT because there is substantial performance. There will not be a situation where it is possible to argue for the charge to tax not arising until 'completion', i.e. the time when the mortgage is discharged and the property conveyed by the parents into the name of the son or his children on his death or divorce. Substantial penalties are likely to have been incurred as well as a substantial amount of interest because of the long delay in drawing the matter to the attention of HMRC Stamp Taxes.[33] It may be possible to argue in these circumstances that because the arrangement is domestic there is no intention to create legal relations[34] or the arrangement is so uncertain that it cannot form the basis of a contract[35] but such arrangements are also likely to give rise to disputes within the family and part of the costs of resolving these disputes could be the payment of a substantial amount of SDLT, late payment interest and penalties for failure to file a return at the appropriate time.

10.6 VOLUNTARY ASSIGNMENTS

The vast majority of trusts and settlements are created voluntarily (i.e. without consideration). On the basis that there is a general exemption (subject to certain exclusions) for transactions where there is not chargeable consideration,[36] it might

---

[32] Who may be at risk in signing off the first time buyer relief.

[33] The limited evidence in practice suggests that a delay of two years is sufficient for the full tax-related penalty to be levied.

[34] *Parker* v. *Clark* [1960] 1 All ER 93.

[35] *Yeoman's Row Management* v. *Cobbe* [2008] 4 All ER 713; *Scammell* v. *Ouston* [1941] AC 251; *Sweet & Maxwell* v. *Universal News Services* [1964] 3 All ER 30.

[36] FA 2003, Sched.3, para.1; see also Sched.4, paras.16A and 16B where there are certain tax indemnities.

be thought that there were no significant SDLT issues in respect of trusts. However, this is not an entirely accurate appraisal of the situation: there are problems in relation to SDLT. Not all dealings in trust assets or interests are voluntary in the sense that there is no consideration. Where there is consideration such as the mutual exchange of equitable interests upon the variation of a trust or an estate, such deeds of family arrangement were not liable for stamp duty in general because they were not sales.[37] This analysis is no longer relevant because of the much broader basis of SDLT which is not limited to 'sales' in the general meaning of the term. In consequence, a much wider range of transactions involving trusts and estates is potentially within the charge to tax in the SDLT regime.

10.7   EXCHANGES AND TRUSTS

Moreover, there is an increased risk that the variation or partition of a trust or an estate may be an exchange possibly attracting two charges to tax where land is involved on both sides of the transaction. There are also anti-avoidance provisions such as the connected company charge pursuant to FA 2003, ss.53 and 54 which include transfers of land into and out of the settlement, with very limited exemptions applying to dealings with or by trustees. These charges may apply upon the transfer or leasing of property into a trust, dealings in equitable interests and transfers of property out of the settlement.[38]

10.8   RESULTING AND OTHER SIMILAR TRUSTS

Constructive trusts creating equitable interests which may arise and may in certain cases create a 'valid contract'[39] notwithstanding the absence of writing in any form are not the only problems. These raise the question as to whether 'informal arrangements' can operate to 'create' equitable interests or trusts in some form and whether the actions relied upon to create the constructive trust are chargeable consideration within the extended definition. Other forms of trust can arise because of the lack of formality or because of the special circumstances of the case when equitable presumptions can apply. Certain of these have been referred to above in relation to the rules of 'accidental vesting' where trusts can arise because an imperfect gift becomes effective if the legal title to the relevant property vests in the

---

[37]   *Henniker* v. *Henniker* (1852) 1 E&B 54.

[38]   Moreover where, as is probable, the estate of the deceased or the trust fund includes or may receive interests in shares and loan stock of companies, questions of the much wider liability to the directly enforceable stamp duty reserve tax can arise (see FA 1986, s.87 and following), it having been from time to time the view of HMRC Stamp Taxes that the definition of 'chargeable securities' contained in FA 1986, s.99 (as amended) is probably sufficiently wide to encompass interests in shares and other securities held as part of a trust fund; however it appears that at present this view which would in many cases be incorrect is not taken.

[39]   *Yaxley* v. *Gotts* [1999] 3 WLR 1217.

persons who would have been the trustees of the gift. There is a retrospective equitable intervention with numerous problems as to when the charge to tax and the notification obligations arose and whether there was chargeable consideration because of the 'reliance' upon the imperfect gift that makes it 'perfect'.[40] These other forms of equitable intervention are important in determining what interests are 'acquired' by any person as part of the arrangement and whether there are creations of other interests which may either change the nature of the transaction from a 'imperfect gift' into a land exchange with additional charges and notification obligations or leave property in an inappropriate place which requires further steps to resolve the situation and bring about the result that the parties intended.[41] These principles are important for determining what interests have been created and whether there is consideration or the value of the interest in question where market value principles are the basis of the charge.

There are situations where there may be some form of 'resulting trust' imposed upon the person who is subjected to equitable obligations by reason of informal arrangements. Moreover, there will be some fundamental technical issues of principle depending upon the nature of the implied trust and the circumstances giving rise to the trust. For example, certain 'resulting trusts' arise because the person concerned has failed to make an effective disposition of the entire equitable interest in the property.[42] This raises certain issues as to whether the entire equitable interest leaves upon the effective date and the balance reverts to the transferor or only the relevant part of the equitable interest passes and the balance remains. In the latter case there is only one possible chargeable transaction. In the former case there are two chargeable transactions, namely there are reciprocal movements of the equitable interest; this being so, the question arises whether they are 'consideration' for each other so that a land exchange arises pursuant to FA 2003, s.47. It will become an important issue of principle about whether the attempt to transfer a partial interest in property is a transfer of a limited interest with a reservation (i.e. a single transaction) or an outright transfer of the whole with a re-transfer of a limited interest back (i.e. a land exchange with two chargeable transactions). Much may turn upon the structuring of the arrangement and whether in law it is possible to reserve or except the interest in question or a regrant is required. To some extent it may be possible to overcome these difficulties by utilising nominees whose

---

[40] See *Henry* v. *Henry* [2010] 1 All ER 988; *UK Housing Alliance* v. *Francis* [2010] 3 All ER 519.

[41] See, for example, *Vandervell* v. *IRC* [1967] 1 All ER 1; but note the possibility that the principles developing from *Re Hastings Bass* [1974] STC 211 and cases upon rectification such as *Re Slocock's Will Trusts* [1979] 1 All ER 358 and *Re Butlin's Settlement* [1976] 2 All ER 483 may apply to cancel or modify the transaction producing a different SDLT result. These principles are particularly important since they may be limited to situations where there is a trust or possibly fiduciary or equitable relationship between the parties with the consequence that equitable duties owed to another person may impose restrictions upon the decision-making power of the relevant party and therefore because the party acted outside the scope of the powers delegated to him his decision is invalid in some way.

[42] *Vandervell* v. *IRC* [1967] 1 All ER 1.

existence is generally ignored for the purposes of SDLT;[43] but increasing anti-avoidance legislation is restricting the scope for such simple mitigation of a possibly unnecessary charge which only arises by reason of the lack of flexibility in general property law.[44] It is considered that, in general, such a resulting trust does not give rise to a chargeable transaction. However, in some situations there will be a potentially chargeable transaction such as where equitable interests are acquired because of contributions to the acquisition and maintenance of the property or where a person has acted upon the oral promises of the other party when there may be an actual increment from the promisor or other person who becomes a trustee as in *Yaxley* v. *Gotts*.[45] There is the technical question as to whether a resulting trust involves merely the reservation of the limited interest or whether, as is likely to be the view of HMRC Stamp Taxes, there is the disposal of the whole interest and a transfer back of the balance of the interest because this has not been disposed of correctly in accordance with the legislative provisions such as Law of Property Act 1925, s.53(1)(c).[46] There are, as indicated elsewhere, problems about 'excepting and reserving' and whether this involves an outright transfer plus the grant of rights back with a land exchange[47] or is simply a restriction upon the interest passing. There may be difficulties because the labelling of the concept as 'resulting trust' suggests that there must be something that goes and something that 'results' or passes back to the person as opposed to something that is excluded from the transaction initially, i.e. 'retained trust interest'. This may raise questions as to whether there is a land exchange and, therefore, two transactions for chargeable consideration which will fundamentally change the whole SDLT profile of the arrangement.

However, such cases may differ from those where there is some form of implied trust or resulting trust in a particular form. There may be a difference between those cases where the property is transferred upon the basis that certain interests will 'belong' to the transferor[48] and those where property is acquired but put in the name of a nominee or other person. In certain of those cases the trust may be 'implied' because, for example, the property is assumed to belong to the person providing the consideration or there may be minors involved. Alternatively there may be no trust because there may be presumptions of an intention to advance the entire interests of

---

[43]   FA 2003, Sched.16, para.3.

[44]   But also the comments of Megarry J in *Sargaison* v. *Roberts* [1969] 3 All ER 1072 that the limitations and requirements of property law should not produce unintended tax consequences.

[45]   [1999] 3 WLR 1217.

[46]   Although strictly it would seem that this provision applies only to interests in land but the definition of 'equitable interest' contained in s.205(1)(x) thereof has been overlooked by counsel who argued the key cases upon this provision. It is probably too late to argue that the errors of counsel and the lack of knowledge of the judiciary can be used as a basis for ignoring decisions of the House of Lords although in *Neville* v. *Wilson* [1997] Ch 144 the Court of Appeal dealing with the matter as a conveyancing issue effectively overruled the decision of the House of Lords in *Oughtred* v. *IRC* [1960] AC 206 which was concerned with stamp taxes and therefore involved a judiciary unlikely to be sympathetic to the taxpayer.

[47]   FA 2003, s.47.

[48]   *Re Park* [1970] 1 All ER 611.

the person to whom the legal title is transferred. In this situation the court is simply declaring where the beneficial interest in the property lies, not whether it has moved and returned in whole or in part. The analysis of the interest is, therefore, a key factor in determining whether there is a chargeable consideration or a movement of an equitable interest in the form of a transfer and a regrant. The nature of the tax is, therefore, that many professional advisers will have to return to their student textbooks in order to produce a decent technical analysis of the transaction which their clients have entered into and hope that this will produce a reasonable SDLT result without excessive interest and penalty issues.

10.9 TRUSTS, FORMALITIES AND TRANSACTION TAX

The formalities for the creation of a trust of land do not affect the creation or operation of resulting, implied or constructive trusts.[49] By their very nature such trusts arise without the formality of documentation recording their existence, but as they invariably attach themselves silently, the transaction itself will bear any tax payable. The difficulty of such trusts arising by operation of law rather than by specific action of the parties, although it may be the actions of the parties that enable the law to create such trusts, is identifying the effective date, i.e. the date at which the tax charge and the notification obligations arise. As there is likely to be an oral arrangement it may be difficult for HMRC Stamp Taxes to establish that there is an effective binding contract between the parties that provides for completion by a conveyance so that the effective date will be 'completion' whatever that may mean in the current context since FA 2003, s.117 is silent on the subject.

Many such implied trusts are really remedies imposed by equity to counteract improper conduct such as breaches of trust and fiduciary duties. Such remedial arrangements are usually intended to prevent the equitable interest from passing from the original owner so that any transferee acquires only the legal title in a fiduciary capacity. Consequently, such arrangements are unlikely to involve chargeable acquisitions.

10.10 TRUSTS: GENERAL

The draftsman's view of equitable interests behind trusts and similar arrangements as chargeable interests and the extension of chargeable consideration mean that there has been a significant increase in transactions where trusts and estates are involved which are subject to the full impact of SDLT as compared with the former stamp duty regime.

---

[49] Law of Property Act 1925, s.53(2).

10.10.1 Terminology: classification of trusts

Two types of trust situation exist in the SDLT provisions,[50] namely:

- a bare trust; and
- a settlement.

These are usually created expressly; but implied, resulting and constructive trusts are nevertheless indirectly important both for their direct and indirect effect because they may result in the acquisition of a chargeable interest and they may affect the identity of the vendor and/or the purchaser. Such trusts which can arise notwithstanding the absence of writing[51] may mean that a totally oral transaction can be effective even though the conditions of LP(MP)A 1989, s.2 are not satisfied because, according to Walker LJ, the equitable treatment of the transaction overrides the statutory requirements for writing.[52] They are also important for compliance reasons in identifying the purchaser or the vendor for the purposes of paying the tax and completing the land transaction return (SDLT 1 and 2) since the legal title and land register are no longer conclusive for these purposes. The existence of fiduciary obligations such as in the case of agents who are affected by the implied trust rule may affect who can sign the return.[53] The relevance of the legal title and registration is much diminished and the significance of beneficial ownership is much increased. Accurate analysis of the legal relationship between the various interested parties and the land is now fundamental to the compliance regime if taxpayers and their advisers are to avoid penalties for incorrect returns and assisting in the preparation thereof. Whilst professional advisers may be liable only for 'knowing' assistance, pleas of ignorance of the underlying law as meaning there is no 'knowledge' of the incorrect facts in the return may be less convincing and certainly embarrassing.[54]

10.10.2 Settlement or bare trust

The distinction between a bare trust or nominee situation[55] and a settlement is important since in the case of a bare trust except where new leases are involved the existence of the trust is ignored and all transactions in relation to the land are treated as having been performed by the beneficial owner.[56] In consequence, transactions

---

[50] Statutory trusts such as those arising upon joint ownership do not have their own separate category or regime, although there are certain compliance issues (see, for example, FA 2003, s.103). There may also be questions whether such joint ownership creates a partnership, see **Chapter 12**.

[51] LPA 1925, s.53(2); see *Neville* v. *Wilson* [1997] Ch 144 criticising *Oughtred* v. *IRC* [1960] AC 206 and effectively reversing it on the relationship between LPA 1925, s.53(1)(c) and (2).

[52] *Yaxley* v. *Gotts* [1999] 3 WLR 1217; *UK Housing Alliance* v. *Francis* [2010] 3 All ER 519; *RTS Flexible Systems Ltd* v. *Molkerei Alois* [2010] 3 All ER 1.

[53] See FA 2003, s.106.

[54] FA 2003, ss.95 and 96.

[55] Which may be important in deciding whether there should be two nominees in order to give a valid receipt pursuant to LPA 1925, s.27.

[56] FA 2003, Sched.16, para.3(1).

involving nominees such as a change of nominee[57] will not normally incur any liability to SDLT but, contrary to this general principle, an increasing number of such situations are attracting tax consequences. Where there is the grant of a lease to a nominee this is now fully taxable;[58] however, such transactions are not without consequences. A lease granted between July 2004 and March 2005 to a nominee may not attract a charge to SDLT, but any subsequent assignment of the lease is treated as the grant of a new lease by the assignor[59] which will include the beneficial owner of the lease.

On the other hand, the 'purchaser' is the beneficial owner who, subject to limited exceptions, is the only person who can sign the declaration on the land transaction return or self-certificate (see **Chapter 17**). There can no longer be any secrecy such as a person acting as agent for an undisclosed principal. The signing of the return by the agent will be invalid and a return will not have been filed on time. This will, of course, frequently produce situations where there is a divergence between the persons identified as vendors and purchasers and signing the land transaction return and included in the SDLT 5 certificate and those on the Land Registry documentation. For example, where parents combine with a child to purchase property jointly and beneficially but the property is to be registered solely in the name of the child, the SDLT 1 and SDLT 5, to be correct, should refer to the three parties, but the Land Registry transfer will be in the child's name.[60] The Land Registry now recognises these and other problems where there is a potential mismatch between the SDLT documentation and the Land Registry requirement. It is possible, but not guaranteed, that the Land Registry will accept without challenge documentation presented upon the basis that there can be no Revenue certificate (SDLT 5) and is prepared to act on the basis of an explanatory letter. Similar problems will apply to partners and others and may affect even vendors where the property is held by a nominee or pursuant to an uncompleted sale contract, such as a subsale arrangement. These principles mean that it is no longer permissible to rely solely upon the land register or the parties to the contract who may be acting in an undisclosed fiduciary capacity.

These look-through rules which affect liability to pay and the compliance obligations mean that it is, therefore, necessary to be able to recognise which situation is relevant.

---

[57] The position of nominees and the connected company charge (FA 2003, s.53) has not been expressly dealt with but as there is no transaction it seems that the connected company charge does not apply. The Government indicated that as only the legal title passed there was no significant market value for the purposes of the tax so that no charge arises. Unfortunately, the official view means that an SDLT 1 is required because there is chargeable consideration.

[58] FA 2003, Sched.16, para.3(3).

[59] FA 2003, Sched.17A, para.11 (as amended).

[60] Key areas for investigation for first time buyer relief: FA 2003, s.57AA.

10.11   BARE TRUSTS

A bare trust is a trust under which property is held by a person as trustee,[61] either:

- for a person who is absolutely entitled as against the trustee;[62] or
- for two or more persons who are or would be jointly[63] so entitled.[64]

10.11.1   Person absolutely entitled as against the trustee

A person is treated as absolutely entitled to property as against the trustees if he has the exclusive right, subject only to satisfying any outstanding charge, lien or other right of the trustee to resort to the property for payment of duty, taxes, costs or other outgoings or to direct how the property is to be dealt with[65] or who would be so entitled but for being a minor or other person under a disability. The distinction turns upon whether the beneficial interest is held absolutely without successive interests and, in particular, whether the holder of the legal title has any powers or discretions of his own or subject to the statutory definition and questions of disability[66] is totally controlled by the beneficial owner.[67] General law would indicate that a nominee is a person who merely holds the legal title for some person absolutely and has no power or discretion but must act under the direction of the absolute beneficial owner. Successive, as opposed to joint, interests such as to A for life and then to B absolutely will be a 'settlement' and not a bare trust notwithstanding that both A and B are of full age and capacity and between them absolutely entitled to the property[68] and the nature of the property held by the trustees may preclude persons from becoming absolutely entitled.[69] The ability of the owner of the legal title to take decisions on his own initiative would point towards a 'trust'.

---

[61]   It is important for trustees and personal representatives to note that their status may change where interests change such as where a person becomes absolutely entitled on the death of the life tenant or a power of appointment or advancement is exercised but the legal title is not immediately transferred. Appropriation by executors may have similar consequences.

[62]   This is the same terminology as that for capital gains tax. Presumably the cases in that area such as *Crowe* v. *Appleby* [1975] STC 502 will be useful aides in applying this legislation to SDLT.

[63]   FA 2003, s.121.

[64]   FA 2003, Sched.16, para.1(2).

[65]   FA 2003, Sched.16, para.1(3).

[66]   In some situations a vendor may be acting as a nominee for the purchaser; but the existence of unpaid vendors' liens may affect the passing of full equitable interests and may produce the bare trust arising; see, for example, *Musselwhite* v. *Musselwhite* [1962] Ch 964; *Langen and Wind Ltd* v. *Bell* [1972] Ch 685; *Michaels* v. *Harley House (Marylebone) Ltd* [2000] Ch 104; *Walsh* v. *Lonsdale* (1882) LR 21 Ch D 9; *Re Kidner* [1929] 2 Ch 121.

[67]   See e.g. *Brown* v. *Cork* [1985] BCLC 363; *Cowan de Groot Properties Ltd* v. *Eagle Trust Plc* [1991] BCLC 1045.

[68]   *Saunders* v. *Vautier* (1841) 4 Beav 115.

[69]   *Lloyds Bank* v. *Duker* [1987] 3 All ER 193.

10.11.2　Two or more persons who are or would be jointly entitled

This will apply to many domestic or family transactions such as purchase by husband and wife or partners where statutory trusts may apply;[70] but joint ownership of a concurrent nature may mean that the individual beneficial owners are eligible for a minority discount from the proportionate share of the market value of the entire property.[71]

10.12　TRUSTS AND SDLT

SDLT (and where shares and other notifiable securities and interests in certain partnerships are involved stamp duty reserve tax or stamp duty) arises in relation to trusts upon:

- the establishment of the trust;
- the initial vesting of property;
- the appointment and retirement of trustees;
- vesting assets in the trustees;
- changes of investments by trustees;
- dealings in equitable interests in the trust; and
- distribution by trustees to beneficiaries including exercises of powers of appointment and revocation.

10.13　SETTING UP A TRUST

The mere declaration of an express trust or a deed of nomineeship will not, of itself, be a chargeable transaction for the purposes of SDLT.[72] It may set out the terms upon which the parties intend to hold the property but it does not, of itself, necessarily transfer interests in property. However, as indicated above, where the trust is not an express trust but some form of equitable principle or relief such as a constructive or resulting trust the trust taking effect may itself be an event that is related to the passing of property. The implied trust or proprietary estoppel may operate as some form of contract for value notwithstanding the absence of writing.[73] The creation of the trust and the property movements are essentially the same event

---

[70]　Trusts of Land and Appointment of Trustees Act 1996.

[71]　*Re Wight* [1982] 2 EGLR 236.

[72]　But note that the choice of trustee is important for SDLT. Trustees may be connected companies (FA 2003, ss.53 and 54). Trustees are not 'individuals' but bodies of persons: *Jasmine Trustees* v. *Wells & Hind* [2007] STC 660 (but see the special definitions in FA 2003, Sched.15, Part 3).

[73]　*Yaxley* v. *Gotts* [1999] 3 WLR 1217.

and are therefore potentially chargeable transactions with notification and payment obligations; but legislative provisions such as LPA 1925, s.53, may prevent full title vesting.[74]

10.14 PROPERTY INTO TRUST

Property may become part of the trust assets in various ways:

- the trustees may purchase the property; or
- the settlor may transfer the property into the trust, usually but not invariably by way of gift;[75] or
- there may be an appointment by the trustees of one settlement into a new trust or a subtrust.[76]

However, the exemption for gifts is subject to the connected company charge[77] and certain dealings involving partnerships and connected persons.[78] Trustees are connected with the settlor and, it seems, with other trustees so that the appointment and changes of trustees as well as vesting property in a corporate trustee upon the initial creation of the settlement may be within the charge. The Government has accepted that a transfer (but not the granting of new leases)[79] to a bare trustee does not attract a significant charge to SDLT[80] because the legal title itself is of negligible value. It remains to be seen whether it will accept that the connected company charge has no application upon the wider basic principle that there is no change of beneficial ownership such as occurs on the change of trustees; it is expected that this view will be adopted in practice.

10.15 'SUBGIFTS'

As indicated above, the 'gift' to the trustees may be subject to SDLT as it may complete more than one transaction. A classic illustration would be where the settlor has agreed to purchase the property and directs the vendor to transfer the property directly to the trustees. Such a purchase and 'subgift' may escape SDLT as a 'subsale' since the second limb (i.e. the gift to the trustees) is not a sale for the market value of the property.[81] The effect of FA 2003, s.45 is that if the two

---

[74] *Vandervell* v. *IRC* [1967] 1 All ER 1.
[75] Undertakings to pay any inheritance or capital gains tax arising may not be chargeable consideration: FA 2003, Sched.4, paras.16A and 16B.
[76] See e.g. *Pilkington Brothers Ltd* v. *IRC* [1982] STC 103.
[77] FA 2003, s.53.
[78] FA 2003, Sched.15, para.25 (as amended).
[79] FA 2003, Sched.16, para.3 (as amended).
[80] Pursuant to FA 2003, s.53.
[81] There is, however, a technical argument on the legislation that in order to obtain subsale relief, the 'subsale' arrangement must be for consideration. The view of HMRC Stamp Taxes on this point

transactions are substantially performed or completed at the same time, the original purchaser escapes liability notwithstanding that he pays the contract price in full, and possibly receives a transfer. This is upon the basis that the contract between A and B and the arrangements between B and the trustees are completed at the same time but the relieving provisions in s.45 refer to the second contract. It may be that HMRC Stamp Taxes will attempt to establish that this requires the second movement of the property to be for a consideration so as to constitute a contract. The effect of this would be that subsale relief would not be available in the case of a purchaser and subgift. However, subject to this potential argument by HMRC Stamp Taxes it would appear possible to vest the property in the trustees free of tax provided that the trustees are not within the connected company charge.

10.16 PURCHASE OF LAND

Where trustees of a settlement purchase land they are deemed to be purchasers of the whole of the interest acquired, including the beneficial interest and are taxable upon general principles save that the return or self-certificate may, it seems, be given by one or more of the trustees.[82]

10.17 INITIAL VESTING OF TRUST ASSETS

Different considerations arise where it is intended that the nominated trustees shall take over the control and management of the property to give effect to the trust. In these circumstances, notwithstanding the presence of the three certainties, the trust will be imperfectly constituted until such time as the property is properly vested in the trustees by the manner appropriate to the nature of the property and this may be relevant for determining the effective date of the transaction. Until this happens and the property is in their hands, the trustees are trustees of nothing.[83]

---

is not known, but, although a weak argument, there is a significant risk that it may make it. Payment of a few pounds may be prudent protection in this situation.

[82]   FA 2003, Sched.16, paras.5 and 6; SDLT 6.

[83]   *Richards* v. *Delbridge* (1874) LR 18 Eq 11. Cash and goods can be transferred by delivery, but land must be conveyed or assigned by deed, shares by a stock transfer form or directives through CREST where the default liability to the principal charge to stamp duty reserve tax will apply unless appropriate steps are taken to enable the utilisation of those transaction indicators or 'flags' which indicate that the transaction is for one of the relevant reasons not liable to stamp duty reserve tax and for the obtaining of a stamp duty relief at fixed rate of £5 which cancels the charge to stamp duty reserve tax. But note the nil rate for share transactions where the consideration for the transaction does not exceed £1,000 and an appropriate certificate of value is included in the transfer document. Solicitors should note that stamp duty reserve tax is directly enforceable and it is required under penalty that appropriate records are maintained so that upon audit by HMRC the parties can substantiate their utilisation of the particular flag and reporting the tax.

It would seem from the definition of 'conveyance' for certain purposes in relation to the effective date[84] that it is intended that any written instrument which creates the trust (or which is treated as creating it) could be treated as a 'conveyance', possibly triggering the payment and notification obligations, if any, but these are likely to be rare circumstances because of the exclusions for gifts or other transactions where there is no chargeable consideration[85] and such transactions are usually relieved from the need to notify.[86]

A written assent by personal representatives in favour of themselves as trustees of the will is required in order to prove that they have ceased to act as personal representatives and are acting as trustees of the land,[87] but there is unlikely to be chargeable consideration unless it is a part of a larger transaction.[88]

If, on the other hand, the settlor first conveys the property to trustees on trusts yet to be declared, no beneficial interest passes as there is an immediate resulting trust back to the settlor.[89] The conveyance or transfer will not give rise to a tax charge because there is no change of beneficial ownership and the legal title is held on a bare trust,[90] unless it involves a lease to a nominee.[91] In such a situation subsequent attempts to create an effective trust are likely to be required to be in writing in order to comply with LPA 1925, s.53(1)(c). The trust instrument, when executed, will have the effect of shifting the beneficial interest away from the settlor and into the hands of the beneficiaries, and thus bear the full charge to SDLT but only if for a chargeable or deemed consideration.[92]

10.18 DISPOSITIONS OF TRUST PROPERTY: DEALINGS IN EQUITABLE INTERESTS

The area of dealings in equitable interests and lack of formality may be important since LPA 1925, s.53(1)(c) requires most dealings to be in writing and, *prima facie*, in the absence of writing there is no transaction. For example, if instead of transferring the beneficial interest direct to the intended donee, the donor orally instructs his trustees to hold the donor's beneficial interest for the donee in lieu of the donor, this is in substance also a disposition of the equitable interest, since it is an

---

[84] FA 2003, s.119.
[85] But note transfers subject to mortgage (FA 2003, Sched.4, para.8) and to connected companies (FA 2003, ss.53 and 54).
[86] FA 2003, s.77A; but see **17.7**.
[87] Administration of Estates Act 1925, s.36(4) and (7); *Re King's Will Trusts* [1964] Ch 542; *Re Hodge* [1940] Ch 260; but not it seems if they purport to sell as personal representatives (*Re Ponder* [1921] 2 Ch 59).
[88] Consideration, however, is not unknown in the shape of a financial inducement to persuade the tenant in tail in remainder to bar the entail, and resettle on further trusts.
[89] See *Vandervell v. IRC* [1967] 1 All ER 1.
[90] FA 2003, Sched.16, para.3.
[91] See FA 2003, Sched.16, para.3(3) (as amended); but see *Ingram v. IRC* [1999] STC 37.
[92] FA 2003, Sched.3, para.1.

equitable assignment[93] and the direction to the trustees must be in writing if it is to be effective.[94] If as a result of the interaction of such legislation there is no effective transaction there is no charge to tax.

Since 'acquisition' includes not merely assignments but also the creation of interests as well as releases and surrenders, but not disclaimers, many dealings in interests in trusts will be subject to SDLT if done for consideration.[95] For example, an assignment by a life tenant of all or part of his interest will require the purchaser of that interest to pay SDLT and make a return. Similarly, the release of a life interest or the appointment or advancement of capital or including new beneficiaries[96] if done for consideration will be chargeable as will be a surrender of an interest if done for consideration.

A somewhat more frequent occurrence will be an arrangement whereby one party releases or assigns his interest in favour of the other party for some consideration probably consisting of other property held within the trust. This will be a straightforward transfer of an interest in land in consideration of the interest in the other property being received. It will be taxable upon the open market value of the property or interest therein received where there is a land exchange or upon the value of the other property received as consideration in kind.

10.19 APPOINTMENT AND RETIREMENT OF TRUSTEES

There is no specific provision dealing with appointments and retirement of trustees, but normally such transactions will not be for consideration and so not subject to tax pursuant to FA 2003, Sched.3, para.1. It may be that land held by the trustee is subject to a charge or mortgage and so the change of trustee involving a transfer or a vesting order[97] would appear to be vulnerable to a claim pursuant to FA 2003, Sched.4, para.8, but since this charge requires the assumption of a personal liability by the trustee which may not be forthcoming and there is no fundamental change of the ownership of the property[98] it seems that HMRC Stamp Taxes will not normally seek tax.[99] However, it seems that HMRC Stamp Taxes intends to impose a charge when the change of trustee is in connection with the transfer of the property between specific trusts or where there is no change of trustee but some form of appropriation

---

[93] See *Re Tyler* [1967] 3 All ER 389; *Letts* v. *IRC* [1957] 1 WLR 201.

[94] *Grey* v. *IRC* [1960] AC 1; *Oughtred* v. *IRC* [1960] AC 206 but note *Neville* v. *Wilson* [1997] Ch 144 and see *Yaxley* v. *Gotts* [1999] 3 WLR 1217; *Henry* v. *Henry* [2010] 1 All ER 988.

[95] Assuming that such exercises are not tainted as frauds on the power.

[96] Note *Pilkington Brothers Ltd* v. *IRC* [1982] STC 103.

[97] Pursuant to Trustee Act 1925, s.40 which is a potentially taxable event because it is either by court order or by operation of law: FA 2003, s.43.

[98] The attitude of HMRC Stamp Taxes may differ where the transfer is to a new subtrust or other settlement arising pursuant to an advancement (*Pilkington Brothers Ltd* v. *IRC* [1982] STC 103).

[99] But note the potential charge if the rights or liabilities of the parties to the mortgage are changed in connection with the transfer: FA 2003, Sched.4, para.8 (as amended).

and apportionment to themselves as trustee of a separate settlement,[100] and the
liability to repay the mortgage changes.

Should the connected company charge be applied by HMRC Stamp Taxes to
changes of trustees the exclusions contained in s.54 will apply. Transfers to
corporate trustees carrying on the business of managing trusts or which are
otherwise unconnected with the settlor apart from the settlor–trustee relationship
will be exempt. For the time being, however, appointments or changes of trustees
where the trustees are family companies[101] will be vulnerable to attack and should
be avoided until some guidance of the official view has been provided from practice.
This will be a particular problem where there is an advancement or appointment
into a new trust with corporate trustees, notwithstanding the exemption since
HMRC Stamp Taxes will almost certainly seek to apply the connected company
charge even though it is essentially merely a change of trust interests. The reallocation of assets with consent is *prima facie* a chargeable transaction, otherwise the
specific relief for such transactions would not be necessary.[102]

10.20 INTERESTS OF BENEFICIARIES

A trust arises whenever one person holds property subject to an obligation, enforceable by equity, to use the property in whole or in part for another; and, as indicated
above (see e.g. **10.8**), equity may create such relationships in a variety of
circumstances. The classic example is where the legal estate or interest in, say, land
or shares is vested in the trustee or trustees with a direction to hold upon stated trusts
for the beneficiaries. It has long since been recognised that the rights of the
beneficiaries, though originally *in personam* only against the trustees, have
acquired the status of interests in property enforceable historically against the
whole world, save for the time-honoured bona fide purchaser for value of the legal
estate without notice, actual or constructive, of a prior equitable interest in the
property, or those deriving title through such a person.[103] Nevertheless, pending
overreaching, the equitable rights arising out of the trust remain firmly interests in
property, as illustrated with a vengeance by the House of Lords in its decision in
Williams & Glyn's Bank Ltd v. Boland.[104] This aspect of the decision is reinforced
by LP(MP)A 1989, ss.1(6) and 2(6), both of which defined an interest in land for the
purposes of the sections as 'any ... interest ... in or over land or in or over the
proceeds of sale of land'. It was apparently thought necessary to make the extension
of the basic definition.

Although these provisions have not been expressly included in FA 2003 this view
has been adopted and extended by the draftsman of the SDLT legislation. By

---

[100] Note FA 2003, Sched.16, para.8.
[101] And so are likely to be 'connected companies'.
[102] FA 2003, Sched.16, para.8.
[103] See also LPA 1925, s.2; but note that there may need to be at least two trustees: ibid., s.27.
[104] [1981] AC 487.

necessary implication from other provisions it is clearly his view that beneficiaries interested in trusts governed by English law have interests in land, i.e. their interests are chargeable interests and this would apply to trusts which hold a mixture of investments such as shares and land, and the interests of the beneficiaries may change or vary in size as investments are sold and purchased.

Unfortunately, most trust funds are not simply land but consist of a wide mixture of investments.[105] This means that the interests involved in the variation will involve interests in land and other property. There will, in consequence, be a completely mixed arrangement involving mutual transfers or acquisitions of a mixed fund only part of which is land. Unless the transaction is carefully structured, there will not be a straightforward exchange of minor interests in land with tax only upon the equality adjustment; there is a significant risk that HMRC Stamp Taxes will take the view that each individual interest in land is being separately transferred for consideration in kind, with the relevant proportion of the consideration provided being allocated between the land and other assets pro rata. It will be difficult to persuade HMRC Stamp Taxes to isolate the two land interests into two separate transactions for mixed considerations not a 'land exchange' treatment; each equal interest is transferred for mixed consideration of the other interest not a simple land-for-land exchange with an adjustment for equality. The beneficiaries may both be faced with arguments for tax because there is not a simple land exchange of minor interests with equality. This may mean a double charge upon the apportioned consideration and not a single charge upon the equality adjustment, if any.[106] It may be necessary to fragment the transaction so that one equitable interest consists solely of minor interests in land 'exchanged' for the other minor interests in land and a balancing interest of other assets.

10.21 FOREIGN TRUSTS

In consequence, equitable interests in trusts including foreign trusts[107] where the trust fund includes land in the UK are regarded as chargeable interests. This emerges impliedly from the rules dealing with certain types of trust. Although foreign trusts may differ from English trusts in the sense that the beneficiaries may not have some form of equitable interest in the underlying property, i.e. a proprietary interest that may entitle them to trace the property to a certain extent but have merely a personal right against the trustees to compel proper administration of the trust and to sue for breach but without any rights of a proprietary nature in relation to

---

[105] Which is, of course, an argument that the equitable interest is a separate chose in action and not a bundle of interests in the individual trust assets which is the view of the draftsman.

[106] See FA 2003, s.47, Sched.4, paras.5 and 6.

[107] The legislation specifically creates such a direct interest for such trusts and overrides issues such as *Baker* v. *Archer Shee* 15 TC 1; and *Archer Shee* v. *Garland* 15 TC 693; see FA 2003, Sched.16, para.2.

the underlying property,[108] the fact that the foreign law merely gives an *in personam* right is overridden by legislation.[109] Therefore, interests in foreign trusts are treated as though the trust was governed by English law,[110] i.e. if the English law would give the beneficiary in a similar English law trust some form of proprietary interest in the underlying property then notwithstanding the trust is governed by foreign law and administered by trustees outside the UK, the interest of the beneficiary, who may be non-resident, is a chargeable interest and dealings in that interest for consideration will be subject to SDLT.[111]

As a consequence of this, variations of foreign trusts involving disposals of a beneficial interest where the trust assets include land in the UK held directly will involve potentially chargeable transactions (see **2.12**) if done for consideration notwithstanding that the trust assets are held by non-resident trustees under a trust created by a non-resident settlor and all of the relevant beneficiaries are resident offshore holding under a trust governed by foreign law which does not give them a proprietary interest in the land.[112] In such situations it would seem prudent for the trustees to hold any chargeable interests in UK land through an offshore company the shares in which may be dealt with free of stamp duty, if this does not lead to adverse tax consequences in other areas.[113]

---

[108] See Archer Shee v. Garland 15 TC 693; Baker v. Archer Shee 15 TC 1.

[109] FA 2003, Sched.16, para.2.

[110] Scots law may differ but they have to apply English law notions no matter how inappropriate.

[111] The assumption of the draftsman that the tracing remedy of beneficiaries under English trusts is an interest in land in the general sense is questionable, but with the legislation having been prepared on the basis that it is a chargeable interest it will be difficult to persuade the current judiciary that the legislation was prepared on a false premise. The argument will be that by necessary implication for the purpose of SDLT the interest of the beneficiary is a chargeable interest. However, the question then arises as to whether the interest of the beneficiary is a 'major interest' since it is neither a leasehold nor a freehold interest in equity but is a limited interest. This will be important in relation to the rules for calculating SDLT upon exchanges of interests and reporting obligations.

[112] An interest in a trust fund is a chose in action, enforceable only by court action against the trustees at the instance of a beneficiary. A purchaser or an assignee of a chose in action must remember to protect his interest by giving notice to the person obliged to distribute the property. There may, of course, be questions whether such notices are in substance equitable assignments (see e.g. *Brandt's (Wm)* v. *Dunlop Rubber Co* [1905] AC 454). It is thought that in order to be an equitable assignment the notice would require to be signed by at least the transferor or vendor. In the case of a legal chose in action, express written notice must be given to the debtor, trustee or other person from whom the assignor would have been entitled to claim the debt or chose in action. An equitable interest in a trust fund should be protected in exactly the same way under the rule in *Dearle* v. *Hall* (1828) 3 Russ 1. Since 1925 the notice to the trustees must be in writing (LPA 1925, s.137) and to give maximum protection should be served on all the trustees (*Re Wasdale* [1899] 1 Ch 163). Failure to serve notice may cause the donee to lose priority in the event of a subsequent dealing with the same interest. However, SDLT is not affected by issues of priority or the potential loss of the interest purchased. Tax will be payable by reference to substantial performance or completion in the sense of the delivery of the assignment notwithstanding that full title does not pass because the requisite notice has not been given. There will be no right to reclaim the tax if the transaction proves to be valueless through loss of priority because this is not the annulment or rescission of the contract within FA 2003, s.44(9).

[113] But note FA 2003, Sched.4, paras.16A and 16B.

10.22 DISCRETIONARY TRUSTS

Beneficiaries of discretionary and similar trusts do not have interests in the underlying property.[114] There are merely personal rights against the trustees for proper administration. In consequence, in general, dealings in such interests are not dealings in chargeable interests even if done for consideration and this is not universally changed by the legislation. In consequence interests in foreign trusts of a similar nature[115] will not involve the ownership of chargeable interests by the beneficiaries.

10.22.1 Anti-avoidance

It would appear, therefore, that the purchase of an interest in a discretionary trust is not as such taxable. However, it is specifically provided[116] that where a chargeable interest is acquired pursuant to the exercise of a discretion or power of appointment vested in the trustees of a settlement, the acquisition is treated as being made for a sum equal to any consideration that was given by the person in whose favour the appointment or discretion was exercised before becoming an object of the power or discretion. Therefore, if a person pays a sum of money whether to the trustees or to the settlor or to any other party in order to be included within the class of discretionary beneficiaries or appointees, that money will rank as chargeable consideration in respect of any land transferred out of the trust.[117] This charge is, however, not limited to discretionary trusts but appears to be intended to apply to situations where rather than purchasing an equitable interest in a fixed interest trust, which is potentially taxable, the money is paid to be included within the class of persons to whom an appointment can be made which, apart from this provision, would not appear to be taxable.

10.23 CREATION OF DERIVATIVE TRUSTS

As an alternative to disposing of his equitable interest outright (see **10.11**) which is the acquisition of a chargeable interest (see **10.18**) or persuading the trustees to exercise their powers to appoint or advance trust assets upon trust for other beneficiaries within their power, the assignor may care to create a derivative or subtrust, leaving himself as a buffer between the head trustees and the ultimate beneficiary who may not be a person within the prescribed class in the original headlease to whom the trustees may appoint or advance the property.[118] Thus if a

---

[114] *Gartside* v. *IRC* [1968] AC 553; *IRC* v. *Holmden* [1968] AC 685; but query the position, for example, where there is only one discretionary beneficiary and no power to accumulate the income.
[115] Compare *Baker* v. *Archer Shee* 15 TC 1; *Archer Shee* v. *Garland* 15 TC 693.
[116] FA 2003, Sched.16, para.7.
[117] Assuming that the exercise is not tainted as a fraud on a power or similar breach of trust.
[118] See *Pilkington Brothers Ltd* v. *IRC* [1982] STC 103.

beneficiary has, say, a life interest in property which he wishes to sell to another, instead of assigning the interest outright he can convey it to a new set of trustees to hold on the stated trusts, or continue to hold it himself as trustee, having moved the beneficial interest down one step by a declaration of trust. In either case the original trustees will remain owners of the legal estate and interest, and liable to account for the income to the new trustees of the life interest or the original life tenant, as the case may be. They or he in turn must pass the income down the line to the beneficiary. If trustees of the life interest are to be appointed, exactly the same principles as above apply in properly constituting the trust, but as the subject-matter of the conveyance to the trustees is a subsisting equitable interest, the conveyance must be in writing to satisfy LPA 1925, s.53(1)(c), or pass the equitable interest by constructive trust where this is permitted without writing.[119] This applies even though the property in the hands of the head trustees consists of property capable of transfer by delivery.

Where, however, the former beneficial life tenant chooses himself to remain trustee, he can make the declaration of trust orally, at least if the property out of which the trust has been created is personalty. If the trust is of land, unless a bare trust or a strict settlement governed by the Settled Land Act 1925 is involved, the legal estate will be held on trust for sale by the original trustees. As such but subject to any implications of the Trusts of Land and Appointment of Trustees Act 1996 the property is treated by equity as personalty by the application of the doctrine of conversion. Nevertheless, the safer view appears to be that the beneficial interests are still in land until sale actually takes place and certain definitions of 'land' include the proceeds of sale of land. Certainly the interest of a tenant in common in equity under a trust for sale was held in *Cooper* v. *Critchley*[120] to be an interest in land for the purpose of LPA 1925, s.40(1), before its repeal by LP(MP)A 1989, s.2, although these principles of 'part-performance' may have been resurrected in the guise of equitable principle by *Yaxley* v. *Gotts*.[121] LPA 1925, s.53(1)(b), governing the formation of trusts in land (which has not been repealed) is very similar in wording and purpose to the old s.40.

10.24 INTERNAL REARRANGEMENT OF BENEFICIAL INTERESTS

Frequently there will be consideration for the adjustment in the rights of beneficiaries since it will be part of a variation of the trust under which interests are exchanged such as where a life tenant and remainderman agree to combine their interests in order to partition the fund.[122] This arrangement will not qualify for the special

---

[119] See *Neville* v. *Wilson* [1997] Ch 144; 'overriding' (i.e. reversing on correct analysis) *Oughtred* v. *IRC* [1960] AC 206; *Escoigne Properties Ltd* v. *IRC* [1958] AC 549.
[120] [1955] Ch 431.
[121] [1999] 3 WLR 1217.
[122] There is a highly technical but ultimately less than convincing argument that certain arrangements converting a beneficial joint tenancy into a tenancy in common are land exchanges

treatment for partitions[123] since the interest will not be jointly owned, i.e. the parties are not joint tenants or tenants in common but hold interests in succession.[124] In such a situation the life tenant and remainderman will be 'exchanging' interests[125] in land so that charges to SDLT will arise.[126]

It should be remembered that a release of a beneficial interest under a trust will amount to a disposition if in writing and if its effect is to move or create a beneficial interest in favour of another and will constitute an 'acquisition' for the purposes of SDLT by the person benefiting from the transaction. Thus, if instead of a life tenant selling his interest to the remainderman, he purports for consideration to surrender or release it, the effect is the same: the reversion is accelerated and falls into possession immediately.[127] In the case of a gift, the desired result could be achieved by the trustees exercising their powers of advancement under powers conferred upon them by the trust instrument[128] or the Trustee Act 1925, s.32, with the requisite consent of the life tenant. The consent of the life tenant to the arrangement is not a release of an interest[129] but issues may arise where there are reallocations of the trust interests which are *prima facie* taxable unless within the exemption.[130] The statutory powers are limited to the advancement of one half only of the actual or presumptive entitlement of the reversioner, but in a properly drawn trust deed these powers can and should be enlarged. The exercise of a power of advancement may be a dutiable transaction when the power is exercised in favour of a connected company which can include a corporate trustee of a derivative settlement because of the connected company charge[131] or where the person benefiting has provided consideration in order to become an object of the power.[132] Where the alteration of the equitable interest is effected with the assistance of the court pursuant to the Variation of Trusts Act 1958 the court order[133] is potentially subject to SDLT if there is consideration provided for the variation. Acquisitions include transactions effected by a court order so that these variations can be chargeable transactions if the conditions are satisfied. Such arrangements are not normally transactions for

---

because the parties are acquiring rights to the property not affected by the *jus accrescendi*. This turns upon the technical interpretation of FA 2003, s.47. This will not be a 'partition' since the land is not physically divided. As these interests will usually exist in relation to freeholds and leaseholds the beneficial interests 'exchanged' will be 'major interests' with two market value charges (FA 2003, Sched.4, para.5). The issue is whether the arrangement is 'contractual'. In so far as the situation is dealt with by one party serving the appropriate notice (LPA 1925, s.36(2)), it is arguable that there is no contract; but a mutual agreement to bring about this result could be vulnerable to attack. At present, fortunately, HMRC Stamp Taxes has not shown any intention to take this point.

[123]   FA 2003, Sched.4, para.6.
[124]   FA 2003, s.121.
[125]   Compare *Oughtred* v. *IRC* [1960] AC 206.
[126]   FA 2003, s.47.
[127]   *Platts Trustees* v. *IRC* (1953) 34 ATC 292.
[128]   See *Pilkington Brothers Ltd* v. *IRC* [1982] STC 103.
[129]   Re Pauling's Settlement [1962] 1 WLR 86.
[130]   FA 2003, Sched.16, para.8; see **10.19**.
[131]   FA 2003, ss.53 and 54.
[132]   FA 2003, Sched.16, para.7.
[133]   FA 2003, s.43; *Terrapin International* v. *IRC* [1976] 1 WLR 665.

consideration[134] and so will not normally attract SDLT but this is not a universal principle and tax may arise in the particular circumstances where there is chargeable consideration.[135]

Instead of one party wishing to rearrange the beneficial interests so that an advantage is conferred on another, there may be a rearrangement of the interests under which neither party gains.[136] But if there is chargeable consideration moving between the parties the transaction may be caught as chargeable[137] and it seems that even a reallocation of the trust investments between the various beneficial interests is taxable, at least in those cases where the beneficiary consents to the reallocation. Fortunately, there is a specific albeit limited relief from this charge.[138]

The same problems arise where interests in land are involved in the exchange or variation. In such case the structure of the variation of the equitable interest is important because the transaction may be either land exchange or transfer of a chargeable interest for consideration in money's worth where the computational rules differ significantly. An illustration likely to be quite common in practice would be where land is held for A for life remainder to B and the beneficiaries agree to divide the land between themselves. Such an arrangement is not a partition because the interest is not held 'jointly',[139] i.e. concurrently, but consecutively. In consequence, there are exchanges of interests in land. However, since these, like most interests in trusts are merely limited interests in freehold land and leaseholds, this will be an exchange of minor interests. In consequence, although the parties become entitled to a freehold interest in their respective part of the land, the tax is chargeable only upon any consideration provided by way of equality,[140] but, as considered above, in other situations the issues as to whether HMRC will argue for two 'sales' are more complex and structuring issues may arise.

10.25 COMPUTATIONAL ISSUES

Two areas of computation problems arise.

10.25.1 Apportionment

In so far as the trust fund consists of a mixture of investments including both shares and land, and only one interest includes land such as where the life tenant surrenders

---

[134] *Henniker* v. *Henniker* (1852) 1 E&B 54; see also FA 2003, Sched.4, paras.16A and 16B.

[135] See e.g. *Oughtred* v. *IRC* [1960] AC 206; but see the effective and correct overruling of this case by the Court of Appeal in *Neville* v. *Wilson* [1997] Ch 144.

[136] In some situations all parties may lose; see *Lloyds Bank* v. *Duker* [1987] 3 All ER 193. This may be a reason for the trustees and others refusing to co-operate in what may be a breach of duty by them.

[137] *Oughtred* v. *IRC* [1960] AC 206.

[138] FA 2003, Sched.16, para.8.

[139] FA 2003, s.121.

[140] FA 2003, Sched.4, para.6; but note the special rules where partnerships are involved: FA 2003, Sched.15, para.16 (as amended).

his life interest in the land and possible other assets in return for the remainderman surrendering him interests in other assets, presumably, it will be necessary to apportion any cash consideration paid upon an assignment of the interest between the interest in the land and the interest in the other assets on a just and reasonable basis.[141] Only the consideration properly apportioned to the former would appear to be within the charge to SDLT.

10.25.2 'Exchanges'

More frequently, however, the arrangement will involve mutual transfers of benefi-cial interests which may include land on one side or the other or both. The computation rules will differ depending upon whether there is an exchange of interests in land or there is only one interest in land and the property being received does not include any land interest such as where a life tenant agrees to transfer the interest including the interest in any land held in the trust by the remainderman in consideration of becoming absolutely entitled to shares held by the trustees.

In the case where only one side of the bargain involves the acquisition of an interest in land, the SDLT will be charged upon the consideration, i.e. the appor-tioned value of the shares or other assets relevant to the proportion of the land interest being 'acquired' which are received from the trustees at the direction of the remainderman. However, where the interests being exchanged both involve inter-ests in land the land exchange rules[142] may apply if HMRC Stamp Taxes, contrary to its expected position set out above, treats the arrangement as two disposals for mixed consideration because both sides of the transaction include non-land assets and the parties have not sought to separate out the different assets and consideration in their documentation. This gives rise to a conceptual difficulty as to the nature of the interest of the particular beneficiary. A major interest is defined[143] as being a freehold or leasehold interest whether subsisting at law or in equity. The interest of the beneficiary in a trust is only a limited interest in such land and, *prima facie*, would appear not to be a 'major interest'. In consequence, where the exchange does not involve the acquisition of a major interest on either side then the chargeable consideration is the amount or value of any consideration provided other than the disposals that are given.[144] This would appear to limit the charge to any considera-tion that represents equality or other adjustments. The value of the interests in land being mutually exchanged is ignored.

---

[141] See FA 2003, Sched.4, para.4.
[142] FA 2003, s.47.
[143] FA 2003, s.117.
[144] FA 2003, Sched.4, para.5(4)(a) and (b).

10.26 POWERS OF APPOINTMENT AND ADVANCEMENT

Chargeable interests include powers over land[145] and there is no reason why this should not include powers of appointment or advancement and possibly powers of revocation exercisable by trustees or other persons who may have power to direct interests whether by deed or will. Given the general exemption for gifts,[146] except where special rules apply such as where connected companies or partnerships are involved,[147] the normal exercise of powers by trustees is unlikely to give rise to a charge to SDLT because there will be no chargeable consideration.

However, where a chargeable interest is acquired by virtue of the exercise of a power of appointment and the person in whose favour the appointment is made gives consideration to become an object of the power, the chargeable interest is taxed as if that consideration was consideration for the appointment.[148] Where consideration is provided, assuming that this does not constitute some form of fraud on a power, then in so far as the property appointed or advanced out of the settlement includes land there will be a chargeable transaction as far as the appointee is concerned. Where the property appointed is subject to a mortgage[149] there is a potential charge to tax if the transferee assumes personal liability for the mortgage.[150] However, if the transferee while taking the property subject to the charge does not assume personal liability, i.e. there is no personal covenant to repay the mortgage or a recharging of the property (as banks are unfortunately prone to requiring) which does not include such a personal covenant, there is no charge because there is no assumption within the charging provisions; but if as part of the arrangements there is a variation of the rights and liabilities of the parties there is a deemed assumption of the liability and this is deemed to be chargeable consideration producing a chargeable transaction.[151]

10.27 RESERVATION OF BENEFIT

A difficult area arises where the settlor wishes to vest the property in the trustees while reserving some benefit for himself whether by way of contract or otherwise, or wishes to dispose of only a partial interest in the property.[152] Here the conveyancing mechanics imposed by the general law or the machinery adopted by the parties

---

[145] FA 2003, s.48(1)(a).
[146] FA 2003, Sched.3, para.1.
[147] FA 2003, ss.53 and 54 where the previous stamp duty exemption for distribution out of trusts contained in FA 2000, s.120 has not been continued in relation to SDLT, and Sched.15, para.24 (as amended). The provision relating to transfers into partnerships consisting of bodies corporate has been repealed as it is no longer relevant following the restriction of the sum of the lower proportions (SLP) relief to cases where the partners are 'individuals'.
[148] FA 2003, Sched.16, para.7.
[149] FA 2003, Sched.4, para.8.
[150] FA 2003, Sched.4, para.8.
[151] FA 2003, Sched.4, para.8A.
[152] Note *Vandervell* v. *IRC* [1967] 1 All ER 1.

and the apparent attitude of HMRC Stamp Taxes to excepting and reserving (see **4.24**) can affect the SDLT costs significantly since 'land exchanges', which are widely defined,[153] are potentially subject to a double charge[154] upon market value.[155] It is not always possible to transfer land reserving an interest or simply gifting a partial interest; the transaction may have to take the form of a transfer and a regrant of the retained interest (see also **4.24**). This type of problem will frequently arise where the settlor wishes to transfer the freehold of his home to the trustees but retain the right to continue to reside there for his lifetime or that of his widow,[156] or is entering into some form of equity release or home annuity arrangement where there may have to be an outright transfer of the main interest and the grant of some form of right of occupation that has the appropriate value. Such arrangements are likely to create leases for life[157] rather than licences[158] and there may be an intention to grant or reserve a lease for a fixed term for the settlor. HMRC Stamp Taxes takes an aggressive position in this area and has contended that where there is a transfer of the title to trustees who agree to delay delivery of vacant possession indefinitely this is a lease for life[159] and is not a licence to occupy since it confers exclusive possession upon the transferor/donor. HMRC Stamp Taxes may take the view that there is a sale and leaseback rather than just the gift of a reversionary interest.[160]

Pursuant to FA 2003, s.47, the SDLT upon the transfer will be charged upon its market value and the leaseback will be taxable upon a deemed premium equal to its market value and upon a rent reserved.[161] HMRC Stamp Taxes, after long resistance, is beginning to accept that the land transferred is to be valued subject to the obligation to grant the leaseback.[162]

---

[153]   FA 2003, s.47.

[154]   But note the comment of Megarry J in *Sargaison* v. *Roberts* [1969] 3 All ER 1072 to the effect that taxation should not rely upon old fashioned conveyancing principles such as these.

[155]   But note the possibility of a 'minority discount' or other limits upon the position of the co-owner as in *Re Wight* [1982] 2 EGLR 236.

[156]   See, for example, *Kildrummy* v. *IRC* [1990] STC 657; *Ingram* v. *IRC* [1999] STC 37; *Lloyds Bank* v. *Duker* [1987] 3 All ER 193.

[157]   For the purposes of SDLT a lease for life is treated initially as a lease for one year but which grows annually respectively if the occupation continues beyond the first or any subsequent anniversary; see FA 2003, Sched.17A, para.4; see **Chapter 8**.

[158]   Skipton Building Society v. Clayton (1993) 66 P&CR 223.

[159]   Treated initially as a lease for one year but increasing each year for the purposes of the charge upon any rent reserved during which the lease continues; becoming a two-, three- or four-year lease, etc.

[160]   There are issues as to whether there is a contractual relationship between the settlor and the trustees. See *Nichols* v. *IRC* [1973] STC 497; [1975] STC 278; *Re Park (No.1)* [1970] 1 WLR 626; *Re Park (No.2)* [1972] Ch 385.

[161]   It may be helpful to investigate in any particular case whether the exemption for a sale and leaseback or the alternative finance regime apply: FA 2003, ss.57A and 71A and following.

[162]   It was formerly possible to mitigate these multiple charges by arranging for the first stage to be the grant of the lease to a nominee followed by a sale of the reversionary interest to the third party subject to and with the benefit of the lease. However, it is now provided that where a lease is granted to a nominee or by a nominee to the beneficial owner it is taxable.

CHAPTER 11

Estates of deceased persons

11.1 GENERAL

Death, as such, is not a chargeable event for stamp duty land tax. It may have other tax obligations such as inheritance tax. Lifetime arrangements may have included undertakings to pay any inheritance tax or capital gains tax but these may not be chargeable consideration.[1] There is no specific general exemption for property passing on death but as such arrangements will normally, but not invariably, be for no chargeable consideration they will not be chargeable transactions.[2] However, the deceased may have been part-way through a contract for the acquisition of land which has to be completed by the personal representatives and these will, of course, become liable for any SDLT arising upon the transaction[3] and they may be liable for any unpaid SDLT in respect of transactions recently completed by the deceased where the appropriate filings have not been made and the tax paid. The death may operate to 'protect' earlier transactions where equity would not protect them such as in *Strong* v. *Bird*,[4] and there may be a *donatio mortis causa* that could fall into charge. It may also be the occasion when certain arrangements between the deceased and members of the family are completed.[5] It may be an occasion when certain issues relating to the SDLT have to be dealt with but these arise largely because of the open-ended nature of much of SDLT itself. As indicated below, there may open contractual positions such as purchases by the deceased with earnouts or clawbacks and these will have to be resolved because there is an attendant SDLT liability in respect of the contingent consideration. This may have been properly dealt with and the tax postponed at the appropriate time or the parties may have failed to deal with the situation or taken the view that no money would be payable. In consequence, the vesting of the land in the personal representatives whether pursuant to the will or an intestacy or its overseas equivalent which may include the

---

[1] FA 2003, Sched.4, paras.16A and 16B.
[2] FA 2003, Sched.3, para.1, s.77A. However, it must not be overlooked that the terms of a will may render the taxpayer ineligible for first time buyer relief; see **4.3.4**.
[3] FA 2003, s.106(3); on limitation periods see Sched.10, para.31(4).
[4] (1874) LR 18 Eq 315.
[5] *Henry* v. *Henry* [2010] 1 All ER 988.

principle of universal succession by operation of law where the deceased was domiciled abroad will not be a chargeable event.

Numerous SDLT events may arise during the course of the administration of the estate such as rent reviews or payments of instalments of any overage consideration and the adjustment of the SDLT position consequent thereon. Similarly, there would not normally be a charge to tax upon the vesting of the assets in the beneficiaries since these will be transactions for no chargeable consideration although there are special reliefs and exemptions available including special rules for dealing with property that is subject to a mortgage.

However, arrangements taking effect on death may be chargeable transactions for a variety of reasons. As a *donatio mortis causa* will normally be a 'gift' it will be exempt notwithstanding that it takes effect outside any will or intestacy. Other extra-testamentary dispositions becoming effective on death may, however, be taxable, e.g. constructive trusts (such as where, for example, the house is to pass to the carer) which arise because the satisfaction of the condition (here, of caring for the landowner) is the performance of consideration which creates a contractual type of relationship. On the other hand, there may be issues where a promise was made to effect a gift which was not perfected during the lifetime of the promisor but became effective on death by reason of the rules of accidental vesting which depend upon the identity of the personal representatives.[6] There will also be issues for 'carers' and others who entered into an understanding that if they looked after the house owner the property would be theirs[7] or similarly if they had paid the mortgage instalments prior to the death.[8]

Provisions within the will also raise issues. For example, it may be provided that, in broad terms, the matrimonial home is to pass to the surviving spouse subject to some arrangement such as the payment of an amount equal to the nil rate band of inheritance tax possibly charged upon the property and the surviving spouse may provide a loan note on the assumption of liability. There are many such arrangements but the general view of HMRC Stamp Taxes is that such arrangements are taxable as 'sales' for the amount of the 'debt'.[9] It is far from obvious that its analysis is correct in all cases; but, since it accepts that it is possible to transfer property subject to a mortgage without incurring a charge provided that no personal liability for the debt is assumed, this seems, for the time being, to offer a relatively unprovocative method of dealing with the situation free of tax for the time being.

11.2 DECEASED'S LIABILITIES TO TAX

When the deceased has entered into a chargeable transaction, the responsibility for payment and clearly the SDLT will pass to the personal representatives who become

---

[6] *Strong* v. *Bird* (1874) LR 18 Eq 315.
[7] See *Henry* v. *Henry* [2010] 1 All ER 988.
[8] Errington v. Errington and Woods [1952] 1 KB 290.
[9] See Guidance Note 12 Nov. 2004.

personally liable (not merely accountable) for the tax but with a right to deduct the tax paid out of the assets and effects of the deceased.[10] There is, of course, no provision dealing with the position where the estate is insolvent such as limiting the liability to the assets received by the personal representatives. In consequence, the indemnity may be valueless. Frequently the deceased will have entered into a transaction but not postponed the tax. The personal representatives will, it seems clear, be liable for the tax, interest and tax-related penalties which may exceed the value of the estate or they will be too late to make an application to postpone the tax.[11] The legislation seems to impose an unlimited liability upon personal representatives who may not wish to take up the appointment.

11.3 TAX DURING ADMINISTRATION

It might be thought that this is unlikely to be a significant problem but the assumption is incorrect. In addition to incomplete transactions of purchase there are many structures where there are outstanding taxation liabilities and until these have been resolved it will not be possible to complete the administration of the estate. Typical structures will include, *inter alia*:

- leases with reviewable rents where there may be an obligation to make a further notification upon review and at the end of the fifth year of the term of the lease; or
- any subsequent review or increase of rent reserved by a lease owned by the deceased after the expiration of the fifth year producing an abnormal increase; or
- acquisition of land where the consideration is variable within FA 2003, s.51 where instalments of the overage or other payment are outstanding.[12] Where the variable payment is a premium in connection with the grant of the lease,[13] the liability passes to an assignee of the lease, but in all other cases the obligation to resolve the taxation issue remains with the original purchaser of the land unless there is an effective exit strategy included in the contract of acquisition (see **4.40**); and
- where there are arrangements for SDLT upon a prior transaction these are payable by instalments.[14]

These outstanding liabilities can delay the administration of the estate for many years and will require careful planning when disposing of or assenting the land in

---

[10] FA 2003, s.106(3).
[11] FA 2003, s.80; Stamp Duty Land Tax (Administration) Regulations 2003, SI 2003/2837, Part 4.
[12] FA 2003, s.80.
[13] FA 2003, s.81A; Sched.17A, para.12.
[14] FA 2003, s.90; Stamp Duty Land Tax (Administration) Regulations 2003, SI 2003/2837.

question.[15] Where, in the course of the administration of the estate, the personal representatives discover that the deceased made an error in a land transaction return, it seems that there is an open issue of principle as to whether they are under a duty to correct that error within a reasonable time or suffer a tax-related penalty.[16]

11.4 FOREIGN ESTATES

The SDLT legislation applies to estates of persons domiciled outside the UK where the assets include chargeable interests in the UK. Such persons should consider holding UK land interests through offshore companies.[17] The estates of such deceased individuals who held land or trust interests in the UK, whether testate or intestate, are potentially taxable; administration of such estates must also deal with the outstanding liability for transactions entered into by the deceased in his lifetime mentioned above.

11.5 WILLS AND INTESTACIES

The SDLT areas relating to wills where tax may arise are:

- transfers of assets to specific legatees and devisees;
- appropriation of assets in satisfaction of legacies;
- dealings in interests in the estate after a variation;
- variations of the estate of the deceased.

11.6 INTERESTS OF BENEFICIARIES

A key problem likely to be faced by all persons administering the estate of a deceased individual as well as the beneficiaries themselves, especially where there is a plan to vary the estate, will be the nature of the interests of the potential beneficiaries, which include beneficiaries of estates of persons domiciled outside the UK. It would seem that interests in the estates of deceased parties may amount to chargeable interests[18] in land in the UK. If this were not the assumption in the legislation variations of estates would not be taxable so that there would be no need for the reliefs for such transactions. A specific devisee would have such an interest, assuming that the estate was not insolvent when he might not receive anything at all.

---

[15] See, for example, the need for 'exit strategies' at **4.40**.

[16] FA 2003, Sched.10, para.8 provided such an obligation but there is no express replacement of the obligation after the substitution of this duty to rectify by Sched.10, paras.31 and 31A.

[17] Such companies would also offer potential benefits for sharing tax savings on the sale of the company rather than the land.

[18] But possibly minor interests depending upon the terms of the will.

Residuary estates may be more difficult since until the residue has been administered and all creditors and liabilities have been provided for, the residuary beneficiaries do not have any interest in the underlying assets.[19] However, it would seem
that when the administration is complete an interest in the property vests and a
chargeable interest arises. There would seem to be no reason why the estates of
persons dying non-domiciled or not resident in the UK may not produce chargeable
interests where the estate holds land in the UK. The overseas factor does not appear
to affect the situation so that the tax applies.[20] It will, however, be necessary to
analyse the rights of the various devisees and residuary beneficiaries under the law
governing the administration in order to determine the nature of their rights. It
seems that HMRC Stamp Taxes takes the view that the *Livingston* principle[21]
applies to all cases and not merely residuary interests. In consequence, in practice
the interests of beneficiaries of the estates of deceased individuals may not become
chargeable interests until the administration of the estate is well advanced. It seems
that the provisions applying to trusts will not, as such, apply to the estates of
deceased persons during the administration. However, there seems to be no reason
why the provisions affecting foreign trusts should not apply to trusts arising under
wills or intestacies of persons non-domiciled or not resident in the UK.

11.7 TESTAMENTARY TRUSTS

Testators frequently leave all or part of their estates subject to trusts and statutory
trusts may arise upon intestacy. It seems that trusts created by the wills of deceased
persons are governed by the basic trust regime, although there may be some
questions as to when the land ceases to form part of the estate of the deceased person
or becomes trust property or the person's representatives become nominees[22] with
all of the compliance issues related to the change of status, and whether an assent or
other appropriate vesting arrangement has been entered into by the executors,
particularly where these are the same persons as the trustees of the testamentary
settlement. Such trusts arising upon death will usually be for no consideration and
therefore exempt from SDLT[23] and not notifiable.[24] The vesting of the land in the
trustee or the personal representative becoming a trustee will not be a notifiable
transaction.

One issue of compliance arises. At this stage there is a change of status: the
personal representatives become trustees and different principles apply.[25] Normally

---

[19] Commissioner of Stamp Duties (Queensland) v. Livingston [1964] 3 All ER 692 (PC).

[20] There may, therefore, be benefits in holding land in the United Kingdom through a company,
preferably incorporated abroad so that its shares can be dealt in generally without the payment of
stamp taxes; but note Stamp Act 1891, s.14(4).

[21] [1964] 2 All ER 692.

[22] FA 2003, Sched.16, para.1.

[23] FA 2003, Sched.3, para.1.

[24] FA 2003, s.77A.

[25] FA 2003, s.106(3); Sched.16, para.5.

executors will be the vendors so that their identification on the land transaction return may not be a significant issue in practice. However, it remains to be seen whether, although there is no tax loss HMRC Stamp Taxes will, as seems likely, seek to impose a penalty for an incorrect return upon the 'purchaser'.

11.8 ASSENTS AND APPROPRIATIONS

However, persons other than specific devisees of land may be affected by SDLT. For example, a pecuniary legatee may enter into an arrangement with the personal representatives that a particular parcel of land be appropriated to him in satisfaction of his right to the pecuniary legacy.[26] However, frequently wills provide that the personal representatives may appropriate property in satisfaction of other types of legacy without the need for the consent of the beneficiary.[27] Specific exemptions have been subsequently introduced as FA 2003, Sched.3, para.3A, whereby the acquisition of property by a person in or towards the satisfaction of his entitlement under or in relation to the will or intestacy of a deceased person is exempt such as where the matrimonial home is appropriated towards the interests of the surviving spouse.[28] The exemption applies where the property is assented subject to a mortgage; but the acquirer must not give any other consideration. However, where there is any other consideration such as where the legatee may have to make a payment because the value of the property exceeds the amount of his legacy, the charge is limited to the amount of the actual consideration.[29] As the relief is included in Sched.3, there is no notification obligation regardless of the value of the property where there is a transfer of a major interest, i.e. a freehold or a lease unless it relates to land in a disadvantaged area[30] and would be exempt by reason of those provisions.

11.9 VARIATION OF ESTATES OF DECEASED PERSONS

It has long been possible for beneficiaries under a will or on intestacy to rearrange by agreement between themselves their respective testamentary or statutory entitlements.[31] In so far as the interest of any of the parties to such a transaction is a chargeable interest then such an arrangement will, *prima facie*, give rise to a charge to SDLT if done for consideration. Much may depend upon the circumstances of the arrangement. For example, a disclaimer of a legacy which would usually be without

---

[26] *Jopling* v. *IRC* [1940] 2 KB 282.

[27] Compare Administration of Estates Act 1925, s.46, which was not regarded as a sale for stamp duty purposes; but the current charge applies to transactions pursuant to powers, statutes and by operation of law.

[28] FA 2003, Sched.3, para.3A.

[29] FA 2003, Sched.4, para.8A.

[30] FA 2003, Sched.6, para.13.

[31] Inheritance Tax Act 1984, s.142; Taxation of Chargeable Gains Act 1992, s.62.

consideration should not give rise to a charge to SDLT even though the interest vests in some other person. Moreover, even if there is consideration, it is considered that no charge to tax arises since a disclaimer is not within the definition of an acquisition. However, there may be some other form of disposition within the definition of 'acquisition' whether a release, surrender or otherwise in return for some reciprocal arrangement or the payment of consideration directly. In so far as the consideration for the disposal of the chargeable interest in land consists of consideration[32] other than entering into another land transaction in the land exchange provisions,[33] the SDLT upon the person acquiring the interest will be by reference to the amount or value of the consideration provided. However, where there is some form of reciprocal arrangement where issues similar to those considered in relation to trusts (see **Chapter 10**) arise such as arrangements whereby interests in one property are released or surrendered in consideration of other interests being released or surrendered so that the parties are in effect exchanging interests in land then the land exchange provisions will apply.[34] In this situation the question as to whether the particular devisee has a major or non-major interest will be important. For example, where there is a specific devise of a freehold interest to A it would seem that, *prima facie*, A has a major interest albeit his interest subsists in equity.[35] However, where the interest is part of some form of testamentary trust or a limited interest is granted such as a right to occupy for life[36] the interest may not be a major interest. This affects the computation and notification obligations.

In so far as there is an exchange involving one or more major interests such as where one beneficiary is exchanging the freehold land left to him for freehold land devised to some other beneficiary then there will be two charges to SDLT based upon the market value of the interest being acquired. Any equality adjustment would appear to be ignored.[37] However, where the transaction involves 'exchanges' of interests all of which are not major interests the mutual exchange of interests is ignored in determining the extent of the chargeable consideration which is limited to any other consideration provided such as any equality payment or other consideration providing such an adjustment.[38]

However, SDLT may be payable on any element of consideration in kind deemed to be dutiable,[39] as, for example, a mutual transfer of an interest in land for an interest in shares. For example, where the family home is demised to the children jointly, one child may wish to take the house absolutely and the other children are agreeable to this provided that they are appropriately compensated such as by receiving the assets in the estate or possibly a cash payment by the acquiring party

---

[32] Compare FA 2003, Sched.16, para.8.
[33] FA 2003, s.47.
[34] FA 2003, Sched.4, para.5.
[35] FA 2003, s.117.
[36] Which may be a lease for life see *IRC* v. *Lloyds Private Banking* [1998] STC 559 and see FA 2003, Sched.17A, para.4 and **Chapter 7**.
[37] FA 2003, Sched.4, para.5(3).
[38] FA 2003, Sched.4, para.5(4).
[39] FA 2003, Sched.4.

who borrows the cash from a bank or other lender, i.e. the cash is not part of the estate assets. *Prima facie* there is a chargeable transaction (which may be a linked transaction because all of the parties are 'connected') involving an acquisition of land for a consideration in kind consisting of the compensation adjustment. The liability to *ad valorem* stamp duty on such rearrangements with other arrangements is relieved by FA 2003, Sched.3, paras.3A and 4.

11.10 RELIEF

There is a limited exemption from SDLT in respect of certain variations of the estates of deceased persons. No charge to SDLT [40] arises in respect of the variation of an estate of a deceased person, provided that:

- the deceased was competent to dispose of the chargeable interest in question. This means that the deceased was not acting as trustee or had a special power of appointment over the property. It would seem that where the deceased had a special power of appointment over the property whether exercisable by deed or will, he is to be regarded as competent to dispose for these purposes;[41]
- the transaction is carried out within the period of two years after the death;
- no consideration in money or money's worth[42] other than the making of a variation of another such disposition is given for the variation.

It is immaterial whether or not the administration of the estate is complete or the property has been distributed in accordance with the original dispositions, provided that the consideration if any consists solely of other interests in the estate.

If the variation is made for any consideration in money or money's worth other than consideration consisting of the variation in respect of another of the dispositions, such as might be the case if the child receiving the house has to resort to borrowing from a bank to provide all or even part of the compensation, the relief remains available but on a restricted basis. The tax is charged upon the external consideration but the benefit of the lower rates is available by reference only to such external consideration.

---

[40]   FA 2003, Sched.3, para.4.
[41]   He may be competent to dispose where he had a general power of appointment, see e.g. *Re Penrose* [1933] Ch 793.
[42]   See *Secretan* v. *Hart* 45 TC 701; but note the probably erroneous comments of 'services' as money's worth because the service cannot be sold in the open market. This is supported by the inclusion of FA 2003, Sched.4, para.11 specifically dealing with services.

11.11 RELIEF FOR PURCHASERS OF LAND FROM PERSONAL REPRESENTATIVES

In order to facilitate the administration of estates, a relief is provided for a property trader whose business includes purchasing dwellings from personal representatives where the deceased individual occupied the property as his only or main residence at some time in the two years preceding his death. The property trader must acquire by transfer a major interest; the grant of a new lease is not exempt. The land must not exceed 0.5 hectare and such larger area as is reasonable for the property. The property trader must not spend more than a limited amount on refurbishment (i.e. £10,000 or 5 per cent of the consideration paid up to a maximum of £20,000). The property trader must be a company, a limited liability partnership, or a partnership comprised solely of companies, and must not permit its employees to occupy the premises nor grant a lease or licence. If the conditions are subsequently breached the tax is clawed back.[43]

---

[43]   FA 2003, Sched.6A, paras.3, 8, and 11(3).

CHAPTER 12

Partnerships

12.1 GENERAL

Partnerships are governed by complex stamp tax regimes, namely:

- a regime for ordinary acquisitions of chargeable interests from or disposals to unconnected persons.[1] So-called ordinary acquisitions of assets by partnerships are governed by the normal principles of stamp duty, stamp duty reserve tax and SDLT, although there are certain modifications for compliance in the last case;
- a special SDLT regime for acquisitions of chargeable interests from and transfers to persons connected with the partners;[2] and
- a complex regime for transfers of interests or shares in partnerships.[3] For example, where there are transactions which constitute transfers of interests in a partnership there is a relief to the extent that the assets of the firm are free of stamp taxes such as book debts, a charge of 0.5 per cent where there are shares or marketable securities and a charge to SDLT where the partnership property includes land by reference to the market value of such land.

12.2 TERMINOLOGY

Certain issues arise as to the terminology since the same terms such as 'transfer' can bear different meanings in different parts of FA 2003, Sched.15, and possibly meanings that may differ also from other parts of the SDLT regime and from the ordinary English or dictionary definition of the term. Also there are rumours of a possible change of practice as to what will be accepted by HMRC as a partnership (see **12.2.1**).

The following comments are offered as a form of general guidance on the possible meaning of the terms in question but as there can be no certainty how HMRC Stamp Taxes will interpret the provisions the comments are put forward

---

[1] FA 2003, Sched.15, Part 2.
[2] FA 2003, Sched.15, Part 2.
[3] FA 2003, Sched.15, paras.14, 17, 17A and 23; see **12.18**.

more in hope than a confident expectation that a reasonable approach will be adopted. The key issues will be applied in their 'plain English' – traditional legal meanings though these may not be compatible with the views of HMRC Stamp Taxes.

12.2.1 'Partnership'

'Partnerships' are to some extent widely defined as regards the type of business vehicles taxed as if they were 'partnerships' but there is no specific definition as such; although anything that is a 'partnership' is excluded from the definition of 'company'.[4] The definition of those partnerships within the SDLT regime includes all forms of partnership formed or established in the UK including general partnerships under the Partnership Act 1890, limited partnerships under the Limited Partnerships Act 1907 and limited liability partnerships under the Limited Liability Partnerships Act 2000.[5] 'Partnership' also includes a firm or entity formed or established abroad having a similar character to any of those formed under English law;[6] but no guidance is provided as to the possibly relevant criteria.[7] Clearly limited liability and corporate personality are no longer major criteria since it is expressly provided that the legal personality of a partnership is disregarded to the extent that the chargeable interest held by or on behalf of the partnership is treated as held by or on behalf of the partners and the land transaction is treated as having been entered into by or on behalf of the partners as such[8] but the partnership is deemed to continue notwithstanding changes in the membership. For foreign business structures it seems that much may turn upon the description of rights of membership such as whether there are numbers of separate units of small uniform amounts other than one single holder.

12.2.2 'Business'

It seems that the basic definition will be that contained in Partnership Act 1890, s.1. It is a key element in the statutory definition of partnership[9] that the partnership is carrying on a 'business'[10] which may be a factor in whether the chargeable interest is partnership property[11] and whether there is a 'transfer' of a chargeable interest to a partnership. It is provided that there is a 'transfer' where the chargeable interest

---

[4]   FA 2003, s.100(1).

[5]   The legislation indicates that the charge for the tax overrides any such limited liability at least in cases where there is a purchase from or by or lease by or to the partnership.

[6]   See e.g. *Dreyfus* v. *IRC* 14 TC 560.

[7]   The treatment of the vehicle by the foreign jurisdiction for tax purposes is irrelevant.

[8]   FA 2003, Sched.15, para.2.

[9]   Partnership Act 1890, ss.1 and 45.

[10]   There may also be issues as to whether it should be carrying on a 'business' with a view to profit, etc.

[11]   FA 2003, Sched.15, para.34; see **12.5**.

becomes or ceases to be partnership property.[12] This leaves open the question whether there is a chargeable transaction only where there is an appropriation to or from business assets so that actual transfers are not as such taxable unless the asset is appropriated or whether there is in addition to an actual 'transfer' a deemed transfer on any such appropriation. There has for some time been a residual worry that where the vehicle was essentially an investment structure such as a joint venture which acquires/develops land and receives the rent this is a 'business' or whether it is simply an investment vehicle. In practice, hitherto, HMRC has been prepared to accept any description that the parties make. If the participants describe their vehicle as a 'partnership' HMRC would apparently be prepared to accept this at face value, although where the parties stated that they did not intend to create a partnership this was not conclusive and HMRC might challenge the treatment.[13] It is, however, rumoured that HMRC and, in particular, HMRC Stamp Taxes may be reconsidering the situation and the fact that the parties have either described their structure as a partnership or have even registered under the various Partnership Acts will no longer automatically ensure that the treatment is conclusive. In consequence there are two fundamental unanswered questions as to the official views in this area, namely:

- whether the activities are sufficiently businesslike for the vehicle to be regarded as a partnership; and
- even if the vehicle is a partnership because it is registered as such, whether the transaction falls within the scope of what HMRC Stamp Taxes regards as its 'business' or whether it is not a business activity and so is deemed not to be an acquisition or is a deemed disposal or some other form of unfavourably taxed activity.

12.2.3 'Partner'

No explanation is given of who is to be treated as a partner for these purposes. This, too, may be a matter of the general law of partnership. Persons who are 'salaried partners' as opposed to equity partners may not be partners in law;[14] but they may be liable as partners by reason of estoppel or holding out,[15] or because they have not given notice of their retirement or seen to the removal of their names from the

---

[12] FA 2003, Sched.15, paras.35 and 37.

[13] It should be noted that the label attached by the parties to their transaction is not conclusive and it is a matter of detailed analysis of the rights and liabilities created; but where the factors are evenly balanced the parties' stated intention might tip the balance in favour of their label: *Ready Mixed Concrete (South East) Ltd* v. *Minister of Pensions* [1968] 1 All ER 433; *Ogwr* v. *Dykes* [1989] 2 All ER 880; *BSM (1257) Ltd* v. *Secretary of State for Social Services* [1978] ICR 894; *Massey* v. *Crown Life* [1978] 2 All ER 576.

[14] *Stekel* v. *Ellice* [1973] 1 All ER 465.

[15] See e.g. Partnership Act 1890, s.14; note also the effects of s.43 thereof.

notepaper.[16] It seems probable that HMRC Stamp Taxes will seek to rely upon these principles in order to collect the tax.[17]

12.3 OTHER UNDEFINED TERMS: PARTNERSHIP SHARES AND INTERESTS

There are some half definitions of certain key terms but these lack any really helpful precision and the plain English drafting has produced many specialised if unusual meanings of routine terminology that have to be noted. In particular there is a very important set of provisions based around a partner's 'share' which is different from a partnership 'interest'. Thus the transfer of an 'interest' may trigger a tax charge but the chargeable amount is related to the 'share'.[18] No explanation is provided of a partnership 'interest' and how this differs from a partner's 'share'. The latter is defined by reference to a partner's right to participate in the income profits of the firm. This is, however, as far as it goes. A 'partnership share' is the share in the income profits of the partnership to which the person is entitled at the relevant time[19] which, as mentioned below, is itself a problem (see **12.3.1**). It has no relevance to his capital.[20] This raises a whole range of problems and the current indications are that these many ambiguities are intended to be exploited by HMRC Stamp Taxes.

12.3.1 Partnership 'share'

This is defined as the person's share in the 'income profits' of the firm.[21] There may be a fixed entitlement, but the legislation does not deal with the situation that apart from many family partnerships the profit allocation may include some form of discretionary or bonus pool. In none of these cases is there any indication as to how, on the effective date for the transaction, the partner's share is to be determined. It will be many months after the end of the financial year before the final payout is known and that it is clear that the partner's 'share' is not related to his capital. There may also be particular issues where in the case of certain types of limited partnership there may be a managing or general partner who receives a fixed fee or a percentage of capital under management plus a share of the profits or income arising.

---

[16]   *Tower Cabinet* v. *Ingram* [1949] 2 KB 397.
[17]   They may, however, be less willing to press the argument simply for the purpose of imposing penalties such as for submitting an incorrect land transaction return by not including such persons as 'purchasers'.
[18]   See e.g. FA 2003, Sched.15, para.34(2).
[19]   See e.g. FA 2003, Sched.15, paras.14(7), 17(5); 12(1), Step 4.
[20]   But note the flexibility when determining the sum of the lower proportions; see **12.11**.
[21]   FA 2003, Sched.15, para.34(2). A change in profit-sharing ratios is regarded officially as a 'transfer': FA 2003, Sched.15, para.36 (as much amended) but 'profits' may be widely interpreted as described below in this section.

12.3.2 Partnership 'interest'

In other cases, the legislation refers to a partnership interest but without any explanation or guidance as to its intended scope or meaning. The above problematic approach to partnership 'shares' raises the question as to whether a partnership 'interest' is to be treated as the capital or economic participation in the firm. The current approach of HMRC Stamp Taxes is that partnership 'interest' is the interest in the net assets of the firm, but without indicating whether the 'net' position is arrived at by deducting or ignoring partners' loans to the firm (possibly including undrawn profits[22]). Since these are not 'liabilities' of the firm they are likely to be treated as assets rather than liabilities when calculating the percentage involvement of the partner and any interest is a profit share. This means that the 'repayment' of 'loan accounts' can reduce 'interest' payments and so involve a change in profit-sharing ratios which, in the official view, produces a transfer of a partnership 'share' potentially subject to tax. There is also the question, given the amendments contained in Sched.15, para.17A relating to repayment of loan accounts, as to whether a partner's interest will be not merely his participation in capital but his entire economic involvement with the firm such as any partner loan account including monies advanced to the firm or possibly including undrawn shares of profits, although the amendments in para.17A suggest that these latter items would not be included since this could incorporate an element of double counting, particularly where partnership shares are concerned.

12.3.3 Partnership profits

The 'income profits' of partnerships are a key factor in the process of determining the sum of the lower proportions (SLP) deduction. Notwithstanding its importance, there is no definition of 'income profits' of the firm and there are fundamental issues of applying the concept of share of profits which is an overall annual concept to a single land transaction event. Neither 'income' nor 'profits' are defined. For example, presumably HMRC Stamp Taxes will have to operate on the basis of the partnership accounts as drawn since this will represent the income or profits of the partnership in a reasonable form. HMRC Stamp Taxes is taking a wide view apparently approaching this more consistently with the income tax profits of the firm. In consequence, included in a partner's share are not only the profits ultimately allocated but also there are questions of possibly added back prior allocations of profits such as special remuneration and possibly interest on partnership loan capital. The final profit shares in the agreement may not be the correct figures to apply. These rules are unworkable in the context of a transaction-based tax since profits and profit shares are fixed on an annual basis. While a prior charge of X per cent of profits to one partner can be determined and added back to modify the agreed division of the ultimate profits, this cannot work where a partner is entitled to a fixed

---

[22] Which may depend upon whether HMRC Stamp Taxes accepts the technical difference between a 'loan' and a 'debt' and the terms of the partnership agreement on these issues.

amount payable whether or not there are profits or there are special arrangements for dealing with rent if any property of the firm is sublet again regardless of profits for the year. No guidance as to how to deal with such issues has been provided by HMRC Stamp Taxes, which appears to be unaware of the defects in this legislation.

The question of shares and interest are complex; the main safeguard, in practice, is that for most of the partnerships within the special regime there is unlikely to be much in the way of fluctuating income shares. However, since there are rules concerned with the merger and demerger of partnerships[23] which operate under the guise of transfers between partnerships, there will be many situations where a partnership owns freehold land and as part of some restructuring or pension operation the land is transferred to a new vehicle which is leased back to the existing or any new partnership. In these situations while there is no guarantee of total identity between the various merging or demerging vehicles there will be a signifi-cant overlap so that the reduction for the sum of the lower proportions which is based upon income shares will be a major problem. In consequence, there will be potential problems for professional partnerships as well as for investment vehicles.

12.4 'TRANSFER' OF CHARGEABLE INTERESTS AND PARTNERSHIP INTERESTS

The special charges are based upon 'transfers' which are defined in terms similar to 'acquisition';[24] but there are extensions to the definition such as 'transfer' includes property becoming or ceasing[25] to be partnership property which includes, in the official view, chargeable interests being utilised by licence in relation to 'partner-ship property'; and there are transactions deemed to be transfers of partnership interests. Unfortunately the draftsman has not made it clear whether the definition of 'transfer' in the latter case is in addition to the general definition of transfers or is in substitution for it.

12.4.1 'Transfer'

There are several definitions of 'transfer' for the purposes of the special regime:

• a general definition equivalent to 'acquisition' of a chargeable interest as regards 'ordinary' acquisitions. This does not apply to transfers of partnership

[23] FA 2003, Sched.15, para.23.
[24] FA 2003, s.43, Sched.15, para.9.
[25] FA 2003, Sched.15, paras.34(1), 36 and 37. It remains to be seen how HMRC Stamp Taxes intends to treat termination of leases by lapse of time particularly where the tenant might be in a position to hand over the lease by operation of law, but declines to do so. Fortunately these will rarely be for actual consideration, and so not taxable, but they may have to be notified by SDLT 1: FA 2003, s.77 (as amended).

interests[26] and possibly not to acquisitions from connected parties within the special acquisitions regime;

- a definition of transfers to or by a partnership in terms of a chargeable interest becoming partnership property.[27] There is the issue as to the interaction of this provision and the general definition of 'transfer' considered in the preceding bullet point. It seems that on one view there is a transfer to a partnership only where the chargeable interest becomes 'partnership property', i.e. is used for the purposes of the partnership. In these situations transfers of land into a partnership that is not used for the partnership business would not become 'partnership property' and therefore there would be no transfer for these purposes. However, the contrary view is that the preceding bullet point represents the basic definition of 'transfer' which includes the various listed events and that this definition is extended so as to apply where the property becomes partnership property by being used for the purposes of its business.

This is an important practical issue since the same difficulties arise in relation to transfers out of a partnership. It is provided that there is a 'transfer' where property ceases to be used for the purposes of the partnership business[28] and this could give rise to significant difficulties where property is appropriated out of the mainstream partnership business such as where land held as part of a farm is set aside and is to be developed and leased. There will, of course, be issues as to whether, in this situation, the setting aside is establishing a new business or is an extension of the existing business of the partnership but, as indicated above, there are potential problems as to whether a joint venture is a partnership because it is a pure investment vehicle or whether there is an appropriation of land from business activities to what is a pure investment activity.[29] Moreover, there is a special definition of 'transfer' for the purposes of the charge upon dealings involving a partnership 'interest'.[30]

The particular meaning has to be noted in each separate context with the question as to whether the differences with so-called definitions represent different meanings and provide some guidance on the meaning in each case, or, as is more likely, it is simply bad drafting upon the basis that consistency is not a reasonable drafting objective.

---

[26] FA 2003, Sched.15, para.9(2); s.43.
[27] FA 2003, Sched.15, paras.35 and 37.
[28] FA 2003, Sched.15, paras.35 and 37.
[29] Compare *Baytrust Holdings Ltd* v. *IRC* [1971] 1 WLR 1333 where 'trade investments' were held not to be part of the undertaking of the company and *E. Gomme* v. *IRC* [1964] 3 All ER 497 to the effect that not every asset owned by a company is part of its business or undertaking.
[30] FA 2003, Sched.15, para.36.

12.5 PARTNERSHIP PROPERTY

Although the provisions refer to 'transfers' and 'chargeable interests', there is a definition of 'partnership property'[31] as an interest[32] held by or on behalf of a partnership, or one or more of the members of a partnership or for the purposes of the partnership business, and there is a transfer of a chargeable interest to a partnership whenever a chargeable interest becomes partnership property and a transfer by a partnership, *inter alia*, where a chargeable interest ceases to be partnership property.[33]

These definitions are widely but not necessarily consistently interpreted by HMRC Stamp Taxes. For example, HMRC Stamp Taxes has, on occasion, expressed the view that where a partner who owns land grants a licence to the partnership his whole freehold interest becomes partnership property with a full charge upon the market value of the land in question; but if he actually transfers a chargeable interest such as where he grants a tenancy at a rent (which rent acts as 'actual consideration') the partnership property is the tenancy interest. This transaction would not on general principles be taxable because there is no 'transfer' of a chargeable interest, but on HMRC Stamp Taxes' argument the freehold becomes partnership property because it is utilised for the purposes of the partnership business and is, in consequence, transferred. This difference between what is 'acquired' and what becomes 'partnership property' has to be noted because, in addition to the general definition of 'transfer' in terms of 'acquisition', there is also for the purposes of the special regime a transfer by a partnership when a chargeable interest ceases to be partnership property,[34] or an interest is created out of partnership property.[35] It is, therefore, a major question whether this provision brings the whole freehold value into charge upon the grant, variation or termination of a licence to use or occupy the land. It seems that these provisions are intended to maximise the scope of the charge by maximising the extent of the property acquired in order to enhance the chargeable consideration where there is a transfer of a partnership share.[36] Since the charge upon 'transfers' of partnership interests is related to the market value of the partnership property, the question of the extent of the partnership property is crucial in many cases. Where a partner has granted a short lease at a rent to the firm,[37] the chargeable amount is related to the actual lease but if he merely grants a rent-free licence, albeit of a limited nature, the entire freehold interest or the entirety of the chargeable interest is owned by the licensor.

---

[31] FA 2003, Sched.15, para.34(1).
[32] Note, not a 'chargeable interest'.
[33] FA 2003, Sched.15, paras.34, 35 and 37.
[34] FA 2003, Sched.15, paras.35 and 37(a).
[35] FA 2003, Sched.15, para.37(b).
[36] FA 2003, Sched.15, para.14.
[37] Which is unlikely to be excluded from the computation by FA 2003, Sched.15, para.15.

12.6   STAMP TAXES AND PARTNERSHIPS

Partnerships are subject to a variety of charges to stamp taxes, for example:

- Basic rules of stamp duty continue to apply to acquisitions of shares and marketable securities by partnerships,[38] but there are difficulties since the language is not consistent even within FA 2003, Sched.15.
- There is a charge to stamp duty at the rate of 0.5 per cent on acquisitions by a partnership of shares or marketable securities and if such stamp duty is not paid then there will be a liability to the principal charge to stamp duty reserve tax at the same rates.
- There is a charge to SDLT on land acquisitions outside the special regime;[39] the so-called ordinary acquisitions regime.
- There is an exemption from both the above charges for the acquisition of property including land on the initial incorporation of an existing partnership into a limited liability partnership.[40]
- Where there is an instrument operating as a 'conveyance' or a written agreement[41] to 'transfer' an interest in a partnership there is now an obligation to apportion the consideration between non-chargeable assets, shares and marketable securities, and land.[42]
- The consideration attributable to non-chargeable assets such as goodwill,[43] book debts and intellectual property of the firm is not subject to stamp taxes in any form.[44]
- To the extent that the consideration for the transfer of an interest in a partnership relates to stock or marketable securities owned by the partnership the consideration allocated will be subject to stamp duty at the rate of 0.5 per cent.[45] It seems that HMRC Stamp Taxes does not regard this aspect of the transaction as being within the charges to stamp duty reserve tax.
- The SDLT charge upon the part of the consideration for the 'transfer' attributable to any chargeable interest in land that is 'partnership property' is up to 4 per cent and is considered in more detail below (see **12.18**).

It will be obvious that this apportionment will involve a valuation of each individual asset in the partnership and an apportionment of the consideration to each, which may be a difficult matching exercise because the consideration may well take account of the liabilities of the firm.[46] There may also be problems because of the

---

[38]   FA 2003, Sched.15, para.31. HMRC Stamp Taxes does not seek to apply stamp duty reserve tax to dealings in partnership interests even in relation to limited liability partnerships.
[39]   FA 2003, Sched.15, paras.5 and following.
[40]   FA 2003, s.65.
[41]   FA 1999, Sched.13, para.7.
[42]   FA 2003, Sched.15, paras.31 and following.
[43]   But note the problem of whether it is goodwill or land value; see **2.15.2**.
[44]   FA 2003, s.125 and Sched.15, paras.31 and following.
[45]   Finance (No.2) Act 2005, Sched.10, para.21; FA 2003, Sched.15, para.33 (as amended).
[46]   Note the provision dealing with liabilities in FA 2003, Sched.15, para.32.

way in which professional and other firms treat 'goodwill' (see **2.15.2**) which are unsecured general liabilities not charged upon specific assets and may not be business goodwill but a key element in the valuation of the partnership's land. It remains to be seen how willing HMRC Stamp Taxes is to act upon the basis of the partners' valuation which may depend upon whether it is supported by independent advice or arm's length negotiations. However, the actual consideration may be influenced by the provisions in the partnership deed as to how matters are to be dealt with or that provide arbitrary procedures for calculating 'values' or attributing assets, such as relating to 'goodwill' to previous years' average profits or to future profits.

The situation is not simplified by the fact that different principles apply for each of the taxes involved and different rules for computing and reporting the tax are applicable. Valuation exercises will frequently be required, which are likely to involve costs disproportionate to the tax involved, particularly at the rate of 0.5 per cent. Regrettably, the desire to avoid such extra costs is likely to expose the taxpayer's advisers to allegations of negligence and extended discovery assessment periods which will involve even higher costs and interest and penalties.

12.7 SDLT: ORDINARY TRANSACTIONS – NON-CONNECTED COUNTERPARTIES

Basically the ordinary rules of SDLT which apply to all persons apply to 'partnerships' in relation to acquisitions from unconnected parties. Given the provisional nature of much of SDLT and the continuing nature of the partnership notwithstanding the changes in the membership,[47] there will be difficult questions for incoming and outgoing partners as to the liability to the tax in relation to acquisitions and disposals of chargeable interests and interest and penalties which may need to be resolved because there are certain modifications to the general compliance regime for ordinary transactions involving partnerships.

12.7.1 Liability: responsible partners

An ordinary acquisition by a partnership is treated as being made by the partners. In consequence, the liability falls upon the 'responsible partners' who are the partners as at the effective date and any person who becomes a partner after that date.[48] Retirement does not appear to relieve a partner from liability.[49] Anything done or to be done is a matter for the responsible partners; liability for the tax, penalties and interest can be enforced against the partners individually on a joint and several basis[50] it seems, notwithstanding that this liability may exceed the limited input

---

[47] FA 2003, Sched.15, para.3.
[48] Such partners are also liable to penalties but with limitations in respect of periods prior to their admission: FA 2003, Sched.15, para.7.
[49] Compare *Tower Cabinet v. Ingram* [1949] 1 All ER 1033.
[50] FA 2003, Sched.15, paras.6 and 7.

capital contribution of the partner to the firm.[51] However, tax and interest may not be recovered from responsible partners who were not partners as at the effective date. Penalties may be recovered against new partners where these accrue on a daily basis after their admission or where the act or default occurred after their admission even where the effective date predates such admission.[52]

12.7.2 Compliance: representative partners

Acquisitions by a partnership must be dealt with by means of a land transaction return (SDLT 1) which must be signed by the appropriate persons. Strictly, this is all of the partners, not merely the persons to whom the legal title passes such as the first four named persons who will be acting effectively as nominees for all of the partners as beneficial owners.[53]

However, it is provided that the administration of compliance with the tax (and the initial liability to pay) can be dealt with by representative partners.[54] These are persons who are nominated by the majority of the partners whose nomination has been approved in advance by HMRC Stamp Taxes, who must also sanction any changes in the list of representative partners.[55] In practice, however, HMRC Stamp Taxes treats a partnership as a single purchaser so that when inserting the name of the vendor or purchaser in the land transaction return (SDLT 1 and 2) only the partnership name is required.[56]

12.8 SDLT: SPECIAL TRANSACTIONS

There is a group of transactions entered into after 22 July 2004 subject to special charges, where the counterparty to the transaction is a partner or a person who is connected with the partner[57] whether as 'vendor' or 'purchaser' and the chargeable interest becomes or ceases to be utilised as partnership property (i.e. 'used' for the purposes of the partnership business in whole or in part). Special charges also apply to persons about to become a partner and it seems possibly retired as well as retiring partners.

Special transactions in relation to partnerships can be divided into five broad areas:

---

[51] It is assumed but not confirmed by HMRC Stamp Taxes that where the partners have to contribute additional funds to include liabilities for SDLT this will not be regarded as an adjustment in the rights of the partners for the purposes of, *inter alia*, the anti-avoidance provisions of FA 2003, Sched.15, paras.17 and 17A.

[52] FA 2003, Sched.15, para.7 (as amended).

[53] FA 2003, Sched.16, paras.1 and 3 (as amended).

[54] FA 2003, Sched.15, para.8.

[55] FA 2003, Sched.15, para.8.

[56] Notes for Guidance (SDLT 6).

[57] A person may be connected with a partner without necessarily being a connected company.

- 'transfers'[58] of chargeable interests to partnerships from partners or connected persons, whether for cash or in consideration of the issue of shares or the increase of shares in partnerships;[59]
- 'transfers' of interests in a property investment partnership[60] which can include, in the view of HMRC Stamp Taxes, a wide range of transactions;[61]
- certain adjustments in the partnership structure;[62]
- the transfer of partnership property from a partnership to partners or persons connected with them such as the withdrawal or repayment of capital *in specie* on retirement or where the partnership leases or sells land to one of its members or a connected person;[63] and
- transfers between partnerships which will usually apply to mergers and demergers of partnerships.[64]

12.9 GENERAL PRINCIPLES

The legislation relating to dealings between partners and connected persons within the special regime, i.e. transfers of chargeable interests into and out of partnerships, is complex but the broad policy appears to be that no charge to tax should arise in so far as the land remains owned by the same connected individuals[65] or connected partner or in certain cases connected persons (i.e. persons who are not connected simply by reason of being partners). A similar but not identical policy applies to the removal of land from partnerships, unless there is 'actual consideration' moving between connected persons. To some extent fiction prevails over reality in coping with transactions that are not intended to be taxed but consistent application of this policy has proved to be beyond the skills of those structuring and drafting the legislation.

This treatment, however, does not extend to transfers of partnership interests but, in general, tax arises only where there is a property investment partnership.[66] Professional and other partnerships are not within this charge but extended anti-avoidance provisions[67] frequently apply to such firms. Where a charge arises, the chargeable consideration is, broadly, not the actual consideration where rent is involved but a proportion of the market value (whatever this may be).

Unfortunately the discrepancy between the treatment of partnership capital and partnership income profits provides a trap for the unwary unless the allocations

---

[58] Defined in FA 2003, Sched.15, para.9(2) but note paras.35 and 36, and compare s.43(3).
[59] FA 2003, Sched.15, para.10.
[60] Defined in FA 2003, Sched.15, para.14 (as amended).
[61] FA 2003, Sched.15, para.36; see **12.18**.
[62] FA 2003, Sched.15, paras.17 and 17A.
[63] FA 2003, Sched.15, para.18; see **12.15**.
[64] FA 2003, Sched.15, para.23; see **12.17.1**.
[65] Jasmine Trustees v. Wells & Hind [2007] STC 660.
[66] FA 2003, Sched.15, para.14.
[67] FA 2003, Sched.15, paras.17 and 17A; see **12.25**.

made for the purposes of the charging formula described below are carefully considered and appropriately applied.

12.10 ACQUISITIONS OF CHARGEABLE INTERESTS FROM CONNECTED PERSONS

There is a chargeable transaction where there is what is effectively an acquisition of a chargeable interest by a partnership from a partner or connected person.[68] This applies where there is a 'transfer',[69] i.e.:

- a transfer of a chargeable interest by an existing partner into the partnership; or
- a transfer by a person who becomes a partner such as on the initial contribution of capital; or
- a transfer by a person connected with an existing partner; or
- a transfer by a person connected with a person who becomes a partner.

These provisions will apply to situations where an owner of property who is either a partner or connected with partners sells or leases land or possibly, in the view of HMRC Stamp Taxes where the owner grants a licence to the partnership on an arm's length basis. The provisions will also apply where a person contributes land to the partnership as his initial contribution of capital on being admitted to partnership or as an *in specie* increase of his partnership share when he is already a partner.

The chargeable consideration for any transaction not involving the grant of a lease is the market value or a proportion thereof; any actual consideration is ignored. Where there is the grant of a lease the charge is upon the net present value of actual rent or a proportion thereof plus a deemed premium related to market value (or a proportion thereof) taking account of the actual rent. There is a reduction in the charge to market value where the partners are individuals connected with the transferor, lessor or grantor of the chargeable interest. The percentage reduction is determined in accordance with the formula:

$$(MV \times (100 - SLP)\%)$$

where:

MV is market value;
SLP is the sum of the lower proportions.

If there is a lease the rent (i.e. any actual consideration) is taken into account but any actual premium is ignored and there is a deemed premium of market value[70] (taking into account the rent). This is designed to deal with leases at below the market rent.

---

[68] FA 2003, Sched.15, para.10.

[69] 'Transfer' is defined in the same manner as 'acquisition' within the basic charging provisions: FA 2003, Sched.15, para.9(2); compare s.43(3).

[70] On the determination of market value of leases note the provision in FA 2003, Sched.15, para.38.

Tax is charged upon the proportion of the deemed market value premium, if any, and the net present value of the rent pursuant to the formula:

$$(MV \times (100 \, SLP)\%) + ((NPV \, rent) \times (100 - SLP)\%)^{71}$$

where:

MV is the deemed premium (if any);
NPV is the net present value of the actual rent; and
SLP is the sum of the lower proportions.

12.11 SUM OF THE LOWER PROPORTIONS (SLP)

Having determined the market value or premium and the net present value of the lease as the basic chargeable consideration, it is then necessary to reduce this by reference to the sum of the lower proportions (SLP). The policy is to avoid a charge to SDLT where there is, in effect, no real change of ownership. The following principles may be disapplied by a property investment partnership making an appropriate election,[72] which reinstates the full market value for the acquisition and cancels the reduction for the SLP. There is, therefore, an increased charge on the acquisition because the reduction for the SLP is not available but this election[73] reduces the charge upon transfers of interest in the partnership (see **12.21**); but effectively excluding the value of the land from the chargeable consideration.

The key issue in ascertaining the chargeable amount is determining SLP. To do this it is necessary to apportion the interest in the land of the transferor among relevant partners connected with him provided that either he is one of the partners or the connected partners are individuals[74] connected with him (see below). For these purposes the relief is available where the transferor is a partner even where it is a body corporate but for connected persons the relief is available only if they are individuals or deemed individuals.[75]

The issue is how the value is to be allocated between the relevant parties in order to determine the degree of certainty of ownership. This is the aggregate of the lower of two percentage figures which are allocated to each eligible partner, namely:

- his percentage share of income profits; or
- the percentage chosen by the parties who are free to choose any figure not necessarily capital share.

The lower proportion is the proportion so allocated[76] or the proportion of the property measured by that partner's income share. In practice this means that the

---

[71]   It should be noted that although the same formulae apply to disposals of land by partnerships, the SLP is determined in a different way; see **12.16**.
[72]   FA 2003, Sched.15, para.12A; see **12.12**.
[73]   FA 2003, Sched.15, paras.12A and 14.
[74]   Note the problems of trustees as in *Jasmine Trustees* v. *Wells & Hind* [2007] STC 660.
[75]   FA 2003, Sched.15, para.12(3).
[76]   It is not possible to transfer one partner's share to another partner.

partner's income profit share will be chosen since this represents the maximum relief. The greater the sum of the lower proportion (i.e. the share of the property retained by the transferor and connected partners) the smaller the market value falling into charge; but the chargeable actual consideration will increase. It seems to be the official view that where the parties are dealing with unconnected persons, the whole value of the property will be subject to charge by reason of the market value charge and the actual consideration is ignored but it is difficult to support this by reference to the legislation.

It is, in consequence, important to understand the complex process to determine the SLP but, as indicated above, if all of the parties are individuals who are 'connected' or any corporate partner is also the transferor no market value charge should arise because there is no charge where such a connection exists.[77] In such a situation, where the SLP is 100 there will be no chargeable consideration; but because the exemption pursuant to FA 2003, Sched.3, para.1 does not apply, the transaction will be notifiable upon a land transaction return (SDLT 1).[78] HMRC Stamp Taxes has difficulty in coping with a return which shows zero in the chargeable consideration box following the cancellation of self-certificates designed to deal with these situations. For example, in order to determine sum of the lower proportions (SLP) it is necessary to identify the owner of the chargeable interest and the persons who are connected with him and who are individuals and are partners who together with the transferor where he is a partner are known as 'corresponding partners'.

The owner's interest in the chargeable interest is apportioned between the corresponding partners who are individuals[79] and the owner if he is involved in the partnership. This apportionment can, in the view of HMRC Stamp Taxes, be made in whatever proportions produce the lowest tax for the parties. The apportionment does not have to be made by reference to shares in the partnership income; it can be made by reference to capital interests to deal with situations where there is a difference between income entitlement and level of capital. The parties may even choose to allocate on a totally unrelated basis. However, since the maximum reduction is limited to the partner's income share, allocations on this basis will normally produce the best result; but, given that profits are not always on a simple fixed basis (see **12.3**), this is not an easy test to apply as at the effective date. For each partner the 'lower proportion' is the lesser of the proportion of the chargeable interest apportioned to him and the proportion equivalent to his 'partnership share' (i.e. his share in the income profits – not capital – of the firm)[80] immediately after the transaction. The sum of the lower proportions is the aggregated lower proportion for each connected partner.

---

[77] FA 2003, Sched.15, para.12.
[78] FA 2003, Sched.15, para.30.
[79] *Jasmine Trustees* v. *Wells & Hind* [2007] STC 660; FA 2003, Sched.15, para.12(1), Step 2.
[80] FA 2003, Sched.15, para.34(2).

For example, H and W own land equally and are entering into partnership with their son and daughter, S and D who are individuals. All parties are connected. The capital shares are H and W 50:50; the profit shares are H:W:S:D – 10:10:60:20.

Allocating on the basis of capital shares produces H:W:S:D – 50:50:0:0 but the lower proportions, i.e. income shares, are 10 (income share):10:0 (allocated share):0 i.e. 80 per cent of the market value is chargeable (because the allocated shares of S and D are below their income shares and those allocated to H and W exceed their income shares).

Allocating on the basis of income shares produces a 100 per cent SLP reduction.

For example, A and B are unconnected parties entering into a partnership whereby A contributes land and B contributes cash.[81] Assuming that the profit and capital shares are 50:50, the maximum SLP will be 50 (i.e. A's share of the income profits) so that there is a charge upon 50 per cent of the market value. This applies even where A receives cash from the partnership intended to balance the capital share; this will be actual consideration which has to be ignored.

Where corporate bodies are involved as partners the reduction for the body corporate's share of the income profits will be available only where it is the transferor or lessor of the property i.e. it is the same person on both sides of the transaction. The reduction is not available where the company is not the transferor but merely a connected person who is a partner. However, there is a reduction for certain companies which are acting as nominees.[82]

12.12 PROPERTY INVESTMENT PARTNERSHIPS ELECTIONS

Property investment partnerships are defined[83] as partnerships whose sole or main activity is investing or dealing in chargeable interests whether or not that activity involves the carrying out of construction operations.[84] There is a special regime for the transfer of interests in these partnerships (see **12.18**). However, the charge upon the transfer can be modified by the exclusion of certain chargeable interests where the partners make an election to disapply the special charge upon the acquisition of the property.[85] Where the election is made the charge upon the acquisition is based upon the full net present value of any rent and/or the market value of the land. There is no reduction for the SLP. There is, therefore, a major strategic issue of when to make the election. In broad terms, there is no benefit and only an increased tax liability if the purpose of the partnership is to acquire, develop and lease the land to produce an income. Since the participants do not intend to transfer interest there will be no charge pursuant to para.14 and the normal rules will apply upon the

---

[81]   It seems that these arrangements are not affected by FA 2003, Sched.15, para.17A which may not apply to the 'debt' arising upon the initial contributions of capital; but for the time being pending clarification of the policy behind these provisions it seems prudent to pay cash at once.

[82]   FA 2003, Sched.15, para.12(3).

[83]   FA 2003, Sched.15, para.14(8).

[84]   FA 2004, s.74.

[85]   FA 2003, Sched.15, para.12A.

ultimate disposal of the chargeable interest. In consequence, there will be no benefit in the longer term to compensate for the enhanced charge and loss of the deduction for the SLP on the initial acquisition. Essentially the para.12A election is worth considering only in cases where it is intended that there will be numerous changes in the membership of the firm as investors come in and/or leave.

12.13 ANTI-AVOIDANCE PROVISIONS

There are obvious temptations for parties to establish an initial partnership structure that has favourable income-sharing ratios since capital participation is irrelevant. This could produce a situation where the land is transferred into the partnership with a total or substantial reduction for the SLP but there is a major change in the capital ownership of the asset. Variations in the income shares of the partners in non-property investment partnerships are not transfers;[86] the effect would be that the land could be transferred through a partnership paying little or no SDLT on the way. However, HMRC Stamp Taxes has introduced anti-avoidance provisions designed to deal with these situations; namely:

- variations of interests and changes to the partnership;[87] and
- returns of capital and withdrawal of funds.[88]

12.14 REMOVAL OF LAND FROM PARTNERSHIP

There are many ways in which property can be taken out of a partnership. There are *prima facie* no special rules for transfers or disposals or leases to unconnected third parties; but it appears that HMRC Stamp Taxes is extremely anxious to prevent the parties from using the reliefs from the market value charge as a means of incorporating the partnership and its land, i.e. converting the land into shares.[89] As with transfers into partnerships where the partners include bodies corporate there is an increasing number of restrictions upon the reductions in the market value chargeable consideration although there appear to be significant errors in the drafting which may offer the opportunity of incorporating a partnership business. There are two basic charging regimes for acquisitions from partnerships and five main areas for investigation namely:

- whether there is an ordinary acquisition[90] or a special regime acquisition[91] by a person connected with the transferee or lessee;

---

[86] As defined by FA 2003, Sched.15, para.14; see **12.18**.
[87] FA 2003, Sched.15, para.17.
[88] FA 2003, Sched.15, para.17A.
[89] FA 2003, s.53; Sched.15, para.10 but see **12.26**.
[90] FA 2003, Sched.15, Parts 1 and 2.
[91] FA 2003, Sched.15, para.18.

- when a charge arises;
- the chargeable amount;
- transfers between partnerships such as mergers and demergers;[92] and
- whether partnership consists solely of bodies corporate.[93]

12.15 TRANSFERS OUT OF A PARTNERSHIP

There are many ways in which there can be a 'transfer' by a partnership such as a sale or lease, a return of capital to a partner, a transfer in satisfaction of a partner loan and, presumably, appropriations of a lease to 'non-business' purposes, i.e. situations where the property ceases to be within the definition of partnership property[94] because, for example, it ceases to be utilised for the purposes of the partnership business without an actual transfer or disposal of the land. For example, there may be a transfer, if the view of HMRC Stamp Taxes should be correct, upon the termination of a licence[95] to use land held by one of the partners or while the chargeable interest remains partnership property an interest is carved out of it, such as by the grant of a lease or a sublease or creation of an easement or profit. As no specific provisions are made for winding up of partnerships these rules apply to distributions of land to the members in such circumstances. There is a possible transfer of partnership property if it ceases to be partnership property or ceases to be used for the purposes of the partnership business or a sub-interest such as a lease or sublease is created out of the partnership property and this sub-interest does not itself become partnership property.

As indicated above, where the partnership utilises land for its business which is owned by one of the partners otherwise than pursuant to a lease at a rent such as a licence, the whole interest of the licensor/parties becomes partnership property. The termination of the 'licence' will, in the official view, result in the 'transfer' of the entire chargeable interest already owned by the transferee.

Transfers of the partnership property out of the partnership take a variety of legal forms, such as where partners may wish to reduce their capital or to retire and take the repayment of their capital *in specie*.[96] Alternatively, the partnership may be dissolved and the land distributed to the partners either pro rata or in accordance with some form of liquidation agreement whereby certain assets are allocated to particular partners and others are distributed elsewhere.[97] There may also be

---

[92] FA 2003, Sched.15, para.23.

[93] FA 2003, Sched.15, para.24.

[94] FA 2003, Sched.15, paras.37 and 34(2).

[95] It is currently totally uncertain how HMRC Stamp Taxes intends to react where the relevant holding over involves a partnership and, in particular, where the partnership does not hold over and does not take advantage of any relevant legislation.

[96] Note also the trap where a relevant partner withdraws cash from the business pursuant to FA 2003, Sched.15, paras.17 and 17A.

[97] Although there are special rules for dealing with partitions of chargeable interests held by partnerships in FA 2003, Sched.15, para.16, there is a fundamental question, where the land held by

'removals' of assets from the partnerships by reasons of partnership mergers and demergers.[98] Unfortunately, many of these transactions are governed by different principles and it is necessary to identify into which category the transaction falls.

12.16 COMPUTATION

The rules for calculating the tax charge are similar in concept to those concerned with land going into a partnership (see **12.10**) and the same formulae apply but the data to be inserted in the formula differs. The policy appears to be that to the extent that the property remains vested in persons who are partners or persons connected with partners or possibly former partners, the market value charge is reduced and tax in respect of any rent payable will be computed on a proportion of the net present value,[99] if any. To the extent that the property vests in persons who are partners or a person who is connected with the transferor partners are either the transferee or are individual partners connected with the transferee. The relief will be available where the company is on both sides of the transaction in any other manner than being partners, the market value charge will arise and the amount of chargeable consideration will be correspondingly reduced. In this situation the connected party issue it seems refers to 'persons' rather than individuals[100] which includes connected companies, so may provide some reduction in the chargeable amount that would otherwise arise on an incorporation. Appropriate proportions of the net present value of the rent passing under a lease that is granted out of the partnership are included in the chargeable amount.

---

the partnership is divided among the partners, whether this is in fact a 'partition' within the general rules or is some form of complicated land exchange provision. This affects the application of the charging provisions which differ between partitions and land exchanges in FA 2003, Sched.4, paras.5 and 6. Although there is some doubt upon the point, it seems that in practice HMRC Stamp Taxes is inclined to the view that a division of a pool of assets rather than the physical division of a single asset held under a single title can constitute a partition.

[98] It seems that FA 2003, Sched.15, para.16 may have some relevance in such cases because it refers to the acquisitions (although not referred to as a transfer this is presumably intended to bring in the full definition of 'acquisition' which is the same for most purposes as 'transfer') and a chargeable interest in a partnership in consideration of entering into a land transaction. However, since a partnership interest as such is not a chargeable interest notwithstanding the look-through provisions, it seems that entering into partnership would not be a land exchange; but an assignment of a partnership interest in return for land would be a land exchange for these purposes. This narrow interpretation gives a correspondingly narrow application for the modification of the rules relating to exchanges and partitions.

[99] The special rules also apply where the person 'has been' a partner or is connected with a 'has-been' partner. There is no obvious time limit on the separation of the former partner from the firm. For example, there is no suggestion that the transaction has to be in connection with ceasing to be a partner. It seems odd that there should be a special charge when the person acquiring the chargeable interest ceased to be a partner for bona fide commercial reasons unconnected with the current transaction several years previously; but the legislation could be utilised to support such a charge.

[100] The reference to 'individuals' is to the partners transferring rather than the transferee.

12.16.1 Sum of the lower proportions (SLP)

The key issue in computing the charge is again SLP reducing the amount of the market value or proportion of the net present value of any actual rent brought into charge. It is necessary to apportion the proportion of the chargeable interest held by the connected transferee after the transaction among the partners who are the transferees and persons connected with them provided that the transferor partners are individuals.[101] This applies to connected 'persons' which includes companies and is not limited to individuals;[102] but there are issues where bodies corporate are involved. The reduction for the sum of the lower proportions applies only where the corporate partner is the transferor or lessor. The relief will not otherwise be available in other cases since the connected partners have to be individuals.[103]

This allocation can be made on the most favourable basis as with acquisitions (see **12.11**). SLP is the aggregate of the lower of either the proportion so allocated or the partner's income share (see **12.3**). In consequence, in practice, it will usually be beneficial to reduce the market value charge to allocate on the basis of income share since this represents the maximum extent of the relief.

The formulae for determining the chargeable amounts which are described above (see **12.10**) apply but only with the modification that when determining SLP[104] it is necessary to identify the interest of each partner or a person connected with the partner in the chargeable interest in question prior to the transaction. The interest held by the 'transferee' of the chargeable interest after the transfer is then allocated to him and partners connected with him. The SLP is the lower of the interest as so allocated to him and each connected partner or each partner's share in the income profits of the firm.

Where there is a transfer of chargeable interest out of a partnership which consists wholly of bodies corporate and the SLP is 75 or greater, the charge is essentially upon the market value of the interest transferred[105] although relief for intra-group transfers may be available.[106]

---

[101] There are certain harsh transitional rules which treat the share as nil where the land was vested in the partnership after 19 October 2003 and before July 2004 unless *ad valorem* stamp duty was paid (the fixed £5 is not sufficient) or an SDLT charge has been incurred and tax paid if any tax was due: FA 2003, Sched.15, para.21. The partners' SLP is restricted to zero where certain transactional provisions apply; namely where the effective date of the transfer was on or after 20 October 2003 and the instrument did not bear *ad valorem* stamp duty or was not chargeable to SDLT the proportion allocated to the partner is zero. This is a major practical issue since most routine transfers of land to partnerships attracted only the fixed duty or the partners relied upon a non-stampable contract and did not convey the legal title or grant the lease; but note FA 1999, Sched.13, para.14 and FA 1984, s.111, FA 1994, s.204 (now repealed but may be relevant for transactions during the relevant period); FA 2003, Sched.19, para.8.

[102] But note *Jasmine Trustees* v. *Wells & Hind* [2007] STC 660 and trustees and partnerships which are bodies of persons but not bodies corporate (FA 2003, Sched.15, para.20(3)); but there are special rules for transfers between partnerships such as mergers and demergers.

[103] But note the different drafting for transfers out of partnerships pursuant to FA 2003, Sched.15, paras.20 and 21.

[104] FA 2003, Sched.15, para.20.

[105] FA 2003, Sched.15, para.24.

[106] FA 2003, Sched.7, Part 1; note especially Sched.15, paras.27 and 27A.

12.17 DISSOLUTION

12.17.1 Transfers between partnerships: mergers and demergers

Where there is a transfer from one partnership to another partnership and there is at least one person who is a partner in both firms or there are persons in the transferee or lessee firm who are connected with the members of the transferor or lessor partnership such as a merger or demerger or incorporating a limited liability partnership (where the incorporation relief[107] is not available), the tax is calculated upon the basis of an acquisition by a partnership or a disposal by a partnership whichever produces the higher charge.[108]

It might be thought that, since the charge on transfers into a partnership and transfers out of a partnership are based upon essentially the same formula of the net present value of any rent and/or market value reduced by the sum of the lower proportions to the extent that the parties on both sides of the transaction are the same or are connected, there would be little difference between the two charges. However, there are certain important differences between the two sets of provisions and, in general, it seems that the treatment of the transaction as being a transfer out of a partnership may contain certain benefits but there are certain disadvantages. For example, when calculating the charge on the basis that there is a transfer into the new partnership the reduction for the SLP is available only where the partners in the new firm are individuals. On the other hand, where there is a transfer out of a partnership there may be a reduction for the sum of the lower proportions where the transferee partnership includes bodies corporate. There are also certain restrictions where the transferor partnership consists solely of bodies corporate.[109] In addition, there are certain anti-avoidance provisions. These are, essentially, transitional provisions which are related to the announcement of the changes to be made in relation to partnership transactions on 19 October 2003. These rules are designed to deal with changes in the partnership share between 19 October 2003, if a partner was a partner on that date or such later date as he became a partner.[110] The effect is that where the transfer into the partnership took place on or before 22 July 2004 there is no increase in the share unless *ad valorem* stamp duty was paid on the transfer in. This is a particular problem since most transfers of land into a partnership were taxable only with the fixed duty because they were contributions to capital and not transfers on sale. Also, there may not have been a transfer in the strict sense but simply an agreement to contribute with the parties intending to rely upon subsale or other reliefs when it became necessary to move the legal title. Where the transfer of the land into the partnership took place after that date then there is no increase in the partner's share unless SDLT, if any, has been paid. These provisions are complicated and apply only to a limited range of transactions but there are

---

[107] FA 2003, s.65.
[108] FA 2003, Sched.15, para.23.
[109] FA 2003, Sched.15, para.24.
[110] FA 2003, Sched.15, para.22.

dangers that the share allocated to a partner will be zero unless substantial tax was paid on the land going into the partnership. Each case will have to be investigated on its own merits and facts.

There is, in addition, a major issue of principle where there is a possibility that the transfer will be regarded as a transfer into the new partnership within para.10. Where there is a transfer within para.10 there are various anti-avoidance provisions.[111] However, these only apply where there is a charge within para.10. The draftsman has, however, failed to make it clear whether where the special charge arises on transfers between partnerships which are taxed as if para.10 applied with modifications this is to be treated as being within para.10 so that the anti-avoidance provisions apply as regards any subsequent changes in the partnership membership or there are returns of capital to payments of partners who have transferred the land in or made loans to the partnership whether on a long-term or on a bridging basis (see **12.25**). It is considered that this is a special charge where the sole impact of para.10 is for computational reasons and that it is not a charge pursuant to para.10 so that the anti-avoidance provisions do not apply.

12.17.2 Property investment partnerships: mergers and demergers

One area where the draftsman has considered the possible implications of the alternative bases for charge is in relation to property investment partnerships. Such partnerships are, *prima facie*, within the special charging regime but the partners are given power to disapply the special regime upon the acquisition of property and pay tax by reference to the market value.[112] This has certain implications for the computation of the tax upon changes in the partners. The rules have the effect that where there is a reorganisation of a partnership whether a merger or demerger there are alternative bases for taxation. It is provided that where an election is made pursuant to para.12A for the purposes of the charge upon the entry into the partnership this also has effect for the purposes of the application of the rules should HMRC Stamp Taxes seek to treat it as being a transfer out of a partnership.[113] In consequence, an election on a similar reconstruction of this nature can disapply the special regime for the purposes of a potential charge under para.10 and this will also protect, for what it is worth, the transferee partnership as if the transfer had been taxed under para.10 as opposed to para.18. Since it is by no means obvious that making a para.12A election is necessarily beneficial where there is a partnership merger or demerger or similar reconstruction then the parties must think equally hard in order to determine whether to make the election since this may have to be done before HMRC Stamp Taxes intervenes and challenges the return upon the basis that the charge should be calculated upon the potentially higher basis of

[111] FA 2003, Sched.15, paras.17 and 17A.
[112] FA 2003, Sched.15, para.12A.
[113] FA 2003, Sched.15, para.37.

para.18 rather than para.10. This seeking to anticipate the reaction of HMRC Stamp Taxes is important since, once made, an election that para.12A applies cannot be revoked.

12.18 TRANSFERS OF PARTNERSHIP INTERESTS

12.18.1 General

There have been considerable difficulties for many decades with HMRC Stamp Taxes in relation to changes in partners. This can apply to situations where a new partner is introduced or a partner retires or there may be a combination of both the admission of new partners and simultaneous retirement of existing partners. Usually there is a programme, quite often built into the partnership agreement, for simultaneous admissions and retirements and for these to take place at an appropriate point in the tax year applicable to the partnership if only for the purpose of simplicity of accounting and shares of profits. The major difficulties have been twofold:

- the nature of the interest in the partnership; and
- what constitutes a 'transfer' of an interest in a partnership.

Obviously, a 'transfer' of an interest in a partnership applies to the situation of where one partner assigns all or part of his share in the income and capital or other economic involvement in the partnership to another person whether an existing partner or not. However, there are certain restrictions upon the ability to assign to third parties since other partners may wish to have some control over who is a partner in the firm. The normal situations where changes in the partnership participation rights or voting power arise are those where a partner retires and withdraws his capital or reduces his participation by reducing his capital and profit share in the form of semi-retirement. Partnership interests also change where a new partner is brought in and he becomes entitled to a share of the profits which may or may not be related to a contribution of new capital. The two events may be related so that the incoming partner may contribute capital which contributes in whole or in part to the capital withdrawn by any retiring partner or partners. Such arrangements operate to move interest in the partnership between the partners coming in or retiring and the continuing partners but there is no formal 'assignment' or transfer of their interests as such.

There are also issues concerning the nature of the interest 'transferred'. HMRC Stamp Taxes has taken the view that transfer includes the simultaneous injection of new money and the withdrawal of capital by incoming and outgoing partners even where these are part of routine changes pursuant to the partnership agreement. It seems that its view is that it is sufficient if these two events are contemporaneous although there will usually be some form of 'causal' link in the sense that the transactions are related because they are pursuant to the arrangements in the partnership agreement. The statutory definitions in FA 2003, Sched.15, as they have been amended from time to time reflect HMRC Stamp Taxes' uncertainty in this area and some of the issues are discussed later (see **Chapter 15**).

There are also issues as to the nature of the participation in the partnership that is being transferred. This can include a variety of interests such as the right to a share in the profits, the participation in the capital as well as loans and other economic involvement. Technically partners cannot be their own creditors and so 'partner loans' are not necessarily debts for the purposes of stamp taxes but may represent some other form of economic involvement. However, HMRC Stamp Taxes has never raised any particular issues on this score although there may be questions of adding back interest on any such 'loan' as being really an allocation of the profits of the firm which would be a crucial factor in deciding what is the partner's 'share' since this is defined as his participation in the income profits of the firm. None of these concepts are defined. As regards the interest as a partner, i.e. the share in capital or income HMRC Stamp Taxes has fluctuated between treating the interests of the partner as being a bundle of separate equitable undivided interests in the partnership assets and treating the interest as being a separate item of property in its own right. It is clear that any principle that seeks to treat it as being a bundle of individual rights could be a particular problem, but the current regime for partnerships[114] does operate on this basis. It provides that on the transfer of an interest in a partnership it may be necessary to separate out the land interests where SDLT issues arise, interests in shares and marketable securities when stamp duty (but not necessarily stamp duty reserve tax) may apply and other assets that are not subject to stamp taxes when no charge will arise. It may be necessary to apportion the consideration between these various interests or have regard to market value of certain property for the purposes of determining whether there is a charge and if so the chargeable amount.

At other times HMRC Stamp Taxes has claimed that the right of a partner is some form of equitable interest and so subject to the numerous restrictions dealing with such property such as Law of Property Act 1925, s.53(1)(c).[115] This question of whether the interest is an equitable interest as opposed to a legal chose in action or contract would be important if documentation were necessary for passing title but it seems that as long as there is an effective passing of title documentation is not necessary for the purpose of the charge to SDLT.[116] In addition there is the basic underlying law as to partners, partnerships and the transfer of their interests and whether related injections of new money and the withdrawal of capital are 'transfers' and whether there can be such a 'transfer' where one partner withdraws cash

---

[114] FA 2003, Sched.15, paras.14, 31, 32 and 36.
[115] But note *Neville* v. *Wilson* [1997] Ch 144, effectively overruling the House of Lords erroneous decision in *Oughtred* v. *IRC* [1960] AC 206. Moreover, neither decision paid any attention to the definition of equitable interest for the purposes of LPA 1925 which is defined in terms of equitable interests in land so that equitable interests in non-land assets are not within s.53(1)(c). Unfortunately, it is now probably far too late to make an effective challenge on these decisions that were manifestly decided *per incuriam*.
[116] FA 2003, ss.42 and 43.

and another contributes assets in kind or the cash for the retirement is derived by new or existing bank funding arrangements. There are many other technical problems. Unfortunately, those responsible for drafting the partnership provisions which have been changed on many occasions have operated on a patchwork basis rather than trying to achieve consistency and so there are many problems around what is the transfer of a partnership interest. It will be noted that the charge is based upon the transfer of 'interests' which are not defined, although the chargeable amount is by reference to the 'partnership share'. In relation to property investment partnerships there are special rules as to which property is brought into charge to tax and which can be ignored for the purposes of calculating the liability to SDLT.

12.18.2 Partnership interests as 'chargeable interests'

While there is a lifting of the corporate veil for those partnerships that have the status of a corporate entity[117] and there is a limited degree of transparency for the purposes of compliance and collection of the tax[118] there is no complete look-through. In consequence, the share or interest of a partner is not a collection of individual interests in the underlying assets but is a separate item of property. As noted above, HMRC Stamp Taxes has fluctuated between seeking to argue that a share of a partner is a separate interest or item of property.[119] It would seem that the current theory that has to be derived from the recent legislation is that a partner's interest or share in the partnership is, in general, a separate chose in action and not a collection of individual items or part-interests in the partnership assets. Were the latter the correct analysis, the situation would not need the fragmentation of the charge when dealing with partnerships that have non-taxable assets, shares and marketable securities or land.[120] The effect is that notwithstanding that the partnership effectively owns only land[121] as a general principle an interest in the partnership is not a chargeable interest in land. Consequently, in general an agreement to 'transfer' an interest or share in a partnership would not be a chargeable transaction. There are, however, complex rules dealing with situations where such a transaction is chargeable.

---

[117] FA 2003, Sched.15, para.2.

[118] FA 2003, Sched.15, paras.6 and 7.

[119] It has, rather misguidedly, sought to treat this as being an equitable interest whereas it is an item of property based upon contract and is therefore a legal chose in action. In consequence, the mechanics for dealing with this are governed by Law of Property Act 1925, s.136 and not s.53(1)(c) and this has important implications for the possible charge upon any contracts to sell a partnership interest pursuant to FA 1999, Sched.13, para.7 where the partnership has assets that include shares and marketable securities; see **12.6**.

[120] FA 2003, Sched.15, paras.31 and following; see **12.6**.

[121] Although this may raise important questions as to whether it is a property investment partnership or indeed, whether it is a partnership at all because it is holding land and not carrying on a business as required by Partnership Act 1890, s.1; see **12.2**.

12.19 PARTNERSHIP INTERESTS AS CHARGEABLE INTERESTS: SPECIAL SITUATIONS

There are specific situations (see **12.18.2**) where the legislation expressly provides that for certain limited purposes an interest in the partnership is to be treated as if it were a chargeable interest.

The effect of these provisions providing for a degree of transparency and fragmentation and deeming for interests in partnerships means the transfer of 'an interest' in a partnership is a complex and usually expensive stamp tax calculation because certain of the consideration will be apportioned to partnership assets that are not subject to tax such as 'goodwill' unless the 'goodwill' is land value (see **2.15.2**) and book debts which are tax free, or shares held by the partnership where a charge to stamp duty of 0.5 per cent may arise on the apportioned consideration for the 'transfer' and chargeable interests in land where there is a potential charge of up to 4 per cent upon the market value rather than the actual consideration. It must, however, be noted that the circumstances where a 'transfer' or stamp tax event may occur differs as between the various stamp taxes.[122]

12.20 THE CHARGE ON TRANSFER: PROPERTY INVESTMENT PARTNERSHIPS

There is a chargeable transaction where there is a transfer of an interest in a property investment partnership for consideration and the partnership property includes a chargeable interest in land.[123] The extent of the charge will depend upon whether a para.12A election has been made on any acquisition of the land (see **12.21**). These issues are, in general, limited to property investment partnerships so that, *prima facie*, there may appear to be relatively few issues for professional and other partnerships where land may be involved. A key point to note is that this charge applies to partnership 'interests' rather than 'shares' which latter is limited to profit shares. This has the effect that where there is a transfer of an interest in a partnership (whatever that may mean) there is a charge although the charge is calculated by reference to partnership 'shares' which are the income participation arrangements (see **12.3.1**) since it seems that 'interests' in a partnership may include loan accounts as well as capital involvement; dealings in these may amount to a 'transfer' (as discussed below) but the charge is calculated upon a totally different basis. It is important to note that notwithstanding the existence of a form of look-through, the effect of these provisions is not such as to convert a partnership interest itself, in whole or in part, into a chargeable interest.

---

[122] For example, the charge to stamp duty requires an instrument of transfer which is not the case for SDLT.

[123] FA 2003, Sched.15, para.14.

This charging provision does contain a number of problems but it is provided[124] that a chargeable acquisition of a partnership interest can occur only pursuant to FA 2003, Sched.15, paras.10, 14 and 17.

12.20.1 'Transfer'

There has to be a 'transfer' of whatever may be an 'interest' in a partnership and which may be different as between the various relevant taxes. This definition for SDLT[125] has been subject to various changes. Currently it is provided that where a person acquires[126] or increases a partnership share there is a transfer of an interest in the partnership to that partner and from the other partners. This is extremely ambiguous drafting since it is a deemed transaction that is not, *prima facie*, a transfer in plain English, i.e. a direct assignment from one partner to another which was one of the former definitions.[127] It remains to be seen whether HMRC Stamp Taxes will seek to argue that this is simply an extension of the normal meaning of the word 'transfer' to include variations in the profit-sharing ratios. It has for many decades been the view of HMRC Stamp Taxes that there is a 'transfer' or 'convey-ance' of a partnership interest where one partner contributes additional capital or an incoming new person contributes capital and there is at the same time a withdrawal of capital by another partner. This was applied on an entirely arbitrary basis because it could give rise to difficulties where there was the usual arrangement for admis-sions and retirements of partners to take place on the same day. It also ran into particular problems where a partner or incoming partner contributed additional capital or new capital which was used to repay the loan capital of other partners and there are potential major issues where the two events do not involve cash such as where the retiring partner withdraws cash but the incoming partner contributes additional land.

12.20.2 Partnership share

It will also be noted that there is deemed to be the transfer of an 'interest' in a partnership where there is a variation in the 'share'. There is a basic question as to the grammatical construction of the words used. There is a situation where a partner varies his share and there is a different situation where the share of a partner 'is varied'. For example, the basic aspects of the drafting of the legislation appear to require some form of subjective involvement so that the partner agrees to the change

---

[124]   FA 2003, Sched.15, para.29.
[125]   FA 2003, Sched.15, para.36 (as much amended). The history of the definition and the several variations may provide some guidance on the construction of the definition in force from time to time.
[126]   It seems that this does not require an existing partner to reduce his interest or share. An 'acquisition' or transfer may arise where a new or incoming partner subscribes additional capital, the existing partners do not withdraw capital but their share will be adjusted to allow for the new partner.
[127]   Which, unfortunately, remain relevant as historical evidence as to the possible meaning of the term.

in the profit-sharing ratio as such. This will be important since in many situations a partner's share in the profits of the firm 'is varied' as a consequence of transactions that are not, as such, designed to deal with profit-sharing ratios. These can include situations where a partner retires and as a result the interests of the continuing partners are effectively increased. Obviously, where a partner retires and a new partner is admitted the profit-sharing ratios of the two may be different. For example, a retiring partner with a significant share in the profits of the firm may mean that the incoming partner acquires an interest in the profits but as a consequence of the arrangement because his share is lower than the share of the retiring partner the shares in the continuing partners increase automatically. The adjustment in the profit-sharing ratios was not the prime objective of the transaction. Also there may be some form of 'step lock' arrangement whereby the share of a partner increases automatically over time. It may, for example, be provided that on admission a partner's share is 5 per cent of the profit but this will increase by 2.5 per cent per annum over the following five years.[128] In these situations the share of the partner 'is increased' in the sense that it follows the pattern laid down in the partnership agreement but there is no separate agreement; it is part of the original arrangements and is automatic. The share may fall into the category of 'is increased' rather than a partner increasing or acquiring a share as a totally separate event outside the partnership agreement.[129]

In addition, the draftsman has overlooked the question of 'take home pay'. There are many circumstances where the amount of the profits actually received by or allocated to a partner[130] produces a different figure from the percentage share. For example, there may be an existing partnership for members where there is an equal participation of 25 per cent of the profits. However, the parties may admit one or two new partners who contribute substantial capital and business to the firm. In such circumstances the additional partners may acquire equal shares in the profits of the firm so that each partner will find that his notional share of the profits (subject to any adjustments and writebacks) will reduce from 25 per cent to 20 per cent or 16 per cent. However, because of the additional capital or business or land contributed to the firm there will be an increase in the amount of the profits to be shared. It is not impossible that a partner who was entitled to 25 per cent of the profits of the firm may find that, notwithstanding the nominal reduction in his profit share to 16 per cent, he receives a larger payout at the end of the period because of the success of the new venture. On the other hand, the removal of a less than efficient partner from the firm may mean that notwithstanding the reduction of capital the amount available for distribution is larger and so the take home pay of the existing members is greater. There are many situations, therefore, where the facts of the actual payout and

---

[128] There may also be related 'bonus arrangements' whereby the profits paid to a particular partner may increase by reason of a pot being retained from the distributable profits in order to reward outstanding performance.

[129] Compare the drafting in provisions such as FA 2003, Sched.15, paras.36 and 17(2)(a)(ii).

[130] Which may have to be left behind as some form of partner loan and funding of the firm and may not be withdrawn in whole or in part for some years.

distribution of the profits may produce an increase or reduction that is not necessarily a consequence of the adjustment of the profit shares but simply a result of
changes in the structure of the partnership, its capital and the overall business. This
raises the question as to whether HMRC Stamp Taxes will accept that the provision
is limited to changes in the profit-sharing ratios, which is the definition of a
partnership 'share'.[131] The question will be whether any of the other adjustments in
a partner's participation in the profits will be a 'transfer'. For example, variations in
the capital-sharing ratio which do not necessarily affect the income shares where
there is a repayment of a partner's loan capital may be 'transfers' of interests but
they do not affect the partner's 'share'.

Moreover, as indicated above, there are fundamental problems with the inept
drafting of the legislation in relation to what is a partner's 'share'. There are
potential problems where there is a 'flexible' profit-sharing basis such as where
there is a reserved fund out of profits that is designed to provide for bonus or other
payments, or where there are partners who are upon a fixed amount since, as
indicated above, there may be considerable doubt for many many months after any
relevant event as to whether there has been a change in the 'share', i.e. the
percentage in terms of take home pay of the particular partner. However, for
property investment partnerships there will frequently be a general or managing
partner who may be paid a 'management fee' plus a further payment. This payment
may be linked to the capital value of the partnership assets or a percentage of the
rents and income received from the property. There will, therefore, be the fundamental question as to whether the basic fee or management charge is an allocation of
the profits of the firm in which case the percentage share may differ depending upon
the profitability or otherwise of the partnership during any particular period. The
recession or certain properties becoming vacant could have quite a dramatic effect
upon the 'share' of the profits of the firm for partners in these situations.

12.20.3 Subjective, objective and initial contract

There will be a question of whether the use of the word 'acquires' requires an active
step by the relevant person or whether it is passive in the sense that it applies where
an interest is acquired or increased by a partner as a result of the actions of other
parties without his own intervention such as where there is an increase of his income
share by reason of the retirement of another partner. His share is increased but
arguably *he* does not increase his share.[132] It seems likely that the uncertainties of
this drafting mean that notwithstanding the clearly narrow scope of the current
provisions particularly in the context of the paragraphs which have been repealed
and replaced there may be a potential charge where there is:

• an outright assignment from A to B of his partnership share;

---

[131] FA 2003, Sched.15, para.34(2).
[132] See also FA 2003, Sched.15, para.36.

- the retirement of A linked with a withdrawal of his capital from the partnership related to a transaction whereby B is admitted into partnership and contributes capital. It has for decades been the view of HMRC Stamp Taxes (albeit one that was not generally accepted) that a withdrawal of capital by one partner as part of a commercially related transaction whereby another partner contributes capital may be an assignment of a partnership interest and for certain purposes this has been given statutory effect[133] and extended;[134]
- a withdrawal of part of his capital by A related to a transaction whereby B contributes new capital or increases his capital;
- the routine admission of a new partner who contributes capital without there being any related retirement or withdrawal of capital by the existing partners. This will almost inevitably affect profit-sharing ratios, because of the participation of the new partner who acquires a share in the profits of the firm but where his share is less than the share of the outgoing partner, the shares of the other partners are increased although they may not increase them; and
- the retirement of a partner and withdrawal of capital without any related admission of new partner or increase of capital by the existing partners who may provide the funding for the repayment of capital through bank borrowing rather than injecting new capital.[135] As with the preceding point, the change in profit-sharing ratios will arise because of the retirement of the particular partner so that although the partner's share is 'increased' he does not 'increase' it as such.[136]

12.21 COMPUTATION OF THE CHARGE UPON TRANSFER: PROPERTY INVESTMENT PARTNERSHIPS

A key issue of principle is that the charge arises by reference to 'interests' but the chargeable amount is related to 'shares'. This will be important where there is a change in the 'interest' such as a variation of capital or repayment of loan accounts which may affect so-called 'interest payments' but which may not affect the 'share' as nominal participation of the partner in the profits. Also there are detailed problems of the assets to be included in the chargeable amount which may depend, *inter alia*, upon whether a para.12A election has been made and whether there is a Type A or Type B transfer.[137]

---

[133] FA 2003, Sched.15, para.36.

[134] FA 2003, Sched.15, paras.17 and 17A. HMRC Stamp Taxes is also of the view that giving guarantees of borrowings by the partnership and leaving profits undrawn can constitute relevant consideration in the context of transfers of partnership interests.

[135] It will be noted that there may be problems related to the anti-avoidance provisions of FA 2003, Sched.15, paras.17 and 17A which do not require any causal link or tax avoidance purpose.

[136] See FA 2003, Sched.15, para.36.

[137] FA 2003, Sched.15, para.14.

12.21.1 Transfers: type A or B?

The chargeable amount, which is the amount upon which the person who acquires an increased share or becomes a partner is liable to tax depends upon the nature of the transfer. There are, essentially, two types of transfer, as follows.

12.21.1.1 Type A transfer

Two categories of Type A transfers exist, namely:

- where there is an arrangement entered into under which the whole or part of a partner's interest as partner is acquired by another person who may be an existing partner and consideration in money or money's worth is given on behalf of the person acquiring the interest;[138] and
- where there are arrangements entered into under which a person becomes a partner and the interest of an existing partner in the partnership is reduced or an existing partner ceases to be a partner and there is a withdrawal of money or money's worth from the partnership by the existing partner (other than money or money's worth paid from the resources available to the partnership prior to the transfer).[139]

12.21.1.2 Type B transfer

Any other transfer of a partnership interest is a Type B transfer.

12.21.2 Chargeable amount

The chargeable consideration for the transaction is an amount equal to a proportion of the market value of the relevant partnership property. The proportion is dependent upon whether the person was or was not a partner before the transaction. Where the person acquiring the interest was not a partner before the transfer the proportion is his partnership share (i.e. share of the partnership income profits) immediately after the transfer. Where the person concerned was a partner before the transfer the proportion is the difference between his partnership share before and after the transfer.

---

[138] FA 2003, Sched.15, para.14(3A).

[139] This question of previously available resources is a matter of some obscurity. Clearly it is intended to deal with situations where new property is injected into the partnership such as new capital being subscribed or possibly loans being made by the partners to the partnership in order to fund the withdrawal of capital. However, there will be significant issues where the partnership has, for example, a pre-existing overdraft facility with the bank and this is drawn on in order to provide the repayment of capital. In a sense the overdraft facility is a 'resource' available to the partnership and it was previously available notwithstanding that the amount involved has increased. Other issues around this type of construction are likely to arise in many cases.

394

12.21.3 What assets?

Having determined the proportion that is to provide the basis for the charge, which is related to the partnership 'share' rather than the 'partnership interest', it is important to note that although it is the transfer of a partnership 'interest' that triggers the charge to tax the chargeable amount is calculated by reference to the partnership 'shares' (see **12.3**). The chargeable amount depends upon whether there is a Type A or a Type B transfer.

12.21.3.1 Type A transfer

In relation to a Type A transfer the relevant partnership property is every chargeable interest held by the partnership as partnership property[140] immediately after the transfer other than:

- any chargeable interest that was transferred to the partnership in connection with the transfer. This would appear to exclude from the charge any land contributed by the incoming partner as his capital;
- any market rent lease falling within Sched.15, para.15;[141] and
- any chargeable interest that is not attributable economically to the interest in the partnership that is transferred. This would seem to be intended to deal with particular partnership structures where there are arrangements relating to the capital where the assets of the partnership are divided into various bundles possibly described as 'A assets' and 'B assets'. In these situations the 'A assets' may be allocated to some of the partners but not all of them and the 'B assets' may be allocated to other partners. In this situation the cellular structure of the partnership would mean that the 'B assets' are not attributable economically to the 'A shares' or interests and will be excluded from the charge upon the transfer of an 'A interest'.[142]

12.21.3.2 Type B transfers

In relation to a Type B transfer the relevant partnership property is every chargeable interest held as partnership property[143] immediately after the transfer other than:

- any chargeable interest that was transferred into the partnership in connection with the transfer such as the contribution of land by way of new capital;
- any lease that falls within the exclusion of market rent leases;[144]

---

[140]   Which raises questions as regards investments held by the partnership that are not used for the purposes of the partnership business; see FA 2003, Sched.15, paras.35 and 37.

[141]   See also FA 2003, Sched.15, para.38.

[142]   FA 2003, Sched.15, para.14(5).

[143]   Again the problem arises as to whether an asset held by the partnership but as an investment and not as part of its business is partnership property for these purposes: FA 2003, Sched.15, paras.34(2), 35 and 37.

[144]   FA 2003, Sched.15, para.15.

- any chargeable interest that is not attributable economically to the interest in the partnership that is transferred;
- any chargeable interest that was transferred to the partnership on or before 22 July 2004;
- any chargeable interest in respect of whose transfer to the partnership an election has been made under para.12A. Since this will have borne SDLT upon the full market value without the benefit of the reduction for the sum of the lower proportions it would seem to be inappropriate that it is taxed again on changes in the partnership structure;
- any other chargeable interest whose transfer to the partnership did not fall within the special regime for the injection of property into the partnership. This will presumably include land acquired from unconnected parties under the ordinary transaction principles. Since these will have paid full SDLT upon acquisition it would seem to be inappropriate that they are brought into charge to tax upon any changes in the partnership.

12.22 TRANSFERS OF INTERESTS IN NON-PROPERTY INVESTMENT PARTNERSHIPS

For firms that are not property investment partnerships, there is a 'transfer of an interest' giving rise to the application of anti-avoidance provisions.[145] It would seem that where there is a 'transfer of an interest' for the purposes of these anti-avoidance provisions, although these are not necessarily arrangements within the special charge upon transfers of interests in property investment partnerships, they have to be noted and they cannot be protected by the making of a para.12A election.

12.23 EXEMPTIONS AND RELIEFS FOR TRANSFERS OF PARTNERSHIP INTERESTS

The market value charges override the exemption for gifts producing a reporting obligation even in relation to gifts of land or partnership interests, but all other reliefs apply in respect of contributions of land into or out of the partnership or transfers of partnership shares. Charity relief applies to transfers of partnership shares to charities and intra-group relief is available for transfers of land into and out of partnerships and the reliefs for company reconstruction apply. These reliefs are subject to the usual clawbacks relevant to the particular relief.[146]

---

[145] FA 2003, Sched.15, paras.17 and 17A.
[146] FA 2003, Sched.15, para.27.

12.24 TRANSFERS OF INTERESTS IN NON-PROPERTY INVESTMENT PARTNERSHIPS: ANTI-AVOIDANCE

Where a partnership includes chargeable interests among its assets changes in the partnership such as the retirement of partners, the admission of new partners or variations in the partnership shares may have SDLT implications. In broad terms, where the partnership is a professional partnership the basic charge applies only in relation to dealings with interests in a property investment partnership so that in professional partnerships or partnerships where there may be substantial land but the land is used for the purposes of the business rather than constituting the business itself such as farming or retail partnerships there is no direct charge, i.e. the 'transfers' are not within FA 2003, Sched.15, para.14.

However, certain anti-avoidance provisions have become more important. These were designed to supplement the original charges upon the transfers of interests in partnerships which own land which applied to all forms of partnership. However, notwithstanding the reduction in the scope of the charge upon transfers of interests in partnerships, so that it is now limited to property investment partnerships, these anti-avoidance provisions have not been reduced in scope and can apply where there is a transfer of land into a partnership that falls within FA 2003, Sched.15, para.10 because the transferor is either a partner or is connected with the partnership or there is, possibly, some form of merger or demerger where HMRC Stamp Taxes applies the charge upon the entry into the partnership as opposed to the charge upon land leaving the existing partnership. Subsequent changes in the partnership or capital or funding structures may give rise to a charge.[147]

Fortunately, in practice, for many professional partnerships this should not be an issue since the partners will not be connected. Any reduction for the sum of the lower proportions is likely to be negligible. Nevertheless, there are frequently situations where land is owned by some of the partners and leased into the partnership. It may be operating as some form of pension fund. In these situations there will be a total or substantial overlap between the members in the various partnerships[148] so that the para.10 regime may be applicable and subsequent dealings will be affected by the anti-avoidance rules depending upon the construction of the specific charging provisions.[149]

---

[147] Which, of course, raises the question of whether the special provisions for transactions between partnerships is an application of the para.10 charge, where applicable, or it is a separate charge outside para.10 so that paras.17 and 17A cannot arise.

[148] If accepted by HMRC Stamp Taxes as a business vehicle as opposed to a mere investment vehicle.

[149] FA 2003, Sched.15, para.23.

12.25 ANTI-AVOIDANCE FOR SPECIAL TRANSACTIONS

Anti-avoidance legislation means that other situations are brought into the charge to tax. These chargeable situations include:

- situations where there is a transfer of land to a partnership and there is a subsequent transfer of a partnership interest which is not otherwise a chargeable transaction; for the purposes of FA 2003, Sched.15, para.17, this is a chargeable transaction effected for a chargeable consideration equal to a proportion of the market value of the chargeable interest transferred previously into the partnership;[150] or
- where, within the three years after the transfer of a chargeable interest to a partnership, there is:
  - a withdrawal of money from the partnership which is not a distribution of income such as a person contributing land, withdrawing capital; or
  - a partner reducing his interest or ceasing to be a partner; or
  - a repayment of a loan made by the person contributing the land or a connected person.[151]

It is an open question whether HMRC Stamp Taxes intends to apply this provision to delayed payment of any money owing in respect of the initial establishment of the firm such as where one of the partners contributes land as capital and a balancing adjustment is made to reflect the intended capital and/or income interests.

These anti-avoidance provisions are designed to bring into the charge to tax transactions whereby a person contributes land to the partnership, subsequently another person becomes a partner and eventually the original contributor retires so that the 'new partner' effectively becomes the owner of the land. There are, of course, many variations upon this theme intended to be entrapped by this legislation so that, in general, retirements and admissions will henceforth require careful scrutiny taking into account these provisions. The acquisition of the land and the deemed transfer are linked transactions.

The effect of these provisions has to be noted because they can apply to commercial partnerships where there are the usual annual retirements and admissions to partnership. These are regarded by HMRC Stamp Taxes as 'arrangements' notwithstanding that they are unconnected with the acquisition of the land and are pursuant to the usual typical provisions in professional partnership agreements. Technically these could be treated as transfers of partnership interests to the extent that the partnership has a chargeable interest in land,[152] but it is believed that there may be an informal concession to be operated where the 'arrangements' are routine provisions in the partnership deed. Transfers of partnership shares are not notifiable

---

[150]   FA 2003, Sched.15, para.17.

[151]   FA 2003, Sched.15, para.17A.

[152]   This applies to all chargeable interests in land including leases other than certain leases granted solely for a full reviewable market rent where the rent has to be reviewed at least once every five years: FA 2003, Sched.15, para.15.

if the consideration (or deemed consideration) for the transaction does not exceed the nil rate threshold. This will protect most commercial partnerships unless the chargeable consideration exceeds the nil rate threshold. This also ignores the amount of any 'actual consideration' or deemed consideration for the transfer. The level of the contribution or withdrawal of capital is not, of itself, relevant for these purposes. The nil rate band is usually £150,000 (upon the basis that this is the relevant nil rate because the land held by the partnership is usually non-residential). In so far as certain of these provisions depend upon the existence of 'arrangements', it is believed that HMRC Stamp Taxes is contemplating operating an unofficial concession that normal retirements and admissions pursuant to the terms of the partnership deed will not be arrangements and so outside the scope of the tax – details are awaited.

12.26 INCORPORATION OF PARTNERSHIP

There are no specific reliefs for the incorporation of businesses whether in the form of sole traders or partnerships (see **Chapter 13**). In consequence, an attempt to convert a partnership into a body corporate will not be eligible for a simple relief. This seems to be part of a general policy of HMRC Stamp Taxes to prevent parties from converting land into shares which can be dealt with on a much more stamp duty efficient basis.

However, there are two possible areas where some reduction in the stamp tax charge may be available:

1. There is a specific relief for the conversion of an existing partnership into a limited liability partnership.[153] This provides the parties with the benefit of corporate personality and limited liability but without necessarily incurring all of the potential tax disadvantages of operating through a body corporate.[154] There are numerous conditions that have to be satisfied before the relief is available including an administrative one that the transfer of the business must be within one year of the date of the incorporation of the limited liability partnership. Care will, therefore, be needed in order to avoid unnecessary delays. There must be total identity between the members of the existing partnership and the members of the limited liability partnership.[155] The existing partners in their capacity as members of the new limited liability partnership must have their interests in the same proportions. The provisions do not, therefore, provide any relief where the limited liability partnership is formed to acquire the land from an independent party as the commencement of a totally new business or investment vehicle.

---

[153] FA 2003, s.65.
[154] See Technical Bulletin 50 (2000).
[155] However, HMRC Stamp Taxes has indicated that where the incorporation or conversion takes place at the same time as the routine retirements and new admissions at the end of any particular financial year this may not be an insuperable problem; see Technical Bulletin 50 (2000).

2.   There is a market value charge where land is transferred from a partnership to a connected person but in some situations this may qualify for a reduction by reference to the sum of the lower proportions (SLP).[156] In this situation it would seem that the reduction for the SLP is available for connected 'persons' and unlike the relief for transfers into a partnership is not limited to partners who are 'individuals'.[157] It may, therefore, be the situation that where a partnership which includes individuals,[158] is incorporating there may be a connected company. In this case it can be argued that the specific charge for transfers out of partnerships prevails over the normal connected company charge so that although these both impose a charge by reference to market value the partnership rules prevail and provide a possible reduction for the SLP.

12.27 PARTNERSHIPS AND GROUPS

Frequently the partners in a partnership will be bodies corporate that may be members of the same SDLT group. Problems arise as to the nature of partnership participation and the group structure (see **13.24**), and whether transfers into or out of the partnership qualify for the relief and, if so, how the provisions for the relief apply.[159]

---

[156]   FA 2003, Sched.15, paras.18 and 21; see **12.15**.

[157]   There are restrictions upon the reduction where the partnership consists solely of corporate members: FA 2003, Sched.15, para.24.

[158]   Note FA 2003, Sched.15, para.24 dealing with the relief where the partnership consists of bodies corporate.

[159]   FA 2003, Sched.15, paras.27 and 27A.

CHAPTER 13

Corporate transactions

13.1 BACKGROUND

Although the primary focus of this book is on acquisitions of land, there are problem areas for property transactions where bodies corporate are involved as vendors or purchasers of land[1] as well as where their shares are the subject-matter of the contract because the complexities of and lack of finality in the tax. A major review of warranties and indemnities is required, linked with previous reviews thereof since there are frequently significant changes in the structure of the tax which create long-term problems for corporate taxpayers and which will inevitably pass with the company to purchasers of its shares. In consequence since property lawyers are likely to encounter transactions involving companies an understanding of the issues arising would seem to be prudent.[2] HMRC Stamp Taxes intended to introduce a charge to SDLT upon dealings in shares and interests in 'land rich companies'. Like many jurisdictions outside the UK which have failed to produce a workable regime for such companies, HMRC Stamp Taxes has abandoned this attack on companies and their shareholders, but only 'for the time being'.

The problems involved include:

- whether the vehicle is a body corporate or a partnership or a deemed individual;[3]
- acquisitions of land by a company where, for example, the connected company charge applies;[4]
- the frequent practice of using companies as nominees or bare trustees may involve special charges;[5]
- acquisitions of land from companies where, in addition to the problems that generally affect persons acquiring land who are forced by statute to take over

---

[1]   Such as the need to file SDLT 4 (as amended) in virtually every case no matter how straightforward.

[2]   Note the comments of Lightman J in *Hurlingham Estates* v. *Wilde* [1997] STC 627 on the expected tax knowledge of property lawyers.

[3]   Jasmine Trustees v. Wells & Hind [2007] STC 660.

[4]   FA 2003, ss.53 and 54; see **13.4**.

[5]   FA 2003, Sched.16, para.3 (as amended) including a special charge for certain transactions between 22 July 2004 and 19 March 2005.

the provisional tax liabilities of the vendor,[6] there are special rules, imposing anti-avoidance provisions for reliefs available only for bodies corporate.[7] These are particularly important in practice, where special charges may arise where the vendor is a body corporate and reliefs for companies may have been obtained on a previous transaction (see **8.61**);

- new areas for due diligence and contractual warranties and indemnities for share purchases because of the primary clawback and secondary tax liabilities which may arise upon a sale of shares or a change of control, which are not the same type of event (see **Appendix C**); and
- a new set of related problems for valuing the securities in a body corporate because of the lack of finality in many areas of SDLT where 'time bomb' situations exist which may not be obvious from the accounts.

These special rules have long-term risks for purchasers from the company, purchasers of shares in a company, the company itself and the shareholders and directors who may be personally liable for the tax.[8]

13.2 'COMPANY'

13.2.1 'Company' and 'body corporate'

It is first necessary to identify those entities which are affected by these provisions since there are different definitions of 'company' and the meanings vary within the charging and compliance regimes. Detailed scrutiny of the relevant definitions is essential. There are long-term subtle practices of HMRC Stamp Taxes which frequently lie dormant but, from time to time, resurface to trap the unwary and it must not be assumed that 'company'[9] and 'body corporate' necessarily mean the same thing to HMRC Stamp Taxes,[10] although the EU rules against discrimination are having an impact in this area.[11] It seems, in practice, that HMRC Stamp Taxes may have abandoned this distinction between a 'body corporate' and a 'company'.

---

[6] See, for example, FA 2003, Sched.17A, para.11.

[7] FA 2003, Sched.17A, para.12.

[8] See, for example, FA 2003, Sched.7, paras.5 and 12.

[9] HMRC has also been known to take the point that 'company' in UK legislation means a registered company and does not include organisations such as local authorities and industrial and provident societies which are made bodies corporate by the ruling legislation, and Royal Charter corporations. These views are generally regarded as incorrect.

[10] For decades the view of HMRC Stamp Taxes has been that while 'body corporate' includes foreign vehicles, 'company' is limited to companies registered under the companies legislation; see *Nestle* v. *IRC* [1953] 1 All ER 877; *Chelsea Land* v. *IRC* [1978] 2 All ER 113.

[11] Note *Ministre de Finances* v. *Weidert* [2005] STC 1241; see also FA 2006, ss.169 and 172.

13.2.2 Basic definition

The basic definition for SDLT is that a 'company' means any body corporate or unincorporated association but not a partnership,[12] but this applies mainly for compliance purposes and is frequently modified for charging and exempting provisions such as those affecting unit trusts and open-ended investment companies. It will include for certain purposes clubs and similar organisations even where these are not bodies corporate by their controlling legislation.[13] Partnerships that are bodies corporate such as limited liability partnerships are not treated as companies.[14]

13.3 ACQUISITIONS BY COMPANIES: GENERAL POSITION

In general, the acquisition of a chargeable interest by a company is subject to SDLT by reference to the actual consideration and subject to the normal rules for specific performance. This can give rise to an immediate charge upon the incorporation of businesses, i.e. when the directors resolve to allot the consideration shares or the company takes effective possession of the land which will include the use of new or existing companies in connection with a corporate reorganisation or reconstruction. Moreover, it must be noted that HMRC Stamp Taxes has an adverse view towards the conversion of land into shares because of the possibility of a lower tax charge upon dealings in shares.[15]

13.4 SPECIAL CHARGES: CONNECTED COMPANIES

Three areas of special charge apply,[16] where:

- an estate or interest in land is acquired by a company which is connected with the person transferring or vesting the estate or interest;[17] or

---

[12] FA 2003, s.100.

[13] See now Co-operative and Community Benefit Societies and Credit Unions Act 2010.

[14] FA 2003, s.100(1); Sched.15, Part 1.

[15] But note potential traps on share sales such as where the vendor requires the purchaser to procure the repayment of any indebtedness of the target company since HMRC Stamp Taxes has long sought to argue that pursuant to Stamp Act 1891, s.57 the debt to be repaid is part of the stampable consideration, although this is a very dubious argument; see *Spectros International Plc* v. *Madden* [1997] STC 114.

[16] FA 2003, s.53.

[17] FA 2003, ss.53 and 54.

- an estate or interest in land is transferred to or vested in a company and some or all of the consideration for the transfer or vesting consists of the issue or transfer of shares or securities issued by a company with which the 'vendor' is connected;[18] or
- there is a transaction between a partnership and a connected company.[19]

The acquisition is deemed to be for a consideration not less than the market value of the chargeable interest immediately before the effective date, i.e. the chargeable consideration is the higher of the actual consideration or the market value of the chargeable interest. Where the transaction involves the grant of the lease at a rent the tax is charged upon the market value of the lease and the rent or the actual premium and net present value of the rent if greater. Where the transaction involves the grant of a lease, or possibly a deemed grant of a new lease,[20] there is a charge upon a deemed premium equal to the market value of a lease at that rent plus the net present value of the actual rent. It is specifically provided that this charge overrides the exemption for gifts and other transactions for non-chargeable consideration so that the transaction is fully notifiable.[21]

13.5   EXEMPTIONS FROM CONNECTED COMPANY CHARGE

FA 2003, s.54 provides that the connected company charge does not apply to acquisitions by connected companies where the consideration, if any, does not consist of or include shares or securities in the following cases.

13.5.1   Corporate trusts

Settlors (and certain members of their family) are connected with the trustees of the settlement. This means that, *prima facie*, a market value charge arises upon transactions whereby property is vested in corporate trustees except where the connected company which is to hold the estate or interest as trustee:

- is a person carrying on a business which consists of or includes the management of trusts; and
- is to hold the estate or interest as trustee acting in the course of that business; and

---

[18]   It seems that for these purposes the company must be connected with the other party (the vendor) prior to the transaction. The charge does not apply where the vendor becomes connected only as a consequence of the transaction.

[19]   FA 2003, Sched.15, Part 3.

[20]   Such as pursuant to FA 2003, Sched.17A, para.12A.

[21]   FA 2003, s.53; but this does not apply where the transaction is excluded from the connected company charge pursuant to s.54 thereof; different rules apply to transactions between partnerships, partners and connected companies; see **Chapter 12**.

- apart from Income Tax Act 2007, ss.993 and 994 and Corporation Tax Act 2010, ss.1122 and 1123 (trustees as connected persons), would not be connected with the 'vendor', i.e. is not a family owned company.

It should be noted that these exemptions do not protect companies controlled by trustees. For example, where trustees, whether corporate or individual, decide to transfer UK land into a company of which they are the sole shareholders there will be a market value charge notwithstanding that the company is incorporated outside the UK.

13.5.2 Nominee or bare trustee companies

These provisions are essentially aimed at settlements and there is no specific exemption for transfers to nominee companies. However, the Government stated in the debates on the Finance Bill 2003 that because no beneficial interest vests in the nominee company the value of the interest which it acquires, i.e. the bare legal title, is valueless so that no charge arises in practice. Since all acquisitions other than certain dealings in leases[22] by a nominee are treated as acquisitions by the beneficial owner and there cannot be an acquisition from oneself, a transfer between a nominee and the beneficial owner is not an acquisition or chargeable transaction[23] in any event.

This has, however, been modified subsequently. FA 2004 imposed charges upon the first assignment of leases granted by nominees,[24] but this was replaced by provisions in FA 2005 treating the grant of the lease as a fully chargeable transaction. These latter provisions also apply a full charge to a lease by the nominee company to the beneficial owner. Conveyancers will need to investigate whether the tenant selling the lease is a nominee or beneficial owner or trustee of a settlement and the dates on which the lease was granted or the agreement for lease was substantially performed.[25]

---

[22] FA 2003, Sched.16, para.3 (as amended); see **8.14** and **10.11**.

[23] However, there is a charge upon the first chargeable assignment of the lease: FA 2003, Sched.17A, para.11.

[24] FA 2003, Sched.17A, para.11.

[25] The key dates currently are 22 July 2004 and 19 May 2005. This may also raise the conveyancing issue of whether a receipt from two trustees is required pursuant to LPA 1925, s.27 since there will be actual knowledge of the trust and this may affect the overreaching principles.

13.5.3 Distribution by companies

Dividends *in specie*,[26] distributions by liquidators[27] and purchases and redemptions of share capital *in specie*,[28] are *prima facie* exempt because there is no chargeable consideration.[29] However, where the distribution is to a connected company the market value charge would *prima facie* apply;[30] but there is an exemption[31] for such acquisitions unless the chargeable interest being distributed was acquired by an exempt intra-group transaction within the preceding three years. However, there may be relief for intra-group transactions but there are problems over beneficial ownership and other restrictions where liquidations are involved.[32]

13.6 PARTNERSHIPS AND COMPANIES

Dealings between partnerships and companies where there is a degree of identity between the partners and the shareholders in the company can be complicated. It would seem that notwithstanding the potential significant overlap between the partners and the shareholders in the company the connected company charge[33] is replaced by the special regime for dealings between partnerships and persons connected therewith. In consequence, there are two potential areas of special charge, as follows.

---

[26] Which are in general law transactions for no consideration see *Wigan Coal and Iron* v. *IRC* [1945] 1 All ER 392; *Associated British Engineering* v. *IRC* [1940] 4 All ER 278; there may be issues where the dividend is declared as a cash sum to be satisfied by the transfer *in specie* whether there is a transfer in satisfaction of a debt pursuant to FA 2003, Sched.4, para.8; but see *Re Bradford Investments (No.2)* [1991] BCLC 688; note the possible benefits of such resolution where 'valuations' are concerned; *Stanton* v. *Drayton Commercial Investment Co. Ltd* [1982] STC 585.

[27] Frequently distributions by liquidators are subject to the shareholders taking over liabilities such as mortgages on the company's land. This creates a sale within the basic connected company charge and outside the distribution for no chargeable consideration exclusion therefrom (FA 2003, Sched.4, para.8). There are difficult issues where the shareholders give the usual indemnity to the liquidator at the end of the liquidation dealing with possibly undisclosed liabilities. This may be an uncertain consideration but it seems to take the transaction out of the exclusion.

[28] A return of share capital whether on the redemption of shares or a reduction of capital is a transfer in satisfaction of the rights of members and so is for a consideration (see *Re Bradford Investments* (No.2) [1991] BCLC 688). However, this is not a chargeable consideration because it falls outside FA 2003, Sched.4 and within the exclusions from the connected company charge pursuant to FA 2003, s.54.

[29] A charge to tax may arise where the property distributed is subject to a charge and the persons acquiring the land assume or are deemed to assume the liability in respect of the mortgage: FA 2003, Sched.4, para.8.

[30] The charge may be relieved if the conditions for exemption for intra-group transactions can be satisfied.

[31] FA 2003, s.54; note that transactions within these exemptions may not be notifiable because s.53 notification requirements apply to transactions chargeable pursuant to s.53 itself.

[32] See *Ayerst* v. *C&K (Construction) Ltd* [1976] AC 167; **13.8.**

[33] FA 2003, s.53.

13.6.1 Transfers from companies to partnerships

Where there is a transfer to a partnership by a person who is either a partner or a person connected with the partners the actual consideration is ignored and there is a special charge by reference to market value.[34] The charge is, however, reduced where the partners in the transferee or acquiring firm are either the person making the disposal such as the vendor or lessor or are individuals connected with the person making the disposal. Clearly, the restriction to 'individuals' as partners is significant. However, it does mean that there are possible reductions in the tax charge in this context. The reduction is by reference to the sum of the lower proportions which is basically designed to prevent a charge to tax where there is no real economic change in the ownership of the asset. This reduction in charge will, in effect, not apply where there is a transfer by a company to a partnership where the company is itself a partner or, it seems, the controlling shareholders in the company are individuals who are also partners. There will, however, be no reduction in the charge upon the market value or the proportion of the market value where the company is not a partner or the partners are themselves corporates and possibly trustees[35] who are not individuals who are shareholders in the relevant companies so as to be connected.[36]

13.6.2 Transfers from partnerships to companies

A similar situation arises where there is a transfer of a chargeable interest from a partnership to a body corporate. Similar rules apply where there is a transfer from a partnership to a 'person' connected with the partnership.[37] It is provided that there is a market value charge where there is a transfer of land out of a partnership to a person who was a partner or a person connected with the partners.[38] This is modified, however, where there are transfers out of partnerships that consist solely of bodies corporate[39] or between partnerships whether consisting of individuals or bodies corporate.[40] The details of these arrangements and the various reliefs are discussed further in relation to partnerships (see **Chapter 12**). However, it is provided that where the acquisition is made by a 'person' connected with the partners who are individuals or the acquiring body corporate is itself a partner the charge upon the market value or the proportion of any rent being derived where a lease is granted is reduced by the sum of the lower proportions, which is calculated

---

[34] FA 2003, Sched.15, para.10; see **Chapter 12**.
[35] Jasmine Trustees v. Wells & Hind [2007] STC 660.
[36] But note *Steele* v. *EVC* [1996] STC 785.
[37] This appears to be a drafting oversight in the legislation which was designed to prevent the use of partnerships for incorporating land and converting it into shares. Unfortunately, the draftsman appears to have overlooked the structure of the legislation. In consequence, any 'creative construction', i.e. judicial legislation, may provide a charge where the legislation indicates that there should be a relief.
[38] FA 2003, Sched.15, para.18.
[39] FA 2003, Sched.15, para.24.
[40] FA 2003, Sched.15, para.23.

by reference to the profit share entitlements in the income profits of the firm of the relevant partners. In consequence, where a partnership is seeking to incorporate there is a potential market value charge upon any land transferred from the partnership to the body corporate but this may be reduced where the company into which the business is being transferred is itself one of the partners or is connected with individuals who are partners in the firm.

13.7 PURCHASES FROM COMPANIES

Particular issues arise as regards the investigation and due diligence in connection with acquisitions from bodies corporate. Not all of these charges are unique to companies and, therefore, these issues may apply to acquisitions from other persons, but are more likely to arise with companies because of the tendency to utilise companies as nominees or bare trustees or other convenient vehicles for joint ventures.

The problem areas for investigation are:

- acquisitions of leases from nominees granted between 22 July 2004 and 19 May 2005; these may be taxable as the grant of new leases;[41]
- assignments of leases which are subject to special charges on the assignee[42] because the leases were exempt when granted pursuant to:
  - sale and leaseback arrangements;[43]
  - group or reconstruction relief.[44] This differs from clawback relief and applies even where the chargeable interest is acquired as part of the assets in an undertaking or business as a going concern. It will, in consequence, not always be obvious that this provision might apply so that it must become routine for questions to be asked;
  - relief for charities which can include charitable companies,[45] including corporate charities.

    There is no time limit on this charge upon assignment, nor is it a consideration for the application of these special charges that the grant of the lease and its subsequent assignment are either connected or part of some scheme or arrangement for the avoidance of tax.

---

[41] FA 2003, Sched.16, para.3; Sched.17A, para.11 (before the latest amendments).
[42] This overrides the exclusion of the usual indemnities on assignments pursuant to FA 2003, Sched.17A, para.17.
[43] FA 2003, s.57A (as amended).
[44] FA 2003, Sched.7, Parts 1 and 2.
[45] FA 2003, Sched.8; see **5.27**.

13.8 ROUTINE TRANSACTIONS

13.8.1 Liquidation

The liquidation of the company does not involve a disposal or acquisition of assets but it may operate to cause a clawback of some previously obtained exemption for intra-group transactions or company reorganisations.[46]

13.8.2 Receiverships

The appointment of receivers and similar arrangements such as administrators does not cause the same degrouping as liquidations and so does not pose the same risk of clawback. However, a sale of a subsidiary company by the receiver may trigger a clawback of previously obtained relief.[47]

13.9 CORPORATE REORGANISATIONS

There is no 'look-through' in relation to land rich companies so that transfers of shares and marketable securities are not, as such, subject to SDLT,[48] or a higher rate of stamp duty or stamp duty reserve tax. Nevertheless, many transactions involving shares in companies are affected, directly or indirectly, by SDLT. A corporate reorganisation may *inter alia*:

- involve clawback implications for previous transactions and possible warranty or indemnity claims for primary or secondary liability for the tax clawback in share sale contracts;[49]
- have problems of its own as regards reliefs because, for example, there are 'arrangements';
- encounter difficulties where the parties believe that the transaction is a transfer of a going concern for the purposes of VAT (see **4.30**);
- set up new clawback charges;
- create the risk of any assignment of a lease being taxed as the grant of a new lease so that there may be claim against the company by the assignee for an indemnity;[50]

---

[46] See *Ayerst* v. *C&K (Construction) Ltd* [1976] AC 167 on loss of beneficial ownership; FA 2003, Sched.7, para.3 but note paras.4(4) and 4ZA.

[47] FA 2003, Sched.7, para.3; but note paras.4(4) and 4ZA.

[48] It should also be noted that where the first step in an assignment is a 'transfer' of shares this is not included in the tax charge pursuant to the statutory general anti-avoidance provisions; see FA 2003, s.75C(1).

[49] See e.g. FA 2003, Sched.7, para.4(6).

[50] FA 2003, Sched.17A, para.12.

- create 'time bomb' situations such as future rent reviews within the company that may have a bearing upon share sales in the future (see **Appendix C**);
- be subject to the payment of tax deferred from previous acquisitions.[51]

The availability or usefulness of the reliefs from SDLT[52] may be dependent upon whether there is to be an immediate clawback of any intra-group relief obtained within the preceding three years.[53] In consequence, when planning a reconstruction of a company or a group and the possible utilisation of these reliefs it is now necessary to consider whether the proposed transaction will:

- trigger a clawback of previously obtained reliefs;[54] or
- set up a new three-year period in relation to land in the UK involved in the reconstruction; or
- involve a roll-over of previously obtained relief so that the clawback risk passes into the new group for the balance of the three-year clawback period.[55]

13.10   WAIT-AND-SEE PROBLEMS

Corporate reorganisations usually involve several steps which take time to be implemented. The SDLT issues on such reorganisations are complicated by the facts that SDLT arises on a transaction basis (see **1.18**) and that in the view of HMRC Stamp Taxes there may be two or possibly more effective dates.[56] Other events also may retrospectively adjust the circumstances so that there will be a lack of finality as at the date for testing whether the conditions for relief are satisfied. This gives rise to a fundamental problem of whether the relief is available at substantial performance where the condition was not to be satisfied until completion. For example a company may take possession to fit out before the obligation to issue shares arises and the shares are actually registered (i.e. 'issued'). HMRC Stamp Taxes seems, by long tradition, to have had difficulty understanding these issues but has not taken these points in practice.[57]

---

[51]   Which raises difficulties as to whether this statutory novation of the tax liability is excluded from the chargeable consideration as an assumption of liabilities within the relief or is a potential cash payment outside the relieving provisions.

[52]   Or their equivalent for stamp duty. The clawback and exclusion events will be related to share transactions and so within the realms of stamp duty and its reliefs such as FA 1930, s.42 and FA 1986, ss.75 and 77. As the clawback is related to a company leaving the group or a change of control, the relieving events for the clawback will be linked to the share transfers. Both sets of relieving provisions must, therefore, be noted.

[53]   FA 2003, Sched.7, para.4.

[54]   Including a relief from stamp duty obtained within the preceding two or three years (depending upon the date of the instrument for which the relief was obtained) since such relief remains subject to clawback (see FA 2003, Sched.19, para.6).

[55]   See e.g. FA 2003, Sched.7, para.4(6) and (7).

[56]   FA 2003, s.44(8) and Sched.17A, para.12B.

[57]   The author is aware of many cases where HMRC Stamp Taxes granted the relief notwithstanding that the consideration shares were not registered until several years after the execution of the

13.11   RELIEFS

In addition to the limited relief for transactions between members of the same SDLT tax group[58] there are two areas of relief available in relation to corporate reorganisations involving the 'acquisition' of chargeable interests in land, namely:

- total exemption for a limited range of corporate reconstructions;[59] and
- a reduced rate of 0.5 per cent for certain types of corporate reorganisations.[60] The conditions are less stringent than for 'reconstructions' but different anti-avoidance provisions apply.

13.12   IMPORTANCE OF STAMP DUTY RELIEFS

The SDLT reliefs are similar to those that applied and, to some extent, continue to apply in relation to stamp duty[61] although the importance of stamp duty reliefs has been reduced because of the reduction of stamp duty (and stamp duty reserve tax) to transactions involving shares and marketable securities and the lower rate of 0.5 per cent.[62] However, these stamp duty reliefs are important in two respects:

- the legislation is very similar, although not identical, so that the former decisions and practices in relation to stamp duty reliefs may be of direct relevance in relation to the meaning and interpretation of the SDLT reliefs; and
- in some situations the obtaining of relief from stamp duty pursuant to these various provisions, although related to shares, may have the effect of avoiding or postponing the clawback charge that arises where certain events have occurred. Although the reliefs from stamp duty pursuant to provisions such as FA 1986, s.75 are not directly, as such, applicable to SDLT the reorganisation of a company involving arrangements that qualify for stamp duty relief pursuant to these provisions may mean either that the SDLT relief taken in respect of some earlier transaction or even an earlier part of the transaction is not clawed back or such relief may be rolled over for the balance of the three-year clawback period.[63]

---

document for stamp duty. There is no evidence of the point being taken – few SDLT Enquiries have been initiated in this context.

[58]   FA 2003, Sched.7, Part 1; see **13.24**.
[59]   FA 2003, Sched.7, para.7; see **13.14**.
[60]   FA 2003, Sched.7, para.8; see **13.20**.
[61]   FA 1986, ss.75–77.
[62]   In consequence, certain aspects of these reliefs are effectively redundant.
[63]   See, for example, FA 2003, Sched.7, paras.4(6), 10(4) and (5) and 11.

13.13 PROFESSIONAL AND PRACTICE ISSUES

In consequence, property practitioners will need to have an awareness of the stamp duty reliefs available for share transactions in order to determine[64] whether their property transaction and reorganisation is one that will trigger an immediate clawback of previously obtained relief or is not such an immediate problem. Similarly, company and commercial solicitors will need to be aware of the potential consequences of these share and other transactions for SDLT.

13.14 RECONSTRUCTIONS

FA 2003, Sched.7, para.7 relieves chargeable transactions in land entered into in relation to certain types of company reconstructions.

A relief (i.e. no SDLT is initially chargeable) is available where a chargeable transaction is entered into 'pursuant to or in connection with'[65] a scheme[66] for reconstruction of a body corporate (which includes foreign incorporations but not partnerships),[67] whereby another body corporate, including foreign companies, acquires the whole or part of the undertaking[68] of the other body corporate for a consideration as below.

The consideration for the acquisition (which may include third party inducements)[69] must consist either:

- wholly of the issue[70] of non-redeemable shares[71] in the company acquiring the undertaking all of the target company's shareholders; or
- partly of the issue of non-redeemable shares to the shareholders and the balance being the assumption or discharge of the liabilities of the company whose undertaking is being acquired.

This limitation on the type of consideration permitted means that it is important to ensure that the transfer of the undertaking escapes the charge to VAT as a transfer of

---

[64]   And to avoid a possibly unnecessary charge to stamp duty reserve tax; FA 1986, ss.86 and 92.

[65]   *Clarke Chapman John Thompson Ltd* v. *IRC* [1975] STC 567, holding that these are wide words including matters not directly part of the scheme.

[66]   The author has had difficulties with HMRC Stamp Taxes on the meaning of the word 'a' and whether there are two schemes or larger arrangements; see, for example, *Crane Fruehauf* v. *IRC* [1975] STC 51.

[67]   FA 2003, s.100.

[68]   See, for example, *Baytrust Holdings Ltd* v. *IRC* [1971] 1 WLR 1333; *E. Gomme* v. *IRC* [1964] 3 All ER 497.

[69]   *Crane Fruehauf* v. *IRC* [1975] 1 All ER 429; *Central and District Properties* v. *IRC* [1966] 1 WLR 1015.

[70]   This requires registration; see *Oswald Tillotson* v. *IRC* [1933] 1 KB 134; *Brotex Cellulose Fibres Ltd* v. *IRC* [1933] 1 KB 158; *Murex* v. *IRC* [1933] 1 KB 173; *National Westminster Bank* v. *IRC* [1995] 1 AC 119.

[71]   Difficulties may be encountered with foreign incorporates where the capital structure and the process of the 'creation' or the equivalent of 'varying' shares because of the local law.

a going concern. Should there be a payment of cash[72] such as VAT or arrangements for dealing with VAT should the transaction not be the transfer of a going concern, this may take the transaction outside the scope of the exemption from stamp duty.

13.15 CONSIDERATION ISSUES

Various issues arise on this question of the consideration in addition to the registration of shares, including those discussed below.

13.15.1 The identification of the consideration

There are numerous problems in what appears to be a simple matter of the law of contract. It is frequently the situation that the acquiring purchaser or company may have to make arrangements for the indebtedness of the target company.[73] It is provided that the assumption of liabilities is not to be regarded as disentitling the acquirer from the relief. It would seem, therefore, that arrangements whereby the transferee of the undertaking agrees to assume the liabilities or agrees to indemnify the existing company against these liabilities or, it would seem, makes a payment of cash in order to enable the target company to discharge its liabilities will remain eligible for the relief. However, this last point concerning cash payments is one where there are potential difficulties. Technically, it seems that the relief should not be available because there is a payment of cash rather than the assumption of liabilities although this is an arrangement designed to enable the acquiring company to deal with the liabilities related to the target company. HMRC Stamp Taxes has, from time to time sought to argue that cash payments are not the assumption of liabilities although it has also on numerous occasions accepted that a cash payment is the assumption or 'discharge' of liabilities within the relieving provisions.

13.15.2 VAT complications

The question of VAT is not so easily dealt with. Clearly, where the acquiring company agrees to indemnify the existing company against liability for previously unpaid VAT (as opposed to paying the VAT upon the immediate transaction) this is an assumption of liabilities within the relief. The problem is how to deal with any VAT that will or may arise in relation to the reconstruction. This is, obviously, a point that needs to be addressed commercially and as a matter of contract since the existing company may be liable for VAT in respect of the transaction should it not qualify for treatment as a transfer of a going concern.

Where the parties believe that the transaction involves a transfer of a going concern but make the usual provision that should the transaction not qualify as a

---

[72] Note the drafting issues of debt and set-off which are crucial in this context; *Coren* v. *Keighley* 48 TC 370.

[73] Note the drafting issues such as in *Spectros International Plc* v. *Madden* [1997] STC 114.

transfer of a going concern the purchaser will pay the VAT upon delivery of an appropriate tax invoice, such payment in cash must inevitably exceed the permitted 10 per cent limit. There is little evidence of the approach of HMRC Stamp Taxes in practice because the current Enquiry procedure is not being operated at the level intended. In so far as extra consideration is required, it could consist of an obligation to issue further shares but this still leaves liquidity problems. Moreover, an undertaking to issue shares is not the issue of shares nor the payment of cash; it is a separate chose in action in the form of a right to be allotted[74] and so outside the scope of the eligible consideration for the relief. The most prudent course is to provide that the consideration consisting of the issue of shares is inclusive of VAT, if any is payable. This avoids the possibility that HMRC Stamp Taxes might refuse the relief upon the ground that the obligation to issue shares in satisfaction of the VAT was not an issue of shares within the relieving provisions.[75] Hopefully, since the relief requires a transfer of an undertaking the transaction may qualify for exclusion from VAT as a transfer of a going concern.

13.15.3   Third party participation

The area of inducements to parties to enter into transactions is one that causes considerable fiscal difficulties. There may be general taxation issues as to whether the agreement to accept the inducement is the performance of services which may affect the taxation liability.[76] There is considerable technical difficulty in this area which depends upon the facts and structuring of the documentation as to whether the offering of inducements by, for example, a third party such as an offer to purchase the consideration shares, where the vendor requires cash whereas the purchaser prefers to issue shares,[77] is a separate offer or is an inducement that is part of the arrangement.[78] This can be a major problem where there are arrangements for the onward sale of the shares (see **13.18**) or there is some form of reconstruction which involves the formation of a new company and, particularly in times of

---

[74]   Which is not the same as a right to an allotment of shares. The issue of shares by a company is complex and raises many issues for SDLT. There are key distinctions between the contractual right to be allotted (a future share transaction), a right to an allotment (the directors have acted) and the issue of the shares (i.e. registration): *Letts* v. *IRC* [1957] 1 WLR 201; *Pye-Smith* v. *IRC* [1958] 1 WLR 905; *Oswald Tillotson* v. *IRC* [1933] 1 KB 134; *Brotex Cellulose Fibres Ltd* v. *IRC* [1933] 1 KB 158; *Murex* v. *IRC* [1933] 1 KB 173. These may be key issues not only on the question of eligibility for relief but also on the fundamental question of the effective date and the charge to tax.

[75]   Note the issues of whether there is a 'wait-and-see' principle in SDLT; see **1.24**.

[76]   See, for example, the problems of reverse premiums and VAT and issues in relation to income for services in e.g. *Gleneagles Hotel* v. *Customs and Excise* [1986] VATTR 196; *Russell* v. *Customs and Excise* [1987] VATTR 194; *Customs and Excise Commissioners* v. *Cantor Fitzgerald International (C-108/99)* [2001] ECR I-7257; *Trinity Mirror* v. *Customs and Excise* [2001] STC 192; *Ridgeons Bulk* v. *Customs and Excise* [1994] STC 427.

[77]   Obviously there are complex company law issues as to whether this is an indirect issue of shares to a third party for cash, sometimes described as a 'backdoor rights issue' which may be subject to restrictions.

[78]   See, for example, *Crane Fruehauf* v. *IRC* [1975] STC 51; *Central and District Properties* v. *IRC* [1966] 2 All ER 433; *Shop and Stores Developments* v. *IRC* [1967] 1 All ER 42.

recession or insolvency, a third party is to inject funds into the new company in order to deal with its liabilities. There is a very fine line according to Scarman LJ[79] between an arrangement where new funds are injected or shares being issued as within the consideration package are to be acquired by a third party so that these inducements are part of the scheme of reconstruction which is the whole arrangement or scheme or where they are part of a larger arrangement of which the scheme or reconstruction is itself only a part, i.e. they operate outside the reconstruction scheme although commercially linked. There would seem to be a major drafting issue for professional advisers, to decide between situations where there is a single agreement under which a company is to be reconstructed and new money to be injected whether by way of subscription for capital in the new company or to purchase shares being issued and situations where the injection of the new funds is subject to and conditional upon the reorganisation taking place. In the latter case HMRC Stamp Taxes has for several decades accepted that the relief is available although in the former case the relief has been refused.

13.16 SHARE REGISTERS

Additionally, immediately after the acquisition each shareholder in the register of members in the target company must also appear in the register of members of the new company holding shares in the same proportion or as near thereto as is possible. Underlying beneficial ownership of the shares is irrelevant. The share register controls the exemption and not necessarily the underlying beneficial ownership. For example, if A and B each own one share in the target company and B holds that one share as nominee for A who is the sole beneficial owner, the relief is available only if, after the transaction, the shares in the acquiring company are registered equally in the name of the two members; the relief is refused if only one share is issued to the nominee notwithstanding that this reflects the underlying beneficial ownership. Subscriber shares can easily upset the proportions of the registration of the consideration shares. It is possible to reduce the number of shares to be issued to any of the subscribers so that after the transaction the correct proportions are maintained. In relation to the equivalent reliefs from stamp duty, strict observance of the conditions was insisted upon so that a divergence in shareholding percentages that emerged only at the seventh place of decimals could lead to a rejection of the relief. It can therefore be expected that an approval will be similarly difficult for SDLT, although changes in the legislation requiring that shareholder identification must be as nearly as possible indicate that rounding up or down need not proceed with too many decimal places.

---

[79] *Crane Fruehauf v. IRC* [1975] STC 51.

13.17 BONA FIDES AND TAX AVOIDANCE

The acquisition must be effected for bona fide commercial reasons and must not form part of a scheme of arrangement of which the main purpose or one of the main purposes is the avoidance of liability to stamp duty, income tax, corporation tax, capital gains tax or SDLT. This is usually established by producing a copy of any clearance letter from HMRC in relation to capital gains tax,[80] but the preparation of the clearance application may require careful drafting since such correspondence has been utilised by HMRC Stamp Taxes to refuse the relief.[81]

There have been numerous practical difficulties with HMRC Stamp Taxes on these issues. The test has now been converted into two separate tests: tax avoidance and commerciality. As regards the first condition, it must be shown that the transaction is not intended[82] to achieve one of the listed or prescribed tax benefits. This is, of course, a matter of evidence but it is not easy to persuade HMRC Stamp Taxes as to the parties' motives or purposes.

13.17.1 Multiple purpose or serendipity

Also, there have been considerable difficulties in persuading HMRC Stamp Taxes that the taxation benefit in question is one that is an incidental benefit and is not a prime objective of the reorganisation.[83] There may be commercial reasons for the reorganisation which do not include taxation matters such as the need to segregate certain key assets of the company from the financial risks associated with its involvement in the business. For example, a property holding company may be formed as part of the reorganisation process to acquire land which will be leased to the trading company so that in the event of trading difficulties the land is fully protected. This may mean that there are incidental taxation benefits.[84] There will, therefore, be a major need to present matters to HMRC Stamp Taxes in such a way that it can be established that any taxation consequences are incidental and not the sole or primary purpose of the arrangement. Also, the bona fide commercial purpose is a separate test from that involving tax avoidance.

There are two problems in relation to the scope of the test what is 'commercial' and whether the test applies to the overall arrangement or each individual step. This is a key issue since stamp taxes apply to individual steps ignoring the overall

---

[80] HMRC Stamp Taxes tends to rely upon capital gains tax clearances rather than those obtained or not obtained in relation to other taxes.

[81] See e.g. *Swithland Investments* v. *IRC* [1990] STC 448.

[82] There are, however, subtle differences between 'intention', 'purpose' and 'motive' such as what is the reason (motive) for the purpose. The purpose for acquiring the gun is to carry out the 'intention' to kill X because he is a love rival (motive). These fundamental issues are usually not understood by the current judiciary normally because they are not properly presented by counsel in argument.

[83] *Moody* v. *Cox and Hatt* [1917] 2 Ch 71.

[84] Although there may be taxation disadvantages because what was formerly a single trading enterprise may now be two separate enterprises for the purposes of inheritance tax only one of which is trading and the main asset-owning company is an investment company outside the various reliefs.

planning. HMRC Stamp Taxes appears to take the view that when looking at the tax avoidance test it is necessary to look at the overall arrangement and not necessarily the individual steps. However, it seems that in relation to the bona fide commercial test each step has to be viewed separately and justified as a proper commercial arrangement. In consequence, there have been problems with arrangements where there are interest-free loans or leases at a low rent being granted. Establishing bona fides is not always particularly easy and there will need to be substantial contemporaneous corroborative evidence to back up any claims for the relief.

In addition, HMRC Stamp Taxes takes the view that where there are certain aspects of tax efficiency in the transaction whether a primary purpose or an incidental consequence, this can affect the availability of the relief because the tax efficiency means that there is not a bona fide commercial purpose. For example, relief has been objected to by HMRC Stamp Taxes in relation to reorganisations where there are possibilities of mitigation of a tax other than those on the prescribed list. A reorganisation may have certain inheritance tax benefits or may have foreign tax advantages. Although these are not prescribed taxes for the tax avoidance test HMRC Stamp Taxes takes the view that if one of the factors driving the decision is a desire to mitigate other taxes this renders the decision not bona fide commercial. This is clearly a wrong approach as a matter of basic principle.[85]

As there is no advance clearance procedure for SDLT and there are increasing indications that HMRC Stamp Taxes is less willing to rely upon clearances for other tax purposes notwithstanding that these apply a similar test,[86] there are practical difficulties for the adviser who must take a decision as to whether he thinks the relief is available when structuring the transaction and, importantly, when completing the return and deciding how much tax to pay and whether to claim the relief.

13.18 'RECONSTRUCTION' DEFINED

It is a condition of the relief that there is a scheme of reconstruction which requires that an existing company transfers its undertaking to another company which carries on substantially the same activities and that both companies are owned by substantially the same shareholders. Although total shareholder identity is an express condition for this relief[87] and the test for reconstruction requires only 'substantial identity', merely satisfying the former condition is not necessarily sufficient to satisfy this test. There may be situations where, notwithstanding the mirror share capital condition is satisfied, there may not be a scheme of reconstruction and the relief will be lost. For example, where there is a pre-sale reorganisation and there are plans for the onward movement of the shares in the acquiring company

---

[85] *IRC* v. *Brebner* 43 TC 705; *IRC* v. *Willoughby* [1997] STC 995.
[86] The author has encountered several cases where HMRC Stamp Taxes has refused to co-operate in a pre-transaction ruling because the issues are 'too difficult'.
[87] FA 2003, Sched.7, para.7(4).

to a third party[88] which have become so integrated into the contracts that they are part of 'the scheme' or the scheme itself where the related arrangements are outside the scheme, the onward sale can affect what is the consideration and/or whether there is shareholder identity.[89] Where there are plans for the injection of fresh outside capital into the acquiring company the documentation relating to and the timing of such contributions can affect whether there is a scheme of reconstruction.[90] The word therefore raises a larger timeframe in testing for the entitlement to the exemption. In addition such arrangement may also be a key issue as to whether there is consideration being provided by a third party which jeopardises the exemption.

13.19   ACQUISITION OF 'UNDERTAKING'

There must be the acquisition of the whole or part of an undertaking,[91] i.e. the assets transferred must constitute a 'business' or 'part of a business' of the transferring or target company. Not every asset of the company will be an undertaking.[92] There is accordingly a question of fact in each case, whether the assets concerned formed part of a business or were mere investments not constituting a business as such.[93] The holding of investments for example by owning land and receiving the rent can itself constitute a business[94] and be an undertaking. There is, therefore, a potential problem where the assets concerned are shares[95] or land if HMRC Stamp Taxes contends that, essentially, holding investments is not necessarily a 'business' and does not involve an undertaking for these purposes. It will be necessary to take a firm line to persuade HMRC Stamp Taxes with suitably weighty support for the taxpayer that an undertaking is involved. It will, however, be important to ascertain the degree of investment holding in any particular case and the nature of the activities of the company.

A particular area of difficulty is where the land has been occupied for the purposes of the business such as a factory and the objective of the arrangement is to segregate the ownership of the assets from the business. There may, therefore, be the incorporation of two new companies to one of which the business activities are

---

[88]   Normally, the scheme ends when the consideration shares are registered: *Crane Fruehauf* v. *IRC* [1975] STC 51; but see also *Snell* v. *HMRC* 78 TC 294; *Swithland Investments* v. *IRC* [1990] STC 448.

[89]   Central and District Properties v. IRC [1966] 2 All ER 433.

[90]   See the discussion in *Crane Fruehauf* v. *IRC* [1975] 1 All ER 429.

[91]   See also R v. Industrial Dispute Tribunal ex p Courage and Co. Ltd [1956] 1 WLR 1062.

[92]   See also *E. Gomme Ltd* v. *IRC* [1964] 1 WLR 1348.

[93]   *Baytrust Holdings Ltd* v. *IRC* [1971] 1 WLR 1333.

[94]   See e.g. *IRC* v. *Tyre Investment Ltd* 12 TC 646.

[95]   Although shares are outside the charge to SDLT. The inclusion of shares in one or more subsidiary companies and/or the inclusion of land interests may, on the basis of practices of HMRC Stamp Taxes which lack consistency in this area, produce an initial return that the whole operation is not a reconstruction or an undertaking regardless of the nature of any other assets involved. The relief from stamp duty may provide a roll-over of the clawback provisions; see e.g. FA 2003, Sched.7, paras.4(4) and (6) and 10(4) and (5). It may matter whether the shares are part of an undertaking.

transferred and to the other of which the land constituting head office or factory premises or retail outlets is transferred and these are leased back to the other new company to occupy for the purchase of the business. HMRC Stamp Taxes may seek to refuse the relief in respect of both land movements, by arguing that the transfer of the freehold or reversionary interest is not part of the undertaking because the business carried on by the new company in relation to the land is not the same as the business carried on by the original company. However, there is no requirement in the legislation or previous related case law for the undertakings to be the same in the transferor and the transferee companies. A situation as outlined above will frequently arise where there are rationalisations of the business in the new company or where the assets acquired are absorbed into the activities of an existing company. Such an approach by HMRC Stamp Taxes would have little merit and should be resisted by reliance on the legislation and the case law.

There are technical issues in relation to the question as to whether there is some form of reconstruction or amalgamation (which latter is not within the relief) where a company that has its own trade or business acquires all or part of the trade of another company because there is not the necessary underlying ownership at shareholder level in relation to the business at the operating level as the new business represents an amalgamation of two or more different businesses that go into common ownership rather than continuing in separate ownership. However, this is not the same question. The pooling of business may constitute an amalgamation but it is not a reconstruction. Any authorities on the point of 'amalgamation' are not relevant in relation to 'reconstruction' and what is required is that what passes to the new company is part of what used to be the undertaking of the existing company.

Similarly, in situations such as that illustrated above of segregating the land from the business activities,[96] HMRC Stamp Taxes may challenge the relief in respect of any lease from one new company to another new company notwithstanding that the lessee is carrying on the same trading activities as the existing company. Its argument is that this is not part of the undertaking of the company to which the reversionary interest was transferred in order to enable it to grant the lease. However, the drafting of the reliefs from SDLT have seriously undermined this type of analysis for HMRC Stamp Taxes. It is simply required that the various dealings in the chargeable interest are 'in connection with'[97] the transfer of the undertaking, etc. They do not have to form part of the undertaking. In consequence, it would seem that the plain English drafting has enlarged the scope of the relief so that it is no longer necessary to have to resist the argument of HMRC Stamp Taxes so strenuously that there must be the carrying on of the same business and any lease between the new companies cannot be part of an undertaking. Such arrangements are 'in

---

[96] Which may be challenged by HMRC Stamp Taxes as not being a bona fide commercial purpose.

[97] See *Clarke Chapman John Thompson Ltd* v. *IRC* [1975] STC 567, and to apply a restrictive construction in this context would cause difficulties for HMRC Stamp Taxes in relation to the statutory general anti-avoidance provisions of FA 2003, ss.75A–75C.

connection with' the reconstruction of the company and therefore the relief has been (probably inadvertently) potentially significantly relaxed and enlarged.

13.20 PARTITIONS AND REORGANISATIONS OF COMPANIES: REDUCED RATE

There is a relief in the form of the reduced rate of 0.5 per cent[98] where the conditions for the full relief for 'reconstructions' are not satisfied. This is available where there is a family disposal requiring the company's activities to be split; in very limited circumstances it may also be available for contributions of assets into a joint venture vehicle but this is a situation where fears of tax avoidance have overruled the need for reliefs for commercially desirable arrangements. There are numerous conditions that have to be fulfilled. However, where the terms and conditions are the same as or similar to those for reconstruction relief they should bear the same meaning as set out above.

13.20.1 Qualifying conditions for the 0.5 per cent rate

A reduced rate of SDLT of 0.5 per cent (but without any adjustment to the chargeable consideration) is available where a body corporate (which now includes foreign companies) acquires the whole of part of the undertaking of another body corporate (which can include foreign companies) for a consideration as below.

The consideration must consist either:

• wholly of the issue of non-redeemable shares in the acquiring company; or
• partly of the issue of non-redeemable shares in the acquiring company and partly of either the assumption or the discharge of liabilities of the disposing company and/or cash not exceeding 10 per cent of the nominal value of the non-redeemable shares issued as part of the consideration. This can include VAT if the transaction does not constitute a transfer of a going concern which clearly cancels the relief (see **4.30**).

Such consideration shares must be 'issued' either:

• to the company whose undertaking is being acquired; or
• to all or any of the shareholders in the company whose undertaking is being acquired.

These terms, in general, are the same as those utilised for the similar relief for reconstructions and, in practice, bear the same meaning.

---

[98] It must be noted that there is a risk that where the relief is clawed back this is at the full rate relevant to the transaction without credit for the 0.5 per cent tax paid initially. The issues are complex but the risk of 'double taxation' has to be noted.

13.20.2 Disqualifying conditions

13.20.2.1 Associated companies and share arrangements

The relief is not available unless the acquiring company is not associated with another company that is a party to arrangements with the target company relating to shares of the acquiring company issued in connection with the transfer of the undertaking or part.[99] For these purposes companies are 'associated' if one has control of the other[100] or both are controlled by the same person or persons,[101] and 'arrangements' includes any scheme, agreement or understanding whether or not legally enforceable.[102] This condition will preclude the relief where, as part of the arrangement, there is a plan for the consideration shares to be sold to a third party.[103] It would also appear to strike down the relief in cases where the transaction for which the relief is being sought is a preliminary step to injecting the business into a joint venture. The terms of the articles of association of the joint venture company and any shareholder agreements[104] may make the claim for relief vulnerable to these provisions. It remains to be seen how aggressive HMRC Stamp Taxes intends to be where bona fide commercial arrangements of this nature are involved.

This condition does not apply where the relevant arrangements are not with a body corporate but with individuals or possibly partnerships even where these include corporate partners. It must, however, be noted that limited liability partnerships are, in general, bodies corporate and arrangements with these may fall within this restriction upon the relief notwithstanding that for certain SDLT purposes the legal personality of such a partnership is to be ignored.[105]

13.20.2.2 Restricted undertaking

There must be the acquisition of an undertaking or part of an undertaking which has been described above (see **13.19**); but there are restrictions upon the type of land activities that can be undertakings within the relief. The relief is not available in those cases where the undertaking or part of the undertaking acquired by the acquiring company has as its main activity the carrying on of a trade that does not consist wholly or mainly of dealing in chargeable interests. For these purposes 'trade' has its meaning for the purposes of income tax.[106] This, of course, relates to attempts to deal with the undertaking of companies that are essentially land

---

[99]   FA 1986, s.76(3A).
[100]   As defined by Corporation Tax Act 2010, ss.449 and following.
[101]   FA 1986, s.76(6A)(a).
[102]   FA 1986, s.76(6A)(b).
[103]   Although this might also give rise to a clawback problem where the onward sale arises spontaneously subsequently in the same way that an inappropriately drafted onward sale of shares or injection of new funds cancels the previously mentioned relief for reconstruction.
[104]   See e.g. *Steele* v. *EVC* [1996] STC 785; *Irving* v. *Tesco Stores (Holdings) Ltd* [1982] STC 881.
[105]   FA 2003, Sched.15, para.2.
[106]   FA 2003, Sched.7, para.8(5A).

investment companies and to allow the relief only where the land is simply one of the assets used in the course of the business and does not represent the main business.[107]

This disqualifying condition raises many issues where a company wishes to separate its land from the risks of its business carried out on the land. Obviously, in this situation land occupied as a factory or office or retail premises or for the purposes of a farming business will meet the conditions since the undertaking of the existing company will consist of the carrying on of a trade that is not just property investment or development. However, as far as the acquiring company is concerned, its business or undertaking will be the holding of land with a view to leasing it to the associated trading company. While this provision may provide useful ammunition in relation to the argument for the relief considered above, since it indicates that there can be the acquisition of part of an undertaking that is not itself a business, it seems that HMRC Stamp Taxes might seek to refuse the less stringent relief where there is the segregation between the ownership of the land and the carrying on of the business thereon.

13.21 CLAWBACK OF BOTH OF THESE RELIEFS FOR CORPORATE REORGANISATIONS

Clawback of both of these reliefs within FA 2003, Sched.7, Part 2, can occur where:

- relief has been obtained under either of the above provisions; and
- control of the acquiring company changes before the end of the period of three years beginning with the effective date of the transaction[108] or more than three years after that date where the change of control is in pursuance of or in connection with 'arrangements', which include any scheme, arrangement or understanding whether or not legally enforceable[109] made before the end of the three-year period; and
- at that time the acquiring company still holds the interest that was acquired by the exempt transaction or an interest derived therefrom and that interest has not subsequently been acquired at market value under a chargeable transaction in relation to which relief pursuant to FA 2003, Sched.7, paras.7 or 8 was available but was not claimed then.

It is important to note in this context that there may be a 'change of control' without a change of control. It is possible for more than one person or group of persons to have separate control of a company at the same time because there are many criteria

---

[107] Compare the definition of property investment partnerships pursuant to FA 2003, Sched.15, para.14 (as amended).

[108] Since there may be two or more effective dates for the same transaction (see **3.3**) it seems that the later of these dates will be the commencement of the clawback period. In consequence, there should be no delay between substantial performance and completion in order to avoid re-starting the ticking of the three-year clock to the disadvantage of the client.

[109] FA 2003, Sched.7, para.9(5)(a).

for testing whether a particular person or group of persons exercises 'control'.[110] There can, it seems, be the acquisition of control by a person without the former controllers losing 'control' within any of the particular aspects of the definition. In consequence, an arrangement whereby a White Knight agrees to subscribe for share capital in the new vehicle may mean that he has control and there is a 'change' of control notwithstanding that the original shareholders continue to retain control because they have, for example, more than 51 per cent of the votes.

13.22 TAXABLE AMOUNT

Where the clawback applies the relief in relation to the exempt transaction or an appropriate proportion of it is withdrawn and SDLT becomes chargeable.[111] The amount of tax payable is the tax that would have been chargeable in respect of the exempt transaction but for the relief if the chargeable consideration for that transaction had been an amount equal to the market value of the chargeable interest and any related property.[112] The appropriate proportion means an appropriate proportion having regard to the subject-matter of the relevant exempt transaction and what is held at the time of the change of control by the acquiring company or by that company and any relevant associated companies.[113]

13.23 EXCLUSIONS FROM CLAWBACK

The exemption for land acquired in connection with a scheme of reconstruction is not withdrawn where the change of control arises as follows:

- as a result of a transaction in shares that is between one party to a marriage and the other party which is effected in connection with a transaction that qualifies for the matrimonial breakdown relief;[114]
- as a result of a transaction varying a disposition following a person's death that is within the relief for variations within two years after the death;[115]
- where the control of the company acquiring the land changes as a result of an intra-group transfer of shares which qualifies for exemption pursuant to Finance Act 1930, s.42 or Finance Act (Northern Ireland) Act 1954, s.11;

---

[110] Note the problems of two or more persons acting together or as parties to some joint venture arrangement having combined 'control' for these purposes.

[111] FA 2003, Sched.7, para.9.

[112] This is an odd provision since, in most cases on such a reconstruction, it is likely that the companies will be 'connected companies' when the transaction will be deemed to be at not less market value in any event (see FA 2003, s.53). This charge appears to restrict the amount of charge pursuant to the connected company provisions.

[113] FA 2003, Sched.7, para.9(3).

[114] FA 2003, Sched.3, para.3.

[115] FA 2003, Sched.3, para.4.

- as a result of a transaction in shares which qualifies for exemption pursuant to Finance Act 1930, s.42;[116] the clawback is not terminated but merely held over for the balance of the three-year period. In consequence, the clawback applies where there is a 'degrouping' of the relevant companies during the unexpired portion of the three-year period which is not itself excluded from the clawback under the provisions mentioned in this and the surrounding paragraphs;
- where the control of the company acquiring the land changes as a result of transfer of shares to another company in relation to which relief pursuant to Finance Act 1986, s.77 applies because essentially this relief is available only where the ultimate shareholders remain unchanged.

13.24   RELIEF FOR INTRA-GROUP TRANSACTIONS

An exemption from SDLT is available for chargeable transactions if both parties are bodies corporate within the same SDLT group as at the effective date[117] of the transaction which includes unlimited companies, foreign incorporations, certain local authorities, charter corporations and other bodies provided that they have the necessary share capital structure and are the parent company of the group. This relief is similar to but not identical to the relief from stamp duty (and indirectly stamp duty reserve tax) for share transactions. While the former cases and practices may provide some guidance as to the availability of this relief they are not guarantees that the relief will be available but they may help to avoid or to defer clawback charges.

---

[116]   Or Finance Act (Northern Ireland) 1954, s.11.

[117]   Since there may be more than one effective date for the transaction it is necessary to satisfy the conditions for exemption at both effective dates, i.e. substantial performance and completion. If the conditions for relief are satisfied as at substantial performance there is no automatic carry forward of the relief to completion where this is a separate effective date. Conversely, where the conditions are satisfied as at completion but not as at substantial performance there is no carrying back of the relief. In addition, where reliefs are obtained but are subject to clawback if events happen within three years after the effective date the three-year period will commence as at the date of substantial performance but the clock will stop running and a new three-year clawback period will commence if there is subsequent completion. HMRC Stamp Taxes has not yet addressed the issue of where a chargeable transaction is notified and takes effect by reference to substantial performance but there is an appropriate change more than three years after the effective date so that, *prima facie*, the clawback does not arise. However, the parties may decide to tidy up the title by proceeding to a formal completion after the operation of the clawback event. It would seem, in these circumstances, that the conditions for the exemption cannot be satisfied and the tidying-up of the title is fully taxable notwithstanding that as at substantial performance the relief was available and intervening events have not produced a clawback of the charge.

13.24.1 Group structure

13.24.1.1 Seventy-five per cent subsidiary

This relief requires that the companies are associated as part of what may broadly be described as an SDLT tax group. This requires that:

- one body corporate is the 75 per cent subsidiary of the other; or
- both are 75 per cent subsidiaries of a third company.

The 75 per cent shareholding test requires that the parent company is the beneficial owner of not less than 75 per cent of the ordinary share capital of the subsidiary, i.e. all the issued share capital, by whatever name known, of the company other than capital, the holders of which have a right to a dividend at a fixed rate but have no other right to share in the profits of the company. This test can be satisfied by both direct and indirect shareholdings through other companies.[118]

This means that there can be two types of group structure. There can be a direct or linear group where A owns the whole of the share capital of B which owns the share capital of C and so on.[119] Also there may be a triangular structure or pyramid where A owns the share capital of B which owns the share capital of D and A owns the share capital of C which owns the share capital of E. In these situations B and C and D and E are members of the same group provided that the various shareholding and economic conditions are satisfied.

13.24.1.2 Seventy-five per cent economic interest

In addition to the 75 per cent share holding in nominal terms, group relief applies if the parent company has a 75 per cent economic interest in the subsidiary company, i.e. 75 per cent of the assets in a winding up and 75 per cent of the dividend.[120]

This primarily applies to shares, but certain types of loan capital such as convertible loan stocks, certain limited recourse finance, and profit-sharing loans are treated as shares for the purpose of the economic interest test. In consequence, the rights of creditors of the subsidiary company must be investigated to determine whether they affect the group structure. It will be noticed that these conditions are essentially incompatible with the nature of SDLT. The relief is tested by the circumstances as they exist as at the relevant effective date or dates. Unfortunately, many of the conditions, particularly those relating to economic interests, can only be satisfied on an annual basis. Rates of interest may fluctuate and the company may make a loss over the year. It seems that HMRC Stamp Taxes takes a crude approach to the legislation. Essentially, if it looks as though the conditions are satisfied as at the effective date then the relief will be obtained. The fact that the conditions could not be satisfied at the end of the year sometime after the effective date does not

---

[118]   See, for example, FA 2003, Sched.7, para.1(4).
[119]   Compare *Rodwell Securities Ltd* v. *IRC* [1968] 1 All ER 257.
[120]   FA 2003, Sched.7, para.1(3).

retrospectively cancel the relief although, technically, it might give rise to a clawback issue because the shareholding structure will change as economic circumstances change. Conversely, if the conditions do not look as though they are satisfied as at the effective date or dates the relief is not retrospectively obtained if the conditions are subsequently satisfied as at the year end. This is the result of crude legislative preparation. The tests are based upon those that apply for annual taxes such as corporation tax and have been taken across into other taxes such as stamp taxes without any proper consideration of the fact that the two tests and taxes are mutually incompatible.

13.24.2 Control test

The parent company must also have 'control' of the relevant subsidiaries and there must be no arrangement in place whereby another person could acquire control of the acquiring company but not of the vendor company.[121]

13.25 ANTI-AVOIDANCE PROVISIONS

There are two sets of provisions designed to restrict the availability of the relief:

- there are certain disqualifying conditions which prescribe certain arrangements so that the relief is not available; and
- there are certain clawback provisions whereby the relief having been obtained is forfeited if within three years or possibly longer certain events occur.

13.25.1 Disqualifying 'arrangements'

Notwithstanding that the parties have satisfied or avoided the above qualifying and disqualifying provisions, the relief is not available where there are 'arrangements' which meet certain conditions in the transferee company.[122] It is necessary for HMRC Stamp Taxes to reject the relief where there are arrangements and to show that the types of transaction within those arrangements fall within the prescribed restrictions.

13.25.1.1 'Arrangements'

'Arrangements' include any scheme, agreement or understanding whether or not legally enforceable. It is necessary for there to be some involvement with a third

---

[121] FA 2003, Sched.7, para.2; but intra-group reliefs are potentially available where the intra-group transaction is a preparatory move for a larger reconstruction of the company.

[122] There are also issues as to whether the shares are beneficially owned by the appropriate person for the relief.

party such as a purchaser of the shares.[123] It is difficult to have a unilateral arrangement no matter how strong the intention to sell or to bring about the desired result may be, but it seems that the practice may continue to be based upon the views set out in relation to stamp duty in Statement of Practice SP3/98. As regards the provision and receipt of the consideration and ceasing to be associated, the practice set out in that Statement of Practice will be applied in relation to SDLT. One area of uncertainty is the provision excluding the relief where there is an arrangement whereby the consideration or part thereof is to be received by a non-associated person, such as where an intra-group lease is granted prior to the sale of the reversionary interest whereby rent becomes payable to a non-group landlord. Hitherto this has not proved an obstacle to obtaining the relief.[124]

13.25.1.2 Prescribed arrangements

The types of arrangement leading to the non-availability of the relief are that:

- the consideration, or any part of the consideration for the conveyance or transfer is to be provided or received, directly or indirectly by an outsider, i.e. a person other than an appropriately associated body corporate; or
- the disposing company and acquiring company are to cease to be associated by reason of the acquiring company ceasing to be a 75 per cent subsidiary;[125] but there may be relief where this is merely a step in a larger arrangement.[126] Reorganisations by liquidators transferring assets into a new clean subsidiary company will be outside the relief since a company in liquidation is not the beneficial owner of shares in its subsidiary companies. The appointment of a receiver or administrator does not affect beneficial ownership;[127] but hiving down assets or businesses by a receiver to a new subsidiary is unlikely to qualify for the relief because there may be arrangements to degroup the subsidiary company or the relief, if obtained, will be clawed back within three years although in certain situations the relief may not be clawed back for preparatory moves for larger reconstruction of the company.

The relief is also not available where the intra-group transaction is a subsale or an assignment of a contract with a vendor who is not a member of the SDLT group.[128] Alternative finance arrangements relating to a sale and sale back affect the availability of the relief.[129]

---

[123] *Times Newspapers* v. *IRC* [1971] 3 All ER 98.
[124] However, such an arrangement faces other problems such as clawback charges and special charges on assignment, pursuant to FA 2003, Sched.7, Part 1 and Sched.17A, para.11.
[125] FA 2003, Sched.7, para.2.
[126] FA 2003, Sched.7, para.2(1).
[127] Ayerst v. C&K (Construction) Ltd [1976] AC 167.
[128] FA 2003, s.45(5A)(a); cf. *Escoigne Properties Ltd* v. *IRC* [1958] AC 549.
[129] English Sewing Cotton Co Ltd v. IRC [1947] 1 All ER 679.

13.25.2 Clawback of intra-group relief

13.25.2.1 Clawback event

The intra-group exemption is withdrawn and the SDLT becomes payable where, within three years after the effective date,[130] the acquiring body corporate while still holding the land ceases to be a member of the same group as the vendor/lessor. The clawback also applies where the land is held by a relevant associated company[131] to which the original acquiring company has transferred the property, and that associated company leaves the group at the same time as the degrouping of the initial transferee or lessee company, while the relevant associated company holds the chargeable interest or an interest derived from a chargeable interest that was acquired by such exempt intra-group transaction and has not subsequently been acquired at market value under a chargeable transaction for which group relief from SDLT was available but was not claimed (i.e. attempts to exploit the intra-group relief to escape the clawback are vulnerable to attack).

There are numerous points that need to be noted in relation to the operation of the clawback provisions:

- the degrouping does not require a disposal of all or any of the shares which form the basis of the group structure as at the relevant effective date.[132] It can arise where new shares are issued so that the shareholding is reduced below the 75 per cent level or dividend rights or rights on a winding up are varied or certain types of loan capital are issued which mean that the economic 75 per cent requirement cannot be satisfied;
- the test is purely chronological. There is no requirement for 'arrangements' nor need the original transaction be in connection with the subsequent degrouping; and
- a company ceases to be the beneficial owner of shares in its subsidiary companies when it goes into liquidation[133] but not receivership. This will *prima facie* apply to the liquidation of various companies, although there are certain exclusions for certain types of liquidation and reconstruction considered below. However, in times of recession the provision can result in clawback charges notwithstanding that there is a bona fide commercial attempt to rescue the company's business and save jobs.

---

[130] Or longer if arrangements are in place for degrouping during the three-year period such as negotiations for the sale of the company starting within the three-year period.

[131] A 'relevant associated company' means a company that is controlled by the company that acquired the land pursuant to the exempt transaction immediately before the control of that company changes and of which control changes in consequence of the change of control of that company: FA 2003, Sched.7, para.9(4).

[132] i.e. the later of the two effective dates of substantial performance and completion; see **3.3**.

[133] Ayerst v. C&K (Construction) Ltd [1976] AC 167.

13.25.2.2   Taxable amount

The amount of tax chargeable is the tax that would have been chargeable in respect of the transaction for which the exemption was obtained for the intra-group transaction. This is on the basis that the chargeable consideration for that transaction being between connected companies would have been an amount not less than the market value of the chargeable interest acquired by that transaction[134] together with any interest or right appurtenant or pertaining to the chargeable interest that is acquired with it.

13.25.2.3   Degrouping associated companies

It is a requirement of the clawback that the transferee company continues to hold the chargeable interest or an interest derived from it at the time of the clawback event. In order to counteract certain avoidance devices that involve movement of assets between associated companies which degrouped at the same time, the clawback charge applies to a relevant proportion of the value of the land where the land has become fragmented. The tax can be recovered not only from the company that holds the chargeable interest or any property derived from it at the time of the degrouping event.[135] The charge may also be recovered from the vendor, or any company that at the relevant time (i.e. at any time during the clawback period between the original transaction and the degrouping event) was a member of the same group as the purchaser company and was above it in the group structure.[136] This means that warranties and indemnities relating to clawback charges within the target company are not necessarily sufficient since there are the secondary liabilities for other members of the group which need to be expressly provided for. Also the tax due in respect of the clawback can be recovered from any person who at any relevant time was a controlling director of the purchaser or of a company having control of the purchaser.[137]

13.25.3   Exclusions from clawback

The exemption for intra-group transactions is not withdrawn where the purchaser/lessee ceases to be a member of the same group as the vendor/lessor as a result of:

- a transaction in shares of the vendor company[138] whereby the vendor leaves the group; but subsequent dealings in the shares of the acquiring or 'purchaser' company causing it to leave the group[139] can produce a clawback charge;[140]

---

[134]   FA 2003, s.53.
[135]   FA 2003, Sched.7, paras.4, 4ZA and 4A.
[136]   FA 2003, Sched.7, para.5.
[137]   See *Hely Hutchinson* v. *Brayhead Ltd* [1968] 1 QB 549 on the duty of directors to investigate the affairs of companies to the boards of which they are elected prior to the date of their election.
[138]   FA 2003, Sched.7, para.4ZA(1).
[139]   Including a change of control.
[140]   FA 2003, Sched.7, para.4ZA(4).

- anything done for the purposes of or in the course of winding up the vendor/lessor or another company that is above the vendor/lessor in the group structure.[141] A company is 'above' the vendor/lessor in the group structure if the vendor/lessor or another company 'above' the vendor/lessor is a 75 per cent subsidiary of the company;[142]

- an acquisition of shares by another company, in relation to which the share transfer is exempt from stamp duty pursuant to FA 1986, s.75, immediately after which the purchaser/lessee is a member of the same group as the company acquiring those shares.[143] However, in this case the exclusion of the clawback is not on a permanent basis: the position is merely held over. SDLT is clawed back if:

  - the purchaser/lessee ceases to be a member of the same group as the company acquiring the relevant shares within three years of the effective date of the transaction for which the intra-group exemption was obtained (or after the three-year period when in pursuance of or in connection with arrangements made before the end of this period); and

  - at the time it ceases to be a member of the same group, the purchaser/lessee (or any company that ceases to be a member of the same group as the company acquiring the shares in consequence of the purchaser/lessee ceasing to be a member) holds a chargeable interest acquired under the transaction for which the intra-group exemption was obtained, or derived from an interest so acquired, but not subsequently at market value, under a chargeable transaction for which intra-group exemption was obtained[144] but not claimed.

The clawback is not excluded where the transferor leave the group prior to the degrouping of the transferee or lessee company,[145] but subsequent dealings in the shares in or a change of control of the transferee or lessee company may trigger a clawback.

13.26 PROCEDURE FOR 'CLAIMING' OR ACQUIRING EXEMPTIONS FOR CORPORATE RECONSTRUCTIONS AND INTRA-GROUP TRANSACTIONS

As with all reliefs from SDLT,[146] there is no formal procedure for applying to HMRC Stamp Taxes 'claiming' the reliefs pursuant to Sched.7 as with equivalent

---

[141] FA 2003, Sched.7, para.4(4).
[142] FA 2003, Sched.7, para.4(5).
[143] FA 2003, Sched.7, para.4(6).
[144] Pursuant to FA 2003, Sched.7, para.1.
[145] FA 2003, Sched.7, para.4ZA.
[146] See **Chapter 5**; there is, as a result of amendments, currently a procedure for claiming repayment of overpaid tax set out in FA 2003, Sched.11A. It is essential that the company has all relevant materials and records to support a claim for repayment of overpaid tax but note the problem of claiming repayment of tax where there is a valid amendment of the return within the restrictive 12-month period pursuant to FA 2003, Sched.10, para.6.

stamp duty reliefs. The parties simply take the relief by making appropriate entries in the land transaction tax return and not self-assessing any tax or paying the lower amount of SDLT and hoping that any subsequent HMRC Stamp Taxes Enquiry agrees with their views.[147] The usual range of penalties and interest will apply if the interpretation adopted by the parties proves to be incorrect, but provided that they have considered all relevant matters properly and can prove this by having made and retained contemporaneous written records they may not be subject to the extended limitation periods[148] and additional penalties[149] for 'negligence' or 'fraud' or 'carelessness' in making the return.

13.27 SHARE TRANSACTIONS, DUE DILIGENCE, WARRANTIES AND 'TIME BOMBS'

Share acquisitions and valuations may be adversely affected by the company's position since, as described elsewhere, much of the tax is provisional and it is difficult to achieve finality. Purchasers of shares need to be aware of these long-term open tax positions including clawback payments or forfeiture of reliefs or subsequent rent reviews or linked transactions and other situations which are lying dormant but likely to 'explode' like a time bomb at any time within the company. Not all of these have a time limit when the tax risk expires and even the expiration of a lease is no guarantee that the potential problems have ceased. There is also a fundamental question as to whether the company has appropriate records and all other information that it may require for dealing with an Enquiry or discovery assessment and any of its own tax events (see **18.17**).

Reliefs are available for reconstructions but these are subject to numerous conditions and long-term problems such as clawback or special charges upon later unrelated transactions. These long-term issues affecting provisional tax positions may have a significant impact upon the company's assets. Clawbacks entered into on the acquisition of land (i.e. additional consideration payable upon the happening of a specified event at some future date which may not occur for 80 years) can leave the company with an open tax position for many years with a serious risk that the original provisional return was underestimated as well as an open tax position where the tax may have been postponed or not properly declared which has to be resolved before the company can be reconstructed or dissolved. It seems that such deferred or potential tax charges are not being adequately reflected in companies' accounts by the auditors who are apparently signing off accounts without recognising these issues of deferred or potential tax liabilities as well as the contractual risks in the notes to the accounts. For example, the company's base cost for capital

---

[147] Any title registered upon the basis that the relief was available cannot be challenged by HMRC Stamp Taxes or the Land Registry notwithstanding the relief is rejected by HMRC Stamp Taxes.

[148] FA 2003, Sched.10, para.31.

[149] FA 2003, s.87; Sched.10, para.31A.

allowances will not be properly dealt with and should the tax not be taken into account profits will be overstated and excessive dividends and directors' bonuses may be improperly declared.

In consequence, it is not sufficient merely to ask for warranties and indemnities to the effect that the company is up to date with its SDLT. As with all aspects of the self-assessment tax regime the possibility of Enquiries which may challenge a relief that has been claimed or disposals at market value[150] included in the self-assessment and any related penalties and interest will have to be taken into account. Deferred tax issues in relation to postponed payment of tax or the enforced assumption of tax liability in relation to the assignment of leases will require investigation. In addition, SDLT like other taxes can arise as a 'secondary tax liability', i.e. a company may become liable for the tax of another company.[151] In consequence, warranties and indemnities should extend to such secondary liabilities by expressly including liability for specified taxes arising in such circumstances. However, it should be noted that where such secondary liabilities arise there is an obvious risk that any indemnities may be valueless since HMRC is unlikely to pursue such secondary liabilities unless the company primarily liable is insolvent. For example, as there is power to recover the clawback amount from other companies in the same group as the acquiring company or lessee body corporate, the potential impact upon the proposed arrangements has to be investigated possibly where there are plans for the liquidation of any company liable directly or indirectly for the clawback amount. There will need to be careful planning of any arrangements to fund any SDLT[152] actually clawed back since this may involve a payment in cash as part of the reconstruction which is not permitted by the terms of the section granting the relief intended to be relied upon, thereby destroying the exemption being sought. The possible roll-over of the clawback into the new group will also need to be investigated where the particular stage is merely one step in a much larger reconstruction involving onward movement of shares which may be inconsistent with the roll-over treatment of the clawback.

13.28 SHARE SALES, WARRANTIES, INDEMNITIES AND DUE DILIGENCE

The following is not intended as a comprehensive review of the warranties and indemnities required in share purchase agreements which have never been regarded as being within the scope of this book. This is merely a review of the problem areas that need to be drawn by property solicitors to the attention of their corporate colleague when carrying out due diligence for consideration by them when acquiring shares (see **Appendix C**).

The change to SDLT from stamp duty and, in particular, that it is a self-assessment tax that is directly enforceable with severe penalties for non- (or inadequate)

---

[150] Note *Langham* v. *Veltema* [2004] STC 544.
[151] See, for example, FA 2003, Sched.7, paras.5 and 6; see **Chapter 7**.
[152] Or stamp duty from the previous regime.

compliance and the fact that there is no finality until at the earliest the end of the Enquiry period (which, in certain circumstances, may run for 21 years from the effective date of the transaction) has introduced whole new areas of due diligence in relation to share sales. These include the 'time bombs' mentioned above.

Unlike adjudication for stamp duty, obtaining the SDLT 5 is merely the start of the process; it is not a guarantee that the correct amount of SDLT has been paid. HMRC can challenge an SDLT 1 on the basis that:

- the figure inserted as market value was not correct;[153]
- the estimates of possible future payments with prior transactions were not properly prepared;
- the exemption claimed was not available; or
- the transaction was linked or was affected by later linked transactions and the initial return may have been provisional and requires a subsequent retrospective adjustment possibly producing additional tax.

Also as mentioned previously there might be problems with the Land Registry where employees have asserted a statutory duty[154] to refuse registration even where there is a Revenue certificate (SDLT 5) if they believe the relief claimed was not available,[155] or where they believe that the exemption is being utilised for what the Land Registry employee regards as tax avoidance.

It remains to be seen whether assignees taking an exempt lease that is subject to a special charge upon assignment[156] as part of the purchase of the business will insist upon some adjustment in the price or some reverse payment in respect of the additional stamp duty cost of the transaction. This may mean that certain leases could have a 'negative value' in that it may cost money to dispose of them.

The problems of proper compliance, leases of negative value, subsequent adjustments for variable payments such as rent and overages, etc., remain within the company and are not, as such, affected by the change of ownership of its shares although the share transaction may trigger a clawback of reliefs previously obtained or possibly roll-over the clawback. Purchasers of shares will therefore need to investigate the SDLT position of the company in depth in order to discover what current and long-term problems may be locked within the company and adjust the price and/or take suitable warranties and indemnities.

The lack of finality in relation to much of SDLT can be regarded as a ticking time bomb for persons acquiring shares in a company. Where there is a direct purchase of land the lack of finality can be dealt with. Either it is a problem for the vendor who retains it and must therefore take appropriate steps which will be drawn to the attention of the purchaser or they will by law be passed to the purchaser or assignee who, if properly advised, will be able to take appropriate steps for his protection.

---

[153] *Langham* v. *Veltema* [2004] STC 544.

[154] Based upon a misreading of FA 2003, s.79(1) (as amended); see **1.10.2**.

[155] Notwithstanding that even HMRC Stamp Taxes does not have express power to refuse to act upon a land transaction return and to require the parties to prove that the claimed relief is available.

[156] FA 2003, Sched.17A, para.12; see **8.60**.

However, when purchasing shares in a company that has an open-ended SDLT liability the due diligence process will require looking through the company to see what its property position may be. The open-ended nature of the taxation liability may be because of the structure of the tax such as where the company has bought land with a variable consideration where the tax may have been deferred; or it may be as a result of a failure to provide for an appropriate exit strategy in the contractual arrangements and the parties have embarked upon some form of 'cascade of covenants' as described by some solicitors where there is a potential liability that can extend for up to 100 years. The situation is, however, not limited to purchases of land with some form of overage or clawback arrangement; it may also extend to routine transactions such as where there is a lease granted on commercial terms with a variable rent. As a result of changes to the legislation the problem of reviewable rents is not limited to the first five years of the term but can extend to periods after the expiration of that period.[157] It may apply to situations where there are options to renew the lease[158] or there may be a holding over pursuant to the Landlord and Tenant Act 1954 (see **8.47**) or there may be a routine variation of a lease that involves some form of express or implied surrender and regrant where the existing lease had an open-ended tax position because of the variable nature of the rent or premium. All of these liabilities lie within the company and will not emerge into 'real issues' until the appropriate events happen. However, the impact of these real issues emerging upon the position of the company will be reflected in the value of the shares of the company so that these issues have to be dealt with by way of proper investigation into the affairs of the company supported by suitable warranties and indemnities that are established in such a way that they can be enforced or any appropriate security in relation to them is valid should there be any problems in tracing the vendors of the shares when the problems emerge many years into the future. The due diligence process of asking for suitable warranties must be designed to produce the appropriate responses from the vendor in a disclosure letter or appropriate warranties and indemnities being insisted upon by the purchaser.

13.29 POTENTIAL PROBLEM AREAS

These situations include the following.

13.29.1 Variable rents: first five years

In the case of leases with variable rents, as described elsewhere, the tax position has to be reviewed at some stage during the first five years of the term of the lease. This may result in increased taxation being payable or a refund of tax already paid. Purchasers of shares in a company will require protection against the company having seriously underestimated the tax charge with the problems of related interest

---

[157]   FA 2003, Sched.17A, paras.13, 14 and 15.
[158]   See the issues of successive linked leases pursuant to FA 2003, Sched.17A, para.5; see **4.13**.

and penalties with the consequent significant reduction in its assets. Indeed, even the current owners of the shares at the time when the company enters into the relevant land transaction or is subject to a rent review or begins holding over will need to know the position and what tax should be provided for in the company's accounts. Failure to recognise the full extent of the liability could mean that the company's profits are overstated, negligently, and any dividends paid or directors' bonuses declared could be either returns of capital or unlawful or commercially inappropriate or even beyond the powers of the directors leaving them with a personal liability to reimburse the company for the overpayment. This will apply even where the lease has been assigned and appropriate contractual arrangements have been entered into with the assignee.

13.29.2　Variable rents: after five years

Variable rents raise problems beyond the expiration of the fifth year of the term of the lease. All leases with variable rents are potentially vulnerable to the special charge that arises on the basis of a deemed new lease where any subsequent increase represents an abnormal increase in the rent. While it may prove commercially difficult to safeguard the purchaser of shares against the full consequences of a potential subsequent increase in the rent giving rise to such a charge, the purchaser of shares may find it prudent to obtain the full SDLT history of all leases granted on or after 1 December 2003 within the SDLT regime and discover their SDLT position including the base rent for abnormal increases, namely the highest rent paid during any 12 months during the first five years of the term.

13.29.3　Clawback: change in share ownership/control within a three-year period

Other forms of relief[159] are subject to clawback if there is a change in the share ownership or control within a three-year period. The details of these clawback provisions are considered elsewhere but share purchasers will need appropriate warranties that neither the immediate transaction nor any previous transaction will give or has given rise to a clawback. This may go beyond the immediate company since in some situations, although there may have been a change of ownership or control, the relief is not immediately clawed back but the liability continues to follow the company under its new ownership for the balance of the three-year term.

13.29.4　Effect of other subsequent events

Other forms of relief are subject to withdrawal by reference to subsequent events.[160] In other cases[161] a relief may be cancelled by the imposition of a special charge upon subsequent dealings in the property and a well-advised third party may depress the

---

[159] See, for example, FA 2003, Sched.6A; Sched.7.
[160] See, for example, FA 2003, Sched.6A.
[161] FA 2003, Sched.17A, para.12.

price of the asset or seek a reverse indemnity not subject to tax[162] thereby depriving the company of assets and taking value from the shares.

13.29.5 Open-ended nature of the compliance regime

The timing problems are not limited to the open-ended substantive taxation liabilities. The long-term issues include the open-ended nature of the compliance regime which potentially extends beyond the 21-year period to over a century given the current practices related to certain types of consideration. With the aim of facilitating e-conveyancing and title issues by seeking to remove stamp taxes from title problems and attempting to put SDLT issues behind the land register, HMRC Stamp Taxes created a longer-term problem in many situations such as sales or companies where the tax issue is not closed because the land transaction return can be challenged with consequent costs even where the challenge or Enquiry or discovery assessment is totally unjustified. In consequence, it is no longer possible because of the provisional nature of the tax structure to deal with the situation by means of a simple warranty that all of the company's documents are duly stamped;[163] the fundamental changes made in relation to both the charge to SDLT and its administration mean that there is no finality in most cases because using an SDLT 5 is not the equivalent of adjudication and HMRC Stamp Taxes has up to 21 years to investigate the transaction. An Enquiry or discovery assessment can produce costs even where unjustified or where justified there will be additional tax, interest and penalty charges. Provision for them has to be made, particularly since a successful Enquiry does not necessarily preclude a subsequent discovery assessment.[164]

13.30 COMPLIANCE SITUATION FOR WARRANTIES ON SHARE PURCHASE

A purchaser of a company will require appropriate warranties that the company is up to date with its SDLT compliance if only to deal with the problem that the mere filing of a land transaction return may be open to challenge for a period of 21 years.[165] Undertakings should be obtained to the effect that:

- all forms that should have been filed have been filed;
- the correct forms have been lodged;
- the information contained within the forms was correct; and
- the forms are not open to challenge. There must also be some contractual provision that there are no current Enquiries in progress and that there are no

---

[162] FA 2003, Sched.4, para.16; Sched.17A, para.17.
[163] Which might be void pursuant to Stamp Act 1891, s.117.
[164] FA 2003, Sched.10, paras.30(3) and 12(2A).
[165] FA 2003, Sched.10, para.31.

reasons to believe that if there is an Enquiry launched[166] in relation to any particular transaction undertaken by the company this will lead to the imposition of extra tax, interest and penalties. As with all taxes based upon self-assessment, these warranties will need to be wide-ranging since self-assessment requires the parties to form a view as to matters such as market value or present and future market rents and, in relation to SDLT, the fundamental problem of 'cost' for the supplies of services and works all of which can be challenged by HMRC.

The company may have bought land on some overage or earnout basis where the tax was originally dealt with on an estimated basis. This will require investigation of whether the tax has been appropriately guestimated and deferred on a proper basis. There must also be a review as to when instalments and any tax deferred in relation to such payments[167] are payable.

There may also be a risk of penalties and interest for the company should a land transaction return be challenged.

13.31 DEFERRED OR PROVISIONAL TAX

A major problem of SDLT is that it lacks finality and this problem of open tax positions will run with the company notwithstanding any change in the ownership of shares in the company (see **13.27** and **Appendix C**). In certain situations, particularly those related to variable payments, whether by way of premium or rent, the original tax calculation is provisional only and in many cases payment of estimated tax can be deferred. The first SDLT 1 will have been filed on the basis of estimated payments. In many cases the taxpayer company may have been able to defer the payment of the tax on the variable amount.[168] Details of these matters will be required to be disclosed and taken into account in fixing the price, as well as undertakings that the amount in respect of which the tax has been deferred is the correct amount. Also, warranties should be obtained to the effect that no additional tax over and above that estimated and postponed will fall due; that the company has made adequate provision in its accounts for the payment of the deferred tax; and that this has been correctly reflected in its dividend policy and the payment of directors' bonuses.[169]

---

[166] An Enquiry may be launched without HMRC Stamp Taxes having any reason to suspect errors in the land transaction return (SDLT 1). It is a random process.

[167] FA 2003, ss.53, 80, 87 and 90; Stamp Duty Land Tax (Administration) Regulations 2003, SI 2003/2837, Part 4.

[168] FA 2003, ss.53, 80, 87 and 90; Stamp Duty Land Tax (Administration) Regulations 2003, SI 2003/2837, Part 4.

[169] As an incidental point since this tax is purely estimated and the figures may prove to be higher as circumstances develop, particularly over a long period of time, the question of the level of the provision may have to be reviewed from time to time and this may have important consequences as to the level of the company's distributable profits and reserves for dividend policy. Discussions with the company's auditors would seem to be appropriate.

No doubt the selling shareholders may take the view that the company may have overestimated and over-provided for this postponed tax. They may want some provision for the adjustment of the consideration, i.e. a repayment in the event of the company receiving a refund or paying less tax than that predicted and/or postponed.

There are, however, considerable practical difficulties in these arrangements. Given the nature of many types of deferred or variable consideration which may extend over an 80-year period (see **4.40**) and where the challenge may extend to 21 years beyond that date[170] there is a significant risk that when either the vendor or the purchaser of the shares believes that a claim can be made there may be considerable difficulties in tracing the counterparty. Even where there may be time limits upon the warranty there have been considerable difficulties of dealing with situations where vendors or purchasers have emigrated, died or are generally not available to act as payers of consideration that is due or they cannot be served as defendants in any litigation. In these situations the normal types of time limit of six or 12 years upon warranties and indemnities or other arrangements dealing with fluctuations in what is effectively the consideration are completely irrelevant. There have been difficulties in finding the relevant counterparty or someone who is liable. Where the potential contractual liability and the related tax charge period is a century the difficulties are manifestly greater. As the above indicates traditional time limits upon warranty claims are inappropriate.

Additionally, this possibility related to deferred taxation may apply to land that is no longer owned by the company. As described elsewhere, transfers of land subject to overage and clawback arrangements do not pass the liability to deal with the tax in respect of the initial transaction, unless perhaps[171] it is some form of variable premium or variable rent in the lease where the liability passes to the assignee.[172] The original contract may not contain a suitable exit strategy (see **4.40**). In such cases there may be long-running contractual arrangements between the company and the purchaser or assignee of the property concerning the tax situation. For example, the company, when assigning a lease, may have given a warranty to the assignee that the amount of tax paid to HMRC is the correct amount and, if it is insufficient, the company may have to indemnify the assignee. All such indemnities and similar arrangements for outstanding possible tax charges (including exit strategies or a 'cascade of covenants' or any undertakings to provide or receive information affecting outstanding tax liabilities for variable consideration) will need to be disclosed, and appropriate warranties and indemnities obtained,[173] where proper provision for the ultimate liabilities has not been made in the accounts of the target company by the auditors of the company.

---

[170] FA 2003, Sched.10, para.31.

[171] It is currently an open question whether there is a statutory novation involving the release of the taxpayer or there is a form of joint and several liability with the possibility of an implied indemnity if the lawyers have failed to include express provision to this effect in the contract.

[172] FA 2003, s.81A; Sched.17A, para.12.

[173] Including security for the warranties and indemnities of any payments that may be required pursuant thereto because of the widespread problem of effectively valueless rights to compensation because the counterparty is not available or is insolvent.

CHAPTER 14

Liability for the tax

14.1 GENERAL

All taxes require provisions identifying the person who is responsible for dealing
with the tax. Frequently, and this applies to some extent in relation to SDLT, there
may be a difference between the person who is liable for the tax and the person who
is accountable for the tax. This will usually involve a person having to pay the tax of
another person but who will be entitled to an indemnity or reimbursement, assuming that the true taxpayer, i.e. the person liable, has the resources to pay the tax
which is not always the case.[1] These issues and additional complications apply in
relation to SDLT in that although there are rules identifying the person liable to the
tax, usually referred to as 'the purchaser', there are some highly complex rules
which make this a very significant practical area. For example:

- There are certain persons who are accountable for the tax of another person
  such as liquidators of companies[2] and personal representatives.[3]
- There are numerous legislative provisions for SDLT which actually impose the
  liability for tax upon a person who is not a party to the transaction. For example,
  in relation to the assignment of leases the assignee may become liable in
  respect of any open tax positions of the original tenant.[4] This is an actual
  shifting of liability not a mere accountability problem.[5]
- A person may be personally liable in respect of a transaction but his taxation
  liability may be influenced by the taxation history of some predecessor in title.
  For example, when dealing with certain variations of rent after the expiration of
  the fifth year of the term the current tenant will be liable for the tax but the
  computation thereof and the question of whether there is a liability depends

---

[1]   The terms of the statutory indemnity may be limited requiring appropriate drafting of the
contracts and agency agreements.
[2]   FA 2003, s.100(7); see **Chapter 13**.
[3]   FA 2003, s.106(3); see **Chapter 11**.
[4]   FA 2003, Sched.17A, paras.12 and 12B.
[5]   It is an open question whether this novates the liability which involves relieving the original
taxpayer and making the assignee solely liable, or creates some form of joint and several liability
with an implied right to an indemnity; see **14.7**.

upon the taxation history of the original tenant and any successors in title prior to the tenant at the time of the relevant review.[6]

• Purchasers of shares in a company may find themselves indirectly liable for the tax falling upon the company where proper enquiries have not been carried out (see **Chapter 13**).

• In some situations controlling directors of companies may be liable for the clawback of tax.[7]

14.2 ACCOUNTABILITY: PROFESSIONAL ISSUES

In addition, HMRC Stamp Taxes originally hoped to introduce a tax where there was a strict separation between liability (i.e. the taxpayer) and accountability (i.e. some person who had to pay the tax on behalf of the taxpayer). This was modelled upon the provisions of stamp duty reserve tax. In these situations certain persons have to account for the tax of other persons but subject to rights of indemnity or excuses if they are unable to recover the tax from the person liable.[8] This works reasonably well in relation to a tax where there are relatively few accountable persons such as market-makers, operators or computerised systems on stock exchanges. However, it is potentially a major problem where the accountable person is the solicitor acting in the transaction and seeking to record the transaction at the Land Registry on behalf of the purchaser. There will be major issues of client relationships should HMRC Stamp Taxes introduce the arrangement and provision is made for this to be implemented in the legislation. FA 2003, s.76(2) enables HMRC Stamp Taxes to reduce the period for filing and payment from 30 days to instant settlement. The objective is to require the tax to be paid at the time the parties seek to implement the registration process at the Land Registry. This will require major funding arrangements and HMRC Stamp Taxes has as part of the planning considered the possibility that solicitors should maintain appropriate accounts which, like the CREST system for stock exchange transactions, automatically through the Land Registry computer transfer funds to HMRC Stamp Taxes when an application is made for registration. Clearly this will require significant changes in funding and client account arrangements. At present, because of the delays in computerised title matters the issue has not attracted a great deal of attention. However, it will be necessary for practitioners to monitor proposed changes by HMRC Stamp Taxes and the Land Registry in relation to computerised title matters and e-conveyancing and the related obligation to pay the SDLT before the registration process can continue.

It is not surprising that the so-called simplification of stamp taxes has produced a compliance regime that contains an amount of legislative materials about 10 times larger than the actual charging and relieving provisions. While it may be possible to

---

[6] FA 2003, Sched.17A, paras.13, 14 and 15.
[7] FA 2003, Sched.7, paras.5 and 12.
[8] Stamp Duty Reserve Tax Regulations 1986, SI 1986/1711, regs.2 and 4.

discover what to do if a charge arises by working through the legislative maze, the imbalance in the legislation means that it is not so easy to determine whether a charge arises and how to self-assess the tax. Nor is there clear guidance on what procedures need to be adopted in order to produce a land transaction return SDLT 1 based upon guestimates, that is not vulnerable to discovery assessments and is not 'negligent' so that a possible 21-year opportunity exists for HMRC Stamp Taxes to issue a discovery assessment.[9]

14.3 SELF-ASSESSMENT

The payment and compliance regime for SDLT is based upon self-assessment, subject to a somewhat long-term open-ended regime for HMRC Stamp Taxes to challenge the return.[10] This regime requires the person identified by the legislation as a party to the actual or deemed or notional transaction, usually referred to as 'the purchaser', to provide prescribed information by means of completion of one or more of the land transaction returns (SDLT 1–4 (as amended)), to calculate and pay the tax (frequently on a 'guestimated' and provisional basis) and to arrange for the keeping of records. Moreover, much of SDLT even in the case of routine house purchases or leases of flats[11] is of a provisional nature, so that there are:

- continuing obligations upon the purchaser to file and pay for many years after the effective date, possibly to the consternation of personal representatives and liquidators who cannot complete the liquidation or administration;
- the purchasers of shares in companies which have acquired land on the basis of a provisional tax position;
- problems of building into the contract a workable exit strategy (see **4.40**);
- difficulties for purchasers who may have to take over the open tax charge.[12]

Each component in this process has its own detailed provisions.

---

[9]   FA 2003, Sched.10, para.28.

[10]   On the absence of 'finality' in SDLT, see **Chapter 1**.

[11]   The current fashion for 'in-fill development' and other arrangements means that even house purchases have a 'hope value'. There are obvious difficulties in allocating a firm figure to such hope value. There are, therefore, general practices for ignoring hope value and substituting some form of earnout, overage or clawback or attempts to capture other benefits that may be derived by the purchaser from acquiring a property and turning it quickly or developing it at a profit at some long-term date in the future. This has produced a practice of asking for an 80-year perpetuity period for these arrangements. There are, however, many major tax problems for a vendor entering into such an arrangement including the potential loss of principal private residence relief and converting what will be a capital gain into taxable income. Solicitors who advise vendors to enter into such arrangements need to deal with the tax downside of these arrangements and the commercial problems associated therewith. Similarly, those advising purchasers who agree to such arrangements are creating long-term SDLT problems for the purchaser as well as difficulties about base cost, capital allowances and the computation of VAT.

[12]   FA 2003, s.81A; Sched.17A, para.12.

14.4 THE TAXABLE PERSON: 'THE PURCHASER'

There is a misleading drafting style of defining the taxpayer and by implication the nature of the transaction in terms of 'the purchaser'[13] and a 'purchase'. 'Purchaser' can include lessees or assignees and others who bear various titles such as appointees or donees or parties to an 'exchange' who are not 'purchasers'[14] and their transactions are not 'purchases' in the sense of the general meaning of the term of someone who acquires an asset for a cash payment. In addition, the legislation itself contains some 'definitions' of 'purchaser'[15] that are not necessarily models of clarity or totally consistent with each other. This is unfortunate since the identification of the 'purchaser' and the related 'vendor' is particularly important for a whole range of reasons. For example:

- there are special charges where the vendor and the purchaser are so related that the connected company rules apply;[16]
- there may be reliefs available where companies are associated within the same SDLT group or there is a scheme of reconstruction which requires identity of the various parties and of the business;[17]
- special rules apply where there are dealings between partnerships and vendors or purchasers who are 'connected';[18] and
- there may be difficult issues as to whether a person acquiring property in a fiduciary capacity is a trustee or a personal representative since different consequences apply (see **Chapters 10** and **11**).

The issue is, therefore, not a simple one of deciding who is 'acquiring' the property or who as 'purchaser' is responsible for paying the tax and filing the return. This, itself, may be a problem since there could be questions of joint acquisitions of property and whether these require the filing of an additional land transaction return form (SDLT 2) identifying the 'true purchasers' as opposed to any nominees or front person who is acquiring for a beneficial owner absolutely entitled.[19] There are also situations where the legislation, in effect, relates to the identity of the 'purchaser' as taxpayer to the land in a sense that the liability as 'purchaser' runs with the land and does not stay with the original or true taxpayer.[20]

There are certain legislative starting points but these do not provide the total answer to the problem. For example, in relation to the basic chargeable event of the acquisition of a chargeable interest it is provided that 'the purchaser' in relation to a

---

[13] Which is also utilised as the basis for the first time buyer relief so that it is not limited to buyers in the sense of general English: FA 2003, s.57AA.

[14] Compare the construction of 'sale', etc. for stamp duty.

[15] FA 2003, s.43(4) and (5).

[16] FA 2003, ss.53 and 54.

[17] FA 2003, Sched.7, Parts 1 and 2; see **Chapter 13**.

[18] FA 2003, Sched.15, Part 3; see **Chapter 12**..

[19] FA 2003, Sched.16, para.3; see **10.11**.

[20] FA 2003, Sched.17A, para.12.

land transaction is the person acquiring the land.[21] The related 'vendor' who is a key person in relation to the availability of various reliefs or connected company charges or the special charges in relation to partnership and so on is defined as the person disposing of the subject-matter of the transaction. It will be immediately obvious that these are not necessarily the same as the person described as 'V' and 'P' for the purposes of the notional transaction within the general statutory anti-avoidance provisions.[22] It is, however, provided that notwithstanding the reference to the parties as 'purchaser' and 'vendor' the definitions apply even though there is no consideration given for the transaction.[23] Obviously, this is meant to cover the deficiencies in the drafting in the sense that the person defined as, for example, 'purchaser' is the person acquiring the land who may be acquiring it as a donee or other party in circumstances where a notification is required notwithstanding, for example, FA 2003, Sched.3, para.1 (see **5.7.2**). Moreover, having referred to a person as being a purchaser or vendor even though there is no consideration it is provided[24] that a person is not to be treated as a 'purchaser' unless he has given consideration for or is a party to the transaction. This spills over into the concept of 'chargeable consideration' which is key to the charge to tax[25] since it is provided that unless there are special rules applying, the chargeable consideration for a transaction is, in general,[26] consideration in money or money's worth[27] given for the subject-matter of the transaction directly or indirectly by the purchaser or a person connected with him.[28] In other words, there are certain circularities in the arrangement in that a person is not a 'purchaser' unless he has provided consideration but it is not expressly stated whether this is limited to 'chargeable' consideration although the consideration is not 'chargeable consideration' unless it is provided by 'the purchaser' (i.e. the person who is providing the consideration). There are, therefore, potentialities for great confusion and problems with related penalties in identifying the relevant 'taxpayer' in many transactions, particularly in those where there are arrangements to have money paid by third parties or guarantees given and similar arrangements or inducements are provided.[29]

The first step is to identify the party to the transaction within the definition of 'purchaser'. This not only goes to the question of who is liable to pay the tax and the chargeable amount, but may affect whether there is chargeable consideration

---

[21] See e.g. FA 2003, s.43(4).
[22] FA 2003, ss.75A–75C.
[23] FA 2003, s.43(4) and (5).
[24] FA 2003, s.43(5).
[25] FA 2003, Sched.3, para.1; s.77A.
[26] FA 2003, Sched.4, para.1; subject to special rules such as paras.10 and 11 thereof.
[27] See, for example, *Secretan* v. *Hart* 45 TC 701.
[28] FA 2003, s.43(4) and (5) and Sched.4, para.1(1); on third party provisions of the consideration see, for example, *Crane Fruehauf* v. *IRC* [1975] STC 51; *Shop and Stores Developments* v. *IRC* [1967] 1 All ER 42.
[29] See, for example, *Crane Fruehauf* v. *IRC* [1975] STC 51; *Central and District Properties* v. *IRC* [1966] 2 All ER 433; *Shop and Stores Developments* v. *IRC* [1967] 1 All ER 42; see **13.18**.

provided by the right person[30] and the nature of the transaction. Other issues turn upon the identity of the purchaser such as linked transactions since these apply only to transactions between the same parties or persons connected with either of them[31] and various reliefs[32] and who may sign the return.[33]

14.5 SIGNIFICANCE OF IDENTIFICATION OF 'PURCHASER'

The purchaser is a key figure upon whom the liability to pay[34] and the compliance obligations[35] are initially but only *prima facie* imposed. In particular, at present, the purchaser is important for many reasons other than payment of the tax, the most important of which in practice are as follows.

14.5.1 Signature of land transaction return

Only the purchaser is permitted to sign the land transaction return but special rules apply.[36]

Even where other persons are entitled to sign the land transaction return the identity of the purchaser has to be disclosed on SDLT 1.[37] The signature of the return has been modified in major respects. There were clearly inconveniences in the basic land transaction return which could only be signed by 'the purchaser'. This included the signature in a declaration as to the effective date of the transaction. This meant that the return could not be prepared in advance of completion or substantial performance because the effective date might precede completion or the planned completion date might slip thereby invalidating the return. Consequently the client would be required to attend either at completion or shortly thereafter in order to complete the land transaction return so that filing and payment could be made within an appropriate time and title obtained at the Land Registry in order to satisfy mortgagees.[38] It is now provided that the return is in two parts. There is the bulk of the return containing the basic information as to price, identification of property and identification of purchaser which can be signed off by the 'purchaser'. The provisions segregate out the declaration as to the effective date which is an item that can

---

[30]   FA 2003, Sched.4, para.1(1) requires chargeable consideration to be provided by the purchaser or a person connected with the purchaser. The absence of chargeable consideration for this reason means that the transaction is exempt pursuant to FA 2003, Sched.3, para.1 and is, in general, not notifiable: FA 2003, s.77A; see **17.17**.

[31]   FA 2003, s.108; see **4.6**.

[32]   FA 2003, Sched.7; see **Chapter 13**.

[33]   FA 2003, Sched.10, para.1(1)(c); see also paras.1A and 1B; also ss.103–106.

[34]   FA 2003, s.85.

[35]   FA 2003, s.76.

[36]   FA 2003, s.81B; Sched.10, paras.1A and 1B.

[37]   And SDLT 2 where there are more than two purchasers.

[38]   There have been serious errors by solicitors usually acting for the mortgagee and the purchaser in not getting the forms duly signed so that titles have become blocked by their negligence to the annoyance of their mortgagee clients whose security cannot be perfected.

be signed by the professional adviser. This clearly removes the practical difficulties of having the client to attend at completion or shortly thereafter. However, this does not simplify the problem but increases the difficulties for the professional adviser who must be aware that the effective date is not necessarily the same as completion because of the many special rules that apply.[39] Unlike processed conveyancing it is necessary to monitor events between contracts and completion in order to determine whether there may be actions of the parties that amount to 'substantial performance' giving rise to an effective date with a second effective date requiring a subsequent filing at completion (see **3.3**). Failure to make the appropriate enquiries could expose the taxpayer to liabilities and penalties because the return has been prepared negligently.[40] However, in other respects HMRC Stamp Taxes has adopted a rather generous view. Frequently land is held by a nominee who is to be entered on the land register[41] and may be the person involved in signing the Land Registry transfer. Technically, except where leases are involved and the nominee is deemed to be the grantee of the lease[42] the actions of the nominee are deemed to be the actions of the beneficial owner. Technically the beneficial owner should be identified as the purchaser of the property and sign the return. However, HMRC Stamp Taxes has accepted in practice that the signature of the nominee is deemed to be the signature of the beneficial owner and therefore the declaration has been properly completed upon the land transaction return (SDLT 1). An explanatory letter may help with the Land Registry.

14.5.2 Consideration

Consideration is not chargeable consideration, i.e. the transaction is outside the scope of the tax,[43] unless the consideration is provided by the purchaser or a person connected with him[44] and this may also affect the taxation of subsales and assignments.[45] This is likely to give rise to difficulties in identifying the relevant party where there is a multi-party transaction such as where third parties provide inducements or where A agrees to transfer property to B in return for which B agrees to transfer or lease property to C or to release a restrictive covenant over C's land.

---

[39]   FA 2003, s.119(2); see **3.5** and following.

[40]   In this context it should be noted that the liability of the professional adviser may not be limited to reimbursement for penalties and there are suggestions that new penalties should not be increased or imposed where the liability is the fault of a professional adviser. However, it must be noted that the existence of a tax penalty upon a taxpayer's record may have much wider implications. For example, it may be a factor that is taken into account by the Immigration Department of overseas countries in refusing applications for visas to enter or to work in the country. There could, therefore, be substantial claims for loss of job opportunity and future earnings notwithstanding that penalties may be imposed for a very simple error such as being late in payment.

[41]   But query whether a single nominee who is not a trust corporation is sufficient for the purpose of passing a valid title.

[42]   FA 2003, Sched.16, para.3(3); see **10.11**.

[43]   FA 2003, Sched.3, para.1.

[44]   FA 2003, Sched.4, para.1(1).

[45]   FA 2003, ss.45(3) and 45A (as amended).

Because this is a 'land exchange',[46] special computational rules apply if a charge arises which may override the question of whether C has provided consideration relevant for determining whether there is a chargeable transaction and/or the chargeable amount.[47] The attitude of HMRC Stamp Taxes is currently unknown but although the drafting is possibly technically defective, challenges may arise.[48]

14.5.3 Connected persons

It is necessary to identify the 'purchaser' because many provisions depend upon whether other parties involved in the transaction are connected with the purchaser such as the connected company[49] charge, the special partnership regime[50] and certain reliefs for residential property.[51] Possession can be taken by the purchaser or a person connected with him so as to constitute substantial performance of the contract to purchase.[52] Linked transactions are restricted to transactions between the vendor and the purchaser or persons connected with either of these (see **Chapter 3**).

14.5.4 Penalties

The 'purchaser' or any person required to deliver a land transaction return is liable to any penalties imposed[53] although other persons such as subsequently admitted partners may be made liable.[54] It is, however, not clear whether HMRC Stamp Taxes believes that it has statutory power to impose penalties incurred by the default of the original taxpayer where the tax liability is passed by statute to third parties who are not in default in relation to their own obligations.

14.5.5 Record keeping

The 'purchaser' is subject to special obligations to keep records.[55]

---

[46] FA 2003, s.47; see **Chapter 7**.

[47] See, for example, *Crane Fruehauf* v. *IRC* [1975] STC 51; *Central and District Properties* v. *IRC* [1966] 2 All ER 433; *Shop and Stores Developments* v. *IRC* [1967] 1 All ER 42; see **13.15** and **13.18**.

[48] See further **Chapter 3** on third parties and chargeable consideration.

[49] FA 2003, s.53.

[50] FA 2003, Sched.15, Part 3.

[51] FA 2003, Sched.6A.

[52] FA 2003, s.44.

[53] FA 2003, Sched.10, paras.3–5.

[54] FA 2003, Sched.15, para.7.

[55] FA 2003, Sched.10, para.9.

14.5.6 Reliefs

The identity of the vendor and the purchaser is important for certain reliefs such as intra-group transfers and leases, company reconstructions and reorganisation.[56] The identity of the purchaser may also affect whether building work and fitting out are taxable or are exempt.[57]

14.6 BASIC DEFINITIONS

14.6.1 'Purchaser'

Since chargeable transactions include transactions other than sales, it is clear that 'purchaser' must include persons other than a buyer of property in its normal meaning, and 'vendor' must mean something other than the person selling the property.

A 'purchaser' is defined as the person acquiring the subject-matter of the transaction,[58] i.e. the person who becomes entitled to the interest being created or the person whose interest is benefited or enlarged by reason of the surrender or release of a chargeable interest or the person benefiting from a variation of a chargeable interest which in the case of a lease may be either the landlord or the tenant.[59] A person so acquiring is a purchaser even if there is no consideration – which may seem strange, especially since if there is no actual or deemed consideration there is no chargeable transaction.[60] It is, however, necessary to have a 'purchaser' so that there is a person who may sign the return (SDLT 1 to 4) and be the target for all of the compliance obligations. However, a person is not to be treated as a purchaser unless he has given consideration for or is a party to the transaction.[61]

14.6.2 'Vendor'

The identity of the vendor is not always vital to enforcement of the tax but the vendor's identity may be important for the purposes of computing the charge where certain provisions apply, such as the connected company provisions, linked transactions, some partnership arrangements and various reliefs such as intra-group transactions. It remains to be seen whether HMRC Stamp Taxes will take a strict line in relation to penalties where the vendor is not correctly identified or some only of the vendors are disclosed upon the land transaction return, where, as will usually be the case, there is no loss of tax, but there may be issues as to whether appropriate

---

[56] FA 2003, Sched.7.
[57] FA 2003, Sched.4, para.10(2).
[58] FA 2003, s.43(4).
[59] Certain variations of leases are deemed to create a new lease in which case the purchaser will be the tenant.
[60] FA 2003, Sched.3, para.1.
[61] FA 2003, s.43(5).

records have been prepared and retained by the true vendor. The 'vendor' is defined as the person disposing of the subject-matter of the transaction.

Although it is a general requirement for there to be a chargeable transaction there is no requirement that consideration is received for a person to be a vendor as it may be provided by the purchaser to a third party. Thus a donor will be a vendor for the purposes of completing returns where there is a deemed consideration such as a gift to a connected company[62] including a corporate trustee.

As with the purchaser, the nominee rules[63] apply to vendors so that the registered title is not conclusive nor is the contract since the apparent vendor may hold the legal title as a nominee for an undisclosed principal and it is theoretically necessary to investigate the underlying ownership where the vendor is or may be holding in a fiduciary capacity such as a nominee, trustee or personal representative and especially on the issue of whether there are linked transactions because there may be connected vendors (see **4.6**). The investigation of the status of the apparent vendor by the purchaser's advisers is becoming more important in practice because certain transactions involving nominees are taxed in special ways. For example, transfers of leases originally granted between July 2004 and March 2005[64] to a nominee may be taxable as if the assignment were the grant of a new lease which may produce a tax surprise for the assignee, who may also be affected by later linked transactions relating to land other than that which he has acquired entered into by persons of whose existence he might be unaware if the appropriate due diligence has not been exercised (see **4.10**).

14.7 'PURCHASER' AS TAXPAYER: A MOVING TARGET

The legislation refers throughout to the 'purchaser' although this must generally mean the 'taxpayer', i.e. the original acquirer of the property;[65] but it has to be noted that there is no total identification of the 'purchaser' as the 'taxpayer'. This is because the legislation provides that persons who are not parties to the transaction and are, in consequence, not 'purchasers'[66] may nevertheless become 'taxpayers' in the full sense of the term. This includes both compliance and payment for transactions where they have no direct involvement in the original transaction but are involved with the chargeable interest as successors in title, actual or deemed, because the liability for any tax adjustments passes by legislation to them.

Numerous key points of practical importance, therefore, have to be noted.

1. SDLT, unlike the traditional stamp duty which it replaces and which attached to documents, does not automatically follow the land (but see point 3); it

[62] FA 2003, ss.53 and 54.
[63] FA 2003, Sched.16, para.3 (before latest amendment).
[64] FA 2003, Sched.16, para.3 (before latest amendments); Sched.17A, para.11 (as amended).
[65] FA 2003, s.43(4).
[66] FA 2003, s.43(4); Sched.4, para.1.

basically attaches to persons rather than documents and the persons liable for the tax may change over time.

2. However, unlike stamp duty when any person could pay the tax to unblock title this is not possible in SDLT since HMRC Stamp Taxes will not accept payment and issue a Revenue certificate (SDLT 5) enabling the Land Registry to act on the title unless there is a declaration duly signed in the SDLT 1 by the person identified as the appropriate party by the legislation.

3. Although the tax does not attach to the land[67] as such, it may follow the land to some extent so that other persons such as assignees of leases become responsible for another person's tax.[68] This does not represent a title issue in quite the same way as stamp duty, but there is a need for title investigation and due diligence, including the provision for completion and contractual terms for dealing with the situation where the vendor does not have registered title and the release of funds by mortgagees (see **Chapter 1**).

4. The provisional nature of much SDLT, particularly in relation to variable payments and rents and linked transactions when the initial tax return is usually prepared upon an estimated basis and has to be revised from time to time, means that the original taxpayer has an open or unfinalised tax position which may continue for many years.

5. In some cases involving the assignment of leases, the open tax position and related notification obligations[69] pass to the assignee so that, notwithstanding the above comments, the tax liability passes to the assignee.[70]

6. In other cases, such as sales of freehold land with a clawback arrangement, the open tax position remains with the original taxpayer indefinitely unless resolved at the time of the sale. This will clearly affect persons such as personal representatives, liquidators and receivers of companies as well as the warranties and indemnities for both land and share sales and the valuation of shares in corporate taxpayers.

In consequence, these mobile liability and compliance obligations require professional advisers to undertake a major re-think of conveyancing practices and due diligence in order to protect the interests of their clients (see further **Chapter 1**). Even where the outstanding tax liability may not pass with the land on the particular transaction, the full SDLT history of the property will be relevant to the third party whose future tax position may be affected (see **8.61**). One of these issues is determining where the liability to pay (or reclaim) tax and compliance obligations lie at any particular time. Another is whether future events will need to be notified, particularly by or to the unfortunate third party compelled to take over the taxation liability.

---

[67] At present there is no 'HMRC charge' upon the land for unpaid or underpaid tax, interest and penalties, i.e. the tax follows persons not the property.

[68] See e.g. FA 2003, Sched.17A, para.11.

[69] FA 2003, s.81A; Sched.17A, para.12.

[70] FA 2003, Sched.17A, para.12.

14.8 CONNECTED PARTIES

There are various situations where the taxation of the transaction depends upon where the dealings are between connected persons or other transactions are between connected parties. In consequence, although in general, connected parties are not as such liable for another person's tax, a key issue around the identity of 'vendor' and 'purchaser' is that of 'connected persons'. Such persons are important in order to identify:

- whether any consideration is chargeable; this depends upon whether it is provided by the purchaser or a person connected with him;[71]
- whether there is a connected company charge;[72]
- whether the transactions are linked because the linkage applies not only where the transaction is between the same parties but also where the parties are connected with the vendor or the purchaser;[73]
- whether the special regime for partnerships applies.[74]

Persons are connected[75] by reference to 'persons', 'individuals', and sometimes 'companies'. It is important to note the precise meaning of these words. Individuals do not include trustees[76] and are not bodies corporate or companies. A 'person' *prima facie* includes both bodies corporate and individuals and may include a 'body of persons' with special rules for partnerships and other unincorporated joint structures. These provisions have the following consequences.

- A 'person' (i.e. a 'company' or an individual) is connected with an individual if that person is the individual's spouse or civil partner or is a relative or the spouse or civil partner of a relative of the individual or of the individual's spouse or civil partner. Although the reference is to a 'person' being connected with an individual the connection is all in terms of individuals.
- A trustee of a settlement is connected with an individual who is the settlor or who is connected with or a person (query whether this includes bodies corporate as well as individuals) who is connected with such an individual or any body corporate which is connected with the settlement or any trustees of subfund settlements. This is, however, modified in relation to corporate trustees for the purposes of the connected company charge when a corporate trustee is not connected with the settlor simply by reason of the settlor–trustee relationship but will be connected if the settlor or relevant persons have sufficient shareholding in the corporate trustee.

---

71 FA 2003, Sched.4, para.1.
72 FA 2003, ss.53 and 54.
73 FA 2003, s.108.
74 FA 2003, Sched.15, Part 3.
75 See, for example, FA 2003, ss.53 and 108; Income Tax Act 2007, ss.993 and 994; Corporation Tax Act 2010, s.1122.
76 Jasmine Trustees v. Wells & Hind [2007] STC 660.

- A body corporate is connected with a settlement if it is a close company or would be a close company if it were resident in the United Kingdom and the participators include trustees of the company, or it is controlled[77] by a close company.
- A partner is connected with any other person with whom he is in partnership and with the spouse or civil partner or relative of any individual with whom he is in partnership except in relation to acquisitions or disposals of partnership assets pursuant to bona fide commercial arrangement.[78]
- A company is connected with another company if the same person has control of both or a person has control of one company and a person connected with him has control of the other.[79]
- A company is connected with another person if that person has control of it or that person or persons connected with him together have control of it.
- Two or more persons acting together to secure or exercise control of a company are to be treated in relation to that company as connected with one another and with any person acting on the directions of any of them to secure or exercise control of the company.[80]

For these purposes 'relative' means brother, sister, ancestor or lineal descendant.

14.9 PURCHASER: SPECIAL CASES

Special rules apply to particular categories of purchaser. These rules need to be noted since they affect the issue of who is liable for the tax and/or who may sign the land transaction return and/or who is otherwise subject to the compliance obligations.

14.9.1 Joint purchasers

Where two or more people acquire land jointly, i.e. as joint tenants or tenants in common, or their equivalents in Scotland and Northern Ireland,[81] unless special rules apply such as in respect of partners and trustees, all must sign the return and any liability for payment of the tax or penalties is a joint and several liability of the

---

[77] See Income Tax Act 2007, ss.993 and 994; Corporation Tax Act 2010, s.1122

[78] This would mean that where some of the partners, for example, enter into various acquisitions as investments in their private capacity they may be connected parties for the purposes of the linked transaction rules.

[79] This may well include persons who are 'shadow directors' who are exercising *de facto* control and this may affect the residence of the company; *Unit Construction Ltd* v. *Bullock* [1959] 3 All ER 831; *Untelrab Ltd* v. *McGregor* [1996] STC (SCD) 1.

[80] This may involve issues of shadow directorships and joint venture agreements; see, for example, *Steele* v. *EVC* [1996] STC 785.

[81] FA 2003, s.121.

purchasers[82] but may be discharged by any of them[83] such as in the case of purchases of matrimonial homes and other similar jointly occupied premises. The test is, however, based upon beneficial or equitable ownership, not the legal title as such. All beneficial owners must sign even though only one is taking the legal title.[84]

14.9.2 Agents

The basic principle is that individuals must sign personally and there are only limited situations where an agent can sign the return on their behalf.

- A person authorised to act on behalf of an individual by a written power of attorney[85] signed by the individual can sign the declaration. As the power of attorney must authorise the person to act in relation to the matters to which the return (SDLT 1) relates, it seems to be the view of HMRC Stamp Taxes that the power of attorney must refer to the particular transaction. General powers of attorney, other than lasting powers of attorney for persons under a disability to which special rules apply,[86] may not be adequate.

- In order to avoid the need for the client to attend completion meetings an individual purchaser, or each of them, may authorise an agent to complete the form provided that they or each of them make a declaration that with the exception of the effective date, the information in the land transaction return is to the best of his knowledge correct and complete. The return must be in the special prescribed form which contains the special declaration by the agent that the effective date is to the best of his knowledge correct,[87] which may require him to ensure that the client informs him of all dealings in relation to the property such as fitting out, investigating minerals or carrying out repairs before formal completion(see **Chapter 3**). Lack of knowledge through lack of attention leading to a failure to ask the right questions is likely to expose the adviser to problems with HMRC Stamp Taxes.[88]

- In some situations HMRC Stamp Taxes has been prepared to accept a land transaction return (SDLT 1) signed by a nominee or bare trustee[89] although the beneficial owner should sign the declaration. This is on the basis that the acts of the nominees except where the granting of leases is involved are deemed to be the acts of the beneficial owner. In consequence HMRC Stamp Taxes accepts that the signature of the nominee is the signature of the taxpayer so that the return is properly executed on this point.

---

[82] FA 2003, s.103(2)(c).
[83] FA 2003, s.103(2)(a) and (4).
[84] See also LPA 1925, s.27.
[85] In Scotland a factory and commission.
[86] FA 2003, s.106(1).
[87] FA 2003, Sched.10, para.1A.
[88] *Slattery* v. *Moore Stephens* [2003] STC 1379.
[89] As a desperate measure a vendor who has been paid may be a bare trustee for the purchaser (see e.g. *Re Kidner* [1929] 2 Ch 121) and his signature may be acceptable to HMRC Stamp Taxes in order to unblock the title.

However, these rules merely relate to the signing of the form. The purchaser, not the agent, remains liable for the tax and all other compliance obligations such as notifying later linked transactions or relevant rent reviews and paying any extra tax.

14.9.3 Nominees and bare trustees

Where the person involved in the transaction is a nominee or bare trustee,[90] the transaction is treated as being carried out by the beneficial owner and not by the bare trustee.[91] This will include situations where the transfer or lease is taken in the names of four individuals which is the maximum number permitted by LPA 1925, s.34 who hold upon trust for themselves and the other beneficial owners. It will also apply to other forms of joint purchases such as where parents and child combine to purchase a house which is to be taken in the name of the child who may, depending upon the facts, be a bare trustee for himself and the parents. All three are 'purchasers' and must be identified in and sign the land transaction return. In such a situation, therefore, the person liable to the tax is the beneficial owner and, importantly, the only person who can sign the declaration included in the land transaction return is the beneficial owner or his duly authorised agent as considered above. Signature by the nominee would not in theory be a valid declaration and penalties could be imposed for an incorrect return,[92] but HMRC Stamp Taxes has stated that since any action of the nominee is, in general, deemed to be the action of the principal,[93] signing of the declaration by the nominee will be treated as signing by the beneficial owner and will be accepted as valid.

There is an increasing number of situations where transactions entered into by nominees may be subject to a special tax regime as far as the purchaser is concerned such as the assignment of leases.[94]

14.9.4 Companies and bodies corporate

For these and most other purposes companies[95] can act only through human agency and this requires special rules as to both liability and compliance, particularly since the tax applies to companies incorporated and/or resident, i.e. centrally managed and controlled outside the UK, and unit trust schemes and open-ended investment companies[96] but not partnerships since these are excluded expressly from the definition of 'company'. This has the following consequences.

---

[90]   FA 2003, Sched.16, para.1.
[91]   FA 2003, Sched.16, para.3.
[92]   FA 2003, Sched.10, paras.3–5.
[93]   FA 2003, Sched.16, para.3(1).
[94]   FA 2003, Sched.17A, para.11 (as amended).
[95]   Defined for these purposes by FA 2003, s.100.
[96]   For the position of special companies such as unit trusts and open-ended investment companies, see FA 2003, s.101.

14.9.4.1 Liability

The liability to pay the tax falls initially upon the 'proper officer' of the company (i.e. the secretary or the person acting as secretary) or any person having actual or apparent authority to act for the company[97] or a liquidator or an administrator, but he may retain[98] out of money he receives on behalf of the company sufficient to pay the tax and if this is insufficient he is entitled to be indemnified by the company.[99] This may be of little comfort if the company is insolvent and there is a large penalty and interest charge which also appear to be his liability. In relation to foreign companies the tax can be recovered from the proper officer.

14.9.4.2 Compliance

The compliance obligations are the primary responsibility of the proper officer.

14.9.5 Unincorporated associations, clubs and societies

Unincorporated associations, other than partnerships, are treated as companies. It should be noted that many 'associations' such as industrial and provident societies now redefined by recent statute[100] are bodies corporate by their governing legislation and so they fall within the preceding paragraph. These provisions will, in consequence, apply to clubs and similar organisations. Moreover, since the tax applies to unincorporated collective enterprises established abroad but having similar characteristics, it will be necessary to investigate this legal status under the foreign law of the association or syndicate in question. This will be a particularly important investigation for foreign associations that at first sight appear to be similar to partnerships formed or established under English law.[101]

The treatment of non-partnership associations as bodies corporate may affect the identity of the owner of the property, i.e. who or what is the vendor or purchaser but this will mean that the taxpayer is the statutory quasi-entity not the committee. Unfortunately for such associations that may not be deemed to be bodies corporate there is, at present, no clear or simple answer and the issue of beneficial ownership and the question of whether the members are 'absolutely entitled' as against the trustees or the committee[102] and the powers of the members to intervene will be areas of considerable difficulty that may have to be investigated.

---

[97] Specific board resolutions may be helpful on this point.

[98] But note that his personal liability is not limited to the assets of the company.

[99] Which assumes that the company has sufficient resources to meet this liability which is a major risk for property companies in a recession.

[100] . See e.g. Co-operative and Community Benefit Societies and Credit Unions Act 2010.

[101] Once again, lawyers in Scotland are badly served by the draftsman who pays little regard to Scots law where, *inter alia*, partnerships are treated differently. He regards all foreign lawyers as being sufficiently familiar with English law so as to realise that special rules apply to their client, and that English and Scottish lawyers understand foreign law sufficiently to spot these problems when dealing with an overseas investor in land in the UK.

[102] See e.g. *Neville Estates* v. *Madden* [1962] Ch 832.

Although in general liability and compliance are normally imposed upon the same person, in the context of special situations this unity of the obligations is not always clearly observed and there is an open question of whether the fiction of corporate personality applies to shield the individual members or the committee from personal liability for penalties and interest for late payment.

Where the taxpayer is an unincorporated association which is treated as a body corporate such as a club taking a lease of premises, the person primarily liable for the tax and compliance is the person who is:

- the secretary or is acting as the secretary; or
- the person acting as treasurer; or
- any person who for the time being has the express, implied or apparent authority of the association to act on its behalf for the purpose of SDLT; or
- a liquidator if one has been appointed.

In practice, a resolution of the committee nominating the appropriate person is likely to avoid any uncertainty. The proper officer, i.e. the treasurer or the secretary or other person held out by the committee as having authority is personally liable for any tax due but he is given a right of indemnity[103] for what that may be worth in a recession or other case where the cash funds of the association are insufficient to pay the tax so that his personal liability is called upon by HMRC Stamp Taxes.

14.9.6   Partnerships

Separate rules apply to partnerships, which are expressly stated as not being within the definition of 'company' and this is reinforced by a provision which specifically lifts the corporate veil of partnerships such as limited liability partnerships. There are numerous special provisions applicable to partnerships arising pursuant to FA 2003, Sched.15 (as amended) where there are detailed rules as to the identity of the 'purchaser' for each category of transaction (see **Chapter 12**).[104] The immediate difficulty is the problem of determining whether non-English business associations are to be treated as partnerships or as bodies corporate.[105]

Two compliance regimes apply to partnerships involving two definitions, i.e. responsible and representative partners.

---

[103]   FA 2003, s.100(4).
[104]   See, for example, FA 2003, Sched.15, paras.10(7), 17(3) and 17A(5).
[105]   No statutory criteria are provided and it is unclear what relative weight has to be attached to the various possibly relevant factors such as limited liability, corporate personality, participation in management or existence of a general unlimited partner; see **12.2**.

14.9.6.1 Ordinary transactions

LIABILITY: RESPONSIBLE PARTNERS

Where a partnership is subject to SDLT upon an acquisition of land in the ordinary course of business, i.e. outside the special regimes, from persons other than partners or persons about to become partners or persons connected with either of these, the 'purchaser' for the purposes of SDLT is all of the 'responsible partners' who are defined as the persons who are partners as at the effective date of the transaction.[106] Any person who becomes a member of the partnership after the effective date of the transaction is not liable for unpaid tax, penalties and interest on penalties. As regards the payment of tax or interest on unpaid tax or any penalty or interest on a penalty the liability of the responsible partners is a joint and several liability of those partners.[107]

COMPLIANCE: REPRESENTATIVE PARTNERS

The land transaction return and the related SDLT 2 should identify all partners and be signed by them. However, provision is made for the return to be signed only by some of the partners (known as 'representative partners'). These are partners who are nominated by the firm and approved in advance by HMRC Stamp Taxes. HMRC Stamp Taxes in the Notes for Guidance (SDLT 6), by concession, will accept the firm's name as purchaser or vendor and does not require details of all of the partners on numerous SDLT 2s.

14.9.6.2 Special transactions

There are broadly five areas of land transactions involving partnerships where special rules apply (see further **Chapter 12**) and these have their own rules for liability and compliance:

- Acquisitions of chargeable interests from persons connected with partners. In such cases the responsible partners (i.e. the persons who are partners as at the effective date of the transaction and persons who become partners after the effective date who include any partner who is the vendor as regards the transaction) are liable for the payment and compliance obligations including interest and penalties on a joint and several basis. The partners may nominate one or more partners to deal with the compliance obligations in advance of the transaction provided that such person(s) has been approved by HMRC Stamp Taxes,[108] but this does not affect liability.

---

[106] FA 2003, Sched.15, para.6(2) (as amended).
[107] FA 2003, Sched.15, para.7(1) and (1A).
[108] FA 2003, Sched.15, paras.8 and 10(7).

- Transfers and deemed transfers of partnership 'interests' where there is a property investment partnership.[109] In these cases the purchaser is the person who acquires a partnership interest[110] such as by becoming a partner or when he increases his partnership share.[111] This person will be fully liable for the tax and compliance obligations.[112]
- Changes in the membership or constitution of the partnership or return of capital or repayment of loans which fall within the scope of certain anti-avoidance provisions.[113] The persons liable are the responsible partners[114] and include, broadly, the partners at the date of the transaction and any person who becomes a partner as a result of the transaction.
- Acquisitions of land from partnerships by persons who are or were partners or persons connected with the partnership, including another partnership. In these situations it seems that the normal definition of 'purchaser' as the person benefiting from the transaction applies for both payment and compliance obligations.[115]
- Transfers between partnerships such as mergers and demergers but no specific guidance is provided as to liability or duty to notify.

14.9.7   Liquidators and administrators

If a liquidator or an administrator has been appointed for the company or an association or body of persons that is treated as a company then the liquidator or the administrator is the proper officer.[116] If two or more administrators are appointed to act jointly or concurrently then the proper officer is such one of them as is notified to HMRC Stamp Taxes by those persons or, if HMRC Stamp Taxes is not so notified, such one or more of those persons as HMRC Stamp Taxes itself may designate as the proper officer.[117]

14.9.8   Receivers

A receiver appointed by a court in the UK having the direction and control of any property is responsible for discharging any obligations in relation to SDLT in relation to a transaction affecting that property as if the property were not under the

---

[109]   Not defined but the view of HMRC Stamp Taxes appears to be that it is not limited to the share in the capital of the firm but applies also to 'loans' by partners to the firm including, *inter alia*, undrawn profits, which, in the unlikely event of its being held to be the correct approach, will involve consideration problems where there is simply a repayment of such 'indebtedness' of the firm.
[110]   FA 2003, Sched.15, para.14(3).
[111]   Which is defined as the share in the income profits of the firm.
[112]   FA 2003, Sched.15, para.14(3).
[113]   FA 2003, Sched.15, paras.17 and 17A; see **12.22** and **12.24**.
[114]   FA 2003, Sched.15, paras.17(1)(f) and 17A(6).
[115]   FA 2003, Sched.15, paras.18 and 23.
[116]   FA 2003, s.100(7)(a).
[117]   FA 2003, s.100(7)(b).

direction and control of the court.[118] Since specific provision is made for receivers and others acting for persons suffering from some incapacity these provisions would seem to be intended to apply to commercial or insolvency arrangements providing a different regime from that applicable to administrators and/or liquidators. This would appear to impose a personal liability upon such a receiver to pay the tax, interest and penalties due from the company including, it seems, tax and penalties owing in respect of transactions entered into prior to the appointment. There is no statutory reference to any indemnity for payments made on account of the purchaser's liability.

14.9.9 Trustees

Trustees are not, in general law, individuals.[119] The payment of tax, penalties or interest may be recovered from one or more of the 'responsible trustees' who are defined as the persons who are trustees at the effective date of the transaction or any person who subsequently becomes a trustee.[120] However, no amount may be recovered in respect of a penalty or interest on a penalty from a person who did not become a responsible trustee until after the time at which the penalty accrued. In relation to any daily penalty or interest the liability in respect of such penalty or interest does not apply to trustees appointed after the effective date except to the extent that the penalty or interest accrues after the date of their appointment.[121] Different principles apply to nominees and bare trustees (see **10.11**).

14.9.10 Persons acting in a representative capacity other than trustee or agent and nominee

14.9.10.1 Incapacity

The person having the direction, management or control of the property of an incapacitated person is responsible for the obligations of the purchaser in relation to SDLT, i.e. he is required to file any returns, pay the tax personally and is presumably subject to penalties. He may be indemnified in respect of any payments made on behalf of such a person.[122] This will usually be the person holding the lasting power of attorney; different rules apply to receivers appointed by the court[123] and to situations where the Official Solicitor is involved.[124]

---

[118] FA 2003, s.106(4).
[119] Jasmine Trustees v. Wells & Hind [2007] STC 660.
[120] FA 2003, Sched.16, para.5(3).
[121] FA 2003, Sched.16, para.5(2) and (4).
[122] FA 2003, s.106(1).
[123] FA 2003, s.106.
[124] FA 2003, s.81B (as amended); Sched.10, para.1B.

14.9.10.2 Minors

The parent or guardian of a minor is responsible for discharging any obligation where the minor is a 'purchaser',[125] i.e. is responsible for the payment of the tax, filing returns, keeping records and is in consequence liable to the appropriate penalties.

14.9.10.3 Deceased persons

Personal representatives of deceased individuals are affected by SDLT in many situations. For example:

- They may be liable for any SDLT outstanding pursuant to any uncompleted contracts or contracts entered into by the deceased such as earnout or clawback agreements. Even where there is no immediate outstanding liability of the deceased there may be contractual arrangements arising from previous acquisitions of chargeable interests, or potential liabilities in respect of reviews of rent such as where the deceased was carrying on a business.
- Personal representatives may be involved with SDLT issues in relation to the administration of the estate such as in connection with assents or appropriations of property to beneficiaries and variations of the dispositions pursuant to the will or intestacy.[126]
- They may be required to investigate whether they are at the relevant time personal representatives or bare or other trustees of the chargeable interest involved (see **Chapter 10** and **11**).
- The personal representatives of a person who was the purchaser under a land transaction are responsible for discharging the obligations of the 'purchaser' such as payment and filing of the returns in relation to the transaction. Such personal representatives are liable for the tax but have a right of indemnity from the estate. They may reimburse themselves for the tax out of the assets, if any, of the estate of the deceased person.[127] No relief appears to be provided. It seems that they are also liable for any interest or penalties arising on a personal basis but it is not clear whether they are entitled to be indemnified in respect of such liabilities. This apparently simple situation hides a mass of complex issues largely arising from the lack of finality of the tax, although certain HMRC powers are limited to four years after the individual's death.[128] However, it must not be overlooked that the obligations to pay tax may be deferred over a long time such as where the deceased purchased land with a clawback or overage consideration, or his business includes a lease with a reviewable rent. There are potential tax liabilities in such situations that have to be dealt with as part of the administration of the estate (see **Chapter 11**).

---

[125] FA 2003, s.106(2).
[126] FA 2003, Sched.3, paras.3A and 4 (as amended).
[127] FA 2003, s.106(3).
[128] FA 2003, Sched.10, para.31(4).

14.10 ASSIGNEES OF LEASES

14.10.1 General position

Assignees of leases will be 'purchasers' and, in general:

- the charge to tax is limited to a charge upon the price that the assignee is paying for the lease;
- no charge to tax arises upon any amount that is justly and reasonably allocated to the purchase of chattels including equipment attached to the land that for whatever reason has not lost its character as a chattel (see **Chapter 2**);
- there may be issues as to whether any payment described as 'goodwill' is really additional chargeable consideration for the land itself (see **2.15.2**); and
- it is specifically provided that undertakings to pay future rent, certain indemnities for breaches of covenant and reverse premiums such as sums paid by the assignor/original tenant to the assignee to compensate for excessive rents or outstanding obligations relating to dilapidations are not subject to tax.[129]

See further **Chapter 8**.

14.10.2 Special situations

This simple approach is complicated by various less than obvious problems.

14.10.2.1 Variable premiums and rent

Transactions with variable consideration or variable rent are initially assessed upon a provisional or 'guestimated' basis (see **8.33**). The taxpayer's position is, therefore, left open to be retrospectively adjusted in the light of subsequent events. However, in certain situations, assignees of leases become responsible for reporting and paying any tax arising in relation to the original chargeable transaction. The legislation is drafted on the basis of various obligations passing to the assignee and there is no reason to believe that HMRC Stamp Taxes intends this to be limited to reporting obligations. The provisional nature of the original tenant's tax return means that the assignee is required to deal with the final resolution of the original tenant's open tax position,[130] i.e. is substituted for the original purchaser, in the following situations.[131]

---

[129] FA 2003, Sched.17A, paras.10 and 17.

[130] But also, it seems, become entitled to reclaim any tax initially overpaid by the assignor. There is no indication whether this is a joint and several liability with a possible indemnity or whether it is the sole responsibility of the assignee and a release of the original taxpayer when an express contractual warranty would seem prudent.

[131] Also, there are possible issues of taking over the SDLT upon the original agreement for lease where this is assigned prior to substantial performance of that agreement by the original tenant: FA 2003, Sched.17A, para.12B.

- Where any contingent or uncertain premium becomes payable or ascertained,[132] the obligations to deal with subsequent payments of the variable sum have to be satisfied by the current tenant.
- Where there is a later linked transaction[133] including a successive linked lease[134] pursuant to the exercise of an option to renew,[135] the original calculation of the tax on the rent, including where necessary the allocation of the nil rate slice between linked leases, has to be revised to take account of the linked transaction. This has to be carried out by the current tenant of each of the leases. This does not appear to be limited to transactions involving the assignee whose tax position may be affected by transactions between other persons (see **Chapter 4**). He will, in consequence, require undertakings for information potentially relevant to his tax position to be provided.
- Where a periodic tenancy continues or there is a holding over by operation of law there is a deemed extension of the original term. The original tenant should have dealt with the tax as of the effective date but this has to be revised retrospectively as the tenancy continues because the length of the term in the equation has increased. The obligation to deal with this revision of the original tenant's tax position passes to the assignee of the lease.[136]
- Where during or at the end of the first five years of the term of the lease the variable rent becomes 'certain',[137] the original assessment has to be revised. This revision must be carried out by the tenant at the time who may be an assignee of the lease.

14.10.2.2 Exempt leases

Certain leases are exempt from tax when granted (see **8.59**). However, since such reliefs were utilised for aggressive tax planning anti-avoidance provisions were introduced.[138] These impose a charge upon the assignment of a lease as if it were the grant of a new lease so that, for example, the assignee becomes liable for tax upon the future rent so that he is, in effect, paying the tax that the original tenant would have paid but for the relief.[139]

---

[132] FA 2003, s.80 and Sched.17A, para.12(1)(c).
[133] FA 2003, s.108.
[134] FA 2003, Sched.17A, para.5.
[135] FA 2003, Sched.17A, para.12(1)(b).
[136] FA 2003, Sched.17A, paras.3, 4 and 12(1)(c).
[137] FA 2003, Sched.17A, paras.8 and 12(1)(d).
[138] FA 2003, Sched.17A, para.12.
[139] These problems for assignees paying the assignor's tax charge are considered in detail elsewhere; see **8.61**.

14.11 ACCOUNTABILITY FOR THE TAX

At present there are no general provisions for any person other than certain assignees of leases to be liable to account for the tax owed by some other person. However, for certain persons in fiduciary positions such as personal representatives[140] there are some limited provisions imposing an obligation to pay the tax of another person (subject to an indemnity, for what that may be worth in practice). Their accountability rules are considered elsewhere for each person but for the moment solicitors and other professional advisers are not personally accountable for the client's tax. This is, however, expected to change as e-conveyancing is introduced, as HMRC Stamp Taxes is given power to reduce the return period from 30 days to nil so that some form of banking arrangements or accounts will be required for money to be transmitted instantly the land transaction return is filed whether physically or electronically.

14.12 PAYMENT OF THE TAX

Initially the tax had to be paid when filing the return. However, in order to permit electronic filing it was necessary for HMRC Stamp Taxes to amend the legislation which now provides that that payment may be made separately from the filing within 30 days after the effective date.[141] However, the Revenue certificate (SDLT 5) is issued by reference to the land transaction return (SDLT 1) so that the necessary paperwork for obtaining registration of title[142] (SDLT 5) may be obtained notwithstanding that payment has not and may never be made. Registration obtained in such circumstances cannot be challenged by HMRC Stamp Taxes or amended by the Land Registry (see **1.11.2**).

14.13 THE REVENUE CERTIFICATE (SDLT 5)

The SDLT 5 was originally intended as a receipt for the filing of the form (SDLT 1) and payment.[143] This is no longer the case. The SDLT 5 merely acknowledges that what superficially appears to be a valid and correct return has been received by HMRC Stamp Taxes; payment may be made separately.

The incentive to obtain such a certificate is that entry may not be made upon the land register in respect of a notifiable transaction unless it is supported by the sole

---

[140] FA 2003, s.106.
[141] The relevant payment obligations were removed by the repeal of FA 2003, s.76(3)(b); see also Stamp Duty Land Tax (Electronic Communications) Regulations 2005, SI 2005/844 (as amended).
[142] FA 2003, s.79(1) (as amended).
[143] FA 2003, s.76 (as originally enacted).

remaining certificate, namely the certificate (SDLT 5).[144] The practical problem is that, as mentioned elsewhere (see **1.10.2**), the Land Registry sometimes challenges applications upon the basis that they are not notifiable. The exemption from the fixed duty certificates that used to appear on Land Registry documentation has been removed.[145] Previously, between the self-certificate (SDLT 60) and the certification of a transaction as being exempt from the fixed duty, the Land Registry had considerable indications as to the nature of the transaction and sanctions could be imposed upon parties who misused, whether wilfully or negligently, any of these certificates. The Land Registry did have statutory power if not a duty pursuant to Stamp Act 1891, s.17, to investigate any certificates or stamping of documents. Fixed duties have been removed from land transactions[146] and such powers have, *prima facie*, been taken away from the Land Registry but certain employees believe that they have even more extensive powers pursuant to FA 2003, s.79(1). There is, therefore, a potential problem that the Land Registry may insist upon the production of a Revenue certificate (SDLT 5) in respect of a transaction that is not notifiable. This will, of course, expose purchasers or tenants to the costs of filing an unnecessary land transaction return (SDLT 1) with a potential penalty if the return is regarded as being out of time[147] and expose the parties to the risk of an expensive and time-consuming Enquiry which is not strictly justified by the legislation. Enquiries into self-certificates terminated when self-certificates were abolished[148] but there is a power for HMRC Stamp Taxes to enquire into a transaction where a land transaction return (SDLT 1) is filed. Alternatively, the Land Registry may request that a letter is obtained from HMRC Stamp Taxes confirming the situation.[149]

14.14 SELF-ASSESSMENT

When completing the land transaction return (SDLT 1) the taxpayer has to give details of the amount and nature of the chargeable consideration (see also SDLT 4). On the basis of this information, he must calculate the tax due and arrange for payment of that amount to HMRC Stamp Taxes.

Where the taxpayer considers that an exemption or relief is available, the tax is self-assessed upon the basis that the relief is available. HMRC Stamp Taxes will not generally question the SDLT 1 at this stage since it has only limited powers to

---

[144]   The former self-certificate for transactions that were not subject to tax and are now in the broad non-notifiable category, was removed.

[145]   FA 1985, s.87; Stamp Duty (Exempt Instruments) Regulations 1987, SI 1987/516.

[146]   FA 2008, Sched.32; but note para.22 thereof, which suggests that such fixed duties have not been removed entirely.

[147]   Although there should be no tax-related penalty since no tax is payable.

[148]   FA 2003, Sched.11 was substantially repealed.

[149]   It seems that certain employees informally transmit the documents to HMRC Stamp Taxes for guidance. On the use of information submitted to Land Registries in the United Kingdom see FA 2003, s.78A.

'correct' the return for 'obvious' errors and omissions[150] and will be lacking relevant information to challenge 'obvious' errors of principle. HMRC Stamp Taxes on its computer will issue the SDLT 5 on the basis that the exemption or relief has been correctly taken. The land register can then be altered. The availability of the exemption or relief taken in the return reducing the tax initially payable may be tested subsequently upon an Enquiry. If the relief is not available, the appropriate amount of SDLT together with penalties and interest will become payable. However, the entries on the land register are not affected by this so that, for example, mortgagees do not need to retain funds to cover the possibility that the relief will not be available, once the title has been registered (see **1.11.2**).

---

[150] FA 2003, Sched.10, para.7.

CHAPTER 15

Consideration in kind, values, apportionments and related computation issues

15.1 GENERAL

While, in general,[1] SDLT works upon the basis of calculating the tax by reference to the actual cash consideration, which in the current global economy is likely to consist of or include foreign currency,[2] there are, unfortunately, many situations where the consideration is something other than cash.[3] Also the contract may relate to a mixed consideration some of which may be chargeable and the assets being acquired by the purchaser[4] or tenant may include assets other than land not subject to SDLT such as purchases of land and goodwill (see **2.15.2**) or there is a related building contract (see **Chapter 9**), or there is a variation of a trust where the assets are not solely chargeable interests (see **Chapter 10**). In such cases there will usually be a need to apportion consideration between the various assets involved or the different taxable and non-taxable elements in the consideration.[5] The consideration may consist of shares which can be important in computational issues[6] in relation to company reorganisations and reconstructions that do not qualify for relief or where such relief is subject to clawback.[7] Moreover, there has been a considerable

---

[1] See **Chapter 4** for the general provisions regarding the calculation of the SDLT and situations where the actual consideration is ignored completely and/or there is a different deemed consideration.

[2] FA 2003, Sched.4, para.9; see **4.36**.

[3] FA 2003, Sched.4 and numerous very specific provisions scattered throughout the legislation and regulations; see **Chapter 4**.

[4] In this context it should be noted that 'purchaser' in the legislation means 'taxpayer' and can include persons who do not provide consideration such as donees: FA 2003, s.43(4); see **14.4**.

[5] FA 2003, Sched.4, para.4.

[6] And very importantly timing issues because of the process of satisfying the contractual obligation to provide shares; see *Letts* v. *IRC* [1957] 1 WLR 201; *Pye-Smith* v. *IRC* [1958] 1 WLR 905 and *Oswald Tillotson* v. *IRC* [1933] 1 KB 134; *Brotex Cellulose Fibres Ltd* v. *IRC* [1933] 1 KB 158; *Murex* v. *IRC* [1933] 1 KB 173; *National Westminster Bank* v. *IRC* [1994] STC 580. This may also be a key factor in whether certain reliefs are available.

[7] FA 2003, Sched.7, paras.3 and 9; but this clawback is based upon market value rather than the connected company rules of 'not less than the market value' which could exclude the actual consideration.

expansion of the charge to tax beyond the cash and shares that form the basis of the traditional stamp duties to include many forms of consideration in kind. There are certain specific provisions that replace the actual consideration with a consideration calculated by reference to market value.[8] Although the current judiciary have expressed extremely critical views of solicitors who embark the dangerous area of fiscal valuations or valuations for other purposes such as landlord and tenant, the professional adviser must be aware of situations where there may be a charge by reference to market value if only to be in a position to advise the client that it would be a prudent course of action to seek appropriate specialist advice.[9]

15.2 APPORTIONMENT

Where there are acquisitions of mixed assets such as a purchase of a business which has land, trading stock and goodwill, or there is an acquisition of an interest in land with a related building contract there will, of course, be questions as to what is a chargeable interest in what is being acquired and whether there is a charge upon the related assets.[10] This problem of mixed consideration and mixed acquisitions can become extremely complicated in numerous situations such as the variation of estates or variations of trusts where the parties are 'exchanging' interests in 'mixed funds'. This problem of apportionment or attribution of the consideration and of the assets being acquired can be important. It may affect the question as to whether there is some form of 'exchange' for the purposes of SDLT[11] or whether there is simply a transfer of some of the assets for part of the consideration.

It is provided that where there is consideration attributable in part to chargeable consideration and in part to other matters (but not necessarily in relation to the assets being acquired) there must be an apportionment on a 'just and reasonable basis'.[12] Where there is an acquisition of mixed assets for a mixed consideration which may include non-chargeable elements there is a problem of considerable complexity. Moreover, any attempt to manipulate the SDLT charge by inappropriate allocation of the consideration in the contract is fraud, forgery and tax evasion.[13]

There is no guidance as to how the 'just and reasonable' provisions are intended to operate. It must, therefore, be a matter of intense negotiation between the taxpayer's advisers and HMRC Stamp Taxes or any person to whom it delegates the

---

[8]   See, for example, FA 2003, s.53; Sched.15, Part 3; Sched.4, para.5.

[9]   There is a major issue of professional advice in continuing to act where the client refuses to accept such advice; see, for example, FA 2003, ss.95 and 96.

[10]   The linked transaction rules do not apply to aggregate the acquisition of chargeable interests in land with non-chargeable interest. In consequence, when determining the rate applicable to land the linked transaction rules apply only to aggregate the consideration paid for land transactions under associated contracts and arrangements; see **4.6**.

[11]   FA 2003, s.47; see **Chapter 7**.

[12]   FA 2003, Sched.4, para.4.

[13]   *Saunders* v. *Edwards* [1987] 2 All ER 651; *Lloyds & Scottish* v. *Prentice* 121 SJ 847; *Re Wragg* [1897] 1 Ch 796 which may involve issues of money laundering.

matter such as the Shares Valuation Division or the District Valuer as to how the assets being acquired and/or the consideration being provided therefor is to be allocated.[14]

15.3 PRICE ALLOCATION

Key issues in this area will mainly but not solely arise in relation to the sale of land with fixtures or equipment attached to the land (see **2.15.1**) and situations where parties are acquiring a business and there is goodwill (see **2.15.2**). In these situations the consideration must be apportioned on a just and reasonable basis[15] between the land and those items attached to the land that retain their character as chattels, or items that are described as 'goodwill', or related building contracts not part of the land transaction (see **Chapter 9**) which are in fact true goodwill and not simply premium value for the land taking into account its situs, planning consents and other matters. In this situation it is also important to note that the apportionment issues, as regards the allocation of value between the various items, may depend upon the subsequent actions of the parties. For example, persons seeking to argue that the payments are for true goodwill and not the land may be vulnerable if there is a subsequent change in name, logo and employees and the scope or nature of the business. Failure to advise at the pre-contract stage that these issues could arise involves a massive risk for the solicitor.

15.4 CONTEMPORANEOUS EVIDENCE

The actions of the purchaser may be very important in deciding whether there has been a transaction involving true goodwill or there is simply embedded goodwill in the land. For example, a person may acquire a business and agree to purchase the 'goodwill'. However, goodwill may depend upon the existing employees, such as in relation to nursing homes or the chef in relation to some forms of catering establishment. Also there may be issues as to the products sold. For example, where there is a disposal of a supermarket with a well-known brand the inevitable change of brand, logo styles, store decoration and fittings, fascia and the 'own products' sold will be crucial in deciding whether what the purchaser hopes would qualify as tax-free goodwill is not really goodwill because there is no trace of the old business in the new business. There may, therefore, be important issues in disputes with HMRC Stamp Taxes and its valuation advisers within HMRC on these matters and

---

[14] This differs markedly from the stamp duty treatment where it was provided (Stamp Act 1891, s.58(1)) that the consideration was to be allocated upon such basis as the parties thought fit. There were arguments by HMRC Stamp Taxes as to how this applied and how subjective it might be. HMRC Stamp Taxes has clearly taken the opportunity of the introduction of a totally new tax to introduce a more 'objective' basis.

[15] FA 2003, Sched.4, para.4.

the instructions given to the valuers in fixing the price for the transaction could be crucial. A professional adviser will have a duty to his client when advising upon the preparation of the contract to draw his or her attention to the need for taking suitable advice,[16] to ensure that third party valuers, etc. are competent and properly instructed[17] since there is overwhelming evidence in practice that such advisers are resisting liability for poor advice on the basis that they were not properly instructed. In such a context it is important to be aware of the valuation issues including *inter alia* which are the cases where valuation is required and what is to be valued. In practice, since the amounts of tax are, usually, relatively small HMRC Stamp Taxes is likely to be influenced where there is independent professional advice as to value that is up to date, i.e. within the timeframe of the transaction such as during the negotiation phase.

It appears that some of the current judiciary have queried the role of professional advisers in asking appropriate questions as to the relevant facts.[18] Since the other party is asked to supplement the solicitor's advice the role requires asking for the relevant information and supporting evidence. The solicitor, because he is seeking help, is indicating he needs advice on what is or is not relevant which passes the obligation to the person instructed. This will be an important issue since, as indicated in *Langham* v. *Veltema*,[19] it is easy for HMRC to challenge a land transaction return (SDLT 1) on the basis of making a discovery where the issue involves valuations and HMRC Stamp Taxes is not made aware of the principles upon which the valuations were carried out.

15.5   INSTRUCTING THE VALUER

However, when seeking to obtain such advice the solicitor should be aware of certain issues and draw these to the attention of the relevant advocate. These issues are, of course, entirely different from the problems arising. The problems arise because many land transaction returns (SDLT 1 to 4) have to be submitted on a provisional or 'guestimated' basis (see **1.24**, **4.21** and **4.38**), where there are problems of 'guestimating' what is being acquired or what is the consideration for the charge to tax because of the prevalence of e.g. variable consideration and rent reviews affecting the charge to tax.

---

[16]   There are also professional issues should the client refuse to seek such advice and require the solicitor to sign off the returns on unsupported valuations and apportionment.

[17]   Note comments in cases such as *Hurlingham Estates* v. *Wilde* [1997] STC 627 regarding the expectation that the client is receiving appropriate advice from a competent source.

[18]   But note *Slattery* v. *Moore Stephens* [2003] STC 1379.

[19]   [2004] STC 544.

15.5.1   Chargeable consideration

It is often prudent to obtain advice on SDLT issues such as what is the chargeable consideration. In the author's long experience solicitors expose themselves to unnecessary but expensive risks by not seeking advice or, where they do seek timely advice, by believing that the obtaining of counsel's advice is a complete protection. Unfortunately, this approach and the belief that reliance upon accountants and tax advisers is a protection is misconceived. Currently tax counsel are arguing that they are not liable for bad advice because they are not properly instructed. Many current tax counsel do not appear to consider that their obligation to the client involves investigation and determination of relevant facts.[20] Also part of counsel's risk shifting is to blame solicitors for bad implementation notwithstanding that counsel did not advise on the potential risks and requirements of good implementation.

15.5.2   What has to be valued?

The question of the chargeable consideration by reference to value frequently moves between the items to be valued. As indicated above, there are problems of apportionment and the chargeable consideration is not the same as the actual consideration. In general, where property is transferred for a consideration in kind other than another chargeable interest in land the tax will be calculated by reference to the market value of the asset provided by way of consideration. However, where the consideration for the transaction consists of or includes an interest in land there may be issues of exchange.[21] In this situation the chargeable amount is not the value of the consideration provided but the value of the interest in land acquired.[22] In consequence, the item to be valued is very different in the case of the parties exchanging or partitioning land from that which will arise where there is a transfer as part of the breakdown of a non-marital relationship or non-civil partnership where there is a transfer of an interest in the house in consideration of a transfer of other property such as an insurance policy.

15.5.3   The chargeable interest acquired

In some situations such as exchanges and connected companies, the valuation is the interest acquired not the consideration provided.

---

[20]   But note *Slattery* v. *Moore Stephens* [2003] STC 1379 and *Hostgilt Ltd* v. *Megahart Ltd* [1999] STC 141 on the need to ask the right questions. Correct answers to the wrong questions are of no assistance.

[21]   FA 2003, s.47.

[22]   FA 2003, Sched.4, para.5; see **Chapter 7**.

15.5.4 Non-land transaction

There are complex rules and practices relating to the valuation of property other than land such as shares.[23] These special valuation principles may arise because in some situations the actual consideration is disregarded and the charge is by reference to the market value of the interest being acquired not the value of those interests or assets to the vendor or lessor. There is, therefore, a major issue of valuation principle in cases where property is transferred to an unconnected company for a consideration that includes shares where the consideration is the value of the shares being issued,[24] or property is transferred to a connected company when the charge to tax is upon not less than the value of the land being acquired.[25] This can apply, *inter alia*, to:

• acquisitions by connected companies;[26] or
• dealings between partners and persons connected with them;[27]
• land exchanges.[28]

15.5.5 Leases and rents

The transaction may consist of the grant or disposal of a lease where there is an actual rent. HMRC Stamp Taxes has not attempted to pursue its former misguided policy of taxing 'future rents' by claiming that future rents are scientifically ascertainable and can be predicted with total certainty decades in advance as occurred pursuant to FA 1994. The current legislation works upon the basis that the lease is granted for the current passing rent and reviews or other arrangements and the market value is the value of the lease upon the terms actually granted including the rent. In consequence, where there is a full rack rent reviewable under normal commercial circumstances there is unlikely to be a market value (i.e. deemed premium).[29] However, where the rent is for some reason below the market rent[30]

---

[23] But note the comments of Russell LJ in *Crane Fruehauf* v. *IRC* [1975] STC 51 that the parties must do the best they can!

[24] But note the problems that can arise where the share issue is not on the effective date: *Crane Fruehauf* v. *IRC* [1975] STC 51.

[25] FA 2003, s.53.

[26] FA 2003, ss.53 and 54.

[27] FA 2003, Sched.15, Part 3.

[28] FA 2003, Sched.4, para.5.

[29] However, it seems that the Shares Valuation Division and the District Valuer may seek to argue that the absence of rent review and appropriate provisions dealing with the allocation of expenses means that the rent is not a full market rent. Also the inexperienced have been unnecessarily trapped by the valuation argument that there is a capital value to a lease between rent reviews where there is a difference between the current rent as reviewed and the possible market rent if there were an immediate review.

[30] Although there may be difficulties in determining what would be the market rent for the purposes of making the valuation.

HMRC Stamp Taxes may seek to argue that the low rent gives the lease a capital value which can be taxed as a deemed market value premium.[31]

15.5.6 Equality and other payments

In some situations such as exchange of minor interests[32] or partitions[33] the charge is upon any consideration provided by way of equality.

15.6 AREAS WHERE SPECIAL CIRCUMSTANCES ARISE

The relevant circumstances where valuations and apportionment are required include:

- where goodwill is relevant: 'true' goodwill and 'embedded' goodwill need to be distinguished where only the latter is taxable (see **2.15.2**);
- where there are fixtures or chattels (see **2.15.1**);
- land exchanges;[34]
- any situation where there is consideration in kind such as shares or insurance policies;
- situations where 'works' or 'services' are involved because these are taxed by reference to 'open market cost'.[35] This is a new and somewhat bizarre basis for fiscal valuation;
- situations where the actual consideration is replaced by a charge to market value which include:
  - transactions involving dealings with connected companies;[36]
  - transactions between partnerships and partners or connected persons.[37]

---

[31] There is a perennial difficulty with HMRC Stamp Taxes and, to some extent, District Valuers and the Shares Valuation Division in relation to rent holidays. This will normally involve the grant of a lease at low rent. It is frequently difficult to persuade those advising HMRC Stamp Taxes that a low rent is a proper market rent. For example, it may take into account the fact that tenants incur substantial expenditure on fitting out (although this may be taxable as a premium in its own right – see **4.29** and **8.27**).

[32] FA 2003, Sched.4, para.5(4).

[33] FA 2003, Sched.4, para.6; but see **7.8** on what is a 'partition'.

[34] FA 2003, s.47; Sched.4, para.5.

[35] FA 2003, Sched.4, paras.10 and 11.

[36] FA 2003, ss.53 and 54; see **13.4**.

[37] FA 2003, Sched.15, Part 3; see **Chapter 12**. It will, of course, be for the solicitor who undertakes an obligation to prepare the return to ensure that only the relevant market values are obtained and 'true goodwill' has been isolated, and reductions or reliefs such as the sum of the lower proportions (SLP) are properly applied.

15.7 FUTURE VALUES AND RENTS

As indicated elsewhere (see **1.24** and **4.38**) much of SDLT is initially dealt with on a provisional or 'guestimated' basis. The returns have to be filed and tax paid[38] and these returns have to be retrospectively corrected in the light of subsequent events. In these situations the estimated figures are replaced by the actual outcome which may be more or less than the figures included in the guestimated original return. There is no general statutory provision dealing with the question of 'guestimates'. The taxpayer and his advisers must do the best they can.[39] Unreasonably, it is necessary that these 'guestimates' are reasonably accurate. In some situations actual tax has to be paid on the basis of the guestimates[40] and parties are effectively commercially penalised by overestimating. In all situations where there is an underestimate, even where there is a power to defer the payment of the tax, the party can be penalised by way of an interest charge upon the tax underestimated and HMRC Stamp Taxes has not issued any denial that it will seek penalties where parties have made a bona fide attempt but have proved to be incorrect because circumstances such as the credit crunch and recession have dramatically affected the estimates.

This is an unreasonable requirement for taxpayers, particularly since it seems that it will not be applied on a reasonable basis. HMRC Stamp Taxes has for almost 20 years taken the view that it is possible to predict on a scientific basis precisely what rent levels will be many years into the future or what will be the impact of a new planning permission upon land values into the future. It is, therefore, unlikely to be sympathetic to claims that the parties have done the best they can.[41]

This means that in many cases the solicitor preparing the land transaction return (SDLT 1) will be left exposed. The client will not necessarily be in a position to provide any assistance. In some situations where there is a relatively sophisticated business client who has a business plan that includes the projection of future profits and costs including expected levels of future rental payments for the premises there may be some assistance. In other cases, the parties may seek advice from suitable professionals as to the availability of capital allowances and other matters where there is some attempt at apportioning the consideration or its current value, etc. Reliance upon such advice will not, of course, necessarily protect the client from potential interest and penalties but it may provide a degree of comfort for the

---

[38] Possibly with the benefit of the deferral of tax on the estimated element in the consideration; see FA 2003, ss.51, 80, 90 and Stamp Duty Land Tax (Administration) Regulations 2003, SI 2003/2837, Part 4; see **4.38.1**.

[39] Compare Russell LJ in *Crane Fruehauf* v. *IRC* [1975] STC 51.

[40] See, for example, dealings involving rent reviews: FA 2003, s.51; Sched.17A, paras.7 and 8.

[41] Many professional property advisers are, wisely, refusing to co-operate in this exercise and HMRC Stamp Taxes has been suspected of giving inappropriate advice on the helpline by suggesting that the parties ignore the question of future values or future rents and just deal with the return on the basis of the current rent. Unfortunately, there are suggestions that, in practice, HMRC Stamp Taxes may be seeking penalties where the parties have acted on this advice and not sought to predict the impact of future rent reviews.

solicitor preparing the land transaction return (SDLT 1), provided, of course, that he does actually seek to take the benefit of such advice when preparing the return.

The difficulty is seeking to predict the future. This is a particular problem when concerned with rent reviews during the first five years of the term, etc. Currently, the recession and the cancellation or postponement of rent reviews have meant that there have been overestimates but equally this is evidence that attempts to predict the future are clearly a matter of pure speculation. These can be major issues for solicitors without the appropriate 'back-up' advice of relevant property specialists. Nevertheless, there must be some limited obligation to the client to deal with the problems.[42] The important thing is to produce contemporaneous records of the attempts to obtain the information, deal with the question as to whether the 'deferred tax', i.e. the charge upon the deferred consideration can be postponed and show that appropriate steps have been taken to obtain the postponement since this will reduce the risks of penalty and interest for the client.[43] However, the position is essentially untenable in relation to arrangements such as those involving earnouts, overages and clawbacks where the consideration may be linked to projections of potential market value in the light of uncertain planning consent obtained at some uncertain date within the next 80 years.[44]

15.8 PROFESSIONAL DUTIES

There are considerable duties owed to clients by solicitors who are or should be aware that valuation issues are involved,[45] appreciate the broad nature of these issues and the basic principles of fiscal valuation that are likely to arise. These duties clearly involve giving proper advice or instructions as to what is required from the professional valuer who, in the experience of the author, will be only too anxious to pass the risk back to the solicitor on the basis that he was not properly instructed.[46]

There is, therefore, a preliminary question that needs to be drawn to the attention of the adviser as to what is to be valued, i.e. which items he needs to identify and value and those which he can ignore. There are also certain professional obligations to draw the attention of such a professional adviser to any special provisions relating to the property such as covenants that may affect the valuation of the interest[47] or the

---

[42] Such as the statutory duty to prepare a non-negligent, non-fraudulent return: FA 2003, Sched.10, para.31A.

[43] FA 2003, ss.80, 87, 90 and Stamp Duty Land Tax (Administration) Regulations 2003, SI 2003/2837, Part 4.

[44] Unlike *Akasuc Enterprise* v. *Farmar* [2003] PL SCS 127, there may need to be a decision that solicitors who put clients into these situations are themselves negligent.

[45] *Bilkus* v. *Stockler Brunton (A Firm)* [2010] 3 All ER 64.

[46] It may eventually be necessary to question whether the valuer is under some level of duty to discuss his instructions so that he can act properly.

[47] See especially FA 2003, Sched.17A, para.10(1)(c). Surveyors, wealth advisers, estate agents and accountants are not necessarily well versed in the legal issues relating to the property issues such as rights, covenants and special purchaser issues arising from negligent advice (see e.g. *Alexander* v. *IRC* [1991] STC 112 and the technical issue of 'comparables' which are usually completely irrelevant

scope of the charge to tax e.g. upon the transfer of interests in property investment partnerships[48] which identifies particular property the market value of which may be relevant. This is a particularly acute problem in relation to partnerships because of the triple regime for the taxation of transfers and their interests, namely SDLT upon the transfer of interests in property investment partnerships, stamp duty upon transfers of interests in partnerships that own shares and transfers in partnerships where the interest relates to property that is not subject to stamp tax.

15.9 PROFESSIONAL RISK

The issues of fiscal valuation are themselves complex and to a large extent outside the scope of this book since the participation in fiscal valuations is not an area into which professional advisers who are not specialist valuers may enter without fear of a significant risk to their professional indemnity insurance and severe criticism by the judiciary. The solicitor advising on a transaction needs to be aware of those situations where the tax will be charged by reference to the market value of some asset (not necessarily the land interest involved) rather than the actual consideration so that he can advise the client to seek proper or qualified advice[49] but to embark upon an exercise of predicting the likely outcome of any dispute as to market value or market cost is a somewhat precarious activity.

This has, however, become an acute issue in relation to variable rents (see **8.27**). Since the rules relating to variable rents and certain types of variable consideration[50] require 'guestimated' figures when preparing the initial return it may be difficult to advise a client. Surveyors and other specialist property advisers are reluctant to embark upon this exercise and it seems that their professional bodies may be encouraging them not to get involved in such situations. Their view is that they are valuers and not fortune tellers which is perfectly correct and is a massive

---

for land values). It would seem to be a fairly heavy contractual obligation for the solicitor to be aware of these issues and to give the appropriate advice and suitable instructions to the relevant party advising on these issues. There is a vital need for the solicitor to be aware of the problems otherwise he cannot give competent instructions to other professionals who, if not properly instructed, cannot give competent advice. This, of course, raises questions as to how far such other professional advisers should provide assistance for the benefit of the client to negotiating their retainer letter before undertaking the work.

[48] FA 2003, Sched.15, para.14.

[49] Merely advising the client to seek advice on values or other issues does not, of itself, mean that the solicitor has fully discharged his obligations to his client. He is, in effect, underwriting the quality of the advice received. In other words, it is not sufficient to suggest obtaining advice on the issue, it is necessary to recommend a competent adviser. This is not limited to recommending a person believed to be competent but requires a person who is objectively competent. This is usually a problem for insurers. Solicitors who instruct professional negligence counsel rather than tax counsel may find that the advice that they received is little protection for them because counsel were not competent to advise that tax was not payable or that additional tax was payable. The advice received must therefore be scrutinised to determine whether it is relevant and competent.

[50] FA 2003, s.51 and Sched.17A, para.7.

indictment of those persons representing professional bodies who advise HMRC.[51] There will be important issues as to how the principles which HMRC Stamp Taxes may wish to apply to valuations are relevant for stamp tax issues. As Russell LJ indicated in *Crane Freuhauf*,[52] because the legislation is unhelpful and there is no relevant sensible material upon which a debate can be based, the parties must 'do the best they can'.

15.10 PROFESSIONAL ADVICE: OTHER ADVISERS

Frequently the parties may have some form of advice in fixing the price for the transaction. This advice can be extremely helpful in the event of fiscal disputes, provided that the valuers are properly instructed. There is a major risk area for solicitors in their choice of other advisers. This, of course, makes the rash assumption that other apparently qualified professionals are sufficiently misguided to become involved in these areas. Not only must they be objectively competent, but there must be no personal or professional conflict on the issue.

15.11 STAMP TAXES VALUATION LEGISLATION

There is little statutory guidance in relation to valuation for the purposes of SDLT although there are certain provisions dealing with values for other related taxes.[53] The primary provisions are those indicating that the matters are to be governed by questions of market value[54] or market cost.[55] In so far as wider principles are involved there are indications that matters are to be governed by the legislation provided for in the Taxation of Chargeable Gains Act 1992.[56]

15.12 SPECIFIC PROVISIONS

There is a general provision referring to the capital gains tax legislation and there are a few badly drafted provisions dealing with certain situations, for example:

- annuities[57] although these are extremely crude where the annuity provided is variable;[58]

---

[51] On the questionable practices in the consultation process see **Chapter 1**.
[52] [1975] STC 51.
[53] See, for example, Stamp Act 1891, s.6; FA 1986, ss.69(4), 72(2), 94(3).
[54] FA 2003, Sched.4, para.7.
[55] FA 2003, Sched.4, paras.10 and 11.
[56] FA 2003, s.118.
[57] FA 2003, s.52; see **4.31.5**.
[58] FA 2003, s.52(3).

- variable payments including rent;[59]
- services;[60]
- building works.[61]

15.13 BASIC VALUATION ISSUES

Many issues will need to be addressed in any proper negotiations with HMRC Stamp Taxes apart from the above questions of ensuring that any valuers engaged in connection with the acquisition of the business are instructed on a proper basis to produce the data required and to ensure that their data is properly prepared and up to date. There will be various stages in this process:

- negotiating strenuously and hopefully agreeing with HMRC Stamp Taxes without too much delay and cost what is the appropriate situation for the hypothetical transaction in the open market;
- ascertaining whether there is a totally hypothetical contract or whether the valuation process has to be carried out upon the basis of the actual terms between the parties which may leave the vendor or lessor open to a very difficult argument as to what is 'hypothetical', e.g. whether there has to be an assumption of different parties. This can be a key factor where, for example, there is a special price because of speedy completion or the purchase of several flats from plan;[62]
- identifying the parties to the hypothetical open market transaction. This can be a difficult issue in the current SDLT legislation, i.e. whether there is a hypothetical transaction between the original vendor, lessor or grantor and a hypothetical third party or a hypothetical sale or assignment by the actual purchaser or lessee to a hypothetical third party. For example, where there is a market value charge upon a lease because connected companies or partnerships[63] are involved, it is necessary to establish whether the market value is to be determined upon the basis of a hypothetical lease upon the same or similar terms to a third party (i.e. not the actual tenant) who may include a hypothetical tenant (including a hypothetical special tenant or a sitting tenant extending his term) and it assumes a sale of the actual lease by the actual tenant who immediately sells the lease on to a hypothetical third party. To a large extent this may depend upon what is to be valued, i.e. whether there is a deemed grant to a third party by the vendor, or a deemed onward sale by the purchaser or lessee (see **8.12**);

---

[59]   FA 2003, s.51; Sched.17A, paras.7 and 8.
[60]   FA 2003, Sched.4, para.11.
[61]   FA 2003, Sched.4, para.10.
[62]   Compare *Duke of Buccleuch* v. *IRC* [1967] AC 506 and Taxation of Chargeable Gains Act 1992, s.272(2); *Cowan de Groot Properties Ltd* v. *Eagle Trust Plc* [1991] BCLC 1045.
[63]   FA 2003, s.53; Sched.15, Part 3.

- identifying the 'willingness' of the actual or hypothetical parties. It appears to be necessary to assume that the hypothetical seller in the open market and the hypothetical purchaser are not under any pressure to sell, such as might be the case with personal representatives or liquidators anxious to wind up the estate or company,[64] or where there is a pressing need to raise cash urgently.[65] It is not sufficient that the actual parties are at arm's length, they must also be 'willing' to sell;
- identifying the property to be valued and deciding which, if any, of the covenants, restrictions and other arrangements affecting the land are to be taken into account;[66]
- having identified the various factors finding the data to supply the information necessary to fill out the details; and
- agreeing with HMRC Stamp Taxes the relative weight to be attached to each of the various factors.

There is no standard procedure for resolving all of these issues.

15.14 'OPEN MARKET'

Having identified the situation where a valuation of some asset whether land or other property may be required it is then necessary to identify the relevant legislative provisions dealing with how that valuation has to be approached. It is generally expressed to be on the basis of open market value[67] or the open market cost of certain services.[68] These bases make certain major assumptions, not necessarily justified, that the interest can be sold in the open market. However, for example, many minor interests can exist only as part of another interest and cannot be separately sold in the market. There may be a 'nuisance value'[69] but this is not an open market value because the nuisance party cannot sell his interest since only the landlord can pay him.

Unfortunately, while the legislation refers to concepts such as 'open market value' or 'open market cost' it does not really provide much in the way of guidance[70] as to the factors to be taken into account in deciding what is an open market transaction, nor where the parties possibly after debate with HMRC have identified the relevant factors, is there guidance as to the weight or significance that should be applied to them. This is a matter of detailed negotiation and ultimately is likely to result in a dispute involving some form of judiciary who tend to apply the judgment

---

[64] Lap Shun Textiles Industrial Co v. Collector of Stamp Revenue [1976] AC 530.
[65] Cowan de Groot Properties Ltd v. Eagle Trust Plc [1991] BCLC 1045.
[66] FA 2003, Sched.17A, para.10; Sched.15, para.38.
[67] FA 2003, Sched.4, para.7.
[68] FA 2003, Sched.4, paras.10 and 11.
[69] *Alexander* v. *IRC* [1991] STC 112.
[70] *Lynall* v. *IRC* [1972] AC 680. There may be certain situations where legislation has intervened for other taxes. It will be a matter of potentially protracted and expensive disputes for the inexperienced to determine whether those provisions apply to the particular SDLT situation.

of Solomon and determine the market value at roughly half-way between the values being put forward by HMRC Stamp Taxes and the taxpayer.

15.15 HYPOTHETICAL SALE AND PURCHASE

The question of determining what is to be valued for the purposes of the hypothetical sale in the open market involve many issues such as:

- whether there is an open market;
- the terms of such a hypothetical sale[71] and whether these are the same as the actual transaction and if not what modifications thereto are appropriate;
- the identities of the parties to the hypothetical sale or lease. This is a particular issue since in some situations the property to be valued is that being disposed of and in other situations it is the value of the property being received.

There is, therefore, a fundamental question in any particular case depending upon the precise scope and terms of the relevant charging provisions as to who is or might be the vendor in the open market because the interest to be valued is not the same as the interest received. For example, where there is the grant of a lease and market value premium issues become important there would be the question as to whether the interest to be valued is the new lease granted or the old lease exchanged (depending upon how the charge arises, for example, as part of a land exchange). HMRC Stamp Taxes seems to have had particular difficulty with land exchanges where there is an obligation to 'regrant' a chargeable interest or other right. It seems that it is, albeit reluctantly, abandoning its basic position that the valuation of the interest acquired has to ignore the obligation to grant the rights back which can make a major difference (see **4.24**). Looking at the purchaser or lessee the valuation might be of the interest received, whereas for the vendor or lessor it might be the interest received or the price/rent that an independent third party might pay. In the case of a connected company or partnership, the open market value is to be determined on the basis of the price that could be obtained by the landlord when dealing with another hypothetical tenant which may include a 'special purchaser'.

On the other hand, in some situations where the tax is charged by reference to the value of the property received, then where there is some form of land exchange involving a lease, for example, the value of the property received is what the purchaser or tenant may be receiving and is the price that he could expect on a sale of the actual interest that he receives in the open market. The issue would, therefore, include a certain preliminary debate as to the identity of the parties and the identity

---

[71] Such as the effect of leases; the assignment or subletting or allowing other persons into possession are subject to the requirement that the landlord may have to consent and whether such consent can be assumed but the valuation has to take account of the possibility that any onward sale may be opposed (compare *IRC* v. *Crossman* [1937] AC 26); i.e. it has to be assumed that someone will be rash enough to buy the property but will fix the price on the basis he may not be allowed to sell on.

of the parties might affect the hypothetical terms of sale. For example, where it is a question of the market value as far as the tenant is concerned he would be selling the lease as it exists, with all the covenants and restrictions therein; however, where the issue is whether the valuation is to be determined by the price that a landlord might get if dealing with a hypothetical third party then there will be a question as to whether the valuation has to be carried out upon the terms of the actual lease or whether, the open market arrangements being met, any special or relevant covenants such as restrictive covenants or user covenants are to be ignored when carrying out the valuation.[72]

15.16 COMPARABLES AND ACTUAL TRANSACTIONS

HMRC through the District Valuer tends to look for comparables. However, in relation to land or unlisted securities and similar items of property not widely traded publicly there is no true comparable because each parcel of land or shares in a private company or insurance policy will have different aspects and these will be sufficient to mark it off from other apparently similar property. Previous sales, etc. are clearly totally irrelevant.[73]

15.17 THE SPECIAL PURCHASER ARGUMENT

The relationship of the parties may provide special circumstances since this may mean that levels of information as to intention and degrees of co-operation could be influenced significantly,[74] usually to the taxpayer's disadvantage.

There may be issues as to special purchasers such as sitting tenants who may not have an interest that can be sold in the open market but have a 'nuisance value'[75] or there is a marriage value or hope value,[76] notwithstanding that in practice these issues have been replaced by overage, clawback and similar arrangements (see **4.38.2**). This is, however, usually a specious argument because the special purchaser may exist but only as a potential bidder for other property. He will frequently as a hypothetical party not have any interest in the property in question and there will be fundamental questions as to whether the property can be acquired and rapidly sold in the open market at a profit in the circumstances. Unfortunately the legislation imposes the assumption that there will be a sale in the open market

---

[72] Note the issues for valuation of leases where certain assumptions are made such as FA 2003, Sched.15, paras.15 and 38; and note the rather cryptic provision in Sched.17A, para.10(1) relating to a covenant that might affect the rent.

[73] *Salvesen's Trustees* v. *IRC* (1930) 9 ATC 43.

[74] See, for example, the partnership valuation issues where the landlord was connected with the partners and could be expected to co-operate with them: *Walton* v. *IRC* [1996] STC 68.

[75] *Alexander* v. *IRC* [1991] STC 112.

[76] Although these have been replaced by attempts to protect vendors by overage and clawback arrangements.

notwithstanding that there is no realistic or commercial prospect of anyone bidding for the property. It must, therefore, be assumed that there is a 'commercial madman' prepared to bid for the property and an attempt made to guess what this commercial madman would be prepared to pay the price.

The open market value or open market cost test assumes that the relevant transaction is something that can be dealt with in the open market. However, restrictions upon assignment or subletting or other dealings in relation to the property are relevant.[77] The chargeable interest may be non-assignable but the particular party may have a nuisance value[78] or may be in a close relationship with some other party to the property interests[79] and these may provide the basis for reducing the impact of any restrictions upon the saleability of the property. These are issues for detailed and hard negotiation with HMRC Stamp Taxes and those members of HMRC Valuation Sections who are assisting them in these matters.[80]

15.18 OPEN MARKET COSTS

In some situations the tax is charged upon the open market cost of the provision of the consideration such as where the consideration consists of or includes 'works'[81] or 'services'.[82] There is a major difference between actual cost and open market cost, i.e. what it actually costs the taxpayer to supply the consideration and the costs which at arm's length the party would incur. In the former context there is no question of costs being equivalent to a price including a profit element. It is assumed that 'cost' will not include 'opportunity cost' or income or profits forgone such as would arise where a child gives up employment to care for an elderly parent on the promise that he or she will receive the house.[83] HMRC Stamp Taxes has indicated that it will deal with the tax on the basis that VAT can be ignored rather than a proper legislative basis,[84] i.e. its view appears to be that the actual or potential VAT on market value and open market costs will be ignored.

---

[77] *IRC* v. *Crossman* [1937] AC 26; *Alexander* v. *IRC* [1991] STC 112. HMRC Stamp Taxes has for over half a century strenuously argued that contractual restrictions should be totally disregarded because contracts can be varied even where the parties are at arm's length and a variation would shift substantial value between the parties and require major financial adjustments between the parties.

[78] *Alexander* v. *IRC* [1991] STC 112.

[79] *Walton* v. *IRC* [1996] STC 68.

[80] It should, however, be noted that the author was advised by a member of HMRC Stamp Taxes that valuation exercises can be difficult because there is only a limited budget for such matters. They also require quite senior approval before instructing counsel.

[81] FA 2003, Sched.4, para.10.

[82] FA 2003, Sched.4, para.11.

[83] This is an area fraught with problems for the practitioner since it taints first time buyer relief and raises issues of 'cost'. Attempts to deal with the arrangement as part of the estate will involve inheritance tax and capital gains tax issues and are probably fraud upon the Revenue because the arrangement may be a contract taking effect outside the estate and failure to deal with the arrangement on the correct basis involves supplying incorrect information to numerous divisions of HMRC.

[84] FA 2003, Sched.4, paras.2, 10 and 11.

This question of an 'open market' for services raises fundamental questions for many transactions particularly those of a domestic nature or where specialised services are involved. In order to have an 'open market cost' (which is manifestly not the same as the actual cost, if any) the services have to be generally available, i.e. they are supplied in an 'open market'. This is a problem for carers who have been promised the house or flat as a reward for that service.[85] As discussed previously there will be questions as to whether the 'services' have to be treated as a 'package', or fragmented and a 'cost' allocated separately (see **Chapter 4**). It is possible there should be no open market cost unless HMRC Stamp Taxes contends that 'cost' includes the earnings forgone by the carer.[86]

15.19 VAT: VALUES AND COSTS

There are, however, some very significant practical issues in determining the market value and the market cost of services and works. In some situations questions of VAT may arise. For example, there may be a transfer of land where the option to tax has been exercised or the parties believe that it may be a transfer of a going concern although there are risks that VAT may subsequently be payable and the contract makes appropriate provision (see **4.30**). The legislation refers to the price or cost that would be obtained or payable in such situations in the open market. This would suggest that it may be necessary to look at the particular circumstances of the vendor or landlord or the provider of service and whether the transaction is actually potentially subject to VAT because the 'vendor' may or may not be a taxable person for VAT. This involves investigating whether all options to tax have been exercised. It might also mean that there could be wait-and-see issues where there is a potential transfer of a going concern and problems as to whether the actual sale would attract tax because of some defect in relation to the application of the transfer of a going concern provisions (see **4.21** and **16.7**). This does, of course, go to the fundamental question as to how far the actual transaction circumstances and terms of contract and terms of sale apply or whether these are to be replaced by some totally different hypothetical transaction.[87]

It seems that, in practice, HMRC Stamp Taxes is prepared to ignore the question of VAT and not investigate questions as to whether the vendor has to charge such tax or whether the purchaser or tenant would be in a position to obtain full input tax credit or, because of the purchaser's partial exemption position, he may recover only part of the VAT so that the 'cost' to him is higher or lower depending upon these factors. Obviously, from the vendor's point of view, he would receive the full

---

[85] *Henry* v. *Henry* [2010] 1 All ER 988.

[86] However, since this is likely to impact to a major extent on HMRC generally, the manifest conflict of interest suggests that these issues would not be well received or pressed by HMRC.

[87] Compare *Duke of Buccleuch* v. *IRC* [1967] 1 AC 506 where the actual sale could be ignored and the hypothetical sales in the open market fragmented the land because this would produce a better price overall; but see Taxation of Chargeable Gains Act 1992, s.272(2).

amount which would have to go into his VAT computation at the end of the appropriate return period. It seems that these are issues to be ignored as part of the valuation process although the precise extent and consistency of this apparent position remains to be determined in practice over time.

15.20 TIME OF VALUATION

Those responsible for drafting the legislation have failed to deal with a key issue in valuation disputes, namely the time at which valuation has to be carried out. To some extent these issues have been evaded by those responsible by dealing with the tax on a provisional basis subject to retrospective adjustment in the light of subsequent events. In some situations the need for valuation may mean that the consideration is technically 'unascertained', i.e. the information is available but has not been processed. The effect of this is[88] that the parties have to act upon the basis of an estimate of what the final figures will be and then adjust these in the light of the actual situation. This may not be too significant a problem because whether negotiations are for market value or square footage of buildings or other dealings with the relevant balance sheets and figures the parties will have a broad idea as to the likely outcome of the discussions between the relevant advisers. Unfortunately, in these situations the tax has to be paid with the initial return upon the basis of the estimated figures. If the parties have produced the correct figures by luck or they have produced a figure that is above the final outcome there will a possible recovery of tax overpaid together with interest and no penalty or other charges. However, if the parties have made the wrong guess there will be tax underpaid with interest and possible penalties for 'negligence' in not making a proper attempt at arriving at the figures.[89]

Subject to such special provisions the relevant date for carrying out valuations will be the 'effective date'. This may, of course, be a date when all of the relevant data is potentially available but this is not necessarily the case. For example, where there is the grant of a reversionary lease to a connected company there will be a question of whether there is a deemed premium because of the rent levels. This will depend upon 'guestimates' as to whether the rent is likely to be appropriate for the time when the lease takes effect in possession. This may or may not be the case. Should the situation be that the rent agreed is something other than the 'market rent when the lease takes effect in possession' type of formula there would be the question of the parties having to decide whether to declare in the return a potential deemed premium pursuant to FA 2003, s.53.

The position is made even more complicated by the fact that HMRC Stamp Taxes takes the view that for most transactions there will be not one but two effective dates, i.e. substantial performance is an effective date as well as the subsequent grant of

---

[88] FA 2003, ss.51(2) and 80.
[89] FA 2003, Sched.10, para.31A.

lease or conveyance between the same parties.[90] The implications of this for valuation are enormous and to consider all of the possible problems facing professional advisers would extend the scope of this book enormously. For example, there may be the grant of a lease to a connected company. There may also be dealings between owners of land and partnerships of which they are members. In these situations the transaction makes an assumption that the rent could be below the market rent as at the relevant effective date and in such situations there is a deemed market value premium. The problem is that the rent may be appropriate at the time when the lease becomes effective in practice (i.e. the relevant company or partnership enters into possession, starts paying rent and so substantially performs) but it may be below the market rent at the time when the lease is granted some years later. If, as contended by HMRC Stamp Taxes and is likely to be accepted by the current judiciary, there are two effective dates then this could become a major problem. The parties' advisers must, therefore, consider very carefully the dates of allowing the parties to substantially perform their contract and the actual completion thereof. They must also advise the clients that where there is a delay between substantial performance of the contract and completion the parties will be put to considerable expense in obtaining up-to-date valuations as at completion and possible penalties and interest for under-declaring tax on a previous occasion.

15.21 JOINT OWNERSHIP

Where there are dealings in part-interests of jointly owned property, there is a possibility of a minority interest discount for equitable interests.[91]

15.22 OTHER TAXES AND OTHER LEGISLATION

There are numerous cases largely of interest only to specialists in fiscal valuation in other areas of taxation; but, given the tendency for HMRC Stamp Taxes to turn towards the capital gains tax section of HMRC for such advice as they may be able to provide[92] those principles relating to capital gains tax have been included, to some extent, in the provisions for the valuation of assets which may provide a degree of consistency between taxes.

---

[90] FA 2003, s.44(8); Sched.17A, para.12A.
[91] *Re Wight* [1982] 2 EGLR 236.
[92] However, see the savage criticism of the chargeable gains approach in *Balloon Promotions Ltd* v. *Wilson* [2006] STC (SCD) 167 as incorrect; this required a back-down by HMRC.

15.23 NON-LAND VALUATION

The problems are not related solely to the fiscal valuation of chargeable interests in land. There are considerable issues of valuation principles for property other than land where the special rules do not apply. These include the valuation of shares.[93]

15.24 STAMP TAXES VALUATION: PRACTICE

In practice stamp taxes valuation is largely a question of 'nerve' by the taxpayer and the relevant experience of the adviser. HMRC Stamp Taxes tends to start the process with a degree of aggression but this is a fragile approach where the appropriate response from experienced advisers is received. HMRC Stamp Taxes as presently constituted appears to rely upon other divisions of HMRC for advice. Valuation disputes, therefore, represent a bad image for HMRC Stamp Taxes both internally and externally, affect the tax recovery and, importantly, add to the costs thereby reducing the net tax yield. It is usually effective, to curtail valuation disputes, to produce a certificate signed by independent professional advisers and dated within a few months preceding the effective date stating that, in the opinion of the advisers, the property is worth 'not more than' a specified amount. For the vast majority of transactions HMRC Stamp Taxes tends to accept that it is not economic for it to challenge this figure.

---

[93]   But note the less than helpful comment of Russell LJ in *Crane Fruehauf* v. *IRC* [1975] STC 51 that the parties must do the best they can without real hope of judicial support (see Lord Hoffmann in *IRC* v. *Mitsubishi Motors New Zealand* [1995] STC 989).

CHAPTER 16

SDLT and other taxes

16.1 GENERAL

SDLT interacts with other taxes in several ways:

- it may be charged upon other taxes which form part of the consideration for the transaction;[1]
- other taxes such as capital allowances, capital gains tax and income tax may need to take into account the SDLT charge in order to compute the base or acquisition cost or the disposal proceeds which may be relevant for the amount of gains or profits subject to tax;[2]
- changes in the rate of other taxes may themselves give rise to charges to SDLT or refunds of tax already overpaid;[3] and
- the impact of other taxes may be relevant when determining market values and costs for SDLT.[4]

Many of these interactions are complex and long-term problems inevitably arise because of the provisional or 'guestimated' nature of much of SDLT and related filing or returns and the need for retrospective adjustment (see **1.24** and **8.33**). In consequence, the figures involved in relation to SDLT may not be final at the time when claims in respect of other taxes or liabilities to other taxes arise. The question is whether the provisional nature of the SDLT has the consequential effect that other tax computations are themselves provisional and can only be retrospectively finalised or require adjustment from time to time. There are no express provisions dealing with many of these situations and the matter has to be decided as one of general principle.

---

[1] FA 2003, Sched.4, para.2.
[2] See, for example, Taxation of Chargeable Gains Act 1992, s.38(2) (as amended); Capital Allowances Act 2001, ss.345 and following.
[3] See statement on changes in VAT on rents February 2009.
[4] FA 2003, Sched.4, paras.7, 10 and 11; see **Chapter 15**.

16.2 SDLT AND OTHER TAXES

In general SDLT differs from most other taxes in that it is a charge on the costs of acquisition by a purchaser, grantee or tenant whereas most other taxes are charged upon the profits or gains of the vendor.[5] In consequence, there will not be a charge to SDLT upon any corporation tax charges arising in relation to any particular transaction, but the SDLT will be an item of 'cost' or expenditure deductible in computing the profit or loss on the transaction. However, other taxes may affect the cost; for example if a successful challenge by HMRC Customs and Excise of the VAT treatment increases the consideration so the SDLT charge will increase.

There is one other major tax which is a charge upon the acquisition cost namely, VAT,[6] but to some extent unlike SDLT, this tax may be recovered by the taxpayer because the purchaser or tenant may be entitled to some form of input tax credit in respect of the tax paid upon his acquisition of the chargeable interest.[7] Stamp taxes have always been charged upon VAT[8] and this position is continued by statute.[9] It is provided that SDLT is chargeable upon any VAT actually payable otherwise than pursuant to the exercise of the option to tax taking place after the effective date of the transaction.[10] This means that, *prima facie*, where there is an exempt land transaction such as the grant of a lease where the landlord does not exercise the option to tax and there is no mandatory standard rate charge as in relation to newly constructed buildings, etc. the SDLT will be charged upon the basic price. The fact that, as in relation to leases, the position may be changed (because of the subsequent exercise of the option to tax or the price and the related VAT varies by reason of clawback, overage or similar adjustments in the consideration or rent review) is ignored in relation to the initial calculations and any retrospective adjustments thereof which relate back to the original transaction when no VAT was payable. However, subsequent changes in the rate of VAT or the exercise of the option to tax may give rise to taxation consequences in their own right as considered below (see **16.5**).

16.3 OTHER TAXES AND SDLT

While SDLT is not charged upon taxes other than VAT it does have an impact upon the computation of profits and gains so that the final figure, when available, may be a tax deduction or cost. It is provided[11] that the acquisition or base cost of the land

---

[5] A potentially key issue in the application of certain tax avoidance approaches, i.e. cost reduction is not tax avoidance in the general meaning of the term.

[6] FA 2003, Sched.4, para.2; see **4.30**.

[7] Value Added Tax Act 1994, ss.24 and following.

[8] Glenrothes Corporation v. IRC [1993] STC 74.

[9] FA 2003, Sched.4, para.2.

[10] Which is an ambiguous provision in many respects such as whether VAT arising pursuant to rate changes in tax chargeable and whether the subsequent exercise of the option to tax is a chargeable transaction in its own right; see **16.5** and **8.38**.

[11] Taxation of Chargeable Gains Act 1992, s.38(2) (as amended).

includes any SDLT payable. Similar principles would appear to apply in relation to capital allowances in so far as these are available in relation to land although it can include fixtures and buildings[12] and the cost of trading stock for developers and others may be influenced by stamp taxes upon the acquisition particularly following the virtual abolition of subsale relief for developers and house builders.

16.4 UNCERTAIN COSTS

It might seem a potentially simple exercise to add the SDLT to the relevant cost or expenditure incurred. Unfortunately, as indicated above frequently the SDLT cost may not be finalised at any particular time or prior to or as at the relevant SDLT effective date. This uncertainty may frequently arise because of the self-assessment basis of SDLT (see **17.1**). The filing of the land transaction return (SDLT 1) and payment of the tax shown therein may produce a Revenue certificate (SDLT 5) but it is no guarantee that the tax position is correct. HMRC Stamp Taxes may challenge a return basically for six years but this may apply for up to 21 years.[13] It may also challenge transactions accepted by the Land Registry as non-notifiable for a like period.[14] The *prima facie* tax position may therefore change retrospectively. Similarly many reliefs may be retrospectively cancelled by HMRC Stamp Taxes, or clawed back or forfeited by reason of subsequent events. For example, where the acquisition of the land is subject to VAT there may be issues as to whether subsequent fluctuations in the rate of VAT upon the purchase price, which may itself be variable, will increase or reduce SDLT and in many other cases the tax is probably still on a provisional basis and subject to retrospective adjustment. The SDLT may subsequently increase because of later linked transactions. Where the land acquired is affected by the VAT Capital Goods Scheme the VAT cost may fluctuate from year to year and this is recognised for the purposes of capital allowances.[15] However, since SDLT is chargeable upon the VAT payable and not the net figure after taking any input tax credit against output tax such fluctuations by reason of the Capital Goods Scheme should not affect the SDLT computation; but the fluctuations in the SDLT whether arising by reason of changes in VAT or otherwise are not provided for in the capital allowances legislation.

However, where there is deferred consideration of a contingent or uncertain nature the rate and/or amount of VAT may change during the period over which the tax is to be adjusted and the final SDLT figure may only be known many years in the future.[16] For example, where there is the sale of land with a clawback should planning permission be obtained within the following 80 years then, potentially, the

---

[12] See, for example, Capital Allowances Act 2001, ss.345 and following.
[13] FA 2003, Sched.10, para.31.
[14] FA 2003, Sched.10, paras.25 and 28.
[15] See Value Added Tax Act 1994, s.24; Value Added Tax Regulations 1995, SI 1995/2518, Part XV; Capital Allowances Act 2001, ss.345 and following.
[16] FA 2003, s.51; see Value Added Tax Regulations 1995, SI 1995/2518, Part XV.

final consideration and any VAT in respect thereof will not be known for 80 years and therefore the total 'tax cost' will be uncertain when dealing with capital allowances or capital gains tax including situations where there is a roll-over of capital gain upon the replacement of business assets.[17]

These issues have not been considered or dealt with by HMRC Stamp Taxes in the legislation and it may mean there will be complex negotiations with other divisions of HMRC because of the absence of relevant legislation, lack of finality and the fluctuating nature of SDLT arrangements (see **1.11**).

16.5 CHANGES IN OTHER TAX RATES

Difficult issues arise, which are at present not fully resolved as to their solution or possibly correct treatment, where SDLT is charged upon other taxes and the rates of tax change. This is particularly a problem in relation to VAT, especially in the case of rent. It is the view of HMRC Stamp Taxes (see **8.21**) that where there is a rent that is subject to VAT this is a variable rent so that subsequent fluctuations in the rate of VAT during the first five years of the term may mean that additional tax is payable or the taxpayer may be entitled to a refund where the rate reduces[18] when the rent is to be reviewed at the end of the five-year period.[19] This raises practical issues such as whether subsequent fluctuations in the rate of VAT represent VAT payable as at the effective date but it would seem that HMRC Stamp Taxes is strongly of the view that it is such a tax because it is VAT not arising by reason of the subsequent exercise of the option to tax.[20]

Other issues will arise by reason of fluctuations in tax rates such as where there is an increase in the rate of VAT after the expiration of the fifth year of the term of the lease and whether this is a chargeable increase or reduction in the rent[21] which counts towards the calculation of whether there is an 'abnormal' increase in the rent.[22] In general such fluctuations in the rate of VAT are not, of themselves, likely to give rise to a charge to tax because the rate is unlikely to move by such an amount as to constitute an abnormal increase in the rent in its own right although there is the outstanding question of whether it may be a factor in deciding whether the relevant abnormality threshold has been exceeded. A more significant problem is where the lease was exempt when granted and at some stage the landlord exercises the option to tax notwithstanding the effective exclusion for the exercise of the option to tax after the effective date because this is not VAT that was payable as at the effective date.[23] It is questionable whether this affects the rent during the first five years of the

---

[17] Taxation of Chargeable Gains Act 1992, ss.152 and following.
[18] HMRC Guidance Note 30 January 2009; STI 2009, p.460.
[19] FA 2003, Sched.17A, paras.7 and 8; see **8.33**.
[20] FA 2003, Sched.4, para.2.
[21] See FA 2003, s.43(3)(d); Sched.17A, paras.13, 14, 15 and 15A.
[22] FA 2003, Sched.17A, paras.14 and 15.
[23] But note the potential trap where there may be more than one effective date for the same commercial transaction pursuant to FA 2003, s.44(9) and Sched.17A, para.12A; see **8.9**.

term because this is chargeable only in respect of the VAT upon the rent actually payable at the time of the effective date.[24] Certainly the exercise of the option to tax after the expiration of the fifth year of the term would not be taken into account in the review at the end of the first five-year period. However, the question arises in both cases whether the exercise of the option to tax is, in its own right, an increase in the rent giving rise to a charge to tax and therefore creating a new chargeable transaction with its own effective date at which point the new amount of VAT would be actually payable within FA 2003, Sched.4, para.2 (see **4.30**).

16.6 OTHER TAXES, MARKET VALUES, MARKET COSTS AND DRAFTING

On various occasions (see **Chapter 15**) SDLT is chargeable upon market value rather than the actual consideration and consideration consisting of or including 'services' is taxable upon open market cost.[25] The market value or market cost is defined as the price or amount that would be paid for the acquisition or disposal of the asset or services in the open market.[26] It seems that the 'price' in the open market does not include 'costs' so that stamp taxes are ignored.

However, this does not mean that SDLT may not form a component in computing the chargeable consideration. For example, in many cases the premium or the rent for a lease is linked to the costs of the development such as where a developer who is entitled to an agreement for lease enters into a funding arrangement with some institution which funds the development by loan and which will take an assignment of the lease in due course for a consideration[27] that essentially involves the satisfaction of any monies borrowed in the form of development costs. The loan may be on special terms but include a notional figure for interest.[28] Frequently such costs are defined as including stamp taxes incurred by any relevant party. The drafting problem is that, *prima facie*, such costs will include stamp taxes; but the amount of the stamp taxes cannot be determined until the amount of the consideration is fixed, i.e. the costs including the SDLT are finally determined. This can be a particular problem because of the circularity of the arrangements;[29] namely the 'price' which includes the costs will not be known until the SDLT is determined which in turn will not be known until the costs are determined. The problem of what is, effectively, SDLT upon SDLT that operates as a cost[30] will have to be addressed.

---

[24] FA 2003, Sched.4, para.2. Although the review at the end of the fifth year is retrospective (FA 2003, Sched.17A, para.8) the VAT is to be ignored because it arises pursuant to the exercise of the option to tax after the effective date.

[25] FA 2003, Sched.4, para.11; see **4.37** and **15.18**.

[26] FA 2003, Sched.4, paras.7 and 11.

[27] But note the problems for loans and deposits in this area: FA 2003, Sched.17A, para.18A.

[28] See, for example, *Re EuroHotel (Belgravia)* [1975] STC 682; *Chevron Petroleum* v. *BP* [1981] STC 689.

[29] See, for example, *Re Hollebone's Agreement* [1959] 2 All ER 152.

[30] See also problems for draftsmen in dealing with costs in the form of interest or notional interest which are not interest for tax purposes as in *EuroHotel (Belgravia)* [1975] STC 682; *Chevron Petroleum* v. *BP* [1981] STC 689.

In many cases the SDLT will be of a provisional nature and subject to subsequent review which means that the final figures cannot be known for many years and, where there is some form of clawback arrangement that extends over a period of 80 years, the final figures may not be known for several generations and numerous dealings in the property. Services which are chargeable consideration[31] in the open market may be subject to VAT but the particular taxpayer may be entitled to an input tax credit that means he may be able to recover all or part of the VAT. His market 'cost' is, therefore, possibly less than the actual outlay that will be subject to SDLT upon the basis of an actual transaction where the VAT was actually payable as at the effective date. It seems, however, that HMRC Stamp Taxes takes the view that the market value or market cost is to be determined upon the basis that no VAT is chargeable.[32] In consequence, it would seem that it would not be necessary to investigate whether a vendor or landlord has or has not exercised the option to tax and whether the transaction is exempt nor whether the prospective purchaser or tenant is wholly taxable or is in an exempt or partially exempt situation when he may lose all or part of the input tax credit. In these situations it is the figure net of any potential VAT charge that HMRC Stamp Taxes appears to expect the taxpayer to use as the basis for computing his liability.

16.7   TRANSFER OF GOING CONCERN

A key problem area for SDLT is an acquisition of land that may or may not be a transfer of a going concern for the purposes of VAT. In such situations it is not possible to charge VAT.[33] To charge VAT where there is a transfer of a going concern is regarded by HMRC Customs and Excise and the relevant Tribunals as not creating a true charge to VAT. In consequence, it is not a true input tax as far as the purchaser of the chargeable interest is concerned. Generally HMRC Customs and Excise does not take the point and allows the credit for the input tax but, on occasion, usually where the transferor has not accounted in full for the VAT charged, HMRC Customs and Excise has refused to allow the purchaser to claim credit for the improperly charged tax. In such situations it is necessary for the purchaser to proceed against the vendor in ordinary civil litigation for the recovery of money paid under a mistake of law.[34] In consequence, it is usual to provide, subject to various indemnities and counter-indemnities, that should the transaction not be a transfer of a going concern the vendor will issue a VAT invoice and the purchaser

---

[31]   FA 2003, Sched.4, para.11; compare *Secretan* v. *Hart* 45 TC 701.
[32]   See SDLT Manual 4140.
[33]   Unless the parties deliberately do not include the required certificate so that the transaction cannot qualify as a transfer of a going concern: Value Added Tax (Special Provisions) Order 1995, SI 1995/1268, art.5.
[34]   See, for example, *Woolwich Equitable* v. *IRC* 65 TC 265.

will pay the additional price.[35] In this situation it would seem that because there is an obligation to pay the VAT this may be VAT that is actually payable[36] at the effective date for the transaction; but this raises the fundamental question of whether it is VAT payable where the tax point for VAT[37] is later than the effective date for SDLT or falls between the two effective dates for substantial performance and completion.[38] There are, of course, many issues as to whether VAT that is payable only if certain events occur is VAT actually payable within the charge[39] and falls within a variable consideration regime.[40] Potentially, therefore, the possible VAT in the event of the transaction not being accepted as a transfer of a going concern is subject to SDLT and potentially part of the cost of the purchaser for other tax purposes. The arrangement would, therefore, seem to bring the transaction within the variable consideration provisions.[41] It would seem that when making the initial computation of the tax the taxpayer will have to assume that the transaction is not a transfer of going concern and the VAT is part of the chargeable consideration. It should be relatively easy to make the necessary estimate since the rate of VAT will be that in force at the relevant date although it should be noted that there are many difficulties arising because the effective date for SDLT is not the same as the tax point for VAT.[42]

The question then arises as to whether the taxpayer can defer the SDLT in respect of the potential VAT. HMRC Stamp Taxes has from time to time advanced the view that such consideration is 'unascertained' because of the situation of whether the transaction is or is not a transfer of a going concern is known by circumstances as they exist as at the effective date. This means that the consideration being unascertained[43] cannot be deferred.[44] However, although the amount is potentially fixed it is by no means certain that all relevant data as to whether the transaction is or is not a transfer of a going concern for the purposes of VAT will be in place as at the effective date since the tax point for VAT may be later than the effective date for SDLT and may be calculated upon a different basis. Actions of the purchaser after the effective date may mean that the conditions are subsequently not satisfied because of his

---

[35] For some of the VAT complications arising out of such arrangements see, for example, *Higher Education Statistics* v. *Customs and Excise* [2000] STC 332; *Wynn Realisations Ltd* v. *Vogue Holdings Inc* [1999] STC 524; *Hostgilt Ltd* v. *Megahart Ltd* [1999] STC 141.

[36] It seems that HMRC Stamp Taxes regards 'actually payable' as meaning any VAT that arises because the price was subject to VAT at the effective date. It is not apparently restricted to VAT at the rate in force as at the effective date; but this may not be a valid view where the chargeable consideration is a periodical payment where this is to be 'capitalised' as at the effective date; see FA 2003, s.52; see **4.31.6**.

[37] Value Added Tax Act 1994, s.6.

[38] FA 2003, s.44(8) and Sched.17A, para.12A; see **3.3** and **8.9**.

[39] FA 2003, Sched.4, para.2; but see *Eastham* v. *Leigh London and Provincial Properties Ltd* [1971] 2 All ER 887 on conditions and consideration.

[40] FA 2003, s.51.

[41] FA 2003, ss.51 and 81A; Sched.17A, para.12 affecting third parties such as assignees of leases.

[42] Compare FA 2003, s.119 and the special provisions and Value Added Tax Act 1994, s.6 so that the VAT rate may not be known until some time after the effective date for SDLT purposes.

[43] FA 2003, ss.51 and 80.

[44] FA 2003, s.90; see also s.87(5) and Stamp Duty Land Tax (Administration) Regulations 2003, SI 2003/2837, reg.7.

change of user of the asset or the modifications in the business. It is considered that in most circumstances the VAT will be an uncertain consideration because the relevant data will only arise after the effective date for SDLT and will not necessarily be in place as at the effective date as a retrospective review of data. In the circumstances, therefore, while the taxpayer will have to fix the rate by reference to the figure including potential VAT he will be able to defer the payment of the SDLT in respect of the VAT that might arise. Where the effect of the VAT is to increase the chargeable consideration above a SDLT rate threshold the higher rate would have to be paid upon both the basic price and the potential VAT; but, as and when it becomes clear that the transaction is accepted by HMRC Customs and Excise as a transfer of a going concern, the final consideration will be known and the rate of SDLT will be correspondingly reduced below the threshold. In such circumstances the taxpayer will be entitled to make a claim for the repayment of the overpaid tax. However, this higher rate will initially apply even where the taxpayer had successfully deferred the tax upon the VAT amount.

CHAPTER 17

Notifiable transactions and filing returns

17.1 SELF-ASSESSMENT

SDLT is essentially a self-assessment tax which requires the first stage to be the taxpayer and his advisers coping as best they can with the less than satisfactory legislation in order to determine whether there is a charge and, if so, the amount of such charge, filing the necessary return and making payment of the tax due, i.e. the amount shown as payable in the land transaction return (SDLT 1). There have been significant changes in relation to the initial structure since 2003 so that filing and payment are no longer simultaneous transactions.[1] The filing[2] is, essentially, a precondition to obtaining a Revenue certificate (SDLT 5) which is required for production to the Land Registry in support of applications to register notifiable transactions[3] although there have been difficulties with the Land Registry in relation to the presentation of applications for changes in the register where the parties believe the transaction is not notifiable notwithstanding the basic requirement is filing in relation to a notifiable transaction.[4]

Notification obligations raise three issues in practice; namely:

- when is notification required;
- who is responsible, under penalty, to make the return, i.e. who is liable for failure to notify or making an incorrect return; and
- the problems of dealing with the Land Registry in relation to non-notifiable transactions, i.e. where there is no SLDT 5.[5]

---

[1] FA 2003, s.76 (as amended); the filing and payment conditions were repealed; see also Stamp Duty Land Tax (Administration) Regulations 2003, SI 2003/2837, Part 1 (as amended).

[2] Payment is no longer a precondition to obtaining the SDLT 5; see **14.12**.

[3] FA 2003, s.79 (as amended).

[4] There is a key practical issue arising out of the problems of dealings with particular employees within the Land Registry in exercise of their 'local discretion'. HMRC Stamp Taxes may enquire into notifiable transactions but the removal of the self-certificate has taken away its power to enquire into transactions that are not notifiable transactions (FA 2003, Sched.10, para.12(1); relevant parts of Sched.11 repealed). On difficulties with the Land Registry see **Chapter 1**.

[5] FA 2003, s.79(1) (as amended); see **1.10.2**.

17.2 NOTIFIABLE TRANSACTIONS

It is therefore necessary to know when an SDLT 1 is required. Notifiable transactions are those where a land transaction return (SDLT 1 together with the supplementary forms SDLT 2 to 4 (as amended)) is required.

The definition of what is a notifiable transaction was completely recast by FA 2008, s.94; it starts by, in effect, making every transaction notifiable unless excluded. The current starting situation is that, subject to the exclusions (see **17.7**), a notifiable transaction is:

- any acquisition of a major interest in land,[6] which includes[7] the creation, variation, surrender or release of a major interest unless excluded from notification pursuant to FA 2003, s.77A;
- any acquisition, including creation, release, surrender and variation, of a minor interest where there is chargeable consideration in excess of the nil rate band from time to time applicable;[8]
- a deemed chargeable transaction pursuant to FA 2003, s.44A (e.g. where there are building works; see **Chapter 9**); and
- the notional transaction pursuant to the general statutory anti-avoidance provisions;[9] notification is required in addition to any notification required by any actual acquisition by the person eventually identified as the purchaser, notwithstanding that it is expressly provided that the actual transactions are to be 'disregarded'.[10]

17.3 OTHER NOTIFIABLE TRANSACTIONS

This is a less than comprehensive list. There remain, therefore, many situations where there is a specific or implied obligation to notify whether in respect of the current transaction or as a retrospective adjustment of a previous transaction. This list, which has been added to constantly, includes:

- grant and substantial performance of a lease for seven years or more for a chargeable consideration;[11]
- grant and substantial performance of a lease for less than seven years where either the premium or the rent exceeds the nil rate band. In the case of non-residential property a rent of £1,000 per annum cancels the nil rate band for

---

[6] FA 2003, s.117.
[7] FA 2003, s.43 (as amended).
[8] Notification is required where the threshold is exceeded notwithstanding the tax is not payable because of a relief. Where there is an 'exemption' there may be no obligation to notify because there is no chargeable consideration: FA 2003, Sched.3, para.1; but this is subject to situations where notification is required.
[9] FA 2003, ss.75A–75C.
[10] FA 2003, s.75A; see **1.33**.
[11] A peppercorn rent is not chargeable consideration, but £1 is.

the premium making the lease notifiable if there is a premium, which includes backdated rent.[12] Notification is required even where the lease is exempt such as a lease to a charity;

- the assignment of a lease if either a notional grant of the lease at the time of the assignment[13] would be notifiable or the assignment is for a consideration which is taxable at 1 per cent or higher or would be so taxable but for exemption;

- substantial performance of contracts for and completion of the acquisition of freeholds unless either there is an exemption pursuant to FA 2003, Sched.3 (as amended; see **17.7**) or the land is residential property and the chargeable consideration is less than £40,000;[14]

- acquisition of minor interests (i.e. all interests in land other than freeholds and leases) where the consideration falls outside the nil rate band;[15]

- rent reviews during or after the expiration of the first five years of the lease which require retrospective recalculation of the initial 'guestimated' assessment in the first return;[16]

- abnormal increases in rent after the fifth year of the term which involve the deemed grant of a new lease;[17]

- when unascertained consideration or premium becomes certain;[18]

- as and when contingent or uncertain consideration becomes certain or instalments are paid;[19]

- where there is a later linked transaction;[20]

- if treatment as a transfer of a going concern is not granted by HMRC Customs and Excise for the purposes of VAT (see **4.30**);

- intra-group transactions and company reconstructions;[21]

- where any relief is granted subject to clawback, such as transactions involving charities, intra-group transactions and company reconstructions and the relief is clawed back;[22]

- the forfeiture of the special reliefs for residential property pursuant to FA 2003, Sched.6A;

- where any chargeable interest other than a lease is varied[23] for a sufficiently large consideration such as the extension of an option exercise period;

- where a lease is varied.[24]

---

[12] FA 2003, Sched.5, para.1A.
[13] FA 2003, Sched.17A, para.11; see **8.62**.
[14] FA 2003, s.77A.
[15] FA 2003, s.77A.
[16] FA 2003, s.50; Sched.17A, paras.7 and 8; see **8.34**.
[17] FA 2003, Sched.17A, paras.13, 14 and 15; see **8.37**.
[18] FA 2003, s.80.
[19] FA 2003, s.80.
[20] FA 2003, s.81A; Sched.17A, para.11.
[21] FA 2003, Sched.7; see **Chapter 13.**
[22] FA 2003, Sched.7, paras.3 and 9; Sched.8, para.2.
[23] FA 2003, s.43(3).
[24] FA 2003, s.43(3)(d); Sched.17A, para.15A.

This list is, however, somewhat less than complete or even basically helpful. It essentially states that all chargeable transactions are notifiable subject to exclusions. However, there are notifiable transactions that are not within the list because they are deemed transactions or the consideration is deemed to be at a certain level. For example, certain variations of rent or assignments of leases are deemed to be the grant of new leases[25] and many partnership transactions have their own rules and specify persons responsible for notification and payment (see **Chapter 12**). It is, therefore, necessary to plough through the legislation to discover various areas of compliance. These include:

- situations where a transaction that is, *prima facie*, notifiable is not notifiable;
- deemed transactions where notification is required; and
- situations where there is an open-ended tax liability initially reported on a provisional or guestimated basis which requires a retrospective notification in the sense of an adjustment of the earlier guestimated return upon the basis of the actual information or subsequent events.

17.4 NOTIFYING PERSONS

In addition, there is the question as to who is to notify in respect of particular transactions. This has been considered elsewhere (see **Chapter 14**) but it is necessary to bear in mind that persons other than the taxpayer as a party to the original transaction may be required to notify[26] in respect of the original taxpayer's outstanding obligations or subsequent linked transactions although they are not parties thereto.[27] This can apply, for example, to third parties who are by statute responsible for certain aspects of the original transaction including notification and dealing with what is the open tax position of a third party.[28] This may also apply to subsequent linked transactions.[29] It might be thought that because the linked transaction provisions only apply to subsequent related transactions between the same parties or persons connected with either of the parties to the transaction independent third parties would not be affected by the situation. Unfortunately, owing to drafting and structuring oversights unconnected third parties will be affected by linked transactions notwithstanding that they are unconnected with the parties to the original transaction and they may not be parties to the subsequent linked transaction. For example, where there are linked leases of different premises the nil rate slice for rent has to be apportioned between the leases. Later linked arrangements are retrospectively reducing the nil rate allocated to prior leases increasing the tax charge which has to be paid by the current tenant.[30]

---

25   See, for example, FA 2003, Sched.17A, paras.11 and 14.
26   See, for example, FA 2003, Sched.17A, para.12.
27   FA 2003, ss.108, 81A, Sched.17A, para.11.
28   See, for example, FA 2003, Sched.17A, para.12.
29   FA 2003, s.81A.
30   FA 2003, s.81A; Sched.17A, para.12.

17.5   MAJOR INTERESTS: SPECIAL NOTIFICATIONS

Major interests are defined[31] as being freeholds or terms of years absolute.[32]

Certain transactions that are *prima facie* non-notifiable are made indirectly notifiable because they are excluded from the exclusions. In consequence, 'notifiable transactions' involving major interests in land include any transactions that are *prima facie* exempt from charge pursuant to FA 2003, Sched.3 because there is no chargeable consideration which relates to:

- certain dealings involving connected companies;[33] but these notification obligations do not apply to transactions excluded from the connected company charge pursuant to FA 2003, s.54;[34]
- dealings between partnerships and connected persons within FA 2003, Sched. 15, Part 3;[35]
- any dealings within the special reliefs for PFI projects;[36] and
- any residual transactions that remain within the transitional provisions relieving from charge pursuant to the disadvantaged land regime.[37]

There is power to extend the list of transactions falling within Sched.3.[38] Any transactions that are listed pursuant to the exercise of these powers are, *prima facie*, notifiable.[39]

17.6   MINOR INTERESTS

'Minor interests' are, in effect, all chargeable interests that are not 'major interests'. A chargeable transaction relating to a minor interest where the chargeable consideration exceeds the nil rate threshold is notifiable.[40]

---

[31]   FA 2003, s.117.

[32]   Note that this may not be the same as the definition of 'lease' for the purposes of SDLT; note FA 2003, Sched.17A, para.1 which suggests that any interest in land that is for a fixed term may be a 'lease'. It would not, however, convert the interest into a major interest because it would not be a term of years absolute which, presumably, relies upon the definitions in Law of Property Act 1925, s.205, etc.

[33]   FA 2003, s.53(4).

[34]   They are excluded from the charge pursuant to FA 2003, s.53.

[35]   FA 2003, Sched.15, para.32.

[36]   FA 2003, Sched.4, para.17.

[37]   FA 2003, Sched.6, para.13.

[38]   FA 2003, Sched.3, para.5. This exclusion of additional transactions has been exercised only in relation to the temporary so-called SDLT holiday arising by reason of the increase in the nil rate threshold for residential property from £125,000 to £175,000 during 2008 and 2009; see the Stamp Duty Land Tax (Exemption of Certain Acquisitions of Residential Property) Regulations 2008, SI 2008/2339 (now repealed).

[39]   FA 2003, s.77A(1), item 1 (as amended).

[40]   FA 2003, s.77(1)(b); see **17.7.2**.

17.7 NON-NOTIFIABLE TRANSACTIONS

There is no general list of transactions that are non-notifiable. These arise largely by inference from the exclusions or other factors relating to notifiable transactions such as FA 2003, s.77A. Taxpayers must nevertheless preserve adequate records to establish to the satisfaction of HMRC Stamp Taxes that the transaction was not notifiable.[41] The main practical difficulty is persuading certain employees of the Land Registry that the transaction is non-notifiable and they are required to register it without a Revenue certificate (SDLT 5).[42]

The list of non-notifiable transactions applies to the following transactions.

17.7.1 Major interests

17.7.1.1 Schedule 3

The non-notifiable transactions include transactions in FA 2003, Sched.3[43] which include:

- transactions for no chargeable consideration;[44]
- certain tenancy agreements entered into by registered social landlords;[45]
- transactions in connection with the breakdown of marriage or civil partnerships;[46]
- the acquisition of property by a person in satisfaction of his entitlement to property in relation to the estate of a deceased person whether dying testate or intestate;[47]
- transactions for the variation of the estate of a deceased individual entered into within two years of the death.[48]

17.7.1.2 Consideration below £40,000 threshold

There is a *de minimis* threshold saving small transactions from the need to incur the costs involved in notification. These include acquisitions of chargeable interests other than the grant, assignment or surrender of a lease where the interest is a major interest and the chargeable consideration for that transaction, including any linked transactions is less than £40,000. The provision will apply to those rare situations where there is an acquisition of a freehold for less than £40,000 and possibly the variation of a lease where the consideration for the variation is less than £40,000.

---

[41] FA 2003, s.77A; Sched.11 (as amended).
[42] FA 2003, s.79(1) (as amended).
[43] FA 2003, s.77A.
[44] FA 2003, Sched.3, para.1; see **5.7.2.1**.
[45] FA 2003, Sched.3, para.2; see **5.7.2.2**.
[46] FA 2003, Sched.3, paras.3 and the second para.3A; see **5.7.2.3**.
[47] FA 2003, Sched.3, the first para.3A; see further **Chapter 11**.
[48] FA 2003, Sched.3, para.4; see **Chapter 11**.

However, since many variations of leases are either surrenders and regrants by operation of law or are deemed to be the grant of new leases any variation within those categories would appear to be governed by the different notification rules relating to the 'grant' or deemed grant of leases.

17.7.1.3 Leases for low premium and rent

The grant of a lease for a term of seven years or more is not notifiable where the premium for the lease is less than £40,000 and the relevant rent is less than £1,000.[49] It will, however, be remembered that in relation to non-residential property there is no nil rate for the premium where the rent exceeds £1,000.[50] This exclusion will not apply in such situations since there is a chargeable premium, i.e. outside the nil rate.[51] This could be a major problem because of the provision that the backdating of rent produces a charge upon the amount involved not as rent but as a premium.[52] In consequence, since there are many situations where the parties may 'backdate' the commencement of the rent arrangements as opposed to creating a prior term commencement date, and commercial rents are unlikely to be less than £1,000 even where these are ground rents, such backdated rent could attract a significant charge to tax. However, where there are holding over and similar arrangements and certain variations of leases that involve surrenders and regrants the backdated rent may, if carefully organised, retain its character as rent and not be a deemed premium.[53]

17.7.1.4 Grant of short leases

The grant or deemed grant[54] of a lease for a term of less than seven years where the chargeable consideration does not exceed the zero rate threshold is not notifiable. The legislation does not clarify whether the question of the nil rate threshold is that applicable to rents or to consideration other than rent namely premium payments.[55] The removal of the former nil rate threshold for residential property where the ground rent exceeded £600 per annum means that most leases for a small premium and the low ground rent are unlikely to be taxable. In consequence, they would seem by reason of this provision to be non-notifiable. However, leases of non-residential property do not have a nil rate for any premium where the ground rent exceeds £1,000 per annum.[56]

---

[49] FA 2003, s.77A.
[50] FA 2003, Sched.5, paras.9 and 9A.
[51] It is assumed that the first time buyer relief will not affect this notification obligation.
[52] FA 2003, Sched.5, para.1A; but subject to relief for holding over: FA 2003, Sched.17A, paras.9 and 9A.
[53] FA 2003, Sched.17A, paras.9 and 9A.
[54] FA 2003, Sched.17A, para.12A.
[55] On the first time buyer relief see FA 2003, s.57AA.
[56] FA 2003, Sched.5, paras.9 and 9A.

17.7.1.5 Assignment of longer lease

The assignment or surrender of a lease where the lease was originally granted for a term of seven years or more and the chargeable consideration for the assignment or surrender is less than £40,000 is not notifiable.[57] However, it must be noted that certain assignments of leases are taxed as if they were the grant of a new lease.[58] In such cases it seems that the notification arrangements will be those applicable to the grant of a new lease and not the assignment of a term which is the real transaction.

17.7.1.6 Assignment of short lease

The assignment or surrender of a lease where the lease was originally granted for a term of less than seven years and the consideration for the assignment or surrender does not exceed the nil rate threshold is not notifiable. It must be noted that this applies only where the original term was less than seven years. Assignments of leases granted for a longer term are notifiable in accordance with the preceding paragraph notwithstanding that the unexpired term is less than seven years.

17.7.2 Minor interests

There is no notification obligation where there is a dealing in a chargeable interest that is not a major interest unless the consideration exceeds the 1 per cent threshold.[59] This means that most dealings in options, easements, restrictive covenants, rights to light and, perhaps, many interests in trusts (see **Chapter 10**) will not be notifiable. These are minor interests and any consideration related to them or their value in terms of market value is likely to be small. Most minor interests can only exist as part of some dominant land. They cannot have a separate existence or represent rights in gross. Since they cannot have a separate existence the rights themselves are not capable of sale in the open market and, therefore, although they may be valuable[60] because almost every right or restriction has at least a nuisance value, they do not have an 'open market' value because they cannot be separately sold.

---

[57] FA 2003, s.77A(1), item 4.
[58] FA 2003, Sched.17A, para.11; see **8.61**.
[59] FA 2003, s.77(1)(b).
[60] Compare *Alexander* v. *IRC* [1991] STC 112.

CHAPTER 18

HMRC powers and enforcement

18.1 GENERAL

Traditional stamp duties were frequently described as a voluntary tax for a variety of reasons, one being that with limited exceptions HMRC Stamp Taxes could not enforce the payment of tax and the tax was collected 'indirectly' as a title issue. That has been fundamentally changed by SDLT,[1] which is no longer a title issue as such.[2] The tax is directly enforceable and the powers of HMRC Stamp Taxes are being continuously enlarged by every Finance Act. The counterpart to the self-assessment regime shifting the obligation, under severe penalties, to the taxpayer to calculate accurately the tax liability is the conversion of HMRC Stamp Taxes generally from tax inspectors to a form of auditors with extensive powers to collect the tax directly and to reopen transactions for up to 21 years in the many cases which will arise, inevitably, because of the defects in the self-assessment regime and the limitations of the presented forms. This will make it unbelievably easy for HMRC Stamp Taxes to issue a 'discovery assessment'.[3] Other divisions of HMRC have signed up to a statement of practice that indicates this power will be exercised with a 'soft pedal', but HMRC Stamp Taxes did not participate. In consequence, it can be expected that this 'discovery power' will be exercised aggressively. Moreover, to make good the deficiencies in the powers of HMRC Stamp Taxes to investigate transactions there is an obligation unlimited in time under tax-related penalties, imposed upon taxpayers to report any errors in their return, in many cases even where the return was not made negligently or fraudulently, when they become aware of them.[4]

---

[1]   And stamp duty reserve tax; FA 1986, s.86 and Stamp Duty Reserve Tax Regulations 1986, SI 1986/1711, reg.4.

[2]   Although the Land Registry seems to have taken upon the role of tax collector by requisitioning a full SDLT analysis of transactions. This is probably beyond the powers of the Land Registry but is proving a major obstacle to efficient title registration, which is its function.

[3]   *Langham* v. *Veltema* [2004] STC 544.

[4]   FA 2003, Sched.10, para.31A.

18.2 ENFORCING FILING OF THE RETURN

18.2.1 Direct intervention

HMRC Stamp Taxes is given extensive powers to deal with the situation where no return has been filed.[5] However, there is a fundamental practical problem for HMRC Stamp Taxes as to how it may discover the happening of a chargeable transaction where there has been no filing. This, of course, assumes that it becomes aware of a transaction by other means.

18.2.2 Land Registry

To a large extent the enforcement is indirect though the Land Registry[6] refusing to register title changes. The Land Registry has taken on this role of enforcing the tax with surprising enthusiasm (see e.g. **1.12**).

18.2.3 Whistleblowers

In consequence, in practice, there may be situations where, notwithstanding the alleged policies behind the legislation of raising tax on e-conveyancing and expediting registration and easing title investigation the less than successful attempts at changing the title investigation issues still mean third parties may have difficulties in registering their title where the individual has not filed or paid his tax and so cannot register his interest.[7] No doubt there may be situations where there are interested 'whistleblowers'. For example, a person being granted a subtenancy which requires registration and who has paid his SDLT and obtained his Revenue certificate (SDLT 5) will be somewhat irritated to discover that he cannot obtain registration since his immediate landlord is not the registered owner because he has refused to pay the SDLT and cannot produce the certificate that the Land Registry will require for him to be registered.[8] In these circumstances the only effective method for the subtenant to protect his interest would be to inform HMRC Stamp Taxes and hope that it will issue some form of proceedings or notices in respect of the landlord to obtain the necessary payment and eventually issue the necessary certificate (SDLT 5).

---

[5] FA 2003, Sched.10, Parts 4 and 5.

[6] FA 2003, s.79(1) (as amended); see **1.12**.

[7] FA 2003, s.79(1) (as amended). However, note that, because of the changes in making filing, payment and issue of a Revenue certificate separate events even this section is severely limited in practice. It is now possible to file and register title, but not pay. As with stamp duty, therefore, HMRC Stamp Taxes is heavily dependent upon the problems of third parties who cannot obtain registration because the original taxpayer has not obtained registration, or because e.g. the third party's tax position requires them to take over and revise the tax position of the original tenant. These title issues mean that the third party, if properly advised, will not accept a title where the essential and fundamental SDLT information is not produced by the vendor or landlord.

[8] FA 2003, s.79(1) (as amended).

However, since HMRC Stamp Taxes has consistently maintained that it does not have power to issue a certificate or co-operate in changes in registration until the tax has been paid and the declaration signed[9] should the relevant landlord have disappeared or prove unco-operative it may be many years before the title issues related to the headlease are satisfactorily resolved. While there are powers of 'care and management' these are applied in an extremely limited fashion.[10] Penalties are imposed for failure to file a return within the prescribed period[11] and HMRC Stamp Taxes has consistently refused to provide helpful decisions in situations such as that described; it appears to be relying extensively upon the Land Registry to refuse applications to change the register.

18.3 ENFORCING PAYMENT

The primary obligation was on the taxpayer to enclose payment with the land transaction return; the obligation now is to pay within the 30-day period, and HMRC Stamp Taxes is given wide powers to sue for any part of the tax unpaid,[12] interest and penalties.[13] This applies even where the tax arises as a result of its own assessment such as determining on an Enquiry that tax has been unpaid, or where it discovers that insufficient tax has been paid.[14] It may also assess and sue for tax where no land transaction return has been produced.[15]

18.4 CHALLENGING A LAND TRANSACTION RETURN

In the converse situation of dealing with a return that is filed but may be incorrect the powers of HMRC Stamp Taxes are similarly constrained. The idea or policy is that there is, as such, no power set out in the legislation to reject a return. However, should the return be defective, for example because it lacks an appropriate signed declaration or does not include relevant information such as the amount of the chargeable consideration HMRC Stamp Taxes is likely to reject the return.[16] There may, therefore, be some important issues in practice as to when a return is a return or when a return is so defective that it is not a return.

A key practical problem in this area arises in relation to the failure of HMRC Stamp Taxes to deal with the problem of zero chargeable consideration. The

---

[9] FA 2003, Sched.10, para.1(1)(c) or the two declarations of para.1A thereof.
[10] FA 2003, s.42(3).
[11] FA 2003, Sched.10, paras.2–5; see also s.76 (as amended).
[12] FA 2003, s.91.
[13] FA 2003, ss.87 and 88; FA 2009, Sched.56.
[14] FA 2003, Sched.10, para.26.
[15] FA 2003, Sched.10, Parts 4 and 5.
[16] It seems that in practice HMRC Stamp Taxes may not regard all of the entries on the form as being compulsory fields for entry but it is not clear which are regarded as essential or compulsory boxes and which are in a sense 'optional' and can be ignored without risk of rejection.

original plan was that where there was no chargeable consideration the transaction would be 'exempt' within the beneficial provisions of FA 2003, Sched.3, para.1 and the transaction would be notified indirectly by the filing of a self-certificate (SDLT 60) with the Land Registry which would be made available to HMRC Stamp Taxes. However, this facility has been affected in two major respects, which have created practical problems:

- the decision of the Land Registry to remove the exempt instruments certificates[17] although it seems that the fixed duties may not necessarily have been removed from all land transactions;[18]
- the provisions requiring certain transactions for no chargeable consideration to be notified notwithstanding they are 'exempt', such as dealings between partnerships and connected persons, dealings involving connected companies and the run-off of transactions relating to disadvantaged land.[19]

It seems, however, that the Revenue computers are unable to cope with a land transaction return (SDLT 1) filed electronically showing zero consideration. It will reject the return causing delay and cost to the parties who are effectively required to resort to manual filing. While it may be a preferred route to file the return in hard copy with a covering letter, there may be advantages, where appropriate, of inserting a chargeable consideration of £1 and leaving it for HMRC Stamp Taxes to claim that this was an over-market value.

18.4.1 Nature of 'challenge'

Rather than conferring a power to reject a return[20] that was in some way defective, the legislation confers upon HMRC Stamp Taxes a limited power to 'correct' a return.[21] This power to correct returns may be transferred by regulation to the various land registrars in England and Wales, Scotland and Northern Ireland. The power to correct a return applies to 'obvious errors or omissions in the return (whether errors of principle, arithmetical mistake or otherwise)'. Obviously, this power to correct a return would be important during the course of an Enquiry but does not appear to justify significant intervention in the initial filing of a return where there are errors such as the parties adopting what HMRC Stamp Taxes regards as an unacceptable basis for valuing assets or claiming an exemption to which they may ultimately prove to be not entitled. This is, in practice, largely because HMRC Stamp Taxes, and especially its computers, will not have the information necessary to challenge the form for 'manifest' errors of fact or principle. To permit an in-depth investigation of the return on filing would be a

---

[17] Stamp Duty (Exempt Instruments) Regulations 1987, SI 1987/516.
[18] FA 2008, Sched.32, para.22.
[19] See FA 2003, s.53(4); Sched.15, para.30; Sched.6, para.13.
[20] However, certain employees of the Land Registry claim power to reject transactions which, in many situations, is wider than the powers conferred upon HMRC Stamp Taxes.
[21] FA 2003, Sched.10, para.7 (as amended).

return to the former time-consuming adjudication process and would be contrary to the alleged policy of expediting registration of title in order to speed up and reduce the costs of the conveyancing process.

The overall position appears to be, therefore, that provided the boxes contain some form of entry and the arithmetic appears to be correct HMRC Stamp Taxes is not in a position to reject the return. Moreover, at this stage especially where the filing is made electronically, HMRC Stamp Taxes will not have any information on which to base a challenge, certainly in the area of errors of principle. The extension of electronic filing, and the division of the declaration into two parts for signature by the client and the professional adviser who deals with the question of the effective date, has meant that the Revenue certificate (SDLT 5) is returned by the computer more or less instantaneously. Indeed, now that there is separation of filing and payment the SDLT 5 is frequently obtained before payment has been made.

18.5 NON-NOTIFIABLE TRANSACTIONS

HMRC Stamp Taxes' power is limited to Enquiries into land transaction returns; there is no longer power to investigate non-notifiable transactions as a result of the changes made by FA 2008 (see **1.3**). However, where a party files a return unnecessarily whether as a result of dubious pressure from the Land Registry or otherwise, he confers on HMRC Stamp Taxes a power to enquire.

18.6 ENQUIRIES INTO LAND TRANSACTION RETURNS (SDLT 1)

Since, as indicated above, HMRC Stamp Taxes has virtually no power to reject the initial filing of the return, which policy is designed to facilitate registration of title and e-conveyancing, the key weapon in enforcing the tax in practice will be the Enquiry which is the main means for HMRC Stamp Taxes to investigate the transaction. It differs in theory from the traditional adjudication of stamp duty, although currently these Enquiries seem to be conducted in the same way as adjudications, i.e. by correspondence asking the same questions as for the equivalent stamp duty, with little explanation or justification by reference to the legislation. However, it seems that certain tax mitigation schemes have provoked HMRC Stamp Taxes into asserting its information gathering powers against the promoters of these schemes and their associates. It is, in consequence, proving to be an expensive process for taxpayers, although there is a power for taxpayers to appeal to the First Tier Tribunal[22] for an order requiring the Enquiry to be completed within a set time because HMRC Stamp Taxes is being dilatory or inefficient or, possibly, asking irrelevant questions and not justifying its claims for tax on a proper

---

[22]   Replacing the Special Commissioners.

basis.[23] The only practical benefit is that taxpayers can claim a relief and, subject to the Land Registry, obtain registration at once and do not have to wait until HMRC Stamp Taxes has adjudicated the claim and any appeals have been finally resolved.[24]

An Enquiry into a land transaction return can be launched:

- in relation to a land transaction return, during the period of nine months after the filing date if the return was delivered on or before the date;
- nine months after the date on which the return was delivered if the return was delivered late;
- where the return was amended, nine months after the date of the amendment.

It is not final and conclusive for at least three reasons:

- There can be an Enquiry into a land transaction return that is effectively provisional such as where there is an initial return for variable rent and a further return is required after the rent review date. A further Enquiry can be launched into the second and subsequent returns.[25]
- Where there is a later filing for the transaction this may enable HMRC Stamp Taxes to make an Enquiry into an earlier filing.[26]
- HMRC Stamp Taxes can issue a discovery assessment notwithstanding that there has been a previous Enquiry,[27] and there are restrictions upon what it is deemed to know at the end of the Enquiry.[28] Therefore, although HMRC Stamp Taxes may have accepted the land transaction return and possibly corrected it and issued the appropriate certificate (SDLT 5), it can launch an Enquiry or issue a discovery assessment in respect of it for potentially up to 21 years after the effective date.[29]

HMRC Stamp Taxes has extensive powers to 'discover' information during[30] the course of an Enquiry. Where it has given a notice of Enquiry into a land transaction return (SDLT 1) it may by written notice require the taxpayer to produce such documents in his possession or power[31] and to provide such information in such form as it may reasonably require for the purposes of the Enquiry. The taxpayer is

---

[23]   FA 2003, Sched.10, para.24.

[24]   FA 2003, Sched.11, Part 1 was repealed thereby cancelling the power to launch an Enquiry into a non-notifiable transaction at least where no unnecessary land transaction return (SDLT 1) has been filed: FA 2003, Sched.10, para.12(1).

[25]   FA 2003, Sched.10, para.12(2A).

[26]   FA 2003, Sched.10, para.12(2A).

[27]   FA 2003, Sched.10, para.12(3); but see para.30(3)(b).

[28]   FA 2003, Sched.10, para.30.

[29]   The problem will be how, in practice, HMRC Stamp Taxes will be in a position to obtain information sufficient for it to make a discovery, but see the situation in *Langham* v. *Veltema* [2004] STC 544.

[30]   These powers may not exist outside an Enquiry so that there may be limits on the power of HMRC Stamp Taxes simply to derive advice from persons in general; but see FA 2003, Sched.13 (as amended and replaced); see **18.19**.

[31]   But note the limitations imposed upon these words by the House of Lords in *Lonrho* v. *Shell* [1980] 1 WLR 627.

given power to submit 'copies' of documents but these must be photographic or other facsimiles and not duplicates. HMRC Stamp Taxes may require the originals to be produced. It may take copies of or extracts from any document produced. There does not appear to be any restriction upon the uses to which HMRC Stamp Taxes may put such copies and information. It seems that these documents may be made available in relation to challenges to or enquiries into transactions involving other taxpayers. It is possible to appeal against a notice to produce documentation or information[32] although a person who fails to comply with a notice to produce documents or information is subject to penalty.[33]

18.7 AMENDING RETURNS DURING ENQUIRIES

18.7.1 HMRC Stamp Taxes

HMRC Stamp Taxes is given power to amend a land transaction return (SDLT 1) during the course of an Enquiry where it appears that the amount stated as tax due in the return is insufficient and unless the assessment is immediately amended there is likely to be a loss of tax.[34]

18.7.2 Taxpayer

Also the taxpayer may amend a return during the course of an Enquiry.[35] Such an amendment does not restrict the scope of the Enquiry which terminates only when the closure notice is issued by HMRC Stamp Taxes.[36] During the course of an Enquiry any issues may be referred to the appropriate Tribunal[37] for determination.[38] Where there is such a referral or appeal during the Enquiry no closure notice may be given.[39]

18.8 FINALITY OF ENQUIRIES AND DISCOVERY ASSESSMENT

A land transaction return or a self-certificate that has been the subject of one Enquiry, *prima facie*, may not be the subject of another except in the case of a return that has been amended by the taxpayer.[40] However, this does not mean that there can be only one Enquiry into the same transaction. The provisional nature of the tax means that several separate returns may be required for the same transaction and the

---

[32]   FA 2008, Sched.36, para.1 as extended to SDLT by FA 2009, s.96(1)(g).
[33]   FA 2009, s.96(1)(g) and Sched.55; FA 2008, Sched.36.
[34]   FA 2003, Sched.10, para.17.
[35]   FA 2003, Sched.10, para.18.
[36]   FA 2003, Sched.10, para.23.
[37]   Which replaces the General and Special Commissioners.
[38]   FA 2003, Sched.10, para.19.
[39]   FA 2003, Sched.10, para.21.
[40]   FA 2003, Sched.10, para.12(3).

legislation empowers HMRC Stamp Taxes to launch Enquiries into those subsequent returns in certain circumstances,[41] notwithstanding that it has already launched an Enquiry into and agreed and settled the Enquiry and tax due for the earlier returns. Moreover, the subsequent Enquiry may provide information upon which a discovery assessment can be issued. Indeed, in many cases HMRC Stamp Taxes can effectively reopen a transaction notwithstanding a previously completed Enquiry.[42]

An Enquiry extends to anything contained in the return or required to be contained in the return that relates either to the question of whether the transaction to which the return or certificate relates is chargeable or to the amount of tax chargeable.[43] If the notice of Enquiry is given as a result of an amendment to a land transaction return by the taxpayer and the Enquiry period relevant to that return has expired or after an Enquiry into the return has already been completed, the new Enquiry is limited to matters to which the amendment relates or to matters that are affected by the amendment.[44]

18.9 APPEALS

At any time when an Enquiry into a return or a self-certificate is in progress, any question arising in connection with the subject-matter of the Enquiry may be referred to the First Tier Tribunal for determination.[45] The determination of a question is binding on the parties and has to be taken into account by HMRC Stamp Taxes in reaching its conclusions.

18.10 COMPLETION OF ENQUIRY

An Enquiry is completed when HMRC Stamp Taxes delivers a notice informing the purchaser that it has completed its Enquiries and stated its conclusions.[46] Such closure notice must state whether in the opinion of HMRC Stamp Taxes no amendment of the return is required or make such amendments to the return as may be necessary or state that the self-certificate was correct, and if not correct, whether the transaction to which it relates was chargeable or notifiable.[47]

Except where a referral or a question has been made to the First Tier Tribunal for determination and this is still outstanding, the purchaser may apply to the appropriate Tier Tribunal for a direction that HMRC Stamp Taxes gives a closure notice within a specified period. Such notice must be given unless the relevant Tier

---

[41] FA 2003, Sched.10, para.12(2A).
[42] FA 2003, Sched.10, para.30(3).
[43] FA 2003, Sched.10, para.13.
[44] FA 2003, Sched.10, para.13(2).
[45] FA 2003, Sched.10, para.19.
[46] FA 2003, Sched.10, para.23; or the relevant Tribunal has directed closure; see para.24.
[47] FA 2003, Sched.10, para.23.

Tribunal is satisfied HMRC Stamp Taxes has reasonable grounds for not giving a closure notice within a specified period.[48] This may depend upon the degree of co-operation shown by the taxpayer.[49]

18.11 DETERMINATIONS BY HMRC STAMP TAXES

In a case where no land transaction return (SDLT 1) has been delivered HMRC Stamp Taxes may[50] make a determination of the tax at any time within the six years following the effective date of the chargeable transaction calculating the tax to the best of its information and belief.[51] A determination is to have the same effect as a delivery of a land transaction return (SDLT 1) self-assessment by the taxpayer for the purposes of enforcing the tax liability.[52] This tax, so assessed, forms the basis for interest and penalties. However, after the service of such a determination the taxpayer may deliver a land transaction return with a self-assessment and this takes over the process from the determination.[53]

18.12 DISCOVERY ASSESSMENTS BY HMRC STAMP TAXES

HMRC Stamp Taxes may, upon 'discovery' that tax that ought to have been assessed has not been assessed, or an assessment is or has become insufficient or that a relief or exemption claimed is or has become excessive, make an assessment for what, in its opinion, is the correct amount of the tax still outstanding.[54] This includes a power to reclaim any tax that has, in its view, been incorrectly repaid.

This is a potentially powerful tool. It enables HMRC Stamp Taxes to extend time limits beyond the basic Enquiry period and to enlarge its powers to issue discovery assessments into the nature of the chain of title. While conducting an Enquiry into a particular chargeable transaction HMRC Stamp Taxes may claim that it is necessary to inspect or investigate documents relating to other transactions because these somehow impact upon the title or transaction in question which will provide it with ample opportunities to make discoveries relating to those other transactions, since the immediate transaction may depend for its effectiveness on the analysis of its precise legal effect upon the title of one or other of the parties to that transaction. Even a vendor may be vulnerable because he and his advisers can be required to

---

[48]   FA 2003, Sched.10, para.24.

[49]   See e.g. *Gould* v. *HMRC* [2007] STC (SCD) 502 where the comments of Dr Avery Jones seem to impose stringent obligations upon taxpayers to pay the maximum tax claimed by HMRC without protest.

[50]   The problem in practice is how HMRC Stamp Taxes will obtain the information suggesting that there may have been a non-notified chargeable transaction; see **Chapter 17** and **18.5**.

[51]   FA 2003, Sched.10, para.25.

[52]   FA 2003, Sched.10, para.26.

[53]   FA 2003, Sched.10, para.27.

[54]   FA 2003, Sched.10, para.28. See FA 2003, Sched.10, Part 5 generally on discovery assessments.

produce both documents and oral information which may provide sufficient information for HMRC Stamp Taxes to challenge his acquisition of the chargeable interest in question.[55] Since it appears to take the view that non-payment of tax is at least proof of negligence, if not fraud, there is a serious risk of a minimum 21-year period of risk for taxpayers.

Moreover, these problems for taxpayers are likely to increase as the amount of information that has to be disclosed to the Land Registry also increases. All such information will be available to HMRC Stamp Taxes[56] in the same way that every transaction in shares effected through CREST is passed on to it providing it with ample opportunity to make a discovery in relation to transactions other than the one for which the entry in the land register is being sought. HMRC Stamp Taxes is empowered to conduct an Enquiry into the return and the transaction which it reports. It is also entitled to conduct an Enquiry into self-certificates.

18.13 DISCOVERY AFTER ENQUIRY

Such a discovery assessment may only be made if there was fraud or negligence causing the underpayment of the tax or at the end of the Enquiry period HMRC could not on the basis of the information made known to it have been aware of the underpayment of the tax. There are certain statutory assumptions as to the information available to HMRC Stamp Taxes.[57] This is limited to information produced to it 'for the purposes of an enquiry' which suggests that it is entitled to ignore information supplied to it voluntarily in a covering or explanatory letter sent with the land transaction return.[58] It should be noted from these conditions that a discovery assessment can be issued notwithstanding that there has been an Enquiry and the information in question was not available because HMRC Stamp Taxes failed to ask the right questions.

In practice, this open-ended nature of Enquiries and the related powers to demand information give HMRC Stamp Taxes virtually unlimited power to issue discovery assessments[59] whether or not there has been an Enquiry if only because there is no 'white space' for the official disclosure of relevant information that those

---

[55] It also seems highly probable that in any such Enquiry or request for information HMRC Stamp Taxes will take any stamp duty objection available to it (Stamp Act 1891, s.14; *Parinv* v. *IRC* [1998] STC 305) in order to require the payment of additional tax, interest and penalties.

[56] See FA 2003, s.78A (as amended); but given the practice of certain employees of the Land Registry of voluntarily handing over files to HMRC this statutory provision appears to be unnecessary in practice. This practice is a clear indication that covering letters should not be sent to the Land Registry since it has been officially stated to the author that such a letter will almost certainly lead to problems and the files being passed to HMRC for investigation.

[57] FA 2003, Sched.10, para.30.

[58] HMRC Stamp Taxes has stated officially from time to time that it is its policy to ignore such letters, implying that its employees are not authorised to read them so as not to bind HMRC Stamp Taxes; see e.g. *R* v. *IRC ex p Matrix Securities Ltd* [1993] STC 773; *J Rothschild Holdings Plc* v. *IRC* [1988] STC 645 (on appeal [1989] STC 435).

[59] Note *Langham* v. *Veltema* [2004] STC 544.

responsible for the design of the return omitted or overlooked. There is a severe restriction upon the finality of Enquiries[60] because there is no real method of disclosing the full facts with the original return. For example, the boxes in the land transaction return (SDLT 1) relating to the consideration require the taxpayer to insert market value or reasonable estimated future rent but there is no way to disclose the methodology adopted to determine that value or 'guestimate'. Similarly, many boxes in the return forms although listing code numbers for various transactions usually contain a code '0' for other transactions so that the relief taken cannot be fully disclosed.

Attempts to pre-empt the situation and reduce costs for the client by submitting a detailed covering letter setting out all information will be unavailing since the general policy of HMRC Stamp Taxes is not to refer to such letters so that it is not restricted by them. Even if it can be established that the correspondence was read HMRC Stamp Taxes may contend that the employee in question did not have the authority to deal with these issues.[61] HMRC Stamp Taxes seems to take the view that the persons receiving such letters are authorised only to deal with the land transaction returns[62] as required by the legislation. Also, such a letter is not within the prescribed list of information treated as being available to HMRC Stamp Taxes[63] and, according to the advice received by the author from senior employees in the Land Registry, such an explanatory letter (which may be more relevant after the redesign of Land Registry forms) is more likely to be regarded as an opportunity to exercise their 'local discretion' and require that the files be handed over to HMRC Stamp Taxes on the grounds that the transaction is unusual.

18.14 TIME LIMITS

A discovery assessment may be made at any time up to six years after the effective date, unless there is fraud or negligence involved when the time limit is extended to 21 years.[64] As negligence includes not merely errors as to the analysis of the basic legislation but also incorrect preparation of the land transaction return such as not taking proper or officially approved steps to make an estimate of future value of the rent or property, there will be ample opportunity for this longer period to be applied in practice. Moreover, it must not be overlooked that much of SDLT is of a provisional nature with subsequent returns being required, each of which starts a new time period for these and other compliance purposes.

---

[60] See, for example, FA 2003, Sched.10, para.30(4) on discoveries after an Enquiry.
[61] See the successful argument for the Inland Revenue to this effect in *Matrix Securities* v. *IRC* [1994] STC 272.
[62] Which has in effect been delegated to computer through electronic filing.
[63] FA 2003, Sched.10, para.30(4).
[64] FA 2003, Sched.10, para.31.

18.15 POST-TRANSACTION RULINGS

Although HMRC Stamp Taxes has stated that it will give post-transaction rulings, it has restricted the scope of this obligation. Where the application for the ruling is made at the same time as or subsequent to the filing of the land transaction return, it will not give a ruling but will automatically open an Enquiry. Given that there are normally only 30 days for filing of the return and, in practice, even less where the taxpayer is affected by the time limits for the lodging of documents with the Land Registry and requires his certificate, SDLT 5, in time to comply with the Land Registry timetable, the idea of a speedy post-transaction ruling must be rejected in favour of a slow and expensive Enquiry.[65]

18.16 INFORMATION POWERS ON AN ENQUIRY

HMRC Stamp Taxes may give notice in writing to the purchaser to produce to it such documents in his possession or power and to allow it such information in such form as it may reasonably require for the purposes of the Enquiry.[66] The notice must specify the time within which the purchaser is to comply. Such compliance may be satisfied by the giving of copies of documents unless HMRC Stamp Taxes requires the original to be produced. There is a right of appeal against a notice requiring the taxpayer to produce documents or provide information to the Commissioners.[67] A person who fails to produce documents or information as required is liable to a penalty fixed by legislation but possibly subject to mitigation.[68] If during an Enquiry into a return HMRC Stamp Taxes forms the opinion that the amount stated in the self-assessment is insufficient and that unless the assessment is immediately amended there is likely to be a loss of tax, it may by written notice amend the assessment to make good the deficiency.[69]

18.17 RECORD-KEEPING OBLIGATIONS

The need to produce information is supported by the obligation to maintain records. It must, however, be noted that the scope of the powers to seek documents and information from persons other than the taxpayer means that other parties to the transaction and their advisers must keep comprehensive records. Unfortunately, the record-keeping obligations are far wider than those specifically listed in the

---

[65] HMRC Stamp Taxes has declined to give pre-transaction rulings because the issues are 'too difficult' notwithstanding its public stated commitment to CCP10.

[66] FA 2003, Sched.13.

[67] FA 2009, s.96(1)(g); FA 2008, Sched.36, Part 5.

[68] FA 2009, Sched.56.

[69] FA 2003, Sched.10, para.17.

legislation and are inadequate to provide the information that is frequently likely to be required as proof of acceptable title by a well-advised purchaser.

There is an obligation upon a purchaser to keep such records as may be needed to enable him to deliver a complete and correct land transaction return[70] or to support his claim that a transaction is non-notifiable.[71] These records must be preserved for a period of six years after the effective date and until any later date on which either an Enquiry into the return is completed or if there is no Enquiry, HMRC Stamp Taxes no longer has power to enquire into the return.

18.18   IDENTIFYING RECORDS REQUIRED

The legislation contains an illustrative list of records that must be maintained, namely relevant instruments relating to the transaction such as any contract or conveyance and any supporting maps, plans or similar documents and records of relevant payments, receipts and financial arrangements.[72] However, this list is merely illustrative and is far from exhaustive and does not attempt to deal with the 'records' of the transaction and tax computation that have been effectively converted into documents of title (see **1.14**). The general obligation to make a complete return and meet the reasonable requirements of a later purchaser means that much other documentation will be required such as valuations and surveys since these may, *inter alia*, contain information relevant to the allocation of the consideration between the land and chattels and goodwill. Mortgage reports and offering particulars will be necessary and HMRC Stamp Taxes has asked for details of bank accounts and ledgers to show the flow of funds. Indeed, it seems that printouts of any attempt to utilise the calculation or abnormal increase facilities provided online by HMRC Stamp Taxes will be essential since HMRC Stamp Taxes imposes penalties for errors unless the taxpayer can show the error was, as often happens, produced by the online facility and the correct data was inserted. The records, therefore, should include a copy of the calculation of the net present value of the rent so that it can be shown that the correct data was inserted.[73]

Moreover, current Enquiry practice seems to be to ask for the commercial background to the transaction, so correspondence and expert reports as well as any instructions to valuers, who may be required to act on a different basis from the general principles of fiscal valuations, will be essential records. This list will undoubtedly be extensive in commercial transactions especially where goodwill or equipment that may be a fixture is involved; but even routine residential transactions will require significant retention of documents such as estate agents' and

---

[70]   FA 2003, Sched.10, para.9.
[71]   FA 2003, Sched.11, para.4.
[72]   FA 2003, Sched.10, Part 2; Sched.11, Part 2.
[73]   Assignees of a lease, if properly advised, will also require the document (see **8.60**) as a key title document and almost certainly the details of the data inserted and how this was produced and compiled.

mortgagees' correspondence. For example, a valuer advising either a mortgagee considering lending money to the purchaser or a vendor as to a price for the property is vulnerable to demands from HMRC Stamp Taxes for documentation and information. Records should be preserved for the prescribed period.[74]

18.19   POWERS TO CALL FOR INFORMATION INCLUDING NON-ENQUIRY SITUATIONS

The powers of HMRC to obtain information are in a constant state of change being frequently upgraded and extended and HMRC Stamp Taxes is frequently the beneficiaries of these enhanced powers.[75]

In addition to the powers to demand information when conducting an Enquiry into a land transaction return or self-certificate, HMRC Stamp Taxes may give a written notice requiring taxpayers or third parties including professional advisers to produce such documents in their possession or power[76] and to provide it with such information in such form as it may reasonably require for the purposes of the Enquiry,[77] which is supported by the imposition of penalties including a daily penalty of up to £150 per day during which the default continues where this penalty is determined by the court.[78]

There is power to request 'information', which includes both documentation and oral testimony, from the groups below.

18.19.1   The taxpayer

In addition to the power to require information from the taxpayer during an Enquiry described above an officer of HMRC may, at any time (i.e. apparently not only during an Enquiry thereby effectively enlarging the powers to investigate a chargeable transaction and to issue a discovery assessment), by notice in writing require a person to deliver documents in that person's possession or power which may contain information relevant to any tax liability of that person.[79] There does not appear to be any time limit whatsoever to this power; but the approval of the appropriate Tier Tribunal[80] is required for the giving of such notice[81] and a summary of the reasons for applying for such consent must be supplied to the taxpayer.[82]

---

[74]   FA 2003, Sched.10, para.2(2); Sched.11, para.4(2); Sched.11A, para.3.
[75]   See FA 2009, Part 7.
[76]   Note *Lonrho v. Shell* [1980] 1 WLR 627.
[77]   FA 2009, s.96 and FA 2008, Sched.36, Part 1.
[78]   FA 2008, Sched.36, Part.7.
[79]   FA 2009, s.96 and FA 2008, Sched.36, Part 1.
[80]   Transfer of Tribunal Functions and Revenue and Customs Appeals Order 2009, SI 2009/56, replacing the Special and General Commissioners.
[81]   FA 2009, s.96 and FA 2008, Sched.36, para.3.
[82]   FA 2009, s.96 and FA 2008, Sched.36, para.3(4).

The power to demand information does not apply to:

- documents that are personal records or journalistic records or any information contained therein;[83]
- documents or information relating to the conduct of any pending appeal.[84]

Copies may be delivered rather than the originals.[85]

Where there are reasonable grounds for believing that a taxpayer may have failed or may fail to comply with the provisions relating to SDLT and such failure is likely to have led or to lead to serious prejudice of the proper assessment or collection of the tax, HMRC may by notice in writing require a taxpayer to deliver such documents as are in that person's possession or power which contain or may contain in HMRC's reasonable opinion information that may be relevant to the tax liability of that person or to supply any relevant information;[86] this power does not apply to documents that are personal or journalistic records.[87]

18.19.2 Third parties

An officer of HMRC may for the purpose of an Enquiry[88] into the tax liability of any person require some person other than the taxpayer[89] to deliver such documents as are in that person's possession or power which may contain in the officer's reasonable belief, information relevant to the tax liability.[90] It will be necessary to consider the extent of these powers as they are changed from time to time since HMRC Stamp Taxes may wish to embark upon a general fishing expedition which may be *ultra vires*. This applies to any person such as vendors, landlords, mortgagees, valuers of either party and their respective advisers including accountants advising upon the accountancy treatment of the transaction in the accounts of the taxpayer or vendor or landlord. It also extends to persons not involved in the ultimate transaction. For example, a person who made an offer for the property which is rejected and his advisers may be called upon to provide information if HMRC Stamp Taxes forms the opinion that this may have some relevance to the background to the actual chargeable transaction. Persons invited to submit tenders for property and their advisers may need to consider what records they ought to maintain as a matter of self-preservation.

---

[83] FA 2008, Sched.36; FA 2009, s.96; Police and Criminal Evidence Act 1984, ss.12 and 13.
[84] FA 2009, s.96 and FA 2008, Sched.36, para.19.
[85] FA 2003, Sched.13, para.23 (as amended).
[86] FA 2008, Sched.36; FA 2009, s.96.
[87] FA 2008, Sched.36; FA 2009, s.96; Police and Criminal Evidence Act 1984, ss.12 and 13.
[88] This is ambiguous. It may refer to the purpose of conducting an Enquiry or merely for the general purposes of enquiring or investigating into the liability of a taxpayer. It is considered notwithstanding the deficiencies in the drafting that the latter wider meaning is the one likely to be adopted in practice.
[89] Which appears to include promoters of tax schemes who are also subject to obligations to disclose SDLT avoidance schemes.
[90] FA 2009, s.96 and FA 2008, Sched.36, paras.2 and 3.

The consent of a member of the appropriate Tier Tribunal[91] is required before such a notice can be issued.[92] A copy of the notice must be given to the taxpayer to whom it relates[93] although there is power for a Tribunal member to give consent to the issue of a notice without naming the taxpayer to whom the notice relates under prescribed circumstances.[94] The taxpayer must be supplied with a written summary of the reasons for applying to the relevant Tier Tribunal for consent to the issue of the notice.[95]

A notice may not require production of:

- documents or information relating to personal records or journalistic material;[96]
- documents relating to the conduct of a pending appeal by the taxpayer;[97]
- certain documents that may be legally privileged. Notices may be given to barristers, advocates and solicitors only by the Board and not by an authorised officer thereof.[98] However, delivery of such a notice does not apply to a barrister, advocate or solicitor so as to require him to deliver or make available without the client's consent any document with respect to which a claim to legal privilege[99] could be maintained;[100]
- documents originating more than six years before the date of the notice unless the relevant Tier Tribunal[101] has given consent to the extension of the period which may only be given if the Tribunal members are satisfied that tax has been or may have been lost owing to the fraud of the taxpayer;[102]
- certain documents in the possession of auditors. A person who has been appointed as an auditor cannot be required to deliver or make available documents that are his property and were created by him or on his behalf for or in connection with the performance of his functions under the statutory provisions controlling his appointment as auditor;[103]
- certain documents in the possession of tax advisers. A tax adviser, i.e. a person appointed to give advice about the tax affairs of another person[104] is not obliged

---

[91]   Transfer of Tribunal Functions and Revenue and Customs Appeals Order 2009, SI 2009/56; replacing the Special and General Commissioners.
[92]   FA 2009, s.96 and FA 2008, Sched.36, para.3.
[93]   FA 2009, s.96 and FA 2008, Sched.36, para.4.
[94]   FA 2009, s.96 and FA 2008, Sched.36, para.5.
[95]   FA 2009, s.96 and FA 2008, Sched.36, para.3.
[96]   FA 2003, Sched.13, para.20; Police and Criminal Evidence Act 1984, ss.12 and 13.
[97]   FA 2009, s.96 and FA 2008, Sched.36, para.19.
[98]   FA 2003, Sched.13, para.22.
[99]   As defined by FA 2003, Sched.13, para.35.
[100]   FA 2003, Sched.13, para.25.
[101]   Transfer of Tribunal Functions and Revenue and Customs Appeals Order 2009, SI 2009/56; replacing the Special and General Commissioners.
[102]   FA 2009, s.96 and FA 2008, Sched.36, para.20.
[103]   FA 2009, s.96 and FA 2008, Sched.36, paras.23 and following.
[104]   FA 2009, s.96 and FA 2008, Sched.36, para.25; this may not be the same as a promoter of tax avoidance schemes who is required to make disclosure and provide a focal point for HMRC Stamp Taxes to demand information that may provide the basis for finding the information necessary to make a 'discovery'.

to deliver or make available documents that are his property and consist of communications between the tax adviser and the person in relation to whose tax affairs he has been appointed or any other tax adviser of such a person the purpose of which is the giving or obtaining of advice about those tax affairs.[105] This is now, however, subject to the obligation to disclose details of 'tax schemes', and there may be difficulties in deciding whether the document or information belongs to the professional adviser who instructed the legal adviser or to the lay client.

Where a document relates to activities as auditor or tax adviser and contains:

- information explaining any information, return or other document that the person to whom the notice is given has, as tax accountant, assisted his client in preparing for or delivering to HMRC Stamp Taxes; or
- information as to the identity of unnamed taxpayers that has not otherwise been made available to HMRC Stamp Taxes;

then the person to whom the notice is given must, if he does not deliver the document or make it available for inspection in accordance with the notice, deliver a copy of any parts of the document that contain such information as is referred to and make available for inspection such parts of the original document which contain such information.[106]

18.19.3 Tax accountants

Where a person who has stood in relation to others as tax accountant is convicted of an offence in relation to tax by or before a court in the UK or has a penalty imposed upon him for assisting in the preparation of an incorrect return,[107] an officer of the Board may by notice in writing require him to deliver such documents as are in his possession or power which may contain information relevant to the tax liability to which any client of his is or has been or may be subject.[108] No notice may be given for so long as an appeal is pending against the conviction or penalty[109] and the consent of the appropriate judicial authority is required for the giving of such notice.[110] Copies may be produced initially rather than originals.[111]

Such a notice may not require the production of documents or documents that:

- contain personal records or journalist material;[112]
- relate to the conduct of a pending appeal relating to tax by the taxpayer;[113]

---

[105] FA 2009, s.96 and FA 2008, Sched.36, paras.24, 25 and 26.
[106] FA 2009, s.96 and FA 2008, Sched.36, paras.24, 25 and 26.
[107] FA 2003, s.96.
[108] FA 2003, Sched.13, para.14.
[109] FA 2003, Sched.13, para.15.
[110] FA 2003, Sched.13, para.16.
[111] FA 2003, Sched.13, para.23 (as amended).
[112] FA 2003, Sched.13, para.20; Police and Criminal Evidence Act 1984, ss.12 and 13.
[113] FA 2003, Sched.13, para.21(3).

- are legally privileged. A notice may not be given to a barrister, advocate or solicitor by an authorised officer but only by the Board[114] and such a notice does not oblige a barrister, advocate or solicitor to deliver or make available without his client's consent any document with respect to which a claim to legal privilege could be maintained.[115] Legal privilege is defined as[116] communications between a professional legal adviser and his client or any person representing his client in connection with giving legal advice to the client or made in connection with or in contemplation of legal proceedings and for the purposes of such proceedings. It extends to items enclosed with or referred to in such communications made for the purposes of giving legal advice or in connection with legal proceedings when they are in the possession of the person entitled to them. This does not apply to items held for the furthering of a criminal purpose, which may include non-payment of SDLT if it amounts to tax evasion or money laundering.

Regulations have been issued to establish a procedure for the purpose of determining whether a document or part of a document is entitled to legal privilege.[117]

18.19.4   Taxpayers and other persons and fraud

Where there are reasonable grounds for suspecting that an offence involving serious[118] tax fraud in relation to SDLT has been or is about to be committed, and that documents that may be required as evidence for the purpose of any proceedings in respect of such an offence, are or may be in the possession or power of any person, whether or not the taxpayer, the Board of HMRC may apply to an appropriate judicial authority to make an order requiring that person to produce the documentation.[119] A person who is the object of such an intended notice is entitled to receive a notice of the intention to apply for an order and to be heard at the hearing of the application unless the appropriate judicial authority is satisfied that this would seriously prejudice the investigation of the offence.[120] Persons who have received a notice of intention to apply for such an order must not seek to destroy any such evidence.[121]

If there are reasonable grounds for suspecting an offence involving serious fraud in connection with or in relation to tax, not just SDLT, an officer of the Board may apply for an order to the appropriate judicial authority for the issue of a warrant in writing authorising an officer of the Board to enter the premises if necessary by

---

[114]   FA 2003, Sched.13, para.22.
[115]   FA 2003, Sched.13, para.25.
[116]   FA 2003, Sched.13, paras.35 and 25 as amended.
[117]   FA 2003, Sched.13, para.36; Stamp Duty Land Tax (Administration) Regulations 2003, SI 2003/2837.
[118]   Query whether price manipulation is sufficiently 'serious' for these purposes; see *Saunders* v. *Edwards* [1987] 2 All ER 651. See also FA 2003, ss.95 and 96.
[119]   FA 2003, Sched.13, para.32.
[120]   FA 2003, Sched.13, para.33.
[121]   FA 2003, Sched.13, para.34.

force and search them.[122] Such an application may only be made if there are reasonable grounds for believing that the use of an application for an order for the delivery of documents might seriously prejudice the investigation. Items that are subject to legal privilege may not be seized under this procedure.[123] This is governed by the same principles as those described above.

Failure to comply with an order to produce information is treated as contempt of court.[124]

---

[122] FA 2009, s.96 and FA 2008, Sched.36, Part 2; paras.10 and 13.
[123] FA 2009, s.96 and FA 2008, Sched.36, para.13.
[124] FA 2003, Sched.13, para.40.

APPENDIX A

Land areas for investigation

A.1 SOME SUGGESTIONS FOR DUE DILIGENCE, TITLE INVESTIGATION AND RECORD KEEPING

This and the following appendices are a broad summary of the major areas for title issues, due diligence and, mainly, the effective performance of obligations owed to clients as professional advisers, certain aspects of which have been described in the main text; but they are not intended as a comprehensive guide to requisitions, completion arrangements, client handling between contract and completion, etc. Contrary to the statements to Parliament by HMRC, at the time of the introduction of the tax, that there would *inter alia* be no changes as regards the conveyancing process because the new legislation would not affect title issues, the new regime has given rise to a wholly new set of problems to be investigated by the conveyancer, particularly as the Land Registry has recently emerged as a rather zealous collection agency for HMRC Stamp Taxes. These problems fundamentally affect not only title issues, but also the extent of documents of title, i.e. what may be needed to prove title, and create a need to be more closely involved and proactive with the client as a matter of self-preservation. For example it is necessary to ascertain whether the client has substantially performed between contract and completion or is entering into other transactions, whether past, concurrent or future, that may be linked which have to be disclosed on the return. Client care has become a major long-term issue for professional firms. The explanations of the problems outlined below and the 'answers' thereto are described in more detail at relevant places within the main text.

A.2 GENERAL ISSUES FOR CONTRACTS

It has to be acknowledged that as the scope of stamp taxes has moved increasingly from a documentation- to a transaction-based tax, there has also been an expanding subjectivity in relation to attacks upon steps to mitigate the impact of the tax. See for example the condition for certain reliefs that the transaction was entered into for bona fide commercial reasons and not for the avoidance of tax, whatever that may mean,[1] particularly as it may include steps taken to reduce other non-stamp tax charges. Circumstances relating to exemptions become uncertain because of the subjective element in an area such as the commercial justification for the transaction where HMRC generally does not have an impressive reputation and there is little guidance. A key area for requests for disclosure by purchasers will be delivery of any clearance applications for previous transactions, particularly significant clearances where there is no clearance procedure or even the safeguard of rapid adjudication of the new tax. As described elsewhere (see **1.11** and **1.24**), there are issues arising for the provisional nature of most SDLT. For example, purchasers may have to require the inclusion of an 'exit strategy' when entering into a contract and the issues frequently relate to the actions of a vendor or

---

[1]   FA 2003, Sched.7 ;see **Chapter 13**.

landlord but affect a purchaser or lessee (see **4.40**). This need for an exit strategy is a more difficult issue where leases are involved since many SDLT problems run with the lease.[2]

Purchasers will require full SDLT histories of the chargeable interest including details of the data behind the return. This may involve the disclosure of commercially sensitive information to competitors in order to meet the purchaser's reasonable requirements; but failure to obtain such information will not be regarded by HMRC Stamp Taxes as a reason for mitigation of penalties or a defence to any allegations of negligence where the taxpayer submits what turns out to be an incorrect return, or fails to submit a return, or is unaware that a tax charge has arisen, because he does not have access to the necessary information which is controlled by the other parties.[3] This is particularly harsh since, although HMRC Stamp Taxes has power to demand documents and information from persons other than the taxpayer, the taxpayer does not have power to require co-operation from other persons to make available information in their possession such as their files and records including tax returns and correspondence with HMRC because of 'taxpayer confidentiality'.[4] Vendors will increasingly be put under pressure to give extended warranties and indemnities. The scope of 'requisitions' is changed because different and more information is required. This need to require information is crucial to share sales as well as land transactions because of the ???note of outstanding tax liabilities of the company and any related disclosure letter will be far more difficult to prepare properly which might provide some assistance for SDLT. This applies, for example, where the subjective element in stamp taxes has increased but the vendor has not obtained a clearance for other taxes,[5] especially where the tax risk passes directly or indirectly to the purchaser. In practice, clearances given in relation to capital gains tax[6] tend to prevail. Such clearance applications and their responses, even if unsuccessful, or if the proposed transaction is abandoned, are effectively documents of title since they may be necessary evidence in an Enquiry or when dealing with a discovery assessment in relation to a claimed exemption especially where companies are involved. They may also be key indications as to the overall relationship with HMRC.

There will be a significant problem for fiduciaries such as personal representatives, liquidators and receivers (see e.g. **Chapter 11** and **Chapter 13** respectively). The issues include not only questions of whether there is some liability for the tax in any potential transaction such as where the liability is by statute transferred to a third party who must be made aware of the potential problems and related future costs, but also situations where a personal liability is imposed. Investigating the history of the overall context may lead to a nasty shock of obligations to pay another person's tax, including interest and penalties, where, although there may be a statutory indemnity,[7] this may not be adequate to recoup the personal liability because the relevant party does not have sufficient assets.

---

[2] See, for example, FA 2003, Sched.17A, para.12.

[3] Such persons may, however, be under obligations to disclose such confidential information to HMRC Stamp Taxes to aid it in the pursuit of taxpayers.

[4] This has been an issue for shared ownership leases where it is necessary to produce the original documents to show that the relevant statements are included in the documents including stamp duty transactions prior to 1 December 2003 (FA 2003, Sched.19, para.7(2) and Sched.9, para.2(2)).

[5] But note *Swithland Investments* v. *IRC* [1990] STC 448 where a clearance application for other taxes was utilised to attack stamp tax reliefs.

[6] Such as pursuant to Taxation of Chargeable Gains Act 1992, ss.137–139, which are preferred to income tax clearances pursuant to e.g. Income Tax Act 2007, ss.701 and 752; Corporation Tax Act 2010, s.818 the latter being particularly important for land transactions.

[7] See, for example, FA 2003, ss.100(5) and 106.

A.2.1 Which regime?

Although many years have elapsed since the tax was introduced, there are transactions which remain within the stamp duty regime.[8] This frequently arises notwithstanding that much of the SDLT is 'retrospective' but it cannot relate back to stamp duty arrangements, although there are rules for altering the rate of SDLT where the current chargeable transaction applies to a lease that was initially subject to stamp duty.[9] This is important for certain transactions relating to leases within the former disadvantaged land regime. It is necessary to consider the following:

- Whether the completion or other arrangement is pursuant to a contract entered into prior to 1 December 2003 when the transaction may be subject to a stamp duty regime. However, there are many statutory provisions which subject pre-1 December 2003 contracts to SDLT.[10]
- Whether the lease was initially taxed within the stamp duty or the SDLT regime. This affects the basis of the issues but is also important since different rules apply to certain SDLT transactions affecting stamp duty leases. For example:
    - there is no tax charge on holding over a stamp duty lease;
    - there is no credit against the SDLT charge for stamp duty paid in respect of rent when there is a surrender and regrant of a stamp duty lease;
    - payments in respect of variable consideration such as overage and rent reviews under pre-1 December 2003 agreements may not be taxable;
    - different rules apply for linked transactions where certain of the transactions are or were subject to stamp duty such as the exercise of pre-SDLT options and renewals of leases;[11]
    - in the case of leases, the charge to stamp duty is usually significantly lower than its equivalent to SDLT. The search for whether the stamp duty regime applies is usually a good investment for the client; and
    - there are issues where there is an exercise of an option to renew a stamp duty lease.[12]

Notwithstanding the possible extra charge pursuant to the transitional provisions it is crucial that a stamp duty lease is not converted into an SDLT lease and that any variations in the lease adopt basic techniques that do not involve surrender and regrant.

A.3 PURCHASER ('TAXPAYER')

The identity of the 'purchaser' is important, for various reasons. It is necessary to ascertain:

- whether the purchaser is a company to which special rules may apply;
- who is the true purchaser, e.g. whether he is a nominee[13] or there are larger arrangements relating to the property such as a gift to trustees;
- whether he is a person representing the purchaser, such as a receiver, a liquidator or the Official Solicitor.

---

[8] See FA 2003, Sched.19 in general.
[9] FA 2003, Sched.19, para.8; note para.7 thereof in relation to shared ownership transactions pursuant to Sched.9 thereto.
[10] FA 2003, Sched.19 (as amended).
[11] FA 2003, Sched.19 (as amended) including retrospective amendments.
[12] FA 2003, Sched.19, para.9.
[13] FA 2003, Sched.16, para.3.

A.3.1 Purchase of property

A.3.1.1 General

Consider whether the purchaser or tenant has entered into the property to carry out 'works' including fitting out during the negotiation process prior to contract (see **Chapter 9**).

A.3.1.2 Freeholds

(Dealings in existing leases – as opposed to the creation of a new lease or new leases – raise separate issues which are commented upon below.)

The following points need to be considered.

- Whether the registered owner or the person appearing as vendor in the contract is beneficially entitled or a nominee or bare trustee or whether some other person may be the actual settlor such as the beneficial owner or there is a subsale in whole or in part.[14] This is relevant for identifying the 'vendor' for completing SDLT 1 and SDLT 2 and whether the vendor is connected with the purchaser for the purpose of reliefs, connected company charges, the special partnership regime and linked transactions.
- Where there are several acquisitions, whether there is a single vendor or separate vendors; whether the vendors are connected for the purpose of the linked transaction rules,[15] and whether the separate purchasers or lessees are connected with each other.
- Whether any party to a transaction is a fiduciary such as a trustee, personal representative or undisclosed agent.[16] There is a need to investigate the beneficial interests because there is a question whether a party's status has changed such as to a nominee or bare trustee as a consequence of an assent or appropriation, deed of appointment or a death of the life tenant so that the true vendor or purchaser can be identified for the above purposes. Letters to the Land Registry explaining the differences between the SDLT 5 and TR1 may be required.
- What documents including any SDLT 5 from other parties may be required by the Land Registry to give effect to the documents presented to it, especially where the transaction is believed to be non-notifiable (see **1.12**).
- Whether there is variable consideration such as an overage or clawback payment affecting the land and whether this is somehow 'charged' upon the land such as by way of a restrictive covenant or ransom strip,[17] or other arrangement that involves a 'chargeable interest' that is a taxable acquisition by the vendor (see **2.12** and following) or whether the legislation novates the liability to an assignee.[18]
- Whether the vendor's tax position is provisional only and, if so, whether the liability for the outstanding tax passes to the purchaser (see **1.24**, **8.60** and **Chapter 14**).

---

[14] The Land Registry may ask for details of beneficial joint tenancies or beneficial tenants in common even though these are not relevant requests for SDLT.

[15] *Brewer Street Investments Ltd* v. *Barclays Woollen Co. Ltd* [1953] 2 All ER 1330; *Yaxley* v. *Gotts* [1999] 3 WLR 1217; *Re McArdle* [1951] 1 All ER 905; *Branca* v. *Cobarro* [1947] 2 All ER 101; *Winn* v. *Bull* (1877–78) LR 7 Ch D 29.

[16] The rules as to nominees mean that, in practice, there can be no undisclosed agency or nominee arrangement. This raises problems in relation to the position of single nominees and LPA 1925, s.27.

[17] The legal validity of many such arrangements has been questioned because of the lack of benefit to dominant land or even the lack of dominant land to be benefited but which may nevertheless create a chargeable interest and a land exchange (FA 2003, ss.47 and 48(1)(b)); see **Chapter 7**.

[18] See FA 2003, s.81A; Sched.17A, para.12 and note para.12B thereof.

- Whether any estimates such as future value, or rents, or the amount expected to become payable have been prepared by the vendor upon a proper basis, probably requiring independent professional advice. The original purchaser's or tenant's (i.e. the vendor's) open tax position may pass to a third party.[19] Failure to obtain proper advice is negligence or fraud.
- Whether payment of all or any part of the tax upon the variable consideration can be deferred.[20]
- Whether contractual provisions described as 'conditions' are in law consideration within the charge to tax.[21]
- Where the chargeable consideration consists of property other than cash or debt, whether the market value thereof has been prepared on a proper basis.[22]
- Whether the consideration has been apportioned on a just and reasonable basis between the land interests and other property being acquired;[23] failure to do so is easily open to allegations of fraud and criminal sanctions pursuant to FA 2003, s.95. To assist in the preparation of a return in such circumstances could expose the adviser to a £3,000 penalty.[24]
- Whether there have been prior or may be subsequent linked transactions which might impact upon the purchaser's tax position.[25]
- Whether the appropriate information has been received from the vendor that the conditions for the special reliefs for residential property[26] have been satisfied.

A.3.2 Completion arrangements for freeholds: client care

Completion arrangements require that the purchaser obtains all necessary documentation so that he can deal with the Land Registry[27] which may require information to deal with HMRC Stamp Taxes (see e.g. **1.12**). Consider the following.

- So as to avoid allegations of negligent failure to deliver requisite the land transaction return (SDLT 1) or fraudulent returns,[28] whether the taxpayer has been properly advised as to his future compliance and payment obligations and appropriate machinery has been put in place to ensure that the taxpayer complies with the outstanding obligation in the future where the initial land transaction return is not final in relation to such items as rent review and variable consideration.
- Whether there is more than one 'true purchaser' because all purchasers must sign the return.[29]
- Whether there has been earlier substantial performance of an agreement which in the view of HMRC Stamp Taxes occurs if the purchaser obtains the key before completion so that a return should already have been filed and tax paid or the taxpayer has entered into possession of the land to fit out.

---

[19]   FA 2003, s.81A; Sched.17A, para.12.

[20]   FA 2003, ss.51, 80, 90 and Stamp Duty Land Tax (Administration) Regulations 2003, SI 2003/2837.

[21]   *Eastham* v. *Leigh London and Provincial Properties Ltd* [1971] 2 All ER 887.

[22]   FA 2003, Sched.4, paras.4 and 7; *Langham* v. *Veltema* [2004] STC 544; see **Chapter 15**.

[23]   FA 2003, Sched.4, para.4.

[24]   FA 2003, s.96.

[25]   FA 2003, s.108.

[26]   FA 2003, Sched.6A; **5.17**.

[27]   And obtain satisfactory title to provide the promised security to the mortgagee.

[28]   Or suggestions that the professional adviser was a party aware of a tax fraud (FA 2003, ss.95 and 96; *Saunders* v. *Edwards* [1987] 2 All ER 651).

[29]   FA 2003, s.103.

- Whether all information concerning the 'vendor' has been obtained for the completion of the land transaction return which includes identifying the true vendor or vendors which may be relevant, *inter alia*, for linked transactions.
- Whether the owner registered at the Land Registry and/or person(s) appearing in the contract as seller are the true vendor as required by SDLT 1.
- Whether the 'vendor' is the registered owner of the property; if not, what is the status of his application to register and filing of his SDLT 1. Undertakings may be required as to production of an SDLT 5 to the purchaser so that he may apply to be registered. Covering letters explaining the differences between SDLT 5 and TR1, etc., to the Land Registry may be required including details of the vendor's position.
- Whether the persons whose names are to appear in the Land Registry documentation as transferor and transferee or lessor and lessee are the same as those appearing as 'vendor' and 'purchaser' in the SDLT 1 and SDLT 5. If not, an explanatory letter may be required by the Land Registry.
- Whether the vendor is seeking to rely upon subsale relief or the relief for leases granted directly to third parties[30] so that he will not be producing an SDLT 5, but the purchaser's tax position may be affected.
- Whether these subsale or equivalent reliefs will take the form of a direct transfer from the original seller to the purchaser at the direction of the intermediate vendor or the intermediate vendor does not have power to direct a subsale and so will be taking a transfer. In the latter case, the intermediate vendor may be entitled to the relief for subsales (but not leases) notwithstanding that he receives a conveyance or Land Registry transfer.[31] This requires the ultimate purchaser to produce two such transfers but only one SDLT 5 since the intermediate vendor may not be filing any SDLT 1.[32] Full details will be required from the intermediate vendor to enable the required covering letter for the Land Registry to be submitted explaining that no SDLT 5 is required because of subsale relief.
- Where there is a clawback or variable consideration such as an overage required by the vendor, whether there is a prudent exit strategy.
- Where there is a pre-existing clawback arrangement, whether the exit strategy is acceptable and how this affects the purchaser.[33]
- Whether the necessary declarations and prescribed form SDLT 1 and any powers of attorney[34] or board minutes or approval of representative partners have been obtained to permit someone other than the taxpayer to sign the SDLT 1[35] upon which the vendor's or landlord's title depends. If the vendor is a company, trustee, club or association or is not the registered owner details will be required at completion because there is almost certainly a total mismatch between the Land Registry transfers (TR1, etc.) and the Revenue certificate (SDLT 5) at least in those cases where the land transaction return (SDLT 1) has been completely and correctly prepared. Mortgagees will need to be advised where there may be a delay in registration because, *inter alia*, of SDLT 5 delays.
- Whether appropriate steps have been taken by the vendors and their advisers to produce and preserve the required records of the transaction where these may be the basis of the purchaser's own tax liability in due course.[36] These include not merely the transaction

---

[30] FA 2003, s.45; Sched.17A, para.12B.

[31] FA 2003, s.45; Sched.17A, para.12A.

[32] This is a matter of debate with HMRC Stamp Taxes because FA 2003, s.45 states that the first transaction is to be 'disregarded' but it contends that this word has a special unplain English meaning; see also FA 2003, s.75A.

[33] FA 2003, s.81A and Sched.17A, para.12.

[34] FA 2003, s.81A; Sched.10, Part 1 (as amended).

[35] See e.g. FA 2003, ss.81B, 100(2)(b), 103(4).

[36] FA 2003, Sched.10, Part 2 and Sched.11 (as amended).

documents, but all relevant documents such as valuations, including apportionments, the initial offer such as estate agents' advertising, correspondence with mortgagees and details of negotiations with the vendor. Where leases are the subject-matter of the acquisition a printout of the online SDLT calculation produced by HMRC Stamp Taxes should be obtained.

- Whether the taxpayer has been properly advised as to the future obligations in relation to any arrangements whereby tax payments have been deferred and any taxation issues remain open and the related obligation to retain the necessary details since these may be required by third parties involved in any subsequent purchase.
- Where market value may be an issue, whether there may be a discount for bulk purchase or a quick completion which discount is not accepted by HMRC Stamp Taxes as being the market value.[37] Details of the original offer price should be obtained.
- Whether the transaction is linked to other contemporaneous or prior transactions since the taxpayer may be instructing other solicitors on those transactions.
- Whether the transaction may be potentially linked with subsequent transactions since these may require appropriate undertakings by both parties to supply the necessary information to each other.
- Whether the transaction falls within the wide definitions of 'land exchange' when the special rules may apply for computation and reporting; key areas are deeds of variation of leases which may be surrenders and regrants, 'excepting and reserving' and sale and leaseback transactions.
- Whether the vendor is a body corporate which may raise technical problems as to the charge to tax, e.g. on the assignment of leases.[38]

A.3.3   Leases

A.3.3.1   Purchase of existing leases

- It is necessary to ascertain when the lease was actually granted and the agreement for lease was substantially performed because this affects the calculation of the first five years of the term for rent reviews (including the relief for 'backdating' to a term commencement date), and whether two full land transaction returns are required and, if so, whether the first return has been filed. Details of the assessment are required to calculate the rent credit for the formal grant (see **8.26**).
- Many tax problems are passed over to purchasers of existing leases[39] such as:

  – dealing with open tax positions of the original tenant (see **8.61**); and
  – tax issues such as abnormal rent increases which depend upon the SDLT history of the lease (see **8.37** and following).

In consequence, a full SDLT history will be required[40] to enable the purchaser to know when a tax charge may arise and to deal properly with his liability to pay and to file land transaction returns. In this situation the records or documents of title are more extensive than the records illustrated as necessary by the legislation. The SDLT returns are less than helpful since these do not contain the detailed breakdown of the data required and the format is of little use to the purchaser (see e.g. **1.14** and **8.60**). Written evidence is

---

[37]   This is likely to prove a major problem in practice as HMRC Stamp Taxes is treating 'exceptions and reservations' as being regrants creating new rights and producing a land exchange taxable at market value; see **Chapter 7**.

[38]   See, for example, FA 2003, Sched.17A, para.12.

[39]   Different issues arise in relation to these problem areas where there is the grant of a new lease.

[40]   There is no statutory power to demand such information; this must be stipulated for in the contract notwithstanding that it might lead to confidentiality issues for the vendor.

required as to how the information inserted in the return was obtained and processed, relating to matters such as:

- variable premiums where payments remain outstanding;[41]
- variable premiums and the exit strategy if any;[42]
- variable rents including reviewable rents because of reviews during the first five years and abnormal increases thereafter;
- whether the lease was exempt when granted in circumstances where the assignment is to be taxed as the grant of a new lease.[43] The assignee may require some form of contribution to the additional tax charge arising;[44]
- the background to the lease such as whether it is linked with other leases or may be linked with future possible leases or lease renewal and whether the negotiations relating to the option to renew make it vulnerable to the successive linked lease provisions.[45] Undertakings to supply background information to the original transaction may be required but such undertakings are commercially vulnerable should the vendor, etc. die, be liquidated or otherwise not be available when problems with HMRC Stamp Taxes arise which can be up to a minimum of six years after the event;
- whether there are existing leases or may be future leases or leases renewable that might be linked transactions[46] which may affect the tax position of the assignee, e.g. whether the amount of nil rate applied to the net present value of the rent reserved by that lease is to be carried forward and whether additional tax arises in respect of his lease because of the allocation of different amounts of the nil rate for rent to other linked leases;[47]
- turnover and profit-sharing leases: details of the turnover and profits of the prior tenants where there is a turnover or profit-sharing rent, and sums of rent paid where the five-year period has not expired.

For these purposes a copy of the land transaction return (SDLT 1) filed by the original taxpayer will be inadequate because the information included therein will be on a global basis and not on a monthly basis which the legislation requires (see **8.29**, **8.30** and **8.37**).

- Undertakings are required to supply information where the vendor or his successors in title may enter into transactions that may be linked with the particular lease since this may affect the tax position of the assignee because he takes over the open tax position of the original tenant in relation to the assigned lease which requires retrospective adjustment (see **8.60** and **Chapter 14**).
- Indemnities are required to deal with the possibility that the original self-assessment was too low because it is not clear that there is a joint and several liability and there is no express statutory indemnity. Where the assignor's open tax position is passed to the assignee by statute he is protected against liability. Assignors will require indemnities against the assignee's windfall if the initial tax assessment was high and tax is repayable to the assignee. Currently, this is likely to be the case because the recession means that reviews are not taking place or are being deferred, which in turn means that the original 'guestimated' land transaction return (SDLT 1) included too high a figure and tax repayment claims may be in order (see **8.29**).

---

[41] FA 2003, s.80.
[42] FA 2003, s.81A.
[43] FA 2003, Sched.17A, para.12.
[44] Which may be a tax-free payment: FA 2003, Sched.17A, para.18.
[45] FA 2003, Sched.17A, para.5; Sched.5, para.2(5).
[46] FA 2003, s.108; Sched.17A, para.5 and Sched.5, para.2(5).
[47] This applies notwithstanding the principle that linked transactions can arise only between the same parties.

A.3.3.2   New leases

- Where there is an agreement for lease and the lease is to be granted directly to the taxpayer who is a third party (i.e. is not a party to the agreement for lease but is an 'assignee' of the right to the lease),[48] details will be required from the original tenant of his position including whether he has substantially performed the original agreement for lease since the taxpayer's position is totally dependent upon the original tenant's tax position and there may be additional tax payable.[49] The amount of the charge to tax upon the purchaser depends upon whether FA 2003, Sched.17A, para.12B, or s.45 thereof or neither applies. An indemnity against additional tax will be prudent.[50]
- Parties to new leases, as with parties to other transactions, need to consider not only the information they may require for their own tax purposes but what information they may be required to produce to prospective purchasers of their interests in due course as part of the SDLT history of the lease. Such information includes:

    - details of the tenant's plans and obligations in relation to fitting out, taking possession or subselling or other possible substantial performance;
    - whether items of additional rent such as service charges or VAT are separately reserved;[51]
    - detailed records of negotiations leading to the term of the lease and options to renew for linked transaction purposes especially concurrent linked leases;[52]
    - whether there are or may be linked concurrent leases which can include the possibility of subsequent grants of leases[53] which can reduce the amount of the nil rate slice for leases;[54]
    - whether there are potential successive linked leases[55] which may require the assignee to make notification[56] and pay additional tax because the nil rate slice allocated to the lease rent is reduced requiring the payment of additional tax.[57]

A.3.4   Options and pre-emption rights

Details of the background to the grant of options whether put, call or cross and including options to renew leases are now relevant since the exercise of the option may be a linked transaction[58] with the grant of the option or lease being renewed. This will be important to:

- the original grantee for retrospective taxation of the option when exercised;
- assignees who, depending upon the official view, may be subject to the linked transaction rules or affected by lease renewal;
- assignees or purchasers whose tax position might be affected by the exercise of an option by other persons; and
- persons advising how to deal with the linked transactions.

---

[48]   Who may not be the same as a person to whom the original tenant directs the grant of the lease.

[49]   FA 2003, Sched.17A, para.12B; see **8.12**.

[50]   Which may not be taxable adjustments; see FA 2003, Sched.17A, paras.17 and 18.

[51]   FA 2003, Sched.17A, paras.6 and 10.

[52]   FA 2003, Sched.5, para.2(5).

[53]   Which problem of retrospection is complicated by the fact that there may be two separate effective dates for leases (see **8.9**) and the proportion of the net present value can change by reason of rent reviews and other variations.

[54]   FA 2003, Sched.5, para.2(5).

[55]   FA 2003, Sched.17A, para.5.

[56]   FA 2003, s.81A; Sched.17A, para.12.

[57]   FA 2003, Sched.5, para.2(5).

[58]   FA 2003, ss.46 and 108; Sched.17A, para.5; Sched.19, paras.8 and 9.

A.4 TITLE ISSUES

The following need to be obtained:

- details of the effective date of the original acquisition of the land by the vendor or whether the transaction was not subject to SDLT[59] since this may be a key date, along with the details of the tax calculation, etc. for the purchaser because of the retrospective nature of much of the tax such as holding over expired leases;
- confirmation whether the vendor/lessor is the registered or beneficial owner of the property. It is necessary to identify the 'true vendor' for SDLT purposes (see **14.4**);
- details of whether the true vendor is the registered owner. If not, suitable confirmation of the ownership is required in order to explain the difference between the Land Registry documents (i.e. registered parties) and the Revenue certificate (SDLT 5) which deals with the 'true' sellers and purchasers who may not be the registered owner;
- a comprehensive SDLT history (see e.g. **8.60** and following and **14.7**).

A.5 SPECIAL REGIMES

In many cases there are special rules affecting the tax charge for the 'purchaser' or lessee, e.g. where:

- the purchaser is a company connected with the vendor;[60]
- the purchaser is a partnership or person connected with the partnership.[61]

Enquiries are necessary to determine whether the arrangements are required to be notified to HMRC as a tax avoidance scheme.

A.6 ADVISER'S POSITION

Advisers acting for a purchaser are at great risk for serious penalties including imprisonment.[62] They are subject to risk if they do not ask the correct questions of the client before completing the return.[63]

---

[59] See for example, FA 2003, Sched.9.
[60] FA 2003, s.53; see **Chapter 13**.
[61] FA 2003, Sched.15, Part 3; see **Chapter 12**.
[62] FA 2003, ss.95 and 96; *Saunders* v. *Edwards* [1987] 2 All ER 651.
[63] *Slattery* v. *Moore Stephens* [2003] STC 1379; *Stone & Rolls Ltd* v. *Moore Stephens* [2009] 4 All ER 431.

APPENDIX B

Particular problems for the vendor

It may seem bizarre that professional advisers need to know the identity of the 'vendor' as identified for the purposes of SDLT when they are acting for the seller or the landlord; but their client may not be the real 'vendor'. However, such information is crucial to the other party to the transaction (see **Appendix A**) and the vendor's adviser will find from time to time that he is required to provide information on this issue and that failure to do so may lead to a well-advised purchaser abandoning the transaction. Moreover, these issues may need to be investigated twice because of the possibility of two or more effective dates and the identity of the vendor or his relationship with the purchaser may have changed in the interim (see **3.3**, **Chapter 11**) or companies may be liquidated (see **Chapter 13**).

B.1 VENDOR IDENTITY

Point to consider:

- Who is the true vendor? The identity of the 'true' vendor may affect not only the details to be added in the land transaction return (SDLT 1) and whether this may be a linked transaction but also the tax charge because of e.g. the principles for dealings between partnerships and connected persons, transactions involving connected companies, corporate reconstructions.
- Whether the vendor is the correct party for various reliefs.[1]
- Whether the vendor is a charity when special charges may apply to the assignment of a lease.
- Whether the vendor is a company. This may have an impact on:

    - connected company charges;[2]
    - whether intra-group reconstruction reliefs are subject to clawback or may be available or subject to roll-over;[3]
    - whether any of the special charges upon the assignment of leases apply.[4]

- The vendor will require undertakings and indemnities from the purchaser since subsequent events may affect his tax liability and reporting obligations or the purchaser may obtain a tax windfall because the vendor's overestimate of tax means that a tax refund is due (see **1.24** and **4.38**).
- Whether there is a reservation of an interest or a transfer and regrant so that the transaction is a land exchange[5] since this involves the vendor in a potential tax charge

---

[1] Such as FA 2003, s.45(3) and (5A), ss.57A and 73A; Sched.17A, paras.9 and 16.
[2] FA 2003, s.53; see **Chapter 13**.
[3] FA 2003, Sched.7.
[4] FA 2003, Sched.17A, para.12.
[5] FA 2003, s.47.

and reporting obligation. This is an area becoming significant in practice because of the approach of HMRC Stamp Taxes to 'excepting and reserving' as involving regrants of new rights.

- Whether the vendor is 'connected' with any other parties involved in the arrangements since dealings with connected persons can affect the tax[6] e.g. in linked transactions.
- Whether any steps taken to protect the interests of the vendor involve the creation ('regrant') of chargeable interests[7] and, in consequence, a land exchange with a potential tax charge for the vendor either at once or at some stage in the future (see **Chapter 7**).
- Whether the vendor is in a position to enable registration of the purchaser's/lessee's interest by supplying the necessary SDLT records.
- Whether the vendor for the purposes of SDLT is the registered owner of the land otherwise there may be a mismatch between the SDLT 5 if the transaction is correctly reported and the Land Registry document. Appropriate confirmations may be required at completion to satisfy the Land Registry.
- Whether the vendor is relying upon subsale relief not affecting leases since this may affect the tax payable and the reporting of the transaction as well as the documentation required for the Land Registry.
- Whether the grantor of a new lease is relying upon the special relief for agreements for lease[8] since this affects the tax liability of the third party grantee as well as the registration process.[9]
- Whether the vendor has exercised the VAT option to tax.[10]
- Whether the vendor/landlord is a party to a building contract.[11]
- Whether the vendor is the appropriate person for dealings with the Land Registry.
- Whether it is necessary to file the amended SDLT 4 (see **Appendix D**).

B.2   OPTIONS

- Details of the exercise of the option are required since the exercise of the option may be linked with the grant and other transactions such as renewals of other linked leases granted by the seller who may be contractually bound to supply information to third parties potentially affected by the exercise.
- Are there cross-options having value within the exchange provisions?[12]
- Is the person against whom an option is exercised the same person as or connected with the grantor?

B.3   VARIABLE CONSIDERATION

- Consider:
    - whether there are any outstanding taxation liabilities in respect of the previous

---

[6]   See e.g. FA 2003, s.44(5) (substantial performance); Sched.4, para.1 (provision of chargeable consideration).
[7]   FA 2003, s.48(1)(b).
[8]   FA 2003, Sched.17A, para.12B.
[9]   FA 2003, s.45; Sched.17A, para.12B; see **8.12**.
[10]   Which affects the tax computation: FA 2003, Sched.4, para.2.
[11]   FA 2003, Sched.4, para.10(2)(c).
[12]   FA 2003, s.47; Sched.4, para.5; see **Chapter 6**.

acquisition of the property which remain with the vendor and the terms of any exit strategy (see **4.40**) including the particular problems for lease provisions;[13]

– whether the proposed transaction requires payment of tax and/or reporting to be made in respect of any prior acquisition of the chargeable interest or the part thereof being disposed of because payments have to be made in respect of tax on a previous acquisition where the payment of part of the tax has been deferred;

– whether these outstanding tax liabilities are affected by any of the proposals for dealing with any such outstanding consideration and clawback arrangements, or as a novation of the liability (i.e. is there an acceptable 'exit strategy' which deals with the vendor's liability which might be a problem for the purchaser).

- Details of later payments made by the purchaser to third parties may be required because these may affect the vendor's open SDLT position for the original payment.
- Indemnities may be required should the initial tax payment on the vendor's acquisition have been overestimated, otherwise the purchaser receives a windfall profit e.g. on a rent review during the first five years of the lease and other cases where the legislation transfers his liability to the assignee of the lease.[14]

B.4   LINKED TRANSACTIONS

Undertakings may be required from the vendor and his successors in title to supply information relating to previous or later transactions entered into by the vendor/lessor such as leases of different properties, lease renewals or holding over, which may be linked with other transactions to which the vendor is a party. This may affect the liability to tax of assignees of the lease by for example reducing the amount of the nil rate slice allocated to any lease which he retains or which he may have previously assigned and may be linked with the leases being currently assigned. It is not necessary that the purchaser/lessee/grantee is a party to the later linked transaction.

B.5   MISCELLANEOUS

- When the vendor is asked to assist in or to agree to the apportionment of the consideration, consider whether the apportionment has been prepared by the purchaser on a proper basis to avoid suggestions of assisting in a conspiracy to defraud HMRC Stamp Taxes.[15]

---

[13]   FA 2003, s.81A; Sched.17A, para.12.
[14]   This may represent additional chargeable consideration payable by the purchaser.
[15]   Note the width of the comment on conspiracy in *Saunders* v. *Edwards* [1987] 2 All ER 651.

APPENDIX C

Share purchase issues for investigation

C.1 INTRODUCTION

While this book is intended for property practitioners there is a special set of problems for corporate transactions which are relevant for property transactions. However, other transactions are primarily the responsibility of company lawyers who need an awareness of the issues[1] and a recognition of a need to seek advice from their property colleagues who, in turn, need to know how a property tax can interact with what appear to be essentially corporate matters. This Appendix is, therefore, intended to provide some guidance for this necessary co-operation between property and company lawyers.

Transactions involving companies involve many issues, namely:

- acquisitions of chargeable interests by bodies corporate: consider whether these are connected with the vendor[2] or whether special reliefs may be available;[3]
- disposals by or acquisitions from companies whether or not to or by connected parties;
- dealings in shares in a company;
- dealings between companies and partnerships.

C.2 ACQUISITIONS BY COMPANIES: GENERAL

In most respects corporate acquisitions are governed by the normal principles but there are certain special issues to consider, such as:

- whether the vendor and the company are connected;[4]
- whether there are reliefs for associated companies available;[5]
- who are the relevant parties to 'represent' the body corporate for payment and compliance;[6]
- whether the special reliefs for residential property are available.[7]

---

[1] Because of the problems of not obtaining appropriate protection for the purchaser by way of warranties, etc. Also advisers to vendors need to be aware of the issues because of what should appear in detail in any disclaimer letter, etc.

[2] FA 2003, ss.53 and 54.

[3] FA 2003, Sched.7; see **Chapter 13**.

[4] FA 2003, s.53; see **13.4**.

[5] FA 2003, Sched.7; see **Chapter 13**.

[6] FA 2003, s.100.

[7] FA 2003, Sched.6A.

C.3 ACQUISITIONS OF SHARES AND TIME BOMB SITUATIONS

Although sales of shares in companies holding land are subject only to stamp duty or stamp duty reserve tax,[8] SDLT issues arise, albeit indirectly, but they may be vitally important to the value of the company. Points to consider include:

- Whether the share transaction is the first step and so outside the statutory general anti-avoidance provisions.[9]
- Whether the company is up to date with its filing of SDLT 1 and paying the tax, and whether all land transaction return certificates (SDLT 5) have been received and submitted to the Land Registry.
- Whether there are any Enquiries proceeding and whether the company is potentially vulnerable to an Enquiry in the future since this may produce additional tax liabilities, interest and penalties.
- Whether there are any SDLT issues outstanding, including relevant transactions not notified.
- Whether the company may be vulnerable to the risk of a Notice of Assessment for a discovery over the 21-year period.
- Whether the company has fully provided for all tax in respect of variable payments including correctly returning the situation and any arrangement for dealing with the postponement of the deferred contingent tax. This applies not merely to the initial estimated self-assessment but in respect of the tax charge arising in respect of later payment and adjustments. Assurances are required that the initial assessment was prepared on a proper basis, i.e. sufficient tax was paid.
- Whether the company is affected by any open SDLT liability such as variable consideration and reviewable rents during the first five years.
- Whether payment of any part of the tax has been deferred and whether the amount so deferred is sufficient to cover the potential tax liability.
- Whether all payments have been made punctually for deferral arrangements.
- Whether the company is subject to a primary or secondary liability in respect of the clawback of tax relief.
- Whether the potential liability either for postponed tax or for tax on variable payments in relation to acquisitions by the company has been recognised in the company's accounts and subsequent dividend policy. It may be necessary for assurances to be given that nothing has subsequently occurred that might affect the amount of consideration expected to be paid which has not been notified to HMRC.
- Whether there are any chargeable building works or services being undertaken by the company which are taxable consideration for any acquisition. Obtain details of the costs and consider whether these are consistent with any deferral arrangements agreed with HMRC.
- Whether the company is a tenant of a lease that may be vulnerable to liability in the future pursuant to the abnormal increase in rent rules.
- Whether the company is a tenant of a lease that was exempt when granted but which will be subject to charge upon assignment as if it were the grant of a new lease since the assignee may require a reverse payment as compensation, i.e. the lease may have a negative value.[10]
- Whether the company is the owner of a chargeable interest that may be vulnerable to the linked transaction rules such as apply to leases with options to renew or leases that are

---

[8] There are no land rich company provisions at present and share transactions may be outside the statutory general anti-avoidance provisions: FA 2003, s.75C(1).

[9] FA 2003, s.75C(1).

[10] FA 2003, Sched.17A, para.12.

linked with other actual or future or renewed leases. This may affect the liability of the company in respect of its leases because of the amount of nil rate slice for rent allocated to it from the initial charge, i.e. there is a potential retrospective liability for future events such as rent reviews and abnormal increases.

- Whether full details of the SDLT history of all chargeable interests are contained in the company's records since these will be vital for future transactions such as holding over or assignment and calculating liability and meeting its obligations to preserve proper records.
- Whether the company has prepared correct accounts for capital allowances and VAT taking proper account of the potential SDLT charges.
- Whether the company has been a party to a chargeable transaction which was exempt but is vulnerable to clawback as a consequence of either the current transaction or future transactions.
- Whether the company has a residual liability for clawback in respect of other companies with which it has been associated should those other companies fail to pay the tax relief clawed back even though it was not a party to those transactions.
- Whether the company has been a party to a transaction where its acquisition was treated as a transfer of a going concern for the purposes of VAT; full details are required of how the SDLT issues were dealt with.
- Whether the company has participated in a notifiable tax scheme and whether HMRC has been notified.

C.4   DISPOSAL BY COMPANIES

In general disposals by companies are taxable to the purchaser in the normal way, but special rules apply:

- where the counterparty is a connected company;[11]
- where the counterparty is a partnership, in which case the special regime applies;[12]
- where there is a disposal of a lease that was exempt within the corporate reorganisation reliefs[13] or sale and leaseback relief[14] when granted;[15]
- where the company is a charity.[16]

These are issues for the purchaser but require companies to preserve adequate documentation so as to provide title assurance to the purchaser.

C.5   COMPANIES AND PARTNERSHIPS

- Is the company a partner in or otherwise 'connected' with the partner or the partnership?[17]
- Does the partnership consist solely of corporate partners?[18]

---

[11]   FA 2003, ss.53 and 54.
[12]   FA 2003, Sched.15, Part 3.
[13]   FA 2003, Sched.7; Sched.17A, para.11(3)(b).
[14]   FA 2003, s.57A; Sched.17A, para.11(3)(c).
[15]   FA 2003, Sched.17A, para.12A dealing with two effective dates.
[16]   FA 2003, Sched.8; Sched.17A, para.11(3)(d).
[17]   FA 2003, Sched.15, Part 3, paras.10 and 18.
[18]   FA 2003, Sched.15, para.24.

Completing the tax return (SDLT 1 to 4)

D.1 GENERAL

There are many questions to address on the completion of the land transaction return (SDLT 1) arising from factors such as poor drafting of the legislation and the form, and the requirement of much information that is not directly relevant to the tax assessment but would appear to be merely data gathering for purposes other than collection of SDLT. There are, in consequence, numerous issues on what data should be inserted in the SDLT 1 and, of particular importance, the obtaining and the preparation of the data to be inserted in the return.[1]

HMRC Stamp Taxes has published Notes for Guidance (SDLT 6) on its views as to the completion of the land transaction return which also contain relevant code numbers and certain comments on substantive tax issues. However, it is uncertain how far it is safe for a taxpayer to rely upon the Notes, particularly as they are somewhat selective and lacking in detail. Filing is now possible electronically with payment being made separately.

The following is intended to provide assistance in certain aspects where the official guidance is less than clear or non-existent, or possibly incorrect. On this last point, there are significant doubts as to whether HMRC Stamp Taxes will necessarily regard itself as bound by any guidance which it has given. The helpline, which appears to be primarily intended to deal with compliance issues rather than substantive matters, is not intended to bind HMRC Stamp Taxes and it has been judicially stated that reliance upon a telephone discussion such as with the helpline or other persons will not bind HMRC.[2] It also seems that such reliance on the helpline will not be taken into account in deciding whether there is fraud or negligence and is not a matter to be taken into account in relation to the possible mitigation of penalties. It will in consequence provide no protection for the practitioner where there is a claim based upon breach of duty.

The land transaction return is not the only official document. It must also be noted that many communications with HMRC Stamp Taxes such as amendments to the form are supposed to be in the form and contain such information as it may require.[3] In many cases prescribed forms have not been issued.

It must be recognised that much of the information required by the forms has no direct bearing on the tax, and much information that is appropriate to the tax cannot be disclosed on the form.[4] This is because the forms are simply collecting information for the Treasury and

---

[1] Note *Langham* v. *Veltema* [2004] STC 544; see also for penalties FA 2003, ss.95 and 96; Sched.10, para.31A; *Saunders* v. *Edwards* [1987] 2 All ER 651.

[2] *J Rothschild (Holdings) Ltd* v. *IRC* [1988] STC 645 (on appeal on other grounds [1989] STC 435).

[3] See the procedure for amending returns during the first 12 months (FA 2003, Sched.10, para.6), and the making of claims such as for repayments of tax pursuant to an error or mistake (FA 2003, Sched.10, para.34 and Sched.11A) and the special documentation requirements when an amendment involves a reclaim.

[4] Hence the ease with which discovery assessments can be issued as in *Langham* v. *Veltema* [2004] STC 544. Covering letters are of no real benefit in this context.

District Valuers. This appreciation of the underlying policy may help to clarify some of the questions on the form. There is, in consequence, an impression that HMRC Stamp Taxes does not regard all of the boxes on the return as obligatory fields; but this practice of allowing partially completed returns to proceed is not consistent nor is there any clear guidance of what may be ignored.

D.1.1 Electronic filing

Facilities supported by numerous regulations have finally introduced electronic filing,[5] after technical issues delayed the programme. Problems arose because HMRC Stamp Taxes and those people commissioned to provide the software support, etc. did not realise the need to separate payment from filing.[6] This has, to some extent, been rectified although there are still defects in that not all of the necessary consequential amendments in the Stamp Duty Land Tax (Administration) Regulations 2003[7] have been made; but it seems that HMRC Stamp Taxes would not wish to take technical points as regards the possible defects in the Revenue certificate (SDLT 5) where this has been obtained bona fide and accepted by the Land Registry.[8]

The separation of filing from payment means that there are certain benefits in filing electronically as there is a relatively speedy response. Obviously, there is no thorough investigation of the land transaction return (SDLT 1 to 4) filed and there are certain difficulties because the various declarations required will not have been 'signed'. It would seem prudent to take a hard printed copy of the return or returns filed and obtain the signature of the client to these forms for the purposes of maintaining records. There is the technical point available to HMRC Stamp Taxes that if there is no signature of the declaration or deemed signature this means that a valid return has not been received and penalties may be imposed for failure to file.

There are, however, practical difficulties in filing electronically. In particular, it seems that there are problems with transfers of freeholds for nil consideration or, indeed, many situations where there are transfers where there is no chargeable consideration to be inserted in Box 10 on the SDLT 1. This arises because situations where there was no chargeable consideration were not within the realms of notifiable transactions originally but exclusions from the rule of zero consideration being non-notifiable have extended so as to include transactions with connected companies, dealings between partnerships and connected persons[9] and certain transactions involving disadvantaged land and private finance initiatives.[10] It seems that there may be difficulties in persuading the computer system that a property can have a nil or even a negative market value, such as where there is the assignment of a headlease where the rents in are the same as or possibly even exceed the amount of rents paid out to the head landlord together with any expenses (as frequently arises in relation to certain types of lease or enfranchisement). In these situations it may be necessary to file manually with all the costs and irritations associated with preparing the over-engineered SDLT 1.

In addition, filing may be a problem if the Land Registry queries transactions presented to it as non-taxable or non-notifiable (see **1.12**) so that registration is delayed, to the irritation of lenders. In these situations the parties may wish to file electronically in order to obtain the Revenue certificate (SDLT 5) as quickly as possible. However, for the reasons indicated in

---

[5]   Stamp Duty Land Tax (Electronic Communications) Regulations 2005, SI 2005/844 (amended by Stamp Duty Land Tax (Electronic Communications) (Amendment) Regulations 2006, SI 2006/3427).

[6]   FA 2003, s.76 (as originally enacted).

[7]   SI 2003/2837, Part 1.

[8]   See Stamp Duty Land Tax (Administration) Regulations 2003, SI 2003/2837, Part 1.

[9]   FA 2003, Sched.15, para.30.

[10]   FA 2003, Sched.6, para.13.

the previous paragraph, electronic filing and rapid response is not always available in the situations where the Land Registry causes difficulty. It may be necessary to file manually or comply with the increasingly frequent requirement of the Land Registry that a letter rather than an SDLT 5 is produced from HMRC Stamp Taxes.

Since electronic filing permits the obtaining of a Revenue certificate (SDLT 5) and therefore registration without payment of the tax there is a growing number of situations where registrations are being obtained but the tax is not paid. Fortunately, this is not a situation which enables HMRC Stamp Taxes or the Land Registry to cancel the registration (see **1.11.2**). However, solicitors who participate in such arrangements may find themselves parties to conspiracies to defraud the Revenue or money laundering or tax evasion as well as the penalties imposed by FA 2003.[11]

D.1.2 Electronic computation

The mathematical formulae scattered throughout the SDLT legislation represent many potential tedious exercises if calculation is carried out manually. In order to ease this process HMRC Stamp Taxes has introduced online computation facilities. These include the formula for calculating the net present value of rent as indicated elsewhere. It is essential that a hard copy of this screen and calculation of the data inserted in the various boxes is preserved because this is now a major document of title for assignees of leases as well as for clients who wish to be in a position to be able to deal with problems arising on holding over or lease renewals in due course. There are also online facilities for applying the formula in order to determine whether any rent adjustment in the period after the expiration of the fifth year of the term including any holding over or renewal period is an abnormal increase.[12] Unfortunately, these facilities have a habit of producing incorrect results. It seems that there is a particularly acute problem in relation to the abnormal rent increase facility. Surprisingly, these errors in the system tend to favour the taxpayer. Fortunately, HMRC Stamp Taxes has indicated that provided the parties can prove that they utilised the facility and inserted the correct data it will not seek to collect any additional tax that might be due or impose any penalties for incorrect or late or non-filing or any interest on the tax that is no longer payable. This obviously increases the need to obtain copies of the information inserted on the screen and print the relevant page or pages. Persons who claim that they have relied upon the facility but cannot produce the hard copy contemporaneous data will be find it difficult to defend their position. The use of the printer is a simple matter of self-preservation.

D.1.3 Identifying the form

The basic forms are prescribed, i.e. only the appropriate form may be utilised. The initial forms in Scheds.1 and 2 to the Stamp Duty Land Tax (Administration) Regulations 2003[13] have been modified. The current list includes the following.

D.1.3.1 Land transaction return (SDLT 1)

This is the basic return and self-assessment. Note that the amendments permitting agents to sign the return[14] require a special version of SDLT 1 to be utilised because this has to contain the modified declaration required by the regulations. Declarations in the new form include

---

[11]   *Saunders* v. *Edwards* [1987] 2 All ER 651; FA 2003, ss.95 and 96; see also *Stone and Rolls Ltd* v. *Moore Stephens* [2009] 4 All ER 431.
[12]   FA 2003, Sched.17A, paras.13, 14 and 15.
[13]   SI 2003/2837.
[14]   FA 2003, Sched.10, para.1A.

reference to 'agent' as the person confirming the effective date.[15] It seems the purchaser's signature confirming that everything except the effective date is correct can be on a copy of the form.

D.1.3.2 Additional vendor/purchaser details (SDLT 2)

This is required where there are two or more vendors or purchasers; particularly important where nominees are involved. Since the vendor and purchaser are not necessarily the legal owners of the property or even the parties to the contract, it is necessary to investigate these issues. The identity of the parties is important for a whole range of reasons including the assessment of the tax and the linked transaction rules. This may pose an acute issue in respect of partnerships as, notwithstanding the rule permitting representative partners to carry out certain functions, HMRC Stamp Taxes, in practice, treats a partnership as a single vendor or purchaser so that only the partnership name is required in Box 36 in SDLT 1. This indicates, but not conclusively, that the names of all of the partners are not required to be disclosed.

Unincorporated associations such as clubs may be a body corporate so that individual identities are not important and the form may not be necessary. It is unclear how many trustees of charities may have to be identified. The rules limiting registration of legal title to the first four trustees does not limit the disclosure if there are other trustees, although one trustee can sign the form.

D.1.3.3 Additional details of the land (SDLT 3)

As the taxpayer may, in order to save costs, include more than one property in the main SDLT 1 (Box 26) this form will be required. The inclusion of several properties in one return will reduce the need for duplication of much of the information and possibly avoid the need for apportioning a global consideration for several properties. However, obstacles exist to the utilisation of this facility; namely:

- the structure of the form SDLT 1 is such that only transactions having the same effective date can be entered upon the form;
- SDLT 6 suggests that the facility should be utilised for linked transactions but this requires not only the same effective date but also the same parties. In consequence, where the linked transactions involved connected persons, whether as 'vendors' or 'purchasers', separate returns will be required;
- SDLT 6 in the preface to Box 16 indicates that only one lease can be included in the SDLT 1, because it specifically excludes linked leases; and
- where the properties are in different land registries there will be a need to request separate land transaction return certificates (SDLT 5) for each property (SDLT 1, Box 27).

It seems that SDLT 6 requires this return in cases where a freehold is acquired subject to pre-existing leases or a new headlease subject to leases or underleases is granted. For some far from obvious reason, HMRC Stamp Taxes requires full details of all such pre-existing leases to be disclosed (see SDLT 6 in relation to SDLT 1 Boxes 16–22). Further information on all new leases is required by SDLT 4.

---

[15] FA 2003, s.81B.

D.1.3.4   Additional details about the transactions (SDLT 4 (as amended))

This form[16] is designed for disposal of land as part of a business sale and, in effect, replaces with amendment the old stamps form 22 and former companies form 88.[17] However, although no separate guidance is provided as to when HMRC Stamp Taxes expects to receive this form, it is probably prudent to assume that this return is required in every case other than routine domestic conveyancing and investigate whether any of the questions are relevant.

Notwithstanding the references to 'chattels', it is not necessary to submit this form where there is a sale of property without a business, such as a sale of a house and chattels unless the purchaser is a company where SDLT 4 may be required in any event because SDLT 1 does not require disclosure of the purchasing company's number.

Looking to the information required by SDLT 4 (as amended), it seems that it will be required where:

- the property is subject to a lease or tenancy;
- the land transaction is part of a sale of a business;
- the land is commercial property;
- the purchaser is a company;
- the consideration is contingent or uncertain, but not perhaps 'unascertained'. There is, however, an ambiguity because the form, but not SDLT 6, refers to dependence upon future events. It is thought that the reference to 'future events' is to factors that change the calculation rather than merely referring to agreements between the parties which determine the facts upon which the calculation is based such as the square footage of an existing building or market value as at the effective date (see **4.38**). However, it has to be noted that the test for the 'certainty' of the consideration has to be applied as at the effective date which is not necessarily the same as formal completion and the pricing mechanism may be fixed by reference to the later date so that when filing the return for the effective date the consideration will be dependent upon future events. Thus at the effective date the building may be only half constructed; at completion it may be constructed but unmeasured. SDLT 4 will be required in the former case because the consideration is uncertain, and in the latter case because the building is commercial;
- mineral rights have been reserved;[18]
- a post-transaction ruling has been received. This will be an unlikely event in practice since to apply for a post-transaction ruling together with or subsequent to the filing of the land transaction return means that there cannot be such a ruling. This will be regarded by HMRC Stamp Taxes as initiating a full Enquiry. SDLT 4 is only required if the application has been made and the ruling has been received prior to filing SDLT 1 which, in practice, is likely to mean that the taxpayer is out of time for filing both the land transaction return and any Land Registry application;
- arrangements have already been 'agreed' for the postponement of the payment of tax. It seems that SDLT 4 is not required merely if an application for postponement has been made, notwithstanding that tax in respect of which an application to postpone has been made is not due and payable until the application has been refused (Stamp Duty Land Tax (Administration) Regulations 2003, SI 2003/2837, reg.15(3)) but it will be necessary to file the form because the consideration will be uncertain.

---

[16]   Stamp Duty Land Tax (Administration) (Amendment) Regulations 2004, SI 2004/3124.

[17]   Which has been separately amended by regulations (Stamp Duty and Stamp Duty Land Tax (Consequential Amendment of Enactments) Regulations 2003, SI 2003/2868); but which is now unnecessary because there are so few situations where the charge on contracts can arise pursuant to FA 1999, Sched.13, para.7.

[18]   One of the very few situations where HMRC Stamp Taxes accepts that interests can be 'excepted and reserved'.

D.1.4   Payslip

It is no longer necessary that the SDLT 1 is accompanied by payment with details contained in the prescribed payslip[19] since payment can be made separately and electronically. If filed in hard copy the payslip bears the same bar code transaction number as the SDLT 1 page 2. Where the payslip is separate because, for example, the taxpayer is utilising electronic forms, it is necessary to ensure that the bar code is entered on the payslip. It is also necessary to write the bar code number on the cheque so that in the not unlikely event of the cheque and the return becoming separated, HMRC Stamp Taxes may be able to rematch the various documents and payment.

D.1.5   Alterations of the form

There are penalties imposed for ill-treating Revenue forms[20] so alterations to the forms are not encouraged.[21] Three main areas require consideration, as follows.

D.1.5.1   Amendments

Certain adjustments in the tax position are required to be dealt with by way of amendment such as repayments of tax paid on substantial performance of a contract where the contract is later rescinded or annulled,[22] or claims for overpaid tax within 12 months after the 30-day filing period which must be accompanied by the documents.[23] Corrections may also be required where the transaction documentation is rectified in the correct sense of the term. Such correction of drafting errors in the transaction documentation is likely to mean that incorrect details were entered in the original return. There may also be 'corrections' from HMRC Stamp Taxes where there have been manifest minor errors or omissions,[24] e.g. arithmetic or obvious omissions, in completing the form. Such corrections to the return may only be made within nine months after the return was filed by written notice which can be challenged by the taxpayer.[25]

'Amendments' can be made only within 12 months after the expiration of the 30-day filing period, and must be by notice in such form and contain such information as HMRC Stamp Taxes may require.[26] No standard form for these amendments has yet been presented by regulations; but frequently a letter setting out the basis of the amendment is more convenient than completing a full return which has no facility for reclaiming tax or cross-referring to the earlier return. HMRC Stamp Taxes has accepted and acted upon such letter.

D.1.5.2   Alterations to return

Errors may creep in during the preparation of the land transaction return and, while it may in many respects be easier to scrap that return, if it is being prepared manually it may be tedious and time consuming (and presumably non-chargeable) to repeat the exercise if the form has been virtually completed, since masking fluids are prohibited and will result in the form being returned as invalid. Notwithstanding that the forms are ultimately to be scanned electronically and the choice of ink is prescribed by SDLT 1 itself and HMRC Stamp Taxes is accordingly not anxious to encourage physical alterations to the form, it is permitted to cross

---

[19]   FA 2003, s.76 (as amended).
[20]   FA 2003, s.82.
[21]   This extends to folding the returns which is prohibited at several places in the return.
[22]   FA 2003, s.44(9).
[23]   For claims after this date see FA 2003, Sched.11A.
[24]   FA 2003, Sched.10, para.7.
[25]   FA 2003, Sched.10, para.7.
[26]   FA 2003, Sched.10, para.6.

out the erroneous entry and put the correct figures underneath the boxes. However, there are problems with amending returns prepared on screen after printing. Manual amendments may not be recognised by HMRC Stamp Taxes processes. If such an amendment is required, it is recommended that the on-screen version is amended and the earlier version deleted.

D.1.5.3   Subsequent adjustments/contingent tax

As described in the main text there are many situations where, notwithstanding the filing of a land transaction return (SDLT 1) and the receipt of the Revenue certificate (SDLT 5), the taxation position is not final and further full returns with signed declarations are required, with fresh self-assessments retrospectively adjusting the initial tax calculation and, where appropriate, any subsequent intermediate revisions thereof. The adjustment has to be made on a totally new return form. Although the particular return relates to the adjustment of a previous return, it cannot be dealt with as an amendment of the original return even when it is filed within the first 12 months after the initial filing. There will be a separate 'transaction number', i.e. bar code which suggests a separate transaction, but there is no provision for a cross-reference to the earlier land transaction return. The point will emerge to the attention of HMRC Stamp Taxes because of the discrepancies between Boxes 10, 14 and 15, i.e. the relevant consideration, the total tax and the tax currently being paid. The last of these will take into account tax paid with the filing of the prior return and will not be 4 per cent of the chargeable consideration, etc.

D.1.6   Overpaid tax

It will also be noted that no provision is made on the land transaction return form for negative tax, i.e. where at the time of the filing of the later return there is a claim for repayment of previously overpaid tax such as might arise where the effect of a rent review was overestimated. This presumably may be dealt with by way of amendment to the original return if within the relevant 12-month period, or more probably pursuant to the claims procedure prescribed in FA 2003, Sched.11A. The requirement for a notice in the prescribed form will be dealt with, initially, by filing the required form showing nil tax payable and an accompanying letter setting out the previous overpayment with a reference to the relevant bar code number which will, hopefully, be accepted by HMRC Stamp Taxes as a notice in the prescribed form but there will, doubtless, be investigation of the details taking time and adding to the cost.[27] Although this might be regarded as an 'amendment' of the original return by bringing it up to date, it has to be treated as a separate return and, although it may involve a claim for repayment of tax previously overpaid, it is not affected by the restrictions upon error and mistake claims, because although there may have been a mistake in the previous reasonable estimate the current context involves not the correction of errors but the revision of guestimates in the light of subsequent events.

D.2   PARTICULAR POINTS ON THE FORMS

Moving on from the requirements to use black ink, capital letters and not folding the form in case the scanners misread the crease as an entry, the following points should be noted.

---

[27]   Fortunately, interest may be payable on repaid tax.

D.2.1 SDLT 1

Box 2 refers to the grant of a lease;[28] where there is more than one lease SDLT 4, Box 11 will be required. It is important to note HMRC Stamp Taxes' view that the effect of FA 2003, Sched.17A, para.12A is that there are two separate chargeable transactions: as at substantial performance of the agreement and as at grant of the lease. Two totally separate returns with two different effective dates will be required. SDLT 4 will also be required unless the two events are within the 12-month period when an 'amendment' may be accepted or even suggested by HMRC Stamp Taxes in practice.

Box 3: it might be thought that this part of the form is concerned with sales of existing interests, such as freeholds or existing leases, but the codes to be inserted in Box 3 refer to transfers of interests that are subject to leases or underleases. Although these are not newly created leases, SDLT 6 indicates in the notes between Boxes 15 and 16 that the return must disclose those leases subject to which the interest is being transferred even if this has no bearing upon the tax charge. It seems that where the interest transferred is the reversion on several leases, a separate SDLT form for each lease will be required, although much of the information on that form is inappropriate to dealings with leases granted long ago. There is some uncertainty as to whether the notes are correct. In dealing with transfers of freehold interests subject to leases, it seems that SDLT 6 would require the disclosure of the details not merely of the headlease but also of each additional sublease. The fact that there is a separate note dealing with the grant of leases subject to existing tenancies requiring details of those tenancies which are accurately described as subleases indicates that the sale and purchase of a freehold reversion requires the purchaser to disclose details of all existing leases subject to which he acquires the interest and any subleases previously granted out of those leases. This will constitute a significant problem where, for example, there is an acquisition of a freehold interest of a large block of flats by a management company controlled by the tenants. Details of every lease in the block will be required, plus details of any sublettings that the tenants may have entered into, whether on a short-term or a long-term basis.

In addition to details of the leases subject to which the interest is acquired, SDLT 4, Box 2 requires details of the actual use of the premises, such as office or warehouse.

Box 4: apart from the special case of leases and FA 2003, Sched.17A, para.12A[29] there is only one effective date for the transaction although subsequent events may give rise to a notification obligation which frequently relates back to the original effective date (see **1.24**) and although each subsequent return bears a different transaction number or bar code they all have to refer to the date entered in Box 4 on the initial SDLT 1.

Box 5 presents a problem both as to what has to be disclosed and as to the amount of detail required. The former practice for PD forms of inserting 'the usual covenants'[30] is probably no longer acceptable but it seems that in practice only limited disclosure seems to be needed without apparent challenge. Initially HMRC Stamp Taxes was contending that a full disclosure of all covenants and restrictions is required, including planning restrictions and both historic and current conditions as well as those created by the transaction.

The width of disclosure of conditions and restrictions including past and newly created circumstances is supposed to be limited by the need for restrictions to affect the value of the land but there is a different explanation in SDLT 6. Since virtually every covenant, restriction and easement may have some effect upon value of the land, it is difficult to see any limitation upon the width of disclosure. However, it is, in practice, rare for the initially agreed price to be adjusted after investigation of title. It can be said that pre-existing restrictions do not affect

---

[28]   Which includes substantial performance: FA 2003, Sched.17A, para.12A.

[29]   But note FA 2003, s.44(8) which is regarded by HMRC Stamp Taxes as creating two separate chargeable events; see **3.3**.

[30]   There may be no 'usual covenants' see *Sweet & Maxwell* v. *Universal News Services* [1964] 2 QB 699.

the value since these will possibly have been taken into account in fixing the offer price, at least where they are fairly standard in content; but HMRC Stamp Taxes draws a distinction between value and price[31] and might argue that although the price was not adjusted the existence of those conditions affected the value because the asking price was determined having taken them into account. Long-standing restrictions will affect the 'value' because they may inhibit the use of the land; but being in place before the transaction they will not affect the 'price' because again the seller will probably have allowed for these issues. It seems that virtually everything is likely to require disclosure. The position is not helped by the fact that the form refers to 'value' whereas SDLT 6 refers to the chargeable consideration. Essentially, the Notes for Guidance are incorrect since the chargeable consideration is not necessarily linked to the value of the property and the 'value' may be affected by the covenants even though historic. Thus a transaction may be at a deliberately low price or one where the actual consideration is ignored for the purposes of the tax. Since the form has statutory authority, unlike the Notes for Guidance which have no authority, the criterion has to be the possible effect on 'value' which will often bear no relationship to the price.

As regards the depth of the disclosure, it seems that all that is required is 'a description'. However, it seems that, in practice, inserting 'see attached photocopy documents' and enclosing copies of the conveyances, leases or other documents has not hitherto been the subject of a challenge or an Enquiry by HMRC Stamp Taxes. This is not possible when filing electronically so that minimal disclosure appears to be acceptable.

Box 6 requires the date of the contract. For option arrangements this will be the date of the exercise of the option. For conditional contracts it is the date when the contract is executed not when it becomes unconditional. This date is important for transitional provisions but has little, if any, other practical effect since, apart from options and pre-emption rights, the entering into a contract is not as such taxable. The date will, however, be important in determining whether the taxpayer has taken possession pursuant to the contract. This can be a significant issue where the taxpayer is already in occupation under an earlier arrangement of the land such as where a tenant renews a lease. However, in these circumstances already being in possession prior to the contract date should not constitute substantial performance.

Box 7 refers to land exchanges. It has to be noted that current practices indicate that in the official view 'land exchange' as defined by FA 2003, s.47 (see Chapter 7) includes 'excepting and reserving interests' because this involves a regrant, i.e. a land exchange. Where the box is relevant the transaction may be taxed upon market value, not the contract price. When completing Box 10 when the sale is subject to mineral rights this may have to be dealt with in SDLT 4.

Box 8 goes to the question of whether the grant of the option and its exercise are linked transactions so that the tax upon the option has to be retrospectively recalculated and any option premium has to be included in determining the rate on the main contract. It will include an option to renew or extend or terminate leases (but not necessarily the implementation of break clauses which may not give rise to a chargeable transaction).[32]

Each subsequent linked transaction, whether relating to the same or other property, will require submission of new SDLT 1s because the total premium shown in the original return will be generally retrospectively incorrect. A full return is required, not an amendment to the form, unless perhaps the linked transaction occurs within the 12-month period during which the taxpayer is permitted to correct a return.

Box 10 is particularly unclear and the official advice fluctuates between setting out the actual consideration and the chargeable consideration. As this seems to be required as a *prima facie* check upon the consideration for calculating the tax, it is generally regarded as

---

[31] But see *Stanton* v. *Drayton Commercial Investment Co Ltd* [1982] STC 585; see also *Dean v. Prince* [1954] 1 All ER 749.

[32] But note the absence of any effect upon the initial length of the term: FA 2003, Sched.17A, para.2; there may be issues on valuation when there are such arrangements in the lease.

being appropriate to insert the chargeable consideration and this appears to be consistent with the general drafting policy that the word 'consideration' when unqualified by any adjective is, *prima facie*, 'chargeable consideration'. This makes the treatment of exemptions particularly important. Thus intra-group transactions have to incur the cost of a valuation notwithstanding that no tax is payable. This means that if there is variable consideration the appropriate maximum contingent sum or reasonable estimate, as required by FA 2003, s.51, has to be inserted. It will also include the VAT that is potentially payable if the transaction is not a transfer of a going concern on the current official practice.

Box 10 is also relevant for leases. Although the basic computation and provisions for leases appear later in the return, it will be necessary to include in Box 10 the aggregate of the chargeable premium and net present value of the rent for leases produced from later entries.

Box 11: although Box 10 would seem to require disclosure of the VAT possibly payable if the transaction is not a transfer of a going concern this is officially regarded as unascertained consideration and has to be included in the chargeable consideration and tax computation and requires delivery of SDLT 4. Box 11 by referring to 'payable' would seem to require this sum to be disclosed. However, SDLT 6 refers to VAT actually paid which may well be a very different amount if the parties are treating the transaction as a transfer of a going concern. Upon this view the entry here is 'nil' if the parties are approaching the transaction as a transfer of a going concern so that no tax is 'paid'. However, as discussed in the main text, there are disputes in practice as to how this should be treated for computation and Box 10 purposes.

Box 12 has an inadequate list of codes in SDLT 6. In particular, contingent consideration does not include unascertained or uncertain consideration but may include potential VAT in relation to transfers as a going concern on the official view, clawback and overage payments and payments for building works and services. These will have to be included under 'other' (34) but further information will be required in Box 4 on SDLT 4, as will details of any deferral arrangements.[33]

Box 13 will initially be completed on a provisional basis because there may not be another transaction with which it is linked at that stage such as the grant of a lease with an option to renew. A later transaction may be linked so that retrospectively this entry becomes incorrect and requires 'amendment' which will probably form part of the necessary new complete return retrospectively recalculating the tax.[34] The retrospective effect of linked transactions is a key factor in completing and submitting multiple returns.

Linked transactions can be included in the same return (Box 26) only if they have the same effective date, and are between the same parties and not connected persons.

Boxes 14 and 15: the Notes for Guidance (SDLT 6) are less than helpful and potentially misleading on these boxes. Box 14 requires disclosure of the total tax, Box 15 requires only the tax paid, which will include the relevant amounts in respect of leases dealt with in later parts of the return, which will have to be 'carried back'. Frequently the amounts shown in these two boxes will differ and not be a precise percentage of the aggregate amount in Box 10 because the land transaction return may be an amending or further return for the same transaction,[35] where a return has been previously submitted. The amount of tax payable with the second or subsequent return will usually be less than the total amount of the tax, for example where an instalment of an overage payment or a rent review during the first five years of the term has to be notified. Box 14 may contain a different figure from its predecessors as the reasonable estimates become replaced by facts. Box 15 deals only with the extra tax but cannot cope with tax refunds, i.e. negative tax.[36] The reference in SDLT 6 to

---

[33]   FA 2003, s.90 and Stamp Duty Land Tax (Administration) Regulations 2003, SI 2003/2837, Part 4.

[34]   FA 2003, s.81A, which may affect third parties, Sched.17A, para.12.

[35]   It will be noted that the bar code refers to the return not the transaction so that there will be several returns with different bar codes but no means of cross-referring is provided in the forms.

[36]   See FA 2003, Sched.11A.

the total amount due must mean the extra tax payable at that stage not the overall total amount. Note that if tax payments have been deferred this must be referred to in SDLT 4, Box 5.

Box 17 requires the disclosure of the term commencement date. The practical significance of this (see **8.50**) is whether the first review falls within the last quarter of the five-year period because of the practice of backdating the term commencement date to the previous quarter day.[37] Unfortunately, the double charge upon leases introduced by FA 2003, Sched.17A, para.12A (see **8.9**) means that if there is any significant delay between the substantial performance of the agreement for lease and the grant of the lease, the first review date will inevitably fall within the first five years because the backdating will be more than the three months before the actual grant of the lease excluded from the charge. There may also be issues as to whether any backdated rent is taxable as a premium.[38]

Box 18 refers to the end of the lease. For periodic tenancies it seems that HMRC Stamp Taxes is expecting a date at the end of the first period or deemed first period.[39] This has to be noted since a periodic tenancy, such as a weekly or monthly tenancy, is treated as being a tenancy for one year. Therefore, although the calculation of the tax and the reporting obligations are dealt with by reference to a one-year period or longer for a tenancy for a fixed period and thereafter from period to period until determined by notice, this will be treated for these purposes as a tenancy up until the end of the fixed period. There is, therefore, in many cases a potential discrepancy between the date or period used for the calculation of the tax and the date required on the return.

Box 18 ignores break clauses and options to renew[40] but SDLT 4, Boxes 10, 11 and 12 require details of break clauses and options to renew.

Box 19 requires details of rent-free periods but these will usually be linked to some form of rent review and details of these are required in SDLT 4, Boxes 12, 13, 14 and 15.

Box 20 requires details of the initial rent, including any actual VAT. If, as is likely, the rent is reviewable, details of the review date are required under the reference to the first review or adjustment date and further details are required on SDLT 4, Boxes 12, 13, 14 and 15.[41] It seems that details of other variable rents such as turnover and profit-related rents are not required unless HMRC Stamp Taxes takes the view that these represent uncertain consideration within SDLT 4. SDLT 6 provides no guidance as to variable rents payable in arrears. For example, there may be a lease where the rent may include a base figure plus a turnover element which is payable in arrears once the figures for the relevant year have been agreed. The calculation of the tax will be upon the basis of a reasonable estimate of the rent payable which will include a 'guestimate' of the turnover for the first five years. No guidance is provided as to whether the estimated rent is to be included rather than the base rent. It would be prudent to include the estimated figure for the first rent period so as to avoid any allegation of attempts to mislead HMRC Stamp Taxes by suggesting that the transaction is smaller than it actually is. Since one of the criteria for initiating an Enquiry is the size of the transaction, a challenge is more likely if a low figure is inserted, although this would be potentially justifiable because of the lack of guidance. Unfortunately, it seems that attempts to rely upon the notes in SDLT 6 will not be regarded as a reason for mitigating penalties for incorrect returns.

In Box 20 it has to be noted that sums described as rent but paid in respect of periods prior to the grant of the lease are potentially taxed as a premium and should be included in Box

---

[37] FA 2003, Sched.17A, para.7A.

[38] FA 2003, Sched.5, para.1A.

[39] FA 2003, Sched.17A, para.4.

[40] FA 2003, Sched.17A, para.2.

[41] Possible changes in the rate of VAT may make the rent variable but do not have a specific 'review date' for these purposes. When the date for rate change has been announced the new rate has to be included in the initial calculation; see **4.30** and **8.21**.

22.[42] Although rents indexed to RPI are treated as fixed rents[43] for the purpose of calculating the tax, they will not be included as rents where the amount is known. This, like so many other aspects of the various returns, requires the actual information and data rather than any deemed arrangements pursuant to the legislation and regulations.

Box 21 is ambiguous. It refers to the amount of VAT but without specifying the appropriate period. It would seem from the context that this is the actual amount of VAT payable upon the initial rent on an annual basis and not the amount of VAT payable over the period of the lease. It would also seem to require the details of the amount of VAT included in the reasonable estimate of the initial rent (see **8.31**).

Box 22 refers to the total premium. This includes all items within the charge to tax other than rent. It would also include rent paid in respect of periods prior to the grant of the lease (see above). It will include payments for building works, services, land exchanges including surrenders and regrants.[44] Details of other consideration such as consideration in kind or periodical premiums (but not premiums payable by instalments) are required to be disclosed in SDLT 4, Box 18. The total premium requires inclusion of any premium, whether in cash or in kind, for the grant of linked leases. This will apply where there is an option to renew a lease which is a linked transaction as well as the grant of other leases as part of the original commercial transaction. The reference to 'other' consideration (Code 04) would seem to include items such as 'additional rents' in the form of insurance premium contributions notwithstanding that these may not be taxable.[45]

The reference to contingent consideration (Code 09) is limited and does not include uncertain or unascertained consideration.[46] A lease granted for a premium that contains some form of overage or clawback arrangement will not be contingent consideration and should, presumably, be entered as 'other' under Code 04. SDLT 4, Box 19 requires disclosure of reverse premium payments by the landlord to the tenant and any other consideration being supplied by the landlord to the tenant notwithstanding that these are not taxable.[47] This requires disclosure of surrenders and regrants but entries to this effect have already been made on SDLT 1, Box 7 by indicating that the transaction is part of a land exchange.

Box 23, dealing with the net present value of the rent, will (because of the prevalence of rent reviews in many cases) be prepared on the basis of reasonable estimates. Rent reviews, turnover rents and other matters will need to be disclosed on SDLT 4. A subsequent return SDLT 1, in full, will be required as and when the estimates unwind and the actual data as required by the legislation emerges. It must be noted that a completely new return will be required, including the appropriate entries on SDLT 4. It is not possible to correct or amend the original return to take account of subsequent chargeable rent reviews.

Boxes 24 and 25 deal with the calculation of the tax; but it has to be noted that the entries made in Boxes 22–25 have to be carried back to Boxes 10, 14 and 15 for the total consideration and tax charge.

Box 26 provides a useful facility for avoiding the duplication of forms where they merely repeat the same information from other forms relating to the same transaction other than details of the land and possibly avoiding the need to apportion global consideration to some extent; although this is not immediately obvious, the benefit of this facility is limited. The impact of Box 4, dealing with the effective date, is that the form can effectively be used for several properties only where these have the same effective date. It is not sufficient that they are all acquired under a single contract since the arrangement may be such that there are

---

[42] FA 2003, Sched.5, para.1A (as amended); but see Sched.17A, paras.9 and 9A.
[43] FA 2003, Sched.17A, para.7(5); but note the problems of VAT and RPI on rents; see **8.31**.
[44] Details of which are required in SDLT 4, Box 9.
[45] But note FA 2003, Sched.17A, para.10.
[46] Compare SDLT 4 which does not refer to 'unascertained consideration' which relates to past circumstances and the tax upon which cannot be deferred.
[47] FA 2003, Sched.17A, para.18.

different effective dates for various properties. This facility also avoids the need for having to file many subsequent land transaction returns where there are later linked transactions or other events such as payments of instalments in respect of overage payments for certain of the properties but not all of them where the uncertainties have yet to be resolved. In all of these cases where several properties have been acquired under linked or simultaneous arrangements, then all of the forms would require amendment because of the need to include the total consideration for all of the related transactions. Where a single return has been submitted for numerous properties, then only one subsequent form will be required in respect of all of them. It is, therefore, important to try to organise matters in such a way that there is only one effective date, although this could be a problem where leases are concerned because the tenant may go into occupation of some of the premises, but not all, for fitting out or other matters or they may be delayed in certain aspects of the construction works. There may also be difficulties where there is a delay between substantial performance and the date of grant now that these are two separate chargeable events pursuant to the official view of FA 2003, Sched.17A, para.12A (as amended) (see **8.9**).

Box 27 represents a necessary facility if advantage is taken of Box 26. A single land transaction return certificate (SDLT 5) could be seriously inconvenient where the properties are in separate Land Registries.[48] One certificate would not necessarily be the best way of dealing with the registrations, particularly if there have been some delays in the turnaround by HMRC Stamp Taxes and the parties are under pressure to meet Land Registry deadlines. It is usually appropriate to ask for a separate certificate for each property in order to facilitate Land Registry dealings.

Where numerous properties are included, then it will be necessary to complete a separate SDLT 3 for each of the properties. SDLT 1 and SDLT 3 both require details of the local authority in Box 29 and Box 2 respectively. Details of the appropriate codes are contained in SDLT 6.

SDLT 4 will be required even where there is only one property involved in the transaction if mineral rights are reserved from the transaction (Box 7). A separate SDLT 1 will be required for the particular land if dealing solely with the mineral rights if more than one property is included in the transaction return. Fortunately, HMRC Stamp Taxes does not currently regard the reservation of mineral rights as a regrant producing a land exchange with a market value charge upon the seller of the land and the need to file a separate SDLT 1.

Box 33 requires a plan if boundaries need to be defined. The bar code reference has to be included on the reverse of the form including details as to the scale of the plan.

Box 34 requires details of the number of vendors. It must be noted that the vendor is not necessarily the owner of the registered title being transferred, or even a person whose name appears on the contract itself. It is, essentially, the beneficial owner of the property.[49] This is an acute problem where nominees are involved or the property is held upon trust by the first full name for others. This can be a problem where the seller is a body of trustees or a partnership. However, SDLT 6 suggests relaxation of this requirement by stating that a partnership is a single purchaser. Presumably, rather than having to file numerous SDLT 2s for each partner, entry of the partnership name will be sufficient identification of both vendors and purchasers. The fact that the partnership has representative partners who are entitled to act in relation to SDLT on behalf of the firm is not a relevant consideration.[50] These persons are only authorised to act in relation to the role of purchaser but they are not the substitute for the vendor or the purchaser. HMRC Stamp Taxes has not indicated that there is to be any relaxation of these disclosure requirements for other bodies of persons not within the definition of 'company' having numerous members. In some situations the body of

---

[48] Which may also affect the approach to electronic filing payment.
[49] FA 2003, Sched.16, para.3(1).
[50] Pursuant to FA 2003, Sched.15, para.8; these are not the same as the responsible partner; see para.6.

persons may be treated as a body corporate, in which case it seems that the name of the association can be inserted as the name of the vendor.

There are difficulties in complying with these requirements since there is no statutory obligation for the person acting as the seller to disclose information. This has to be obtained by request and contractual stipulation. The purchaser is required to exercise his own due diligence in these matters.

Box 38 relating to the vendor's address is a particular illustration of the problems facing purchasers. It is not unknown for vendors to refuse to divulge their address, particularly if they wish to avoid being stalked by a disgruntled purchaser. In such a situation it is not acceptable to HMRC Stamp Taxes for the purchaser to indicate that this information cannot be obtained and an attempt to submit a return on this basis will lead to its rejection. The advice from the helpline is to insert the address of the premises being acquired. This advice is potentially dangerous because, as the parties to the transaction will be fully aware, by the time of completion which will generally be the effective date in this type of case, the vendor will usually have vacated the premises and moved on. Nevertheless, it seems that HMRC Stamp Taxes may not take too aggressive a line in relation to penalties if the purchaser has used reasonable endeavours to obtain the information, although this may create difficulties for it when conducting an Enquiry on a proper basis rather than, at present, as if it were an adjudication for stamp duty.

For companies the address is the registered office of the company even though this may not be the principal place of business. Where a company is incorporated abroad and does not have premises in the UK, it may be that any address for service contained in particulars registered under the Companies Act 2006 will be sufficient to avoid a penalty.

Box 49, dealing with the number of purchasers, requires an accurate analysis as to who is or are the purchasers. This may require the disclosure of details of numerous persons who are beneficially entitled although not appearing on the land register or as parties to the contract. However, as with vendors, there appears to be a relaxation so far as partnerships are concerned. The partnership counts as a single purchaser and an entry of the partnership name would appear to be sufficient in Box 52.

Box 52: where the purchaser is a company, it is obligatory to file SDLT 4, especially where the company is incorporated abroad.

Box 55 deals with settlements. Where the person appearing on the contract or receiving the transfer is a nominee this box will not be appropriate. In such a case the purchaser disclosed on the form will be the beneficial owner. In consequence, this can only be of relevance where there is not a bare trust or nominee or agency relationship in place.

Box 57 requires details of whether the parties are connected. Various illustrations are given in SDLT 6 but it must be noted that companies within the same group are also connected. This means that such transactions will be dealt with pursuant to the connected company charge or the special regime for partnerships so that the figure to be included in Box 10 will be the market value of the property or the reduced amount for partnerships, not the consideration being paid. This requirement will apply even where the transaction is exempt by reason of intra-group relief or, *prima facie*, qualifies for relief as some form of distribution; but note the reliefs possibly available from the connected company charge in relation to dividends and distributions by and out of companies contained in FA 2003, s.54.

Box 58 is of key practical importance where filing is effected manually. Electronic filing usually produces a rapid response and SDLT 5. Given that in England and Wales, but not in Scotland where special practices apply, there will inevitably be several days' delay in the turnaround of the form before the Revenue certificate (SDLT 5) is produced, and as this is essential for the purpose of obtaining any changes in the land register, it is important to ensure that the SDLT 5 certificate is delivered to the person who has the carriage of the registration process. The form should be sent to the appropriate professional adviser. This may be the person who is acting for the mortgagee who has the greatest incentive in ensuring that the title is registered. Delays in transmitting the form may result in delays in submitting documentation to the Land Registry with consequent problems.

Box 59 raises certain issues consequent upon the entries raised in Box 58, where the form is to be received by an agent. The Notes for Guidance (SDLT 6) state that this is to deal with correspondence 'arising from the submission of the return'. While, in general, in order to ensure that matters are dealt with expeditiously, it is probably appropriate for the correspondence dealing with the initial submission of the return to be dealt with by professionals, there is a longer-term issue. It is not clear whether HMRC Stamp Taxes will use the entry in Box 59 as a letterbox for initiating an Enquiry. It is, at present, unclear whether this is its intention, but there is a risk that this may be the case. This can be something of a problem since, after the transaction is completed, the lay client and the professional may cease to deal with each other on a regular basis. Moreover, given that there may be a significant delay before the Enquiry is launched, the professional may be unable to contact the taxpayer. Until this matter is clarified there may, therefore, be certain difficulties in completing Box 59 on the basis that the professional is to deal with all correspondence.

Box 69, dealing with trustees, refers to trustees of settlements. Nominees, bare trustees and other fiduciaries will be required to answer 'no' because they will not be the 'purchaser'. Indeed, such persons should have no involvement with the form whatsoever since the person identified as purchaser and the person to sign the declaration must be the beneficial owner, subject to the special rules for signatures.

Box 71 is a key box and its completion is fundamental. The rules as to who is required or, within certain limited circumstances, permitted to sign Box 71 is a matter of considerable complexity, as is now the form of the declaration because of the powers of agents to sign in relation to matters relating to the effective date (FA 2003, Sched.10, para.1A (as amended)).

D.2.2   SDLT 4 (as amended)

This form is required in virtually every transaction other than routine residential transactions. It will be required in all 'commercial' cases and even in residential transactions where the taxpayer is a body corporate.[51] Since a body corporate does not have a national insurance number[52] it does have a registration number the details of which will be required. Similarly, companies incorporated outside the United Kingdom will need to file. This will apply to residential transactions for a corporate purchaser even where the company is acquiring the property as some form of trustee whether a bare trustee or a trustee of a settlement. It will apply to all acquisitions of businesses.

Many of the questions are, as with SDLT 1, not directly relevant to the tax but require information as to potential ownership of assets – perhaps as a means of discovering items of property and areas of business that are vulnerable to additional taxation.

Box 1 deals with the sale of a business. For older practitioners it will bear certain resemblances to the former stamps form 22 and companies form 88 namely categorising assets into those that are subject to tax and those that are not taxable. The items listed within this box such as stock and goodwill are, *prima facie*, not subject to tax. However, while the reference to 'other' includes intangible property such as patents and trademarks the reference to 'goodwill' is a highly contentious area. There is a significant debate as regards what is 'goodwill' in the strict sense and what is 'embedded goodwill' or premium value for land within the context of the business (see **2.15.2**). An entry indicating that 'goodwill' is included

---

[51]   This is not the original version of SDLT 4. A replacement was issued because of certain defects such as the confusion between chattels and fixtures on the original return requiring totally the wrong information.

[52]   Although one employee of HMRC Stamp Taxes dealing with these issues persistently believed that companies did have such numbers and required details thereof notwithstanding many explanations to the contrary.

within the sale may provoke a request for details as to why a payment for 'goodwill' was contained when this was really, in the view of HMRC Stamp Taxes, a land value and should have been included in Box 10. It raises important issues for preparation of the transaction and the documentation in order to be able to justify the filing of the return upon the basis that the item in question was true goodwill. Similarly, the reference to chattels and movables is deceptive. Unlike the former stamps form 22 it there is no longer a reference to the relevant equipment being in a state of severance at the effective date. It is an attempt to require the taxpayer to justify the allocation of the consideration between items of equipment that are fixtures and therefore taxable as part of the land or are still chattels and therefore not taxable and not included in any linked transaction computation (see **4.6**).

Box 4 refers to certain forms of variable consideration and relates to Box 5 in the situation of whether the tax has been deferred.[53] It is possible to apply in advance for the postponement of tax upon certain forms of deferred consideration so that permission may have been obtained even before the contracts have been exchanged. This is a prudent course because it avoids difficulties with seeking to persuade HMRC Stamp Taxes to extend the deadlines which is not always forthcoming notwithstanding its powers to do so.[54] Box 4 relates only to certain types of deferred consideration, namely 'contingent', i.e. a fixed sum payable or a fixed reduction in the price if an event does or does not happen at some time in the future. Future uncertain events relate to 'uncertain consideration' such as earnouts, overages and turnover figures. It would seem that this box requires an indication that variable figures are included in the purchase price including the assignment of leases, premiums for the grant of leases and variable rent although certain aspects of this have been dealt with in relation to the rent provisions on SDLT 1. It will be noted that this and Box 5 are irrelevant where the consideration is 'unascertained'. This is a situation (see **8.28**) where the price or rent is dependent upon pre-existing factors so that all the relevant information is available but requires to be processed. In this situation tax is paid upon the estimated basis and there is no power to defer. It is, however, not necessary to refer to this type of consideration in Box 4 because the consideration is neither contingent nor dependent upon future events.

Boxes 9 and onwards are largely information gathering and/or a duplication of information that is already included in SDLT 1. This is particularly the case in relation to Boxes 19 to 35. In some respects it may enlarge upon data such as Box 35 which requires details of how the net present value was calculated.

Box 28 may need to be noted since it refers to the surrender of any leases although it does not require these to be surrendered in consideration of or in relation to the grant of any new lease. Such surrenders are, *prima facie*, taxable as land exchanges[55] but subject to numerous reliefs.[56] It would seem that this may refer to some situations where actual surrenders are not involved. Where there has been substantial performance of an agreement for lease there is a deemed surrender of the deemed lease granted.[57] Similarly, where there are certain types of deeds of variation these operate as surrenders and regrants (see **8.58**). It seems that disclosure of these arrangements is required by Box 28.

Boxes 29 and 30 would seem to be potential anti-avoidance measures. The existence of a break clause is essentially to be ignored.[58] Its only significance for the purposes of SDLT is whether it may have impacts upon levels of rents and whether there is a market value premium in those cases where market values are relevant. However, it has effectively taken on a practical significance since break clauses in leases are among the prime targets for the

---

[53] FA 2003, s.90; Stamp Duty Land Tax (Administration) Regulations 2003, SI 2003/2837.
[54] See FA 2003, s.97.
[55] FA 2003, s.47; Sched.4, para.5.
[56] See, for example, FA 2003, Sched.17A, paras.9 and 9A.
[57] FA 2003, Sched.17A, para.12A.
[58] FA 2003, Sched.17A, para.2.

statutory general anti-avoidance provisions.[59] The exercise of a break clause is not, as such, a chargeable event nor does it entitle the tenant to a refund.[60]

Box 30 ignores the fact that there may be break clauses at various intervals. There may be more than one break clause in leases for slightly longer terms.

Box 31 relating to options is somewhat ambiguous. It seemed to be intended to deal with situations where the lease arises by reason of the exercise of the option for the purposes of investigating the linked transaction rules. It does not make clear the situation of where a lease is granted with an option to renew the lease or to purchase the reversionary interest.

Boxes 32 to 34 simply extend the disclosure required by SDLT 1 and are, presumably, intended to provide HMRC Stamp Taxes with certain dates, when they can expect to receive further filings in respect of the lease. The question of such filings after rent reviews is a matter of potential dispute (see **8.32**). HMRC Stamp Taxes appears to require returns to be filed within 30 days of the review date although this is not consistent with the provisions of FA 2003, s.80 and Sched.17A, paras.7 and 8. It may also be relevant in relation to whether any rent reviews after the expiration of the fifth year of a term are abnormal.[61]

Boxes 36 to 39 would appear to be simply data collection for the purposes of providing information on which HMRC Stamp Taxes could base a claim that the consideration has either been reserved as rent[62] or has not been properly apportioned between rent and service charges.[63] It will be noted that service charges and other items referred to in Boxes 38 and 39 are exempt from SDLT if not reserved as part of the rent.[64]

---

[59]   See, for example, the illustrative list of transactions to which these provisions 'may' apply contained in FA 2003, s.75A.

[60]   But see situations where the exercise of a break clause during the first five years of the term may define the basis for a claim for a tax refund.

[61]   FA 2003, Sched.17A, paras.14 and 15.

[62]   FA 2003, Sched.17A, para.6.

[63]   FA 2003, Sched.4, para.4.

[64]   FA 2003, Sched.17A, paras.6 and 10.

Index